PORNOGRAPHY AND SEXUAL REPRESENTATION

VOLUME III

Recent Titles in
American Popular Culture

PORNOGRAPHY AND SEXUAL REPRESENTATION

A Reference Guide

VOLUME III

Joseph W. Slade

American Popular Culture
M. Thomas Inge, Series Editor

GREENWOOD PRESS
Westport, Connecticut • London

Library of Congress Cataloging-in-Publication Data

Slade, Joseph W.
    Pornography and sexual representation : a reference guide / by Joseph W. Slade.
      p. cm.—(American popular culture, ISSN 0193–6859)
    Includes bibliographical references and index.
    ISBN 0–313–27568–8 (set : alk. paper)—ISBN 0–313–31519–1 (vol. I : alk. paper)—
  ISBN 0–313–31520–5 (vol. II : alk. paper)—ISBN 0–313–31521–3 (vol. III : alk. paper)
    1. Pornography—United States—Bibliography. 2. Pornography—United States. I. Title.
II. Series.
Z7164.P84S56 2001
[HQ472.U6]
016.3634'7—dc21   99–085695

British Library Cataloguing in Publication Data is available.

An on-line version of *Pornography and Sexual Representation:
A Reference Guide* is available from Greenwood Press,
an imprint of Greenwood Publishing Group, Inc.
(ISBN 0–313–31536–1)

Library of Congress Catalog Card Number: 99–085695
ISBN: 0–313–27568–8 (set)
      0–313–31519–1 (Volume I)
      0–313–31520–5 (Volume II)
      0–313–31521–3 (Volume III)
ISSN: 0193–6859

First published in 2001

Greenwood Press, 88 Post Road West, Westport, CT 06881
An imprint of Greenwood Publishing Group, Inc.
www.greenwood.com

Printed in the United States of America

The paper used in this book complies with the
Permanent Paper Standard issued by the National
Information Standards Organization (Z39.48–1984).

10 9 8 7 6 5 4 3 2 1

Copyright Acknowledgments

For

Judith, Joey, and Marya

Contents

Preface

This *Reference Guide* is structured around two premises. The first is that regardless of how one may feel about pornography, sexual expression, and representation, it has profoundly enriched American culture. Rather than try to "prove" this assertion, I allow the sources cited to speak for themselves. At the very least, gathering materials together indicates the degree to which pornography has permeated the social, economic, and political life of America, and I am confident that readers of this *Guide* will be just as astonished as I am by the evidence from so many quarters. As members of a culture, we think about pornography in many different ways. The diversity of opinion is a reminder that far from encapsulating dominant or hegemonic ideas and attitudes—as some critics hold—pornography does not compel assent to a particular agenda. Rather, it invites a constant reevaluation that has so far not tapped the secret of its marginality. Sexual expression somehow continuously refreshes itself, so that it *remains* taboo and thus, in a version of cultural thermodynamics, continuously energizes mainstream social and political expression. *How* pornography remains forever at the edge is not always clear; that it does so is manifest in the debate that it engenders.

   The second premise is that pornography and what we say about pornography constitute our principal ways of speaking about sex, one reason that many researchers prefer the neutral term *sexual materials* to the more charged word *pornography*. Traced far enough, all such materials, all such forms of speaking, are rooted in the oral genres of folklore. "All folklore is erotic," said the late folklorist Gershon Legman, who had in mind the speech of the unwashed. But, in a larger sense, pornography and the comment that it generates, some of it sophisticated, much of it carried by advanced communication conduits, are contemporary versions of the same ancient narratives, jokes, and legends that Legman studied. Calling pornography sexual folklore helps to explain its pervasiveness and also its humanity. Pornography can demystify and secularize sexuality and thus weaken the barriers that divide genders and classes of people; it can also betray and shame our erotic longing and thus reinforce those barriers. The sexual discourse of "others" can seem demeaning, dehumanizing, cheap, tawdry, inauthentic, dangerous, commercial, pathetic, or political, while our own seems inspirational, natural, objective, "real," dignified, safe, and spiritual. Agreeing to disagree about sexual expression will probably bring no more permanent peace than agreeing to disagree about religion, politics, or other things we think important, and this *Guide* does not argue that we should.

Comment on pornography—and eroticism—is, without exception, biased along gender, class, racial, religious, aesthetic, and/or ideological lines. My own biases, easily visible, are of the type traditionally called liberal. Moreover, to pretend that my interest is solely academic would be dishonest. Few academics choose to study materials they abhor. The sheer volume of materials I have canvassed has left me largely unaroused, though I do believe that seeking arousal is a perfectly legitimate goal. Every now and then, fortunately, I run across some passage or image that I do find erotic—or, if you will, pornographic—and hope of stimulation can always spring anew. And yes, I am just as often repulsed by what I see and hear and read.

One final observation. When the South African photojournalist Kevin Carter won the Pulitzer Prize in 1993 for his shot of a vulture patiently waiting near a tiny Sudanese child only seconds away from death by starvation, one of my students asked me how a human being who had taken such a photograph could go on living. She received her answer in mid-1994, when Carter committed suicide. Over the years, I have seen in excess of 5,000 pornographic films or videos, and I have looked at perhaps 150,000 pornographic photos in which bodies have been frozen in states of false passion by entirely unrepentant photographers. Not even the most extreme of these have come remotely close to the inhumanity of the scene captured by Carter. The point, made before, though not often enough, is that as Americans we lack a sense of proportion. We are affronted by a picture of an erect penis or a bare breast, but we glance thoughtlessly every day at obscenities that by rights should stop our hearts.

ACKNOWLEDGMENTS

Many people who assisted me in finding material wish to remain anonymous, but I want to thank them anyway. They include writers and fellow academics, casual and professional correspondents, theater owners, bookshop staffs, photographers and publishers, producers and directors, performers and sex workers, and especially collectors; the latter have given me information about, and often access to, some remarkable archives. Of those friends and correspondents I can name, Joe Amato, Bob and Jean Ashton, Bob Barr, Kenneth Bernard, Ruth Bradley, Joan Brewer, Bill Brigman, Joani Blank, Ray Browne, Vern Bullough,

James Card, Greg Crosbie, Bill Dellenback, Paul Gebhard, Jay Gertzman, Larry Gross, Martha Harsanyi, Christie Hefner, Gary Hunt, Tom Inge, Cathy Janes, Walter Kendrick, George Korn, Raoul Kulberg, Gershon Legman, Terence Malley, Ted McIlvenna, J. B. Rund, C. J. Scheiner, Ivan Stormgart, Joan Templeton, and Joseph Vasta all gave generous amounts of encouragement, information, criticism, or time. Graduate assistants Anthony Bush, Usha Zacharias, and Sharon Zechowski have meticulously traced sources and copied articles. Librarians at many institutions here and abroad have been gracious and patient, especially those at the Kinsey Institute for Research in Sex, Gender, and Reproduction; British Film Archives; Long Island University; New York Public Library; George Eastman House; New York University; Ohio University; and University of Texas. I am grateful to three editors at Greenwood Press, Alicia Merritt, Pamela St. Clair, and M. Thomas Inge, the latter the editor for the series of which this *Guide* is a part, for their help and forbearance. Any mistakes in this *Guide* are mine, of course, not theirs.

The influence of two mentors, perhaps visible only to me, has strongly shaped this project. A quarter century ago, long before writing about pornography was commonplace among academics, my first published article on the subject was reprinted in one of those office magazines compiled for doctors by a drug company. In its pages, next to mine, was an article by Margaret Mead (1901–1978), who, to my enormous surprise and pleasure, invited me to tea. A compilation of comment on pornography, she suggested, would be an anthropological treasure. About the same time, my dean at Long Island University, Felice Flanery Lewis, author of *Literature, Obscenity, and the Law* (still one of the best books on literary censorship), shielded me from attacks on my research into sexual expression. That I was granted tenure was due, in large measure, to her principled defenses of faculty. To these two, then, the first an intrepid voyager of cultures, the second a steadfast guardian of intellectual freedom, I owe major debts.

Because immersing one's self in pornography for so long stimulates a sense of the transgressive, I am conscious of having finished this *Guide* with time stolen from my wife and children. I cannot give that time back, but I hope I can repay the affection with which they allowed me to take it.

How to Use This Guide

Organizing the vast comment on pornography and ancillary, but related, representations of sexuality and gender is difficult. The best scheme begins with historical, bibliographic, and broad theoretical approaches, moves to comment on specific genres arranged by communication media, and concludes with overviews of research and policy. Though I hope the merits of this structure will be evident, some redundancy has been inevitable, in part because historians and commentators often make forays into different genres and periods. To assist the reader I have placed "See Also" notations to other chapters where I think they might help.

The *Guide* has been divided into twenty-one chapters arranged in three volumes, with complete table of contents reproduced in each volume. The sequence is roughly from general to specific, with the first volume offering the broadest view. Chapter 1 is a chronology of significant dates in the history of American pornography. Leaving aside a brief introduction and a reflection on the nature of pornography, the first volume begins with a history of American pornography that discusses pornographic media as they become popular: books, art, and magazines precede photography, film, dance, and the Internet. Should you not find what you are looking for at first glance, look further in Chapter 3, **A Brief History of American Pornography**. Bibliographies, indexes, and encyclopedias (Chapter 4) are broken down into categories for convenience, on the assumption that the reader may wish to locate a starting point for research. As Chapter 5 makes clear, context is important; here are other starting points, located in historical commentaries on various issues and sectors of culture. Chapter 6 outlines major theoretical positions (e.g., aesthetic, technological) on the subject of sexual representation.

The remaining sections in volume I are intended as fairly quick references.

Chapter 7 provides information on famous collectors and collections of pornographic materials, on major research libraries, and on important subcollections and archives broken down, when possible, by genres or media. Chapter 8 covers child pornography, a category that our culture has legally and conceptually separated from other forms of erotic expression, even though conservatives try to conflate them. Despite the dangers that Michel Foucault thought inherent in classifications of sexuality and gender, categorizing types of erotic expression counters the American tendency to lump all such expression together and makes exploration possible.

The other two volumes treat specific categories. The first chapter of volume II addresses scholarship on beauty, bodies, clothing, fetishes, genitalia, masturbation, and appliances. The remaining chapters of the volume explore comment on pornographic expression in dramatic, visual, and electronic media. Here are to be found citations to works dealing with performance, art, photography, motion pictures and videotapes, and electronic media such as the Internet. Volume III outlines criticism on oral, print, and journalistic media by treating folklore, books, newspapers, magazines, advertising, and comic books. Also in the final volume are chapters on research into the nature and effects of pornography, law and censorship, and, finally, economics.

If your subject is exploitation films, for instance, you might begin in volume I with chapter 3 **A Brief History of American Pornography**, look next in film bibliographies in Chapter 4, check Chapter 1 (**Chronology**) for useful dates, and then move to Chapter 13 in volume II for the section on **Exploitation Films**, and go from there to Chapter 19 (**Research on Pornography in the Medical and Social Sciences**) of volume III for studies of effects or to Chapter 20 on **Censorship of Film and Video**. Conversely, you might begin with discussion of the films themselves (Chapter 13) and then backtrack to the broader chapters. The table of contents is detailed enough to suggest links. Almost always, finding material on topics requires looking at several chapters. Comment on *Playboy* magazine, for example, appears in chapters on magazines (17, **Playboy and Its Imitators**), on photography (12, **Female Pinups, Centerfolds, and Magazine Pictorials** and **Models and Techniques**), on research, and on economics, as well as in **A Brief History of American Pornography** (volume I, Chapter 3). As another example, a book of photographic studies of striptease dancers is more likely to be covered in the section on photography (12, **Documentary Photographs**) unless it contains significant textual comment, in which case it would appear in the chapter on performance (10, **Erotic Dance**).

Because this *Guide* deals only with American pornography, I have omitted many excellent works (e.g., Graham Greene's *Lord Rochester's Monkey*, a study of John Wilmot, one of the great British pornographers) that deal with artifacts of other nationalities. It hardly needs saying, I hope, that most of the citations here are to materials designed to shed light on pornography, not to titillate in themselves. Referring to a particular artifact in the larger context of the continuing discussion of sexual representation does not imply that the example is itself pornographic, let alone obscene. Even so, the desire to be as comprehensive as possible has led me to include citations to works that someone, somewhere, has called pornographic. It is silly to speak about pornography without providing examples.

The cutoff point for sources gathered here is late 1998, when the *Guide* started on its way to editors and printers, though as it moved along I added a few in the early part of 1999. Those disappointed not to find up-to-date sources must forgive the lengthy time necessary to make ready so large a work.

Introduction: Finding a Place for Pornography

The spirit of liberty is the spirit which is not too sure that it is right.
—Justice Learned Hand, 1944

Intersecting trends continually readjust thinking about pornography. The most important trend is the growing popularity of erotic representations among overworked Americans seeking stimulation in a capitalistic and technological society increasingly characterized as joyless. A second is the fascination that pornography exerts on scholars bent on unraveling the mysteries of gender. One should be careful not to ascribe too much moral weight to the first trend. After all, politicians used to condemn pornography in the name of a majority that was supposed to hate it. To claim that porn is now acceptable because more people apparently enjoy it is to forget the fickleness of the public. Moreover, if pornography is to retain its marginality, the presumed source of an energy that feeds a cultural mainstream, then sooner or later it will have to refresh its oppositional stance, become more offensive, and regain the power that comes with distance from prevailing mores. Besides, plenty of Americans still recoil from what's out there now, and they are unlikely to draw comfort from knowing that their neighbors like it.

Fashion just as clearly governs the fortunes of current academic theories of sexual expression. The *New Yorker* has devoted several pages to academic research in porn,[1] and niche-marketed periodicals are commissioning the copycat articles that diffuse entertaining information among strata of readers. Behind the journalistic notice, always welcome to professors, lie expectations that may be unrealistic. Erotic representation may or may not demonstrate conclusively that sexuality lies between the legs while gender lies between the ears. Like long-held assumptions that pornography causes antisocial behavior, the poststructuralist theories reviewed by the *New Yorker* may turn out to be equally untestable and wrong-headed. The vast number of ill-conceived, even ludicrous quantitative studies purporting to demonstrate that sexual materials lead to violence testifies to pornography's power to shred articles of faith.

Theories mutate quickly. As a case in point, feminist approaches began with strident redefinitions of pornography as the exclusive discourse of males. As an aphorism, that characterization's validity was roughly equivalent to, say, Engels' and Marx's observation that religion is the opiate of the masses. Both encapsulate degrees of truth. The problem, as the Soviet Union discovered, comes when one legislates on the basis of what is, at most, an insight. Religion is much more than a narcotic, and pornography is much more than the discourse of males. Those feminists who led the reexamination of sexual expression should be commended for bringing fresh perspectives to bear, however, and so should those feminists who began immediately to revise what academics call "totalizing metaphors," or attempts to universalize from limited evidence. From these initiatives have come better ideas—some feminist, and others the contributions of different schools of thought—as should be evident from chapter 19.

Thanks to journalistic interest, the sexual language heard in the ivory tower has been filtered and combined with pornographic language itself transmuted by mainstream media to form a reasonably useful discourse of sex and gender. If Americans are less embarrassed to speak of sex these days, they can also thank Kenneth Starr and Republican members of Congress, who have sanitized words such as "penis" and "ejaculate" by repeating them endlessly. Not so oddly, as many Americans learned, being able to make jokes about the president's genitals (and those of other politicians) and Monica Lewinsky's thongs has eased gender tension and stimulated other kinds of dialogue in workplaces across the country.[2] Enhanced vocabulary counts for a lot. Even fundamentalists seem relieved to be able to give names to things they despise and to join academics in interpreting gender codes. How else would we have become aware of the importance of Teletubbies, purple or otherwise?

Despite the centrality of language to so many postmodern theories of representation, scholars have paid scant attention to ancient components of composition. Margaret Mead once told me over tea in the Museum of Natural History that pornography joined the two most powerful human imperatives that an anthropologist could study: the need to reach orgasm and the need to tell stories: "You can't stop people from having intercourse or masturbating, and you can't stop them from talking about it or writing about it and then masturbating or having intercourse as a result. That's all it comes down to, and there isn't anything else you really have to say. But," she admitted with a grin, "neither one of us is likely to leave it at that."

Whether historians call the practice pornographic or obscene, "talking dirty" is as old as language. Sexual stories possess universal appeal, and the spoken word keeps pornographic tropes alive and current when censorship or political correctness throttles other media. The third volume begins with a section on oral forms of sexual expression that is necessarily selective considering the size of the reservoir. To say that we do not understand the erotic nature of oral traditions is to understate: the structures of spoken obscenity and desire are as mysterious as the linguistic architectures postulated by Noam Chomsky and just as protean. (Gershon Legman, greatest of all authorities on erotic folklore, died on 23 February 1999, leaving too much of what he knew unspoken.)

Included also are chapters on **Erotic Literature**, **Newspapers, Magazines, and Advertising**, and **Comics**, also categories usually taken for granted. Browsers in bookstores may be unaware that the erotic impulses bubbling in today's fiction once secretly molded the consciousnesses of American writers, shaped important thematic strands of American literature, and kept American publishers alive during the depression. Breakfasters digesting today's diet of scandal may not know that the sexual peccadilloes of celebrities and politicians have always been important elements of national journalism, just as sex has long figured in magazines and advertising. Fans of raunchy comic books may know little of the Tijuana bibles that gave rise to the gender-bending, politically subversive genres of the present. In an age of electronic media, most Americans merely smile at the notion that printed pages once carried erotic viruses that could infect unwary readers. Moreover, after the *Final Report* of the Attorney General's Commission on Pornography and the report of special prosecutor Kenneth Starr on the Clinton–Lewinsky affair, both of which were published by the government and both of which equal in explicitness any text ever charged with obscenity, the prosecution of printed materials has fallen off sharply. Prosecutors still go after comic books and try to redemonize written expression when it is distributed by electronic means. Under the On-Line Decency Act passed by Congress in 1998, any Web site operator on the Internet who does not ascertain the age of a user before permitting access to the Starr Report on President Clinton could be prosecuted, one of many reasons that lower courts have thus far (May 1999) struck down the law as unconstitutional.

Such ploys are worth noting as reminders that the nation's existing obscenity laws were formulated in the great literary-legal battles that resulted from publication of *Ulysses, Lady Chatterley's Lover, Fanny Hill*, and *Tropic of Cancer*, when politicians believed that printed words, rather than computer glyphs, were major threats to the body politic. "Formulated" may be the wrong word. American jurisprudence usually evolves toward establishing protected domains for individuals, classes, and actions. As several authorities have noticed, however, American practice presumes sexual expression and representation to be vulnerable to sanction. This domain is defined by negatives, not by affirmations or entitlements: what is not specifically prohibited is permitted, albeit grudgingly. Because the courts have rejected most standards for determining what is prohibited, censors at the moment find it difficult to proscribe, but—and it is an important but—the threat remains real. It is as if the culture had adopted a covert and unconscious strategy to institutionalize instability. By keeping sexual discourse off-balance, permanently contested, tilted toward the outlawed and the forbidden, Americans can still draw on that discourse for fresh infusions of moral and intellectual energy.

As indicated in Chapter 20, on **Pornography and Law**, other uniquely American assumptions have influenced the shaping of legal practice. In their concern for constitutional separation of powers, American courts over time have transferred (and in doing so usually diminished) authority to censor among federal agencies such as the Customs Department and the Post Office and among state censorship boards and private special interest groups such as watch and ward societies, religious action groups, and various ideological organizations that have competed for the privilege of suppressing the speech of others. In hearing cases, the Supreme Court still more or less follows the precedent set in 1973 in *Miller*, which allowed individual states to set community standards, so long as the harm those local prosecutions do to the Constitution is not too blatant. In other efforts to maintain fairness, the Court shows signs of reining in the "forum-shopping" (for local hanging judges) tactics employed in recent years by renegade obscenity units of the Justice Department seeking convictions at all costs. At the same time, the Court has endorsed Congress' refusal to allow the National Endowment for the Arts to support sexual expression. Artists excoriate the decision, but denying public funds to unpopular ideas is an improvement on prior practices that enabled zealots to imprison or impoverish individuals whose ideas they disliked.

Several factors explain the current climate of tolerance. The first is the judicial recognition that while children have a right to protection from adult sexuality, adults have a right to protection from those who would set the limits on adult speech at levels appropriate only for five-year-olds. Americans have made it clear that they will not tolerate child pornography, partly to delineate what is *not* acceptable but, much more important (and again the process is negative rather than positive), to define what *is*. A second factor is that decades of research have failed to uncover evidence of significant links between ordinary sexual expression and antisocial behavior, a factor that undercuts the rationale for banning such speech for adults. Arguments equating sex and violence have been muted. Yet a third factor is an awareness that ancillary, rather than direct, effects do matter. The marketing of pornography, for example, can have an impact on quality of life. In this latter regard, legal intervention has been less effective than changing technology. The Supreme Court has allowed municipalities to use zoning ordinances to move adult movie theaters and bookstores to outlying areas to safeguard real estate values, to shield children and churchgoers from blatant representations, and to buffer passersby from the riffraff that such establishments often attract. The damage to free speech implicit in such decisions has been lessened, however, by the proliferation of electronic media capable of delivering erotic representations anywhere to those able to afford VCRs, cable television, and computers. Leaving aside issues of class—always a factor in legal opinions concerning speech—the advent of communication technologies that make spatial considerations irrelevant has caused panic among legislators who wish to suppress speech on the Internet, but the courts have thus far been, well, judicious. Restraint speaks well for a legal system that will eventually have to modify a body of case law built on *Miller.*

A fourth factor is economic clout. As the sources cited in **The Economics of Pornography** (Chapter 21) suggest, growing legitimacy, global competition, falling prices, and increasing taxation are transforming sexual enterprises, especially pornography, into quasi-respectable businesses. Legitimacy, stringent prosecution, and the rise of the Internet (which cannot be easily co-opted) have dislodged organized crime from the distribution of pornography. Global competition has eroded the dominance of American producers of erotic materials, cheapened costs, expanded markets, and encouraged consolidation of small enterprises into larger ones. Western governments now tax the profits of pornographers, regulate some of the traffic, use diplomacy to counter piracy and violation of copyright of sexually oriented media, and keep an eye on the financial contributions that erotic materials make toward favorable balances of trade. So authoritative a source as *The Economist* predicts that pornography in the next century will take its "rightful" place in the global entertainment industry.[3]

NOTES

1. James Atlas, "The Loose Canon: Why Higher Learning Has Embraced Pornography," *The New Yorker*, 29 March 1999, pp. 60–65.

2. Alex Kuczynski, "In Offices, an Excuse to Talk about S*x," *New York Times*, 2 February 1998, pp. B1, B7.

3. "The Sex Industry," *The Economist*, 346 (14–20 February 1998):23.

15

Folklore and Oral Genres

LANGUAGE: OBSCENITY AND DEMOCRACY

Americans may be less inclined to doubt the connections between sexual expression, personal identity, and democratic freedoms after watching a special prosecutor invade the sexual privacy of a president whose own defense of free speech for his fellow citizens had been lax in the first place. The president's enemies attempted to use pornography to achieve political advantage. But pornography is double-edged. As Lauren Berlant argues in *The Queen of America Goes to Washington City: Essays on Sex and Citizenship*, pornography in all its forms, especially those involving marginalized genders, is the key to citizenship, if only because it serves to remind Americans that spheres of privacy are distinct from realms of public life and that a culture can become authoritarian by trivializing the sexuality of its members. According to Berlant, middle-class messages relentlessly attempt to infantilize Americans; pornography has at least the merit of trying to get beyond such messages and thus helps form the basis of a more rational community. Berlant's thesis has much in common with Joss Marsh's *Word Crimes: Blasphemy, Culture, and Literature in Nineteenth Century England*, which details legal and cultural cases in which lower-class, blasphemous, and obscene speech helped secure democratic rights. As Americans have grown genteel, they have forgotten that democracy is, by definition, vulgar. For democracy to function as a social and political system, it must embrace the common, the trashy, the dispossessed, the lunatic—and it must embrace their discourses, which, through their very outrageousness, in turn transform, energize, and advance the growth of the body politic. Considered from an organic or thermodynamic perspective, a society that cannot assimilate the obscene will die. Fed by obscenity or not, pornographic idiom strives deliberately for instability, and its open linguistic valences foster freedom.

On a personal, rather than political, plane, telling sexual stories is a way of constructing a sexual self, as much a form of empowerment as of autobiography, or so says Ken Plummer in *Telling Sexual Stories: Power, Change and Social Worlds*. Plummer uses as examples rape stories, coming-out stories, and recovery stories but covers sexual surveys and therapy goups as well. He is interested in how such stories are constructed, the tropes they employ, the identities they assume, and the roles that such stories play in creating a participatory and democratic culture. He is particulary interested in the creation of a new genre of stories of "women liking pornography" (115), noting that our society ordinarily gives primacy to narratives that denigrate sexual expression and present pornography as invariably "bad." According to Plummer, sexual stories proliferate because they must, because they are our way of establishing intimacy but also of processing experience, especially those aspects of sexuality that are key to developing the personality and finding a place for it in society. The poetics of desire, as revealed in expression, metaphors, stereotypes, and the structure of erotic narratives are the subjects of *Language and Desire: Encoding Sex, Romance and Intimacy*, a collection of essays edited by Keith Harvey and Celia Shannon in an attempt to understand how such messages function.

For *Sex Lives: A Sexual Self-Portrait of America*, Mark Baker invited people to speak about customs and practices in interviews and confessions. Baker's book and other transcripts of oral recitations such as those found in Iris Finz's *Erotic Confessions: Real People Talk about Putting the Spark Back in Their Sex Lives* are similar to narratives in anthologies of explicit writing (see **Anthologies of Heterosexual Erotica** in Chapter 16), but canny publishers also market tapes about "actual," voiced fantasies to satisfy a demand (fostered by telephone sex services and the Internet?) for speech that seems to mark a more authentic sexuality. *Sex: An Oral History*, two audiocassettes edited by Harry Maurer in which fifty-two people speak of their desires, preferences, and experiences, is typical.

OBSCENITY AND ORALITY

Whether or not one acknowledges the social, psychological, and political aspects of "dirty" speech, the study of pornography properly begins with orality, because sexual expression ultimately springs from obscene humor, bawdy songs, risqué and downright smutty stories, ribald verse, puns, insults, and wordplay. These activities can be subsumed under the term *folklore*, but language, of course, is basic to all of them. (Postmodern literary scholars seem bent on redefining folklore as the discourse of subalterns, but anthropologists and ethnographers, who actually study these discourses professionally, resist ideological characterizations.) Folklore has long been associated with what might be called *low* porn, the most vulgar of all crude representations, but in a larger sense most of what passes for sexual information is folklore. As a conduit, pornography carries "myths," the more outrageous the better. Some of these are archetypal themes, familiar formulas, and beloved figures: sex as dangerous knowledge and other variations on the story of the Garden; tales of sexual trickery and come-uppances for cheating spouses; men with enormous penises and women with huge vaginas—all can be found in oral form or modern videotape. The fraud-ulent notion that women secretly hunger for rape is a popular motif, the notion that all men approve of rape is another.

Antiporn folklore is more fradulent still. In "What Is Feminist Porn?," a brief, remarkable essay that distills volumes of human sexual history and endless the-oretical screeds, the articulate and astute sex worker, Veronica Monet, points out that much of our cultural dissonance over pornography stems from the wide-spread belief that accepting a penis, being penetrated, is automatically to become inferior. That notion explains the otherwise bewildering charges advanced by antiporn feminists that sex is literally violence and that pornography enshrines discrimination by depicting it. In their formulation, sex is nasty and degrading because its purpose is not for love or reproduction but the brutal exercise of power. The assumption, says Monet, is that women's positions during sex

are inherently degrading. Bending over to receive a penis or some other object for penetra-tion of the vagina or rectum, and spreading one's legs for penetration of the vagina or rec-tum seem to be the main offenders. Performing a blow job is a close second, but giving a hand job seems more embarrassing to its recipient. This is in stark contrast to the laughs and applause a male can receive for imitating the thrusting and gyrating of performing sexual intercourse on many comedy shows. Our cultural stance seems to be that the person who moves and/or penetrates is powerful and the person who holds still and/or is penetrated is degraded. How convenient for the male power structure. (207–208)

Women are degraded by the lack of free choice, not by kneeling or bending, Monet insists, and feminists making porn must reject patriarchical ideology by avoiding scenarios of control. More important, she says, so warped a mentality could not survive in a culture that worshiped the generative powers, as did earlier societies. Then, the vulva was sacred: "Not something dirty or disgusting or embarrassing. The vagina swallowed and devoured and conquered. It produced life. It was active and alive. Not some dark dead hole, like our culture seems bent on relegating female genitalia to now. One could see the person penetrating the vulva as being in service to the vulva" (208). Now, by contrast, for antiporn feminists, modern puritans, and uptight Republicans, to *be* fucked is to be hurt, to be degraded. That is why the study of language, of symbol, folklore, and myth is so crucial. Pornography, as a species of folklore, replicates and perpet-uates linguistic, cultural, and psychological confusion. Correcting confusion re-quires making pornography that selectively reinvests positions of intercourse with ancient symbolism, reinventing folklore appropriate to an information age.

In another sense, however, as Monet's examples suggest, folklore differs from "real" mythology in ways that we conceptualize in spatial and philosophical terms. The deities, themes, and motifs of mythology (the narratives of great mother goddesses, for instance) constitute a parallel universe, a coherent aesthetic vision of human experience suitable for inspiring a Virgil, a Goethe, or a Wagner.

By contrast, folklore is incoherent, spasmodic, nasty, funny—a substrate for experience. Folklore originally signified oral discourse. Speech is the most primal human technology, easily romanticized as the discourse of lower classes, less fixed than recorded narratives or visual texts. Oral channels, of course, are far older than print and electronic, far more ubiquitous, and, ultimately, far more disturbing, if only because words can still represent what other media cannot. Beyond myth, deeper than legend, language enables us to transgress, if only in our minds. It has always been thus. For lack of a better name, we sometimes call the psychological stratum beneath pornography *obscenity*, a term we are quite simply incapable of defining, to signify the unspeakable. Even so, obscenity leaves linguistic traces, and scholars track them in an effort to understand the origins and meaning of the forbidden.

SLANG AND GRAFFITI

For all practical purposes, the study of obscenity in the English language may be said to begin with the seven-volume *Slang and Its Analogues*, privately published by John S. Farmer and William Earnest Henley at the turn of the century to compensate for the omissions of the staid *Oxford English Dictionary*. Etymologically brilliant, its entries buttressed by literary references and allusions as well as by evidence of popular usage, this dictionary is justly regarded as the masterwork of English slang, though the first edition is rare. More available is the first volume of what was to be a three-volume edition of a revised and enlarged edition of 1903–1909 (the second and third were never printed); the single volume is called *Dictionary of Slang and Its Analogues, Past and Present: A Dictionary Historical and Comparative of the Heterodox Speech of All Classes of Society for More Than Three Hundred Years with Synonyms in English, French, German, Italian, etc.* In 1989 Kraus Reprint Company compressed the original seven volumes into three entitled *Slang and Its Analogues, Past and Present*. Here we learn, for example, that *cunt* was an early English term for the vagina, perhaps being derived from the name of a street frequented by prostitutes in the thirteenth century, that it took on distinctly vulgar connotations by 1500, and that it became legally obscene by 1700. All subsequent dictionaries of English slang have been derived from the efforts of Farmer and Henley. Indeed, Henry N. Cary so closely plagiarized the pioneering lexicographers that his 1916 *The Slang of Venery and Its Analogues* (clearly a contracted and edited version of *Slang and Its Analogues*) is usually listed by bibliographers as by Farmer and Henley, despite Cary's having added philological material at the same time that he omitted chunks from the original Farmer–Henley work that he thought would not interest Americans. Scholars assessing Cary's contributions should consult his manuscripts, the five-volume "Sexual Vocabulary," which formed the basis of *The Slang of Venery*, and the two-volume "Introduction to Sexual Vocabulary," a distillation never published; both are in the Kinsey Institute. Adolph Niemoller also deliberately modeled his *American Encyclopedia of Sex*, a compilation of American expressions, on Farmer and Henley but devoted more pages to medical discussions of sexual syndromes and to essays on sexual practices, noted erotophiles, and other erotic curiosities and allusions than to language and slang.

One of the best essays on the subversive function of taboo words in culture is Allen Walker Read's "The Nature of Obscenity," on the function of taboo words in cutting through reticence, politeness, and fraudulent modesty. Part of the essay is given over to a history of American modesty, which Read thinks was often excessive. The more public the insistence on modesty, the more urgent the need to puncture it. Just how public is evident from Read's critique of "Noah Webster as a Euphemist," a slight, but historically important, essay on Webster's bowdlerization of the Bible and his habit of substituting words like *breast* for *teat* or *smell* for *stink*. Most histories of sexuality in the United States devote a few paragraphs to Webster, who has become a figure of derision, but his influence was considerable, as Mamie Meredith points out in "Inexpressibles, Unmentionables, Unwhisperables, and Other Verbal Delicacies of Mid-Nineteenth Century Americans." Meredith's brief note indicates the incredible dimensions of the bowdlerization of language practiced by Americans. Some were so offended by the word *hole*, as in trousers, that they substituted *broadcloth secession*. (Given the present climate of political correctness and postmodern pretension, such inventiveness today might secure an award from the Modern Language Association.)

Read's "The Nature of Obscenity" is a revision of his Introduction to *Lexical Evidence from Folk Epigraphy in Western North America: A Glossarial Study of the Low Element in the English Vocabulary*. That work deals with graffiti, which is ubiquitous to all cultures but especially pungent in English because, says Read, our language includes a working vocabulary of half a million words (as opposed to, say, Russian, with only 100,000 or so). That argument squelches the reasoning of American moms, who often complain that their children's use of obscenity indicates a poor vocabulary. Because many Americans regard graffiti as a "low" form of expression indeed, Read again discussed its value as sexual and cultural barometer in "Graffiti as a Field of Folklore"; his thesis is that low expressions are more authentic and revelatory than polite discourse.

Largely thanks to Read, other scholars have taken up the study of messages expressed as orthographic and pictorial graffiti. "Here I Sit—A Study of American Latrinalia," by Alan Dundes, and "Social Analysis of Graffiti," by Terrance L. Stocker, Linda W. Dutcher, Stephen M. Hargrove, and several others, speak to ongoing interest in graffiti as sexual and social indices. Rachel Bartlett has gathered caricatures and cartoons, erotic drawings, and pithy comments taken from women's rest rooms in *Off the Wall: A Collection of Feminist Graffiti*. Surprisingly, John A. Bates and Michael Martin conclude in "The Thematic Content of Graffiti as a Non-Reactive Indicator for Male and Female Attitudes" that females are more likely to write graffiti on rest room walls than men and that the content is more likely to express "hostile, sexual, or issue-related content." By contrast, "Defacing the Facts" reports on the research of sociologist Flora Kaplan, whose studies of women's bathroom graffiti during the 1970s and 1980s found that only about 30 percent of what women write on bathroom walls is about sex—as opposed to about 70 percent for males—and is less aggressive, though it may have a similar explicitness. Edward M. Bruner and Jane Paige Kelso offer a portentous analysis of gendered toilet graffiti in "Gender Differences in Graffiti: A Semiotic Perspective"; they construe differences as the poles of a political discourse on the distribution of power, with men emphasizing competition, and women cooperation. In "Writing on the Wall" Elizabeth C. Grant provides some hilarious and colorful examples of women's bathroom graffiti. More pictorial is Jill Posener's *Spray It Loud*, whose photographs reproduce graffiti sprayed on billboards by women, usually as comment on sexual absurdities or injustice to women. Robert Reisner revised his *Graffiti: Selected Scrawls from Bathroom Walls*, which included mostly New York City examples, into the larger *Graffiti: Two Thousand Years of Wall Writing*. Nigel Rees has collected three volumes of *Graffiti* from British and American sites. Finally, Richard Sterba's " 'Kilroy Was Here' " analyzes the sexual symbolism of the nose on perhaps the most famous graffito of all.

A popular treatment of obscene language and humor is *Four-Letter Word Games: The Psychology of Obscenity*, by Renatus Hartogs and Hans Fantel, who observe that these elements make up a word-game, "a ploy, a gambit, a mode of adjustment employing obscene terms. The game has multiple goals: seduction, aggression, or release from sexual anxiety, depending on the story and the teller" (145). In examining national forms, Hartogs and Fantel conclude that Americans are fond of oral-genital and anal jokes. Hartogs himself discusses the relationship between the obscene, the forbidden, and the sacred, pointing out that "the concepts of obscenity and taboo necessarily overlap. Obscenity is that which we are not allowed to say. Taboo is that which we are not allowed to do. By extension, a taboo act is in itself an obscenity. To the extent of their overlap, the two terms may therefore be used interchangeably" (78). Obscenity can touch upon the holy, blending the sexual and the magical, the filthy and the divine; most studies of obscenity expand on these connections. One of the most rewarding is Bruno Bettelheim's *Symbolic Wounds: Puberty Rites and the Envious Male*, which discusses obscenity as an essential element in rites of passage in various cultures. Here they serve as steps to maturation; Bettelheim contrasts these practices with the limited options afforded American youths to explore the forbidden as a way of learning about sexuality. A more recent foray in this direction is Riane Eisler's *Sacred Pleasure: Sex, Myth, and the Politics of the Body*, which covers ancient to modern folklore.

Gershon Legman calls Robert Graves' *Lars Porsena or the Future of Swearing and Improper Language* "the worst book ever written on humor" ("Erotic Folksongs and Ballads," 448), but it is an early treatise on obscenity in English. Edward Sagarin examines the multiple uses of "dirty words" in the English language, discussing their emphatic, pungent, shocking nature in *The Anatomy of Dirty Words*; Sagarin's was one of the first unexpurgated, full-length studies of the subject, and its notes and references are excellent. The psychiatrist Ariel Arango explains the need to use obscenities in *Dirty Words*, explaining motivation in terms of Freudian theory. Psychologists beyond number have considered obscenity as expressions of unconscious fears and desires. Freud takes precedence here, of course, but still worth reading is the Viennese analyst Edmund Bergler's "On Obscene Words." So is "The Use of Obscene Words in the Therapeutic Relationship," in which Marvin J. Feldman argues that a patient's obscenities offer useful clues to problems, provided that the therapist establishes trust. In *Blue Streak: Swearing, Free Speech, and Sexual Harassment*, Richard Dooling, convinced that humans have a need for profanity, looks at biological and linguistic foundations of swearing as the beginning of intellectual discrimination.

Compiling dictionaries of sexual slang has become a popular pursuit. Alan Richter traces the etymology of words like *pussy, hand-job*, and *muff-dive* in *The Language of Sexuality*; the volume features an excellent glossary and is well organized around major sections on the language of intercourse, terms for sex organs, and so on. Richter's *Sexual Slang* appears to be a somewhat more colloquial updating of that volume. Lawrence Paros' *The Erotic Tongue: A Sexual Lexicon* is an especially wide-ranging etymological study of sexual expressions, going beyond the vulgar to the more flowery tropes of erotic discourse. In *The Cyclopedic Lexicon of Sex: Erotic Practices, Expressions, Variations of the Libido*, J. E. Schmidt gathers sexual nomenclature and expression in taxonomies both scientific and vulgar. J. Scheidlower has collected materials on everybody's favorite obscenity in *The F-Word*; etymologies and humorous examples take up most pages. The etymologies of sexual expressions outlined by Duncan MacDougald in "Language and Sex" contain solid historical references. Readers of James Wolfe's *Sex Talk: The Ultimate Collection of Ribald, Raunchy, and Provocative Quotations* will find a pithy, witty, or vulgar quotation appropriate for almost any sexual situation.

Some texts appeal primarily because they print tabooed words. Despite the suspicious character of the author's name, Christina Kunitskaya-Peterson's little book, *International Dictionary of Obscenities: A Guide to Dirty Words and Indecent Expressions in Spanish, Italian, French, German, Russian*, offers what are actually pretty learned etymological comparisons of American expressions with their counterparts in other languages. Another curious work is Elizabeth Claire's *A Foreign Student's Guide to Dangerous English*, an illustrated lexicon of tabooed words and phrases to avoid—or savor. John Trimble mostly lists *5,000 Adult Sex Words and Phrases: A Treatise on Common Sexual Terms in*

Modern English Idiom; the book has no real lexicographical or etymological apparatus. Equally unremarkable is Leonard Ashley's *The Dictionary of Sex Slang*, though it is a workmanlike volume. Similar in approach, intent, and merit is *The Complete Sex Dictionary*, by Paul J. Gillette, who defines hundreds of sexual terms, many of them vulgar. More elevated are those in Roy Goliard's *A Scholar's Glossary of Sex*, which in some ways represents an attempt to fabricate a more comfortable sexual discourse midway between the vulgar and the Latinate, though its real intent is humorous. There are a great many popular texts, lightweight in scholarship, breezy in tone; *Playboy's Dictionary of Forbidden Words*, edited by Robert A. Wilson, can serve as typical. Just as amusing but carrying a novel twist in the form of audiocassettes that offer advice on proper pronunciation, tone, and inflection of expletives is David Burke's *Bleep! A Guide to Popular American Obscenities*. Burke's chapters include guides to visual gestures as well as expressions, insults, slang, jokes, and euphemisms.

By way of charting just how far etymological analysis has come, scholars can make their own comparison of, say, Ashley Montagu's once-novel *The Anatomy of Swearing*, whose thesis was that using obscenities was "liberating," and Timothy Jay's *Cursing in America: A Psycholinguistic Study of Dirty Language in the Courts, in the Movies, in the Schoolyards, and on the Streets*, whose pages roam social avenues of obscenity. Jay covers obscene phone calls, sexual profanity, and gender stereotypes, precisely calibrates degrees of offensiveness from mild insult to fighting words, and constructs statistical frequency charts of selected expressions like *scumbag* and *shithead*. Not surprisingly, *damn* and *fuck* occur far more frequently than other swearwords, says Jay, while *cocksucker* and *motherfucker* rank as the most offensive. Jay calls for careful attention to the settings, speakers, audiences, and circumstances of messages; his bibliography is superb. In *Wicked Words: A Treasury of Curses, Insults, Put-Downs, and Other Formerly Unprintable Terms from Anglo-Saxon Times to the Present*, Hugh Rawson moves away from commonly used English obscenities per se to aggressive language. His etymological entries are more comprehensive on vintage examples than contemporary; as just one instance, the reader will find rewarding material on a classic insult like *asshole*, but nothing on *dickhead*, a put-down that has come into its own only recently. The title of Richard A. Spears' *Slang and Euphemism: A Dictionary of Oaths, Curses, Insults, Racial Slurs, Sexual Slang and Metaphor, Drug Talk, Homosexual Lingo, and Related Matters* covers the content pretty well. Reinhold Aman's yearbook, *Maledicta: the International Journal of Verbal Aggression*, has for almost two decades printed analyses of jokes, graffiti, threats, blasphemies, swearwords, insults, curses, political humor, ethnic and racial slurs, and so on, a good deal of it involving wordplay on sex and excretion. Here scholars wrestle with mysteries such as why scatological terms like *asshole, turd*, and *piece of shit* should be reserved for males, while anatomical terms like *cunt, twat*, and *slit* are so often used to characterize women. Aman has excerpted some of the most pungent material from the journal for *Talking Dirty: A Bawdy Compendium of Colorful*

Language, Humorous Insults and Wicked Jokes and for *The Best of Maledicta*. Less polite and certainly less scholarly is *Horseshit: The Offensive Review*, which lives up to its subtitle; it is edited by Robert Dunker and Thomas Dunker. Easily the most literate comment on invective verse comes from X. J. Kennedy's *Tygers of Wrath*, a magnificent gathering of samples laced with nimble and erudite critiques.

LANGUAGE, GENDERS, AND SUBCULTURES

Gender issues—especially as manifest in pornography—have led theorists in recent years toward reexaminations of sexual language. Foucault's *History of Sexuality* set the pace. The theme of his three volumes is the inescapable tyranny of language and taxonomies that fix sexuality and gender, prescribe what is permitted and what is forbidden, and generally inhibit human sexuality by institutionalizing behavior. Foucault observes that one of the ways in which Western society controls the potentially chaotic force of sexuality is never to cease talking about it. Language, in short, embodies power, especially that which governs the relationship of genders. As Sandor Ferenczi noted early in this century in a study reprinted in his *Sex in Psychoanalysis*, obscene language carries a "visual imperative" that can strip a woman of clothes and defenses. More recently, Catharine MacKinnon, in *Only Words*, invests language with literal power. For MacKinnon, the childhood rhyme about sticks, stones, and words that can never hurt enshrines political servitude; for MacKinnon, there is *no* difference between sexual words and actual aggression, and for that reason the First Amendment is only a shield for males who savage females as part of a day's work. (See MacKinnon in **Language-Based Attacks** in Chapter 6.) MacKinnon's is easily the most extreme position in the debate and should be read with Antony Grey's *Speaking of Sex: The Limits of Language*, a plea for respect for the sexuality of others embedded in an examination of the power of speech and metaphor. Nicholas Wolfson in "Eroticism, Obscenity, Pornography, and Free Speech" argues succinctly that Americans must not confuse speech with action; there is a "fire wall" between the two. Judith Butler's *Excitable Speech* also takes issue with MacKinnon by moving desire and sexuality into the realm of the performative, a direction pioneered by Dianne Chisholm in "The 'Cunning Lingua' of Desire: Bodies-Language and Perverse Performativity" and Robert Scholes in "Uncoding Mama: The Female Body as Text"; both of those works utilize semiotic approaches. (See also Chapter 9, **The Landscape of the Body**.)

Susan G. Cole's *Pornography and the Sex Crisis* finds in the sexism of language a clue to global conspiracy: "Pornography is not a picture, or words or ideas, but a practice of sexual subordination in which women's inferior status is eroticized and thus maintained" (9). Cole advocates inventing a new, nonpatriarchal sexual language in order to make sex less exciting. In other words, she says, people should desexualize women's experience in order to remove from sexual acts all "the thrill of danger, violence and threats" by equating freedom of expression with absolute safety (142), which would seem a little like equating freedom with comfortable predictability, a sort of Eisenhower-era recipe for friendly totalitarianism. It is easy to poke fun at such positions, of course, but scholars will quickly become aware that a genuine fear of the dangers of sexuality for women is a recurrent theme in otherwise conventional feminist remarks on pornography and is doubtless the greatest single barrier to communication between men and women about the subject.

WOMEN'S SEXUAL DISCOURSE

Barrie Thorne and Nancy Henley have gathered essays on *Language and Sex: Difference and Dominance* to explore gender and sexual variations in language and the role these differences play in shaping identity, relationships, and culture. Equally solid essays on similar topics have been collected by Barrie Thorne, Cheris Kramarae, and Nancy Henley as *Language, Gender and Society*; both volumes are starting points for those interested in gender differences in communication. Another collection, *Language, Sexuality, and Subversion*, edited by Paul Foss and Meaghan Morris, contains contributions by scholars such as Umberto Eco, Jean Baudrillard, and Luce Irigaray on the subversive—rather than institutional—aspects of sexual language. Although several essays are too jargon-freighted to be illuminating, the widely reprinted Irigaray piece, "That Sex Which Is Not One" (161–172 in the preceding volume), on a discourse of the clitoris, is fascinating and has become a touchstone for feminist scholarship on a wide range of sexual comment; Irigaray has expanded the essay into a book, *This Sex Which Is Not One*, which can be read with her *Speculum of the Other Woman*. A psychoanalyst influenced by Lacan, Irigaray argues that language and sexuality are inextricable and that women have lost touch with their bodies because of patriarchal definitions of what their sexuality is supposed to be. Women have different libidos and more than one sex organ, unlike men, but sexual discourse is organized around the phallus, so that women need to recover their own sexuality through linguistic invention. Irigaray asks the central question, Is the language of the *unconscious* gendered in some morphological sense? If it is not, then women should be able to define their own desires. Speaking of language, Irigaray contrasts vaginal metaphors—folded, interior labia—with phallic ones—jutting, exterior erections—to suggest that a culture that drew its energy from female, rather than male, anatomy (clits rather than pricks—her terms, translated, of course) would prize different ways of speaking and writing.

Phallocentric language is also the subject of another French thinker, Julia Kristeva; the best introduction to her work is *Desire in Language: A Semiotic Approach to Literature and Art*. While Kristeva does not think that women's sexuality is repressed, she does believe it needs to be defined by a choice of "significance" that involves declining masculine terms. Her analysis of gender assumptions is brilliant. She finds a feminine voice in nonverbal signs, sounds, and other textual indicators. Still more fertile is the work of Hélène Cixous, whose witty (even sexy) "The Laugh of the Medusa" insists that for women to write honestly about their own sexuality is to undermine masculine dominance: "The woman who still allows herself to be threatened by the big dick, who's still impressed by the commotion of the phallic stance, who still leads a loyal master to the beat of the drum: that's the woman of yesterday" (890). Cixous at times seems a prototype of the Riot Grrl, embracing and inhabiting sexual stereotypes in order to invert and subvert them. Her strategy is visible in "Veiled Lips," in which she says that a labial consciousness allows women to derive sensual pleasure from language in speech and writing. Were a male to call women's communication "slit writing" or "cunt talk," he would be denounced as sexist, but Cixous' assertions, delivered almost with a giggle, disarm by means of their very smuttiness.

Deborah Tannen's extremely popular book, *You Just Don't Understand*, theorizes that men and women speak at "different frequencies"; women strive for connection, while males aim at status and dominance in their different "genderlects." Perhaps the most outspoken of gender theorists of language is Cheris Kramarae, whose *Women and Men Speaking* advances a version of muted group theory, whose assumptions are that subordinate groups are rendered silent by male dominance. At the same time, says Kramarae, women have recourse to "back-channels" of communication that include gossip, folklore, songs, graffiti, diaries, letters, books of subversive sexuality, and so on. Kramarae and Paula Treichler have compiled *Amazons, Bluestockings, and Crones: A Feminist Dictionary*, a volume filled with definitions both amusing and trenchant. Muriel Schulz's "The Semantic Derogation of Women" is perhaps the best of several studies suggesting that English designations for women, unlike terms for men, tend over time to acquire pejorative connotations through gender prejudice. *The Intelligent Woman's Guide to Dirty Words*, a volume by the Feminist Writers Workshop, endorses that view and concludes that most linguists, lexicographers, and etymologists have exhibited male bias. In "Paradigmatic Women: The Prostitute," Julia P. Stanley can find only twenty-two labels for promiscuous males (playboy, stud, Don Juan) against more than 200 for promiscuous females (whore, hooker, harlot, concubine, strumpet, and so on), an imbalance that attests to inequality and prurient interest. Ethel Strainchamps' "Our Sexist Language" carefully traces the philology of vulgar expressions such as *fuck, twot*, and *cunt* and notes that their pejorative senses shift over time as gender issues arise.

The contributors to *Women Talk Sex: Autobiographical Writing on Sex, Sexuality and Sexual Identity*, edited by Pearlie McNeil, Bea Freeman, and Jenny Newman, exhibit a surprising range of erotic expression. Interestingly, says William M. Wiest, men and women usually use the same terminology ("to come") to describe orgasm, a conclusion that may reinforce the notion that sex is a form of communication. Wiest's "Semantic Differential Profiles of Orgasm and Other Experiences among Men and Women" studied groups of men and women college students. For that matter, another study, "Male-Female Use of Expletives: A Heck of a Difference in Expectations," by Constance Staley, indicates that men and women use the same type and number of swearwords in a stressful situation. The surprise is that the group of women surveyed thought that men would use more "strong" words, and the group of men thought women would use fewer and milder ones. By contrast, in "More on Women's—and Men's—Expletives," Lee Ann Bailey and Lenora A. Timm report that women do use fewer strong expressions than men but that women increase the number as they grow older. According to N. G. Kutner and D. Brogan, however, when men and women are asked to write down sexual expressions, men can remember more words than women can. Kutner and Brogan's "An Investigation of Sex-Related Slang Vocabulary and Sex-Role Orientation among Male and Female University Students" asserts that male terms are more sexually exploitative also. (Worth noting are the titles of this and other studies of profanity; the language keeps the slang at academic distance). Still more readable is Robert Baker's " 'Pricks and Chicks': A Plea for Persons." The ways in which men conceptualize sexual intercourse ("screw," "bang," "hump") are inherently aggressive and discriminatory, if somewhat understandable because of the male's more kinetic role in intercourse. Baker points out that one of the pioneers in sexual linguistics, James McCawley, often had recourse to the pseudonym "Quang Phuc Dong" (267) to counter rampant Puritanism but also to add to another tradition of sexual folklore, the double-entendre pseudonym (see Kunitskaya-Peterson earlier). Baker refers readers interested in words for copulation to *Studies Out in Left Field: Defamatory Essays Presented to James D. McCawley*, edited by Arnold M. Zwicky and others, a text that takes enormous pleasure in obscene words.

Class, age, regional origin, profession, and ethnicity can be just as important as gender, says Connie C. Eble, whose "If Ladies Weren't Present, I'd Tell You What I Really Think" suggests that while taboo language is more common among males, venues (parties and male bonding sessions) are also important. In common with many female researchers, Eble believes that women tend in their conversations to foreground love and affection rather than sex itself. That assumption, of course, may well reinforce the socially constructed stereotype that women are "nicer," more responsible, and more concerned with interaction than males, whose expression is assumed to be aggressive, sexist, and detached (not to say fixated on snails and puppy-dog tails). Sally Yerkovich's "Gossiping as a Way of Speaking," which asserts that women gossip in order to build relationships and share information rather than to denigrate each other, may suffer from the same syndrome of counterstereotyping. That folklore might persist in the laboratory should surprise no one, and, in the interests of equity, women should be free to construct their own; the irony is that such stereotypes often merely invert those common to male discourse.

GAY, LESBIAN, AND ETHNIC DISCOURSE

The linguistic pools of American gender subcultures have actually lured scholars for several decades. One of the earliest was Gershon Legman, who wrote with his usual panache about gloriously explicit slang in "The Language of Homosexuality: An American Glossary." There followed "A Glossary of Homosexual Slang," by another stalwart in the field of sexology, A. F. Niemoller. Bruce Rodgers' *The Queen's Vernacular: A Gay Lexicon*, also published as *Gaytalk*, is more up-to-date than either Legman or Niemoller. Leonard Ashley's "Dyke Diction: The Language of Lesbians" draws on publications such as *Vice Versa* (1947–1948), the first lesbian magazine in America. The essays in *Gayspeak: Gay Male and Lesbian Communication*, edited by James W. Chesebro, consider oppressive heterosexual "labels" for gays and lesbians, the gender implications of pronouns, the changes in gay and lesbian slang as marginal groups have grown stronger, the nexus of power and language, lexicons of expressions, and the verbal and nonverbal cues by which lesbians recognize each other. Chesebro's is an indispensable volume. A more entertaining approach is *Word's Out: Gay Men's English*, by William Leap, who tries to parse the differences between gay and straight communication. Judy Grahn discusses linguistic signifiers as cultural constructions, as well as other matters of rhetoric and usage, in *Another Mother Tongue: Gay Words, Gay Worlds*. The essays in *Queer Words, Queer Images: Communication and the Construction of Homosexuality*, edited by R. Jeffrey Ringer, argue that language constructs gender and that discourse private and public keeps homosexuality controversial. The premise inherent in such studies is that while sex is a fact, gender is an idea, a construct best explored by the markers we use to designate difference. Gays themselves can be sexist, racist, and demeaning in their language, says Julia P. Stanley in "When We Say 'Out of the Closets,' " which finds that gays cleave to patriarchal practice of reifying other gays. (Any number of articles observe that the same can be said of feminists, of course.) One of the very best essays on the subject of gendered language, however, is Ruthann Robson's "Pedagogy, Jurisprudence, and Finger-Fucking: Lesbian Sex in a Law School Classroom." Robson notes not only that American jurisprudence is "ignorant of lesbian sexuality" (35) but also that the average law student does not understand the sexual terminology of other genders.

Folklorists have also mined the rich veins of black obscene and sexual humor partly because black idiom feeds mainstream linguistic currents, partly because the narratives are fascinating in themselves. Clarence Major traces expressions from various black subcultures (e.g., prison, drug, prostitute, jazz and blues populations) in *Juba to Jive: A Dictionary of African-American Slang* and explores not only historical variations but also the social dynamics of usage. Part of Edith A. Folb's comprehensive *Runnin' Down Some Lines: The Language and Culture of Black Teenagers* is focused on sexual vernaculars of both young men (pejorative for women) and women (explicit but less negative); the bawdiness is quite rich.

PORNOGRAPHY AS SOURCE OF SEXUAL DISCOURSE

Is pornography a representation of unauthorized desire, or does pornography authorize it? Can a woman fantasize about cunnilingus with another woman, or must language first represent the act for her? The issue is complex. Americans have complained for years that sexuality beggars language, that there are few polite terms for intercourse (*fuck* is too harsh for many tastes) and even fewer for specific acts (*fellatio* is stilted, while *blow job* seems too slangy; *cunnilingus* trips the tongue, while *go down on* strikes many as weird, and *suck* or *lick* thus seems to win by default). How many women have missed out on pleasure because they could not bring themselves to use vulgar terms for activities they desired or, perhaps, did not know they desired—or detested, for that matter? If there is no term for the activity, can the activity exist in a postmodern world? What exactly is the "essentialism" involved?

Given the way language works, which is to say collectively and mysteriously, few novelties are more fraught with danger than the postmodern assumption that scholars can invent a universal discourse of sexuality, one reason that opponents use slang like *pomo* to undercut the postmodernist excess of academics unable to curb their dogmas. Pomo arrogance aside, however, we do need extended study of the ways in which levels of sexual discourse intersect, junctures that can be approached from linguistic, anthropological, political—and lots of other—perspectives. It is not simply a matter of the distinctions to be drawn among words like *sodomize, bugger*, and *cornhole*, nor is it a question of linguistic enrichment, as in the adoption of *deep throat* to designate a confidential source. The problems lie in the different *meanings* of messages such as the following: a traditional "filthy" joke and a sanitized version of it on *Playboy*'s "Party Jokes" page; two female roommates swapping information on how to give a boyfriend a proper blow job as opposed to two gay men speaking of the same technique; a lonely female executive on a business trip, talking intimately by long-distance to her husband back home, and a teenager making his first call to a dial-a-porn service; a description of a particular sexual act, in Latin, in an early twentieth-century sex manual, and the description of a similar act in an ad for a porn magazine in 1978, such as this one from Erik Imports ("He fucks her everywhere but in her ears, and she takes it all and asks for more!"); a dominatrix instructing her "slave," and Senator Helms inveighing against homosexuals for the *Congressional Record*; Eysenek's calculus of obscenity, and a courtroom description of an obscene performance; a theologian's characterization of sex as an ideal expression of love and respect, and the radical feminist's depiction of sex as invariably violent and degrading. Every sexual subculture has its own vocabulary, nuanced by and for degrees of pleasure and complicity, as Thomas E. Murray and Thomas R. Murrell make clear in *The Language of Sadomasochism: A Glossary and Linguistic Analysis*.

Madeline Kripke identifies various linguistic and rhetorical elements in a famous pornographic genre in "The Lingo of the Tijuana Bibles." Kripke uses categories such as alliteration, puns, traditional jokes, limericks, doggerel, ersatz regional speech dialects, demeaning racial and cultural stereotypes, occupational jargon, and underworld and sports lingo. The linguistic subworld of the pornographic film can serve as another example. The medium is not noted for its articulateness, since a hard-core sound track is usually filled with monosyllabic grunts of ecstasy. Even so, most Americans know that *deep throat* can refer to an act in which a penis is orally engulfed *or* a hidden source revealing confidential information. Describing the content of triple-X films requires succinct phrasing (e.g., deep throat) that has little in common with medical terms for intercourse. For instance, reviewers of movies for *Adult Video News* need a flexible, colorful idiom. Consider the problem of translating into language a scene in which a man and woman are engaged in anal intercourse: the woman is seated aside the reclining man, facing his legs so that a low camera angle can "read" both her crotch and her face. The official Kinsey Institute notation for that position is rendered as "[female ♀ symbol] sup [male ♂ symbol] dorsal/ventral seated An HT" for "female superior seated back-to-face heterosexual anal intercourse." Simplifying matters, *Adult Video News* calls the position "a reverse cowgirl anal," which is both precise and self-parodic. What is remarkable is that the term has become standard within five years and routinely appears on video box covers so that the customer will know what to expect. For additional information on pornography's generation of idiom, see Joseph Slade's "Inventing a Sexual Discourse: A Rhetorical Analysis of Adult Video Box Covers." Because traditions are fruitful, some scholar will sooner or later tackle the tendency of new pornographic discourses to voice sexuality as alliteration, and thus reproduce patterns identified by Kripke and Read. The captions on box covers that encapsulate sex scenes or accompany other highly explicit video frames, for example, usually describe the action in terms such as: "Jason plumbs her pulsating pussy" or "His ass itches for 12 inches of man-meat." Those expressions beg comparison with examples such as "Tim Tickled Tillie's Tits Till Tillie's Twat Tingled" that take up pages of Read's *Lexical Evidence from Folk Epigraphy in Western North America*. Another area awaiting exploration is the language-generating and altering effects of e-mail and the Internet. Thus far, though academics are fascinated by the new expressions created for on-line discourse, few have looked at electronic neologisms for sexual intercourse.

Pornography engenders anger and confusion when we believe that inappropriate classes are enjoying erotic stimulation—low rather than high, or even vice versa—and language sometimes carries such implications. One of pornography's missions is to tame a sexuality that often defeats language, but the word *pornography* itself means so many things to so many people that those who would study it frequently propose the alternative *sex materials*. Too often, we use *pornography* to anathematize people, behavior, or texts that we do not like; the word itself marginalizes and oppresses. Producers of sex materials have learned more painfully than postmodern theorists that language shapes epistemology; Ralph Ginzburg went to jail not for publishing obscene material but for advertising it in language that "pandered." Our frustration with linguistic slipperiness, however, should not prevent appreciation of the contributions sexual representation can make to language.

FOLKLORE AND OBSCENITY: RHYMES, SONGS, BALLADS, AND STORIES

We can hardly hope to sketch all the types of bawdy, obscene, or porno-graphic songs, jokes, and stories by which Americans have traditionally de-lighted themselves and each other. Folklore is international, and the field is vast. Folklore—the demotic ("low") rendering of a human sexual imagination—serves as the fountainhead of obscenity and pornography, a cultural id inchoate in its fecundity. Much is uncollected, fugitive, ephemeral, and, most important, still alive—a factor that makes field-workers as important as bibliographers and lexicographers. The rise of mass media that eventually recycle every scrap of a culture's discourses makes the folklorist's task more difficult. Folklore, magic, rituals, legends, and stories are everywhere, but some are more authentic than others. In *American Folklore and the Mass Media*, Linda Dégh refers to a con-stellation she calls "folklore-fakelore-folklure" (the terms represent descending degrees of authenticity). Television audiences "can never be certain whether what they perceive as genuine tradition, folk belief, surviving myth debris, or archetypes projected on the television screen by the collective unconscious is or is not the well-tailored product created by Madison Avenue experts on the basis of computerized research results" (42). Ethnographers and anthropologists some-times try to distinguish between pornographic representations advanced by tech-nology and bawdy, ribald, and vulgar expression authenticated by orality.[1] One can trace particular tropes—"women prefer men with large penises"—to tradi-tional sources, but newer myths—"pornography causes rape"—would seem to be just as much authentic expressions of the credulous. "All folklore is erotic," Legman says.[2] If that be true, then virtually every folklorist and historian of subliterary genres has something to contribute.

For a long time, scholars refused to investigate sexual material, and those who did sometimes adopted pseudonyms to protect themselves. Lingering prej-udices stem not just from the usual sexual pathologies shared by Americans but from strong class biases and assumptions. In an important article in the *Journal of American Folklore*, "The Role of Obscenity in the Folk Tales of the 'Intel-lectual Stratum' of Our Society," Richard A. Waterman observes that American academics and intellectuals often classify a story as "folklore" rather than as an aspirant to "literary" status if the narrative contains obscenity. Arguments over whether obscene materials are fit subjects of study and, if so, whether they should be published in unexpurgated form constitute an ongoing debate in the pages of that journal and others.

As Gershon Legman has remarked in the Introduction to his "Erotic Folksongs and Ballads: An International Bibliography," "Folklore is the voice of those who have no other voice, and would not be listened to if they did. Of no part of folklore is this more true—folksongs and ballads, folklife, language, artifacts, dances and games, superstitions and all the rest—than of the sexual parts" (417). In 1962 the *Journal of American Folklore* published the proceedings of a "Symposium on Obscenity in Folklore" organized by Frank Hoffmann and Tristram Coffin. Notable among those papers, all of which deal with how scholars should approach the subject, are "Misconceptions in Erotica Folklore," in which Legman points out that investigators should be motivated not by prurience (though there is nothing particularly wrong with that) but by a genuine need to understand the roots of storytelling and expression; "Folklore and Obscenity: Definitions and Problems," in which Herbert Halpert speculates on just what makes an instance of bawdiness obscene; and "Say Something Dirty!" in which Horace P. Beek argues that dirty language, jokes, and stories are as worthy of analysis as any other kind. The rationale of the symposium is that obscene folklore has merit precisely because it is not nice, not well behaved, not even rational—and is therefore authentic and primal in a way that polished stories and polite jokes are not.

According to Legman, little since the symposium has appeared on the subject ("Erotic Folksongs and Ballads" [454]), although that is not quite the case. In addition to Legman's own account of battles among famous folklorists in his recent "Unprintable Folklore? The Vance Randolph Collection," Rayna Green has challenged biases in her splendid essay, "Folk is a Four-Letter Word: Dealing with Traditional _____ in Fieldwork, Analysis, and Presentation." Frank Hoffmann's *Analytical Survey of Anglo-American Traditional Erotica* remains one of the best book-length treatments of erotic folklore. First Hoffmann deals with erotic elements as they recur in oral traditions as transcribed in various media, then arranges some 400 erotic folklore types keyed to the classification schemes and motif index in *The Types of the Folktale: A Classification and Bibliography* by Antti Aarne and Stith Thompson and *Motif-Index of Folk Literature: A Classification of Narrative Elements in Folktales, Ballads, Myths, Fables, Medieval Romances, Exempla Fabliaux, Jestbooks, and Local Legends* by Thompson (see **Folklore and Humor** in Chapter 4). Hoffmann's enormous erudition is the cornerstone of scholarship in American oral pornography, but the volume can be difficult to find. Hoffmann's "Prolegomena to a Study of Traditional Elements in the Erotic Film" is of particular interest because of his demonstration that folklore both influences the early American stag film and provides narratives, motifs, and characters for the genre. From time to time appears an article like Ronald I. Baker's "Lady Lil and Pisspot Pete," an analysis of a song attributed to Eugene Field. Legman himself, in "A Summer Reading List to End All Summer Reading Lists," recommends a series of classic books on folklore often regarded as pornographic, including Gould and Pyle's *Anomalies and Curiosities of Medicine*, McClure's *Dark Brown*, Abrahams' *Deep Down in the Jungle*, Read's *Lexical Evidence from Folk Epigraphy*, Legman's *The Limerick: 1700 Examples*, Lewin's *Phantastica: Narcotic and Stimulating Drugs*, Bourke's *Scatalogic Rites of All Nations*, Sanford's *Seventy Times Seven*, and La Glannége's *Oragenitalism*.

Even so, the historical scholarship has been erratic. Many of the classic bibliographies devote sections to folklore. (See **Folklore and Humor** in Chapter

4, especially Ashbee; Clowes; Dawes; Hayn, Gotendorf, and Englisch; Kearney (1981); Gay and Lemonnyer; Hickerson; Pia; and the *Bilderlexicon*.) Some histories of pornographic literature begin with folklore; Patrick J. Kearney's *A History of Erotic Literature*, for example, generously samples ancient stories, parodies, and songs. In fact, the standard format for histories of sexual expression used to call for excursions into folklore. By contrast, largely ahistorical poststructuralist commentaries give precedence to typographical sources. For the serious scholar, the point of departure for study of American sexual folklore is the massive work of Gershon Legman, whose own scholarship literally defines the field. Two works are indispensable. The first is Legman's classic *The Horn Book: Studies in Erotic Folklore and Bibliography*, especially the chapter "Toward a Motif-Index of Erotic Humor" (reprinted in the *Journal of American Folklore*). The chapter attempts to lay the groundwork for an erotic index similar to the international bibles of folklorists by Thompson and by Aarne and Thompson. Even more important is Legman's own recent "Erotic Folksongs and Ballads: An International Bibliography" (for Aarne and Thompson, and Legman, see chapter 4, **Bibliographies and Reference Tools**). The real subtext of Legman's massive list—far longer than this chapter of this book—is that there are erotic worlds still beyond our ken.

The authority on erotica in the colonial and revolutionary periods is Peter Wagner. Wagner's *Eros Revived: Erotica of the Enlightenment in England and America* traces the importation of erotic works from England and the Continent to America. Chapter 9, "Erotica in Early America," is invaluable because of its insights and notes. Wagner examined materials in period libraries rather than the speech that enlivened streets, taverns, and blacksmith shops. His "Eros Goes West: European and 'Homespun' Erotica in Eighteenth-Century America" is likewise better on print media, but Wagner acknowledges the importance of folklore and the oral traditions that transmitted stories and songs. *Erotica*, Wagner says in the latter work, means "bawdy, obscene, erotic, and pornographic works, including satire and scatological humour, which often employ sexual elements. The term not only covers prose fiction and poetry but also non-fiction, such as medical and paramedical works (e.g., sex guides and treatises on venereal diseases), 'chroniques scandaleuses' dealing with the love-affairs of the high and mighty, and anti-clerical publications based on fact and fiction" (145–146).

Relevant here are two books by Leslie Shepard, both of which explore transatlantic forms: *The Broadside Ballad: A Study in Origins and Meaning*, which treats the vulgar broadside as an expression of popular obsession and feeling and characterizes the impulse toward obscenity as human and democratic; and *The History of Street Literature: The Story of Broadside Ballads, Chapbooks. Etc.*, which also does not shy away from explicit invective and low types of humor. Cathy Lynn Preston's "The Tying of the Garter: Representations of the Female Rural Laborer in 17th-, 18th-, and 19th-Century English Bawdy Songs" is a sparkling study of the female body as a commodity in bawdy lyrics sung in England and America. Klaus Roth compares some fifty erotic English folk songs on the subject of adultery with a similar number in German in terms of motifs, origins, and function in *Ehebruchschwänke in Lied Form.*

The scholarly work of record on ballads in English, many of which, of course, traveled to America, is Francis J. Child's five-volume *The English and Scottish Popular Ballads*, although the erotic material is expurgated. It should be used in conjunction with Tristram P. Coffin's *The British Traditional Ballad in North America*, which is not so chary of the explicit. For the "real thing," however, scholars must look to the work of John S. Farmer, distinguished lexicographer, linguist, folklorist, cocompiler of the greatest of all dictionaries of English slang but also cheerful hack writer of pornographic works. Among his several volumes on the subject, *Merry Songs and Ballads Prior to the Year 1800 and Musa Pedestris* is the most rewarding. Farmer infuses his collection with commentary on early English obscene ballads and songs, many of which were sung in the American colonies, together with slanging rhymes and other bawdy lyrics drawn from folklore. The 1964 New York edition of this work, originally published privately for fear of prosecution, contains an Introduction by Legman on Farmer's career as pornographer and philologist. The broadside form was kept alive by southerners, at least until the Civil War, as E. L. Rudolph demonstrates in *Confederate Broadside Verse.*

Until the 1920s, scholars were reticent about the raucous, irrepressible sexuality woven into the folklore of so many regions. Beginning in that decade, two trends began to reshape American folklore research. One was the emergence of a bolder school of anthropology whose advocates viewed sexuality as a key to understanding the dynamics of other cultures. The ur-text here was *The Sexual Life of the Savages*, for which Bronislaw Malinowski studied the inhabitants of the Trobriand Islands of Papua New Guinea. It was a publishing sensation, as the "liberated" subjects of Malinowski's research became surrogate objects of intense American interest. Other major studies followed, of which Margaret Mead's *Sex and Temperament in Three Primitive Societies* is representative.

The second trend was the sub-rosa publication of genuinely explicit folklore. In 1927 Joseph Fliesler, writing under the pseudonyms "J. Mortimer Hall" and "William Passemon," published an important, if not always scholarly, study/compilation called *Anecdota Americana, Being Explicitly an Anthology of the Tales in the Vernacular*, originally issued at the Gotham Book Mart in New York (though with the imprint of Humphrey Adams of Boston). Bell Books reissued the original version, slightly altered, in 1981 as *The Classic Book of Dirty Jokes*. A second volume, also purportedly by "J. Mortimer Hall," but not (according to Legman) by Joseph Fliesler, called *Anecdota Americana. An Anthology of Tales in the Vernacular Edited without Expurgation. By J. Mortimer Hall. Second Series*, with another 500 stories, appeared in 1934, published by Vincent Smith, again under the imprint Humphrey Adams. Brandon House in 1968 reprinted that edition in a two volume set as *The Unexpurgated Anecdota Americana*. Samuel Roth sanitized the tales and anecdotes in 1933 as *Anecdota*

Americana: Five Hundred Stories for the Amusement of the Five Hundred Nations That Comprise America on one of his presses and in slightly different form on still others; the book's publishing history is fascinating because it reveals the many enterprises (Faro, Nesor) operated by Roth in vain attempts to escape official scrutiny. Roth revised the text once more in 1944 as *The New Anecdota Americana*. Publishing histories of erotica make for considerable bibliographic confusion, though it has been reduced by Gershon Legman's immensely learned "Erotic Folksongs and Ballads: An International Bibliography" and by C. J. Scheiner's highly valuable *Compendium*, to both of which this account is indebted. The point, lest it be lost, is that the subterfuges, the clandestinity, and the piracies are themselves folkloristic elements.

Almost as important as *Anecdota Americana*, with the same academic reservations, is L. Brovan and C. Brovan's *The Way of a Virgin*, one of the pioneering studies of obscene folklore and humor. It examines stories about virgins and their deflowerings drawn from world literature. According to C. J. Scheiner, it was first published in London in 1922 as *Anthologica Rarissima. Volume I. The Way of a Virgin*, by the "Brovan Society," and reprinted by Jack Brussel in a New York edition in 1927 (but with the same publishing imprints as the original). T. R. Smith, an editor at Boni and Liveright, surreptitiously published *Immortalia: An Anthology of American Ballads, Sailors' Songs, Cowboy Songs, College Songs, Parodies, Limericks, and Other Humorous Verses and Doggerel Now for the First Time Brought Together in Book Form by a Gentleman About Town*. In addition to the material named in the title, it included contributions by Eugene Fields, e. e. cummings, and (questionably) James Joyce. Earlier, Boni and Liveright had put its own imprint on Smith's *Poetica Erotica: A Collection of Rare and Curious Amatory Verse* (not to be confused with a 1938 volume of the same title, an edition of works by Eugene Field, James Whitcomb Riley, and Benjamin Franklin). The volume was heavily indebted to Farmer's *Merry Songs and Ballads*, many of whose lyrics Smith reproduced. *Facetia Americana*, still another privately printed volume, less ambitiously collected "Fireside Conversation," "A French Crisis," "Little Willie," and "The Old Backhouse," fiction by Eugene Field and other Americans. By now, clandestine publishers had appeared in unlikely American cities like Cincinnati, where the "Sinners Club" (William C. Smith) printed *Blue Law Ballads*, a particular species of local Americana; the ballads were aimed at hypocritical Puritans and prohibitionists.

Two foci of interest, authentic anthropological curiosities, on one hand, and low material clandestinely circulated, on the other, converged when marginal publishing houses, emboldened by the semirespectability of books like Malinowski's, began printing quasi-anthropological and quasi-medical texts on unusual sexual practices and preferences and selling them by mail. (For an extraordinarily rich account of these publishers and the legal difficulties they encountered, see Jay Gertzman's *Bookleggers and Smuthounds* in **Publishers and Booksellers** in chapter 16.) A short list of examples from the 1930s could include *Anomalies and Curiosities of Medicine* by George M. Gould and Walter

L. Pyle; *Anthropological Studies of Sexual Relations of Mankind* by Paolo Mantegazza; *Encyclopedia Sexualis*, edited by Victor Robinson; *American Encyclopedia of Sex* by Adolph Niemoller; *Coercion and Perversion: Or Primeval Degenerates* by H. Kincaid Murray; and *Crossways of Sex* and *Untrodden Fields of Anthropology* by the prolific "Dr. Jacobus X." Despite their titillating subject matter, some of these were serious works. H. Kincaid Murray's tome attacked sexual ignorance and the lack of education in the United States, which the author thought led to repression, mental disorders, and personal tragedy.

More important for the discipline of folklore, scholars themselves became more courageous, albeit slowly. Starting in the 1920s, expurgated, asterisked, or highly "selective" collections of nonetheless questionable songs began to appear with cautious commentary. A representative sampling includes *Folk Songs of the South*, a regional grouping compiled by John Harrington Cox; *The Songs My Mother Never Taught Me*, risqué marching, working, and drinking songs compiled by John Jacob Niles, Douglas Moore, and A. A. Wallgren; *My Pious Friends and Drunken Companions* and *More Pious Friends and Drunken Companions*, sentimental, but borderline, drinking songs compiled by Frank Shay; *Iron Men and Wooden Ships*, sea chanteys and sailors' ballads, also compiled by Shay; *American Tramp and Underworld Slang . . . with a Selection of Tramp Songs*, lyrics and verses prized by hobos and wanderers, compiled by Godfrey Irwin; and *The Hobo's Handbook: A Repertory for a Gutter Jongleur*, a similar collection, compiled by George Milburn. All of these were expurgated to one degree or another, could be described now as off-color rather than obscene, but seemed daring at the time. Even the bowdlerized versions articulated what acceptable songs could not. As Sandra Perry points out in "Sex and Sentiment in America or What Was Really Going On between the Staves of Nineteenth Century Songs of Fashion," the general inability of Americans to sing of adult sexual relationships fostered sublimation in themes of death and loss in genteel parlors and music halls. By contrast, bawdy songs affirmed life, but only in less respectable venues more receptive to raucous evocations of intercourse.

John Henry Johnson's *Bawdy Ballads and Lusty Lyrics* was more ribald, as was James R. Masterson's *Tall Tales of Arkansas*, which pushed against limits, though neither went as far as Louis W. Chapple's *Folk-Songs of Roanoke and the Albermarle*, considered a pioneering field-study because it captured items that still reddened the faces of most scholars. Just how risky this was is evident from the history of A. Reynolds Morse's anonymously and privately published *Folk Poems and Ballads: An Anthology: A Collection of Rare Verses and Amusing Folk Songs Compiled from Scarce and Suppressed Books as Well as from Verbal Sources, Which Modern Prudery, False Social Customs and Intolerance Have Separated from the Public and Historical Record*. It was instantly seized by the police, along with a Morse-edited book of limericks, as soon as it appeared in 1948 and was not reissued for another forty years. Highly sanitized anthologies compiled during the late 1950s include Alan Lomax's *The Folk Songs of North America*, a very comprehensive collection with excellent criticism but expurgated examples; Oscar Brand's *Bawdy Songs and Backroom Ballads*, whose contents, despite the title, are pretty innocuous; and Louis Untermeyer's *A Treasury of Ribaldry*, whose good taste renders the comment largely worthless. The Olympia Press in Paris printed about sixty bawdy poems and ribald songs, a few with music, as *Count Vicarion's Book of Bawdy Ballads* in 1959; the edition was compiled by Christopher Logue under the name "Palmiro Vicarion."

The liberalism of the 1960s made things easier in America. Female folklorists began showing an interest in bawdy songs and in reprinting unexpurgated versions for study. Edith Fowke brought out an unbowdlerized *Traditional Singers and Songs from Ontario*. *Songs of the Cowboys*, collected by N. Howard Thorp and edited by Austin Fife and Alta Fife, restored some songs left out of earlier western compilations. *Songs of the American West*, edited by Richard E. Lingenfelter et al., included some very bawdy songs and ballads. The truly raunchy, authentic cowboy song finally appeared in Guy Logsdon's *"The Whorehouse Bells Were Ringing," and Other Songs Cowboys Sing*. Despite these milestones, only a handful of folklorists collected undeniably obscene material, and they could not or did not print it in raw form. Many of these collections, usually in typescript duplicated at several sites to avoid loss, still repose in folklore archives in universities around the United States. In the Indiana University Folklore Archives and other repositories, for instance, are copies of Kenneth Larson's "Barnyard Folklore of Southeastern Idaho: A Collection of Vulgar Verses, Jokes, and Popular Ballads, All of Them Unprintable, Obtained by Word-of-Mouth from Those Who [Were] Entertained by Them (mostly Farmers, Laborers, and Students) . . . during the Years from 1920 to 1952." It and other treasures await publication in a more relaxed climate. One of those troves has just made its public appearance. In the late 1940s, Floyd Shoemaker edited Vance Randolph's *Ozark Folksongs*, leaving out the bawdy and obscene ones. Frank Hoffmann edited a small section of the omitted material a quarter century later as Randolph's *Pissing in the Snow & Other Ozark Folktales*, with an Introduction praising Randolph's stewardship by Rayna Green. Gershon Legman has just edited all of the forbidden files into two volumes, Randolph's *Roll Me in Your Arms: "Unprintable" Ozark Folksongs and Folklore* and *Blow the Candle Out: "Unprintable" Ozark Folklore*.

Tracing editions can be enormous fun for aficionados. For example, in 1965, under the name E. R. Linton, Edward B. Cray compiled *The Dirty Song Book: American Bawdy Songs*, a collection of almost 100 popular bawdy lyrics, for Medco Books, a publisher of pornographic texts. The book was updated as *The Erotic Muse* in 1969. Brandon House, another porn publisher, printed *The Fifteen Plagues of the Maidenhead and Other Forbidden Verse*, another 100 songs and ballads, most from the seventeenth and eighteenth centuries, with historical annotations by Cray under his real name in 1966. Finally, the University of Illinois brought out Cray's *The Erotic Muse: American Bawdy Songs*, with a much more scholarly, critical apparatus as the climate for publication of traditional obscenity improved. Cray's experience as a compiler resembles Legman's own. Several other collections merit attention. Jerry Silverman's *The Dirty Song Book* offers unscholarly comment on what he calls an American heritage of songs, some of which are given music and guitar chords. This is a very popular text, having been featured by Barnes and Noble for years. Timothy D. Gilbert's *The Naughty and the Bawdy* contains lewd songs, rhymes, wisecracks, and limericks, with annotations. John Milton Hagen's *Lecherous, Licentious, Lascivious Lyrics* is just what its title claims.

The earthy aspects of black urban and rural folklore are evident even in a standard volume that does not focus on sexuality, *The Book of Negro Folklore*, edited by Arna Bontemps and Langston Hughes. But explicitness figures heavily in one of the finest examples of scholarship on the subject, Roger D. Abrahams' *Deep Down in the Jungle: Negro Narrative Folklore from the Streets of Philadelphia*, the result of fieldwork that gathered urban tales; Abrahams presents them in unexpurgated form, with anthropological commentary. Daryl Cumber Dance also conducted extensive fieldwork to collect material for her collection, *Shuckin' and Jivin': Folklore From Contemporary Black Americans*. The obscene and the bawdy, she observes, offer ways of coping with stress, loss, and disappointment but also provide avenues of expression for exuberance, aggression, and affection; salty jokes, "toasts," boasts, myths, and so on code for a range of emotions, responses, and information. In *Mother Wit from the Laughing Barrel: Readings in the Interpretation of Afro-American Folklore*, Alan Dundes brings together essays by folklorists on black stories, sexual mythologies (e.g., the legendary size of the black penis), "toasts," jokes, songs, verse, and invective. Herbert L. Foster explores black erotic verse and oral tales in *Ribbin', Jivin', and Playin' the Dozens*. Probably the most comprehensive collection, historically contextualized and culturally analyzed, is Bruce Jackson's masterfully rendered *"Get Your Ass in the Water and Swim like Me": Narrative Poetry from the Black Oral Tradition*; the commentary, quite simply, is magisterial. As the title of another work suggests, Jackson's *"Wake Up Dead Man": Afro-American Worksongs from Texas Prisons* gathers material from criminal strata, as does *The Life: The Lore and Folk Poetry of the Black Hustler*, for which Dennis Wepman, Ronald B. Newman, and Murray B. Binderman recorded the voices of convicted pimps and drug addicts; it is an especially fine study of the bawdy "toast," a mocking form of salute. An exceptional bibliography rounds off the volume. David Evans also explores the form's obscene rationale and meaning in "The Toast in Context."

EROTIC POETRY

William Cole's *Erotic Poetry: The Lyrics, Ballads, Idyls and Epics of Love— Classical to Contemporary* is basically an updating of T. R. Smith's *Poetica Erotica* to include Anne Sexton and other contemporary American poets. Harold H. Hart edited a four-volume *Immortalia*, an anthology of limericks, sexual parodies, songs, riddles, poems, and jokes with a lot of material not in T. R. Smith's *Immortalia*. Hart reissued the work as *The Complete Immortalia*, and it was reissued yet again as *The Bawdy Bedside Reader*. One can find older anthologies of sensual verse, of course, such as G. W. Fitzwilliam's *Pleasures of Love: Being Amatory Poems*, published in 1808. By the late twentieth century, however, fault lines between amusing verse and more serious erotic poetry were visible enough that anthologists began to separate the more self-consciously artistic from the bawdy traditions of folklore and to package the material more tastefully. The title of Wendell S. Johnson's *Sex and Marriage in Victorian Poetry* is self-explanatory. The elegant contents contrast sharply with those of the anonymously collected *Poems Lewd and Lusty*, a volume probably compiled by its publisher, Harold Hart. J. M. Cohen's *The Penguin Book of Comic and Curious Verse, More Comic and Curious Verse*, and *Yet More Comic and Curious Verse* are perhaps the best collections of vernacular verse, according to Legman, who admires Cohen's editing and commentary.

Louis Untermeyer gathered fairly tame erotic poetry from mostly mainstream writers, including Americans such as e. e. cummings, into *An Uninhibited Treasury of Erotic Poetry*. More recent and less bowdlerized are Alan Bold's *Making Love: The Picador Book of Erotic Verse*, Derek Parker's *An Anthology of Erotic Verse*, John Whitworth's *The Faber Book of Blue Verse*, Sam Hamill's *The Erotic Spirit: An Anthology of Poems of Sensuality, Love, and Longing*, Anthony Howell's *Erotic Lyrics*, and Lawrence Sanders' *Thus Be Loved*. The entries in all of these range from ancient examples to modern, and the last volume is illustrated with photographs of women. Ara John Movsesian's interesting *Pearls of Love* is a guide to writing love letters and erotic poems. Lenore Kandel's volume of her own poems, *The Love Book*, is historically important because it was prosecuted in, of all places, San Francisco; its transgression was to combine religion and eroticism.

The ambiguity of poetry has lent itself well to the kind of indirection necessary to speak of homosexuality; anthologies can layer poems archaeologically, so that scholars can unearth homoerotic meaning in poems from the past. Three helpful anthologies of lesbian poems are *The Arc of Love: An Anthology of Lesbian Love Poems*, a knowledgeable history and survey by a psychotherapist and critic, Clare Coss; *Lesbian Poetry: An Anthology*, edited by Elly Bulkin and Joan Larkin, whose Introduction is first-rate; and *Wanting Women: An Anthology of Erotic Lesbian Poetry*, edited by Jan Hardy, who collects poems probably not familiar to modern readers and all the more valuable for that reason. *Articulate Flesh: Male Homoeroticism and Modern Poetry* is a critical history of mostly mainstream American gay poetry by Gregory Woods; Michael Ayres' *English Homosexual Poetry of the 19th and 20th Centuries* is a description and critique of the Timothy d'Arch Smith private collection of poems; Ian Young's *The Male Muse* anthologizes twentieth-century homosexual verse, including poetry by Tennessee Williams, Allen Ginsberg, Christopher Isherwood, and other well-known poets. *The Male Muse: Gay Poetry Anthology*, edited by Robert

Duncan and others, and *Eros: An Anthology of Friendship*, edited by Alistair Sutherland and Patrick Anderson, comment on gay erotic poems, including some drawn from Americans like Hart Crane. Worth noting also are two volumes by the celebrated erotic filmmaker and artist James Broughton: *Ecstasies: Poems, 1975–1983* and *Graffiti for the Johns of Heaven*.

BLUES, JAZZ, AND EARTHY MUSIC

William R. Ferris, now head of the National Endowment for the Humanities, traces a popular form of music to its roots in bawdy songs and black folklore in *Blues from the Delta*, as does Giles Oakley in *The Devil's Music: History of the Blues*. Other good historical commentaries on the sexuality of blues music include *The Poetry of the Blues*, by Samuel Charters; *Ain't Misbehavin'*, by W. T. Kirkeby and Sinclair Traill; and *Aspects of the Blues*, by Paul Oliver. These histories are replete with song titles that reflected the earthiness to be found at lower socioeconomic levels. Until the 1920s, music publishing and recording companies refused to print or record songs with titles like "If You Don't Like My Potatoes, How Come You Dig So Deep?" (1896). Gradually, however, as the 1920s burst into sexual flame, the bolder companies did bring out works such as "Please Warm My Wiener" and "Your Biscuits Are Big Enough for Me," gleefully smutty metaphors instantly recognizable to audiences. Beyond the double entendres were also subversions of gender, expressed as longings for lovers of the same sex. Lillian Faderman documents the lesbian lyrics and the homosexual subculture of the Harlem music scene in *Odd Girls and Twilight Lovers: A History of Lesbian Life in Twentieth-Century America*. "Fearless, unadorned realism is a distinctive feature of the blues," says Angela Y. Davis in "I Used to Be Your Sweet Mama: Ideology, Sexuality and Domesticity in the Blues of Gertrude 'Ma' Rainey and Bessie Smith": "Their depictions of sexual relationships are not distorted by the superficial idealizations of love characteristic of the American popular song tradition. Romantic love is seldom romanticized in the blues" (246). Though often labeled quasi-pornographic, lyrics such as "Need a Little Sugar for My Bowl," according to Davis, demonstrate that "the female characters are clearly in control of their sexuality, articulating it in a way that is exploitative neither of their partners nor of themselves" (240). Hazel V. Carby explores subversion and affirmation in "It Jus Be's Dat Way Sometime: The Sexual Politics of Women's Blues."

It is impossible to overstate the sexuality implicit in all forms of American music from jigs to ragtime. Work crews building mines, roads, canals, railroads, and farms eased their toil with lusty music celebrating a sexual lubricity equal to the energy devoted to creating a nation. The lyrics drew on fantasies that bonded, amusements that relieved toil. Ragtime was always whorehouse music pounded out by black pianists grateful for employment; competition for the jobs fostered talent. The sporting house incubated native American rhythms. The word "jazz," of course, once meant "fuck," and no thorough history of the form

omits discussion of its vulgar essence and powerful sensuality. Harry O. Brunn
tells the ur-story in *The Story of the Original Dixieland Jazz Band*: when Nick
LaRocca's New Orleans band played a Chicago nightclub one night in 1915, a
Mafia hood in the audience, using the local argot for intercourse, yelled, "Jass
it up, boys!" The next day the band renamed itself the Dixie Jass Band, and
imitators misspelled it before settling on *jazz* (21). Tales of jazz's corrupting
influence on youth swelled to legendary proportions. Paula Fass notes the appeal—composed, in part, of such myths—to flaming youth in *The Damned and
the Beautiful: American Youth in the 1920s*, though any history of the period
will expend several pages on the dire consequences attributed to listening to the
pagan, lascivious music. Kathy Peiss' *Cheap Amusements: Working Women and
Leisure in Turn of the Century New York* discusses the music that the lower
classes preferred at the turn of the century, as does Lewis Erenberg's *Steppin'
Out: New York Nightlife and the Transformation of American Culture*.

The irony is that bawdy folk songs have always fueled the American music
industry, a fact explored at length by Sidney Shemel and William Krasilowsky
in *The Business of Music*. Legman recommends the book because it discusses
the process of converting authentic bawdy folklore into sanitized and merchan-
isable songs. Legman himself writes on the commercial and cultural uses of
folklore in two essays in *The Horn Book*: "Who Owns Folklore?" and "Folksongs, Fakelore, and Cash." As an example of what he means, Legman in
"Erotic Folksongs and Ballads: An International Bibliography" calls a book such
as *Rowdy Rhymes and Bibulous Ballads* and others like it "expurgated semiero-
tica for the gifte-booke trade"; one of the volume's songs is "an object-lesson
in folklore faking" (483); that is, it isn't authentic folklore but has been crafted
for publication. In this category are works like *Libertine Lyrics*, a gathering of
songs from the seventeenth and eighteenth centuries, with a few American examples.

FAIRY TALES

Fairy tales have also energized mainstream narratives. In "The Instrumentalization of Fantasy: Fairy Tales and the Mass Media," Jack Zipes points out that
by the end of the eighteenth century the middle class had come to regard fairy
tales as "amoral because they did not uphold the virtues of order, discipline,
industry, modesty, and cleanliness, and they were regarded as particularly harmful for children because their imaginative components might suggest ways to
rebel against authoritative and patriarchal rule in the family" (98). At the same
time, says Zipes, in the hands of rebellious writers fairy tales became narratives
of subversion. Maureen Duffy examines some of the hidden sexual meanings
and implications of fairy tales in *The Erotic World of Faery*, as does Bruno
Bettelheim in *The Uses of Enchantment*. Today scholars are bringing powerful
feminist critiques to bear on folklore in general and fairy tales in particular. So
far, most have focused on mainstream, rather than marginal, examples. Marina

Warner's *From the Beast to the Blonde: On Fairy Tales and Their Tellers* analyzes the shifting images of women in fairy tales and the motives of a culture that produces them, and the chapter on "Beauty, Wealth, and Power: Career Choices for Women in Folktales, Fairy Tales, and Modern Media" (80–109) in Linda Dégh's *American Folklore and the Mass Media* closely examines the sexual lore attached to female celebrities in confession magazines and tabloids. The unique essays on language, orality, and visuality gathered by Thomas A. Sebeok as *Sight, Sound, and Sense* offer fresh insights on sexual aspects of folklore as well.

SEXUALITY, RELIGION, AND BLASPHEMY

Doubtless because early prosecutions for obscenity were actually directed at speech considered blasphemous, religious irreverence has, of course, never disappeared in America. Thomas Jefferson and James Madison, the latter functioning as the former's mouthpiece at the Constitutional Convention, took great pains to ensure that the principles of Jefferson's Virginia Statute for Religious Freedom be woven into the Constitution over the opposition of those who wished that Anglicanism become the national religion. As a consequence, no single church gained ascendancy, and blasphemy for Americans never acquired the cachet of subversion that it holds for other people. That did not forestall interest in scandalous works like Clifford Howard's semischolarly 1909 underground best-seller, *Sex Worship: An Exposition of the Phallic Origin of Religion*, which investigated the sexual roots of religion and organized discussion around a pretty recognizable symbol. Lee Alexander Stone's *The Story of Phallicism* is only slightly more respectable. B. Z. Goldberg's more scholarly *The Sacred Fire: The Story of Sex in Religion* deals at length with sexual energy as the driving force in religion, analyzes the sexual imagery of many creeds, and contains a pretty good bibliography. Best of all is Richard Payne Knight's *A Discourse on the Worship of Priapus* (1786), a small, but famous, text with a strange publishing history[3], it is most easily found in an edition called *Sexual Symbolism: A History of Phallic Worship*, which also includes (under Knight) Thomas Wright's *The Worship of the Generative Powers* (1866); neither makes much reference to America, but they are still interesting on the mythologies and religious practices that have long swirled about the phallus. (See also **Genitals and Their Folklore** in Chapter 9.)

L. J. King's *House of Death and Gate of Hell* is an example of a very limited American genre, the anticlerical "exposé" of convents and churches as hotbeds of desire and perversion; here are randy monks, lascivious abbesses, pregnant nuns, and, though Protestants do not get equal time, hypocritical ministers and inflamed choir singers. Moreover, many Americans have cherished the many salacious passages in the Bible and delight in pointing them out to the devout. *The Bible Handbook*, edited by W. P. Ball and G. W. Foote, is actually in its eleventh edition, a circumstance that attests to the enduring appeal of its comment on absurdities and obscenities in the Bible. B. E. Akerley tries harder to be amusing (and sometimes merely sniggers) in *The X-Rated Bible: An Irreverent Survey of Sex in the Scriptures*, which parades a large array of lewd and lascivious verses before the reader. Thomas M. Horner also mines a lot of Old Testament veins in *Sex in the Bible*, as does Jonathan Kirsch in the similar *The Harlot by the Side of the Road: Forbidden Tales of the Bible*. G. L. Simons explores sexual myths and old wives' tales in *Sex and Superstition*. A focus on magical aids to arousal reaches back at least to Pascal Beverly Randolph, a nineteenth-century American theorist whose *Sexual Magic* influenced the Rosicrucians and the Order of the Golden Dawn. In *Sex and the Occult*, Gordon Wellesley ranges over the sexual elements inherent in magic, witchcraft, and mysticism.

POPULAR SEX MYTHS

The "factual" documentation of popular sexual lore varies according to the skill and intent of compilers, but five books in that category are readable and, in the main, accurate. They are *Sex: Facts, Frauds, and Follies* by Thomas S. Szasc; *The Simons Book of World Sexual Records* by G. L. Simons; *Secret and Forbidden* by Paul Tabori; *The Intimate Sex Lives of Famous People* by the novelist Irving Wallace and his family; and *The World's Most Sensational Sex Lives* by Nigel Blundell. All are sexual histories of events and personalities, some bizarre, some common enough to be found in the *Guinness Book of World Records*; they list oddities and dates and aim deliberately at prurient interest. Exceptionally readable is *Sexual Myths and Fallacies*, by psychologist James Leslie McCary, who lists dozens of firmly held beliefs, from the notion that "there is a difference between vaginal and clitoral orgasms," to the conviction that "homosexuals are more creative than heterosexuals" and the hope that "pornography and obscenity lead to sexual excess and sexual acting out." McCary also quotes Malcolm Muggeridge's famous remark: "if the purpose of pornography is to excite sexual desire, then it is unnecessary for the young, inconvenient for the middle-aged, and unseemly for the old" (161).

Another author to assay legends is Sarah Dening, in *The Mythology of Sex: An Illustrated Exploration of Sexual Customs and Practices from Ancient Times to the Present*, a treatise on the shaping of myths pertaining to homosexuality, polygamy, incest, marriage, divorce, and various sexual behaviors. Myths have a positive function as well, of course. In a deliberate attempt to shore up gay consciousness by providing it with a foundation of tradition, Will Roscoe compiles stories about homosexuality from the world's mythologies and augments them with materials drawn from erotica and mainstream literature in *Queer Spirits: A Gay Men's Myth Book*. Similarly, one can read the interviews and reminiscences gathered by Susan E. Johnson for *Lesbian Sex: An Oral History* as myth, as underground history, as authentic oral expression, or as political speech. (See **Recovering a "Pornographic" Past: Histories of Homosexual**

Subcultures in chapter 5.) Myth segues effortlessly into custom, however, and from there into compilations of behaviors (for texts on sexual practices, see the section on **Sexual Subcultures** in Chapter 4, especially Bloch, Camphausen, Davenport, Goodland, Ellis and Abarbanel, Gelb, Love, Robinson, and Schmidt).

Vern Bullough and Bonnie Bullough chronicle the stranger beliefs of Americans, including misconceptions about pornography, in *Sin, Sickness and Sanity: A History of Sexual Attitudes*; their *Sexual Attitudes: Myths and Realities* is an updating. John C. Burnham's *Bad Habits: Drinking, Smoking, Taking Drugs, Gambling, Sexual Behavior, and Swearing in American History*, whose general thesis is that time makes previously unacceptable sexual behavior and discourse commonplace, is very readable and full of wonderful anecdotes. Richard Zaks draws on diaries, personal confessions, love letters, poems, jokes, and other sources for his *History Laid Bare: Love, Sex and Perversity from the Ancient Etruscans to Warren G. Harding*. The predecessor of these works is *Our Lusty Forefathers: Being Diverse Chronicles of the Fervors, Frolics, Fights, Festivities, and Failings of Our American Ancestors* by Fairfax D. Downey, a very catholic treatment that skates across classes, regions, and occupations. (See also **Scandal Journalism**, in Chapter 17.)

Of immense historical value are Albert Ellis' two spaced volumes called *The Folklore of Sex*. The first, published in 1951, has been reprinted as *Sex Beliefs and Customs*. It is a splendid survey of ribald and scatological attitudes toward masturbation, nudity, abortion, pornography, prostitution, and birth control as manifest in fiction, women's, religious, and general interest magazines, men's magazines such as *Beauty Parade, Detective, Exotic, Eyeful, Flirt, Girl Models, Glance, Pic, Private Detective, Sir!, Uncensored Detective*, scientific journals, plays, newspapers, popular songs, and radio and television programming—on a single day, 1 January 1950. The second volume, published in 1961, is a follow-up study conducted exactly a decade later. The material analyzed here is drawn from newspapers of New York and other major American cities, together with movies, plays, television shows, and magazines for 1 January 1960. Though little known, Ellis' experiment is a fascinating foray into popular culture and American sexual mythology, an unparalleled attempt to sample popular American attitudes over a full ten years. Tristram P. Coffin has collected more gendered narratives in *The Female Hero in Folklore and Legend*, which contrasts legends with historical records regarding women like Susan B. Anthony, Mae West, Lydia E. Pinkham, Belle Starr, Sarah Bernhardt on her American tours, and other notable women sometimes metamorphosed by sexual fantasy. Similar is N. M. Penzer's *Poison-Damsels, and Other Essays in Folklore and Anthropology*, a compilation of sexual tales about femmes fatale. If listening to women talk about sex persuades Kate Fillion that it is false to say that men lust while women love or that women are not sexually aggressive, in *Lip Service: The Truth about Women's Darker Side in Love, Sex, and Friendship*, Naomi Wolf also sifts through folklore in order to understand female desire in *Promiscuities: The Secret Struggle for Womanhood*. Lana Thompson skewers untruths about women's sexuality in *The Wandering Womb: A Cultural History of Outrageous Beliefs about Women*. Any occasion can generate sexual humor. Of a host of instances, Parke Cummings' *The Whimsey Report: or, Sex Isn't Everything*, a parody of the first Kinsey Report, will suffice. Coffin's *A Proper Book of Sexual Folklore* is also highly readable. Deserving special attention is *Tool Box Scandals*, by "Petronius," the pen name of Joyce Greller, who combined explicit illustrations and photographs with jokes and stories because she feared they might be lost.

MYTHS ASSOCIATED WITH PORNOGRAPHY

Myths about pornography are irresistible. In addition to the fable of the Vatican Library's collection of pornography, cherished legends include reports of the circulation of "snuff films" in which women are allegedly literally killed at the climax of intercourse (no authentic snuff film has been uncovered, [4] although there is a mainstream film with *Snuff* as the title, and there do exist filmed records of executions and murders, but *not* coupled with sex); reports that various famous movie actresses started their careers in pornographic movies (various actors and actresses, like Hedy Lamarr in *Ecstasy* or Sylvester Stallone in *Italian Stallion*, have played nude scenes, but no major figure—unless we include Spaulding Gray [star of *Farmer's Daughter*, 1974], which stretches the limits of "major"—has ever appeared in a hard-core movie; various stag films advertised as featuring Marilyn Monroe, Joan Crawford, Barbra Streisand, Chuck Connors, and Ronald Reagan actually star look-a-likes); reports that the Nazis flooded Poland with pornography to destroy the moral resistance of the country (a story that appears to have been made up out of whole cloth); and reports that the American Office of Strategic Services (OSS) dropped pornography on Hitler's headquarters as a way of inducing surrender through masturbation.

In "Methodological and Conceptual Problems in the Study of Pornography and Violence," I. C. Jarvie mentions additional myths: "that the pornography industry is bigger than the film and rock music industries combined" (there are no accurate figures on the size of the "pornography industry," for the simple reason that no two statisticians seem to agree on what products are to be included); "that there is a hidden agenda in pornography which aims to break down sexual taboos and thus keep women in their place"; and "that there is a connection between viewing/producing pornography and crimes against women" (412). There are others. The scholar is advised to study "Sex Premises" by Barbara O'Dair and Abby Tallmer. The list of seventy-three popular assumptions "deconstructs" debate, say the authors, since some are false, and others are misleading. Number one is: "The male characters in pornography accurately portray male sexuality"; number three: "All men instinctively identify with male characters in pornography"; number 53: "Female sexuality is not genitally oriented"; number 60: "Pornography depicts unhealthy acts, and only unhealthy people enjoy it." Such folklore can often be traced to implicit and explicit mis-statements in marriage manuals, sex guides, religious texts, and ideological analyses of sex and gender.

All too often, critics accept bias as fact, as Harry Settani points out in "Pornography," a discussion of the ethical difficulty of separating knowledge and opinion. As a consequence, prevailing tastes, which tend to be middle-class, tend to be oppressive. The matter of taste is, of course, a complex one, since moral, aesthetic and sexual attitudes arise from a host of interacting sources, cultural and psychological. According to Mark Caldwell in *A Short History of Rudeness: Manners, Morals, and Misbehavior in Modern America*, a volume that deals at length with pornography, morality is not the same as manners, not the same as taste. Tastes may decline over time and generations without necessarily damaging the morality of the state or the individual. Apart from noting the aptness of the phrase *de gustibus non disputandem est* ("there is no arguing with taste"), one can roughly categorize tastes as conservative or tolerant. Conservatives as a rule condemn sexual expression because it ventures into areas of human conduct considered private and intimate. The conservative position, often lampooned, is often sincere; genuine conservatives are not hypocritical and do not read or view erotica on the sly. When the conservative links pornography to chaos and disorder, he or she is correct, since disruption is one of the functions of pornography. While liberal critics recognize this function as socially useful and may even want to institutionalize it (something of a contradiction in terms) by removing restrictions, they are often embarrassed by the language, the images, and the vision, all of which are vulgar.

Americans embrace other odd assumptions: that porn is monolithic in character and form; that masturbation is not evil but that it is somehow inauthentic and that porn can be faulted because it stimulates masturbation; that all pornography either degrades women or reflects a fear of women; that heterosexuals cannot understand gay sex but that homosexuals can understand heterosexual sexuality far better than straights themselves; that porn, by definition an expression of the forbidden, the private, and the marginal, is nonetheless central to our culture; and, above all, that people who enjoy reading or watching pornography are spiritually impoverished, politically incorrect, physically inept, psychologically warped, socially maladjusted, or economically swindled. For these reasons, it is probably fair to say that comment on pornography usually reveals as much about the critic as the subject, because, implicitly, the author defends his or her sexual/gender preferences while condemning those of others. Few even of those who defend pornography will publicly admit to enjoying it, just as they decline to admit enjoying intercourse or masturbation: it has always been risky to do so. As a consequence, the folklore with which we mask discussion of sex and its representations is easily perpetuated. Folklore can evince a touching optimism as well, especially when it suggests that the world is transparent to erotic obsession. My favorite examples are those that attempt to find sexual explanations for the sudden insights of human genius, as in the legend that Orson Welles chose "rosebud" to anchor the motifs of *Citizen Kane* because it was the name by which so many variously gendered Hollywood celebrities fondly referred to (William Randolph Hearst's mistress) Marion Davies' clitoris.

HUMOR: JOKES AND STORIES

In a sense, of course, it is pointless to separate folklore and humor, because the two interpenetrate each other. Some scholars treat them as separate categories, while others posit a common heritage. In "The Old Age of American Jestbooks," Paul M. Zall traces strains to European origins: "repartee from classical rhetoricians, exempla from medieval preachers, bawdy stories from Italian Humanists, scatology from German burghers, parables from Eastern sages, and current quips from Drury Lane, Fleet Street, and Windsor Castle" (3). Several historians explore other early manifestations of American humor, some of which were borrowed from England but all of which included elements of the scurrilous, the bawdy, or the off-color. J. P. Siegel's "Puritan Light Reading" finds that early Americans were fond of humorous titillation. William Howland Kenny's *Laughter in the Wilderness: Early American Humor to 1783* is a broad survey of imported and indigenous humor, coarse, rude, and vulgar. Kenny provides a thorough outline of "Satiric Invective in the Revolution" (215–236) and speaks of Franklin's "Advice to a Young Man" but otherwise discusses only a few examples of mildly obscene attacks on individuals and groups. Two dissertations, both written early in this century, contain useful material on salty humor: G. F. Horner's "A History of American Humor to 1765" and T. L. Kellogg's "American Social Satire before 1800." Kellogg studies satire, some of it verging toward the obscene, in representative newspapers, magazines, and miscellaneous works; she is especially insightful on the *American Almanac*. Part of D. J. Hibler's 1970 dissertation, "Sexual Rhetoric in Seventeenth-Century American Literature," covers religious and political features of seventeenth-century marginal literature, while Karl Keller's article, "Reverend Mr. Edward Taylor's Bawdry," grins at the off-color expressions of an early American divine. Leo Lemay catalogs instances of bawdy verse in *A Calendar of American Poetry in the Colonial Newspapers and Magazines in the Major English Magazines through 1765*. B. L. Granger deals with scurrilous and prurient invective in *Political Satire in the American Revolution, 1763–1783* and reminds us that scatological and obscene humor were staples of the political scene. H. C. Carlisle's *American Satire in Prose and Verse* is an anthology of mild material, properly historicized and still redolent of British influence. Paul Tabori's *The Humor and Technology of Sex* laughs at appliances such as dildos and vibrators but explores erotic literary humor and popular jokes as well. Constance Rourke is the authority for the emergence of a more "American" humor, as opposed to the mutations of English and Continental sources. Her classic *American Humor: A Study of the National Character* has little to do with sexually explicit humor per se but is essential background reading. The same holds true for two other pioneering, now standard works: Walter Blair's *Native American Humor, 1800–1900*, which carries a splendid bibliography of nineteenth-century humor; and Blair and Hamlin Hill's *America's Humor: From Poor Richard to Doonesbury*. Again, neither illuminates obscenity or sexual explicitness, but the scholar ignores them at her or his peril. In her *A Treasury of Civil War Humor*, Sylvia Dannett includes a generous sampling of ribald and off-color jokes of soldiers, and Thomas P. Lowry discusses sexual humor, songs, and folklore of the same conflict in *The Story the Soldiers Wouldn't Tell*.

The greatest of all studies of obscene and pornographic humor are Gershon Legman's *The Rationale of the Dirty Joke: An Analysis of Sexual Humor* and *No Laughing Matter: Rationale of the Dirty Joke. Second Series*. The two volumes constitute a brilliant and as close-to-exhaustive analysis of this ribald genre as one is likely to find. Legman unearths hidden meaning everywhere, traces derivations, ferrets out aggressiveness, and does not shrink from judgments such as "venomous," "nasty," and "sexist." At the same time, the material he treats remains well, funny, and that is perhaps the best indicator of Legman's skill. Legman thinks that dirty jokes originate with males, serve them as a form of colorful plumage for public display, and often denigrate women. Such humor, in short, is masculine, the product of a "voice as phallus." Peter Lehman explores the seriousness behind phallic jokes in movies in "I'll See You in Court: Penis-Size Jokes and Their Relation to Hollywood's Unconscious."

Freud's remarks on the sexual basis of humor and its inherent hostility are well known. In *Jokes and Their Relation to the Unconscious*, Freud maintained that smutty jokes target women. He noted that while some males think jokes assist seduction, they are really instruments by which males violate taboo. Sexism aside, the jokes may ease male anxieties, blunt menace, and encourage bonding. Freud seems never to have heard a woman tell a dirty joke. See also "Humor" in *Complete Psychological Works of Sigmund Freud*. In "Laughter and Sex," Martin Grotjahn uses Freudian keys to unlock the meaning of sexual humor; Grotjahn maintains that sexual jokes always hide something and, so cloaked, provoke laughter through indirection. Another Freudian, Baird Jones, has broken out types of sexual humor into motifs in *Sexual Humor*, a fascinating volume laced not only with jokes but with illustrations from Tijuana bibles, sex magazines, and cartoons.

"The Meanings of Comedy," Wylie Sypher's introduction to a famous collection of essays on comedy, argues that theories of humor must inevitably confront the function and meaning of obscenity, including its aggression. By contrast, Gary Fine views obscene humor as a means for dealing with repressions and for establishing bonds among groups, partly through reinforcing norms of sexual conduct and asserting cohesiveness against the disruptive threat of sexual impulses. Fine's "Obscene Joking across Cultures" selects instances at weddings, initiation and puberty rites, and other community celebrations. Friedrich Damaskow also covers the relationships of wit, humor, the vernacular, and psychology in *Der Pornographische Witz: Beispiele u. Analyse*, arguing that context is crucial. The risqué has many uses, says David Segal in "Excuse Me! The Case for Offensive Humor"; it educates and disarms, defuses tension and undermines prejudices, and makes us laugh, the latter no mean trick. Michael O'Donoghue's "Pornocopika" reaches similar conclusions.

The Dicephalous Dictionary, a collection of off-color "definitions," is another of the "Sex-to-Sexty" series, which also includes *Sex to Sexty* and *Super Sex to Sexty*. These were very popular humor magazines published by John Newbern and edited by Newbern and Peggy Roderbaugh under the pseudonyms "Richard Rodman and Goose Reardon." Legman sees these off-color (rather than obscene) verbal humor and cartoon magazines as the successors to midwestern magazines (published from the 1920s through the 1950s) such as *Captain Billy's Whiz Bang* and *Smokehouse Monthly*, Charley Jones' *Kansas City Laff Book*, and the sex-tabloid newspaper *Broadway Brevities*. The tone of "Gawd, These Jokes Were Painful!," Robert Russell's article on the *College Humor* magazine of the 1920s, is more embarrassed than nostalgic but sketches the cultural climate for transgressive humor during the period. Thomas Grant analyzes the often sophomoric, sometimes homophobic, and always tasteless joshing of the *Harvard Lampoon* in "Laughter Light and Libelous: The *Lampoon* from Harvard Yard to Madison Avenue."

Legman's "Erotic Folksongs and Ballads: An International Bibliography" lists samizdat versions, spin-offs, reprints, paperback editions, and other mutations of joke collections such as *Over Sixteen* and *More over Sixteen*, both by J. M. Elgart. In fact, pornographic and scatological jokes fill an endless stream of anthologies. Among the most popular are the eleven volumes of *Gross Jokes*, collected by Julius Alvin, and the eleven volumes of *Truly Tasteless Jokes*, edited by Blanche Knott. Both compilations avoid commentary. Such miscellanies do, however, indicate the circulation of jokes through classes of culture; they are steady sellers for publishers, who merely need to spruce up covers every now and then. Others of no particular merit, some with comment, most without, of interest primarily because their pages chart the longevity of particular examples, include *Sex Over Lightly*, compiled by Gerry Blumenfield and Harold Blumenfield; *Sex Joke Book*, by Max Brodnick; *The World's Dirtiest Jokes*, by "Victor Dodson," another pseudonym of John Newbern and Peggy Roderbaugh; *World's Best Dirty Jokes*, by "Mr. J."; *World's Dirtiest Joke Book*, by Steve Rossi and Ken Friedman; *Official Book of John Jokes*, by Larry Wilde; *Flushed! The W. C. Companion*, by an anonymous editor; *Sexcapades*, by Bill Wenzel; *Raunchy Riddles* and *More Raunchy Riddles*, by Jackie Martling, a columnist for *Penthouse* and sidekick of Howard Stern; and *X-Rated Riddles*, by Matt Phillips. Any number of men's magazines run off-color joke columns.

LIMERICKS

A popular subcategory of sexual humor, long linked to pornographic impulse, is the limerick, favored by Legman and many others, because the form combines intellectual ingenuity with a fondness for obscenity. Legman's two volumes, *The Limerick: 1700 Examples, with Notes, Variants, and Index,* and *The New Limerick: 2750 Unpublished Examples. American and British,* are without peer. Both are compiled with his usual care, divided into categories ("Buggery," "Organs," "Virginity," "Zoophily," "Abuse of the Clergy," "Assorted Eccentricities," etc.), and supplemented by commentary on their themes, origins, meaning, psychological undercurrents, and cultural and class characteristics. The second volume even identifies some of the form's aficionados as members of the Fifth Line Society, which until 1975 published its own *Transactions.* A typical entry in *The New Limerick* is number 2139:

> There once was a young lady of Guelph
> Who would daily assemble herself:
>   Rubber tits, a glass eye,
>   A blonde wig all awry,
> And her cunt which she kept on the shelf.

Legman's annotation is as follows: "Limerick reduction of a famous 19th-century joke or anecdote, first given in George W. Harris' *Sut Lovingood's Yarns* (1867), on which see fuller details in *Rationale II: No Laughing Matter,* 13.VI.3, 'The Mechanical Man,' pp. 649–52. Chaplin's *The Noble 500 Limericks* (1967) p. 69, expurgates 'cunt' to 'denture' (!) in the last line, but the accompanying illustration purposely gives away the real point by showing a *pussy* smiling on the shelf" (661).

Although not in Legman's league, Ray A. Billington attempts to preserve and catalog the form in *Limericks Historical and Hysterical,* an excellent collection of lots of famous, mostly pornographic or obscene examples, with good commentary. Even better are the remarks by Palmiro Vicarion (the English poet Christopher Logue) who collects more than 200 limericks in *Count Vicarion's Book of Limericks.* Norman Douglas was one of the first to collect the form; his Introduction to *Some Limericks* is as amusing as it is informative, and he has a lot to say about the delights of rhyme and wordplay. Probably the "dirtiest" collection is *The Limerick: A Facet of Our Culture,* by A. Reynolds Morse, who insists that the verse form draws its power from the smutty; the book was instantly suppressed and is very rare. More than 500 limericks in English, nicely illustrated by Aubrey Beardsley, Edward Lear, and other artists make up *The Lure of the Limerick,* compiled by William S. Baring-Gould, who has no illusions about the essential vulgarity of the form, though he singles out those that make learned allusions. Fillmore P. Noble's *The Limerick That Has the Appeal* is a collection of some 2,000, all by Noble himself. John Falmouth's *Ninety-Five Limericks,* another vanity effort, is engaging nonetheless. Readers may doubt that content matches title in *The World's Best Limericks,* an anonymously compiled collection. *Grand Prix Limericks,* volume IV of the magazine series *Sex to Sexty,* boasts incorrectly of 1,000 limericks "never before published."

Louis Untermeyer gathered bowdlerized examples for *Lots of Limericks: Light, Lusty and Lasting*; the commentary, by a very knowledgeable poet and anthologist, is helpful nonetheless. The science-fiction writer Isaac Asimov and the poet John Ciardi offer examples of dueling limericks in *Limericks Too Gross, or Two Dozen Dirty Dozen Stanzas.*

CIRCULATING JOKES BY SAMIZDAT AND INTERNET

In *Work Hard and You Shall Be Rewarded* and *When You're Up to Your Ass in Alligators*, Alan Dundes and Carl R. Pagter comment on the circulation of xerox-copied nasty jokes, racy stories, and ethnic or gender slurs that constitute a genre descended from American samizdat, the handwritten or typed manuscripts once passed hand-to-hand in the United States. According to Dundes and Pagter, vast numbers of jokes and stories still move through the culture in this fashion, an assessment corroborated by Cathy Makin Orr and Michael J. Preston, who have edited *Urban Folklore from Colorado: Typescript Broadsides* and *Urban Folklore from Colorado: Photocopy Cartoons: Vol. II*. These are widely copied jokes and narratives, with xeroxed cartoons to match. Paul Smith has also published *The Complete Book of Office Mis-Practice* and *Reproduction Is Fun*, both on xeroxlore, as Gershon Legman calls the sometimes bawdy sheets that circulate between offices and around businesses. The new wrinkle, as explained by a *New York Times* editorial entitled "Sick Jokes," is e-mail. The editorial was occasioned by the jokes circulating as the consequence of the arrest of Pee Wee Herman (Paul Reubens) for indecent exposure at a Florida porn movie house by officers the media promptly dubbed "the masturbation police." More sophisticated yet are sexual humor sites on the Internet. The best of these is *Urban Legends—Sex*, an academic Web site with full citations for the jokes and folklore explicated there.

JOKES AND STORIES BY WOMEN

Most scholars are convinced that sexual humor is inherently sexist. Several studies explore a range of possibilities. Jerry Aline Flieger analyzes gendered jokes, using a Freudian joke triangle, in which smutty humor appears to be directed at women in "The Purloined Punchline: Joke as Textual Paradigm." In "Is Sexual Humor Sexist?" Anthony J. Chapman and Nicholas J. Gadfield conclude that sexual humor is linked to gender *and* personality. Most sexual cartoons shown to different groups in their study elicited no differences in the "funniness ratings" of men and women, but those in which sexist themes (women as butts of the joke) were obvious were less funny to females. More significant were personality factors such as age, political views, and self-esteem. In "What Is Funny to Whom? The Role of Gender," Joanne R. Cantor reports on two linked surveys, the second (1975) based on sixty-eight male and fifty-three female college students, itself a replication of the first study, a 1970 survey

of similar size and results. She concludes that people think sarcasm in males is clever but not in females; females seem funnier as butts of jokes than males.

Another pair of studies, published together by William F. Fry, are "Psychodynamics of Sexual Humor: Men's View of Sex" and "Women's View of Sex." They present what has by now become a common argument: that men tell jokes that dehumanize women to overcome feelings of inferiority and that they cherish a faith in the superiority of the penis. Women, on the other hand, respond more readily to less aggressive humor that nonetheless deflates or twists expectations. Carol Mitchell stresses in "The Sexual Perspective in the Appreciation and Interpretation of Jokes" that factors such as whether a man or woman is telling the joke, the relationship between the teller and the listener, and the social setting in which the joke is told have a lot to do with who laughs. Generally, Mitchell says, men and women will find the same joke funny—she offers examples of those readily appreciated by both—but for different reasons; hers is an exceptionally lucid article. Jokes can bring people together in unpredictable ways. The Clinton–Lewinski scandal, says Alex Kuczynski in "In Offices, an Excuse to Talk about S*x," has allowed men and women who ordinarily shy away from talk of sex for fear of issues of harassment to swap jokes. Frankness that would otherwise seem inappropriate becomes a way of coping with a national crisis, and women can share in the process.

Except for Constance Rourke, female scholars have shied away from what was long perceived as masculine terrain. Nancy A. Walker charts the somewhat halting evolution of American women's humor as it manifests boldness as a defense against subordination in *A Very Serious Thing: Women's Humor and American Culture*. While Walker does not emphasize sexual candor, she discusses at length the subversive nature of feminist and lesbian varieties and concludes with an enviable bibliography. Walker thinks that women's humor "challenges basic assumptions about women that have justified their public and private subordination" and does so on two levels, one of which advances conventional views of women, the second of which undermines a culture that creates such stereotypes; the two levels subvert each other. Emily Toth's "Forbidden Jokes and Naughty Ladies" asserts that women do delight in smutty humor and cites examples. Toth's "A Laughter of Their Own: Women's Humor in the United States" advances the notion that women's "humane humor role" is to zero in on "the social roles which imprison us all" (200). Gloria Kaufman notes that women's humor does not take aim at men but mocks everyone's behavior in *Pulling Our Own Strings: Feminist Humor and Satire*.

Perhaps the most remarkable article by a woman folklorist is Rayna Green's "Magnolias Grow in Dirt: The Bawdy Lore of Southern Women." Green looks at foul-mouthed southern belles from a woman's perspective. She discovers that the jokes and stories are rarely racist and rarely derogatory to either women or men. One of her favorites is the woman who remarks that she gives her husband intercourse "once a week whether he needs it or not." This kind of humor, says Green, is (1) a form of social criticism, (2) a form of socialization according to the hidden agenda in the lives and thoughts of southern women, (3) a form of sex education, and (4) a form of fun. In some respects the humor is a species of artistry in performance, and, authentic folklorist that she is, Green concludes that it is more illuminating to participate as even an amateur ethnographer in the bawdiness than to study it, because at base it is private sharing among friends.

Florence King, a contemporary humorist of the southern persuasion, appears to endorse this position in *Southern Ladies and Gentlemen*. Her hilarious chapter on "Sex and the Good Ole Boy" deals with folklore, language, and general cultural idiocy. Rolande Diot's "Sexus, Nexus and Taboos versus Female Humor: The Case of Erica Jong" discusses the breaking of male taboos through ribaldry by the author of *Fear of Flying*. The psychology of women's wit occupies Regina Barreca in *They Used to Call Me Snow White . . . But I Drifted: Women's Strategic Use of Humor*, whose thesis is that women use humor with great care and deliberation, even precision. The performance artist Holly Hughes discusses the repertoire and delivery of American comedians she thinks important in "Headless Dyke in Topless Bar: A Personal History of Lesbian Comedy." *Lesbomania: Humor, Commentary, and New Evidence That We Are Everywhere* gathers Jorjet Harper's comic columns from lesbian magazines; her jibes send up heterosexuals and lesbians alike and are evidence of an evolving genre of lesbian humor. Susie Bright also brings humor to her perspective on sexuality; typical is her *Suzie Sexpert's Lesbian Sex World*.

JOKES AND STORIES BY CHILDREN

Martha Wolfenstein examines the function of bawdiness in educating and socializing youngsters in *Children's Humor: A Psychological Analysis*, a very basic and informative text on the role of inventive comic play, sexual and otherwise, in the maturation of youngsters and adolescents. Another fine study to deal with folklore as sexual influence on children is *"One Potato, Two Potato": The Secret Education of American Children* by Mary Knapp and Herbert Knapp. Even more oriented toward folklore is Sandra McCosh's *Children's Humour: A Joke for Every Occasion*, which straightforwardly examines obscene and sexually explicit jokes, tales, and stories. Gershon Legman's first-rate analytic Introduction ranges widely over many examples. Rosemary Zumwalt points out in "Plain and Fancy: A Content Analysis of Children's Jokes Dealing with Adult Sexuality" that the jokes children tell each other furnish metaphors by which they learn to cope with adult sexual reticence. The folklorist Ian Turner collected bawdy children's rhymes in English; they are published as *Cinderella Dressed in Yella*, a volume edited by June Factor and Wendy Lowenstein. Perhaps because they irritate adults, Mother Goose rhymes have generated a great many obscene parodies, though it is unlikely that the perpetrators are children; they may, in fact, more often qualify as what Gershon Legman calls "fakelore." Some of these were anonymously collected in the 1920s as *Censored Mother Goose*

Rhymes. Joseph C. Hickerson and Alan Dundes consider some versions in detail in "Mother Goose Vice Verse."

HUMOR: LENNY BRUCE AS AVATAR

Explicit stand-up comedy has made celebrities of Red Foxx, George Carlin, and many other off-color performers. None of them could have risen to such heights, however, without the travail of Lenny Bruce (1926–1966), who opened comic pathways previously interdicted. Lenny Bruce's performances and arrests led to countless newspaper and magazine articles. Since his death, the theater world has made him into a cultural icon, virtually canonizing him in a Broadway play and a film starring Dustin Hoffman, and his influence on contemporary comedians has been profound. His autobiography, *How to Talk Dirty and Influence People*, should be supplemented with John Cohen's collection of his routines, *The Essential Lenny Bruce*, and Albert Goldman's massive biography, *Ladies and Gentlemen, Lenny Bruce*! Goldman also wrote a short piece, "What Lenny Bruce Was All About," to discuss his pathbreaking humor; Goldman speaks of Bruce as a shaman who exorcises the fears and fantasies of Americans and thus fulfills the promise of obscenity. Albert Gerber's account of the prosecutions of Bruce for attacking sacred cows in *Sex, Pornography and Justice* is logical and forceful, but Robert B. Weide's documentary film, *Lenny Bruce: Swear to Tell the Truth*, a study of Bruce's destruction by police and censors intent on prosecuting him for obscenity, is emotional and aesthetic. The film is a cautionary tale not simply of the failure of the American judicial system to protect free speech but also of the cost to society of destroying a genius who understood his culture better than his contemporaries did. Useful also are Larry Siegel's "Rebel with a Caustic Cause," a period piece from the 1950s reprinted in *Playboy*'s thirty-fifth anniversary issue, Jerry Tallmer's "Lenny Bruce," a critic's assessment of his legacy, Kenneth Tynan's chapter on Bruce in *The Sound of Two Hands Clapping*, a sympathetic memoir, and Bruce Weber's "The Iconoclast as Icon: Actors Vying to Be Bruce Stay within the Lines," a recent article on auditions for a show on Bruce to be mounted by the Top of the Gate in New York City, which indicates the comic's enduring appeal and influence. Tracing that influence to contemporary comedians would require more space than this *Guide* affords. Suffice it to say that without Bruce's legacy, HBO would never be able to run *Drop Dead Gorgeous: A Tragi-Comedy of HIV-Positive Thinking*, comedian Steve Moore's explicit show.

NOTES

1. See for example, Margaret Mead, "Sex and Censorship in Contemporary Society," *New World Writing: III* (New York: NAL/Mentor, 1953), p. 23.

2. Legman quoted by Helen Dudar, "Love and Death (and Schmutz): G. Legman's Second Thoughts," *Village Voice*, 1 May 1984, p. 42.

3. See Peter Wagner, *Eros Revived* (London: Secker and Warburg, 1988), pp. 268–269.

4. See *Gods of Death*, by Yaron Svoray with Thomas Hughes, who claim to have ferreted out snuff films in different parts of the world; it disdains documentation.

REFERENCES

Aarne, Antti, and Stith Thompson. *The Types of the Folktale: A Classification and Bibliography*. Folklore Fellows Communication, 184. Helsinki: Suomalainen Tiedekatemia, 1961.

Abrahams, Roger D. *Deep Down in the Jungle: Negro Narrative Folklore from the Streets of Philadelphia*. Hatboro, PA: Folklore Associates, 1964.

Akerley, B. E. *The X-Rated Bible: An Irreverent Survey of Sex in the Scriptures*. Austin, TX: American Atheist Press, 1985.

Alvin, Julius. *Gross Jokes*. 11 vols. New York: Zebra Books, 1983–1991.

Aman, Reinhold, ed. *The Best of Maledicta*. Philadelphia: Running Press, 1987.

———. *Maledicta: The International Journal of Verbal Aggression*. Waukesha, WI, 1974–.

———. *Talking Dirty: A Bawdy Compendium of Colorful Language, Humorous Insults and Wicked Jokes*. New York: Carroll and Graf, 1993.

Anecdota Americana. An Anthology of Tales in the Vernacular Edited without Expurgation. By J. Mortimer Hall. Second Series. Boston [New York]: Humphrey Adams [Vincent Smith], 1934. Rpt. as *The Unexpurgated Anecdota Americana*. 2 vols. North Hollywood, CA: Brandon House, 1968; the latter has introductory essays by Frank Hoffmann and Jack Hirschman.

Anecdota Americana. Being Explicitly an Anthology of the Tales of the Vernacular. Elucidatory Preface by J. Mortimer Hall [Joseph Fliesler]. Boston [New York]: Humphrey Adams, 1927; reset and expanded, same publisher, 1932. 2d. ed. also reset but not expanded, published as *Anecdota Americana, Being Explicitly an Anthology of the Tales in the Vernacular*. [New York: Gotham Book Mart, 1927–1928]; reprinted as *The Classic Book of Dirty Jokes*. New York: Bell, 1981. Sanitized eds. by Samuel Roth: *Anecdota Americana: Five Hundred Stories for the Amusement of the Five Hundred Nations That Comprise America*. New York: William Faro, 1933; also New York: Golden Hind Press, 1933; rpt. New York: Nesor Publishing Company, 1933; rev. ed. *The New Anecdota Americana*. New York: Grayson, 1944.

Arango, Ariel. *Dirty Words*. Northvale, NJ: Jacob Aronson, 1979.

Ashley, Leonard. *The Dictionary of Sex Slang*. Chelsea, MI: Scarborough House, 1988.

———. "Dyke Diction: The Language of Lesbians," *Maledicta*, 6 (1982): 123–162.

Asimov, Isaac, and John Ciardi. *Limericks Too Gross, or Two Dozen Dirty Dozen Stanzas*. New York: Norton, 1978.

Ayres, Michael. *English Homosexual Poetry of the 19th and 20th Centuries*. London: Michael de Hartington, 1972.

Bailey, Lee Ann, and Lenora A. Timm. "More on Women's—and Men's—Expletives." *Anthropological Linguistics*, 18 (1976): 438–449.

Baker, Mark. *Sex Lives: A Sexual Self-Portrait of America*. New York: Pocket Books, 1997.

Baker, Robert. " 'Pricks and Chicks': A Plea for Persons." *Philosophy and Sex*, ed. Robert Baker and Frederick Elliston. Rev. ed. Amherst, NY: Prometheus Books, 1984, pp. 249–267.

Baker, Ronald I. "Lady Lil and Pisspot Pete." *Journal of American Folklore*, 100 (1987): 191–199.

Ball, W. P., and G. W. Foote, eds. *The Bible Handbook*. 11th ed. Chicago: Ares, 1985.

Baring-Gould, William S. *The Lure of the Limerick*. New York: Clarkson N. Potter, 1968.

Barreca, Regina. *They Used to Call Me Snow White . . . But I Drifted: Women's Strategic Use of Humor*. New York: Viking, 1991.

Bartlett, Rachel, comp. *Off the Wall: A Collection of Feminist Graffiti*. New York: Proteus, 1982.

Bates, John A., and Michael Martin. "The Thematic Content of Graffiti as a Non-Reactive Indicator for Male and Female Attitudes." *Journal of Sex Research*, 16:4 (November 1980): 300–315.

Beek, Horace P. "Say Something Dirty!" *Journal of American Folklore*, 75:297 (1962): 195–199.

Bergler, Edmund. "On Obscene Words." *Psychoanalytic Quarterly*, 5 (1936): 246–248.

Berlant, Lauren. *The Queen of America Goes to Washington City: Essays on Sex and Citizenship*. Durham, NC: Duke University Press, 1997.

Bettelheim, Bruno. *Symbolic Wounds: Puberty Rites and the Envious Male*. New York: Collier Books, 1962.

———. *The Uses of Enchantment: The Meaning and Importance of Fairy Tales*. New York: Knopf, 1976, p. 6.

Billington, Ray A. *Limericks Historical and Hysterical*. New York: W. W. Norton, 1981.

Blair, Walter. *Native American Humor. 1800–1900*. San Francisco: Chandler, 1960.

Blair, Walter, and Hamlin Hill. *America's Humor: From Poor Richard to Doonesbury*. New York: Oxford University Press, 1978.

Blumenfield, Gerry, and Harold Blumenfield. *Sex Over Lightly*. New York: Dorchester Publishing, 1976.

Blundell, Nigel. *The World's Most Sensational Sex Lives*. London: Sunburst Books, 1995.

Bold, Alan, ed. *Making Love: The Picador Book of Erotic Verse*. London: Picador, 1978.

Bontemps, Arna, and Langston Hughes, eds. *The Book of Negro Folklore*. New York: Dodd, Mead, 1958.

Bourke, John Gregory. *Scatalogic Rites of All Nations*. Washington, DC: Lowdermilk, 1891; rpt. *A Dissertation upon the Employment of Excrementious Remedial Agents in Therapeutics, Divination, Witchcraft, Love-Philtre, etc. in All parts of the Globe*. New York: American Anthropological Society, 1934; rpt. *The Portable Scatalog*, ed. Louis P. Kaplan. New York: Morrow, 1994.

Brand, Oscar. *Bawdy Songs and Backroom Ballads*. New York: Dorchester Press, 1960.

Bright, Susie. *Susie Sexpert's Lesbian Sex World*. Pittsburgh: Cleis Press, 1990.

Brodnick, Max. *Sex Joke Book*. New York: Dorchester Publishing, 1975.

Broughton, James. *Ecstasies: Poems, 1975–1983*. Mill Valley, CA: Syzygy Press, 1983.

———. *Graffiti for the Johns of Heaven*. Mill Valley, CA: Syzygy Press, 1982.

Brovan, L., and C. Brovan. *The Way of a Virgin*. New York: Jack Brussel, 1927.

Bruce, Lenny. *How to Talk Dirty and Influence People*. Chicago: Playboy Press, 1965.

Bruner, Edward M., and Jane Paige Kelso. "Gender Differences in Graffiti: A Semiotic

Perspective." *The Voices and Words of Women and Men*. Oxford: Pergamon Press, 1980, pp. 239–252.

Brunn, Harry O. *The Story of the Original Dixieland Jazz Band*. Baton Rouge: Louisiana State University Press, 1960.

Bulkin, Elly, and Joan Larkin, eds. *Lesbian Poetry: An Anthology*. Watertown, MA: Persephone Press, 1982.

Bullough, Vern L., and Bonnie Bullough. *Sexual Attitudes: Myths and Realities*. Amherst, NY: Prometheus Books, 1994.

———. *Sin, Sickness and Sanity: A History of Sexual Attitudes*. New York: New American Library, 1977.

Burke, David. *Bleep! A Guide to Popular American Obscenities*. (With audiocassettes). Berkeley, CA: Optima Books, 1993.

Burnham, John C. *Bad Habits: Drinking, Smoking, Taking Drugs, Gambling, Sexual Behavior, and Swearing in American History*. New York: New York University Press, 1993.

Butler, Judith. *Excitable Speech: A Politics of the Performative*. New York: Routledge, 1997.

Caldwell, Mark. *A Short History of Rudeness: Manners, Morals, and Misbehavior in Modern America*. New York: Picador USA, 1999.

Cantor, Joanne R. "What Is Funny to Whom? The Role of Gender." *Journal of Communication*, 26:3 (Summer 1976): 164–172.

Carby, Hazel V. "It Jus Be's Dat Way Sometime: The Sexual Politics of Women's Blues." *Radical America*, 20:4 (1986): 9–24.

Carlisle, H. C. *American Satire in Prose and Verse*. New York: Random House, 1962.

Cary, Henry N. "Introduction to Sexual Vocabulary." 2-vol. unpublished typescript, 1920. Kinsey Institute for Sex, Gender, and Reproduction.

———. "Sexual Vocabulary." 5-vol. unpublished manuscript, c.1916. Kinsey Institute for Sex, Gender, and Reproduction.

———, ed. *The Slang of Venery and Its Analogues*. Chicago: Henry N. Carey, 1916.

Censored Mother Goose Rhymes. New York: Kendall Banning, 1929.

Chapman, Anthony J., and Nicholas J. Gadfield. "Is Sexual Humor Sexist?" *Journal of Communication*, 26:3 (Summer 1976): 141–153.

Chapple, Louis W. *Folk-Songs of Roanoke and the Albermarle*. Morgantown, WV: Ballad Press, 1939.

Charters, Samuel. *The Poetry of the Blues*. New York: Oak, 1963.

Chesebro, James W., ed. *Gayspeak: Gay Male and Lesbian Communication*. New York: Pilgrim Press, 1981.

Child, Francis J. *The English and Scottish Popular Ballads*, 5 vols. Cambridge: Harvard University Press, 1882–1898; rpt, New York: Dover, 1965.

Chisholm, Dianne. "The 'Cunning Lingua' of Desire: Bodies-Language and Perverse Performativity." *Sexy Bodies: The Strange Carnalities of Feminism*, ed. Elizabeth Grosz and Elspeth Probyn. New York: Routledge, 1995, pp. 19–41.

Cixous, Hélène. "The Laugh of the Medusa," trans. Keith Cohen and Paula Cohen. *Signs*, 1:4 (1976): 875–893.

———. "Veiled Lips." *Mississippi Review*, 11 (1983): 93–131.

Claire, Elizabeth. *A Foreign Student's Guide to Dangerous English*. Rochelle Park, NY: Eardley, 1980.

Coffin, Tristram P. *The British Traditional Ballad in North America.* Rev. ed. Philadelphia: American Folklore Society, 1963.

————. *The Female Hero in Folklore and Legend.* New York: Pocket Books, 1975.

————. *A Proper Book of Sexual Folklore.* New York: Seabury Press, 1978.

Cohen, J. M. *The Penguin Book of Comic and Curious Verse, More Comic and Curious Verse,* and *Yet More Comic and Curious Verse.* 3 vols. London: Penguin, 1952, 1956, 1959.

Cohen, John. *The Essential Lenny Bruce.* New York: Ballantine, 1967.

Cole, Susan G. *Pornography and the Sex Crisis.* Toronto: Amanita Enterprises, 1989; Toronto: Second Story Press, 1992.

Cole, William, ed. *Erotic Poetry: The Lyrics, Ballads, Idyls and Epics of Love—Classical to Contemporary.* New York: Random House, 1963.

Coss, Clare. *The Arc of Love: An Anthology of Lesbian Love Poems.* New York: Simon and Schuster, 1995.

Cox, John Harrington. *Folk Songs of the South.* Cambridge: Harvard University Press, 1925; rpt. Hatboro, PA: Folklore Associates, 1963.

Cray, Edward B. *The Erotic Muse: American Bawdy Songs.* Urbana: University of Illinois Press, 1992.

————. *The Fifteen Plagues of the Maidenhead and Other Forbidden Verse.* North Hollywood, CA: Brandon House, 1966.

Cummings, Parke. *The Whimsey Report: or, Sex Isn't Everything.* New York: Crowell, 1948.

Damaskow, Friedrich. *Der Pornographische Witz: Beispiele u. Analyse.* Munich: Heyne, 1972.

Dance, Daryl Cumber. *Shuckin' and Jivin': Folklore from Contemporary Black Americans.* Bloomington: Indiana University Press, 1978.

Dannett, Sylvia, ed. *A Treasury of Civil War Humor.* New York: Yoseloff, 1963.

Davis, Angela Y. "I Used to Be Your Sweet Mama: Ideology, Sexuality and Domesticity in the Blues of Gertrude 'Ma' Rainey and Bessie Smith." *Sexy Bodies: The Strange Carnalities of Feminism,* ed. Elizabeth Grosz and Elspeth Probyn. New York: Routledge, 1995, pp. 231–265.

"Defacing the Facts." *Screw,* 819, 12 November 1984, p. 14.

Dégh, Linda. *American Folklore and the Mass Media.* Bloomington: Indiana University Press, 1994.

Dening, Sarah. *The Mythology of Sex: An Illustrated Exploration of Sexual Customs and Practices from Ancient Times to the Present.* New York: Macmillan, 1996.

The Dicephalous Dictionary. Fort Worth, TX: SRI, 1967.

Diot, Rolande. "Sexus, Nexus and Taboos versus Female Humor: The Case of Erica Jong." *Revue Française D'Études Americaines,* 30 (November 1986): 491–499.

Dodson, Victor [John Newbern and Peggy Roderbaugh], ed. *The World's Dirtiest Jokes.* Los Angeles: Medco Books, 1969.

Dooling, Richard. *Blue Streak: Swearing, Free Speech, and Sexual Harassment.* New York: Random House, 1996.

Douglas, Norman. *Some Limericks.* Philadelphia: privately printed, 1928?

Downey, Fairfax D. *Our Lusty Forefathers: Being Diverse Chronicles of the Fervors, Frolics, Fights, Festivities, and Failings of Our American Ancestors.* Manchester, NH: Ayer, 1959; rpt. New York: Scribner's, 1947.

Duffy, Maureen. *The Erotic World of Faery.* London: Hodder and Stoughton, 1972.

Duncan, Robert, et al. *The Male Muse: Gay Poetry Anthology*. Freedom, CA: Crossing Press, 1973.

Dundes, Alan. "Here I Sit—A Study of American Latrinalia." *Kroeber Anthropological Society Papers*, 34 (1966): 102–104.

———, ed. *Mother Wit from the Laughing Barrel: Readings in the Interpretation of Afro-American Folklore*. Englewood Cliffs, NJ: Prentice-Hall, 1973.

Dundes, Alan and Carl R. Pagter. *When You're Up to Your Ass in Alligators*. Bloomington: Indiana University Press, 1987.

———. *Work Hard and You Shall Be Rewarded: Urban Folklore from the Paperwork Empire*. Bloomington: Indiana University Press, 1978.

Dunker, Robert, and Thomas Dunker, eds. *Horseshit: The Offensive Review*. Hermosa Beach, CA, 1965–1969.

Eble, Connie C. "If Ladies Weren't Present, I'd Tell You What I Really Think." *Papers in Language Variation*, ed. David L. Shores and Carole P. Hinds. Tuscaloosa: University of Alabama Press, 1977, pp. 295–301.

Eisler, Riane. *Sacred Pleasure: Sex, Myth, and the Politics of the Body*. San Francisco: Harper, 1995.

Elgart, J. M. *Over Sexteen*. New York: Grayson, 1951; New York: Signet, 1968. *More over Sexteen*. New York: Grayson, 1953.

Ellis, Albert. *The Folklore of Sex*, aka *Sex Beliefs and Customs*. New York: Charles Boni, 1951; and *The Folklore of Sex*. New York: Grove Press, 1961.

Erenberg, Lewis. *Steppin' Out: New York Nightlife and the Transformation of American Culture*. Westport, CT: Greenwood Press, 1981.

Evans, David. "The Toast in Context." *Journal of American Folklore*, 90 (1977): 129–148.

Facetia Americana. N.p.: Privately printed, 1925.

Faderman, Lillian. *Odd Girls and Twilight Lovers: A History of Lesbian Life in Twentieth-Century America*. New York: Columbia University Press, 1991.

Falmouth, John, ed. *Ninety-Five Limericks*. New York: Limerick Press, 1932.

Farmer, John S. *Merry Songs and Ballads Prior to the Year 1800 and Musa Pedestris*. New York: Cooper Square, 1964. Rpt. London: privately printed, 1897.

Farmer, John S., and William Earnest Henley. *Slang and Its Analogues*. 7 vols. London: privately printed, 1890–1904. Rpt. as *Dictionary of Slang and Its Analogues, Past and Present: A Dictionary Historical and Comparative of the Heterodox Speech of All Classes of Society for More Than Three Hundred Years with Synonyms in English, French, German, Italian, etc. Vol. I*. Rev. and enlarged. New Hyde Park, NY: University Books, 1966. Rpt. *Slang and Its Analogues, Past and Present*. 3 vols. Millwood, NY: Kraus Reprint, 1989.

Fass, Paula. *The Damned and the Beautiful: American Youth in the 1920s*. New York: Oxford University Press, 1977.

Feldman, Marvin J. "The Use of Obscene Words in the Therapeutic Relationship." *American Journal of Psychoanalysis*, 15:1 (1955): 17–23.

Feminist Writers Workshop. *The Intelligent Woman's Guide to Dirty Words*. (First volume of a projected *Feminist English Dictionary*.) Chicago: Chicago Loop YWCA, 1973.

Ferenczi, Sandor. *Sex in Psychoanalysis*. New York: Basic Books, 1950.

Ferris, William R. *Blues from the Delta*. New York: Doubleday, 1978.

Fillion, Kate. *Lip Service: The Truth about Women's Darker Side in Love, Sex, and Friendship*. New York: HarperCollins, 1998.

Fine, Gary. "Obscene Joking across Cultures." *Journal of Communication*, 26:3 (1976): 134–140.

Finz, Iris. *Erotic Confessions: Real People Talk about Putting the Spark Back in Their Sex Lives*. New York: St. Martin's, 1998.

Fitzwilliam, G. W. *Pleasures of Love: Being Amatory Poems*. Boston: Belcher and Armstrong, 1808.

Flieger, Jerry Aline. "The Purloined Punchline: Joke as Textual Paradigm." *Modern Language Notes*, 98:5 (December 1983): 943–967.

Flushed! The W. C. Companion. New York: Kanrom, 1969.

Folb, Edith A. *Runnin' Down Some Lines: The Language and Culture of Black Teenagers*. Cambridge: Harvard University Press, 1980.

Foss, Paul, and Meaghan Morris. *Language, Sexuality, and Subversion*. Darlington, Australia: Feral Press, 1978.

Foster, Herbert L. *Ribbin', Jivin', and Playin' the Dozens*. Cambridge, MA: Ballinger Press, 1974.

Foucault, Michel. *The History of Sexuality*, trans. Robert Hurley. 3 vols. New York: Pantheon, 1978–1987.

Fowke, Edith. *Traditional Singers and Songs from Ontario*. Hatboro, PA: Folklore Associates, 1963.

Freud, Sigmund. "Humor." *Complete Psychological Works of Sigmund Freud*, trans. James Strachey. 24 vols. London: Hogarth Press, 1961, XXI: 159–166.

———. *Jokes and Their Relation to the Unconscious*, trans. James Strachey. New York: Norton, 1960 [1905].

Fry, William F. "Psychodynamics of Sexual Humor: Men's View of Sex" and "Women's View of Sex." *Medical Aspects of Human Sexuality*, 6 (May 1972): 128–131, 133–135.

Gerber, Albert. *Sex, Pornography and Justice*. New York: Lyle Stuart, 1965.

Gilbert, Timothy D., ed. *The Naughty and the Bawdy*. New York: Hart Publishing Co., 1987.

Gillette, Paul J. *The Complete Sex Dictionary*. New York: Award Books, 1969.

Goldberg, B. Z. *The Sacred Fire: The Story of Sex in Religion*. New York: Liveright, 1932; rpt. New York: Grove Press, 1962.

Goldman, Albert. *Ladies and Gentlemen, Lenny Bruce!* New York: Viking Penguin, 1992.

———. "What Lenny Bruce Was All About." *New York Times Magazine*, 27 June 1971, pp. 121–131.

Goliard, Roy. *A Scholar's Glossary of Sex*. New York: Heinemann, 1968.

Gould, George M., and Walter L. Pyle. *Anomalies and Curiosities of Medicine*. New York: Sydenham, 1937.

Grahn, Judy. *Another Mother Tongue: Gay Words, Gay Worlds*. Boston: Beacon, 1984.

Grand Prix Limericks. Fort Worth [Arlington], TX: SRI Publishing, 1966.

Granger, B. L. *Political Satire in the American Revolution, 1763–1783*. Ithaca, NY: Cornell University Press, 1963.

Grant, Elizabeth C. "Writing on the Wall." *Playboy*, 40:2 (February 1993): 82–83, 147.

Grant, Thomas. "Laughter Light and Libelous: The *Lampoon* from Harvard Yard to Madison Avenue." *Markham Review*, 13 (Spring–Summer 1984): 33–40.

Graves, Robert. *Lars Porsena or the Future of Swearing and Improper Language*. New York: Dutton, 1927.

Green, Rayna. "Folk Is a Four-Letter Word: Dealing with Traditional _____ in Fieldwork, Analysis, and Presentation." *Handbook of American Folklore*, ed. Richard M. Dorson. Bloomington: Indiana University Press, 1983, pp. 525–532.

———. "Magnolias Grow in Dirt: The Bawdy Lore of Southern Women." *Southern Exposure*, 4:4 (1977): 32–35.

Grey, Antony. *Speaking of Sex: The Limits of Language*. New York: Cassell, 1993.

Grotjahn, Martin. "Laughter and Sex." *A Celebration of Laughter*. Los Angeles: Mara Books, 1970, pp. 161–172.

Hagen, John Milton. *Lecherous, Licentious, Lascivious Lyrics*. Danbury, CT: Barnes, 1969.

Halpert, Herbert. "Folklore and Obscenity: Definitions and Problems." *Journal of American Folklore*, 75 (1962): 190–194.

Hamill, Sam, ed. *The Erotic Spirit: An Anthology of Poems of Sensuality, Love, and Longing*. Boston: Shambhala, 1995.

Hardy, Jan, ed. *Wanting Women: An Anthology of Erotic Lesbian Poetry*. Pittsburgh: Sidewalk Revolution Press, 1990.

Harper, Jorjet. *Lesbomania: Humor, Commentary, and New Evidence That We Are Everywhere*. Norwich, VT: New Victoria, 1994.

Hart, Harold H., ed. *Immortalia*. 4 vols. New York: Hart Publishing Co., 1970; reissued as *The Complete Immortalia* by the same publisher in 1971; reissued in 1975 by Bell Publishing as *The Bawdy Bedside Reader*.

Hartogs, Renatus, with Hans Fantel. *Four-Letter Word Games: The Psychology of Obscenity*. New York: Dell, 1968.

Harvey, Keith, and Celia Shannon, eds. *Language and Desire: Encoding Sex, Romance and Intimacy*. New York: Routledge, 1997.

Hibler, D. J. "Sexual Rhetoric in Seventeenth-Century American Literature." Ph.D. dissertation, Notre Dame University, 1970.

Hickerson, Joseph C., and Alan Dundes. "Mother Goose Vice Verse." *Journal of American Folklore*, 75: 258–260.

Hoffmann, Frank. *Analytical Survey of Anglo-American Traditional Erotica*. Bowling Green, OH: Popular Press, 1973.

———. "Prolegomena to a Study of Traditional Elements in the Erotic Film." *Journal of American Folklore*, 78 (1965): 143–148.

Horner, G. F. "A History of American Humor to 1765." Ph.D. dissertation, University of North Carolina, 1936.

Horner, Thomas M. *Sex in the Bible*. Rutland, VT: Tuttle, 1974.

Howard, Clifford. *Sex Worship: An Exposition of the Phallic Origin of Religion*. Chicago: Chicago Medical Books, 1909.

Howell, Anthony. *Erotic Lyrics*. London: Studio Vista, 1970.

Hughes, Holly. "Headless Dyke in Topless Bar: A Personal History of Lesbian Comedy." *Village Voice Special Section on Gay Games and Cultural Festival*, 21 June 1994, pp. 7–9, 33.

Irigaray, Luce. *Speculum of the Other Woman*, trans. Gillian C. Gill. Ithaca, NY: Cornell University Press, 1985.

———. *This Sex Which Is Not One*, trans. Catherine Porter with Carolyn Burke. Ithaca, NY: Cornell University Press, 1985.

Irwin, Godfrey. *American Tramp and Underworld Slang . . . with a Selection of Tramp Songs*. London: Scholartis Press, 1931; rpt. New York: Sears, 1934.

J., Mr. *World's Best Dirty Jokes*. Secaucus, NJ: Citadel Press, 1979.

Jackson, Bruce. *"Get Your Ass in the Water and Swim like Me": Narrative Poetry from the Black Oral Tradition*. Cambridge: Harvard University Press, 1974.

———. *"Wake Up Dead Man": Afro-American Worksongs from Texas Prisons*. Cambridge: Harvard University Press, 1972.

Jarvie, I. C. "Methodological and Conceptual Problems in the Study of Pornography and Violence." *Thinking about Society: Theory and Practice*. Dordrecht, Netherlands: Reidel, 1985, pp. 390–475.

Jay, Timothy. *Cursing in America: A Psycholinguistic Study of Dirty Language in the Courts, in the Movies, in the Schoolyards, and on the Streets*. Philadelphia: John Benjamins, 1992.

Johnson, John Henry, ed. *Bawdy Ballads and Lusty Lyrics*. Indianapolis: Maxwell Droke, 1935.

Johnson, Susan E., ed. *Lesbian Sex: An Oral History*. Tallahassee, FL: Naiad Press, 1996.

Johnson, Wendell S. *Sex and Marriage in Victorian Poetry*. Ithaca, NY: Cornell University Press, 1975.

Jones, Baird. *Sexual Humor*. New York: Philosophical Library, 1987.

Kandel, Lenore. *The Love Book*. San Francisco: Stolen Papers, 1966.

Kaufman, Gloria. *Pulling Our Own Strings: Feminist Humor and Satire*. Bloomington: Indiana University Press, 1980.

Kearney, Patrick J. *A History of Erotic Literature*. London: Macmillan, 1982.

Keller, Karl. "Reverend Mr. Edward Taylor's Bawdry." *New England Quarterly*, 44 (1970): 382–406.

Kellogg, Thelma Louise. "American Social Satire before 1800." Ph.D. dissertation, Radcliffe College, Harvard University, 1929.

Kennedy, X. J. *Tygers of Wrath*. Athens: University of Georgia Press, 1981.

Kenny, William Howland. *Laughter in the Wilderness: Early American Humor to 1783*. Kent, OH: Kent State University Press, 1976.

King, Florence. *Southern Ladies and Gentlemen*. New York: Bantam, 1975.

King, L. J., ed. *House of Death and Gate of Hell*. Toledo, OH?: Protestant Book House, 1928.

Kirkeby, W. T., and Sinclair Traill. *Ain't Misbehavin'*. New York: Peter Davies, 1966.

Kirsch, Jonathan. *The Harlot by the Side of the Road: Forbidden Tales of the Bible*. New York: Ballantine, 1997.

Knapp, Mary, and Herbert Knapp. *"One Potato, Two Potato": The Secret Education of American Children*. New York: Norton, 1976.

Knight, Richard Payne, and Thomas Wright, with an Introduction by Ashley Montagu. *Sexual Symbolism: A History of Phallic Worship*. New York: Julian Press, 1957; rpt. New York: Agora, 1966.

Knott, Blanche. *Truly Tasteless Jokes*. 11 vols. New York: Ballantine, 1982–1991.

Kramarae, Cheris. *Women and Men Speaking*. Rowley, MA: Newbury House, 1981.

Kramarae, Cheris, and Paula Treichler, comps. *Amazons, Bluestockings, and Crones: A Feminist Dictionary*. 2d ed. London: Pandora, 1992.

Kripke, Madeline. "The Lingo of the Tijuana Bibles." *Tijuana Bibles: Art and Wit in America's Forbidden Funnies 1930s–1950s*, ed. Bob Adelman. New York: Simon and Schuster, 1997, p. 11.

Kristeva, Julia. *Desire in Language: A Semiotic Approach to Literature and Art*, ed. Leon S. Roudiez, trans. Tom Gora, Alice Jardine, and Leon Roudiez. New York: Columbia University Press, 1980.

Kuczynski, Alex. "In Offices, an Excuse to Talk about S*x." *New York Times*, 2 February 1998, pp. B1, B7.

Kunitskaya-Peterson, Christina. *International Dictionary of Obscenities: A Guide to Dirty Words and Indecent Expressions in Spanish, Italian, French, German, Russian.* Oakland, CA: Scythian Books, 1981.

Kutner, N. G., and D. Brogan. "An Investigation of Sex-Related Slang Vocabulary and Sex-Role Orientation among Male and Female University Students." *Journal of Marriage and the Family*, 36 (1974): 474–484.

La Glannège, Roger-Maxe de [Gershon Legman]. *Oragenitalism: An Encyclopaedic Outline of Oral Technique in Genital Excitation Part 1: Cunnilinctus.* New York: Privately printed, 1940; rep. and exp. (with *Part II: Fellation and the Sixty-Nine*) by Legman under his own name, as *Oragenitalism*. New York: Julian Press, 1969; rpt. London: Duckworth, 1972; rpt. as *The Intimate Kiss*. New York: Paperback Library, 1971.

Larson, Kenneth. "Barnyard Folklore of Southeastern Idaho: A Collection of Vulgar Verses, Jokes, and Popular Ballads, All of Them Unprintable, Obtained by Word-of-Mouth from Those Who [Were] Entertained by Them (Mostly Farmers, Laborers, and Students) . . . during the Years from 1920 to 1952." Salt Lake City, UT, 1952.

Leap, William L. *Word's Out: Gay Men's English*. Minneapolis: University of Minnesota Press, 1995.

Legman, Gershon. "Erotic Folksongs and Ballads: An International Bibliography." *Journal of American Folklore*, 103 (October/December 1990): 417–501.

———. *The Horn Book: Studies in Erotic Folklore and Bibliography*. New York: University Books, 1964.

———. "The Language of Homosexuality: An American Glossary." *Sex Variants*, ed. George W. Henry. 2 vols. New York: Haeber, 1941, Appendix.

———. *The Limerick: 1700 Examples, with Notes, Variants, and Index*. Paris: Les Hautes Etudes, 1953; rpt. New York: Brandywine Press, 1970; rpt. *The Famous Paris Edition of The Limerick: 1700 Entries*. Secaucus, NJ: Citadel Press, 1979.

———. "Misconceptions in Erotica Folklore." *Journal of American Folklore*, 75 (1962): 200–208.

———. *The New Limerick: 2750 Unpublished Examples. American and British.* New York: Crown Publishers, 1977; rpt. New York: Bell, 1980.

———. *No Laughing Matter: Rationale of the Dirty Joke, Second Series.* New York: Breaking Point, 1975.

———. *Rationale of the Dirty Joke: An Analysis of Sexual Humor.* New York: Grove Press, 1968.

———. "A Summer Reading List to End All Summer Reading Lists." *Fact*, 2:4 (July–August 1965): 38–43.

———. "Toward a Motif-Index of Erotic Humor." *Journal of American Folklore*, 75 (1962): 227–248; rpt. *The Horn Book*, pp. 454–494.

———. "Unprintable Folklore? The Vance Randolph Collection." *Journal of American Folklore*, 103 (July–September 1990): 259–300.

Lehman, Peter. "I'll See You in Court: Penis-Size Jokes and Their Relation to Hollywood's Unconscious." *Running Scared: Masculinity and the Representation of the Male Body*. Philadelphia: Temple University Press, 1993, pp. 105–129.

Lemay, Leo. *A Calendar of American Poetry in the Colonial Newspapers and Magazines in the Major English Magazines through 1765*. Worcester, MA: American Antiquarian Society: 1972.

Lewin, Lewis. *Phantastica: Narcotic and Stimulating Drugs: Their Use and Abuse*, trans. P. H. A. Wirth. New York: E. P. Dutton, 1931.

Libertine Lyrics. Mount Vernon, NY: Peter Pauper Press, n.d.

Lingenfelter, Richard E., et al. *Songs of the American West*. Berkeley: University of California Press, 1968.

Linton, E. R. [Edward B. Cray], comp. *The Dirty Song Book: American Bawdy Songs*. Los Angeles: Medco Books, 1965; updated as *The Erotic Muse*. New York: Oak Publications, 1969.

Logsdon, Guy. *"The Whorehouse Bells Were Ringing." and Other Songs Cowboys Sing*. Urbana: University of Illinois Press, 1989.

Lomax, Alan. *The Folk Songs of North America*. New York: Doubleday, 1960.

Lowry, Thomas P. *The Story the Soldiers Wouldn't Tell*. Mechanicsburg, PA: Stackpole Books, 1994.

MacDougald, Duncan. "Language and Sex." *The Encyclopedia of Sexual Behavior*, ed. Albert Ellis and Albert Abarbanel. 2 vols. New York: Hawthorne Books, 1961, II, 585–598.

MacKinnon, Catharine. *Only Words*. Cambridge: Harvard University Press, 1993.

Major, Clarence, ed. *Juba to Jive: A Dictionary of African-American Slang*. New York: Penguin, 1994.

Malinowski, Bronislaw. *The Sexual Life of the Savages*. New York: Liveright, 1929.

Mantegazza, Paolo. *Anthropological Studies of Sexual Relations of Mankind*, trans. James Bruce. New York: Anthropological Press, 1932.

Marsh, Joss. *Word Crimes: Blasphemy, Culture, and Literature in Nineteenth Century England*. Chicago: University of Chicago Press, 1998.

Martling, Jackie. *Raunchy Riddles* and *More Raunchy Riddles*. New York: Pinnacle Books, 1984, 1985.

Masterson, James R. *Tall Tales of Arkansas*. Boston: Chapman and Grimes, 1942.

Maurer, Harry, ed. *Sex: An Oral History*. New York: Viking, 1994; Two audiocassettes. Newark, CA: Passion Press, 1996.

McCary, James Leslie. *Sexual Myths and Fallacies*. New York: Van Nostrand, 1971.

McClure, Michael. *Dark Brown*. San Francisco: Auerhahn Press, 1961.

McCosh, Sandra. *Children's Humour: A Joke for Every Occasion*. London: Panther/Granada, 1979.

McNeil, Pearlie, Bea Freeman, and Jenny Newman, eds. *Women Talk Sex: Autobiographical Writing on Sex, Sexuality, and Sexual Identity*. London/Milford, CT: Scarlet Press/LPC, 1992.

Mead, Margaret. *Sex and Temperament in Three Primitive Societies*. New York: New American Library, 1935.

Meredith, Mamie. "Inexpressibles, Unmentionables, Unwhisperables, and Other Verbal Delicacies of Mid-Nineteenth Century Americans." *American Speech*, 5 (April 1930): 285–287.

Milburn, George. *The Hobo's Handbook: A Repertory for a Gutter Jongleur*. New York: Ives Washburn, 1930.

Mitchell, Carol. "The Sexual Perspective in the Appreciation and Interpretation of Jokes." *Western Folklore*, 36 (1977): 303–329.

Monet, Veronica. "What Is Feminist Porn?" *Porn 101: Eroticism, Pornography, and the First Amendment*, ed. James Elias, Veronica Diehl Elias, Vern L. Bullough, Gwen Brewer, Jeffrey J. Douglas, and Will Jarvis. Amherst, NY: Prometheus Books, 1999, pp. 207–211.

Montagu, Ashley. *The Anatomy of Swearing*. New York: Macmillan, 1967.

Moore, Steve. *Drop Dead Gorgeous: A Tragi-Comedy of HIV-Positive Thinking*. New York: HBO, 1996.

[Morse, A. Reynolds.] *The Limerick: A Facet of Our Culture*. Mexico City: Cruciform Press, 1944 [1948].

———, comp. *Folk Poems and Ballads: An Anthology: A Collection of Rare Verses and Amusing Folk Songs Compiled from Scarce and Suppressed Books as Well as from Verbal Sources, Which Modern Prudery, False Social Customs and Intolerance Have Separated from the Public and Historical Record*. Waukesha, WI: Maledicta Press, 1984.

Movsesian, Ara John. *Pearls of Love*. Fresno, CA: Electric Press, 1983.

Murray, H. Kincaid. *Coercion and Perversion: Or Primeval Degenerates*. New York: Lutetion Society, 1934.

Murray, Thomas E., and Thomas R. Murrell. *The Language of Sadomasochism: A Glossary and Linguistic Analysis*. Westport, CT: Greenwood Press, 1989.

Niemoller, Adolph F. *American Encyclopedia of Sex*. New York: Panurge Press, 1935.

———. "A Glossary of Homosexual Slang." *Fact*, 2:1 (January–February 1965): 25–27.

Niles, John Jacob, Douglas Moore, and A. A. Wallgren. *The Songs My Mother Never Taught Me*. New York: Macauley, 1929.

Noble, Fillmore P. *The Limerick That Has the Appeal*. Detroit: Privately printed, 1976.

Oakley, Giles. *The Devil's Music: History of the Blues*. New York: Harcourt Brace Jovanovich, 1976.

O'Dair, Barbara, and Abby Tallmer. "Sex Premises." *Caught Looking: Feminism. Pornography, and Censorship*, by the Feminist Anti-Censorship Task Force. New York: Caught Looking, 1986, pp. 50–53.

O'Donoghue, Michael. "Pornocopika." *Russell Baker's Book of American Humor*, ed. Russell Baker. New York: Norton, 1993, pp. 216–221.

Oliver, Paul. *Aspects of the Blues*. New York: Oak, 1970.

Orr, Cathy Makin, and Michael J. Preston, eds. *Urban Folklore from Colorado: Typescript Broadsides* and *Urban Folklore from Colorado: Photocopy Cartoons: Vol. II*. Ann Arbor, MI: University Microfilms, 1976.

Parker, Derek. *An Anthology of Erotic Verse*. London: Constable, 1980.

Paros, Lawrence. *The Erotic Tongue: A Sexual Lexicon*. New York: Holt, 1988.

Peiss, Kathy. *Cheap Amusements: Working Women and Leisure in Turn of the Century New York*. Philadelphia: Temple University Press, 1986.

Penzer, N. M. *Poison-Damsels, and Other Essays in Folklore and Anthropology*. London: Charles Sawyer, 1952.

Perry, Sandra. "Sex and Sentiment in America or What Was Really Going On between the Staves of Nineteenth Century Songs of Fashion." *Journal of Popular Culture*, 6 (Summer 1972): 32–48.

Petronius [Joyce Greller]. *Tool Box Scandals*. New York: Cestrum Nocturnum, 1971.

Phillips, Matt. *X-Rated Riddles*. Los Angeles: Price, Stern, and Sloan, 1981.

Plummer, Ken. *Telling Sexual Stories: Power, Change and Social Worlds*. New York: Routledge, 1995.

Poems Lewd and Lusty. New York: Hart Publishing Company, 1976.

Posener, Jill. *Spray It Loud*. London: Routledge and Kegan Paul, 1982.

Preston, Cathy Lynn. "The Tying of the Garter: Representations of the Female Rural Laborer in 17th-, 18th-, and 19th-Century English Bawdy Songs." *Journal of American Folklore*, 105: 417 (Summer 1992): 315–341.

Randolph, Pascal Beverly. *Sexual Magic*, trans. Robert North. New York: Magickal Childe, 1988.

Randolph, Vance. *Blow the Candle Out: "Unprintable" Ozark Folklore*, ed. Gershon Legman. Vol. II. Fayetteville: University of Arkansas Press, 1997.

———. *Ozark Folksongs*, ed. Floyd C. Schoemaker. Columbia: State Historical Society of Missouri, 1946–1950.

———. *Pissing in the Snow & Other Ozark Folktales*, ed. Frank Hoffmann. Urbana: University of Illinois Press, 1976.

———. *Roll Me in Your Arms: "Unprintable" Ozark Folksongs and Folklore*, ed. Gershon Legman. Vol. I. Fayetteville: University of Arkansas Press, 1992.

Rawson, Hugh. *Wicked Words: A Treasury of Curses, Insults, Put-Downs, and Other Formerly Unprintable Terms from Anglo-Saxon Times to the Present*. New York: Crown, 1989.

Read, Allen Walker. "Graffiti as a Field of Folklore." *Maledicta*, 2 (1978): 15–31.

———. *Lexical Evidence from Folk Epigraphy in Western North America: A Glossarial Study of the Low Element in the English Vocabulary*. Paris: Privately printed, 1935; rpt. *Classic American Graffiti*. Waukesha, WI: Maledicta Press, 1977.

———. "The Nature of Obscenity." *Neurotica*, 1:5 (Autumn 1949): 23–30.

———. "Noah Webster as a Euphemist." *Dialect Notes*, 6:8 (July 1934): 384–391.

Rees, Nigel. *Graffiti*. 3 vols. London: Unwin, 1978, 1980, 1981.

Reisner, Robert. *Graffiti: Selected Scrawls from Bathroom Walls*. New York: Parallel Publishing, 1967.

———. *Graffiti: Two Thousand Years of Wall Writing*. Chicago: Henry Regnery, 1971.

Richter, Alan. *The Language of Sexuality*. Jefferson, NC: McFarland, 1987.

———. *Sexual Slang*. New York: HarperPerennial, 1995.

Ringer, R. Jeffrey, ed. *Queer Words, Queer Images: Communication and the Construction of Homosexuality*. New York: New York University Press, 1994.

Robinson, Victor, ed. *Encyclopedia Sexualis*. New York: Dingwall-Rock, 1936.

Robson, Ruthann. "Pedagogy, Jurisprudence, and Finger-Fucking: Lesbian Sex in a Law School Classroom." *Lesbian Erotics*, ed. Karla Jay. New York: New York University Press, 1995, pp. 28–39.

Rodgers, Bruce. *The Queen's Vernacular: A Gay Lexicon*. San Francisco: Straight Arrow Books, 1972; rpt. as *Gaytalk*. New York: Paragon, 1979.

Roscoe, Will. *Queer Spirits: A Gay Men's Myth Book*. Boston: Beacon, 1995.

Rossi, Steve, and Ken Friedman. *World's Dirtiest Joke Book*. New York: Woodhill, 1979.

Roth, Klaus. *Ehebruchschwänke in Lied Form*. Munich: Fink Verlag, 1971.

Rourke, Constance. *American Humor: A Study of the National Character*. New York: Harcourt Brace Jovanovich, 1959.

Rowdy Rhymes and Bibulous Ballads. Mount Vernon, NY: Peter Pauper Press, 1960.

Rudolph, E. L. *Confederate Broadside Verse*. New Braunfels, TX: Book Farm, 1950.

Russell, Robert. "Gawd, These Jokes Were Painful!" *Esquire*, 70 (December 1968): 164–169.

Sagarin, Edward. *The Anatomy of Dirty Words*. New York: Lyle Stuart, 1962.

Sanders, Lawrence, ed. *Thus Be Loved*. New York: Arco, 1966.

Sanford, John. *Seventy Times Seven*. New York: Knopf, 1939; rpt. *Make My Bed in Hell*. New York: Avon, 1941.

Scheidlower, J., ed. *The F-Word*. New York: Random House, 1995.

Scheiner, C. J. *Compendium: Being a List of All the Books (Erotica, Curiosa, and Sexology) Listed in Our Catalogs 1–6 (1978–1988)*. Brooklyn: C. J. Scheiner, 1989.

Schmidt, J. E. *The Cyclopedic Lexicon of Sex: Erotic Practices, Expressions, Variations of the Libido*. New York: Brussel and Brussel, 1968.

Scholes, Robert. "Uncoding Mama: The Female Body as Text." *Semiotics and Interpretation*. New Haven, CT: Yale University Press, 1982.

Schulz, Muriel. "The Semantic Derogation of Women." *Language and Sex: Difference and Dominance*, ed. Barrie Thorne and Nancy Henley. Rowley, MA: Newbury House, 1975, pp. 64–73.

Sebeok, Thomas A., ed. *Sight, Sound, and Sense*. Bloomington: Indiana University Press, 1978.

Segal, David. "Excuse Me! The Case for Offensive Humor." *Utne Reader*, 53 (September/October 1992): 134–135.

Settani, Harry. "Pornography." *What Is Morality? Questions in Search of Answers*. Lanham, MD: University Press of America, 1992.

Sex to Sexty. Fort Worth [Arlington], TX: SRI, 1964–1976? and *Super Sex to Sexty*, Fort Worth [Arlington], TX: SRI, 1967–1986?

Shay, Frank. *Iron Men and Wooden Ships*. New York; Doubleday, 1924; rpt. *American Sea Songs and Chanteys*. New York: Norton, 1948.

———. *My Pious Friends and Drunken Companions*, and *More Pious Friends and Drunken Companions*. New York: Macauley, 1927, 1928; rpt. as one volume, New York: Dover, 1961.

Shemel, Sidney, and William Krasilowsky. *The Business of Music*. New York: N. P., 1964.

Shepard, Leslie. *The Broadside Ballad: A Study in Origins and Meaning*. Hatboro, PA: Folklore Associates, 1962.

———. *The History of Street Literature: The Story of Broadside Ballads, Chapbooks, Etc.* Newton Abbott, Devon, England: David and Charles, 1973.

"Sick Jokes." *New York Times*, national ed., 6 August 1991, p. A10.

Siegel, J. P. "Puritan Light Reading." *The New England Quarterly*, 37 (1964): 185–199.

Siegel, Larry. "Rebel with a Caustic Cause." *Playboy*, 36:1 (January 1989): 105, 340.

Silverman, Jerry. *The Dirty Song Book*. Briarcliff Manor, NY: Scarborough House/Stein and Day, 1982.

Simons, G. L. *Sex and Superstition*. London: Abelard-Schuman 1966.

———. *The Simons Book of World Sexual Records*. New York: Pyramid Books, 1975.

Sinners Club. *Blue Law Ballads*. Cincinnati, OH: The Sinners Club [William C. Smith], 1922.

Slade, Joseph W. "Inventing a Sexual Discourse: A Rhetorical Analysis of Adult Video Box Covers," *Sexual Rhetoric: Media Perspectives on Sexuality, Gender, and Identity*, ed. Meta G. Carstarphen and Susan Zavoina. Westport CT: Greenwood Press, 1999, 239–254.

Smith, Paul. *The Complete Book of Office Mis-Practice*, and *Reproduction Is Fun*. London: Routledge and Kegan Paul, 1984, 1986.

[Smith, T. R.], ed. *Immortalia: An Anthology of American Ballads, Sailors' Songs, Cowboy Songs, College Songs, Parodies, Limericks, and Other Humorous Verses and Doggerel Now for the First Time Brought Together in Book Form by a Gentleman about Town.* [New York]: privately printed, 1927. Rpt. Venice, CA: Parthena Press, 1969.

———. *Poetica Erotica: A Collection of Rare and Curious Amatory Verse.* 3 vols. New York: Boni and Liveright, 1921–1922.

Spears, Richard A. *Slang and Euphemism: A Dictionary of Oaths, Curses, Insults, Racial Slurs, Sexual Slang and Metaphor, Drug Talk, Homosexual Lingo, and Related Matters.* New York: Jonathan David Publishers, 1981.

Staley, Constance. "Male-Female Use of Expletives: A Heck of a Difference in Expectations." *Anthropological Linguistics*, 20 (1978): 367–380.

Stanley, Julia P. "Paradigmatic Women: The Prostitute." *Papers in Language Variation*, ed. David L. Shores and Carole P. Hinds. Tuscaloosa: University of Alabama Press, 1977, pp. 303–321.

———. "When We Say 'Out of the Closets.' " *College English*, 36 (1974): 385–391.

Sterba, Richard. " 'Kilroy Was Here.' " *American Imago*, 5 (1948): 173–180.

Stocker, Terrance L., Linda W. Dutcher, Stephen M. Hargrove, et al. "Social Analysis of Graffiti." *Journal of American Folklore*, 85:3 (October–December 1972): 338–356.

Stone, Lee Alexander. *The Story of Phallicism*. Chicago: Pascal Covici, 1927; rev. *The Power of a Symbol* (1925).

Strainchamps, Ethel. "Our Sexist Language." *Woman in Sexist Society*, ed. Vivian Gornick and Barbara K. Moran. New York: Basic Books, 1971, pp. 240–250.

Sutherland, Alistair, and Patrick Anderson. *Eros: An Anthology of Friendship.* New York: Arno, 1975.

"Symposium on Obscenity in Folklore," ed. Frank Hoffmann and Tristram Coffin. *Journal of American Folklore*, 75 (1962): 187–265.

Sypher, Wylie. "The Meanings of Comedy." *Comedy*, ed. Wylie Sypher. New York: Doubleday, 1956, pp. 193–258.

Szasc, Thomas S. *Sex: Facts, Frauds, and Follies.* Oxford: Basil Blackwell, 1981.

Tabori, Paul. *The Humor and Technology of Sex.* New York: Julian Press, 1969.

———. *Secret and Forbidden.* New York: NAL, 1971.

Tallmer, Jerry. "Lenny Bruce." *Evergreen Review*, 44 (December 1966): 22–23.

Tannen, Deborah. *You Just Don't Understand.* New York: Ballantine, 1990.

Thompson, Lana. *The Wandering Womb: A Cultural History of Outrageous Beliefs about Women.* Amherst, NY: Prometheus Books, 1999.

Thompson, Stith. *Motif-Index of Folk Literature: A Classification of Narrative Elements in Folktales, Ballads, Myths, Fables, Medieval Romances, Exempla, Fabliaux, Jestbooks, and Local Legends.* 6 vols. Bloomington: Indiana University Press, 1955–1958.

Thorne, Barrie, and Nancy Henley, eds. *Language and Sex: Difference and Dominance.* Rowley, MA: Newbury House, 1975.

Thorne, Barrie, Cheris Kramarae, and Nancy Henley. *Language, Gender and Society*, ed. Thorne, Kramarae, and Henley. Rowley, MA: Newbury House, 1983.

Thorp, N. Howard. *Songs of the Cowboys*, ed. Austin Fife and Alta Fife. New York: Clarkson Potter, 1966.

Toth, Emily. "Forbidden Jokes and Naughty Ladies." *Studies in American Humor*, 4: 1/2 (Spring/Summer 1985): 7–17.

———. "A Laughter of Their Own: Women's Humor in the United States." *Critical Essays on American Humor*, ed. William Bedford Clark and W. Craig Turner. Boston: G. K. Hall, 1984, pp. 199–215.

Trimble, John. *5,000 Adult Sex Words and Phrases: A Treatise on Common Sexual Terms in Modern English Idiom*. North Hollywood, CA: Brandon House, 1966.

Turner, Ian. *Cinderella Dressed in Yella*, ed. June Factor and Wendy Lowenstein. Melbourne, Australia: Heinemann, 1978.

Twain, Mark [Samuel Clemens]. "Some Remarks on the Science of Onanism." *The Mammoth Cod, an Address to the Stomach Club*. Waukegan, WI: Maledicta Press, 1976.

Tynan, Kenneth. *The Sound of Two Hands Clapping*. New York: Holt, Rinehart, and Winston, 1975.

Untermeyer, Louis, ed. *Lots of Limericks: Light, Lusty and Lasting*. New York: Doubleday, 1961.

———. *A Treasury of Ribaldry*. New York: Hanover House, 1956.

———. *An Uninhibited Treasury of Erotic Poetry*. New York: Dial Press, 1963.

Urban Legends—Sex. www.snopes.com/sex.

Vicarion, Palmiro [Christopher Logue]. *Count Vicarion's Book of Bawdy Ballads*. Paris: Olympia Press, 1959.

———. *Count Vicarion's Book of Limericks*. Paris: Olympia Press, 1955.

Wagner, Peter. "Eros Goes West: European and 'Homespun' Erotica in Eighteenth-Century America." *The Transit of Civilization from Europe to America: Essays in Honor of Hans Galinsky*, ed. Winfried Herget and Karl Ortseifen. Tübingen: G. Narr, 1986, pp. 145–165.

———. *Eros Revived; Erotica of the Enlightenment in England and America*. London: Secker and Warburg, 1988.

Walker, Nancy A. *A Very Serious Thing: Women's Humor and American Culture*. Minneapolis: University of Minnesota Press, 1988.

Wallace, Irving, et al. *The Intimate Sex Lives of Famous People*. New York: Dell, 1982.

Warner, Marina. *From the Beast to the Blonde: On Fairy Tales and Their Tellers*. New York: Farrar, Straus, and Giroux, 1995.

Waterman, Richard A. "The Role of Obscenity in the Folk Tales of the 'Intellectual Stratum' of Our Society." *Journal of American Folklore*, 62 (1949): 162–165.

Weber, Bruce. "The Iconoclast as Icon: Actors Vying to Be Bruce Stay within the Lines." *New York Times*, 24 July 1992, p. B12.

Weide, Robert B., producer and director. *Lenny Bruce: Swear to Tell the Truth*. New York: Whyaduck Films/HBO Documentary Films, 1998.

Wellesley, Gordon. *Sex and the Occult*. New York: Bell, 1973.

Wenzel, Bill. *Sexcapades*. New York: Dorchester, 1978.

Wepman, Dennis, Ronald B. Newman, and Murray B. Binderman, eds. *The Life: The Lore and Folk Poetry of the Black Hustler*. Philadelphia: University of Pennsylvania Press, 1976.

Whitworth, John. *The Faber Book of Blue Verse*. Boston: Faber and Faber, 1990.

Wiest, William M. "Semantic Differential Profiles of Orgasm and Other Experiences among Men and Women." *Sex Roles*, 3 (1977): 399–403.

Wilde, Larry. *Official Book of John Jokes*. New York: Bantam, 1985.

Wilson, Robert A., ed. *Playboy's Dictionary of Forbidden Words*. Chicago: Playboy Press, 1972.

Wolf, Naomi. *Promiscuities: The Secret Struggle for Womanhood*, aka *Promiscuities: A Secret History of Female Desire*. New York: Random House, 1997.

Wolfe, James. *Sex Talk: The Ultimate Collection of Ribald, Raunchy, and Provocative Quotations*. New York: Carol, 1994.

Wolfenstein, Martha. *Children's Humor: A Psychological Analysis*. Bloomington: Indiana University Press, 1978.

Wolfson, Nicholas. "Eroticism, Obscenity, Pornography, and Free Speech." *Hate Speech, Sex Speech, Free Speech*. Westport, CT: Praeger, 1997, pp. 103–142.

Woods, Gregory. *Articulate Flesh: Male Homoeroticism and Modern Poetry*. New Haven, CT: Yale University Press, 1987.

The World's Best Limericks. New York: Peter Pauper Press, 1951.

X, Dr. Jacobus. *Crossways of Sex*. New York: American Anthropological Press, n.d. [1930s?].

———. *Untrodden Fields of Anthropology*. New York: Falstaff Press, 1937.

Yerkovich, Sally. "Gossiping as a Way of Speaking." *Journal of Communication*, 27:1 (1977): 192–196.

Young, Ian, ed. *The Male Muse*. Trumansburg, NY: Crossing Press, 1973.

Zaks, Richard. *History Laid Bare: Love, Sex and Perversity from the Ancient Etruscans to Warren G. Harding*. New York: HarperCollins, 1994.

Zall, Paul M. "The Old Age of American Jestbooks." *Early American Literature*, 15 (1980): 3–15.

Zipes, Jack. "The Instrumentalization of Fantasy: Fairy Tales and the Mass Media." *The Myths of Information: Technology and Postindustrial Culture*, ed. Kathleen Woodward. Madison, WI: Coda Press, 1980, pp. 88–110.

Zumwalt, Rosemary. "Plain and Fancy: A Content Analysis of Children's Jokes Dealing with Adult Sexuality." *Readings in American Folklore*, ed. Jan Harold Brunvand. New York: Norton, 1979, pp. 345–354.

Zwicky, Arnold M., et al. *Studies Out in Left Field: Defamatory Essays Presented to James D. McCawley on the Occasion of His 33rd or 34th Birthday*. Edmonton Alta/Champaign, IL: Linguistic Research, 1971.

16

Erotic Literature

HISTORIES OF EROTIC BOOKS

Historians of pornography have concentrated on books because until recently they were more accessible than other media. The greatest bibliographies of erotica also deal in the main with printed genres (see chapter 4, **Bibliographies and Reference Tools**, especially Dawes, Fryer, Kearney, Reade, Thomas, Thompson, Wedeck.) Accounts of efforts to suppress books, often arranged historically, provide a good deal of information as well (see Chapter 20, **Pornography and Law in the United States**, especially Fraxi, Giese, Glaser, Gorsen, Guha, Schidrowitz.)

One of the broadest chronicles is H. Montgomery Hyde's *A History of Pornography*; it is very readable but not entirely accurate and contains a small section on art. Paul Englisch's *Geschichte der Erotischen Literatur* is a more solid survey, prized for its comprehensiveness on the eighteenth through the early twentieth centuries; a splendid work of scholarship, it contains excerpts and reprints of title pages from famous works. Englisch's *Irrgarten der Erotik*, also concerned with literature, deals with erotic art as well. *Literatur und Kunst*, the second volume of the six-volume *Bilderlexicon der Erotik*, is extremely valuable, though it is weighted toward German examples. Ian Moulton's "Before Pornography: Explicitly Erotic Writing in Early Modern England" examines the sociopolitical context of erotic discourse in sixteenth-century England with a view to distinguishing it from post-Enlightenment pornographic genres; he finds that Italian eroticism profoundly influenced English genres. Informed by a meticulous scholarship honed on various bibliographies, Patrick J. Kearney's *A History of Erotic Literature* covers the seventeenth to the mid-nineteenth centuries and includes generous reproductions of title pages. The various essays in

Alan Bold's *The Sexual Dimension in Literature* likewise cover Western literature from classical to modern examples, but very cautiously; the eroticism the essays uncover is conventional. Donald McCormick's freewheeling *Erotic Literature: A Connoisseur's Guide* blends broad history and criticism. The four volumes of John Atkins' *Sex in Literature* begin with antiquity and end with the seventeenth and eighteenth centuries; though the comment is tepid, readers will appreciate the attention to evolving genres. Bernhardt Hurwood's *The Golden Age of Erotica*, best on English books of the seventeenth and eighteenth centuries, reaches into the nineteenth as well. *Sexual Underworlds of the Enlightenment*, edited by George Rousseau and Roy Porter, covers many subliteratures of the period.

Scholarly and rewarding studies of Victorian print pornography, with more attention to British than to American examples, are Steven Marcus' *The Other Victorians*, Walter Kendrick's *The Secret Museum*, Ronald Pearsall's *The Worm in the Bud: The World of Victorian Sexuality*, and a brief chapter in Peter Gay's *The Bourgeois Experience: Victoria to Freud*, volume I of his *The Education of the Senses*. Among those concentrating on specifically American pornography during the same period are Milton Rugoff's *Prudery and Passion: Sexuality in Victorian America*, and the more scholarly *Dr. Bowdler's Legacy: A History of Expurgated Books in England and America*, by Noel Perrin. Although Albert Mordell's gloss on sensual expression in *The Erotic Motive in Literature* seems naive by modern standards, it recalls the tentativeness of criticism in the early twentieth century. Ralph Ginzburg's *An Unhurried View of Erotica* and David Loth's *The Erotic in Literature*, both pioneering efforts to introduce more candid analysis, can still be read for their excerpts and for their comment on the cultural reception of pornography in America; both, however, are superficial. Similarly, George N. Gordon's *Erotic Communications: Studies in Sex, Sin and Censorship*, which offers a decidedly American perspective, is too frequently whimsical to be helpful. Much better than one would expect, given the publisher, is Paul Gillette's *An Uncensored History of Pornography*, whose historical narrative is supplemented with chronologies of authors and major pornographic works.

Roland Barthes speaks of reading itself as an erotic act in *The Pleasure of the Text*: "The text is a fetish object, and *this fetish desires me*" (27). An American version of Barthes' contentions that textual analysis is itself erotic and that reading is a fundamentally masturbatory act has been developed by Steven G. Kellman in *Loving Reading: Erotics of the Text*. Kellman's work helps to explain the attention scholars lavish on texts and is a good example both of fevered postmodernism and of genuine efforts to redefine the discourse of sexuality. The "body" of an author's work lies vulnerable to "the wanton touch of a reader" (16), says Kellman; "eroticism is not a quality of objects but of relationships" because any given "content," pornographic or otherwise, is "unstable and culturally conditioned" (12). Such relativism does not prevent his condemning "sadistic" readers who enjoy such American writers as Thoreau, Twain, and Mailer.

Essays in the volume *The Perverse Imagination: Sexuality and Literary Cul-

ture, edited by Henry Buchen, address the dynamics of reading sex material. Contributors to *Perspectives on Pornography: Sexuality in Film and Literature*, edited by Gary Day and Clive Bloom, employ "feminism, post-structuralism, Marxism, Lacanism, psychoanalysis, and film theory" (vii) to construct their perspectives, none of which are particularly persuasive. An interesting Christian approach, *How to Read a Dirty Book or the Way of the Pilgrim Reader*, by Irving Sussman and Cornelia Sussman, discriminates between print and other media and tries as well to distinguish erotic fiction from pornographic; only the latter is truly "dirty" and "unacceptable." The Sussmans argue for an understanding of the human need to use dirty words and discuss sexual behavior, though they clearly prefer that canonical (rather than popular) American writers on the level of Faulkner and Salinger be the ones to do so. Working with American examples such as Henry Miller and Harold Robbins, Hans Giese parses the poetics of obscenity in *Das Obszöne Buch*; his distinctions resemble those of the Sussmans.

PERIOD COMMENTARIES

Dozens of mainstream American writers have walked a narrow line between the erotic and the pornographic, and the annual American Literature Bibliographies of the *Publication of the Modern Language Association* are the best sources of scholarly information about them. As with most pornographic genres, examples of sexual stories fall into high and low categories, though the passing of time and the elevation of print media above other technologies have tended to blur divisions. Some writers, of course, are more celebrated for their sexual themes than others, and any selection of critical works is idiosyncratic, as is this one.

The authority on erotica in the colonial and revolutionary periods is Peter Wagner. His "Eros Goes West: European and 'Homespun' Erotica in Eighteenth-Century America" is a brief, but peerless, study of the importation of erotica to early America and the slow growth of domestic publishing, often of reprints of European classics, with evidence gleaned from library and bookseller catalogs, chapbooks, and contemporary accounts. Wagner's splendid *Eros Revived: Erotica of the Enlightenment in England and America* is a longer study set against a larger canvas. Chapter 9, "Erotica in Early America," is indispensable because of its important observations and its bibliography of sources. Wagner analyzes traffic in pornographic materials in terms of publishers and libraries, noting the provenance of materials and whether they were imported or reprinted on American presses. Another chapter on antiaristocratic erotic genres notes (146) that the term *pornography* is a middle-class label and represents an attempt to consign erotica, previously material prized by aristocrats, to lower-class status. Wagner has also edited a volume called *Erotica and the Enlightenment*, whose various contributors deal with English and Continental erotica of the eighteenth century; all of them exhibit a scholarship so often absent from discussion of the subject, and Wagner's Introduction (9–40) is first-rate. Many of the European works examined in this volume found their way into colonial libraries and are thus of relevance to American history. Wagner has examined catalogs of many early libraries, including those of Jefferson and William Bird II.

Students of American literary erotica should be familiar with the oral traditions and folkloristic elements that figure so prominently in the genesis of literature. (For material on early American subliterary genres such as chapbooks, songbooks, calendars, and oral relics, see **Folklore and Obscenity: Rhymes, Songs, Ballads, and Stories** in Chapter 15.) Salacious Indian captivity narratives of the early 1800s are the principal focus of "American Chapbooks," one chapter of Harry B. Weiss' *A Book about Chapbooks: The People's Literature of Bygone Times*; Weiss thinks the genre was particularly demotic in its appeal. Kate McCafferty marvels at the endurance of the captivity narrative in "Palimpsest of Desire: The Re-Emergence of the American Captivity Narrative as Pulp Romance," which traces the transgressive genre from colonial times to hybrid romances of the present. Christopher Castiglia measures the power of captivity narratives as they mutate across decades in *Bound and Determined: Captivity, Culture-Crossing, and White Womanhood from Mary Rowlandson to Patty Hearst*. Carroll Smith Rosenberg's "Davy Crockett as Trickster: Pornography, Liminality, and Symbolic Inversion in Victorian America" discusses popular Davy Crockett stories as subversive tales that flourished in concert with waxing fears of youthful masturbation during the period 1830–1850; Rosenberg thinks sexual and scatological narratives, reflecting the dominant discourse of bourgeois males, functioned as archetypes of violence directed at women. In "Humor in American Almanacs: From the Colonial Period to the Civil War and After," Robert Secor identifies *Davy Crockett's Almanac of Wild Sports of the West, and Life in the Backwoods* (1835), the progenitor of the stories that disturb Rosenberg, as written by Crockett himself but demonstrates that the fifty or so lusty almanacs subsequently published under his name were by other hands. The crude humor, hyperbole, and bawdiness were common, says Secor, to the almanac as a form; he traces many examples and directs readers to other sources.

Easily the most celebrated early American to dabble in pornography is Benjamin Franklin (also a compiler of almanacs), and his erotic output has received a good deal of attention. His scatological *Letter to the Royal Academy at Brussels* (1770s?), the whimsically fraudulent *The Speech of Polly Baker* (1747), and the charmingly sexist *Advice to a Young Man on Choosing a Mistress* (1745) are discussed in Wagner's *Eros Revived*, David Loth's *The Erotic in Literature*, and Paul M. Zall's *Ben Franklin Laughing: Anecdotes from Original Sources by and about Benjamin Franklin*. Max Hall's *Benjamin Franklin and Polly Baker: The History of a Literary Deception* is the best account of Franklin's amusing 1747 newspaper hoax, a story about a woman accused of fornication, because it sets the event in the larger context of Franklin's sexual humor. Most of Franklin's sexual or scatalogical essays have been reprinted as *Fart Proudly*. Good accounts of the "bagatelles" Franklin wrote to Frenchwomen while ambassador to France, then published on his own press, are Claude-Anne Lopez's *Mon cher papa: Benjamin Franklin and the Ladies of Paris* and Leo Lemay's "The Public Writings and the Bagatelles."

Perhaps the most interesting text on mainstream candor is Joseph B. Urgo's *Novel Frames: Literature as Guide to Race, Sex, and History in American Culture*, whose general thesis is that literature reveals everything we need to know about sex and the other subjects specified in his title. In *Sexual Personae: Art and Decadence from Nefertiti to Emily Dickinson*, Camille Paglia discusses the "decadence" of Poe, Hawthorne, Melville, Emerson, Whitman, and James and draws credible parallels between Emily Dickinson and de Sade. Useful period studies include Charles I. Glicksberg's *The Sexual Revolution in Modern American Literature*, which calibrates shifts among mainstream authors from Dreiser to Mailer; John Cawelti's "Pornography, Catastrophe, and Vengeance: Shifting Narrative Structures in a Changing American Culture," which demonstrates that genre boundaries (from dime novels to mainstream fiction) are not impermeable; Kimberley Reynolds and Nicola Humble's *Victorian Heroines: Representations of Femininity in Nineteenth-Century Literature and Art*, which concludes from texts and images that Victorian women were hardly ignorant of sensuality; Jenni Calder's *Women and Marriage in Victorian Fiction*, which identifies props of the double standard; Bram Dijkstra's *Idols of Perversity: Fantasies of Feminine Evil in Fin-de-Siécle Culture*, which rehearses images of dangerous, menacing, and evil women in literature and art; William Wasserstrom's *Heiress of All the Ages: Sex and Sentiment in the Genteel Tradition*, which deals with fictional female sexuality in the Gilded Age; Leslie Fiedler's now classic *Love and Death in the American Novel*, which delves into dark racial and sexual currents that roiled American letters; and Henry Buchen's *The Perverse Imagination: Sexuality and Literary Culture*, whose contributors dissect thematic elements. Joseph Allen Boone's *Libidinal Currents* also deals extensively with sexual motifs in classic mainstream American literature.

Merely listing the books and articles on Walt Whitman's erotic poetry would fill this entire section. Because canonization has muted the reverberations of Whitman's pen, critics now focus directly on the sexuality that gifted his genius. The range stretches from postmodern investigations such as M. Jimmie Killingsworth's *Whitman's Poetry of the Body: Sexuality, Politics, and the Text*, to Charley Shively's historical explorations, *Calamus Lovers: Walt Whitman's Working Class Camerados* and *Drum Beats: Walt Whitman's Civil War Boy Lovers*. So eager has been the appropriation of Whitman's homosexuality by recent critics and so prolific the number of books and articles on the poet's gayness that Gene Bluestine wonders in "Sex as Literary Theme: Is Whitman the Good, Gay Poet?" if Whitman's gender proclivities matter all that much.

In "The Serious Function of Melville's Phallic Jokes," Robert Shulman argues that the extensive phallic humor in *Moby Dick* should not be associated with Ishmael's creativity but with the whale's awesome "primal, destructive force" (179). While it is hard to miss the homoeroticism of, say, the sperm-squeezing scene in *Moby Dick* ("I wrote a wicked book," said Melville, "and feel as clean as a lamb"), literary critics in recent years have been looking more closely at his lesser fiction. James Creech, for instance, reveals the real "ambiguities" in the title of another novel in *Closet Reading/Gay Reading: The Case of Melville's Pierre*. Here again, the volume of critical attention lavished on Melville's eroticism is best examined with the help of specialized indexes on the author; a writer so fixated on sperm will obviously attract the attention of critics with similar obsessions.

Similarly, the sheer number of books and articles on the homosexuality hidden, visible, or imagined in the works of Henry James would swamp this bibliography; those interested in the subject will find guides to James elsewhere. Besides, even if James' fiction should turn out to be an elaborate erotic code, as some of his admirers think, calling it pornographic would stretch the term to breaking point. The essays in John R. Bradley's *Henry James and Homo-Erotic Desire* will bring scholars up-to-date. By contrast, the clearly pornographic nature of Edith Wharton's "Beatrice Palmato Fragment" has awakened intense interest in her sexual themes; Wharton's brief fantasy of explicit oral-genital sex between father and daughter is reprinted in R. W. B. Lewis' *Edith Wharton: A Biography*. Gloria C. Erlich delves deeply into Wharton's sexuality in *The Sexual Educations of Edith Wharton*.

Harry J. Mooney's "The *Sub Rosa* Writings of Eugene Field" draws on the Field papers in the Denver Public Library and other archives to analyze Field's editing of *The Stag Party* (1888 or 1889), an extremely rare compendium of funny American bawdy, erotic, and obscene stories, including some of Field's own, such as *Only a Boy. Poetica Erotica* (not to be confused with the three-volume anthology of the same title edited by T. R. Smith) includes pornographic works by Field, Franklin, and James Whitcomb Riley. Very much worth consulting is Douglas H. Gamlin's *The Tijuana Bible Reader*, which reproduces the mostly anonymous typescript narratives that, along with pornographic comics, were called "bibles"; they throb with clandestine pulse. Indispensable to an understanding of that pulse in the 1920s and 1930s is Jay A. Gertzman's *Bookleggers and Smuthounds: The Trade in Erotica, 1920–1940*. Gertzman weaves into his account of bold publishers material about the writers who furnished them with stories: Clement Wood, Joe Hanley, Gene Fowler, Paul Little, Frank Harris, and many others. One publisher, Samuel Roth, wrote *The Private Life of Frank Harris*, a study of the English-American *infant terrible* of erotica. Philippa Pullar's *Frank Harris: A Biography* is more authoritative on the author of *My Life and Loves*; she speaks of the relationship between Harris and Roth but devotes more space to Harris' editorship of the *Saturday Review*, to the motives that drove him to notoriety, and to the political exploits of a colorful adventurer. Introducing a reprint of James Gibbons Huneker's *Painted Veils* (privately printed in 1920), Van Wyck Brooks observes that the character "Mona's 'interior monologue' preceded Mollie Bloom's in *Ulysses* by two years" (vi); several scenes, such as those in which prostitutes pick up coins with their labia, are as explicit as some of Joyce's. *Djuna: The Life and Work of Djuna Barnes*, by Phillip Herring, explains why the novelist's satirical *Nightwood* has drawn admirers from the 1930s to the present.

Erotic experiments in poetry by other major American figures of the period are reproduced in Hemingway's *The Suppressed Poems of Ernest Hemingway* and Gertrude Stein's *Lifting Belly*, the latter edited by Rebecca Mark. Kevin Oderman's *Ezra Pound and the Erotic Medium* dissects Pound's sexual themes and the sensuality the poet attributed to the medium. Thomas Simmons describes the erotic curve of friendships, apprenticeships, and marriages as they configure the work of Ezra Pound, Hilda Doolittle, Yvor Winters, Janet Lewis, Louise Bogan, and Theodore Roethke in *Erotic Reckonings: Mastery and Apprenticeship in the Work of Poets and Lovers*.

No discussion of American pornography can omit Henry Miller. Miller's *Tropic of Cancer* is the most censored book in American history, according to Charles Rembar, whose *The End of Obscenity: The Trials of Lady Chatterley, Tropic of Cancer and Fanny Hill* details various prosecutions of the novel before its final clearance by the Supreme Court in 1964. Any modern history of literary censorship will, of course, devote several pages to Miller. Miller himself noted his special status "as one accused of employing obscene language more freely and abundantly than any other living writer in the English language" in a famous essay called "Obscenity and the Law of Reflection," included in his *Remember to Remember* and in *The Air-Conditioned Nightmare*. In that essay, Miller vents exasperation: "The most insistent question put to the writer of 'obscene' literature is: Why did you have to use such language? The implication is, of course, that with conventional terms or means the same effect might have been obtained. Nothing, of course, could be further from the truth. Whatever the language employed, no matter how objectionable—I am here thinking of the most extreme examples—one may be certain that there was no other idiom possible" (144). In a sense, Miller wrote only autobiographical works, none of which aim to arouse and all of which use obscenity to specific metaphysical and moral effect. The most ambitious iteration is *The World of Sex*.

Frank Kersnowski and Alice Hughes have gathered different interviews with the writer in *Conversations with Henry Miller*, in which Miller elaborates on the concept of literary obscenity: "Obscenity has its natural place in literature, as it does in life, and it will never be obliterated. I feel I have restored sex to its rightful role, rescued the life force from literary oblivion" (56). Some of the letters reproduced in *Henry Miller: Years of Trial and Triumph. 1962–1964: The Correspondence of Henry Miller and Elmer Gertz* also discuss the author's intent. Critic Kingsley Widmer says that his defense of writers such as Miller and D. H. Lawrence earned him the title he gives to " 'Professor of Fuck': Some Reflections on Defending Literary Obscenity," an essay in which Widmer defends Miller's subordination of pornography to obscenity: "What we professors of fuck are defending and disseminating is not just personal or literary idiosyncrasy, not just a more open reporting of language and the body and the rest of reality, but some damning responses to a fraudulent culture and society. Hence, I hold that we should not just be totally against censorship, however ideologically proper some fashion of it may appear, but stand for more and better fucking obscenity" (25). Erica Jong makes a similar plea in her " 'Deliberate Lewdness' and the Lure of Immortality": "Without farts, there are no flowers. Without pricks, there are no poems" (xxxvii).

Miller's literary influence, which may someday rival Walt Whitman's, has led to a large body of critical comment. Even Kate Millett, perhaps the most hostile but also one of Miller's best critics, has called him a "major figure" of American literature. Millett astutely observes in *Sexual Politics* that "however attractive our current popular image of Henry Miller the liberated man may appear, it is very far from being the truth. Actually Miller is a compendium of American sexual neuroses, and his value lies not in freeing us from such afflictions, but in having had the honesty to express and dramatize them" (295). In the end, because of the emotional aggression against women that his writing enshrines, says Millett, his influence may be malignant, a criticism quickly taken up by less able feminist critics who merely bash his work out of helpless incomprehension. An example of the latter type is Vivian Gornick's "Why Do These Men Hate Women? American Novelists and Misogyny," which calls Mailer, Bellow, Roth, and Miller vile and dehumanizing in their presentation of sexuality. Many critics have, of course, observed that major American writers have demonstrated sadistic attitudes toward women. Gershon Legman does so in *Love and Death: A Study in Censorship* but attributes the tendency to the cultural suppression of sexual expression, which leads, he argues, inevitably to themes of aggression.

Michael Woolf finesses such issues when he says that the work of both Miller and Millett transcends pornography and politics in "Beyond Ideology: Kate Millett and the Case for Henry Miller." Numerous champions have defended Miller against charges from left and right, chief among them Norman Mailer, whose *Genius and Lust: A Journey through the Major Writings of Henry Miller* praises his courage and explicitness, and Erica Jong, whose *The Devil at Large: Erica Jong on Henry Miller* states the case for Miller as a Whitman-like sexual saint and a stylistic innovator who forever altered the boundaries of American literature. Of the many texts available on Miller, the best biographies are those by Mary V. Dearborn (*The Happiest Man Alive: A Biography of Henry Miller*) and Robert Ferguson (*Henry Miller: A Life*); both are thorough and astute in their coverage of a career that ranged from the slums of Brooklyn and the low haunts of Paris to the cliffs of Big Sur. Jay Martin extracts Miller's optimism and joy from the obscenity in *Always Bright and Merry*. Worth looking at also is *Henry Miller: The Paris Years*, by Brassaï, the photographer, who supplies intimate knowledge of Miller's friendships with Anaïs Nin and Lawrence Durrell and speaks with detailed understanding of Miller's intentions. Provocative as well is Gerhard Schmolze's "Pornographie als ethische Provokation und erotische

Aggression," a study of Miller's ethical challenges to Christian concepts of love and human nature.

Miller's relationship with Anaïs Nin was crucial to his life and career. The two of them wrote pornographic stories on demand for collectors, and, partly as a consequence, Nin became one of the great female erotic writers of her generation. In the absence of a writer's claim to their work, attribution can be difficult; Benjamin Franklin V argues in "Adventures in the Skin Trade; or, the Enigma of *White Stains*" that Nin may not be one of the authors of *White Stains*, as is commonly believed. Some of the stories she admits to having written earlier have been published in Nin's *Delta of Venus* (1977) and *Little Birds* (1979), both of which are routinely offered by book-of-the-month clubs. In "Anaïs Nin: Author(iz)ing the Erotic Body," Karen Brennan analyzes *Delta of Venus*, one of several works written to earn money that have endured. The multivolume *Diary of Anaïs Nin*, the chronicle of her life and work, is an often erotic narrative of great power, full of (sometimes imagined) information about her contemporaries, and about Miller and herself; her *Henry and June* focuses on Nin's relationship with Miller and his wife. Noël Riley Fitch's *Anaïs: The Erotic Life of Anaïs Nin* examines her fiction against the backdrop of actual affairs, as does Deidre Bair's *Anaïs Nin: A Biography*. Claudia Roth Pierpont looks afresh at Nin's *Diaries* in light of the recent appearance of unexpurgated sections that assert that Nin deliberately slept with her father in "Sex, Lies, and Thirty-Five Thousand Pages." A collection of interviews with Nin has been published as *Conversations with Anaïs Nin*, edited by Wendy M. Du Bow; here Nin speaks of using sexuality to reveal the hidden recesses of mind and body. Johanna Blakely establishes lesbianism as one pole of the erotic tension in a Nin novel; Blakely's "Abrotica: The Lesbian Erotic and the Erotic Abject in Anaïs Nin's House of Incest" analysis is relentlessly psychological.

Writers of the Beat Generation titillated Americans with unprecedented candor. An excellent look at Burroughs, Ginsberg, and Kerouac, with due attention to their eroticism, is John Tytell's *Naked Angels: The Lives and Literature of the Beat Generation*. Jennie Skerl and Robin Crydenberg have collected critical and interpretive essays on Burroughs, beginning with the years in which he seemed most outrageous, in *William Burroughs at the Front: Critical Reception 1959–1989*. Other sources on the controversial writer can be found in *William S. Burroughs: A Reference Guide*, by Michael B. Goodman and Lemuel B. Coley, who list an enormous number of interpretive and critical items, important now that Burroughs has found his way into the mainstream through Hollywood adaptation of his work. Ted Morgan seems more interested in the writer's drug habits than in the explicitness of his narratives in *Literary Outlaw: The Life and Times of William S. Burroughs*. Allen Ginsberg's *Journals: Early Fifties, Early Sixties* recounts encounters with Burroughs, Kerouac, and others and includes notes, fragments, and erotic songs. Barry Miles' *Ginsberg: A Biography* discusses the poet's experiments with sex and obscenity. Neeli Cherkovski's

Hank: The Life of Charles Bukowski runs a critical finger over the writer's erotic edges; Bukowski's *All's Normal Here: A Charles Bukowski Primer* anthologizes critical interpretation along with selections from Bukowski's work.

Edgar Mertner and Herbert Mainusch borrow the Kronhausens' concept of "erotic realism" as a baseline for *Pornotopia: Das Obszöne und die Pornographie in der literarischen Landschaft*, which includes lengthy treatment of Henry Miller, Harold Robbins, and Terry Southern. Maurice Charney's "Sexual Fiction in America, 1955–1980" discusses Philip Roth's *Portnoy's Complaint* (1969), Erica Jong's *Fear of Flying* (1973), Vladimir Nabokov's *Lolita* (1955), Terry Southern and Mason Hoffenberg's *Candy* (1958), William Kotzwinkle's *Nightbook* (1974), Gael Green's *Blue Skies, No Candy* (1976), and Scott Spencer's *Endless Love* (1979), all of which have been denounced or praised as pornography. Charney's *Sexual Fiction* covers in addition classics by Miller, Réage, Lawrence, and lots of others. Sohvi Karjalainen's "On Swearwords and Obscenities in Philip Roth's *Portnoy's Complaint*" makes a plausible case for the necessity of obscenity in Roth's messages. Norman Mailer speaks of the sexuality that informs his own writing in *The Prisoner of Sex*. Helen S. Garson observes in "John Hawkes and the Elements of Pornography" that, like D. H. Lawrence, Hawkes seems to find the gothic genre synonymous with the pornographic. In "Robert Coover's *Spanking the Maid*: Determinism and the Indeterminate Text," Robert Morace argues that the sadomasochistic elements of that novel are ideally suited to Coover's postmodern vision.

It would be impossible even to list all the mainstream authors whose works have been called pornographic. Suffice it to note the regular appearance of articles such as "Pious Pornography," in which N. M. Tischler excoriates Sinclair Lewis, John Updike, and William Styron for attributing garish sexual appetites to religious characters. Tischler observes that without a growing tolerance for sexual expression and the elimination of blasphemy as a test of obscenity, none of those writers could have created such works. Larry McMurtry traces erotic fiction from the hard-boiled sexuality of the 1940s to the more explicit novels of the 1970s in "From Mickey Spillane to Erica Jong." While the public easily accepts candor now, he says, the downside is that the sex rarely serves to illuminate character or theme and thus has lost much of its ability to shock or enlighten. Clive Bloom explores pulp literature as it shades into kitsch in *Cult Fiction: The Popular Reading Cultures of America and Britain*, which he has reissued with a more politically correct title as *Cult Fiction: Popular Reading and Pulp Theory*. Bloom is very good on popular genres, especially the marginal.

As in the case of Miller and Nin, the occasional writing of porn novels has sometimes fed writers who could not sell their more serious work. Formulaic pornography has more often attracted lesser authors adept at working within genre constraints. Carolyn See's "My Daddy, the Pornographer" tells the story of her father, who at sixty-seven became "Hardy Peters," writer of seventeen porn novels in two years; he became "the Thomas Edison of sodomy, the

Grandma Moses of smut," working at what to See is unquestionably a "popular art form" (110). In "My Porno Dad," Victoria Stagg Elliot, herself a porn film reviewer, recalls her father's forays into pornography, a sideline for a writer who wrote scripts for *The Guiding Light* and articles for *Newsweek*: "Dad always said that everything he knew about sex, he had learned from his own writings. Having a father who made a living from writing porno books and magazines meant much more than easy access to a lot of air-brushed pictures and dirty words. It meant having parents who were not afraid to discuss sex, sexuality and sensuality, and who also had the necessary language to communicate their point without resorting to blushing and blank spaces in their speech" (11).

The experience has been equivocal for some writers. Two articles by authors disenchanted by pornography assembly lines are "The Reluctant Pornographer," by Burton Wohl, whose tedious labor in a Los Angeles porn publishing house persuaded him that porn formulas are less about sex than power; and "The Working Day in a Porno Factory," by Ron Sproat, a veteran capable of turning out a 200-page erotic novel every week. Having tried his hand at many porn genres, including dirty comics, Bernard Wolfe confesses to burnout in *Memoirs of a Not Altogether Shy Pornographer*, though his narrative contains an insider's valuable reflections on writing per se. In *Story of "J."*, Terry Garrity, the author with John Garrity of *The Sensuous Woman*, (by "J.") recalls often unpleasant effects of writing an enormously popular sexual guide, among which was harassment. Fans and journalists stereotyped her as a devotee of skimpy clothes, masturbation, and orgies to the point where she felt beleaguered. Erica Jong endured similar abuse, especially unwanted phone calls requesting sex after she wrote *Fear of Flying*, or so she tells Steve Chapple and David Talbot, who also interviewed Anne Rice, Nancy Friday, and Susie Bright for *Burning Desires: Sex in America, a Report from the Field*. Some writers called pornographic hardly deserve the title. In this category one can stand as representative. Calvin C. Hernton's "How I Came to Write 'The Filthiest Book Ever Written' " winces at public reaction to his *Sex and Racism in America*, a sociological text, which was suppressed in various communities.

Some who have written unabashedly pornographic works, on the other hand, remain not only unrepentant and undisillusioned but also proud of their efforts. Anne Rice, best known for her vampire novels, writes explicit romances under the pseudonyms A. N. Roquelaure and Anne Rampling. The lubricity of her "Beauty" trilogy (*The Claiming of Sleeping Beauty* [1983], *Beauty's Punishment* [1984], *Beauty's Release* [1985]) appeals strongly to women, as does the fluid sex of the Rampling novels (*Exit to Eden* [1985]). Ron Bluestone's "Interview with the Pornographer" elicits the remark that Andrea Dworkin and Catharine MacKinnon are "fools" for characterizing pornography as exclusively male. The run-of-the mill pornographic novelist is not interested in finding out what women want, Rice says, suggesting that the ordinary male-oriented formulas are cut-and-dried. "To have a pornography for women, somebody would really have to give women what they want, and they'd have to find out what that is. The porn world is just not structured that way," and she writes to redress the imbalance. In any case, Rice says, "Pornography has no value if you are going to be guarded and worried about what people think" (214). Rice expands on the pleasures of writing erotica for audiences she knows will enjoy reading it in Digby Diehl's "Playboy Interview: Anne Rice." In another interview, "Other Incarnations of the Vampire Author," conducted by Stewart Kellerman, she says: "I think pornography is completely worthwhile. I wanted to write the kind of delicious S&M fantasies I'd looked for but couldn't find anywhere. I'm really rather proud of it, shocking though that might be. I feel that if I'm read 200 years from now, it'll be as much for that as anything else" (16). Katherine Ramsland has written *Prism of the Night: A Biography of Anne Rice*, but seems a little bewildered by Rice's "other" persona.

In "Confessions of a Lady Pornographer," Florence King admits to writing erotica before her other books sold well enough to pay bills and twits critics who refer to her more serious work as trashy also. Marilyn Meeske speaks of her career in "Memoirs of a Female Pornographer." The pseudonymous Linda Du Breuil shares sure-fire formulas in *The Girl Who Writes Dirty Books*. Worth reading for the author's reflections on having written more than 300 porn novels (some of which have been distributed in the United States) is Sue Caron's *A Screw Loose: My Story So Far*, an autobiography by a British writer. Angelo d'Arcangelo, the pen name of Joseph Bush, considers his explicit homosexual fiction a valuable counter to repression in *Angelo d'Arcangelo's Love Book: Inside the Sexual Revolution*, a theme also stressed in his *The Homosexual Handbook*, which includes criticism of gay porn by himself and others. Marco Vassi's *The Stoned Apocalypse* and *A Driving Passion* autobiographically scrutinize the career of an American erotic writer determined to push his fiction past boundaries. *The Erotic Comedies*, another volume from Vassi's prolific hand, combines short fiction and essays on erotica; the latter are perceptive, witty, and a little frightening. Mike McGrady, coauthor of Linda Lovelace's *Ordeal*, was also the organizer of a famous erotic hoax. McGrady's *Stranger than Naked* is the account of how various writers for *Newsday*, collectively known as "Penelope Ashe," wrote the best-selling porn novel *Naked Came the Stranger* (1969), which, in turn, became a popular porn film. Kathy Acker speaks of her performances in pornographic movies—she left when the mobsters and the corporate investors began to steal the fun—as possible influences on her fiction in "Punk Days in New York." "The Quest for Love and the Writing of Female Desire in Kathy Acker's *Don Quixote*," by Richard Walsh, indicates the serious critical attention now paid Acker classics such as *Blood and Guts in High School* and *Kathy Goes to Haiti*.

During the 1960s and 1970s, it seemed, every other writer in Greenwich Village tossed off a sleazy paperback to pay the rent. Those interested in the niche markets of today can consult several "how-to" books. Valerie Kelly's *How to Write Erotica* offers detailed advice on various markets: magazines, book publishers, telephone sex services, video companies. She covers researching reader preferences, finding material, writing seductively, using formats and formulas, and negotiating with editors. Says Kelly, "at its very worst, pornography gives a lopsided view of sex and a bad impression of females. At its best it educates and enlightens people to the possibilities of enjoyment" (4). Because of the shortage of material advocating sexual equality, Kelly believes, writers should be bold: "Having struggled through the trials and heartbreak of learning rules for writing children's books, formulas for sitcoms, structure for three-act plays, politics for screenwriting and patience for waiting on novels to be accepted, I can tell you without reservation that erotica is the easiest, most immediately satisfying, best-paying field for a new writer today" (21). Just as engaging is *How to Write Porno Novels for Fun and Profit*, in which the sixty-year-old pulp writer Richard E. Geis admits to exhaustion but is sympathetic to would-be carriers of the erotic torch. Elizabeth Benedict interviews writers and excerpts passages to persuade would-be writers that sex scenes can be made authentic in *The Joy of Writing Sex: A Guide for Fiction Writers*. Three current guides, Mike Bailey's *Writing Erotic Fiction: And Getting Published*, Derek Parker's *Writing Erotic Fiction*, and Pamela Rochford's *Writing Erotic Fiction: How to Write a Successful Erotic Novel*, insist that the market is healthy, but also insist on dealing with editors to assess demand for particular types. Bailey, Parker, and Rochford suggest language, plots, and degrees of explicitness and offer tips on constructing stimulating scenes and couplings. M. Drax annually publishes *Erotic Writers and Collector's Market*, a directory of publishers and distributors of erotica for writers of manuscripts and screenplays. Similar is James N. Goode's *Erotica Markets: Obscure and Profitable Markets for the Sensual Writer*, whose pages proffer advice and list receptive publishers. Perhaps encouraged by the success of its several erotica series, Circlet Press has published *Erotic Writer's Market Guide*, edited by Lawrence Schimel. The great majority of erotic novels and collections are rarely reviewed, save by periodicals such as *Screw*, which has always run a regular review department called "Fuckbooks." *Screw*'s reviews are worth consulting because of their honesty: the editors calibrate the degree of stimulation.

PUBLISHERS AND BOOKSELLERS

As we have noted elsewhere, Benjamin Franklin served as his own publisher in the colonies. Other domestic publishers of clandestine material left few traces other than the artifacts themselves: a few dozen such books trade today on the rare book market or reside permanently in collections. Franklin was one of the first Americans to own a copy of Cleland's *Fanny Hill*. Isaiah Thomas, perhaps the first actual commercial publisher in America and later founder of the American Antiquarian Society, may have pirated *Fanny Hill* in the 1790s or early 1800s; many other American publishers pirated editions over the years, which authorities routinely seized. In his *Index Librorum Prohibitorum* (under the pseudonym Pisanus Fraxi) of 1877, Henry Ashbee marveled that "America, as in other branches of industry, has made of late years great progress in the production of books, and not the least of those of an improper character. Until 1846 the Americans produced nothing, but merely imported such books; when an Irishman, W[illiam]. Haynes, began to publish, and soon became a rich man. Up to 1871 [this entrepreneur] had published not less than 300 different works, and we are told that the number of such books sold annually in New York amounts to 100,000" (xlix–1). Ashbee in the same passage noted that hardened laws in the United States enabled Anthony Comstock to confiscate books by the ton. A former surgeon, Haynes began his career by pirating *Fanny Hill* and European classics, then over time commissioned domestic novels. According to Walter Kendrick's *The Secret Museum* (129–130), Haynes killed himself when Comstock picked up his trail.

Gershon Legman takes up the chronicle where Ashbee leaves off. Legman's historical and interpretive bibliographic work, *The Horn Book: Studies in Erotic Folklore and Bibliography*, provides a foundation for the study of American writers, publishers, and collectors of erotica from the mid-nineteenth to the early twentieth centuries. Legman's Introduction to Patrick J. Kearney's *The Private Case: An Annotated Bibliography of the Erotica Collection in the British (Museum) Library*, revised as "The Lure of the Forbidden" for Martha Cornog's *Libraries, Erotica, and Pornography*, supplies authoritative information on editions, collections, publishers, and ephemera. John Tebbel's *A History of Book Publishing in the United States* makes frequent reference to prosecution of borderline publishers, and J. D. Hart's *The Popular Book: A History of America's Literary Taste* provides good background but few specifics on contraband.

For his *The Media in America*, John Tebbel counted forty-six pornographic books published between 1800 and 1846 (though the provenance of several is shaky) on the shelves of the Kinsey Institute. Many of these are reprints of European classics, marriage manuals of varying degrees of explicitness, quasi-scientific texts, diatribes against masturbation, and bizarre theories by anonymous authors. Tebbel notes that the reputable publisher Appleton printed sensational accounts of a bishop of New York charged with rape and seduction, mentions that Calvin Blanchard published a translation of Ovid's *Art of Love* in 1862, and lists titles (*Confessions of a Washington Belle; Beautiful Creole of Havana; Adventures of Anna P., or the Belle of New York*; and *Child of Passion, or the Amorous Foundling*) turned out by a notorious New Orleans press during the Civil War. Tebbel mistakenly calls *The Libertine Enchantress: or the Adventures of Lucinda Hartley* (1863) the first "native erotic novel," when in reality it was *Venus in Boston* (1843). David Reynolds correctly identifies the latter and says that its author, George Thompson, has "the dubious distinction of having written the most purely disgusting novels in pre–Civil War America" in *Beneath the American Renaissance: The Subversive Imagination in the Age of Emerson and Melville*. Thompson churned out hundreds, some written under the pseudonym "Greenhorn," with titles such as *The G'hals of Boston, Fanny Greely: Or, the Confessions of a Free-Love Sister Written by Herself*, and *The*

Delights of Love, all released in 1850. In his search for dark impulses underneath the traditional literary canon, Reynolds finds other marginal figures lurking in pornographic subcultures.

Timothy Gilfoyle in *City of Eros: New York City, Prostitution, and the Commercialization of Sex, 1790–1920* has identified pornographic entrepreneurs such as Boston's James Ramerio, who published most of Thompson's erotic fiction. Anthony Comstock's *Frauds Exposed: Or, How the People Are Deceived and Robbed, and Youth Corrupted* and *Traps for the Young* are good sources on publishers such as Ramerio. Information on lots of other sleazy book publishers from the 1870s to the 1950s can be found in the *Annual Reports* of the New England Watch and Ward Society and of the New York Society for the Suppression of Vice, as well as the documents of the latter society catalogued under *Names and Records of Persons Arrested Under the Auspices of the Society: 1920–1950*.

Paul S. Boyer's *Purity in Print: The Vice-Society Movement and Book Censorship in America* is a fairly well detailed account of the prosecution of publishers and distributors from the Civil War to the 1930s. *Comstockery in America*, by Robert W. Haney, comments on the state of pulp literature in the first decades of the twentieth century. *Forbidden Books: Notes and Gossip on Tabooed Literature, Bibliographies and Excerpts . . . by an Old Bibliophile*, (probably) by the brilliant lexicographer and perpetually impecunious hack writer John S. Farmer, is really a guide to books published by Charles Carrington in Paris for the American trade. (According to C. J. Scheiner's *Compendium*, Samuel Roth published a New York edition of 1929.) Carrington, perhaps the most notorious of all booksellers, is profiled in "Charles Carrington: The Man and His Books." Scattered information on marginal dealers is available in the occasional memoir, like R. E. Banta's *William C. Smith, Gentleman Bookseller*, a tribute to a clandestine Cincinnati publisher of books such as Twain's *1601* and *Blue Law Ballads*, and in Edwin Wolf's *Rosenbach: A Biography*, a study of A. S. W. Rosenbach, a rare-book dealer who catered to erotica collectors. Rosenbach's Philadelphia company supplied the Kinsey Institute during its early archive-building.

Domestic sexual expression flowered during the liberal 1920s and the depression 1930s, when publishers like Horace Liveright of Liveright and Boni pushed against the envelope of respectability. Walker Gilmer's *Horace Liveright, Publisher of the Twenties* has chapters on Liveright's harassment by John Sumner and the New York Society for the Suppression of Vice, and on two important censorship trials in which Liveright figured. The first was the prosecution for obscenity of Maxwell Bodenheim's *Replenishing Jessica* (1928), the second Theodore Dreiser's *American Tragedy* (1925). Gilmer provides information on Mencken's "Hatrack" story, on Thomas R. Smith, one of Liveright's editors, who secretly published *Immortalia* (1927), and on other marginal endeavors. Mencken's own *My Life as Author and Editor* recounts these and other battles and dilates on his friendship with authors of controversial books. T. G.

Tanselle focuses on a publisher's struggles against the censorship of works such as *Casanova's Homecoming* and *A Young Girl's Diary* in "The Thomas Seltzer Imprint."

Publishers of erotica aimed at several audiences. Some printed beautifully bound classics for an upscale market of bibliophiles, while others sold suppressed texts to the intellectually curious, and still others mass-produced cheap fiction for the undiscriminating. In a notice entitled "Bootleg Literature," *Publishers Weekly* condemned mail-order houses that advertised sexual materials on the grounds that the practice cheapened the industry. To the censor, there was little difference: trash was trash, no matter how elegant the text or its cover. The risk of prosecution, however, varied depending on the publisher's location, reputation, and financial resources. Jay A. Gertzman provides the best map of the period in *Bookleggers and Smuthounds: The Trade in Erotica, 1920–1940*, a masterly discussion of literary censorship in the 1920s, 1930s, and 1940s, involving booksellers such as Ben Abramson (Argus Books, Chicago), Frances Steloff (Gotham Book Mart, New York City), and Harry Schwartz (Casanova Book Store, Milwaukee); marginal publishers such as Esar Levine (Panurge Press), Benjamin Rebhuhn (Falstaff Press), Louis Shomer (American Ethnological Press), and Jake Brussel (Brussel and Brussel); the carriage-trade publishers with occasionally suspect titles such as Bennett Cerf, Horace Liveright, Alfred A. Knopf, and Pascal Covici; and especially the notorious Samuel Roth, whose enterprises are legendary. Gertzman describes these (in the main) Jewish publishers as "pariah capitalists" (i.e., those who serve a marginal, but important, function in a culture that despises them), a circumstance that helps explain the otherwise mean-spirited American predilection for characterizing pornography as "Jewish." Gertzman is also an excellent source for titles of books published by various presses (as are the catalogs of book dealer C. J. Scheiner). Among other items in his richly realized book, Gertzman deals with rumors that John Sumner apparently delivered some of the books he seized to a chosen bookseller, Harry F. Marks of Manhattan, to resell and that Sumner ran a protection racket, asking for donations in return for not prosecuting booksellers. Gertzman demonstrates that respectable publishers could draw on support and funds to defend their questionable publications, while marginal presses could not.

Gertzman categorizes erotic books of the 1920s, 1930s, and 1940s across a spectrum from borderline to obscene by the standards of the time. The major categories are "Gallantiana" (sometimes called "curiosa" or "facetiae"), which mostly included lightly erotic fiction and expurgated classics (e.g., Boccaccio, Rabelais, Aristophanes), ballads, jestbooks, and treatises on women, love, and relationships; "Sex Pulps," which were potboiling romances and mysteries; "Erotology and Sexology," which included anthropological and sociological texts, some authoritative and serious, some designed to titillate, on subjects ranging from hygiene, deviance, marriage, and birth control to prostitution, nudism, and bizarre sexual customs and practices; "Sleaze—'Bibles' and 'Readers,' " which were often pamphlets filled with confessions, anecdotes, and graphic stories of seduction or conquest, or Tijuana bibles, a term applied to explicit comic books or stapled collections of poorly printed stories; and "Classical and Modern 'Flagitous' Pornography," a classification composed of works officially proscribed (*Lady Chatterley's Lover, Tropic of Cancer, 1601, The Autobiography of a Flea, Fanny Hill*, and so on). Gertzman also discusses "booklegging," or the practice of clandestine or pirated printing, lists printers who ran off questionable editions during the period, and covers types of distribution from respectable bookstores, secondhand shops, lending libraries, drugstores, cigar stores, newsstands, and peddlers to backdate magazine storefronts.

Irene Cleaton and Allen Cleaton chronicle sensational cases in *Books and Battles: American Literature 1920–1930*, while Albert Van Nostrand examines the exploitative aspects of early twentieth-century American mainstream publishing in *The Denatured Novel*. Alan Devoe's "Erotic Books and the Depression" deals with erotica as cheap entertainment in hard times, when the depression reduced the price of pulp novels. During the 1930s book outlets sometimes maintained pornographic rental libraries or sold erotic novels for a dollar a copy. Ellis Parker Butler covers this phenomenon in *Dollarature, or the Drug Store Book*, a volume devoted to the surging popularity of the pulp novel, an item dispensed by drugstores during the late 1920s. W. G. Rogers' *Wise Men Fish Here: The Story of Frances Steloff and the Gotham Book Mart* recounts the collisions between the doyenne of American booksellers and John Sumner's New York Society for the Suppression of Vice, who constantly harassed Steloff because she encouraged Anaïs Nin and sold Parisian editions of Henry Miller's *Tropic of Cancer*. Harry W. Schwartz speaks of selling and renting erotic books in the 1930s in his *Fifty Years in My Bookstore, or a Life with Books*, while his *This Book Collecting Racket* provides authoritative American publishing histories of controversial books by Lawrence, Harris, Cabell, Aleister Crowley, Norman Douglas, and Casanova. D. B. Covington's *The Argus Book Shop: A Memoir* recalls censorship attempts at Ben Abramson's Chicago store, which also stocked serious erotica. Eric Dingwall's *Very Peculiar People: Portrait Studies in the Queer, the Abnormal, and the Uncanny* sketches the author's father, Adam Dingwall, a mail-order importer and publisher (Dingwall-Rock, Ltd.) of erotica, and his associates. Jay Gertzman has recently published a fine article based on legal records and extensive interviews with dealers and collectors of erotica as " 'Esoterica' and 'The Good of the Race': Mail-Order Distribution of Erotica in the 1930s." During the depression, only the sale of erotica under the counter kept legitimate bookstores from bankruptcy, points out Robert Thomas in an obituary of Jack Biblo, a Manhattan dealer ("Jack Biblo, Used Bookseller for Half a Century, Dies at 91").

During this period European presses published books that were forbidden in the United States but are regarded as classics of modernism now. These included avant-garde literature by James Joyce and Henry Miller but also pulp fiction and cruder works. Hugh Ford's *Published in Paris* is a good source on books published in Paris when American publishers would not print them; the details on Sylvia Beach, Jack Kahane, Miller, and Nin are wonderful, and Janet Flanner's Introduction to the volume is exceptional. Noël Riley Fitch foregrounds the Paris publisher of *Ulysses* in *Sylvia Beach and the Lost Generation: A History of Literary Paris in the Twenties*. A personal account of the European publishing scene is Armand Coppens' *Memoirs of an Erotic Bookseller*, which comments on the idiosyncrasies of publishers and distributors and also on the economics of the trade.

The most famous Parisian erotic publisher was the Obelisk Press, established by Jack Kahane in Paris in the early 1930s to make available explicit fiction of merit. After World War II, Kahane's son Maurice Girodias took over Obelisk but lost money trying to follow his father's example of printing books of high quality. In 1953 Girodias founded the Olympia Press, whose list included works of talent but also, increasingly, rather sleazy titles. These were bound in distinctive green covers in a series called "The Traveller's Companion." Number 48, for example, was *Sodom, or the Quintessence of Debauchery*, by John Wilmot (Earl of Rochester). Girodias tells the story of his father's enterprises and reflects on erotica publishing in Paris and on the American market for porn from the 1920s through the 1960s in *The Frog Prince: An Autobiography*, taking a leaf from Kahane's own *Memoirs of a Booklegger*, itself an excellent recollection of the cultural climate that led Kahane into various ventures and of the writers he encountered and published. Girodias has also collected some of the press' output in *The Olympia Reader* and *The New Olympia Reader*, both of which contain graphic narratives; of particular interest is Diane di Prima's account of her liaison with Jack Kerouac in the second volume, because it indicates a shared fondness for fictionalizing sex after the fact. *The Best of Olympia* is still another grouping of pieces, here drawn from the press' periodical, *Olympia Magazine*. Geoffrey Wagner resavors the pleasures of the portable little green volumes tucked in the luggage of sophisticates on European trains in "The End of the 'Porno'—Or, No More Traveling Companions?" John de St. Jorre's *Venus Bound: The Erotic Voyages of the Olympia Press* is a history of the publishers (see also Chapter 4, **Bibliographies and Reference Tools**, especially Kearney and Perkins). Not all of the writers were as grateful to Girodias as he seemed to think they should be; Vladimir Nabokov and Girodias quarreled over the publication history of *Lolita*. Nabokov's "Lolita and Mr. Girodias" can be read with Girodias' account, "Lolita, Nabokov, and I." In this regard, Carol Iannone's "From *Lolita* to *Piss Christ*," which focuses on the former rather than the latter, indicates that neoconservatives still condemn Nabokov's *Lolita*; Iannone argues that artistic merit alone cannot justify obscenity.

Just as important is Samuel Roth (1893–1974), critic, publisher, poet, and pirate, whose name has been immortalized in one of the most significant Supreme Court obscenity decisions (*Roth v. United States*, 1957). Roth wrote *Diary of a Smut Hound* under the pseudonym Hugh Wakem, taking the persona of a vice officer, just after one of his several arrests for publishing obscenity. According to C. J. Scheiner's *Compendium*, the narrative provides accurate information about other American booksellers who dealt in contraband despite Roth's lame attempts at disguise (138). In another jail Roth wrote the self-pitying *Stone Walls Do Not: The Chronicle of a Captivity*, in which he pleaded for free speech. Virtually every history of censorship in the United States discusses Roth's case in terms of the evolution of obscenity law, but his literary career is the subject of two articles by Leo Hamalian, who characterizes him as an engine of popular culture in "Nobody Knows My Names: Samuel Roth and the Underside of Modern Letters" and as a symbol of cultural subversion in "The Secret Careers of Samuel Roth." Hamalian calls Roth an "unblushing pirate" and notes that his chameleon-like changes of identity as publisher and writer could not prevent his being jailed several times. Gay Talese also devotes substantial space to Roth's career in *Thy Neighbor's Wife*, as does Edward de Grazia in *Girls Lean Back Everywhere*. By far the most thorough treatment of Roth to date, however, is Gertzman's *Bookleggers and Smuthounds: The Trade in Erotica, 1920–1940*, where Roth appears as a quintessential outsider.

James Jackson Kilpatrick tries to steer a path between censors and the First Amendment in his discussion of pornographic publishers and distributors in *The Smut Peddlers*, which provides information on books and the culture they engendered in the 1950s. Although Michael Perkins provides a brief history of erotic literature beginning with Euripides and Catullus, the real value of his *The Secret Record: Modern Erotic Literature* is its information on American publishers of the 1960s and 1970s. Here the reader will find the history of Brandon House, the Olympia Press after its move from Paris to New York, Collectors' Publications, Essex House, and various other publishers, together with comment on writers ranging from Richard Amory, to Diane di Prima, Mary Sativa, Akbar Del Piombo, Barry Malzberg, Marco Vassi, Perkins himself, Harriet Daimler, Marcus Van Heller, Alexander Trocchi, and many others. More authoritative yet is Daniel Eisenberg's "Toward a Bibliography of Erotic Pulps," a splendid essay on the difficulties of tracking down ephemera, with a lot of information on the pulp phenomenon. Eisenberg lists various imprints. He also says, "Foreign erotica, that aimed at a foreign market and not merely published abroad for American consumption, has little appeal to the average American reader, and presumably the reverse is also true" (178). While there are obvious exceptions (e.g., *Story of O*), there seems to be some truth to this contention, at least where written material is concerned; porn novels draw strength from local cultural specificity.

Miriam Linna's sporadically published zine *Smut Peddler* runs essays and notes on erotic paperbacks published between 1959 and 1965, a period Linna calls the "Golden Age" of pulp fiction. Like other enthusiasts, aficionados of erotic pulps gravitate toward specific periods. Focusing on a slightly earlier one, Lee Server's *Over My Dead Body: The Sensational Age of the American Paperback, 1945–1955* chronicles the appearance of sensational softcover books like John D. MacDonald's *The Brass Cupcake*, Mickey Spillane's *Kiss Me Deadly*, and Jack Kerouac's *On the Road*, as well as the forgotten *White Slave*

Racket, A Swell-Looking Babe, Hitch-Hike Hussy, and other obscure softcovers. The spicing of detective and mystery fiction with sex is one of the running themes of G. O'Brien's *Hardboiled America: The Lurid Years of Paperbacks*, which characterizes Spillane, Cain, Hammett, and Chandler as inheritors and progenitors of sexually veined consciousness. "Disseminating Desire: Grove Press and 'The End[s] of Obscenity' " by Richard Ellis covers the publishing strategy of the New York company in the 1960s and 1970s, during which time Grove became notorious for its list of erotica high and low. A disapproving Cleveland Amory lists "smutty" titles current in the 1960s in "Paperback Pornography." Here he attacks publishers who publish quasi-respectable and sleazy books, calls for renewed prosecution of the latter, and laments the decline of taste.

Though erotic fiction is not their central focus, several general histories contain a lot of information on the production of cheap, sexy paperbacks: Thomas L. Bonn's *Undercover: An Illustrated History of American Mass Market Paperbacks*; Kenneth C. Davis' *Two-Bit Culture: The Paperbacking of America*; and Frank L. Schick's *The Paperbound Book in America*. In "Lurid! Licentious! Collectible! The Flip Side of the 1940's and 50's," William Grimes quotes James Elroy as saying of paperbacks that Americans knew "the dark stuff was out there, but it was contained" in the 1950s; Elroy explains the current nostalgia by saying that "people want to go back into an era when there were shadows." Lawrence Stark's "Pulp Fiction Erotica" carefully outlines genres for which Beacon, Boudoir, Venus, Quarter, Midwood Books, and other publishers intertwined sex and violence in paperbacks such as *Commie Sex Trap, Marijuana Girl, Sin Cruise, I Am a Lesbian, Dance Hall Girl, Love-Hungry Doctor, Commuter Wives*. These digest-sized books, priced at a quarter, their covers luridly illustrated, were aimed at working-class audiences; they poured from presses in a flood. Coteries of authors including Jack Woodford, Harry Whittington, and Orrie Hitt, supplemented by more "serious" writers such as Lawrence Block and Donald Westlake, churned out most of the paperbacks. Stark notes that the lesbian pulp subgenre was spawned after Gold Medal Books brought out Tereska Torres' *Women's Barracks* (1950). When fan mail rose dramatically, other publishers rushed lesbian novels into print, launching the careers of Ann Aldrich, Valerie Taylor, and Ann Bannon. Stark notes that a mint copy of *Reform School Girl* by Felice Swados (Diversey Romance, 1948) now fetches $400 and up; he lists several dealers in vintage paperbacks. Sarah Lyall's "Lost and Found" details the effort and expense that bedevil American publishers, especially Blue Moon, whose books are routinely seized by Canadian Customs as a consequence of that nation's draconian antismut laws. Robert S. Boynton examines the penchant of Routledge for publishing what many call "academic porn" in "The Routledge Revolution: Has Academic Publishing Gone Too Far?" Routledge seems to have inherited the niche of Grove Press in catering to an audience for upscale erotica, gender-bending, and intellectual titillation. Finally, David Hebditch and Nick Anning offer a contemporary overview of publishing and other enterprises in *Porn Gold: Inside the Pornography Business*.

SEX MANUALS AND GUIDES

One way to examine American attitudes toward sex as they shift over time is to peruse the sexual advice of different eras. Moral or medical (or quasi-medical) "authorities" often mixed opinions about erotica with theories of physiology, mental health, and sexual orthodoxy. Americans frequently read those opinions as a species of pornography, one reason they have been prized then and now by collectors of erotica, though they were usually written more to educate than to titillate. Contemporary historians hold that guides and pamphlets have long functioned as forms of sexual programming. Ann Rosalind Jones' important essay, "Nets and Bridles: Early Modern Conduct Books and Sixteenth-Century Women's Lyrics," makes clear that guides to conduct were designed to train women as technicians of sex and that the "folklore" of often misinformed "lessons" crept into traditional oral folklore, especially songs. Our amusement at crackpot manuals of the past should be tempered by the realization that contemporary guides may be just as suspect: the genre still flourishes as a way of reinforcing sexual norms, gender divisions, and "appropriate" behavior. In any case, books of sexual advice are important milestones in the evolution of mores and medical knowledge.

Among the very earliest to appear in America were various editions of sexual guides authored by "Aristotle," the pen name of an anonymous writer. In his "Eros Goes West: European and 'Homespun' Erotica in Eighteenth-Century America," Peter Wagner notes that in 1744 Jonathan Edwards reprimanded young men in Northampton, Massachusetts, for reading Aristotle's sex guides (*Masterpiece, Compleat Midwife, Problems*), a clear indication of their popularity. Wagner's *Eros Revived: Erotica of the Enlightenment in England and America* and his "The Discourse on Sex—Or Sex as Discourse: Eighteenth Century Medical and Paramedical Erotica" examine these and other paramedical texts in colonial America. Vern Bullough examines various editions (in the Huntington and UCLA libraries) of the Aristotle "medical" guides that once circulated in colonial America and compares them to modern versions of the genre in "An Early American Sex Manual, Or, Aristotle Who?" Otho T. Beall's " 'Aristotle's Master Piece' in America: A Landmark in the Folklore of Medicine" also analyzes advice absorbed on the sly by colonists.

Phillip A. Gibbs shakes his head at the advice offered males in "Self Control and Male Sexuality in the Advice Literature of Nineteenth Century America, 1830–1860." For the sudden erections, night sweats, and constant sexual fantasies that always afflict normal males, Gibbs notes, physicians and ministers urged abstinence, cold compresses or showers, and the thinking of pure thoughts. More attention has been devoted to Victorian sex manuals, presumably because Americans regard the period as rife with sexual hypocrisy. Alan Rusbridger's *A Concise History of the Sex Manual, 1886–1986* begins with Victorian examples, as does Sandy Teller's *This Was Sex*; both are humorous accounts, replete with absurd, misconceived, or warped excerpts from vintage guides. One manual to sell more than a million copies in various editions from 1894 on was *Light on Dark Corners* by B. G. Jefferies and J. L. Nichols; it has been reprinted with a historical Preface by J. W. Collins and Edward Spear. William Dwyer's *What Everyone Knew about Sex, Explained in the Words of Orsen Squire Fowler and Other Victorian Moralists* reviews the folklore disseminated by Victorian experts, the most obtuse of whom was Fowler, a phrenologist. A fine resource is Ronald G. Walters' *Primers for Prudery: Sexual Advice to Victorian America*, which bases its case on texts by physicians, ministers, utopians, educators, public health officials, and quacks. John S. Haller and Robin M. Haller's *The Physician and Sexuality in Victorian America* is an especially rich survey grounded on contemporary texts by legitimate mainstream doctors who sought to provide help and advice during a period of sexual ignorance and urgency, with some reference to quacks as well. In *The Destroying Angel: Sex, Fitness, and Food in the Legacy of Degeneracy, Graham Crackers, Kellogg's Corn Flakes, and American Health History*, John Money tells the stories of faddists Sylvester Graham and John Harvey Kellogg, crusaders against masturbation and sexuality, and provides a well-drawn background of the sexual landscape of the period. Kellogg (1852–1943), a physician and disciple of Graham, invented a cracker (named after Graham) that he believed was a sexual suppressant capable of curbing masturbation; wags observed that prohibitions against eating crackers in bed stemmed not from annoyance at crumbs but the fear that others would suspect the reason one was eating them. Granola and Corn Flakes, other Kellogg products, were alleged also to diminish sexual desire. His regimen for patients included sexual abstinence ("an erection is a marker on the grave") and as many as five enemas a day. Kellogg's career inspired a comic novel by T. Coraghessan Boyle, which was made into a mainstream film on the doctor's colonic obsessions, *The Road to Wellness* (1995). Another excellent study is Jayne A. Sokolow's *Eros and Modernization: Sylvester Graham, Health Reform, and the Origins of Victorian Sexuality in America*, which catalogs sexual misconceptions.

In *Dear Dr. Stopes: Sex in the 1920s*, Ruth Hall reproduces documents on "normal" sex authored by physicians in the 1920s. Americans have never shied away from offering sexual advice, but Bernarr Macfadden probably deserves a niche to himself. The journalist and physical faddist published *Manhood and Marriage* (among other books of advice) to warn fellow males of the debilitating effects of masturbation and too-frequent intercourse. His ideas are the subject of William R. Hunt's *Body Love: The Amazing Career of Bernarr Macfadden*, which details his run-ins with Anthony Comstock and other prudes. Many manuals have been aimed at the young; they are skewered by Johnny Marr in *(Anti-) Sex Tips for Teens: The Teenage Advice Book, 1897–1987*, a chronicle of advice narratives intended to persuade young people not to engage in intercourse. The texts Marr covers range from *What a Young Man Ought to Know* (1897) to Pat Boone's *Between You, Me, and the Gatepost* (1960). Though they acknowledge that both males and females suffered from the mythologies and silly theories of moralists and medical authorities, Barbara Ehrenreich and Deidre English challenge the presumption of males' prescribing sexual behavior for women in *For Her Own Good: 150 Years of the Experts' Advice to Women*. "Everything They Always Wanted You to Know: The Ideology of Popular Sex Literature," by Meryl Altman, is a pleasantly paranoid piece on sexual advice for women in manuals by males from Thomas Van de Velde to David Reuben, all of whom tried to promote a masculine "normality" in sexual behavior. Similarly, Michael Gordon and Penelope Shankweiler itemize discrimination against women in terms of expectations of sexual pleasure in "Different Equals Less: Female Sexuality in Recent Marriage Manuals."

A fascinating account of the divergent ways in which orgasm is described for men and women in sex manuals is "Written Descriptions of Orgasm: A Study of Sexual Differences." Here Ellen B. Vance and Nathaniel N. Wagner, noting that manuals published before the 1950s encouraged women to fake orgasms, comment on the implausibility of some of the descriptions of climax. Awareness that women were sexual creatures rather than passive participants came slowly, say M. S. Weinberg, R. G. Swensson, and S. K. Hammersmith. Their "Sexual Autonomy and the Status of Women: Models of Female Sexuality in U.S. Sex Manuals from 1950 to 1980" suggests that while mutual orgasm became something of a fetish, guides to sexuality were short on advice about just how women were supposed to achieve this beatific state. Diana Scully and Pauline Bart examined twenty-five gynecological texts to find that most advocated the medical view that women who could not achieve vaginal orgasms were "frigid" in "A Funny Thing Happened on the Way to the Orifice: Women in Gynecology Textbooks." Finally, Gerald Sussman satirizes the genre in *The Official Sex Manual: A Modern Approach to the Art and Techniques of Coginus*. Because the sex manual will strike some readers as self-parodistic, Sussman's efforts may seem more labored than funny, but the outlines of the more treasured formulas are amusing enough. Although *I Hear America Mating* is more properly construed as a book of comic folklore, Ralph Schoenstein also sends up sex manuals. James R. Peterson suggests that sex manuals tell us a great deal about ourselves in "A Brief History of Sex Tricks."

In a subcategory is the newspaper or magazine column of sexual advice. R. Kent surveys mostly British and American newspaper and magazine advice columns, some of which attend to sexual matters, in *Aunt Agony Advises: Problem Pages through the Ages*. *The Playboy Advisor Revisited* compiles columns that have appeared in the magazine, while Susan Crain Bakos has collected some of her columns from *Playboy* and *Penthouse* in *Dear Superlady of Sex*. These might profitably be compared with *The Advocate Adviser*, a collection of Pat Califia's advice columns in the gay magazine *The Advocate*. Guy Trebay's "Live from the Wet Spot: Dan Savage—Miss Manners He's Not" interviews Don Savage, the sex-advice columnist and author of *Savage Love* (New York: Plume, 1998), a collection of his columns, on the need for good information for all genders.

Earlier editions of *Our Bodies Ourselves*, a self-help text for women assembled by the Boston Women's Health Book Collective, offer detailed information on sexual matters. More recent editions seem circumspect, presumably so as not to offend women opposed to pornography or politically incorrect behavior. (See also **Sex Education** in Chapter 5.)

NARRATIVES OF PROSTITUTION

Although the word "pornography" was introduced into English less than 150 years ago, its etymological construction from the Greek means "writing about whores or prostitutes," and narratives about prostitutes still constitute an important genre. Perhaps the best single background history on the subject is Richard Symanski's *The Immoral Landscape: Female Prostitution in Western Societies*, an excellent survey of trends in familiar cultures, while Timothy J. Gilfoyle's analysis of the representations of prostitution in *City of Eros: New York City, Prostitution, and the Commercialization of Sex, 1790–1920* is more focused on America.

The starting points for the scholar interested in *representations* of prostitutes, however, are the splendid bibliographies on the subject compiled by Vern Bullough and his associates (see chapter 4, **Bibliographies and Reference Tools.**) It is, of course, as literary characters and themes that prostitution has most directly contributed to pornography. The ur-novel, so far as Americans are concerned, is John Cleland's *Fanny Hill, or Memoirs of a Woman of Pleasures*, which was imported and reprinted by colonists as early as 1789. Ralph Thompson traces the publishing history of the novel both here and abroad in "Deathless Lady." According to Thompson, among notable Americans to have cherished copies were Benjamin Franklin, the author, ambassador, and printer; Isaiah Thomas, the Federalist publisher and author of *History of Printing in America*; and Samuel Tilden, governor of New York and presidential candidate. Despite its age, *The Prostitute in Literature*, by Harold Greenwald and Aron Krich, covers still notable examples. A worthwhile anthology of fiction is *Fille de Joie*, a collection of short stories and novel excerpts by Henry Miller, Frank Harris, Alexander Woolcott, and several non-Americans. Innocuous enough now, the stories were explosive for their time. The historian Carl Bode has edited a volume entitled *The Editor, the Bluenose, and the Prostitute: H. L. Mencken's History of the "Hatrack" Censorship Case*, containing documents relating to the April 1926 issue of *The American Mercury*. The journal's editor, H. L. Mencken, in that issue published a vignette by Herbert Asbury (journalist of seamy life in cities) of a small-town prostitute nicknamed "Hatrack." When the New England Watch and Ward Society tried to stop sale of the journal on grounds of obscenity, Mencken wrote his famous essay "Puritanism as a Literary Force," which is included in the volume.

Khalid Kishtainy examines characterizations of prostitutes at the turn of the century in *The Prostitute in Progressive Literature*; Pierre L. Horn and Mary

Beth Pringle include American works such as Stephen Crane's *Maggie, a Girl of the Streets* in their discussion of *The Image of the Prostitute in Modern Literature*. Laura Hapke treats similar works in *Girls Who Went Wrong: Prostitutes in American Fiction, 1885–1917*. Kathleen Kramer explores the roles of sex workers in canonical (Chopin, Wharton, Crane) and popular literature of the period 1890–1929 in "Questionable Characters: Turn-of-the-Century American Fictions, Feminism, and the Fallen Woman." A fascinating, cross-cultural study of a famous text as it migrated across the Atlantic is Nancy Huston's *Mosaïque de la pornographie: Marie-Thérése et les autres*, on Marie-Thérése, author of *Vie d'une prostitueé* (*The Way of a Prostitute*), published by Olympia Press in Paris in 1955 and by Brandon House in California in 1966, with a chronology blending French and American (Miller, Nabokov, Sartre, Bataille) responses. Invaluable to critics is "Notes on Trick," for which Susan Walsh, herself a former massage parlor masseuse, interviews the writer Mary Gaitskill about the novelist's past life as a stripper and hooker. Gaitskill weaves her fiction around female workers in the sex trade and observes that she is often misunderstood: "People, even those who style themselves as very hip, still tend to think of prostitutes stereotypically. They even cherish the stereotype because they have an almost sentimental attachment to the idea of a tough-talking whore who'll blurt out Hard Truths with a capital T. So if I portray prostitutes who are complicated, intelligent, sensitive women I must be lying" (19).

Lisa McLaughlin contrasts representations as forms of narrative in older media and in television programs in "Discourses of Prostitution/Discourses of Sexuality." So does Shannon Bell, whose *Reading, Writing, and Rewriting the Prostitute Body* deals with images of the prostitute in literature and performance, with special attention to contemporary artists like Annie Sprinkle, Veronica Vera, and Bell herself. *Sex Work: Writings by Women in the Sex Industry*, a collection gathered by Frédérique Delacoste and Priscilla Alexander, allows prostitutes, performers, porn stars, and other sex workers to speak for themselves, sometimes in amazingly articulate essays. Though primarily focused on prostitutes, *Live Sex Acts: Women Performing Erotic Labor*, a key text by Wendy Chapkis, draws on interviews with anticensorship feminists and activists such as Annie Sprinkle. Chapkis argues that there is a clear difference between sex that is performance, as in performance art or porn film intercourse, whose mechanics can be detached from the person, and commercial sex that erodes the spirit because it cannot be so distanced. The essays in *Prostitution: On Whores, Hustlers, and Johns*, edited by James E. Elias, Vern L. Bullough, Veronica Elias, and Gwen Brewer, cover lap-dancing, hustling, feminist issues, and various aspects of the sex industry by therapists, academics, and sex workers.

Like successful CEOs, politicians, and generals, celebrated American madams customarily conclude their careers by publishing their memoirs, which rarely fail to mention the famous CEOs, politicians, and generals who patronized their establishments. They are excellent sources of sexual folklore but also of cultural information, since the women sometimes confide the names of authorities they had to pay off, the hypocrites who condemned them, the working conditions, the political climate of the region and period, and so on. A random sampling of largely formulaic works includes Sara Harris' *House of 10,000 Pleasures*, by a New York hostess to the rich and famous, among them King Farouk of Egypt; Sally Stanford's *The Lady of the House: The Autobiography of Sally Stanford*, whose clientele spanned various classes in San Francisco; Pauline Tabor's *Pauline's: Memoirs of the Madam on Clay Street*, which recalls the gangsters and politicians of Chicago; and Serge G. Wolsey's *Call House Madam: The Story of the Career of Beverly Davis*, on the doyenne of several Hollywood houses of prostitution. Of particular interest is *Pleasure Was My Business*, by Madame Sherry [Ruth Barnes], who recalls how King Farouk, one of her steady clients also, would arrive loaded down with pornographic films to show his favorite hostesses (199ff). One ethnic variation became a virtual subgenre, recognizable because of parodies, when in 1953, Polly Adler published the story of her brothel, *A House Is Not a Home*, which quickly became a classic; in 1965 Polly Alderman published *Diary of a Jewish Madam: I Was a Jewish Madam*. The roots of this narrative reach back to turn-of-the-century scandals involving Jewish prostitution in North and South America, the women having been transported to this hemisphere from Eastern Europe.

Research on male prostitutes in America is growing. Joseph Itiel's *A Consumer's Guide to Male Hustlers*, despite its very real how-to aspects, discusses the male prostitute as an independent contractor, and itemizes issues of motivation, health and safety; Itiel draws on personal experience and covers the image of the hustler in media. In *Understanding the Male Hustler*, Samuel M. Steward adopts a more sociological approach and also sketches cultural iconography, as does *Male Prostitution*, by Donald J. West. The operator of a gay bordello, Kenneth Marlow, has published his memoirs as *Mr. Madam: Confessions of a Male Madam*. *The Trade: Gay Male Escorts and Masseurs: Their Private and Working Lives*, by Bobby Hutchison, studies more than fifty escorts and masseurs from all classes. Dane Taylor and Antonia Newton-West interview male prostitutes and the women who patronize them in *Gigolos: The Secret Lives of Men Who Service Women*. All of these works, to one degree or another, contrast literary representations with the real thing.

A more important category is the tale of the reluctant prostitute, of which Virginia MacManus' *Not for Love* is symbolic. MacManus, an underpaid schoolteacher, took up prostitution in order to survive, then wrote about her experience. Writing with Robin Moore and Yvonne Dunleavy, Xavier Hollander, perhaps the best-known contemporary prostitute in America, wrote *The Happy Hooker*, to deny any sort of duress. The book was made into a hard-core porn movie and two mainstream Hollywood films. Several other books elevated Hollander to the status of national sex counselor, and for a time she wrote a monthly column for *Penthouse*. Jan Hutson's *The Chicken Ranch: The True Story of the Best Little Whorehouse in Texas* generated a musical and then a film. Heidi Fleiss and Sydney Biddle Barrows, the "Madam to the Stars" and the "Mayflower Madam," respectively, are still embroidering their publicity. The latter, with William Novak, has published *Mayflower Madam: The Secret Life of Sydney Biddle Barrows*, which draws some of its cachet from the protagonist's blue bloodline, while Heidi Fleiss' mentor, Alex Adams, writing with William Stadiem to trade on her pupil's notoriety, published *Madam 90210: My Life as a Madam to the Rich and Famous*, about her Hollywood call girl service. Much more interesting is Dolores French's perspective in *Working: My Life as a Prostitute*, written with Linda Lee; the happily married French describes the profession as a viable middle-class career option with degrees of personal satisfaction (if no medical plan) and speaks with fond nostalgia of her experiences. French's account makes clear that attitudes toward prostitutes are socially constructed. That is apparent also in the distinctions Americans commonly make between whores, and, say, sexual performers (see chapter 10, **Performance**) or sexual therapists. The clinical treatment of sexual dysfunction over the last couple of decades has generated this latter class of professional. Although an earlier age would certainly have called them prostitutes, surrogates who teach patients to overcome psychophysical problems by engaging in intercourse with them have become commonplace, and they, too, write about their techniques and missions. Two of a significant number are Heather Hill's *Sexual Surrogate: Notes of a Therapist* (written with John Austin) and Amanda Stewart's *Sex Therapist: My Story*.

Closely related are documentaries on sex workers, some objective, some prurient. In the former category, Susan Hall has published two books illustrated with photos by Bob Adelman: *Gentleman of Leisure: A Year in the Life of a Pimp* studies a pimp's environment and the prostitutes who people it, while *Ladies of the Night* lets prostitutes speak for themselves. Gail Sheehy's popular book, *Hustling*, explores linkages between prostitution and pornography. More deliberately titillating are Bernhardt Hurwood's *The Girls, the Massage and Everything: The Naked Truth about Massage Parlors*, on prostitutes who pretend to knead muscles, and Gabriel Vogliotti's *The Girls of Nevada*, on the legalized prostitution at Nevada's Mustang Ranch. Finally, two zines written by and for people in the trade are *P.O.N.Y. X-Press* and *Whorezine*. Both are revelations. So are the accounts by international working women collected by Gail Pheterson as *A Vindication of the Rights of Whores*, an extraordinary anthology and call for organization that is mandatory for scholars in this field. Pheterson has an essay in the special issue of *Social Text* devoted to sex workers; the entire issue is valuable, especially Anne McClintock's Introduction.

SEXUAL THEMES AND FETISHES IN LITERATURE

Hundreds of literary critics have dealt with sexual images and themes in American literature, with the erotic roles of women or homosexuals, or with other signs and symbols of fictional lubricity. Few engage clandestine texts directly, let alone concentrate on acts of intercourse, but those who do can be extraordinarily helpful. Strother Purdy points out that literary eroticism often seems unreal precisely because censorship denies sex a place in a normal life. Purdy laments the lack of scholarly attention devoted to sexual behavior on the page in "On the Psychology of Erotic Literature." In *Vom Elend der Literature: Pornographie und Gesinnung*, an exploration of twentieth-century high pornography, William S. Schlamm reviews theories and issues in mostly European fiction from de Sade to Silone, with excursions into American examples. According to Peter Stallybrass and Alison White, fetishistic and transgressive genres can be directly related to political and economic trends in the larger culture. Stallybrass and White suggest in *The Politics and Poetics of Transgression* that some barriers against mixing genres from low and high porn are strong, others weak; some low genres are truly subversive, while others are easily co-opted. Peter Brooks believes that the sexual body is a generator of symbolization and language. Brooks' *Body Work: Objects of Desire in Modern Narrative* observes that anxieties and hope figure in metaphors of the body, as inscribed in both literature and art.

Among other proposals made by H. J. Eysenck in "A Psychologist Looks at Pornography" is a grading system by which all literature can be ranked in terms of its sexual content. Eysenek devises a "scale of sexual activity" that awards 3 points to "one minute continuous lip kissing," 4–5 points for "manual manipulation of female breast, over clothes," 8 for "sexual intercourse, face to face," 12 to "oral manipulation of male genitals to ejaculation," and so on, all of which he compiles in a wonderfully loony "Pornography Index" that weighs points in terms of nouns, adverbs, adjectives, and verbs (96–97). Sociologist Don D. Smith analyzes the content of adult paperbacks published between 1967 and 1974 in "The Social Content of Pornography" to conclude that most are aimed at males and that in 60 percent "sex episodes are characterized by sex for sex's sake—sheer physical gratification devoid of any feeling toward the partner as a person" (22), a practice to which Smith brings a politically correct dislike, though why sex for its own sake should be reprehensible he does not make clear. Smith says that depictions of particular acts and themes do not vary much with the passage of time, being largely unaffected by events or trends in the outside world; he does not believe that the women's movement has had any effect on content.

Paul Englisch's *Das skatologische Element in der Literatur, Kunst, und Volksleben* covers scatological motifs in mostly European literature, though he takes note of a fascination with such themes in the work of Benjamin Franklin and other colonists. The revised and expanded twelve-volume edition of Ernst Schertel's classic study of the late 1920s, *Der Flagellantismus in Literatur und Bildnerei*, is definitive on whipping as a theme in global literature until the 1950s. Its lavish illustrations attest to flagellation as an iconographic element in visual pornography as well. The recurring image of whipping in mainstream American literature is the focus of Richard H. Broadhead's "Sparing the Rod: Discipline and Fiction in Antebellum America." Incest, masturbation, sexual dominance, and reproduction in fiction of the mid-nineteenth century are the topics covered in G. M. Goshgarian's *To Kiss the Chastening Rod: Domestic Fiction and Sexual Ideology in the American Renaissance*. Many of the examples featured in Gerald Greene and Caroline Greene's *S-M: The Last Taboo* are drawn from literature. Henry Miles' *Forbidden Fruit: A Study of Incest in Forbidden Literature* traverses clandestine examples, among them classic pornographic tales, while James B. Twitchell's *Forbidden Partners: The Incest Taboo in Modern Culture* traces incest as image and theme in mainstream art and literature from the eighteenth century to the present. Laurie Adams Frost selects examples of bestiality in modern American fiction for her "Pets and Lovers: Human–Companion Animal Bond in Contemporary Literary Prose." Since 1974, *Semiotext(e)* has probed sexual recesses. A typical issue is 4:1 (1981) on "Polysexuality," a collection of fiction and manifestos (on fetishes from intercourse with animals to pedophilia), some of which narrowly skirt incomprehensibility. Colin Wilson's *The Misfits: A Study of Sexual Outsiders* covers fairly standard fetishism in literature. Rob Moore has collected erotic stories by eleven women and five men, all with open-air settings and "non-sexist" language, for a volume called *Field Guide to Outdoor Erotica*. Nancy Ellen Talburt singles out the sexual connotations of a familiar fluid in "Red Is the Color of My True Love's Blood: Fetishism in Mystery Fiction."

Several well-known texts outline the sexual anxieties underlying American attitudes toward miscegenation; each deals with the exfoliation of racial fears into fantasies of enormous enduring power. These fall into various categories ranging from the alleged sexual receptivity of black women, a myth perpetuated first by a slavery that institutionalized sexual abuse by white masters and second by a social inferiority that kept women of color vulnerable, to the nightmares associated with black penises and the alleged preferences of white women for them. Calvin C. Hernton's *Sex and Racism in America* contextualizes literary works, as do W. J. Cash's *The Mind of the South* and Eldridge Cleaver's *Soul on Ice*. For a better understanding of the persistence of miscegenational taboo, one need look no further than books such as Jean de Villiot's *Black Lust* and Felix Bryk's *The Sex Life of African Negroes* and *Voodoo-Eros*, all circulated by marginal publishers in the 1930s. Disguised as documentary approaches to the mating habits of Africans, they capitalized on the exotic and erotic appeal of primitivism and miscegenation.

In "Racism in Pornography," Alice Mayall and Diana E. H. Russell analyze conventional pornographic books to demonstrate that African Americans, especially women, are stereotypically depicted as animalistic. More recently, of course, writers of color have begun to affirm sexuality in their own terms, a circumstance that has led critics to study the way sex is handled in such contexts. Ann Ducille's "Blue Notes on Black Sexuality: Sex and the Texts of Jessie Fauset and Nellie Larsen" is a good example, as is Arthur Flannigan-Saint-Aubin's " 'Black Gay Male' Discourse: Reading Race and Sexuality between the Lines," both of which view sexual expression as partly political. *Erotique Noire: Black Erotica*, edited by Miriam Decosta-Willis, Reginald Martin, and

RoseAnn P. Bell, anthologizes Alice Walker, Chester Hines, Trey Ellis, Calvin
Hernton, and others and includes an Introduction by Ntozake Shange. The suc-
cess of that volume led Martin to edit a second, *Dark Eros: Black Erotic Writ-
ings*. Sandra Y. Govan's "Forbidden Fruits and Unholy Lusts: Illicit Sex in
Black American Literature" deals with forays into sexuality by writers from
Richard Wright to the present.

One of the most distinguished African American writers of erotica is Audre
Lorde, whose own defense of pornography, "Uses of the Erotic," is legendary
(see **Mature Feminist Reactions to Antiporn Campaigns** in Chapter 6).
Among several notable critical essays on Lorde, her fiction, and her influence
are Sharon P. Holland's "To Touch the Mother's C(o)untry: Siting Audre
Lorde's Erotics," an appreciation of the pornographic aspects of Lorde's *Zami*;
Katie King's "Audre Lorde's Layered Lacquerings: The Lesbian Bar as a Site
of Literary Production," which views Lorde as a lesbian exemplar; and Claudine
Raynaud's " 'A Nutmeg Nestled inside Its Covering of Mace': Audre Lorde's
Zami," which analyzes the liberating aspects of Lorde's vaginal metaphors.
Black Women Writers at Work, edited by Claudia Tate, interviews Lorde. Em-
manuel Nelson's *Gay and Lesbian Writers of Color* is another good collection.
On a Bed of Rice: An Asian-American Erotic Feast, edited by Geraldine Kudaka,
brings together Asian American erotica by writers of Korean, Filipino, Japanese,
East Indian, Vietnamese, Chinese, and Thai descent. Similarly, *Under the Pomegranate Tree: The Best New Latino Erotica*, edited by Ray Gonzalez, gathers
erotic work by another important American group.

SCIENCE FICTION AND FANTASY EROTICA

Erotic writers over the last several decades have been drawn to science fiction,
and fantasy primarily because sexuality in such forms need not be restricted by
the constraints of realism. Harry Harrison's *Great Balls of Fire! A History of
Sex in Science Fiction* is an amusing survey of the efforts of science fiction
writers to employ bizarrely conceived sexual encounters, as is Thomas Scortia's
Strange Bedfellows: Sex and Science Fiction. Some of the critical essays in
Donald Palumbo's *Eros and the Mind's Eye: Sexuality and the Fantastic in Art
and Film* deal with print media, while those in his *Erotic Universe: Sexuality
and Fantastic Literature* concentrate on erotic roles of technology, imagined
carnal encounters with aliens, and reflections on futuristic conceptions of sex to
be found in fiction; the bibliographies in both volumes are essential to research
in these areas. In contrast to the multiple genders that some critics find so
engaging in these genres are the standard sexual characters that Leslie Friedman
still finds common in works listed in the brief "science fiction" section of *Sex
Role Stereotyping in the Mass Media: An Annotated Bibliography*. In *Alien Sex:
19 Tales by the Masters of Science Fiction and Dark Fantasy*, editor Ellen
Datlow argues that erotic elements are important and enduring components of
science fiction's appeal. Sheldon R. Jaffery's comment in *Sensuous Science*

Fiction From the Weird and Spicy Pulps examines stories drawn from vintage magazines. *Eros in Orbit: A Collection of All New Science Fiction Stories about Sex*, edited by Joseph Elder, *The Shape of Sex to Come*, assembled by Douglas Hill, and *Sex in the 21st Century: A Collection of SF Erotica*, gathered by Michael Parry and M. Subotsky, are anthologies containing information on major and minor writers. As a side note, the "Dr. 'A' " who wrote *The Sensuous Dirty Old Man* is Isaac Asimov, long the dean of American science fiction. Gardiner Dozois' *Dying for It: More Erotic Tales of Unearthly Love* collects sexy ghost stories.

The erotic pulse is one of the subjects in Samuel R. Delaney's splendidly recalled autobiography, *The Motion of Light in Water: Sex and Science Fiction Writing in the East Village, 1957–1965*. In "Pornography/Censorship," Delaney asserts that contemporary publishers are so conservative that pornography today does not have the richness of classics published in the 1960s. Delaney recounts his frustration with his own attempts at writing a pornographic work and in the process refers to pornography as "a practice of writing—i.e., it's a genre, and genres do not yield up their necessary and sufficient conditions, i.e., they cannot be defined" (14). (The novel, *Hogg*, was published in 1996.) He does say that it is enough to think of pornographic works as those that arouse by intent or accident: "I think it is terribly important to have a genre—or genre-set—in which it is possible to say *anything*: true, untrue, or at any level of fantasy, metaphor, violence, or simple outrageousness" (30). As Fred Botting's *Sex, Machines and Navels: Fiction, Fantasy and History in the Future Present* makes clear, science fiction underlines the relationship between bodies and machines and heightens this uneasy affinity as writers drag psychoanalysis into cyberspace. Botting ranges over reengineerings of desire, reworkings of sexual identities and differences, and the power of transformational metaphor in science fiction.

Several anthologies of erotic science fiction are devoted exclusively to gay and lesbian subgenres. The broadest is the second edition of *Uranian Worlds: A Guide to Alternative Sexuality in Science Fiction, Fantasy and Horror*, edited by Eric Garber and Lyn Paleo, who stress that all three genres lend themselves to characterizations of different genders, some only imagined, and to the exploration of alternative sexual identities. Garber's *Embracing the Dark* anthologizes gay erotic horror stories. *Worlds Apart: An Anthology of Lesbian and Gay Science Fiction and Fantasy*, edited by Camilla Decarnin, Garber, and Lyn Paleo, and *Meltdown: An Anthology of Erotic Science Fiction and Dark Fantasy for Gay Men*, edited by Caro Soles, offer intelligent comment. Sword and sorcery stories for gays and lesbians make up *Swords of the Rainbow: Gay and Lesbian Fantasy Adventures*, edited by Garber and Jewelle Gomez. Jeffrey M. Eliot's *Kindred Spirits: An Anthology of Gay and Lesbian Science Fiction Stories* contains stories on homosexual themes, while Pamela Sargent's *Women of Wonder* and *More Women of Wonder: Science Fiction Novelettes by Women about Women* foreground heterosexual and bisexual heroines as well, though eroticism is not the only element of interest. Marleen S. Barr, in *Lost in Space: Probing Feminist Science Fiction and Beyond*, thinks science fiction's penchant for experimentation attracts women. Joanna Russ subjects gender and other assumptions in science fiction to her always skeptical scrutiny in *To Write Like a Woman: Essays in Feminism and Science Fiction*. Robin Roberts insists that science fiction's novel terrain has room for speculation on gender in *A New Species: Gender and Science in Science Fiction*. In any case, the erotic form is exploding. Circlet Press now publishes a women's series edited by the prolific Cecilia Tan: the volumes include *Forged Bonds: Erotic Tales of High Fantasy, Sex Magick, Telepaths Don't Need Safewords, Worlds of Women: Sapphic Erotica*, and *S and M Future: Erotica on the Edge*.

ANTHOLOGIES OF HETEROSEXUAL EROTICA

The erotic anthology is virtually a genre in itself. Anthologies acquaint the casual reader with the enormous variety of erotic poetry and fiction produced by writers celebrated and obscure, and the titles are often revealing, as in *The Mammoth Book of International Erotica* and *The Mammoth Book of New Erotica*, both edited by Maxim Jakubowski. Most aim at a loosely heterosexual audience: if the fantasies of one selection do not appeal, those of another might. Editors introduce the contents with historical, thematic, or biographical commentary, although these remarks vary considerably in depth and interest, and then let the stories or excerpts speak for themselves. The most famous collections gathered low expression: songs, stories, poems, and folktales (see **Folkore and Obscenity: Rhymes, Songs, Ballads, and Stories** in Chapter 15) and are still hard to find. More accessible were compilations that could be characterized as literary erotica. One of the earliest to be published in America, as a slim volume in the Haldeman-Julius series of "little blue books," was Joseph McCabe's *Masterpieces of Erotic Literature*. Another of note is *The Bedroom Companion, or a Cold Night's Entertainment*, popular during the 1930s, which brought together ribald or erotic pieces by William Rose Benet, Marc Connelly, Dr. Seuss, Abner Dean, Philip Wylie, Ogden Nash, Rex Stout, and other notable Americans; according to Gershon Legman, Wylie edited the volume. Similar is *The Playboy's Handbook: In Defense of the Bachelor*, edited by William Allan Brandner, a collection of pieces by Benjamin Franklin, Ben Hecht, Frank Sullivan, James Thurber, and others.

An amusing popular treatment is Robert Reisner's *Great Erotic Scenes from Literature*, which is very similar to his earlier *Show Me the Good Parts: The Reader's Guide to Sex in Literature*; both excerpt classic texts. So does *Banned: Classical Erotica: Forty Sensual and Erotic Excerpts from Aristophanes to Whitman—Uncensored*, whose title says it all. Peter Fryer has edited *The Man of Pleasure's Companion: An Anthology of Secret Victorian Vices*, a volume nicely informed by scholarship. Modest comment shapes Donald Mc-

Cormick's *Erotic Literature: A Connoisseur's Guide*, though the selections (antiquity to modernity) are predictable; the same is true of Roy Harley Lewis' *The Browser's Guide to Erotica*. Nigel Cawthorne's *Secrets of Love: The Erotic Arts through the Ages* draws mostly on literature. George Mair includes synopses of classics such as *The Sex Life of the Foot and Shoe* and *Five Hundred Years of Foreplay* in his *The Sex-Book Digest; A Peek between the Covers of 113 of the Most Erotic, Exotic, and Edifying Sex Books*, whose pages also touch on sex manuals, sexual advice, sexual surveys, manuals of sex devices, and other materials. Not quite so catholic is *Too Darn Hot: Writing about Sex since Kinsey*, for which Judy Bloomfield, Mary McGrail, and Lauren Sanders collect excerpts from mostly American writers from William Burroughs to Scarlot Harlot.

Anthologies stream from presses today. Among the most literate are *The Gates of Paradise: An Anthology of Erotic Short Fiction*, edited by Alberto Manguel; *The Literary Companion to Sex: An Anthology of Prose and Poetry*, edited (more wittily than usually is the case) by Fiona Pitt-Kethley; and *The Bloomsbury Guide to Erotic Literature*, edited by Jane Mills. Such titles suggest upscale eroticism, as does *Tart Tales: Elegant Erotic Stories*, edited by Carolyn Banks. Susie Bright seems bent on defining a national erotica. Her annual volumes of *The Best American Erotica* include stories by Samuel Delaney, Lisa Palac, Anne Rice, Carol A. Queen, Michael Dorsey, Trish Thomas, Nicolson Baker, Chris Offutt, Bart Plantenga, Danielle Willis, and many others. The stories and excerpts called simply *Erotic Tales* are also predominantly American: those represented include Erica Jong, Philip Roth, Frank Harris, Henry Miller, and Mary McCarthy. David Steinberg has edited two volumes, *Erotic by Nature: A Celebration of Life, of Love, and of Our Wonderful Bodies*, a compendium of glossy, elegant writing, art, and photos by American men and women of various genders, and *The Erotic Impulse: Honoring the Sensual Self*, an erotic miscellany that balances fiction with critical and theoretical approaches to sexual explicitness. The similarly upscale *Winds of Love*, edited by Helen Gurley Brown, features erotic fiction by the likes of Judith Rossner, Garson Kanin, and A. Alvarez. In recent years, narratives written by "average" people, a form that was pioneered in the 1950s by men's magazines such as *Mr.* and later stabilized by publications such as *Penthouse* ("Forum"), have begun to appear as books. A typical example is *Good Sex: Real Stories from Real People*, edited by Julia Hutton, who includes sexual memoirs from various genders. Excerpts and reprints of cross-over genres, mixing sex and violence by writers such as Bob Flanagan, Gary Indiana, Dennis Cooper, Mary Gaitskill, Karen Finley, Diamanda Galás, Stewart Home, and many others, are included in *High Risk: An Anthology of Forbidden Writings* and *High Risk 2: Writings on Sex, Death, and Subversion*, both edited by Amy Scholder and Ira Silverberg. Packaging is the most interesting aspect of *Sex Box: Man, Woman, Sex*, three boxed volumes of excerpts from well-known authors such as Acker, Hemingway, Joyce, Nin, and Gaitskill.

GAY EROTICA

Raymond de Becker's *The Other Face of Love* and Cecile Beurdeley's *L'amour bleu*, French texts published in the 1970s and widely circulated in this country since, deal authoritatively with homosexuality as theme and content in Western art and literature. Probably the single most influential work on homosexuality in literature in English, however, is Eve Kosofsky Sedgwick's *Between Men: English Literature and the Male Homosocial Desire*. It argues that the real "subject" of English literature is male bonding, or, as Sedgwick calls it, "homosocial" connections between males "through, around, or over, the body and soul of a woman"; the latter functions as a "conduit" between the real partners, who are men (26). English fiction imitates a patriarchal "traffic in women," a term she borrows from Gayle Rubin. The triangle thus constituted is a defense against the menace of homosexuality, even as it allows for homoerotic symbolism and nuance before ultimately affirming heterosexuality. In the final analysis, says Sedgwick, homosexuality is entirely a matter of definition, and literature is one of the most important grounds for its construction. In her recent *Tendencies*, Sedgwick ranges across Diderot and Jane Austen in her quest to formulate a "queer theory" that can address issues as diverse as effeminacy and AIDS. Earl Jackson's *Strategies of Deviance: Studies in Gay Male Representation* explores the images of gays in several media but is most illuminating on textual narratives from early to modern times. Lee Edelman offers new readings of traditional and contemporary texts in *Homographesis: Essays in Gay Literary and Cultural Theory*, as does Gregory Woods in *A History of Gay Literature: The Male Tradition*.

For much of American history, gays strove to forge a gay identity beneath conventional depictions of homosexuality in a culture that anathematized them as deviant. David Bergman studies the struggles of mainstream authors from Whitman and Melville, to Tennessee Williams and James Baldwin in *Gaiety Transfigured: Gay Self-Representation in American Literature*. Brian Reade's *Sexual Heretics* focuses on homosexual writers in the period from 1850 to 1900. Roger Austen's *Playing the Game: The Homosexual Novel in America* discusses the stances forced on the homosexual writer, who adopted various strategies for disguising and revealing the gay content of his work. James Levin also looks beneath surfaces to find patterns in *The Gay Novel in America*. Both of the latter are excellent on the tension between mainstream and marginal letters. A quest for distinctive attributes animates the essays in *Sexual Sameness: Textual Differences in Lesbian and Gay Writing*, edited by Joseph Bristow.

Scott S. Derrick argues that homosexual writers and early feminists shared anxieties, concerns, and literary strategies in *Monumental Anxieties: Homoerotic Desire and Feminine Influence in 19th Century U.S. Literature*. Mark Lilly treats American writers such as James Baldwin in the larger context of a literary culture marked by Jean Genet, Oscar Wilde, and Christopher Isherwood in *Gay Men's Literature in the Twentieth Century*. Lilly has also edited a series of approaches under the title *Lesbian and Gay Writing: An Anthology of Critical Essays*, as has Stuart Kellogg, whose two volumes are called *Essays on Gay Literature* and *Literary Visions of Homosexuality*. In "Coming Out as Going In: The Image of the Homosexual as a Sad Young Man," Richard Dyer explores the texts and covers of twentieth-century homosexual pulp novels, which emphasized gay sensibility in terms of the tormented psyches of cultural aliens. Literary examples of sodomy are the subject of Lee Edelman's "Seeing Things: Representation, the Scene of Surveillance, and the Spectacle of Gay Male Sex."

Benjamin De Mott writes sympathetically about the condition of the homosexual author in America, with particular attention to how suspicion taints response to the gay writer's talent, in "But He's a Homosexual . . ." The most interesting part of John Preston's two-volume *Flesh and the Word: An Anthology of Erotic Writing*, is Preston's autobiographical "My Life with Pornography," in which he speaks of his own erotic fiction. Preston puts one cultural fact succinctly: "Erotica was never written about gay men. We were, by definition, obscene; therefore, anything written about us had to be declared pornography" (II, 2). Preston and Michael Lowenthal have edited a third volume of *Flesh and the Word*, and Lowenthal himself yet a fourth, both devoted entirely to gay erotica. Preston expands on gay themes in *My Life as a Pornographer and Other Indecent Acts*, whose reflections include musings on the state of sexuality and gender in the United States, his ambitions in writing erotic prose, and the satisfactions it has given him. Like Preston, Stanton Hoffman argues that the only "real" American literature of homosexuality *is* pornography. In "The Cities of Night: John Rechy's *City of Night* and the American Literature of Homosexuality," Hoffman says Rechy's powerful narratives intruded upon middle-class complacency to give gay writers a recognizable voice. Angelo d'Arcangelo writes about himself and other gay porn writers of the 1950s and 1960s who published abroad before transferring their battle flags to the United States in *Angelo d'Arcangelo's Love Book: Inside the Sexual Revolution*. D'Arcangelo thinks that sexual explicitness sharpens a necessary wedge in the struggle for gay identity; otherwise, the middle class can simply pretend to ignore homosexuality.

Classic texts from antiquity forward form the bulk of *The Gay and Lesbian Literary Heritage: A Reader's Companion to the Writers and Their Works, from Antiquity to the Present*, edited by Claude J. Summers. David Galloway and Christian Sabisch also concentrate on more established writers in *Calamus: Male Homosexuality in Twentieth Century Literature: An International Anthology*. Paul Hallam's *The Book of Sodom* anthologizes several centuries' worth of homosexual texts; Hallam draws on books from private collections as a way of illustrating what cultures designate as perverse. David Leavitt and Mark Mitchell include stories of various genres by international authors in *The Penguin Book of Gay Short Stories*. "Lower" genres are well represented in Boyd McDonald's *Smut* and in his six volumes called *True Homosexual Experiences from S. T. H. Writers*. The latter stories, drawn from the magazine *Gay Sunshine*, are arranged

under individual titles (*Cum, Flesh, Wads*, and so on). Haworth Press, in addition
to launching the Harrington Pleasure Press specifically to publish erotic gay
fiction, has also started *Harrington Gay Men's Fiction Quarterly*, for the same
purpose. Finally, Carol Queen and Lawrence Schimel have edited a fascinating
volume of experimental erotica, *Switch Hitters: Lesbians Write Gay Male Erotica and Gay Men Write Lesbian Erotica*. (See also **Period Commentaries** in
this chapter.)

ROMANCES

The 1970 *Report* of the President's Commission on Obscenity and Pornography dismissed the romance novel as outside its purview, though it did provide
content analyses for those unacquainted with the pornographic aspects of romance fiction. Since then romances have become exponentially more explicit.
The romance novel for women annually accounts for a huge percentage of all
books published in the United States. (See Chapter 21, **The Economics of Pornography**.) According to some historians, Harlequin, a Canadian publisher, virtually invented the modern woman's romance; Harlequin's own in-house
chronicle, *Thirty Years of Harlequin: 1949–1979*, accepts the credit. A less-
incestuous history, Margaret Jensen's *Love's Sweet Return: The Harlequin
Story*, agrees that the publisher defined the market. According to Jensen, Harlequin sold 218 million books in twelve languages in ninety-eight countries in
1982 (34). Leslie W. Rabine's *Reading the Romantic Heroine: Text, History,
Ideology* concentrates on classics, but the chapter called "Sex and the Working
Woman in the Age of Electronics: Harlequin Romances" points out that "the
inner conflict of the Harlequin heroines is a more explicitly sexualized version
of feminine conflicts analyzed by authors writing during the Industrial Revolution, like Stendhal or Charlotte Brontë, but places it in a new sociohistoric
context" (176). Rabine praises the Harlequin "author as heroine" writing in the
face of academic scorn to bring happiness to the many.

As publishers other than Harlequin have entered the market, astonishing sales
and cultural impact have led to increased comment. Critics agree that appeal is
sexual but differ over whether the form should be called pornographic, and if
so, what that means. Northrop Frye in *The Secular Scripture: A Study of the
Structure of Romance* observed circumspectly that the pornographic imagination
is "the demonic pole of the vertical structure of romance" (53), and while subsequent critics trace the modern romance to the classical origins that Frye sign-
posts, the force of mass-market eroticism gives them pause. In *Endless Rapture:
Rape, Romance, and the Female Imagination*, Helen Hazen acknowledges the
term that must apply: "male pornography has to do with slippery bodies first
and foremost. Women's pornography or, rather, the literature that provides
women sexual excitement, is romance" (117).

Numerous studies identify subgenres: the Regency romance, set in the nineteenth century and revolving around characters drawn from imagined stereotypes

of the period; the gothic romance, energized by frisson born of fear; and various types of confessional fiction, narratives of unhappy adventures in love. That this list of formulas is not exhaustive is evident from the number of academic articles purporting to discover others. Rachel Anderson's *The Purple Heart Throbs: The Sub-Literature of Love*, for instance, finds many categories. One of the more interesting is the Afro-American romance pioneered by Odyssey Books and, more recently, by Zebra Books' Arabesque line: Edith Updike's "Publishers of Romance Novels Add Color to Their Lines" discusses this development and interviews readers and authors such as Sandra Kitt.

In "Talking Sex: A Conversation on Sexuality and Feminism," Deidre English, Amber Hollibaugh, and Gayle Rubin discuss variations in discourse; they recognize that self-parodistic aspects of romance undermine what they call "the politics of pornography" (76). Because so much antiporn rhetoric follows Victorian ideology of the sort advanced by Elizabeth Cady Stanton, who claimed that "men are brutes," English et al. think the period settings of so many romances are ironic. In a topical essay, "Romance Novels Discover a Baby Boom," Alessandra Stanley notes that formulas constantly mutate. She breaks down women's romance fiction into Regency novels, which are relatively chaste; historical novels, sometimes called "bodice-rippers," because the hero opens the heroine's blouse wider than her skirt; and "category" romances, so called because they focus on contemporary fantasies. The latter type has begun to incorporate pregnancy as the outcome of fevered liaisons and to work child raising into the schedules of busy moms who must find time for passionate sex.

"There are at least four types of category romances," says Jeanne Dubino in an exploration of the links between female sexuality and economics entitled "The Cinderella Complex: Romance Fiction, Patriarchy, and Capitalism": "The sweet, the sensual, the longer and the teen. All varieties of the romance contain the pattern of 'heroine gets rich through love' " (103). The thesis of Jan Cohn's *Romance and the Erotics of Property: Mass-Market Fiction for Women* maintains that issues of power overshadow love: "In the fantasy gratification offered by contemporary popular romance are not only the secret sentimental and sensual delights of love but the forbidden pleasures of revenge and appropriation. In heavily coded structures these stories redistribute not only the power relations that exist within marriage, within the patriarchal family, but through and beyond that threaten existing gender relations in the broadest areas of power in patriarchal society itself" (3).

Gothic novels by and for women make up a genre of considerable pedigree; their blend of prurience and exaltation is the subject of Michelle A. Masse's *In the Name of Love: Women, Masochism, and the Gothic*. Useful also are Eugenia DeLamotte's *Perils of the Night; A Feminist Study of Nineteenth Century Gothic*, Kate Ellis' *The Contested Castle: Gothic Novels and the Subversion of Domestic Ideology*, Elaine Showalter's "American Female Gothic," and Anne Williams' *Art of Darkness: A Poetics of Gothic*, all of which wrestle with definitions, delineate characters, plots, and themes, and explore the form's erotic delights, which spiral out of the constraints of patriarchy and the strictures of domestic life. Some of these critics see the foregrounding of women's sexual fantasies and anxieties as conterminous with the advance of feminism; others trace vectors to and from high and low culture. Joanna Russ' famous "Somebody Is Trying to Kill Me and I Think It's My Husband: The Modern Gothic" explores the characteristics of the typical young heroine menaced in contemporary examples. In her Introduction to *Daughters of Darkness: Lesbian Vampire Stories*, Pam Keesey points out that the sexual symbolism of the vampire can be made far more explicit and that other body fluids may easily take the place of traditional blood. Poppy Z. Brite has gathered differently gendered vampire stories, an offshoot of the gothic, in *Love in Vein: Vampire Erotica*. (See also Anne Rice elsewhere in this section.) Finally, if only because few people seem to know of the curiously cruel pornographic tenor of Andrea Dworkin's fiction, reading novels such as *Ice and Fire* and *Mercy* serves to put her antiporn writings in an ironic light. The latter work Naomi Morgenstern calls "pornogothic" in " 'There Is Nothing Else like This': Sex and Citation in Pornogothic Feminism," where she claims that Dworkin's *Mercy* can be read as pornographic but also as "feminist testimonial" (40). The less charitable Susie Bright puts it differently: "I can't tell you how many women masturbate to the dirty parts of her novel."[1]

"Soft-Porn Culture," by Ann Douglas, maintains that popular culture is out to "get" the liberated woman. Harlequin romances, whose dynamics are a "duel of sexual stupidity" (26), present women as enjoying psychic abuse from males. At the same time, Douglas thinks women have an opportunity to bring "boldness" to traditional forms:

In harvesting the material generated by the new freedom and the new roles open to their sex, women are able to regenerate, free from any effective charges of anachronism, the more traditional forms, like the novel, the memoir, and the narrative, whether in film or fiction, treated as passé by their male contemporaries. Because these forms are dependent for validity on the presence of genuine social change, women, implicated willy-nilly in such change, need not abandon or violently reorder their structure as men, whose status is currently more static, apparently must. Women are able to use forms, in other words, that have long proved both their immense popularity in the marketplace and their place in the halls of artistic fame. (28)

In "Romance Fiction: Porn for Women," Alison Assiter also believes that the genre's stereotypes inevitably reinforce repression of women.

By contrast, Angela Miles' "Confessions of a Harlequin Reader: Romance and the Myth of Male Mothers," an essay with first-rate notes and citations, concludes that the central fantasy in romantic fiction aimed at women is of males as nurturers. If that be true, then the romance would appear to operate as does pornography aimed at males: it collapses the two genders into one. Where male viewers of porn videotapes prize aggressive insatiability in women, women readers of romances prefer men who offer softer degrees of affection and psychic support. Janice A. Radway's *Reading the Romance: Women, Patriarchy, and Popular Literature*, a reader/response, not quite ethnographic study, agrees that such readers do harbor such hopes but finds the fantasies regressive because they serve as an infantile escape from responsibility, the same charge leveled against more traditional porn. The avoidance of responsibility, without the nurturing, is a major theme of male-oriented porn, Radway believes. Radway calls the romance a "feminized discourse" that negotiates the realms of public and private consciousness and states of wealth and power in an effort to assert the value of love.

Ann Snitow's "Mass Market Romance: Pornography for Women Is Different" argues that Harlequin romances, in particular, offer warm, friendly, and respectful fantasies; they exalt sex in the usual contradictions of ravishment and protection. Carol Thurston thinks that the genre requires serious examination because reading romances provides a way for women to discover their own sexuality, as her aptly titled *The Romance Revolution: Erotic Novels for Women and the Quest for a New Sexual Identity* makes clear. Claire Coles and M. Johanna Sharp draw similar conclusions in "Some Sexual, Personality, and Demographic Characteristics of Women Readers of Erotic Romances." Although more concerned with television soap operas, another genre often called porn for women, Tania Modleski's *Loving with a Vengeance: Mass-Produced Fantasies for Women* deplores the contempt of feminist critics for romance; the form has great symbolic value, in particular for mother–daughter relationships. Jayne Ann Krentz's "Trying to Tame the Romance: Critics and Correctness" concludes that efforts to make the romance respectable have fortunately failed; it can and should be vibrantly subversive.

Where the Heart Roams, directed by George Csicsery, documents the journey of the "Love Train," a string of railroad cars carrying authors and fans from Los Angeles to New York for an awards ceremony. Barbara Cartland, author of 360-plus romances, laments on camera that the genre she helped invent is now clearly pornographic, while another writer, more candid, says that the intent in such fiction is to "turn men into sex objects," a goal that has been accelerated by a women's movement that fosters such fantasies. E. Jean Carroll observes that the male characters in the novel represent wish-fulfillment for readers: they are "dark and brooding but glitzy," are "hard-edged but also sensitive," possess "courage," "intelligence," "raw animal magnetism," "money," "good looks," and "flash." The hero must not be "sweet" or "vulnerable." Various authors tell the filmmaker that men's porn, by contrast, is more graphic, full of things that can be touched, while women's porn like their own contains more feeling, more attention to setting. More than a dozen writers have written on the craft they employ in *Dangerous Men and Adventurous Women: Romance Writers on the Appeal of the Romance*, edited by Jayne Ann Krentz. The essays deal with the "codes" and formulas of the romance and with themes like virginity, heroism, seduction, subversion, empowerment, and happiness.

The essays in *Writing Romance Fiction: For Love and Money* (1983), edited by Helene Schellenberg, offer advice to wannabe authors and might be usefully compared to a manual that appeared a decade earlier, Kathryn Falk's *How to Write a Romance and Get It Published* (1983), for a sense of the genitality that publishers now require. Valerie Kelly specifies sure-fire formulas for steamy, satisfying romances in *How to Write Erotica*. Not everyone is happy with the deepened candor. Two librarians, Shirley Moretto and Kathleen Weidenburner, have written "We'll Take Romance" to suggest strategies their colleagues might employ for coping with the wide range of romances and with the diplomacy sometimes necessary to soothe older readers upset by scenes of penetration and oral sex. (See **Erotic Books** in Chapter 4, especially Fallon, Griley, and Ramsdell.)

MORE EXPLICIT WOMEN'S WRITING

There is considerable overlap between more recent, more explicit fictional narratives and the older, more subtle eroticism of traditional categories like the Regency romance. If a questing finger reaches and parts labia, does the narrative cease being a "romance" and become something else? Or is the issue a question of language or formula? A case in point might be *Story of O*, the notorious "letter" to her lover by Dominique Aury, who wrote it under the pen name Pauline Réage. (Though not American, the novel has sold many thousands of copies in the United States and has figured in sociological studies as a touchstone of American attitudes toward porn.[2] It is one of the most explicit novels ever written by a woman, yet it is clearly a part of the tradition called romantic; all that need be said here is that the genre is elastic.

Enrico Badellino's cross-cultural concentration is evident in *Le scrittrici dell 'eros: una storia della pornografia al femminile*, a chronicle of women writers of erotica from Sappho to Anaïs Nin (and other contemporaries, some American). In "The Front-Line: Notes on Sex in Novels by Women, 1969–1979," Ann Snitow tries to isolate trends among authors trying to map sexual territory and finds that while they may emphasize sex as warmth and sharing, they are straightforward in their faith in eroticism. Jeanne De Berg's *Women's Rites: Essays in the Erotic Imagination* argues that women are prone to eroticism that undermines social mores, although this could be a doubly subversive text, since booksellers have long suspected that De Berg is really Allain Robbe-Grillet. Uta West discusses famous pornographic novelists such as Mary Sativa, Lela Seftali, Harriet Daimler, and Diane Di Prima, some of whom wrote for Maurice Girodias, in "Pornography in Petticoats."

The best introductions to what are rapidly emerging as erotic genres for women are the many anthologies of explicit fiction to appear in the last decade. One of the mechanics by which subgenres come to the fore is the practice of anthologizing, which collects sometimes fugitive examples, makes them available for criticism, and, more important, begins to create and widen the audience. Editors of the better anthologies also place the material in a historical, cultural, or artistic context and occasionally analyze persistent themes or single out notable characters. Most contain editorial comment that is less academic than appreciative but that does help position erotic fiction as a form of popular culture. At this stage, what makes anthologies of women's erotica significant is their attempt to map sexual territory both old and new, to experiment with what women—as opposed to men—find titillating, stimulating, and fun. The bolder editors do not mince words: their aim is to moisten their readers' genitals by providing stories to masturbate to. Given rising demand by women for narratives of strong sexuality, many editors now commission fiction directly and do not wait for stories to appear elsewhere first.

The three volumes written by members of a California group called the Kensington Ladies were among the first in the field. The first, *Ladies Own Erotica: Tales, Recipes, and Other Mischiefs by Older Women*, includes reminiscences, drawings, poetry, fiction, even recipes. Pat Adler edited the second, *Erotic Companion: Kensington Ladies' Erotica Society*; the third is *Look Homeward Erotica*. Three other important anthologies allow elegance and vulgarity to collide: *Herotica: A Collection of Women's Erotic Fiction*, which was followed by *Herotica II* and *Herotica III*, the first and third edited by Susie Bright, the second by Bright and Joani Blank, and by *Herotica IV* and *V*, both edited by Marcy Sheiner. Here dozens of women writers launch excursions into bisexuality, lesbianism, and kinky obsessions. Bright's Introduction to the first volume observes that "some women want the stars, some the sleaze," and she guarantees that the contents will prompt masturbation. The sexual therapist Lonnie Barbach has published two collections, *Erotic Interludes: Tales Told by Women* and *Pleasures: Women Write Erotica*, stories of first sexual experiences, lesbian encounters, group sex, public intercourse, and anonymous couplings, as treated by writers such as Susan Griffin, Valerie Kelly, and Tee Corinne.

Similar in intent is *Slow Hand: Women Writing Erotica*, edited by Michele Slung. Slung praises the "equal-opportunity treatment of the issues of age or physical attractiveness" in erotica by women, who are determined "not to have our sexuality be about things that are (often) beyond our control and not to have our sexual selves dictated or defined by others" (xvii). Laura Chester has gathered pieces by Toni Morrison, Kathy Acker, Audre Lorde, and others in *Deep Down: The New Sensual Writing by Women* and pieces by male and female writers for *The Unmade Bed: Sensual Writing on Married Love*. Margaret Reynolds' *Erotica: Women's Writing from Sappho to Margaret Atwood* is similar to *Touching Fire: Erotic Writings by Women*, edited by Louise Thornton, Jan Sturtevant, and Amber Coverdale Sumrall; included are fiction and poetry by Margaret Atwood, Alice Munro, Sharon Olds, Adrienne Rich, Maxine Kumin, Marge Piercy, and Tess Gallagher. Examples of erotica by thirty-nine relatively young female writers and artists fill the pages of *The Girl Wants To: Women's Representation of Sex and the Body*, edited by Lynn Crosbie. Harriet Gilbert's international reach gathers erotica in *The Sexual Imagination from Acker to Zola: A Feminist Companion*. Lest the older generation be slighted, Dena Taylor and Amber Sumrall have provided a forum in *The Time of Our Lives: Women Write on Sex after 40.*

LESBIAN EROTICA

(See chapter 4, **Bibliographies and Reference Tools**, especially Bradley and Damon; Clardy; Damon, Watson, and Jordan; Foster; Kehoe; Olsham; and Roberts.)

A growing subgenre is the lesbian romance, or pulp novel, the subject of Catrióna Rueda Esquibel's "A Duel of Wits and the Lesbian Romance Novel or Verbal Intercourse in Fictional Regency England" and Suzanne Danuta Walters' "As Her Hand Crept Slowly Up Her Thigh: Ann Bannon and the Politics of Pulp." Jean Radford's "An Inverted Romance: *The Well of Loneliness* and Sexual Ideology," an essay (97–112) in *The Progress of Romance: The Politics of Popular Fiction* also edited by Radford, examines what might be called the lesbian ur-romance. The notoriety of Radclyffe Hall's celebrated lesbian novel overshadowed her success as a Hollywood screenwriter. Vera Brittain's *Radclyffe Hall, a Case of Obscenity?* is an early study of the novel's originality, while William Fitzgerald's "Radclyffe Hall's *The Well of Loneliness*: Sources and Inspirations" argues that Hall adapted her story from Richard Von Krafft-Ebing.

Hall was an important progenitor of erotic American fiction. For several decades, lesbian pulps served as one bond between lesbians who were often isolated from each other and certainly from the American mainstream. Here they could learn that others felt similar desires, which seem, in retrospect, very like the romantic longings of their middle-class heterosexual counterparts. The novels celebrate affection, loyalty, and touching as counters for loneliness, but rarely passion, which publishers shied away from. Lillian Faderman discusses male pornographic fantasies of lesbians in fiction as opposed to the fantasies embodied in lesbian literature in her *Surpassing the Love of Men: Romantic Friendship and Love between Women from the Renaissance to the Present.* Faderman's *Odd Girls and Twilight Lovers: A History of Lesbian Life in Twentieth-Century America* is especially good on lesbian pulp fiction of the 1920s and 1930s. Roberta Yusba analyzes those of a later period in "Twilight Tales: Lesbian Pulps, 1950–1960." A most useful reference tool is *Lesbiana: Book Reviews from The Ladder, 1966–1972*, by Barbara Grier (aka Gene Damon), a collection of Grier's criticism of fiction from one of the most important journals of lesbian consciousness during a period when authors were taking tentative steps toward visibility. Grier and Coletta Reid have also put together *Lesbian Lives: Biographies of Women from "The Ladder."* Sonya L. Jones' *Gay and Lesbian Literature since World War II*, while not concerned with erotica per se (aiming instead at such writers as Capote, Whitman, Jane Rule, and Bertha Harris), touches on erotic impulses and is especially useful on the Lavender Archives and the Lesbian Herstory Archives.

Catharine Stimpson's "Zero Degree Deviancy: The Lesbian Novel in English" examines Hall's *The Well of Loneliness*, Barnes' *Nightwood*, and Brown's *Rubyfruit Jungle*, among other modern texts. Bonnie Zimmerman looks at themes, motifs, formulas, and structural elements in *The Safe Sea of Women: Lesbian Fiction, 1969–1988*. The critical comment in *Sweet Dreams: Sexuality, Gender and Popular Fiction*, edited by Susannah Radstone, ranges across high and low gay and lesbian literature. Several writers call for the construction of a lesbian aesthetic by which to evaluate and appreciate an eroticism that lies beyond the experience of heterosexuals. Victoria L. Smith's "Starting from Snatch: The Seduction of Performance in Bertha Harris' *Lover*" is excellent not only on Harris' 1976 novel but also on the responses to lesbian fiction among lesbian readers since. Alison Hennegan's "On Becoming a Lesbian Reader" focuses on standards for the study of texts.

Other well-reasoned approaches include Sally Munt's collection of essays, *New Lesbian Criticism: Literary and Cultural Readings*, on building a specifically lesbian consciousness as distinct from conventional feminist conceptions; Mandy Merck's *Perversions: Deviant Readings by Mandy Merck*, an unapologetic embrace of lesbian consciousness; Judith Roof's *A Lure of Knowledge: Lesbian Sexuality and Theory*, on the shapes of lesbian desire as manifest in mostly modern literature; and Elizabeth Meese's *(Sem)Erotics: Theorizing Lesbian: Writing*, on experimental lesbian works, analyzed in terms of authors' motivations, features of narrative, and other textual considerations. Several collections of essays also attempt to stake out critical ground. These include *Inside/Out: Lesbian Theories, Gay Theories*, edited by Diana Fuss (fiction, film, social and political issues); *Lesbian Texts and Contexts: Radical Revisions*, edited by Karla Jay and Joanne Glasgow (Willa Cather, lesbian subplots, lesbians in black fiction); and *What Lesbians Do in Books*, edited by Elaine Hobby and Chris White (critical examinations of texts classic and modern). Aligning history with criticism, Bonnie Zimmerman's "What Has Never Been: An Overview of Lesbian Feminist Literary Criticism" enumerates claims that lesbians write and read out of a definable aesthetic and emotional sensibility.

JoAnn Loulan's *The Lesbian Erotic Dance: Butch, Femme, Androgyny and Other Rhythms* is a cut above most approaches because it asserts that stereotypes of lesbians have powerful value for narrative purposes and can be inverted or transcended for new meaning. One of the most thoughtful rationales for lesbian porn has been articulated by Dorothy Allison. The chapters on "Sex Writing: The Importance and the Difficulty" and "A Personal History of Lesbian Porn" in her *Skin: Talking About Sex, Class and Literature* make the point that it is important to write pornography in order to make sense of lesbian sexuality, although difficult to get beyond clichés, some of which have been borrowed from male genres. In "Between the Sheets: My Sex Life in Literature," Donna Allegra, a black lesbian, recounts her search for identity and erotic stimulation.

Pride of place as spokesperson for lesbian writing, however, should go to Joan Nestle. Her *The Persistent Desire: A Femme-Butch Reader* anthologizes essays on erotica, fiction, memoirs, poems, photos, and oral history focusing on femmes and butches. More important is her *A Restricted Country*, which contains three stunning essays: "Butch-Femme Relationships: Sexual Courage in the 1950s" (100–109); "My Mother Liked to Fuck" (120–122); and "My History with Censorship" (144–150). (For discussion of the last of these essays, see **Gay and Lesbian Responses to Feminist Antiporn Campaigns** in Chapter 6.) The first of these admires women who followed their desires during a period in which being a lesbian was dangerous; the second celebrates the power of sexuality to give life meaning. Earlier in the volume, Nestle writes: "If [lesbian erotic writers] are the people who call down history from its heights in marble assembly halls, if we put desire into history, if we document how a collective erotic imagination questions and modifies monolithic societal structures like gender, if we change the notion of woman as self-chosen victim by our public stances and private styles, then surely no apologies are due. Being a sexual people is our gift to the world" (10).

Implicit in much of the gay and lesbian fascination with pornographic representations is the recognition of a cultural dynamic by which the marginal moves into the mainstream; heterosexual pornography, long anathematized, has nonetheless emerged as an energizing force in an information economy that consumes everything. The pattern, these critics sense, may well hold true for homosexual pornography, and events appear to support them. The material is proliferating so quickly that we can only hint at the material in anthologies, especially since they vary widely in their critical apparatus and usefulness. We might also observe that any taxonomy or categorization is a form of what information theorists call *preprocessing*, a reduction of rich experience to a set of labels and, as such, involves a destruction of information. To call eroticism heterosexual or homosexual, some critics think, is to perpetuate divisions that work against an appreciation of sensuality that normally flows across sexual and gender barriers and thus to reinforce political labels that fix and rigidify experience. On one hand, such classifications assist in forging sexual identities for minorities such as gays and lesbians; on the other, they may make communication among such groups and other groups of heterosexuals more difficult.

Like the Kensington Ladies mentioned earlier, the Sheba Collective is a joint endeavor. Their two volumes of lesbian erotica are *Serious Pleasure: Lesbian Erotic Stories and Poetry* and *More Serious Pleasure*. Terry Woodrow has edited the two-volume *Lesbian Bedtime Stories*, a title that is almost as catching as the publisher's name (Tough Dove), and Irene Zahava has produced two volumes of *Lesbian Love Stories*, anthologies of works by writers such as Joan Nestle and Jane Rule. Karen Barber has assembled tales under the punning titles *Bushfire: Stories of Lesbian Desire* and *Afterglow: More Stories of Lesbian Desire*, while Carol Allain and Rosamund Elwin have chosen *Getting Wet: Tales of Lesbian Seduction* to indicate the content. *The Penguin Book of Lesbian Short Stories* is an international collection of stories in many genres by authors ranging from Sarah Orne Jewett to contemporary writers, chosen by Margaret Reynolds.

Susie Bright's *Susie Sexpert's Lesbian Sex World* includes fiction as well as advice aimed at lesbians. Pat Califia, the authority on lesbian pornography, probably deserves a bibliographic entry to herself. Volumes such as *Macho Sluts* exhibit her own fiction, while her *Sapphistry: The Book of Lesbian Sexuality* contains self-reflexive comment on erotica. Califia, a champion of pornography as a key to adequately realized sexuality, is probably the most skilled contemporary writer of pornography working today if one measures talent by appeal across genders. Her sexual scenes involve lesbians, to be sure, but her imagination is catholic enough to stimulate almost anyone. Tee Corinne has edited *The Poetry of Sex: Lesbians Write the Erotic*, an anthology laced with her usual gentle reflections. In another lesbian collection, *Riding Desire: An Anthology of Erotic Writing*, Corinne voices her credo: "I write erotica out of a need to share my own kind of story—not high drama sex or wildly acrobatic sex—rather warm, comforting, garden-variety sex that nourishes year after year" (156). It is an accurate description of Corinne's stories in *Dreams of the Woman Who Loved Sex: A Collection*.

New Lesbian Writing: An Anthology, edited by M. Cruikshank, contains prose and poetry on mostly nonerotic themes ranging from loneliness to political activism but boasts a good bibliography of "Recent Lesbian Fiction, 1980–83." The tales collected by Katherine Forrest and Barbara Grier in *The Erotic Naiad: Love Stories by Naiad Authors* are much more explicit. For *The Coming Out Stories*, Julia Penelope Stanley and Susan J. Wolfe have chosen tales of lesbians flushed by desire from the closet. Lady Winston's *The Leading Edge: An Anthology of Lesbian Sexual Fiction* brings together erotic experiences as told by Pat Califia, Dorothy Allison, Chocolate Waters, Jewel Gomez, Noretta Koertge, and others. Joan Nestle and Naomi Holoch have collected short stories by twenty-eight authors (white, black, Hispanic, Jewish) of various classes and experiences in *Women on Women: An Anthology of American Lesbian Short Fiction*. Sara Dunn reviews recent volumes from Pat Califia; the Sheba Collective, and "Cuntissa de Mons Veneris" in "Voyages of the Valkyries: Recent Lesbian Pornographic Writing." Her conclusion is that the stories are welcome but hints that there are too many dildos and appliances for her taste. The *Lambda Book Report* offers bimonthly reviews of gay and lesbian literature.

NOTES

1. Susie Bright, quoted by Steven Chapple and David Talbot, *Burning Desires: Sex in America—A Report from the Field* (New York: Signet, 1990), p. 316.
2. See, for instance, N. M. Malamuth and V. Billings. "Why Pornography? Models of Functions and Effects," *Journal of Communication*, 34:3 (Summer 1984): 117–129.

REFERENCES

"A," Dr. [Asimov, Isaac]. *The Sensuous Dirty Old Man*. New York: Signet, 1972.
Acker, Kathy. "Punk Days in New York." *Fist*, 1 (1988): 9–11.

Adams, Elizabeth "Alex," and William Stadiem. *Madam 90210: My Life as a Madam to the Rich and Famous*. New York: Villard, 1993.

Adler, Polly. *A House Is Not a Home*. New York: Popular Library, 1953.

Alderman, Polly. *Diary of a Jewish Madam: I Was a Jewish Madam*. New York: Samuels Press, 1965.

Allain, Carol, and Rosemund Elwin, eds. *Getting Wet: Tales of Lesbian Seduction*. Toronto: Women's Press, 1992.

Allegra, Donna. "Between the Sheets: My Sex Life in Literature." *Lesbian Erotics*, ed. Karla Jay. New York: New York University Press, 1995, pp. 71–81.

Allison, Dorothy. *Skin: Talking about Sex, Class and Literature*. Ithaca, NY: Firebrand Books, 1994.

Altman, Meryl. "Everything They Always Wanted You to Know: The Ideology of Popular Sex Literature." *Pleasure and Danger: Exploring Female Sexuality*, ed. Carole S. Vance. Boston: Routledge and Kegan Paul, 1984, pp. 115–130.

Amory, Cleveland. "Paperback Pornography." *Saturday Evening Post*, 6 April 1963, pp. 10, 12.

Anderson, Rachel. *The Purple Heart Throbs: The Sub-Literature of Love*. London: Hodder and Stoughton, 1974.

Assiter, Alison. "Romance Fiction: Porn for Women." *Perspectives on Pornography: Sexuality in Film and Literature*, ed. Gary Day and Clive Bloom. New York: St. Martin's, 1988, pp. 101–109.

Atkins, John. *Sex in Literature*. 4 vols. London: Calder and Boyars. I: *The Erotic Impulse in Literature*, 1970; II: *The Classical Experience of the Sexual Impulse*, 1973; III: *The Medieval Experience*, 1978; IV: *The Modern Experience*, 1982.

Austen, Roger. *Playing the Game: The Homosexual Novel in America*. New York: Bobbs-Merrill, 1977.

Badellino, Enrico. *Le scrittrici dell 'eros: una storia della pornografia al femminile*. Milan: Xenia, 1991.

Bailey, Mike. *Writing Erotic Fiction: And Getting Published*. Lincolnwood, IL: NTC Contemporary Publishing, 1998.

Bair, Deidre. *Anaïs Nin: A Biography*. New York: Putnam, 1995.

Bakos, Susan Crain. *Dear Superlady of Sex*. New York: St. Martin's, 1992.

Banks, Carolyn, ed. *Tart Tales: Elegant Erotic Stories*. New York: Carroll and Graf, 1994.

Banned: Classical Erotica: Forty Sensual and Erotic Excerpts from Aristophanes to Whitman—Uncensored. Holbrook, MA: Bob Adams, 1992.

Banta, R. E. *William C. Smith, Gentleman Bookseller*. Hattiesburg, MA: Book Farm, [1945?].

Barbach, Lonnie, ed. *Erotic Interludes: Tales Told by Women*. Garden City, NY: Doubleday, 1986.

———. *Pleasures: Women Write Erotica*. New York: Harper and Row, 1984.

Barber, Karen, ed. *Afterglow: More Stories of Lesbian Desire*. Boston: Alyson, 1993.

———. *Bushfire: Stories of Lesbian Desire*. Boston: Alyson, 1991.

Barr, Marleen S. *Lost in Space: Probing Feminist Science Fiction and Beyond*. Chapel Hill: University of North Carolina Press, 1993.

Barrows, Sydney Biddle, with William Novak. *Mayflower Madam: The Secret Life of Sydney Biddle Barrows*. New York: Arbor House, 1986.

Barthes, Roland. *The Pleasure of the Text*, trans. Richard Miller. New York: Hill and Wang, 1975.

Beall, Otho T. " 'Aristotle's Master Piece' in America: A Landmark in the Folklore of Medicine." *William and Mary Quarterly*, 20 (1963): 207–222.

Becker, Raymond de. *The Other Face of Love*, trans. Margaret Crosland and Alan Daventry. New York: Bell, 1974.

The Bedroom Companion, or a Cold Night's Entertainment: Being a Cure for Man's Neuroses, a Sop to His Frustrations, a Nightcap of Forbidden Ballads, Discerning Pictures, Scurrilous Essays, in Fine, a Steaming Bracer for the Forgotten Male. New York: Farrar and Rinehart, 1935.

Bell, Shannon. *Reading, Writing, and Rewriting the Prostitute Body*. Bloomington: Indiana University Press, 1994.

Benedict, Elizabeth. *The Joy of Writing Sex: A Guide for Fiction Writers*. Cincinnati, OH: Story Press, 1996.

Bergman, David. *Gaiety Transfigured: Gay Self-Representation in American Literature*. Madison: University of Wisconsin Press, 1991.

Beurdeley, Cecile. *L'amour bleu*, trans. Michael Taylor. New York: Rizzoli, 1978.

Bilderlexicon der Erotik. 6 vols. Vienna and Hamburg: Verlag für Kulturforschung, 1928–31, 1963. Edited by Leo Schidrowitz: I: *Kulturgeschichte*; II: *Literatur und Kunst*; III: *Sexualwissenschaft*; IV: *Ergänzungsband*. Edited by Armand Mergen: V and VI: *Sexualforschung: Stichwort und Bild*.

Blakely, Johanna. "Abrotica: The Lesbian Erotic and the Erotic Abject in Anaïs Nin's House of Incest." *Lesbian Erotics*, ed. Karla Jay. New York: New York University Press, 1995, pp. 227–240.

Bloom, Clive. *Cult Fiction: The Popular Reading Cultures of America and Britain*. New York: St. Martin's, 1996; aka *Cult Fiction: Popular Reading and Pulp Theory* (1998).

Bloomfield, Judy, Mary McGrail, and Lauren Sanders, eds. *Too Darn Hot: Writing about Sex since Kinsey*. New York: Persea, 1998.

Bluestine, Gene. "Sex as Literary Theme: Is Whitman the Good, Gay Poet?" *Journal of Popular Culture*, 31:3 (Winter 1997): 153–162.

Bluestone, Ron. "Interview with the Pornographer." *Vogue*, 176:4 (April 1986): 212, 214, 216.

Bode, Carl, ed. *The Editor, the Bluenose, and the Prostitute: H. L. Mencken's History of the "Hatrack" Censorship Case*. Boulder, CO: Roberts Rinehart, 1988.

Bold, Alan, ed. *The Sexual Dimension in Literature*. Totowa, NJ: Barnes and Noble, 1983.

Bonn, Thomas L. *Undercover: An Illustrated History of American Mass Market Paperbacks*. New York: Penguin, 1982.

Boone, Joseph Allen. *Libidinal Currents*. Chicago: University of Chicago Press, 1998.

"Bootleg Literature." *Publishers Weekly*, 28 March 1931, p. 1689.

Boston Women's Health Book Collective (BWHBC). *Our Bodies Ourselves*. 2d ed. Boston: BWHBC, 1976.

Botting, Fred. *Sex, Machines and Navels: Fiction, Fantasy and History in the Future Present*. New York: Manchester University Press/St. Martin's, 1999.

Boyer, Paul S. *Purity in Print: The Vice-Society Movement and Book Censorship in America*. New York: Scribner's, 1968.

Boyle, T. Coraghessan. *The Road to Wellville.* New York: Signet, 1994; film version: Columbia Pictures, 1995.

Boynton, Robert S. "The Routledge Revolution: Has Academic Publishing Gone Too Far?" *Lingua Franca,* 5:3 (March/April 1995): 24–32.

Bradley, John R., ed. *Henry James and Homo-Erotic Desire.* New York: St. Martin's 1999.

Brandner, William Allan. *The Playboy's Handbook: In Defense of the Bachelor.* New York: Knickerbocker, 1942.

Brassäi. *Henry Miller: The Paris Years,* trans. T. Bent. New York: Arcade, 1995.

Brennan, Karen. "Anaïs Nin: Author(iz)ing the Erotic Body." *Genders,* 14 (Fall 1992): 66–86.

Bright, Susie, ed. *The Best American Erotica.* New York: Collier, 1993, 1994, 1995, 1996, 1997.

———. *Herotica: A Collection of Women's Erotic Fiction.* Burlingame, CA: Down There Press, 1988.

———. *Herotica III: A Collection of Women's Erotic Fiction.* New York: Plume, 1994.

———. *Susie Sexpert's Lesbian Sex World.* Pittsburgh: Cleis Press, 1990.

Bright, Susie, and Joani Blank, eds. *Herotica II: A Collection of Women's Erotic Fiction.* New York: Plume, 1991.

Bristow, Joseph, ed. *Sexual Sameness: Textual Differences in Lesbian and Gay Writing.* New York: Routledge, 1992.

Brite, Poppy Z., ed. *Love in Vein: Vampire Erotica.* 2 vols. New York: Harper/Prism, 1996, 1997.

Brittain, Vera. *Radclyffe Hall, a Case of Obscenity?* South Brunswick, NJ: A. S. Barnes, 1969.

Broadhead, Richard H. "Sparing the Rod: Discipline and Fiction in Antebellum America." *Representations,* 21 (Winter 1988): 67–96.

Brooks, Peter. *Body Work: Objects of Desire in Modern Narrative.* Cambridge: Harvard University Press, 1993.

Brooks, Van Wyck. "Introduction." *Painted Veils,* by James Gibbons Huneker. Greenwich, CT: Fawcett, 1964, pp. v–vii.

Brown, Helen Gurley, ed. *Winds of Love.* New York: Cosmopolitan, 1975.

Bryk, Felix. *The Sex Life of African Negroes.* New York: Falstaff Press?, 1930?

———. *Voodoo-Eros.* New York: Privately printed, 1933.

Buchen, Henry, ed. *The Perverse Imagination: Sexuality and Literary Culture.* New York: New York University Press, 1970.

Bukowski, Charles. *All's Normal Here: A Charles Bukowski Primer,* ed. Loss Pequeno Glazier. Fremont, CA: Ruddy Duck Press, 1985.

Bullough, Vern L. "An Early American Sex Manual, Or, Aristotle Who?" *Sex, Society, and History.* New York: Science History Publications, 1976, pp. 93–103.

Burroughs, William. *William Burroughs at the Front: Critical Reception 1959–1989,* ed. Jennie Skerl and Robin Crydenberg. Carbondale: Southern Illinois University Press, 1991.

Butler, Ellis Parker. *Dollarature, or the Drug Store Book.* Boston: Houghton Mifflin, 1930.

Calder, Jenni. *Women and Marriage in Victorian Fiction.* New York: Oxford University Press, 1976.

Califia, Pat. *The Advocate Adviser.* Boston: Alyson, 1991.

————. *Macho Sluts*. Boston: Alyson, 1988.

————. *Sapphistry: The Book of Lesbian Sexuality*. Tallahassee, FL: Naiad Press, 1980.

Cash, W. J. *The Mind of the South*. New York: Vintage, 1960.

Caron, Sue. *A Screw Loose: My Story So Far*. London: B & T Publishers, 1977.

Castiglia, Christopher. *Bound and Determined: Captivity, Culture-Crossing, and White Womanhood from Mary Rowlandson to Patty Hearst*. Chicago: University of Chicago Press, 1998.

Cawelti, John. "Pornography, Catastrophe, and Vengeance: Shifting Narrative Structures in a Changing American Culture." *The American Self: Myth, Ideology, and Popular Culture*, ed. Sam Girgus. Albuquerque: University of New Mexico Press, 1981, pp. 182–192.

Cawthorne, Nigel. *Secrets of Love: The Erotic Arts through the Ages*. San Francisco: Harper, 1998.

Chapkis, Wendy. *Live Sex Acts: Women Performing Erotic Labor*. New York: Cassell, 1996.

Chapple, Steve, and David Talbot. *Burning Desires: Sex in America, a Report from the Field*. New York: Signet, 1990.

"Charles Carrington: The Man and His Books." *A Victorian Sampler*, ed. Richard Manton. New York: Blue Moon Books, 1992, pp. 1–24.

Charney, Maurice. *Sexual Fiction*. New York: Methuen, 1981.

————. "Sexual Fiction in America, 1955–1980." *The Sexual Dimension in Literature*, ed. Alan Bold. Totowa, NJ: Barnes and Noble, 1983, pp. 122–144.

Cherkovski, Neeli. *Hank: The Life of Charles Bukowski*. New York: Random House, 1991.

Chester, Laura, ed. *Deep Down: The New Sensual Writing by Women*. London: Faber and Faber, 1988.

————. *The Unmade Bed: Sensual Writing on Married Love*. New York: HarperCollins, 1992.

Cleaton, Irene, and Allen Cleaton. *Books and Battles: American Literature 1920–1930*. Boston: Houghton Mifflin, 1937.

Cleaver, Eldridge. *Soul on Ice*. New York: Dell, 1968.

Cohn, Jan. *Romance and the Erotics of Property: Mass-Market Fiction for Women*. Durham, NC: Duke University Press, 1988.

Coles, Claire, and M. Johanna Sharp. "Some Sexual, Personality, and Demographic Characteristics of Women Readers of Erotic Romances." *Archives of Sexual Behavior*, 13 (June 1984): 187–209.

Comstock, Anthony. *Frauds Exposed: Or, How the People Are Deceived and Robbed, and Youth Corrupted*. Montclair NJ: Patterson Smith, 1969; rpt. of the 1880 original.

————. *Traps for the Young*, ed. Robert Brenner, 1883; rpt. Cambridge: Belknap Press, 1967.

Coppens, Armand. *Memoirs of an Erotic Bookseller, Assisted by His Tired Wife Clementine and Her Distant Lover*. New York: Grove, 1969.

Corinne, Tee. *Dreams of the Woman Who Loved Sex: A Collection*. Austin, TX: Banned Books, 1987.

————. *The Poetry of Sex: Lesbians Write the Erotic*. Austin, TX: Edward William Austin, 1992.

————. *Riding Desire: An Anthology of Erotic Writing*. Austin, TX: Banned Books, 1991.

Covington, D. B. *The Argus Book Shop: A Memoir*. West Cornwell, CT: Tarrydiddle Press, 1977.

Creech, James. *Closet Reading/Gay Reading: The Case of Melville's Pierre*. Chicago: University of Chicago Press, 1994.

Crosbie, Lynn, ed. *The Girl Wants To: Women's Representation of Sex and the Body*. Toronto: Coach House, 1993.

Cruikshank, M., ed. *New Lesbian Writing: An Anthology*. San Francisco: Grey Fox Press, 1984.

Csicsery, George, director. *Where the Heart Roams*. Point of View documentary series, Public Broadcasting System, first aired 4 August 1991.

d'Arcangelo, Angelo [Joseph Bush]. *Angelo d'Arcangelo's Love Book: Inside the Sexual Revolution*. New York: Olympia Press, 1971.

————. *The Homosexual Handbook*. New York: Olympia Press, 1969.

Darnton, Robert. *Forbidden Best-Sellers of Pre-Revolutionary France*. London: HarperCollins, 1996.

Datlow, Ellen, ed. *Alien Sex: 19 Tales by the Masters of Science Fiction and Dark Fantasy*. New York: NAL-Dutton, 1990.

Davis, Kenneth C. *Two-Bit Culture: The Paperbacking of America*. Boston: Houghton Mifflin, 1984.

Day, Gary, and Clive Bloom, eds. *Perspectives on Pornography: Sexuality in Film and Literature*. New York: St. Martin's, 1988.

Dearborn, Mary V. *The Happiest Man Alive: A Biography of Henry Miller*. New York: Simon and Schuster, 1991.

de Becker, Raymond. *The Other Face of Love*, trans. Margaret Crosland and Alan Daventry. New York: Bell, 1969.

De Berg, Jeanne [Allain Robbe-Grillet?]. *Women's Rites: Essays in the Erotic Imagination*, trans. Anselm Hollo. New York: Grove, 1987.

Decarnin, Camilla, Eric Garber, and Lyn Paleo, eds. *Worlds Apart: An Anthology of Lesbian and Gay Science Fiction and Fantasy*. Boston: Alyson, 1986.

Decosta-Willis, Miriam, Reginald Martin, and RoseAnn P. Bell, eds. *Erotique Noire: Black Erotica*. New York: Doubleday, 1992.

de Grazia, Edward. *Girls Lean Back Everywhere: The Law of Obscenity and the Assault on Genius*. New York: Random House, 1992.

Delacoste, Frédérique, and Priscilla Alexander, eds. *Sex Work: Writings by Women in the Sex Industry*. Pittsburgh: Cleis Press, 1987.

DeLamotte, Eugenia. *Perils of the Night: A Feminist Study of Nineteenth Century Gothic*. New York: Oxford University Press, 1990.

Delaney, Samuel R. *The Motion of Light in Water: Sex and Science Fiction Writing in the East Village, 1957–1965*. New York: Arbor/Morrow, 1988.

————. "Pornography/Censorship." *American Book Review*, 14:1 (April–May 1992): 14, 30.

De Mott, Benjamin. "But He's a Homosexual . . ." *The Perverse Imagination: Sexuality and Literary Culture*, ed. Irving Buchen. New York: New York University Press, 1970, pp. 147–164.

Derrick, Scott S. *Monumental Anxieties: Homoerotic Desire and Feminine Influence in*

19th Century U.S. Literature. New Brunswick, NJ: Rutgers University Press, 1998.

Devoe, Alan. "Erotic Books and the Depression." *Publishers Weekly*, 5 August 1933, pp. 343–344.

Diehl, Digby. "Playboy Interview: Anne Rice." *Playboy*, 40:3 (March 1993): 53–54, 56, 58–64.

Dijkstra, Bram. *Idols of Perversity: Fantasies of Feminine Evil in Fin-de-Siècle Culture*. New York: Oxford University Press, 1986.

Dingwall, Eric. *Very Peculiar People: Portrait Studies in the Queer, the Abnormal, and the Uncanny*. New Hyde Park, NY: University Books, [1962].

Douglas, Ann. "Soft-Porn Culture." *New Republic*, 30 August 1980, pp. 5–9.

Dozois, Gardiner, ed. *Dying for It: More Erotic Tales of Unearthly Love*. New York: Harper/Prism, 1997.

Drax, M. *Erotic Writers and Collector's Market*. P.O. Box 20593, Sun Valley, NV, current.

Du Bow, Wendy M., ed. *Conversations with Anaïs Nin*. Jackson: University of Mississippi Press, 1994.

Du Breuil, Linda. *The Girl Who Writes Dirty Books*. New York: Norton, 1975.

Dubino, Jeanne. "The Cinderella Complex: Romance Fiction, Patriarchy, and Capitalism." *Journal of Popular Culture*, 27:3 (Winter 1993): 103–118.

Ducille, Ann. "Blue Notes on Black Sexuality: Sex and the Texts of Jessie Fauset and Nellie Larsen." *American Sexual Politics: Sex. Gender, and Race since the Civil War*, ed. John C. Fout and Maura Shaw Tantillo. Chicago: University of Chicago Press, 1993, pp. 193–219.

Dunn, Sara. "Voyages of the Valkyries: Recent Lesbian Pornographic Writing." *Feminist Review*, 34 (Spring 1990): 160–170.

Dworkin, Andrea. *Ice and Fire: A Novel*. New York: Weidenfeld and Nicolson, 1987.

———. *Mercy*. London: Secker and Warburg, 1990; New York: Four Walls Eight Windows, 1991.

Dwyer, William. *What Everyone Knew about Sex, Explained in the Words of Orsen Squire Fowler and Other Victorian Moralists*. New York: Bell, 1972.

Dyer, Richard. "Coming Out as Going In: The Image of the Homosexual as a Sad Young Man." *The Matter of Images: Essays on Representations*. New York: Routledge, 1993, pp. 73–91.

Edelman, Lee. *Homographesis: Essays in Gay Literary and Cultural Theory*. New York: Routledge, 1994.

———. "Seeing Things: Representation, the Scene of Surveillance, and the Spectacle of Gay Male Sex." *Inside/Out: Lesbian Theories, Gay Theories*, ed. Diana Fuss. New York: Routledge, 1991, pp. 93–116.

Ehrenreich, Barbara, and Deidre English. *For Her Own Good: 150 Years of the Experts' Advice to Women*. Garden City, NY: Doubleday Anchor, 1979.

Eisenberg, Daniel. "Toward a Bibliography of Erotic Pulps." *Journal of Popular Culture*, 15:4 (Spring 1982): 175–184.

Elder, Joseph, ed. *Eros in Orbit: A Collection of All New Science Fiction Stories about Sex*. New York: Trident Press, 1973.

Elias, James E., Vern L. Bullough, Veronica Elias, and Gwen Brewer, eds. *Prostitution: On Whores, Hustlers, and Johns*. Amherst, NY: Prometheus Books, 1998.

Eliot, Jeffrey M., ed. *Kindred Spirits: An Anthology of Gay and Lesbian Science Fiction Stories*. Boston: Alyson Publications, 1984.

Elliot, Victoria Stagg. "My Porno Dad." *Future Sex*, 4 (1993): 10–11.

Ellis, Kate Ferguson. *The Contested Castle: Gothic Novels and the Subversion of Domestic Ideology*. Urbana: University of Illinois Press, 1989.

Ellis, Richard. "Disseminating Desire: Grove Press and 'The End[s] of Obscenity.' " *Perspectives on Pornography: Sexuality in Film and Literature*, ed. Gary Day and Clive Bloom. New York: St. Martin's, 1988, pp. 26–43.

Englisch, Paul. *Geschichte de Erotischen Literatur*. Stuttgart: Puttman Verlag, 1927.

———. *Irrgarten der Erotik*. Leipzig: Lykeion, 1931.

———. *Das skatologische Element in der Literatur, Kunst, und Volksleben*. Stuttgart: Puttman Verlag, 1928.

English, Deirdre, Amber Hollibaugh, and Gayle Rubin. "Talking Sex: A Conversation on Sexuality and Feminism." *Sexuality: A Reader*, ed. Feminist Review. London: Virago Press, 1987, pp. 63–81.

Erlich, Gloria C. *The Sexual Educations of Edith Wharton*. Berkeley: University of California Press, 1992.

Erotic Tales. New York: Castle, 1991.

Esquibel, Catrióna Rueda. "A Duel of Wits and the Lesbian Romance Novel or Verbal Intercourse in Fictional Regency England." *New Perspectives on Women and Comedy*, ed. Regina Barreca. Philadelphia: Gordon and Breach, 1992, pp. 123–133.

Eysenck, H. J. "A Psychologist Looks at Pornography." *Penthouse*, 3: 8 (April 1972): 95–100, 102.

Faderman, Lillian. *Odd Girls and Twilight Lovers: A History of Lesbian Life in Twentieth-Century America*. New York: Columbia University Press, 1991.

———. *Surpassing the Love of Men: Romantic Friendship and Love between Women from the Renaissance to the Present*. New York: Morrow, 1981.

Falk, Kathryn. *How to Write a Romance and Get It Published*. New York: Crown, 1983; rpt. New York: NAL, 1990.

[Farmer, John S.?] *Forbidden Books: Notes and Gossip on Tabooed Literature, Bibliographies and Excerpts . . . by an Old Bibliophile*. Paris: Carrington, 1902; rpt. New York: [Samuel Roth], 1929.

Ferguson, Robert. *Henry Miller: A Life*. New York: Norton, 1991.

Fiedler, Leslie. *Love and Death in the American Novel*. New York: Criterion, 1960.

Fille de Joie. New York: Grove Press, 1967.

Fitch, Noël Riley. *Anaïs: The Erotic Life of Anaïs Nin*. Boston: Little, Brown, 1993.

———. *Sylvia Beach and the Lost Generation: A History of Literary Paris in the Twenties*. New York: Norton, 1983.

Fitzgerald, William. "Radclyffe Hall's *The Well of Loneliness*: Sources and Inspirations." *Journal of Sex Research*, 14:1 (February 1978): 50–53.

Flannigan-Saint-Aubin, Arthur. " 'Black Gay Male' Discourse: Reading Race and Sexuality between the Lines." *American Sexual Politics: Sex, Gender, and Race since the Civil War*, ed. John C. Fout and Maura Shaw Tantillo. Chicago: University of Chicago Press, 1993, pp. 381–403.

Ford, Hugh. *Published in Paris*. New York: Macmillan, 1975.

Forrest, Katherine, and Barbara Grier, eds. *The Erotic Naiad: Love Stories by Naiad Authors*. Tallahassee, FL: Naiad Press, 1992.

Franklin, Benjamin. *Fart Proudly: Writings of Benjamin Franklin You Never Read in School*. New York: Ariel Press, 1990.

Franklin, Benjamin, V. "Adventures in the Skin Trade; or, the Enigma of *White Stains*." In *Search of a Continent: A North American Studies Odyssey*, ed. Mikko Saikku, Maarika Toivonen, and Mikko Toivonen (Festschrift in Honor of Professor Markku Henriksson's 50th Anniversary). Helsinki, Finland: Renvall Institute for Area and Cultural Studies, 1999, pp. 262–274.

Fraxi, Pisanus [Ashbee, Henry Spencer]. *Index Librorum Prohibitorum; Centuria Librorum Absconditorum; Catena Librorum Tacendorum, Being Notes Bio-Biblio-Iconographical and Critical on Curious, Uncommon and Erotic Books*. 3 vols. London: Privately Printed, 1877, 1879, 1885; rpt. *Index Librorum Prohibitorum; Centuria Librorum Absconditorum; Catena Librorum Tacendorum*. 3 vols. London: Skilton, 1960; rpt. *Bibliography of Forbidden Books*. 3 vols. New York: Jack Brussel, 1962; rpt. *The Encyclopedia of Erotic Literature*. 3 vols. New York: Documentary Books, 1962; *Forbidden Books of the Victorians: Henry Spencer Ashbee's Bibliographies of Erotica*, ed. Peter Fryer. London: Odyssey, 1970.

French, Dolores, with Linda Lee. *Working: My Life as a Prostitute*. New York: Dutton, 1988.

Friedman, Leslie. *Sex Role Stereotyping in the Mass Media: An Annotated Bibliography*. New York: Garland. 1977.

Frost, Laurie Adams. "Pets and Lovers: Human–Companion Animal Bond in Contemporary Literary Prose." *Journal of Popular Culture*, 25:1 (Summer 1991): 39–53.

Frye, Northrop. *The Secular Scripture: A Study of the Structure of Romance*. Cambridge: Harvard University Press, 1976.

Fryer, Peter, ed. *The Man of Pleasure's Companion: An Anthology of Secret Victorian Vices*. London: New English Library, 1969.

"Fuckbooks." *Screw*, 1969–.

Fuss, Diana, ed. *Inside/Out: Lesbian Theories, Gay Theories*. New York: Routledge, 1991.

Galloway, David, and Christian Sabisch, eds. *Calamus: Male Homosexuality in Twentieth Century Literature: An International Anthology*. New York: Morrow, 1982.

Gamlin, Douglas H., ed. *The Tijuana Bible Reader*. San Diego: Greenleaf Classics, 1969.

Garber, Eric, ed. *Embracing the Dark*. Boston: Alyson, 1991.

Garber, Eric, and Jewelle Gomez, eds. *Swords of the Rainbow: Gay and Lesbian Fantasy Adventures*. Boston: Alyson, 1996.

Garber, Eric, and Lyn Paleo, eds. *Uranian Worlds: A Guide to Alternative Sexuality in Science Fiction, Fantasy and Horror*. 2d ed. New York: Macmillan, 1990.

Garrity, Terry, with John Garrity. *Story of "J."* New York: Morrow, 1984.

Garson, Helen S. "John Hawkes and the Elements of Pornography." *Journal of Popular Culture*, 10 (Summer 1986): 150–155.

Gay, Peter. *The Education of the Senses*. 4 vols. I: *The Bourgeois Experience: Victoria to Freud; II: The Tender Passion*. New York: Oxford University Press, 1984, 1986; III: *The Cultivation of Hatred*; IV: *The Naked Heart*. New York: Norton, 1993, 1995.

Geis, Richard E. *How to Write Porno Novels for Fun and Profit*. Port Townsend, WA: Loompanics, 1985.

Gertzman, Jay A. *Bookleggers and Smuthounds: The Trade in Erotica, 1920–1940*. Philadelphia: University of Pennsylvania Press, 1999.

————. " 'Esoterica' and 'The Good of the Race': Mail-Order Distribution of Erotica in the 1930s." *The Papers of the Bibliographical Society of America*, 86:3 (September 1992): 295–340.

Gibbs, Phillip A. "Self Control and Male Sexuality in the Advice Literature of Nineteenth Century America, 1830–1860." *Journal of American Culture*, 9 (Summer 1986): 37–41.

Giese, Hans. *Das Obszöne Buch*. Stuttgart: Ferdinand Erike Verlag, 1965.

Gilbert, Harriet, ed. *The Sexual Imagination from Acker to Zola: A Feminist Companion*. London: Jonathan Cape, 1993.

Gilfoyle, Timothy J. *City of Eros: New York City, Prostitution, and the Commercialization of Sex, 1790–1920*. New York: Norton, 1992.

Gillette, Paul. *An Uncensored History of Pornography*. Los Angeles: Holloway House, 1965.

Gilmer, Walker. *Horace Liveright, Publisher of the Twenties*. New York: David Lewis, 1970.

Ginsberg, Allen. *Journals: Early Fifties, Early Sixties*, ed. Gordon Ball. New York: Grove Press, 1977.

Ginzburg, Ralph. *An Unhurried View of Erotica*. New York: Ace Books, 1958.

Girodias, Maurice. *The Frog Prince: An Autobiography*. New York: Crown, 1980.

————. "Lolita, Nabokov, and I." *Evergreen Review*, 37 (September 1965): 44–47.

————, ed. *The Best of Olympia*. London: Olympia Press/New English Library, 1966.

————, ed. *The New Olympia Reader*. New York: Black Watch, 1970; rpt. New York: Blue Moon Books, 1993.

————, ed. *The Olympia Reader*. New York: Grove Press, 1965.

Glicksberg, Charles I. *The Sexual Revolution in Modern American Literature*. The Hague: Martinus Nijhoff, 1971.

Gonzalez, Ray, ed. *Under the Pomegranate Tree: The Best New Latino Erotica*. New York: Washington Square Press, 1996.

Goode, James N. *Erotica Markets: Obscure and Profitable Markets for the Sensual Writer*. Nashville, TN: Ferret Press, 1988.

Goodman, Michael B., and Lemuel B. Coley. *William S. Burroughs: A Reference Guide*. New York: Garland, 1990.

Gordon, George. *Erotic Communications: Studies in Sex, Sin and Censorship*. New York: Hastings House, 1980.

Gordon, Michael, and Penelope Shankweiler. "Different Equals Less: Female Sexuality in Recent Marriage Manuals." *Journal of Marriage and the Family*, 33 (August 1971): 459–465.

Gornick, Vivian. "Why Do These Men Hate Women? American Novelists and Misogyny." *Village Voice*, 6 December 1976, pp. 12–13, 15.

Goshgarian, G. M. *To Kiss the Chastening Rod: Domestic Fiction and Sexual Ideology in the American Renaissance*. Ithaca, NY: Cornell University Press, 1992.

Govan, Sandra Y. "Forbidden Fruits and Unholy Lusts: Illicit Sex in Black American Literature." *Sexual Politics and Popular Culture*, ed. Diane Raymond. Bowling Green, OH: Bowling Green State University Popular Press, 1990, pp. 68–90.

Greene, Gerald, and Caroline Greene. *S-M: The Last Taboo*. New York: Grove Press, 1973.

Greenwood, Harold, and Aron Krich. *The Prostitute in Literature*. New York: Ballantine, 1960.

Grier, Barbara [aka Gene Damon]. *Lesbiana: Book Reviews from The Ladder, 1966–1972*. Reno, NV: Naiad Press, 1976.

Grier, Barbara, and Coletta Reid, eds. *Lesbian Lives: Biographies of Women from "The Ladder."* Oakland, CA: Diana Press, 1976.

Grimes, William. "Lurid! Licentious! Collectible! The Flip Side of the 1940's and 50's." *New York Times*, 25 July 1994, p. B3.

Hall, Max. *Benjamin Franklin and Polly Baker: The History of a Literary Deception*. Pittsburgh: University of Pittsburgh Press, 1990.

Hall, Ruth, ed. *Dear Dr. Stopes: Sex in the 1920s*. New York: Penguin, 1978.

Hall, Susan, with photos by Bob Adelman. *Gentleman of Leisure: A Year in the Life of a Pimp*. New York: NAL, 1972.

———. *Ladies of the Night*. New York: Trident, 1973.

Hallam, Paul. *The Book of Sodom*. New York: Routledge/Verso, 1994.

Haller, John S., and Robin M. Haller. *The Physician and Sexuality in Victorian America*. New York: Norton, 1977.

Hamalian, Leo. "Nobody Knows My Names: Samuel Roth and the Underside of Modern Letters." *Journal of Modern Literature*, 3 (April 1974): 889–921.

———. "The Secret Careers of Samuel Roth." *Journal of Popular Culture*, 1 (Spring 1968): 317–338.

Haney, Robert W. *Comstockery in America*. Boston: Beacon Press, 1960.

Hapke, Laura. *Girls Who Went Wrong: Prostitutes in American Fiction, 1885–1917*. Bowling Green, OH: Bowling Green State University Press, 1989.

Harlequin Books. *Thirty Years of Harlequin: 1949–1979*. Toronto: Harlequin, 1979.

Harrington Gay Men's Fiction Quarterly. Binghamton, NY, 1999–.

Harris, Sara. *House of 10,000 Pleasures*. New York: Dutton, 1962.

Harrison, Harry. *Great Balls of Fire! A History of Sex in Science Fiction*. London: Pierrot, 1977; aka *Great Balls of Fire: An Illustrated History of Sex in Science Fiction*. New York: Grosset and Dunlap, 1977.

Hart, J. D. *The Popular Book: A History of America's Literary Taste*. Berkeley: University of California Press, 1963.

Hazen, Helen. *Endless Rapture: Rape, Romance, and the Female Imagination*. New York: Scribner's, 1983.

Hebditch, David, and Nick Anning. *Porn Gold: Inside the Pornography Business*. Boston: Faber, 1988.

Hemingway, Ernest. *The Suppressed Poems of Ernest Hemingway*. N.p. [Paris?], n.d.

Hennegan, Alison. "On Becoming a Lesbian Reader." *Sweet Dreams: Sexuality, Gender and Popular Fiction*, ed. Susannah Radstone. London: Lawrence and Wishart, 1988, pp. 165–190.

Hernton, Calvin C. "How I Came to Write 'The Filthiest Book Ever Written.' " *Fact*, 3: 5 (September–October 1966): 36–47.

———. *Sex and Racism in America*. Garden City, NY: Doubleday, 1965.

Herring, Phillip. *Djuna: The Life and Work of Djuna Barnes*. New York: Viking, 1995.

Hill, Douglas, ed. *The Shape of Sex to Come*. London: Pan Books, 1978.

Hill, Heather, with John Austin. *Sexual Surrogate: Notes of a Therapist*. Chicago: Henry Regnery, 1976.

Hobby, Elaine, and Chris White, eds. *What Lesbians Do in Books*. London: Women's Press, 1991.

Hoffman, Stanton. "The Cities of Night: John Rechy's *City of Night* and the American

Literature of Homosexuality." *The Perverse Imagination: Sexuality and Literary Culture*, ed. Irving Buchen. New York: New York University Press, 1970, pp. 165–178.

Holland, Sharon P. "To Touch the Mother's C(o)untry: Siting Audre Lorde's Erotics." *Lesbian Erotics*, ed. Karla Jay. New York: New York University Press, 1995, pp. 212–226.

Hollander, Xavier, with Robin Moore and Yvonne Dunleavy. *The Happy Hooker: My Own Story*. New York: Dell, 1972.

Horn, Pierre L., and Mary Beth Pringle, eds. *The Image of the Prostitute in Modern Literature*. New York: Ungar, 1984.

Hunt, William R. *Body Love: The Amazing Career of Bernarr Macfadden*. Bowling Green, OH: Bowling Green State University Popular Press, 1989.

Hurwood, Bernhardt. *The Girls, the Massage and Everything: The Naked Truth about Massage Parlors*. Greenwich, CT: Fawcett, 1973.

———. *The Golden Age of Erotica*. Los Angeles: Shelbourne, 1965.

Huston, Nancy. *Mosaïque de la pornographie; Marie-Thérése et les autres*. Paris: Editions Denoël/Gauthier, 1982.

Hutchison, Bobby. *The Trade: Gay Male Escorts and Masseurs: Their Private and Working Lives*. New York: Cassell, 1999.

Hutson, Jan. *The Chicken Ranch: The True Story of the Best Little Whorehouse in Texas*. New York: A. S. Barnes, 1982.

Hutton, Julia, ed. *Good Sex: Real Stories from Real People*. Pittsburgh: Cleis Press, 1992.

Hyde, H. Montgomery. *A History of Pornography*. New York: Farrar, Straus, and Giroux, 1965.

Iannone, Carol. "From *Lolita* to *Piss Christ*." *Commentary*, 89:1 (January 1990): 52–54.

Itiel, Joseph. *A Consumer's Guide to Male Hustlers*. Binghamton, NY: Haworth Press, 1998.

Jackson, Earl, Jr. *Strategies of Deviance: Studies in Gay Male Representation*. Bloomington: Indiana University Press, 1995.

Jaffery, Sheldon R., ed. *Sensuous Science Fiction from the Weird and Spicy Pulps*. Bowling Green, OH: Bowling Green University Popular Press, 1984.

Jakubowski, Maxim, ed. *The Mammoth Book of International Erotica*. New York: Carroll and Graf, 1996.

———. *The Mammoth Book of New Erotica*. New York: Carroll and Graf, 1997.

Jay, Karla, and Joanne Glasgow, eds. *Lesbian Texts and Contexts: Radical Revisions*. New York: New York University Press, 1990.

Jefferies, B. G., and J. L. Nichols. *Light on Dark Corners* [1894]. New York: Grove Press, 1967.

Jensen, Margaret. *Love's Sweet Return: The Harlequin Story*. Bowling Green, OH: Bowling Green State University Press, 1984.

Jones, Ann Rosalind. "Nets and Bridles: Early Modern Conduct Books and Sixteenth-Century Women's Lyrics." *The Ideology of Conduct: Essays on Literature and the History of Sexuality*, ed. Nancy Armstrong and Leonard Tennenhouse. New York: Methuen, 1987, pp. 39–72.

Jones, Sonya L. *Gay and Lesbian Literature since World War II*. Binghamton, NY: Haworth Press, 1998.

Jong, Erica. " 'Deliberate Lewdness' and the Lure of Immortality." *1601 and Is Shake-*

speare Dead?, by Mark Twain, ed. Shelley Fisher Fishkin. *The Oxford Mark Twain.* 29 vols. New York: Oxford University Press, 1996, xxvii, xxxi–xlii.

———. *The Devil at Large: Erica Jong on Henry Miller.* New York: Turtle Bay Books, 1993.

Kahane, Jack. *Memoirs of a Booklegger.* London: Michael Joseph, 1939.

Karjalainen, Sohvi. "On Swearwords and Obscenities in Philip Roth's *Portnoy's Complaint.*" Master's thesis, Department of English Philology, University of Helsinki, Finland, 1989.

Kearney, Patrick J. *A History of Erotic Literature.* London: Macmillan, 1982.

———. *The Private Case: An Annotated Bibliography of the Erotica Collection in the British (Museum) Library.* London: Landesman, 1981.

Keesey, Pam, ed. *Daughters of Darkness: Lesbian Vampire Stories.* Pittsburgh: Cleis, 1993.

Keller, Karl. "Reverend Mr. Edward Taylor's Bawdry." *New England Quarterly,* 44 (1970): 382–406.

Kellerman, Stewart. "Other Incarnations of the Vampire Author." *New York Times,* 7 November 1988, pp. C15–16.

Kellman, Steven G. *Loving Reading: Erotics of the Text.* Hamden, CT: Shoe String Press, 1985.

Kellogg, Stuart, ed. *Essays on Gay Literature.* Binghamton, NY: Haworth Press, 1985.

———. *Literary Visions of Homosexuality.* Binghamton, NY: Haworth Press, 1985.

Kelly, Valerie. *How to Write Erotica for Fun and Profit.* New York: Harmony Books, 1986.

Kendrick, Walter. *The Secret Museum: Pornography in Modern Culture.* New York: Viking, 1987.

Kensington Ladies Erotica Society. *Erotic Companion: Kensington Ladies' Erotica Society,* ed. Pat Adler. Berkeley, CA: Ten Speed Press, 1985.

———. *Ladies' Own Erotica: Tales, Recipes, and Other Mischiefs by Older Women.* Berkeley, CA: Ten Speed Press, 1984.

———. *Look Homeward Erotica.* Berkeley, CA: Ten Speed Press, 1990.

Kent, R. *Aunt Agony Advises: Problem Pages through the Ages.* London: W. H. Allen, 1979.

Kersnowski, Frank, and Alice Hughes, eds. *Conversations with Henry Miller.* Jackson: University of Mississippi Press, 1994.

Killingsworth, M. Jimmie. *Whitman's Poetry of the Body: Sexuality, Politics, and the Text.* Chapel Hill: University of North Carolina Press, 1989.

Kilpatrick, James Jackson. *The Smut Peddlers.* Garden City, NY: Doubleday, 1960.

King, Florence. "Confessions of a Lady Pornographer." *Penthouse* 5:1 (September 1973): 129–134.

King, Katie. "Audre Lorde's Layered Lacquerings: The Lesbian Bar as a Site of Literary Production." *New Lesbian Criticism: Literary and Cultural Readings,* ed. Sally Munt. New York: Columbia University Press, 1992, pp. 49–58.

Kishtainy, Khalid. *The Prostitute in Progressive Literature.* New York: Allson and Busby, 1982.

Kramer, Kathleen M. "Questionable Characters: Turn-of-the-Century American Fictions, Feminism, and the Fallen Woman." Ph.D. dissertation, University of Wisconsin–Milwaukee, 1995.

Krentz, Jayne Ann. "Trying to Tame the Romance: Critics and Correctness." *Dangerous*

Men and Adventurous Women: Romance Writers on the Appeal of the Romance, ed. Jayne Ann Krentz. Philadelphia: University of Pennsylvania Press, 1992, pp. 107–114.

———, ed. *Dangerous Men and Adventurous Women: Romance Writers on the Appeal of the Romance*. Philadelphia: University of Pennsylvania Press, 1992.

Kudaka, Geraldine, ed. *On a Bed of Rice: An Asian-American Erotic Feast*. New York: Anchor/Doubleday, 1995.

Lambda Book Report. 1625 Connecticut Avenue NW, Washington, DC 20009.

Leavitt, David, and Mark Mitchell, eds. *The Penguin Book of Gay Short Stories*. New York: Penguin, 1994.

Legman, Gershon. *The Horn Book: Studies in Erotic Folklore and Bibliography*. New York: University Books, 1966.

———. "Introduction." *The Private Case: An Annotated Bibliography of the Erotica Collection in the British (Museum) Library*, by Patrick J. Kearney. London: Landesman, 1981, pp. 3–34; revised as "The Lure of the Forbidden." *Libraries, Erotica, and Pornography*, ed. Martha Cornog. Phoenix, AZ: Oryx Press, 1991, pp. 36–68.

———. *Love and Death: A Study in Censorship*. New York: Breaking Point, 1949.

Lemay, Leo. "The Public Writings and the Bagatelles." *Benjamin Franklin: A Collection of Critical Essays*, ed. Brian M. Barbour. Englewood Cliffs, NJ: Prentice-Hall, 1979, pp. 146–160.

Levin, James. *The Gay Novel in America*. Hamden, CT: Garland, 1991.

Lewis, Roy Harley. *The Browser's Guide to Erotica*. New York: St. Martin's, 1981.

Lewis, R. W. B. *Edith Wharton: A Biography*. New York: Harper and Row, 1975.

Lilly, Mark. *Gay Men's Literature in the Twentieth Century*. New York: New York University Press, 1993.

———, ed. *Lesbian and Gay Writing: An Anthology of Critical Essays*. New York: Macmillan, 1990.

Linna, Miriam. *Smut Peddler*. P.O. Box 646, Cooper Station, New York City 10003, 1993–.

Lopez, Claude-Anne. *Mon cher papa: Benjamin Franklin and the Ladies of Paris*. New Haven, CT: Yale University Press, 1966.

Loth, David. *The Erotic in Literature*. New York: Julian Messner, 1961.

Loulan, JoAnn. *The Lesbian Erotic Dance: Butch, Femme, Androgyny and Other Rhythms*. San Francisco: Spinsters/Aunt Lute, 1990.

Lowenthal, Michael, ed. *Flesh and the Word 4: Gay Erotic Confessionals*. New York: Plume, 1997.

Lyall, Sarah. "Lost and Found." *New York Times*, 20 July 1994, p. B8.

Macfadden, Bernarr. *Manhood and Marriage*. New York: Physical Culture, 1916.

MacManus, Virginia. *Not for Love*. New York: Dell, 1961.

Mailer, Norman. *Genius and Lust: A Journey through the Major Writings of Henry Miller*. New York: Grove Press, 1976.

———. *The Prisoner of Sex*. Boston: Little, Brown, 1971.

Mair, George. *The Sex-Book Digest: A Peek between the Covers of 113 of the Most Erotic, Exotic, and Edifying Sex Books*. New York: Quill, 1982.

Manguel, Alberto, ed. *The Gates of Paradise: An Anthology of Erotic Short Fiction*. New York: Crown Publishing Group, 1993.

Marcus, Steven. *The Other Victorians: A Study of Sexuality and Pornography in Mid-Nineteenth Century England*. New York: Basic Books, 1965.

Marlow, Kenneth. *Mr. Madam: Confessions of a Male Madam*. Los Angeles: Sherbourne Press, 1964.

Marr, Johnny. *(Anti-) Sex Tips for Teens: The Teenage Advice Book, 1897–1987*. San Francisco: John Marr, 1990[?].

Martin, Jay. *Always Bright and Merry*. London: Sheldon Press, 1979.

Martin, Reginald, ed. *Dark Eros: Black Erotic Writings*. New York: St. Martin's, 1997.

Masse, Michelle A. *In the Name of Love: Women, Masochism, and the Gothic*. Ithaca, NY: Cornell University Press, 1992.

Mayall, Alice, and Diana E. H. Russell. "Racism in Pornography." *Gender, Race and Class in Media: A Text-Reader*, ed. Gail Dines and Jean M. Humez. Thousand Oaks, CA: Sage, 1995, pp. 287–297; an earlier version appears in *Making Violence Sexy*, ed. Diana E. H. Russell. New York: Teachers College Press, 1993, Chapter 16.

McCabe, Joseph. *Masterpieces of Erotic Literature*. Little Blue Book B-849. Girard, KS: Haldeman-Julius, 1949.

McCafferty, Kate. "Palimpsest of Desire: The Re-Emergence of the American Captivity Narrative as Pulp Romance." *Journal of Popular Culture*, 27:4 (Spring 1994): 43–56.

McCormick, Donald. *Erotic Literature: A Connoisseur's Guide*. New York: Continuum, 1992.

McDonald, Boyd. *Smut*. New York: Calamus Books, n.d.

———. *True Homosexual Experiences from S. T. H. Writers*. 6 vols. San Francisco: Gay Sunshine Press, 1983–1985.

McGrady, Mike. *Stranger than Naked*. New York: Wyden, 1970.

McLaughlin, Lisa. "Discourses of Prostitution/Discourses of Sexuality." *Critical Studies in Mass Communication*, 8 (1991): 249–272.

McMurtry, Larry. "From Mickey Spillane to Erica Jong." *Washington Monthly*, May 1975, pp. 12–20.

Meese, Elizabeth. *(Sem)Erotics: Theorizing Lesbian: Writing*. New York: New York University Press, 1992.

Meeske, Marilyn. "Memoirs of a Female Pornographer." *Esquire*, 62 (April 1965): 112–115.

Mencken, H. L. *My Life as Author and Editor*, ed. Jonathan Yardley. New York: Knopf, 1993.

Merck, Mandy. *Perversions: Deviant Readings by Mandy Merck*. New York: Routledge, 1993.

Mertner, Edgar, and Herbert Mainusch. *Pornotopia: Das Obszöne und die Pornographie in der literarischen Landschaft*. Frankfurt am Main: Athenaum Verlag, 1970.

Miles, Angela. "Confessions of a Harlequin Reader: Romance and the Myth of Male Mothers." *The Hysterical Male*, ed. Arthur Kroker and Marilouise Kroker. New York: New World Perspectives, 1991, pp. 92–131.

Miles, Barry. *Ginsberg: A Biography*. New York: Simon and Schuster, 1989.

Miles, Henry. *Forbidden Fruit: A Study of Incest in Forbidden Literature*. London: Luxor Press, 1973.

Miller, Henry. *The Air-Conditioned Nightmare*. New York: New Directions, 1947.

———. *Henry Miller: Years of Trial and Triumph, 1962–1964: The Correspondence of*

Henry Miller and Elmer Gertz, ed. Elmer Gertz and Felice Flanery Lewis. Carbondale: Southern Illinois Press, 1978.

―――. *Remember to Remember*. New York: New Directions, 1947.

―――. *The World of Sex*. New York: Grove Press, 1965.

Millett, Kate. *Sexual Politics*. New York: Doubleday, 1969.

Mills, Jane, ed. *The Bloomsbury Guide to Erotic Literature*. London: Bloomsbury, 1993.

Modleski, Tania. *Loving with a Vengeance: Mass-Produced Fantasies for Women*. New York: Methuen, 1984.

Money, John. *The Destroying Angel: Sex, Fitness, and Food in the Legacy of Degeneracy, Graham Crackers, Kellogg's Corn Flakes, and American Health History*. Buffalo, NY: Prometheus Books, 1985.

Mooney, Harry J., Jr. "The *Sub Rosa* Writings of Eugene Field." *Papers of the Bibliographical Society of America*, 75 (1978): 541–552.

Moore, Rob, ed. *Field Guide to Outdoor Erotica*. Moscow, ID: Solstice Press, 1988.

Morace, Robert. "Robert Coover's *Spanking the Maid*: Determinism and the Indeterminate Text." *Markham Review*, 14 (Spring–Summer 1985): 24–27.

Mordell, Albert. *The Erotic Motive in Literature*. New York: Boni and Liveright, 1919.

Moretto, Shirley, and Kathleen Weidenburner. "We'll Take Romance." *Library Journal*, 15 September 1984, pp. 1727–1728.

Morgan, Ted. *Literary Outlaw: The Life and Times of William S. Burroughs*. New York: Avon, 1988.

Morgenstern, Naomi. " 'There Is Nothing Else Like This': Sex and Citation in Pornogothic Feminism." *Sex Positives? The Cultural Politics of Dissident Sexualities*, ed. Thomas Foster, Carol Siegel, and Ellen E. Berry. New York: New York University Press, 1997, pp. 39–67.

Moulton, Ian F. "Before Pornography: Explicitly Erotic Writing in Early Modern England." Ph.D. dissertation, Columbia University, 1995.

Munt, Sally. *New Lesbian Criticism: Literary and Cultural Readings*. New York: Columbia University Press, 1992.

Nabokov, Vladimir. "Lolita and Mr. Girodias." *Evergreen Review*, 45 (February 1967): 37–41.

Nelson, Emmanuel, ed. *Gay and Lesbian Writers of Color*. Binghamton, NY: Haworth Press, 1993.

Nestle, Joan. *A Restricted Country*. Ithaca, NY: Firebrand Books, 1987.

―――, ed. *The Persistent Desire: A Femme-Butch Reader*. Boston: Alyson, 1992.

Nestle, Joan, and Naomi Holoch, eds. *Women on Women: An Anthology of American Lesbian Short Fiction*. New York: Plume, 1990.

New England Watch and Ward Society. *Annual Reports*. Boston: New England Watch and Ward Society, 1905–1939.

New York Society for the Suppression of Vice. *Annual Reports*. New York: New York Society for the Suppression of Vice, 1874–1940.

―――. *Names and Records of Persons Arrested under the Auspices of the Society: 1920–1950*. Library of Congress, Manuscript Division, Microfilm 19:359.

Nin, Anaïs. *Delta of Venus*. New York: Harcourt Brace Jovanovich, 1977.

―――. *The Diary of Anaïs Nin*, ed. Gunther Stuhlmann. 7 vols. New York: Swallow Press and Harcourt, Brace, and World, I: *1931–1934*, 1966; II: *1934–1939*, 1967. New York: Harcourt, Brace, and World, III: *1939–1944*, 1969. New York: Harcourt Brace Jovanovich, IV: *1944–1947*, 1971; V: *1947–1955*, 1973; VI: *1955–1966*, 1976; VII: *1966–1974*, 1980.

———. *Henry and June*. New York: Harcourt, 1986.

———. *Little Birds*. New York: Harcourt Brace Jovanovich, 1979.

O'Brien, Geoffrey. *Hardboiled America: The Lurid Years of Paperbacks*. New York: Van Nostrand Reinhold, 1981; rev. ed. *Hardboiled America: Lurid Paperbacks and the Masters of Noir*. New York: DaCapo, 1997.

Oderman, Kevin. *Ezra Pound and the Erotic Medium*. Durham, NC: Duke University Press, 1986.

Paglia, Camille. *Sexual Personae: Art and Decadence from Nefertiti to Emily Dickinson*. New York: Vintage, 1991.

Palumbo, Donald, ed. *Eros and the Mind's Eye: Sexuality and the Fantastic in Art and Film*. Westport, CT: Greenwood, 1986.

———. *Erotic Universe: Sexuality and the Fantastic Literature*. Westport, CT: Greenwood, 1986.

Parker, Derek. *Writing Erotic Fiction*. New York: Marlowe and Company, 1996.

Parry, Michael, and M. Subotsky, eds. *Sex in the 21st Century: A Collection of SF Erotica*. London: Granada, 1979.

Pearsall, Ronald. *The Worm in the Bud: the World of Victorian Sexuality*. New York: Macmillan, 1969.

Perkins, Michael. *The Secret Record: Modern Erotic Literature*. New York: William Morrow, 1977.

Perrin, Noel. *Dr. Bowdler's Legacy: A History of Expurgated Books in England and America*. New York: Atheneum, 1969.

Petersen, James R. "A Brief History of Sex Tricks." *Playboy*, 43:9 (September 1996): 41–42.

Pheterson, Gail, ed. *A Vindication of the Rights of Whores*. Seattle: Seal Press, 1989.

Pierpont, Claudia Roth. "Sex, Lies, and Thirty-Five Thousand Pages." *New Yorker*, 1 March 1993, pp. 74–80, 82–90.

Pitt-Kethley, Fiona, ed. *The Literary Companion to Sex: An Anthology of Prose and Poetry*. New York: Random House, 1993.

The Playboy Advisor Revisited. Chicago: Playboy Press, 1969.

Poetica Erotica. N.p.: Esoterika Biblion Society, 1938.

"Polysexuality." *Semiotext(e)*, 4:1 (1981). New York, 1974–.

P.O.N.Y. X-Press. 25 West 45th Street, New York City 10036.

Preston, John. *My Life as a Pornographer and Other Indecent Acts*. New York: Masquerade Books, 1993.

———. ed. *Flesh and the Word: An Anthology of Erotic Writing*. Vols. I and II. New York: Plume, 1992, 1993.

Preston, John, and Michael Lowenthal, eds. *Flesh and the Word 3: An Anthology of Gay Erotic Writing*. New York: Plume, 1995.

Pullar, Philippa. *Frank Harris: A Biography*. New York: Simon and Schuster, 1976.

Purdy, Strother. "On the Psychology of Erotic Literature." *The Perverse Imagination: Sexuality and Literary Culture*, ed. Henry Buchen. New York: New York University Press, 1970.

Queen, Carol, and Lawrence Schimel, eds. *Switch Hitters: Lesbians Write Gay Male Erotica and Gay Men Write Lesbian Erotica*. Pittsburgh: Cleis Press, 1996.

Rabine, Leslie W. *Reading the Romantic Heroine: Text, History, Ideology.* Ann Arbor: University of Michigan Press, 1985.

Radford, Jean. "An Inverted Romance: *The Well of Loneliness* and Sexual Ideology." *The Progress of Romance: The Politics of Popular Fiction,* ed. Jean Radford. London: Routledge, 1986, pp. 97–112.

———, ed. *The Progress of Romance: The Politics of Popular Fiction.* London: Routledge, 1986.

Radstone, Susannah, ed. *Sweet Dreams: Sexuality, Gender and Popular Fiction.* London: Lawrence and Wishart, 1988.

Radway, Janice A. *Reading the Romance: Women, Patriarchy, and Popular Literature.* Chapel Hill: University of North Carolina Press, 1984.

Ramsland, Katherine. *Prism of the Night: A Biography of Anne Rice.* New York: Plume, 1992.

Raynaud, Claudine. " 'A Nutmeg Nestled Inside Its Covering of Mace': Audre Lorde's *Zami.*" *Life/Lines: Theorizing Women's Autobiography,* ed. Bella Brodzki and Celeste Schenck. Ithaca, NY: Cornell University Press, pp. 229–238.

Reade, Brian. *Sexual Heretics.* New York: Coward-McCann, 1971.

Reisner, Robert, ed. *Great Erotic Scenes from Literature.* Chicago: Playboy Press, 1972; rpt. *Show Me The Good Parts: The Reader's Guide to Sex in Literature.* New York: Citadel, 1964.

Rembar, Charles. *The End of Obscenity: The Trials of Lady Chatterley, Tropic of Cancer and Fanny Hill by the Lawyer Who Defended Them.* New York: Random House, 1968.

Reynolds, David. *Beneath the American Renaissance: The Subversive Imagination in the Age of Emerson and Melville.* New York: Knopf, 1988.

Reynolds, Kimberley, and Nicola Humble. *Victorian Heroines: Representations of Femininity in Nineteenth-Century Literature and Art.* New York: New York University Press, 1994.

Reynolds, Margaret, ed. *Erotica: Women's Writing from Sappho to Margaret Atwood.* London: Pandora, 1990; Fawcett, 1992.

———. *The Penguin Book of Lesbian Short Stories.* New York: Penguin, 1994.

Roberts, Robin. *A New Species: Gender and Science in Science Fiction.* Champaign: University of Illinois Press, 1993.

Rochford, Pamela. *Writing Erotic Fiction: How to Write a Successful Erotic Novel.* Philadelphia: Trans-Atlantic Publishers, 1997.

Rogers, W. G. *Wise Men Fish Here: The Story of Frances Steloff and the Gotham Book Mart.* New York: Harcourt, Brace, and World, 1965.

Roof, Judith. *A Lure of Knowledge: Lesbian Sexuality and Theory.* New York: Columbia University Press, 1991.

Rosenberg, Carroll Smith. "Davy Crockett as Trickster: Pornography, Liminality, and Symbolic Inversion in Victorian America." *Disorderly Conduct: Visions of Gender in Victorian America.* New York: Oxford University Press, 1985, pp. 90–108.

Roth, Samuel. *The Private Life of Frank Harris.* New York: W. Faro, 1932.

———. *Stone Walls Do Not: The Chronicle of a Captivity.* 2 vols. New York: W. Faro, 1931.

Rousseau, George, and Roy Porter, eds. *Sexual Underworlds of the Enlightenment.* Chapel Hill: University of North Carolina Press, 1988.

Rugoff, Milton. *Prudery and Passion: Sexuality in Victorian America.* New York: Putnam, 1971.

Rusbridger, Alan. *A Concise History of the Sex Manual, 1886–1986.* London: Faber and Faber, 1986.

Russ, Joanna. "Somebody Is Trying to Kill Me and I Think It's My Husband: The Modern Gothic." *Journal of Popular Culture,* 6:4 (1973): 666–691.

———. *To Write Like a Woman: Essays in Feminism and Science Fiction*: Bloomington: Indiana University Press, 1995.

Sargent, Pamela, ed. *Women of Wonder* and *More Women of Wonder: Science Fiction Novelettes by Women about Women.* New York: Vintage, 1970, 1971.

Scheiner, C. J. *Compendium; Being a List of All the Books (Erotica, Curiosa, & Sexology) Listed in Our Catalogs 1–6 (1978–1988).* Brooklyn, NY: C. J. Scheiner, 1989.

Schellenberg, Helene, ed. *Writing Romance Fiction: For Love and Money.* Cincinnati, OH: Writer's Digest Books, 1983.

Schertel, Ernst, ed. *Der Flagellantismus als Literarisches Motiv.* 4 vols. Leipzig: Parthenon-Verlag, 1929–32; rev. and exp. ed. *Der Flagellantismus in Literatur und Bildnerei.* 12 vols. Schniden bei Stuttgart: F. Decker, 1957.

Schick, Frank L. *The Paperbound Book in America.* New York: Bowker, 1958.

Schimel, Lawrence, ed. *Erotic Writer's Market Guide.* Cambridge, MA: Circlet Press, 1999.

Schlamm, William Siegmund. *Vom Elend der Literatur: Pornographie und Gesinnung.* Stuttgart-Dagerloch: Seewald, 1966.

Schmolze, Gerhard. "Pornographie als ethische Provokation und erotische Aggression." *Verbot de Pornographie? Gesellschaftsstruktur und Sexualle Sucht,* ed. Wolfgang Böhme. Stuttgart: Radues-Verlag, 1968, 45–70.

Schoenstein, Ralph. *I Hear America Mating.* New York: St. Martin's, 1972.

Scholder, Amy, and Ira Silverberg. *High Risk: An Anthology of Forbidden Writings* and *High Risk 2: Writings on Sex, Death, and Subversion.* New York: Plume, 1991, 1994.

Schwartz, Harry W. *Fifty Years in My Bookstore, Or a Life with Books.* Milwaukee, WI: N.p., 1977.

———. *This Book Collecting Racket.* Chicago: Normandie House, 1937.

Scortia, Thomas. *Strange Bedfellows: Sex and Science Fiction.* New York: Random House, 1972.

Scully, Diana, and Pauline Bart. "A Funny Thing Happened on the Way to the Orifice: Women in Gynecology Textbooks." *Changing Women in a Changing Society,* ed. Joan Huber. Chicago: University of Chicago Press, 1973, pp. 283–288.

Secor, Robert. "Humor in American Almanacs: From the Colonial Period to the Civil War and After." *American Humor Magazines and Comic Periodicals,* ed. David E. E. Sloane. Westport, CT: Greenwood Press, 1987, pp. 549–562.

Sedgwick, Eve Kosofsky. *Between Men: English Literature and the Male Homosocial Desire.* New York: Columbia University Press, 1985.

———. *Tendencies.* Chapel Hill, NC: Duke University Press, 1994.

See, Carolyn. "My Daddy, the Pornographer." *Esquire,* 78 (August 1972): 110–113, 184–186.

Server, Lee. *Over My Dead Body: The Sensational Age of the American Paperback, 1945–1955.* San Francisco: Chronicle Books, 1994.

Sex Box: Man, Woman, Sex. 3 vols. New York: Chronicle, 1996.

"Sex Workers and Sex Work." Special issue of *Social Text*, 37 (Winter 1993).

Sheba Collective, eds. *More Serious Pleasure.* London: Sheba, 1990.

———. *Serious Pleasure: Lesbian Erotic Stories and Poetry.* London: Sheba, 1989.

Sheehy, Gail. *Hustling.* New York: Dell, 1971.

Sheiner, Marcy, ed. *Herotica 4.* New York: Plume, 1996.

———. *Herotica 5.* New York: Plume, 1997.

Sherry, Madame [Ruth Barnes]. *Pleasure Was My Business*, as told to S. Robert Tralens. New York: Lyle Stuart, 1961.

Shively, Charley. *Calamus Lovers: Walt Whitman's Working Class Camerados.* San Francisco: Gay Sunshine Press, 1987.

———. *Drum Beats: Walt Whitman's Civil War Boy Lovers.* San Francisco: Gay Sunshine Press, 1989.

Showalter, Elaine. "American Female Gothic." *Sister's Choice: Tradition and Change in American Women's Writing.* New York: Oxford University Press, 1994, pp. 127–144.

Shulman, Robert. "The Serious Function of Melville's Phallic Jokes." *American Literature*, 33 (1961): 179–194.

Simmons, Thomas. *Erotic Reckonings: Mastery and Apprenticeship in the Work of Poets and Lovers.* Champaign: University of Illinois Press, 1994.

Slung, Michele, ed. *Slow Hand: Women Writing Erotica.* New York: HarperCollins, 1992.

Smith, Don D. "The Social Content of Pornography."*Journal of Communication*, 26:1 (Winter 1976): 16–24.

Smith, Victoria L. "Starting from Snatch: The Seduction of Performance in Bertha Harris's *Lover.*" *Sex Positives? The Cultural Politics of Dissident Sexualities*, ed. Thomas Foster, Carol Siegel, and Ellen E. Berry. New York: New York University Press, 1997, pp. 68–94.

Snitow, Ann. "The Front-Line: Notes on Sex in Novels by Women, 1969–1979." *Women: Sex and Sexuality*, ed. Catharine R. Stimpson and Ethel S. Person. Chicago: University of Chicago Press, 1980, pp. 158–174.

———. "Mass Market Romance: Pornography for Women Is Different." *Radical History Review*, 20 (Spring/Summer 1979): 141–161; rpt. *Powers of Desire: The Politics of Sexuality*, ed. Ann Snitow, Christine Stansell, and Sharon Thompson. New York: Monthly Review Press, 1983, pp. 245–263; rpt. *Passion and Power: Sexuality in History*, ed. Kathy Peiss and Christina Simmons, with Robert A. Padgug. Philadelphia: Temple University Press, 1989, pp. 259–276.

Sokolow, Jayne A. *Eros and Modernization: Sylvester Graham, Health Reform, and the Origins of Victorian Sexuality in America.* Rutherford, NJ: Fairleigh Dickinson University Press, 1983.

Soles, Caro. *Meltdown: An Anthology of Erotic Science Fiction and Dark Fantasy for Gay Men.* New York: Masquerade, 1997.

Sproat, Ron. "The Working Day in a Porno Factory." *Sexual Deviance and Sexual Deviants*, ed. Erich Goode and Richard R. Troiden. New York: Morrow, 1974, pp. 83–92; rpt. of article in *New York Magazine*, 11 March 1974, pp. 37–41.

St. Jorre, John de. *Venus Bound: The Erotic Voyages of the Olympia Press.* New York: Random House, 1996.

Stallybrass, Peter, and Alison White. *The Politics and Poetics of Transgression*. Ithaca, NY: Cornell University Press, 1986.

Stanford, Sally. *The Lady of the House: The Autobiography of Sally Stanford*. New York: Putnam's, 1966.

Stanley, Alessandra. "Romance Novels Discover a Baby Boom." *New York Times*, national ed., 3 April 1991, pp. A1, A13.

Stanley, Julia Penelope, and Susan J. Wolfe, eds. *The Coming Out Stories*. Watertown, MA: Persephone Press, 1980.

Stark, Lawrence. "Pulp Fiction Erotica." *Gallery*, July 1995, pp. 74–78, 97.

Stein, Gertrude. *Lifting Belly*, ed. Rebecca Mark. Tallahassee, FL: Naiad Press, 1989.

Steinberg, David, ed. *Erotic by Nature: A Celebration of Life, of Love, and of Our Wonderful Bodies*. Berkeley, CA: Shakti Press, 1988.

———. *The Erotic Impulse: Honoring the Sensual Self*. Los Angeles: Tarcher/Perigee, 1992.

Steward, Samuel M. *Understanding the Male Hustler*. Binghamton, NY: Haworth Press, 1991.

Stewart, Amanda. *Sex Therapist: My Story*. New York: Ace, 1975.

Stimpson, Catharine. "Zero Degree Deviancy: The Lesbian Novel in English." *Critical Inquiry*, 8 (1981): 363–380.

Summers, Claude J., ed. *The Gay and Lesbian Literary Heritage: A Reader's Companion to the Writers and Their Works, from Antiquity to the Present*. New York: Holt, 1995.

Sussman, Gerald. *The Official Sex Manual: A Modern Approach to the Art and Techniques of Coginus*. New York: Putnam's, 1965.

Sussman, Irving, and Cornelia Sussman. *How to Read a Dirty Book or the Way of the Pilgrim Reader*. Chicago: Franciscan Herald, 1966.

Symanski, Richard. *The Immoral Landscape: Female Prostitution in Western Societies*. Toronto: Butterworths, 1981.

Tabor, Pauline. *Pauline's: Memoirs of the Madam on Clay Street*. Louisville, KY: Touchstone, 1972.

Talburt, Nancy Ellen. "Red Is the Color of My True Love's Blood: Fetishism in Mystery Fiction." *Objects of Special Devotion: Fetishes and Fetishism in Popular Culture*. Bowling Green, OH: Bowling Green State University Press, 1982, pp. 69–88.

Talese, Gay. *Thy Neighbor's Wife*. New York: Dell, 1981.

Tan, Cecilia, ed. *Forged Bonds: Erotic Tales of High Fantasy*. San Francisco: Circlet Press, 1993.

———. *S and M Future: Erotica on the Edge*. San Francisco: Circlet, 1995.

———. *Sex Magick*. San Francisco: Circlet Press, 1993.

———. *Telepaths Don't Need Safewords*. San Francisco: Circlet Press, 1992.

———. *Worlds of Women: Sapphic Erotica*. San Francisco: Circlet Press, 1993.

Tanselle, Thomas G. "The Thomas Seltzer Imprint." *Papers of the Bibliographical Society of America*, 58 (1964): 400–406.

Tate, Claudia, ed. *Black Women Writers at Work*. New York: Continuum, 1983.

Taylor, Dane, and Antonia Newton-West. *Gigolos: The Secret Lives of Men Who Service Women*. Boston: Mt. Ivy Press, 1994.

Taylor, Dena, and Amber Sumrall, eds. *The Time of Our Lives: Women Write on Sex after 40*. Freedom, CA: Crossing Press, 1993.

Tebbel, John. *A History of Book Publishing in the United States*. 4 vols. New York: Bowker, 1978.

————. *The Media in America*. New York: Crowell, 1974.

Teller, Sandy. *This Was Sex*. Secaucus, NJ: Citadel Press, 1978.

Thomas, Robert McG. "Jack Biblo, Used Bookseller for Half a Century, Dies at 91." *New York Times*, 18 June 1998, p. C20.

Thompson, Ralph. "Deathless Lady." *The Colophon: A Quarterly for Bookmen*, 1:2 (Autumn 1935): 207–220.

Thornton, Louise, Jan Sturtevant, and Amber Coverdale Sumrall, eds. *Touching Fire: Erotic Writings by Women*. New York: Carroll and Graf, 1989.

Thurston, Carol. *The Romance Revolution: Erotic Novels for Women and the Quest for a New Sexual Identity*. Champaign: University of Illinois Press, 1987.

Tischler, N. M. "Pious Pornography." *Christianity Today*, 15 (23 April 1971): 14–15.

Trebay, Guy. "Live from the Wet Spot: Dan Savage—Miss Manners He's Not." *Village Voice*, 13 October 1998, p. 51.

Twitchell, James B. *Forbidden Partners: The Incest Taboo in Modern Culture*. New York: Columbia University Press, 1987.

Tytell, John. *Naked Angels: The Lives and Literature of the Beat Generation*. New York: Grove Press, 1986.

Updike, Edith. "Publishers of Romance Novels Add Color to Their Lines." *New York Newsday*, 25 July 1994, pp. 23–24.

Urgo, Joseph R. *Novel Frames: Literature as Guide to Race, Sex, and History in American Culture*. Jackson: University Press of Mississippi, 1991.

Vance, Ellen B., and Nathaniel N. Wagner. "Written Descriptions of Orgasm: A Study of Sexual Differences." *Archives of Sexual Behavior*, 5 (1976): 87–98.

Van Nostrand, Albert. *The Denatured Novel*. Indianapolis: Bobbs-Merrill, 1960.

Vassi, Marco. *A Driving Passion*. New York: Masquerade Books, 1993.

————. *The Erotic Comedies*. Sag Harbor, NY: Permanent Press, 1981.

————. *The Stoned Apocalypse*. New York: Trident Press, 1972; rpt. New York: Pocket Books, 1973.

Villiot, Jean de. *Black Lust*, trans. Laurence Ecker. New York: Panurge Press, 1931.

Vogliotti, Gabriel. *The Girls of Nevada*. Secaucus, NJ: Citadel, 1975.

Wagner, Geoffrey. "The End of the 'Porno'—Or, No More Traveling Companions?" *Sewanee Review*, 75 (1967): 364–376.

Wagner, Peter. "The Discourse on Sex—Or Sex as Discourse: Eighteenth Century Medical and Paramedical Erotica." *Sexual Underworlds of the Enlightenment*, ed. George Rousseau and Roy Porter. Chapel Hill: University of North Carolina Press, 1988, pp. 9–38.

————. "Eros Goes West: European and 'Homespun' Erotica in Eighteenth-Century America." *The Transit of Civilization from Europe to America: Essays in Honor of Hans Galinsky*, ed. Winfried Herget and Karl Ortseifen. Tübingen: G. Narr, 1986, pp. 145–165.

————. *Eros Revived: Erotica of the Enlightenment in England and America*. London: Secker and Warburg, 1988.

————, ed. *Erotica and the Enlightenment*. New York: Peter Lang, 1991.

Wakem, Hugh [Sam Roth]. *Diary of a Smut Hound*. Philadelphia: William Hodgson, 1930.

Walsh, Richard. "The Quest for Love and the Writing of Female Desire in Kathy Acker's *Don Quixote*." *Critique*, 32:3 (Spring 1991): 149–168.

Walsh, Susan. "Notes on Trick." *Village Voice Literary Supplement*, September 1995, pp. 15–20.

Walters, Ronald G. *Primers for Prudery: Sexual Advice to Victorian America*. Englewood Cliffs, NJ: Prentice-Hall, 1974.

Walters, Suzanne Danuta. "As Her Hand Crept Slowly Up Her Thigh: Ann Bannon and the Politics of Pulp." *Sexual Politics and Popular Culture*, ed. Diane Johnson. Bowling Green, OH: Bowling Green University Popular Press, 1990, pp. 81–101.

Wasserstrom, William. *Heiress of All the Ages: Sex and Sentiment in the Genteel Tradition*. Minneapolis: University of Minnesota Press, 1959.

Weinberg, M. S., R. G. Swensson, and S. K. Hammersmith. "Sexual Autonomy and the Status of Women: Models of Female Sexuality in U.S. Sex Manuals from 1950 to 1980." *Social Problems*, 30 (1983): 312–324.

Weiss, Harry B. "American Chapbooks." *A Book about Chapbooks: The People's Literature of Bygone Times*. Hatboro, PA: Folklore Associates, 1969.

West, Donald J. *Male Prostitution*. Binghamton, NY: Haworth Press, 1993.

West, Uta. "Pornography in Petticoats." *Penthouse*, 1:1 (August 1970): 76–78.

Whorezine. 2300 Market Street, Suite 19, San Francisco 94114.

Widmer, Kingsley. " 'Professor of Fuck': Some Reflections on Defending Literary Obscenity." *American Book Review*, 14:1 (April–May 1992): 15, 25.

Williams, Anne. *Art of Darkness: A Poetics of Gothic*. Chicago: University of Chicago Press, 1995.

Wilson, Colin. *The Misfits: A Study of Sexual Outsiders*. London: Carroll and Graf, 1989.

Winston, Lady. *The Leading Edge: An Anthology of Lesbian Sexual Fiction*. Denver: Lace Publications, 1987.

Wohl, Burton. "The Reluctant Pornographer." *Harper's Magazine*, (December 1976): 91–94.

Wolf, Edwin. *Rosenbach: A Biography*. Cleveland: World Publishing, 1960.

Wolfe, Bernard. *Memoirs of a Not Altogether Shy Pornographer*. New York: Doubleday, 1972.

Wolsey, Serge G. *Call House Madam: The Story of the Career of Beverly Davis*. New York: Matin Tudordale, 1942.

Woodrow, Terry, ed. *Lesbian Bedtime Stories*. 2 vols. Redway, CA: Tough Dove, 1989, 1990.

Woods, Gregory. *A History of Gay Literature: The Male Tradition*. New Haven, CT: Yale University Press, 1998.

Woolf, Michael. "Beyond Ideology: Kate Millett and the Case for Henry Miller." *Perspectives on Pornography: Sexuality in Film and Literature*, ed. Gary Day and Clive Bloom. New York: St. Martin's, 1988, pp. 113–127.

Yusba, Roberta. "Twilight Tales: Lesbian Pulps, 1950–1960." *On Our Backs* (Summer 1985): 30–31, 38.

Zahava, Irene, ed. *Lesbian Love Stories*. 2 vols. Watsonville, CA: Crossing Press, 1989, 1991.

Zall, Paul M. *Ben Franklin Laughing: Anecdotes from Original Sources by and about Benjamin Franklin*. Berkeley: University of California Press, 1980.

Zimmerman, Bonnie. *The Safe Sea of Women: Lesbian Fiction, 1969–1988*. Boston: Beacon, 1990.

———. "What Has Never Been: An Overview of Lesbian Feminist Literary Criticism." *Feminist Studies*, 7 (1981): 451–475.

17

Newspapers, Magazines, and Advertising

NEWSPAPERS

The press has traditionally functioned as a membrane between the nucleus of American culture and its margins. The porosity of the membrane, however, has varied from period to period. Nearly every history of sex in America covers journalistic treatment (or avoidance) of straight, gay, or lesbian issues, though discussion of individual newspapers or magazines will often be subordinated to particular themes or events. Three that discuss print media as purveyors of vulgar messages are *Our National Passion: 200 Years of Sex in America*, by Sally Banes, Sheldon Frank, and Tem Horowitz; *Erotic Communications: Studies in Sex, Sin and Censorship*, by George H. Gordon; and *The Sex Industry*, by George Paul Csicsery. A roundtable discussion by Lester Kirkendall, Gina Allen, Albert Ellis, and Helen Colton published as "Sex Magazines and Feminism" advances the view that pornography can be life-affirming, educational, and necessary. The participants advise sexual experts and feminists to write for newspapers and sex magazines as a way of countering demeaning messages.

Newspaper categories, however, are imprecise. One school of thought, led by historian Timothy J. Gilfoyle, holds that domestic American pornography actually began with what were called "sporting papers" in the late 1830s and early 1840s. Sporting papers—newspapers devoted to masculine pursuits such as gambling, racing, cockfighting, billiards, boxing, wrestling, club-hopping, theater-going, and, above all, women-chasing and politics—grew out of the rough and tumble activism of Jacksonian democracy. Gilfoyle's *City of Eros: New York City, Prostitution, and the Commercialization of Sex, 1790–1920* alludes to early associations between pornography and politics; as one of several examples Gilfoyle cites Henry R. Robinson, a Manhattan printer and Whig political caricaturist who specialized in pornographic etchings and lithographs (145–147). Drawing on what was already an established democratic tradition, Whigs and Democrats alike accused one another of sexual shenanigans as a way of undermining pretence, status, and fitness for office. Gilfoyle and other scholars have examined this type of political attack more fully in files of sporting papers housed at the American Antiquarian Society (Worcester, Massachusetts). Gilfoyle's "Politics and 'Sporting Men': The Birth of Pornography in the U.S.," Patricia Cline Cohen's "Editors and Publishers of the Sporting 'Flash' Press," and Helen Lefkowitz Horowitz's "Understanding 'Obscenity' in the 1840s" all deal at length with tabloids such as the *Whip*, the *Flash*, the *Weekly Rake*, and the *Libertine*. These issued from print shops on Ann and Nassau Streets in lower Manhattan, in what was becoming the penny press district. In some respects, the papers were merely "pleasure guides" to the nightlife and attractions of the city. But while typical issues discussed and even appeared to advertise the charms of showgirls and prostitutes, they usually did so in the guise of excoriating members of the opposite political party who patronized dives and bordellos. Despite its partisanship, the indignation, says Gilfoyle, did not seem feigned. By modern standards, the text and pictures of the sporting papers were mild in their detail and explicit degree. Nevertheless, political foes such as Benjamin Day, publisher of the *New York Sun* (and no stranger to seamy scandal journalism himself), succeeded in suppressing the sporting papers on grounds of obscenity. Thirty years later the *Police Gazette* (1878–1897) merged the genre of the sporting paper and that of sex crime journalism into pages of cartoons, lithographs, and stories of showgirls, prostitutes, detectives, and athletes. This offensive mix led Philadelphia prosecutors to seize the *Police Gazette* in 1889. Sporting papers could easily be classified as scandal types, but I have chosen to categorize their descendants—which include *Screw* magazine in the present— as examples of the politically-driven "alternative and underground press," to be discussed later.

SCANDAL JOURNALISM

If sexual scandal is the criterion, then proto-porn can be traced to the sensational cast of the first issue of the first newspaper printed in the United States. In 1690, the Massachusetts Bay Colony seized *Publick Occurrences*, published by Benjamin Harris in Boston, because he ran on the front page a story about the French monarch's alleged preference for his son's wife. The Sedition Act, one of the four Alien and Sedition Acts of 1798 passed by a Federalist Congress, ostensibly to forestall treason by sympathizers with French Revolutionists, was actually used to jail Jeffersonian editors who charged members of Congress with sexual improprieties and deviant tastes real or imagined. The unpopularity of those Acts helped elect Jefferson President, whereupon Jefferson pardoned all those imprisoned, even though he had been a favorite target of journalists who had printed salacious stories about his alleged affair with Sally Hemings.

Most scholarship on the genre of scandal journalism, however, begins with examples of the early twentieth century. John Tebbel's *The Media in America* points out that Joseph Patterson's *Daily News*, first published in 1919, carried sensationalism so intense that it was called the "servant girl's Bible," a factor that explains its phenomenal circulation of 1 million in 1925, while Bernarr Macfadden's *Evening Graphic* was called the *Evening Pornographic* (362) and enjoyed almost as large a readership. *Jazz Journalism: The Story of the Tabloid Newspapers* is Simon Michael Bessie's history of rowdy papers like the *New York Daily News*, the *New York Mirror*, and the *New York Daily Graphic*, which focused on sex and violence during the 1920s and, to a lesser extent, the 1930s. Lester Cohen's *The New York Daily Graphic: The World's Zaniest Newspaper* deals exclusively with Bernarr Macfadden's sex-drenched tabloid; Cohen finds pertinent Macfadden's relationship with Earl Carroll, the burlesque impresario. The memoirs of Emile Gauvreau, the *Graphic*'s managing editor and the man who masterminded such scandals as the coverage of the Daddy Browning and Peaches case, recalls this affair and many others in *Hot News*. The *Graphic* routinely faked pictures of lechers, miscegenators, criminals, and, above all, undressed women.

Texts speculating on the sexual predilections of public figures or purporting to be first-person accounts of those linked with celebrities have been constants in American history. Such documents amuse and aggrandize and are a species of middle-class porn themselves. *Fall from Grace: Sex, Scandal and Corruption in American Politics, 1702–1987* by Shelley Ross centers on Washingtonian sexual indiscretions that became subjects of parodies, broadsides, and literature, from Alexander Hamilton and Mrs. Reynolds, Jefferson and Sally Hemings, to Gary Hart and Donna Rice (who has since become an antiporn crusader—see **Censorship of Computers and the Internet** in Chapter 20). Nigel Cawthorne's *Sex Lives of the U.S. Presidents* rehearses similar stories and finds peculiar erotic quirks in most occupants of the White House. The chapters of Kevin Mc-Donough's parodic *A Tabloid History of the World* bear titles such as "I Was Jefferson's Love Slave," the alleged memoirs of Sally Hemings. A quick and accurate reference guide to sensational stories from the colonial period to the contemporary Mayflower Madam is George C. Kohn's *Encyclopedia of American Scandal*. The standard work on journalistic scandal-mongering is Suzanne Garment's *Scandal: The Culture of Mistrust in American Politics*. Garment's chapter on the 1970s and 1980s (169–197) provides an amusing account of the bidding wars between newspapers, magazines like *Penthouse* and *People*, and television tabloids such as *Geraldo* and *Entertainment Tonight* for the rights to the stories of Donna Rice and her affair with Senator Hart. Garment's "Afterword" on "Clarence Thomas, Bill Clinton, and the House Bank" (305–344) details the treatment of Thomas' alleged predilection for porn and Clinton's for Gennifer Flowers. Ironically, the *Penthouse* issue in which Flowers posed nude and talked about the size of Clinton's penis arrived in subscribers' mailboxes the day after he was elected president; Flowers' *Passion and Betrayal* contains few other revelations about her special friend. A sampling of scandalous journalism heavily weighted toward the present might range from Paul Leicester Ford's *Who Was the Mother of Franklin's Son?*, on Benjamin Franklin's liaisons; Judith Campbell Exner's *My Story*, on Exner's affair with JFK and her connections with the Mob; and Sharon Churcher's "She's No Barbara Bush," on Patricia Kluge, the British porn queen linked with Virginia governor Douglas Wilder.

Scandal reportage often takes the form of institutionalized gossip. Neal Gabler's biography of Walter Winchell, *Winchell: Gossip, Power and the Culture of Celebrity*, explores the gossip columnist's early career with Macfadden, who helped to invent this titillating genre. The folklore concerning sex in and around Hollywood, some of it false, is fed by "tell-it-all" memoirs, scandal magazines, and gossip columnists. Kenneth Anger's two gossip collections, *Hollywood Babylon* and *Hollywood Babylon II*, offer nitty-gritty stories of sex, drugs, and crime in the movie capital; volume II argues unconvincingly that Joan Crawford starred in a stag film in the days when she was allegedly engaged in prostitution. Columnist James Bacon's *Made in Hollywood* also details salacious rumors. Perhaps the best-known gossip columnist is Earl Wilson, who has published several books covering erotic drama and cinema, of which *The Show Business Nobody Knows* and *Show Business Laid Bare*, both arch and sniggering, are representative. More recent is Mark Drop's *Dateline Hollywood: Sins and Scandals of Yesterday and Today*, a compilation of juicy, if familiar, anecdotes about feuds, romances, divorces, fetishes, and sex drives in tinsel city. Constant compilation of tidbits about stage and screen implies that sexual curiosity underlies America's fascination with performing artists. Yet, as any study of novelist F. Scott Fitzgerald's relationship with the gossip columnist Sheilah Graham makes manifest, the curiosity can be transformed into high art. Moreover, serious biographers agonize over the secret experiences of their subjects. Karen Winkler talks with biographers of Eleanor Roosevelt, Anne Sexton, Arthur Ashe, Paul Robeson, and other Americans in " 'Seductions of Biography': Scholars Delve into New Questions about Race, Class, and Sexuality" in order to ask, "Are private lives always relevant to biography?"

For many cultural critics, journalistic ethics is an oxymoron, but surfeits of scandal have led to public breast-beating by reporters. The *New York Times* ran on its front page "For the Media, an Unsavory Story Tests Ideals and Stretches Limits," an article in which Janny Scott reported on the discomfort that the Clinton–Lewinsky affair was causing reporters who had never used words such as "oral sex" or "semen" in a story before. Probably the best of most recent reflections is Henry Louis Gates' "American Notes: The Naked Republic," which deplores the transformation of America into a "Tabloid Nation" through excessive focus on the sexual peccadillos of Clinton, Thomas, Hart, and others, all of which are injurious to real political debate. "Enough already," says the author (123). The title of David J. Krajicek's *Scooped! Mass Media Miss Real*

Story on Crime While Chasing Sex, Sleaze, and Celebrities is self-explanatory. As a case study, Krajicek offers an analysis of pressures that led to hyping of the Kathy Willets affair, the story of the "Florida Nympho" who managed to bring down hypocritical "Christian" law enforcement officers. The contributors to *Media Scandals*, edited by James Lull and Stephen Hinerman, also take journalists to task for misplaced priorities. Curtis D. MacDougall's *News Pictures Fit to Print . . . Or Are They?* is a now-dated, but still used, guide to the law and journalistic policies involved in deciding whether or not to use photographs depicting nudity, obscene situations, corpses, and other questionable images. The relevant portions of *Photography/Politics: Two*, edited by Patricia Holland, Jo Spence, and Simon Watney, discuss the ethics and politics of depicting bodies in newspapers and magazines, with particular reference to ethnicity, eugenics, youth, disease, and so on. Richard Reeves' *What the People Know: Freedom and the Press* takes stock of an American journalism torn between giving the public what it wants—or what editors think the public wants—and presenting genuinely informative copy.

Modern-day supermarket tabloids traffic in the prurient without the queasiness of their mainstream counterparts, a predilection that for some makes them pornographic. The *Report* of the President's Commission on Pornography and Obscenity (1970) called them "sensational" or "exposé" magazines; the same magazines are now called "supermarket" periodicals. They are literal fountainheads of the sexual folklore, urban myths, celebrity gossip, and bizarre legends that add zest and (sometimes meaning) to culture. Journalists themselves have shied away from reporting on supermarket tabloids, presumably because the more respectable are embarrassed by them. Easily the best study of the genre, S. Elizabeth Bird's *For Enquiring Minds: A Cultural Study of Supermarket Tabloids*, compares mainstream and "sleaze" papers, specifically, the *National Enquirer*, the *Weekly World News*, the *Globe*, the *Sun*, the *National Examiner*, and the *Star*, to find that the stories are often not that different from mainstream papers, that the supermarket tabloids may even be accurate, but that they put a particular spin on the narrative of events for a readership the editors have judged precisely. That readership is the subject of "An Attitude Segmentation Study of Supermarket Tabloid Readers," by Eileen Lehnert and Mary J. Perpich, who divide readers into three types, those reading for fun, those reading carelessly for information, and those reading with a desire to believe. F. E. H. Schroeder is also interested in what audiences find appealing and lists some of the more popular stories in "*National Enquirer* Is National Fetish! The Untold Story!"

J. Ressner's "Enquiring Minds: A Walk on the Sleazy Side with the New Breed of Tabloid Reporters" is less tolerant, as is P. J. Corkery's "*Enquirer*: An Eyewitness Account," which focuses on the notorious *National Enquirer*. Jonathan Alter writes in "Substance vs. Sex" about the *Star*'s zeal in reporting the Gennifer Flowers story, while Pat Jordan's admiring "Hello. This Is Alan Smith of the *National Enquirer*. . . . " points out that the increased quality of reporting at the scandal sheet has forced critics to take "celeb" journalism more seriously. Jordan's "The Trash Collector," a profile of David Perel, editor of the *National Enquirer*, depicts the man as driving reporters relentlessly to plumb depths.

Howard Rudnitsky concentrates on the founder-publisher of the *Enquirer* and how he patterned the tabloid on the *Reader's Digest* in "How Gene Pope Made Millions in the Newspaper Business." Michelangelo Signorile, himself a keeper of a "Gossip Watch," devotes one of his columns to tracing a story about a prominent gay person that appeared first in the *Star*, then in the *National Enquirer*, then in the *New York Post*, as an illustration of how scandalous information circulates, a cultural function of tabloids. Most libraries do not archive tabloids because of the tawdriness and ephemerality of their subjects, but they can index a culture's popular obsessions, says Rebecca Sturm Kelm in "The Lack of Access to Back Issues of the Weekly Tabloids: Does It Matter?"

Scandals that overtake antisex or antiporn crusaders are especially delicious, since they add hypocrisy to spicy narratives. By and large, conservatives are quite sincere in their objections—moral, political, aesthetic, or religious—to forms of expression they think demeaning, destructive, or dehumanizing. Examples of prurience abound, of course, but to build anecdotes of weak-willed, two-faced crusaders into a theory of conservative hypocrisy has the same validity as using isolated instances of aggression to buttress theories that pornography causes sexual violence. In *God's Bullies*, Perry Young dissects the careers of various Elmer Gantries who have tried to impose their morality on others, sometimes promoting themselves by attacking pornography. Charles M. Sennot's *Broken Covenant* is a study of Father Bruce Ritter, head of New York City's Covenant House, a shelter for runaway and homeless children. Ritter, an outspoken critic of pornography, which he called the root of all sexual crimes, served on the 1986 Attorney General's Commission on Pornography and endorsed the repressive tactics employed by that body. Allegations that he sexually molested boys in his care forced his resignation and rustication. Attorney General Meese's own difficulties with the law led critics to assume that the 1986 commission was either evidence of his own hypocrisy or a smoke screen to mask his own transgressions. Charles Keating, another prominent antiporn critic and member of the Meese Commission, went to prison for swindling thousands of Americans out of their savings. In "Double Trouble," L. J. Davis says that Keating actually used his antiporn organization, Citizens for Decency through Law, to dispose of worthless stock; Davis also details the economic cost to the American public.

Charles E. Shepard's *Forgiven: The Rise and Fall of Jim Bakker and the PTL Ministry* details the sexual scandal that overtook another critic of pornography; Shepard thinks that if talk-show hosts had not had Bakker and his wife as figures of fun, Johnny Carson would have had to invent them. Bakker's nemesis, Jessica Hahn, has become a celebrity courtesy of *Playboy* magazine and the *Howard Stern Show*. Articles on the several falls from grace of Jimmy Swaggart, another antiporn crusader, are so numerous as to require no listing; journalists thanked God for the story of Swaggart's riding around looking for prostitutes with a stack of porn magazines in the seat beside him. "Debbie Does Swaggart" is prostitute Debbie Murphree's report on the antiporn evangelist's tastes in sex and pornography. Arthur Frederick Ide denounces the smutty tactics used by fundamentalists like Jerry Falwell and Pat Robertson in their self-proclaimed war against "smut" in *Evangelical Terrorism: Censorship, Falwell, Robertson, and the Seamy Side of Christian Fundamentalism*, though Ide's book suffers from hyperbolic claims similar to those advanced by his opponents. Joe Domanick's "Maybe There Is a God" is an amusing reflection on the punishments meted out to antiporn crusaders Ritter, Swaggart, Meese, Keating, Bakker, and Robert Bauman, the latter arrested for soliciting sex from a boy.

In *Official and Confidential: The Secret Life of J. Edgar Hoover*, Anthony Summers alleges that the Mafia prevented the FBI from prosecuting many Mob activities by blackmailing Hoover with photos of the FBI director engaged in homosexual acts with his longtime associate, Clyde Tolson. As if to give credence to the argument that pornography is a form of political expression, Hoover kept extensive files on pornographers in the hope that he could find links between sexual expression and communist or other "subversive" organizations, or so says Natalie Robins in *Alien Ink: The FBI's War on Freedom of Expression* (67ff). In "The Creep, the Cop, His Wife, and Her Lovers," Pat Jordan tells the story of Doug Danziger, vice-mayor of Fort Lauderdale and a vociferous antiporn crusader, whose career ended when he was discovered on videotape in intercourse with Kathy Willets, wife of a deputy sheriff. Jordan's coverage of the media circus is enlivened by reports that the sheriff's office would auction the lady's nipple ring to compete with street vendors selling T-shirts emblazoned with the words "Kathy Did Fort Lauderdale" and by accounts of the frenzied attempts of tabloid television shows to purchase rights to the videotapes. (Willets herself is now a porn video performer.) Those looking for more of this sort of thing should consult *The Intimate Sex Lives of Famous People*, by the novelist Irving Wallace and other writers in the Wallace family.

A special category of scandal journalism includes magazine layouts featuring (usually) women in the news in the altogether. *Playboy* and *Penthouse* pay large sums for rights to nude photos of the suddenly notorious. A random sampling would include photographic articles on Clinton-linked Paula Jones (*Penthouse*, April 1998); Frank Gifford–linked Suzen Johnson (*Playboy*, November 1997); and O. J. Simpson–linked Faye Resnick (*Playboy*, March 1997), though the number could be much extended. Leaving aside normal appeals to voyeurism, the practice anoints objects of desire and fixes standards of sexual attractiveness for the culture at large. Publishing nude photos of someone without paying the subject, of course, serves to embarrass, an entirely different motive. In "All the Nudes Fit to Print," David Handelman interviews Charlie Malloy, editor of *Celebrity Skin*, which publishes nude movie stills and paparazzi shots of movie stars and famous personalities. To objections that celebrities suffer from such invasions of their privacy, Malloy responds, "If you're that self-conscious, then wear underwear!" (116).

SEX CRIMES IN THE MEDIA

A subcategory of scandalous news is the reporting of sexual crimes, which have sometimes been inflated to enormous proportions. The practice is an ancient one, according to Peter Wagner, who makes no bones about calling it "Pornography in the Courtroom: Trial Reports about Cases of Sexual Crimes and Delinquencies as a Genre of Eighteenth Century Erotica." According to Mitchell Stephens, whose A History of News contains a section on gossip, crime, and scandal, four qualities "beyond mere heinousness" have attracted Americans to crime stories: "a woman or child as victim or suspect; a highborn or well-known victim or suspect; some doubt about the guilt of the suspect; and intimations of promiscuous behavior by the victim or suspect" (108). Andie Tucher's wonderfully titled Froth and Scum: Truth, Beauty, Goodness, and the Ax-Murder in America's First Mass Medium centers on two antebellum New York media scandals, the murders of a prostitute in an upscale brothel and a man beaten to death by the brother of inventor Samuel Colt. The press sensationalized both cases, says Tucher, and set prurient patterns for media successors. Keith Soothill and Sylvia Walby's Sex Crime in the News studies the sensationalizing of sex crimes as a species of "reporting" that frequently shades into pornography, using mostly British examples. Helen Benedict offers case studies of such American instances as the Mike Tyson trial and the Anita Hill affair in Virgin or Vamp: How the Press Covers Sex Crimes. Jane E. Caputi is more interested in the formulas and tropes (gore, victimization, sentimentality) that shape a genre as they emerge from reporting on violent sexual crimes in "The Fetishes of Sex-Crime." More specific is Caputi's The Age of Sex Crime, on the sexualized discourse with which the press treats the serial murders of women.

Estelle B. Freedman's important " 'Uncontrolled Desires': The Response to the Sexual Psychopath" points out that widely reported crimes of sexual pathology may create national panics that, in turn, refocus and redefine issues of sexuality in the culture at large (see **Pressure Groups, the Bifurcation of Feminism, and Moral Panics** in Chapter 5). Like Wagner, Freedman calls sex crime a subgenre of popular journalism; she notes that major periodical indexes such as the New York Times Index and The Readers' Guide created a "sex crimes" category in the 1930s and that women's magazines began to feature articles on sex crimes in the 1950s and 1960s. Freedman appends an impressive bibliography. More recently, Carol Tavris argues in "Beware the Incest-Survivor Machine" that incest stories have become a narrative industry abetted by groups that encourage women to "recover" and even invent memories of childhood abuse; in any case, it is clear that such stories have become a popular pornographic genre akin to the Indian captivity narratives of the colonial period. Somewhat similar is Lawrence Wright's "Remembering Satan: Parts 1 and 2," on the controversial Olympia, Washington, case, in which a whole family succumbed to "memories" of satanic ritual, child abuse, infanticide, and child pornography, apparently as the result of hysteria. The external and internal dynamics that shape stories of rape, coming-out, and recovery are the subject of Ken Plummer's *Telling Sexual Stories*, which examines the tropes and ritualistic aspects of various accounts.

THE ALTERNATIVE AND UNDERGROUND PRESS

Tabloid newspapers, because they can be published quickly and cheaply, have often served as a quasi-demotic alternative press in the United States. In giving voice to the disfranchised, they have sometimes carried sexually explicit messages as expressions of rebellion. Sexual narratives can descend into mere sensationalism, of course, but can also attack prevailing morality and promote unusual alternative lifestyles. One of the best histories is David Armstrong's *A Trumpet to Arms: Alternative Media in America*, a chronicle that begins with revolutionary newspapers in the early republic but that concentrates on the tabloids of the 1960s and 1970s. Sidney Ditzion devotes several pages to the periodicals published by sex radicals in the late nineteenth century in *Marriage, Morals, and Sex in America: A History of Ideas*, as does Milton Rugoff in *Prudery and Passion: Sexuality in Victorian America*, Hal D. Sears in *The Sex Radicals: Free Love in Victorian America*, and Taylor Stoehr in *Free Love in America: A Documentary History*.

Historically very important is *Free Press Anthology*, a group of articles mostly on pornography and censorship compiled from alternative papers by the noted constitutional lawyer Theodore A. Schroeder in 1909. Another excellent source is the two-volume *The American Radical Press, 1880–1960* edited by Joseph R. Conlin, who places sexual expression in political context. That many of the underground tabloids of the 1960s dealt candidly and often lasciviously with sexual matters is clear from Jacob Brachman's survey of "The Underground Press." The casual reader can dip into two anthologies published in 1972: *Underground Press Anthology*, compiled by Thomas King Forcade, and *Underground Reader*, compiled by Mel Howard and Forcade. More critical of the journalists themselves is Laurence Leamer. Leamer's *The Paper Revolutionaries: The Rise of the Underground Press* suggests that the sexual explicitness masked an adolescent political sensibility. Leamer thinks that the pornographic irreverence of the publications was as much a red flag to authorities as the unorthodox politics of the editors. Various attempts to suppress politically and sexually radical papers are the subject of Geoffrey Rips' *The Campaign against the Underground Press*, which has a Foreword by Allen Ginsberg and includes reports by Areyeh Neier, Todd Gitlin, and Angus Mackenzie. Robin Morgan calls radical magazines of the 1960s and early 1970s blatantly sexist. The thesis of her "Goodbye to All That" is that the energy behind the "revolution" was pornographic and that the males who wrote and edited the papers oppressed women even as they politically "liberated" themselves.

Robert J. Glessing's *The Underground Press in America* is comprehensive on counterculture papers like the *East Village Other* and the *Berkeley Barb*, which often mixed political radicalism, opposition to the Vietnamese War, and pornographic rebellion. The sketches of counterculture luminaries are the main appeal of Abe Peck's *Uncovering the Sixties: The Life and Times of the Underground Press*. Ken Wachsberger has collected first-person accounts of what writers tried to accomplish in *Voices from the Underground: Insider Histories of the Vietnam Era Underground Press, Vol. I*, though most of these are concerned with political issues. Scholars seeking primary material (e.g., issues of particular papers) from the period should see **Alternative and Underground Sources** in Chapter 7, especially Case, Danky, Kimball, and Wachsberger. See also **Magazines, Newspapers, and Comics** in Chapter 4, especially *Alternative Press Index* and Committee on Small Magazines and Publishers. *Alternative Press Review* reprints articles from different contemporary presses on a variety of topics, some sexual. The *Underground Newspaper Microfilm Collection* contains 147 reels of papers published between 1965 and 1973, drawn from various archives. In *A Secret Location on the Lower East Side: Adventures in Writing 1960–1980*, Steven Clay and Rodney Phillips chronicle two decades of New York's underground writing and magazine publishing scene. Stephen Duncombe examines primarily political rather than pornographic zines, but with some reference to sexual content, and extends his focus to include the present in *Notes from Underground: Zines and the Politics of Alternative Culture*.

The most outrageous conflation of sex and politics occurred in the underground magazine *The Realist*, whose editor, Paul Krassner, has republished material from 1958 to 1971 as *How a Satirical Editor Became a Yippie Conspirator in Ten Easy Years*; the artwork (*Fuck Communism* and *Disneyland* [depicting favorite cartoon characters madly copulating]) and articles seem tame now. More recently, Krassner has published reminiscences called *Confessions of a Raving, Unconfined Nut: Misadventures in the Counterculture*, which recalls intentions, failures, and successes, including his seven months as publisher of *Hustler*. In Ron Chepesiuk's interview, "Paul Krassner, Father of the Underground Press," Krassner takes credit for coining the phrase "soft-core pornography," which he said "gives you a soft-on" (34). Most famous of the hard-core sex tabloids is *Screw*, published since 1969 by Al Goldstein, who also produces erotic programs (*Midnight Blue*) for Manhattan cable television. *Screw*'s immense sales in the 1960s inspired a host of imitators: *Bang, Kiss, The New York Review of Sex, Luv, Pleasure, Fun, Cocksure, Ecstasy, Desire*, and so on, most published in New York, Los Angeles, or San Francisco. Often attacked, *Screw* survived, in part, because Goldstein combined the salacious with political protest and is indefatigable in insisting that his journal is protected speech: a typical issue is just as likely to savage an agency of the state of New York for some backward social policy as to scream about censorship. Although distinctly in the tradition of the "sporting papers" of the 1840s, the genius of *Screw* was its deliberate mythologizing of the sexuality of the city to suggest that the seamy undergrounds that it so meticulously chronicled somehow furnished the energy that drove the metropolis. *Screw* was widely, if surreptitiously, read as a guide to the sexual consciousness of alternative political subcultures; the magazine helped to construct the "sexual revolution" by shaping its folklore. Few libraries archive the tabloid (the Kinsey Institute has a complete run), but a 1971 collection, *The Screw Reader*, by Goldstein and the original copublisher, Jim Buckley, provides the flavor of the early issues.

Philip Nobile's "Inside *Screw*" quotes Buckley: " '*Screw* isn't a jerk-off paper,' he insists. 'When we have a story on how to give a blow-job, it's a sociological statement' " (163). Goldstein demonstrates his flair for the outrageous in "Playboy Interview: Al Goldstein": "If there's a God, I'm sure he's jerking off to *Screw*" (218). George Frankl insists that sex tabloids have not made the world more progressive or even safer for sexual expression, but he does dilate on political functions of pornography as manifest in tabloids like the British *Oz* and the Dutch *Suck* in his *The Failure of the Sexual Revolution*. So does *The Age of Perversion: A Close-Up View of Sexuality in Our Permissive Society*, by Jason Douglas, a disapproving look at sleazy American, German, Dutch, and British sex tabloids and magazines of the 1960s. Jack Boulware's *Sex American Style: An Illustrated Romp through the Golden Age of Heterosexuality* contains information on sex newspapers, their editors, and investors. In *Politico Frou-Frou: Pornographic Art as Political Protest*, Tuppy Owens traces political pornography of the 1990s to *Suck*, a hard-core tabloid published in Amsterdam beginning in October 1969 (roughly contemporaneously with *Screw* in America), which led off its first issue with "The Gobble Poem," a play on gay blow jobs by W. H. Auden. *The New Sexual Revolution*, edited by Lester A. Kirkendall and Robert N. Whitehurst, contains some material on sex tabloids. Bob Hoddeson interviews Goldstein and also the editors of the *San Francisco Ball*, a sex tabloid modeled on *Screw*, in *The Porn People: A First-Person Documentary Report*. The May issue of *Details* annually lists sex tabloid guides to various cities in the United States; in 1995 those included are *Atlanta Xcitement, Texas Connection* (Dallas), *The Rocky Mountain Oyster* (Denver), *The Oregon T & A Times* (Portland), *The Spectator* (San Francisco), *The Stranger* (Seattle), and *Florida Xcitement* (Tampa Bay).

BORDERLINE MAGAZINES

The standard history, still invaluable, is Frank Luther Mott's five-volume *A History of American Magazines*. It is not particularly concerned with underground magazines, let alone pornographic ones, but is excellent on occasional borderline periodicals. John Tebbel's *The Media in America* sporadically chronicles sex-oriented magazines, as does Theodore Peterson's *Magazines in the*

Twentieth Century. One of the very earliest questionable magazines in North America was the *Onania*, a semisalacious, quasi-medical periodical imported from England and rapidly reprinted in the early 1700s. Peter Wagner discusses its circulation, reprinting, and contents in "The Veil of Medicine and Morality: Some Pornographic Aspects of the *Onania*." If the "medical" magazine was one type, then the lurid "crime" journal was another, the latter a throwback to the *Newgate Calendar* and eighteenth-century London crime sheets. Edward Van Every's *Sins of America as Exposed by the Police Gazette* is a classic exploration of exploitative tabloid "journalism," which helped shape the genre. Gene Smith and Jayne Barry Smith have edited excerpts of articles, graphics, cartoons, illustrations, and advertisements from the magazine from the years 1878 to 1897 into a volume called *The Police Gazette*. Features include stories about prostitutes, crime, chorus girls, actresses, sports figures, and so on. Similar elements still structure modern versions such as *Front Page Detective, Detective Cases, True Police Cases*; they still dote on raunchy tales, sensational narratives, and sleazy photos. Al Rose's *Storyville, New Orleans: Being an Authentic, Illustrated Account of the Notorious Red-Light District*, a history of the district by the man who found the famous Bellocq plates of prostitutes, provides information on *The Mascot*, a Louisiana sporting paper devoted to New Orleans nightlife. Lists of questionable magazines seized in New York and Boston can be found in the *Annual Reports* of the New York Society for the Suppression of Vice and the New England Watch and Ward Society.

Chapter 5 of Frederick Lewis Allen's *Only Yesterday* discusses the revolution in morality that took place in the 1920s, a phenomenon Allen thinks was assisted by newspapers and magazines. The title of *The Tijuana Bible Reader*, edited by Douglas H. Gamelin, refers in this instance to tabloid compilations of erotic stories, frequently illustrated with photos; the term is also used to describe "dirty" comic books as well. Both types, according to Jay Gertzman in *Bookleggers and Smuthounds: The Trade in Erotica, 1920–1940*, were often printed by printers who ordinarily used their presses to run off whiskey labels. Information on specific "girlie" types is available in Mark Gabor's *The Illustrated History of Girlie Magazines*, Harald Hellmann's *The Best of American Girlie Magazines*, and Alan Betrock's *Pin-Up Mania: The Golden Age of Men's Magazines (1950–1967)*. C. G. Martignette and L. K. Meisel have compiled mostly covers in *The Best of American Girlie Magazines*; they provide some bibliographic information, but the volume's chief value is the spectrum of "girlie" types. (See also **Female Pinups, Centerfolds, and Magazine Pictorials** in chapter 12.)

Bernarr Macfadden, who operated the *New York Graphic* newspaper, also published a series of spicy and confession magazines during the 1930s, when censorship in America was commonplace. William R. Hunt's *Body Love: The Amazing Career of Bernarr Macfadden* points out that Macfadden's *True Story* quickly stimulated a host of imitators, which led to Macfadden's trying to outflank his competition by starting *True Experiences* (1922), *Love and Romance*

(1923), *Intimate Stories* (1948), and others, most of which appealed to women readers. *Pulpwood Editor*, written by Harold B. Hershey, one of Macfadden's rivals, is a good source on the genre and its brushes with the law. Greg Mullins reflects on the oblique appeal of the bodybuilding illustrations central to Macfadden's *Physical Culture* in "Nudes, Prudes, and Pigmies: The Desirability of Disavowal in *Physical Culture*." The photos scandalized some readers. Macfadden's obsession with physique, homoerotic and otherwise, receives extended treatment in Robert Ernst's *Weakness Is a Crime: The Life of Bernarr Macfadden*. Postal officials frequently targeted *Esquire* magazine for its breezy ribaldry, which only encouraged the editors. Hugh Merrill's *ESKY: The Early Years at Esquire* deals with the magazine's role as a taste-maker. Sean Nixon's *Hard Looks: Masculinities, Spectatorship, and Contemporary Consumption* investigates advertising and editorial strategies in *Esquire* and other mainstream men's magazines.

Three histories cover the great pulp magazines in detail. Of these, the most venerable is Tony Goodstone *The Pulps: Fifty Years of American Popular Culture*. Chapter 6, entitled "Exploiting the Girls: Innocence," covers "snappy," "saucy," and semisalacious pulps such as *Snappy Stories*, which first appears in 1912. Chapter 7, entitled "Exploiting the Girls: Straight Out Sex," deals with "spicy" magazines, like *Spicy Detective, Spicy Western*, and *Spicy Adventure*, and with the horror magazines that described torture on "every part of the anatomy (excepting the pelvis, of course)" (141). *Cheap Thrills: An Informal History of the Pulp Magazines*, Ron Goulart's account of sensational genres, is only occasionally about genuinely pornographic types. Lee Server's principal interests in *Danger Is My Business: An Illustrated History of the Fabulous Pulp Magazines, 1896–1953* are the often sexy police, detective, and thriller categories, sometimes lumped together by the President's Commission on Pornography and Obscenity as "barber shop magazines." The titles are redolent of earlier eras: *Broadway Brevities, Smokehouse Monthly, Artists and Models, Wow, Hot Dog, Jazza-Ka-Jazza, Zest, Army Fun*. H. A. Otto's 1963 survey of periodicals, "Sex and Violence on the American Newsstand," concluded that detective magazines combined sex and violence to a greater degree than other monthlies. In "Detective Magazines: Pornography for the Sexual Sadist?" Elliott P. Dietz, Bruce Harry, and Robert Hazelwood suggest that detective magazines may contribute to sexual sadism by functioning as "training manuals" and "equipment catalogs" for criminals; the authors note that they are in the tradition of Cesare Lombroso, the nineteenth-century criminologist who thought that scandalous newspapers continuously encouraged deviance in the lower classes (Lombroso is also celebrated for much stranger ideas, of course).

Alan Betrock leads the reader through the pages of *Confidential, Bare, True Life Secrets, Dare, Sir, Pose, Bad Girls, Police Dragnet*, and many others in his *Unseen America: The Greatest Cult Exploitation Magazines, 1950–1966*. Betrock provides a lot of information on Robert Harrison, the notorious if versatile magazine entrepreneur who learned his trade on Macfadden's *New York*

Daily Graphic, moved on to publish girlie magazines such as *Beauty Parade, Eyeful, Flirt, Titter*, and *Wink*, and hit his stride in 1952 with *Confidential*. The popularity of this and other scandal magazines purveying rumors about the alleged sexual habits of screen luminaries peaked in 1955, when *Confidential*'s circulation rose to four million. Scandal magazines purveying rumors about the alleged sexual habits of screen luminaries reached a zenith during the 1950s. In *The Personality Index to Hollywood Scandal Magazines, 1952–1966*, Betrock and Hillard Schneider provide an annotated listing of the celebrities who were subjects of articles and features in journals like *Confidential*; the volume contains commentary on the dimensions and formulas of the genre as well. Steve Govoni's "Now It Can Be Told" is an excellent retrospective on *Confidential*, which staked out territory previously held by periodicals like the *Police Gazette* but preferred scandals among the famous. For *The Folklore of Sex*, a splendid reference tool, Albert Ellis compared images and stories in various media, including men's magazines such as *Male* and *Argosy*, first in January 1950, then again in January 1960 (for detailed discussion see **Folklore and Obscenity: Rhymes, Songs, Ballads, and Stories** in Chapter 15, Ellis). Ed Lange and Stan Sohler have edited a generous sampling of the magazines that afforded many Americans their first glimpse of frontal nudity other than their own in *Nudist Magazines of the 50s and 60s*. The two volumes are good companion pieces to *The Shameless Nude*, for which Charles Cropsey and Jill Browner assembled articles and photos drawn from the magazine *Nude Living*. Nudist magazines appeared in 1931, according to Philip G. Stewart's "The New-Genre Nude: A New Fine Art Motif Derived from Nudist Magazine Photography," and began to reshape the way the culture saw, appreciated, and represented the nude figure. Stewart says that American editors avoided traditional European justifications for nudity as promoting health, beauty, and moral cleanliness, though they did run illustrations and articles on swimming and bathing; instead, they emphasized "real" people, mixed sexes and ages, contemporary settings, and informal poses.

In a special category were journals that marketed high porn under the flag of sophistication. The notorious Samuel Roth edited several periodicals that masqueraded as upscale vessels of taste: *Beau: The Man's Magazine* (1924), *Two Worlds Monthly: Devoted to the Increase of the Gaiety of Nations* (1926–1927), notable for its unauthorized condensation of Joyce's *Ulysses* but also for stories by writers as diverse as Boccaccio and Clement Wood and for erotic illustrations by Austin Spare, Alexander King, and Cecil French; *Casanova Jr.'s Tales* (1929); *American Aphrodite* (1951–1955), a quarterly containing works of erotica by well-known writers such as Henry Miller, G. S. Viereck, Frank Harris, and Roth himself, often illustrated; and *Good Times: A Review of the World of Pleasure* (1954–1956), whose content was similar. Roth's career has been enshrined in a conviction that bears his name. So has that of Ralph Ginzburg, whose prurient merchandising of high-quality fiction and essays resembled Roth's. Successful prosecution of Ralph Ginzburg's magazines sent the publisher to jail. Thomas Whiteside's "An Unhurried View of Ralph Ginzburg" discusses his trial, where Ginzburg was found guilty of pandering in his promotion of materials that themselves were not obscene. Whiteside also examines the magazines *Fact, Avant-Garde*, and *Eros*. (Volume I, number 3 of *Eros* carried Bert Stern's now-classic photos of a nude Marilyn Monroe.) Ginzburg himself wrote "Eros on Trial," devoting an entire issue of *Fact* to the case. While the case was making its way through the courts, Dan Wakefield reviewed Ginzburg's defense and his appeal in "An Unhurried View of Ralph Ginzburg." In "Playboy Interview: Ralph Ginzburg," following the affirmation of his sentence by the Supreme Court, Ginzburg says, "I could have pleaded guilty at the trial and received a suspended sentence. I'd have lost a lot less money and energy, and retained my freedom. But I chose to fight. I lost. I'll abide by the decision [five years in prison, $42,000 in fines]" (47).

(For humor magazines, see **Humor: Jokes and Stories** in Chapter 15.)

PLAYBOY AND ITS IMITATORS

Few magazines have inspired more comment, hostile and otherwise, than *Playboy*. Although scarcely any history of modern sex and eroticism fails to mention it, it is important to remember that to many Americans today, *Playboy* is no more pornographic than, say, *Vogue*. Confirmation is as close as Gretchen Edgren's *The Playboy Book: Forty Years, the Complete Pictorial History*, whose excerpts depict the magazine as both staid and elderly. Founded by Hugh Hefner in 1953, *Playboy* developed a mix of nude pictorials, including the monthly "Playmate," quality fiction, excellent reportage, and sexually liberated "philosophy," whose cultural influence, though editor/publisher Hefner consistently overstated it, was real in the 1960s. Ironically, because the magazine pays extremely well, remains hospitable to women writers, checks its facts rigorously, and chooses its topics carefully, *Playboy*, in fact, offers extraordinary talent, high aesthetic standards, and impeccable liberal credentials. Graphics have won numerous awards; some have been collected by Ray Bradbury as *The Art of Playboy*. Thomas Weyr's *Reaching for Paradise: The Playboy Vision of America* offers the most thorough and balanced examination of the impact of the magazine's utopian sexual vision on American lifestyles. Frank Brady's *Hefner* and Russell Miller's *Bunny*, the first an "unauthorized" biography, speculate on the magazine's cultural role without losing sight of Hefner and his lifestyle.

Hefner himself wrote "On Playboys and Bunnies" to contend that in helping to give women a sexual identity separate from that imposed by husbands and history, he helped to free women for other roles. Given the now hackneyed contention that representation somehow objectifies only women's bodies, it is an argument that deserves more attention. Decoupling women's sexuality from a traditional context, in which men were presumed to own a woman's body or, at the least, her loyalty and devotion, may very well have been a necessary first step before women could assume the multiple roles that men have considered their right. "Objectification," as a form of role playing, becomes a necessary precondition to liberation. Stripped of the mystery that helped keep women property, the body becomes a substrate for a repertoire of other, nonsexual identities that are simply not imaginable when the body is shrouded from view. In company with legions of critics, James M. Ferreira asserts in "Fetishes and Fetishism in Girlie Magazines" that *Playboy*'s ideal of the good life, as measured in money and access to beautiful women, is essentially false. J. Anthony Lukas' "The 'Alternative Life-Style' of Playboys and Playmates" dissects the magazine's orientation in pop-sociological terms. Barbara Ehrenreich's *"Playboy* Joins the Battle of the Sexes" views the magazine's editorial stance as a form of rebellion against commitment. An accurate, but uncritical, look at man and empire generated *Hugh Hefner: Once upon a Time*, a television documentary by the producers of *Twin Peaks*, in which the fading of the Playboy vision seems obvious. A more amusing portrait of Hefner is Joe Goldberg's *The Big Bunny*. The perspective in Gloria Steinem's famous essay, "I Was a Playboy Bunny," reprinted (from *Show* magazine of May 1963) in her *Outrageous Acts and Everyday Rebellions* (29–69) is critical of Hefner's commodification and objectification of women, not to mention his idea of a sexy costume; her complaints were, in fact, the first significant chinks in the *Playboy* pedestal. Stephen Byer is also critical in *Hefner's Going to Kill Me When He Reads This*, a behind-the-scenes exposé of Hefner's idiosyncrasies and autocratic methods.

Critics sometimes construct a folklore at variance with that shaped by *Playboy* itself. The most hostile view is Judith A. Reisman's *"Soft Porn" Plays Hardball: Its Tragic Effects on Women, Children and the Family*, which asserts that *Playboy* and similar "soft-core" magazines are responsible for the breakup of the American family and for most sexual crimes committed in the United States; Reisman also charges Hefner with carrying out an alleged plot by Alfred Kinsey to secularize sex, desanctify religion, and suborn morality. She seems particularly upset by *Playboy*'s cartoons twitting Santa Claus, who should, she thinks, be sacred to children. Catharine MacKinnon blames the magazine not only for objectifying women but also for promoting intercourse, the origin of inequality among men and women, in "More than Simply a Magazine: *Playboy*'s Money." Neil Gallagher's proposal to extirpate pornography, published as *How to Stop the Porno Plague*, calls for a campaign against *Playboy* for having "opened the door to savage sex." *Playboy* has been a favorite target of the censorious for years, most recently of the Meese Commission, whose attorneys tried to pressure convenience stores not to carry it, *Penthouse*, or other magazines that commission members did not like.

A 1988 study of 106 male college students carried out by N. M. Malamuth and R. D. McIlwraith, reported as "Fantasies and Exposure to Sexually Explicit Magazines," advances what may be an awful truth: that males no longer read *Playboy* "primarily for sexual stimulation and fantasy" (though they may still read *Penthouse* for those purposes). Actually, as early as 1971, tests conducted with mechanical devices measuring arousal induced by "erotic" photographs elicited complaints from the male subjects that *Playboy* photographs were "monotonous and tedious" (309), or so says Marvin Zuckerman in "Physiological Measures of Sexual Arousal in the Human." Such results would appear to mean either that *Playboy* is read as much for its fiction and reporting as any other magazine or that its readership is simply aging. I. H. Bernstein and his colleagues tried to determine whether explicit nudity in photos from a collection of magazines ranging from fashion monthlies to *Penthouse* affected male assessments of female beauty. Their only significant finding, as reported in "Effect of Attitudes toward Pornography upon Male Judgements of Female Attractiveness," was that men who preferred the more explicit photographs didn't seem to care whether they saw the faces of the models or not.

Peter Michelson compares the sexual content and editorial strategies of *Playboy* and *Penthouse* in "The Pleasures of Commodity, or How to Make the World Safe for Pornography," and contrasts *Playboy* and *Screw* in *The Aesthetics of Pornography*; his conclusion is that the magazines are pretty innocuous, though *Screw*'s anarchic stance lends it a cachet of political rebellion. Slick magazines market sex tastefully, says Gail Dines in " 'I Buy It for the Articles': *Playboy* Magazine and The Sexualization of Consumerism," and *Playboy* set the pattern. Three chapters of George Frankl's *The Failure of the Sexual Revolution* compare British and American soft-core magazines like *Club* and *Playboy* in terms of content, appeal, and social consequences and make similar points. Such an interpretation—that *pornographic* may be a misnomer where glossiness is concerned—seems borne out by other cultural indicators. Two informative pieces on Hugh Hefner's successors are Roger Cohen's "Ms. Playboy," an article on the efforts of Christie Hefner, daughter of Hugh, to improve the fortunes of Playboy Enterprises, which she now heads, and Douglas Martin's "Family Man. No Mansion. This Guy Really Runs Playboy?," a profile of Michael Perlis, the current unflamboyant publisher of the magazine itself. The magazine's shift in status suggests a relentless cultural dynamic; once reviled as tawdry, *Playboy* now seems securely middle-class. John Brady's "Nude Journalism" sketches *Playboy*'s evolution from outrageous newcomer to stodgy institution. By contrast, says the *Village Voice*'s Michael Musto in "Where the Queers Are," *Penthouse* has become the politically correct magazine for gays and lesbians, yet another indication that politics makes for strange bedfellows. Up-to-date discussions of *Playboy* can be found in *Burning Desires: Sex in America, a Report from the Field* by Steve Chapple and David Talbot, who survey a good deal of far more explicit imagery in other journals. Jack Boulware discusses most of the glossy men's magazines in *Sex American Style; An Illustrated Romp through the Golden Age of Heterosexuality*, as does John Heidenry in *What Wild Ecstasy: The Rise and Fall of the Sexual Revolution*.

Glossy magazines reveal class differences in content and audience. Sari Thomas' "Gender and Social-Class Coding in Popular Photographic Erotica" examines *Blueboy, Cheri, Gallery, Hustler, Mandate, Oui, Penthouse, Playboy,* and *Playgirl* to find that upwardly mobile heterosexual males prefer idealized images in the slicker magazines, while lower-class readers of magazines like

Hustler go for "sexier" pictures, that is, those featuring wider-spread thighs, more pubic hair, pinker labia. Heterosexual women readers of *Playmate* get low-sex-content male nudes, while upscale homosexual males get idealized shots, and so on. Gender figures also in "Male and Female Interest in Sexually-Oriented Magazines," for which John Stauffer and Richard Frost compared reader-responses to *Playgirl* and *Playboy* to conclude that women showed considerable ambivalence toward male nudity, apparently because the contexts for it were so often unreal, whereas men liked pictures of nude women no matter how fanciful the excuse. For "Nude Times: 2," Marcia Seligson interviews Doug Lambert, publisher of *Playgirl*, who insists that women do like seeing pictures of nude men. A companion piece, "Nude Times: 1" by Carolyn See, looks at a variety of men's magazines in terms of the stereotypes they promote. Lee D. Rossi's "The Whore vs. the Girl-Next-Door: Stereotypes of Women in *Playboy, Penthouse*, and *Oui*" distinguishes between the "well-scrubbed sexuality" of *Playboy* and the "decadent sexuality" of the latter two magazines but finds that all of them subordinate and demean women.

Content analyses seem more useful than statistical surveys of photographic elements, which tend to cancel each other out. In their "A Longitudinal Content Analysis of Sexual Violence in Best-Selling Erotica Magazines," Neil Malamuth and Barry Spinner surveyed photos and cartoons in *Playboy* and *Penthouse* from 1973 to 1977 to find that while the photographs reflected some increase in violent elements (setting, costume, interactions between figures), the cartoons did not. A similar study, "Sexual Violence in *Playboy* Magazine: A Longitudinal Content Analysis," by Joseph E. Scott and Stephen J. Cuvelier covered the years 1954 to 1978; their conclusion was that violence as element or theme in pictorials and cartoons was pretty rare and has decreased still further since 1978. The latter statistics indicate that violence as a theme occurred on less than one page per 3,000; fewer than one in four pictorials depicted violence even in subtle kinetic form. Berkeley Kaite's "The Pornographic Body Double: Transgression Is the Law" examines taboos through comparisons of *Penthouse* centerfolds and nude transvestites in other media to insist on the ambivalence of images in porn generally. Kaite speculates on codes of masculinity in soft- and hard-core magazines, although Joe A. Thomas suggests that unwarranted postmodern juxtaposition may have led Kaite astray in "(Over) Theorizing Dirty Magazines." For his study, "The Reader, the Author, His Discursive Woman and Her Lover: A Cyclical Study of the Social Effects Constituted by 'Top-Shelf' Magazines," Simon Hardy says that he interviewed males who read soft-core magazines in order to give voice to an often impugned audience. Hardy found that the young men experienced a sense of transgressiveness, perhaps even greater zest as a consequence of feminist critiques of pornography.

Dennis R. Hall's "A Note on the Erotic Imagination: *Hustler* as a Secondary Carrier of Working-Class Consciousness" maintains that the content and photos of *Hustler*, despite claims as "revolutionary," simply reinforce blue-collar values. Walker Sachs, in "Sex Magazines: No Business like Show Business," calls

Hustler a "comic book," "the McDonald's of sex magazines" (24). A closer reading by Laura Kipnis in "(Male) Desire and (Female) Disgust: Reading *Hustler*" finds that the magazine's lower-class subversion of bourgeois culture, on one hand, is offset by its antifeminist and antiliberal bias, on the other. It is a brilliant paper, sure in its reading of the contradictions inherent in erotic genres. Kipnis revises the argument somewhat in her *Bound and Gagged: Pornography and the Politics of Fantasy in America*. By contrast, Eva Feder Kittay's "Pornography and the Erotics of Domination" rehashes arguments that porn is about power, not sex. Her analysis of the objectification of women in *Playboy, Penthouse*, and *Hustler* presumes agreement that the editors are evil. *The Millionaire Pornographers: Adam Special Report 12* profiles Hugh Hefner, Bob Guccione, Larry Flynt, and Al Goldstein, among others; its value is slight.

When Morley Safer interviewed Bob Guccione for a *Sixty Minutes* segment on "Pornography and the First Amendment," the publisher of *Penthouse* spoke of the need for outrageous expression and defended the graphic display of bodies. Gerry Spence's *Trial by Fire: The True Story of a Woman's Ordeal at the Hands of the Law* is an attorney's account of the suit by Kim Pring against *Penthouse* when the magazine ran an article suggesting that Pring, a former Miss Wyoming, won beauty contests through skill at fellatio. Technically about libel, the volume contains a lot of information on the magazine. An arch look at the personalities behind *Penthouse* is Philippa Kennedy's "A Marriage Made in Sleaze," a *London Express* article widely reprinted. Kennedy focuses on Bob Guccione and his late wife, Kathy Keaton, who together built the $200 million-per-year General Media International; Kennedy quotes Keaton to the effect that "part of being a feminist is sexual freedom and part of that is exploiting your body."

Class—measured, only in part, by assessments of wealth—affects the ways in which Americans look at pornography entrepreneurs. Consider reference tools as a barometer of cultural approval. High school students learn to use *Current Biography* in preparing term papers. *Current Biography* profiled Hugh Hefner in 1968, waited until 1994 to do a biography of Bob Guccione, but has yet to cover Larry Flynt. Guccione has always been careful to present material as upscale, though it would be hard to imagine Flynt's *Hustler* publishing photos of women urinating after the manner of *Penthouse* Pets. *Jerry Falwell v. Larry Flynt: The First Amendment on Trial*, Rodney A. Smolla's account of the legal battle between the televangelist and the publisher of *Hustler* magazine—which printed a salacious parody of the minister in 1983—is definitive on an important libel case dealt with too casually in the movie version of Flynt's life; the book reminds us that libel and obscenity were historically conflated. Smolla's treatment dramatizes the participants, who come to resemble one another in their sleaziness. An early disapproving article was Robert Ward's "Grossing Out with Publishing's Hottest Hustler," on Flynt as he was just beginning his career. Jeffrey Klein interviews staff members at *Hustler*, talks to Flynt about his religious conversion, and elicits the publisher's views on women, the First Amendment, and obscenity in "Born Again Porn." For a recent look at Flynt, scholars should consult Deborah Hastings' Associated Press report, "The Unhappy Hustler." Flynt, paralyzed by an assailant's bullet for publishing photos of a black and white couple in *Hustler*, still controls a $100 million empire of thirty magazines, including *Maternity Fashion* and *Beauty*. Hastings recounts Flynt's battles with Charles Keating, his short-lived religious fundamentalism, and his aims in starting *Hustler*. Flynt himself has written an autobiography, *An Unseemly Man: My Life as Pornographer, Pundit and Social Outcast*, published at the same time that the movie *The People versus Larry Flynt* was released. Laura Kipnis' "It's a Wonderful Life" contrasts man and magazine with the movie version of life and career. Perhaps more than that of any other single individual in recent history, Flynt's career illustrates the cultural dynamics by which society first marginalizes the pornographer/outsider, then rehabilitates and defangs him through capitalistic appropriation and commodification. The process, Kipnis thinks, is the nation's ultimate revenge on Flynt. As always, pornography shapes culture. J. Hoberman calls Milos Forman's film "Capra-porn" and the character of Flynt a "Kmart Libertine" in "Working-Class Heroes," his review of the movie. Challenged by his portrayal as a champion of the First Amendment in the movie *The People vs. Larry Flynt*, the publisher attempted to martyr himself again in Cincinnati by deliberately breaking the city's draconian censorship ordinances, reported Joel Stein in "Larry Flynt, the Sequel." As this *Guide* goes to press, Kenneth Starr, the special prosecutor whose pornographic tactics led to the Clinton–Lewinsky scandal, has done what few others could have done: elevated Flynt almost to the status of a statesman, a role the publisher took on when he began to unearth sexual peccadilloes among Clinton's hypocritical detractors to counter Starr's obsessive search for dirt on the president.

FETISH AND ADULT SPECIALTY MAGAZINES

Though dated, the most comprehensive study of fetish magazines is Gillian Freeman's *The Undergrowth of Literature*, a thorough survey of magazines and journals dealing with sexual predilections of all sorts; no one has sensed more accurately the cultural hierarchy of fetishes in the West. Freeman offers judgments that still hold up; she calls *Rubber International* the most academic of the fetish publications, for example, and brings a precise sense of niche marketing to her assessment of heterosexual and homosexual magazines. Regularly published periodicals, however cheap or sleazy, bestow presence and even legitimacy on fetishes by acknowledging a community of adherents. That is the thesis of Sarah Harris' *The Puritan Jungle: America's Sexual Underground*, based on interviews with gays, vice cops, transvestites, pornographers, performers, and hustlers. Harris recognizes specialized magazines as channels of communication, although her approach is pretty sensational. Michael Leigh also ferrets out subcultures through magazines and newspapers in *The Velvet Underground*, a guide to erotic journalism of the 1960s. More contemporary guides are *Apocalypse Culture*, a collection of essays drawn from fringe publications, edited by Adam Parfrey, and *Beneath the Underground*, an arch insider's view of the world of weird journalism by Bob Black. Various issues of *Semiotext(e)* excerpt bizarre material from zines and small presses, though the result itself often seems the literary equivalent of a train wreck. Issue 4:1 (1981), for example, is appropriately entitled "Polysexuality" but is so incoherent that it has escaped condemnation. A mildly illuminating interview with the editors by Henry Schwarz and Anne Balsamo is called "Under the Sign of *Semiotext(e).*" The two volumes of *Sensoria from Censorium* collect strange material from zines of many kinds, some of them apparently (though not unmistakably) sexual. David Hebditch and Nick Anning devote a few pages to specialty periodicals in *Porn Gold: Inside the Pornography Business*, as does John Heidenry in *What Wild Ecstasy: The Rise and Fall of the Sexual Revolution*. Louis H. Swartz's "Erotic Witness: The Rise and Flourishing of Genitally Explicit and Sex Act Explicit Heterosexually Oriented Photographic Magazines in the U.S., 1965–1985" discusses the difficulties of creating categories for sex magazines and, given their enormous range of fetishes and values, of the difficulties of establishing "connoisseurship" and research methods.

(For other periodicals, see Chapter 4, **Bibliographies and Reference Tools**, especially Attorney General's Commission, Brent, Bud Plant, Committee on Small Magazines and Publishers, Daly and Wice, Freeman, Friedman, Gunderloy and Janice, Husni, Kadrey, Kick, Kinsey, Last Gasp, Lewis, Locke, Loompanics, Milton, Owens, President's Commission on Obscenity and Pornography, and Stang; see also Chapter 7, **Major Research Collections**, especially Berman, Elcano and Bullough, and Gellatly.)

Charles Winick's classic "A Content Analysis of Sexually Explicit Magazines Sold in an Adult Bookstore" identifies themes and formulas and suggests reasons for their appeal and mechanics. According to Winick, only 5 percent of adult magazines employ bondage themes, and only 1 percent sadomasochistic themes; the rest dote on naked women or couples engaged in intercourse. If one specific fetish magazine can be said to have set the pace for others, it was *Bizarre*, published erratically in Canada by John Willie from 1946 to about 1950. (According to C. J. Scheiner, *Bizarre* was based on the British magazine *London Life*, also imported into the United States.[1] All twenty-six issues have been reprinted as Willie's *Bizarre: The Complete Reprint of John Willie's Bizarre*, *vols. 1–13* with Eric Kroll's commentary on the bondage-and-discipline themes, the costume fantasies, and the voluptuous pen of the artist. In second place is *Exotique*, published from 1957 to 1963, similarly saturated with outlandish appliances and claustrophobic sexuality. The first thirty-six issues, most of them featuring the saga of Leonard Burtman, a fictional scientist and photographer as he grovels before a majestic dominatrix, have been reprinted in three volumes as *Exotique: A New Magazine of the Bizarre and Unusual. Exotique*'s successors now occupy niches in a market fragmented by specific tastes. Gini Graham Scott indexes magazines on S/M and bondage and discipline in *Dominant Women,*

Submissive Men: An Exploration in Erotic Dominance and Submission, as do Thomas Weinberg and G. W. Levi Kamel in *S&M: Studies in Sadomasochism*; Weinberg and Kamel are especially informative on periodicals from the 1970s such as *Amazon* (Philadelphia) and *Latent Image, Aggressive Gals*, and *Bitch Goddesses* (Los Angeles). *The Groupsex Tapes*, by H. E. Margolis and Paul Rubenstein, contains a section on swingers' magazines of the 1960s.

William Grimes quotes Alan Betrock, an archivist, as saying that girlie and scandal magazines sold 35 million copies a month in the 1950s in "Lurid! Licentious! Collectible! The Flip Side of the 1940's and 50's." Neil Wexler profiles Elmer Batters, editor and publisher of magazines popular in the 1950s such as *Black Silk Stockings, Thigh High, Leg-O-Rama, Tip Top*, and *Sheer Delight*, all of them catering to leg fetishists, in "The Master of Leg Art." (For more on Batters, see **Fetish Photographs** in Chapter 12.) In "The Mastur Race," Mark Kramer interviews Dian Hanson, the articulate and witty editor of *Juggs, Bust Out, Leg Show*, and *Big Butt*. Hanson, formerly an editor on *Puritan*, slickest of hard-core magazines, moved to fetish soft-core because she was fascinated by specialization. Hanson associates pornography with advances in leisure, self-awareness, and deepening cultural richness. Her success as an editor, she claims, is the result of her encouraging men to tell her what sorts of text and images they enjoy masturbating to. Most of her correspondents, Hanson says, have been taught that sex is sinful, and have learned to masturbate as an outlet, a practice she thinks both moral and practical. Masturbation permits men to pursue diverse sexual dreams, and to do so without bothering others or pestering women who do not share those fantasies. Michael Kaplan elicits ideas from Hanson on how to arouse readers in "Editing by Desire." The veteran writer Valerie Kelly analyzes formulas and themes in periodicals such as *Ass Parade, Bottom, Leggs, Big Boobs, Silky, Pet Pussy, Baby Doll, Naked Nymphs, Roommates, Milk Maids, Bondage Life, TV Tricks, Outlaw Biker, Stallion, Stroke, Leg Parade, Chunky Asses, Lesbian Lovers, Big Mama*, and others for wanna-be writers in *How to Write Erotica for Fun and Profit*. Kelly covers topical orientations, characterization, and plot in heterosexual romances, gay, lesbian, and fetish genres. Kelly recommends that writers draw on sexual surveys for ideas: *The Hite Report* of 1976, she points out, is unusually informative on ways in which women masturbate and the intercourse positions they fantasize about.

Given the reticence that afflicts critics, most hard-core picture magazines have escaped serious attention. These are perhaps the most subversive types of pornography—and not simply because they remain uncredited and even anonymous to the point of going unregistered for copyright purposes. They are often lumped together as so much "smut" or "trash," despite their depiction of a sexuality that defies categorization. They undermine academic theory: symbolic subtexts disappear behind genital explicitness, and images quite literally overwhelm a language often consciously parodied on the page. A Lacanian analysis in which phallus is distinguished as "signifier" from the actual penis glistening in the photo would probably provoke laughter (and some would say that is porn's true purpose). The picture magazines are deliberately, relentlessly crude, cruder than any documentary or vérité photographer would ever be, primitive to a point beyond aesthetics, certainly beyond articulation; that is one reason for their being.

Moreover, soft-core publishers marginalize hard-core magazines out of self-interest. Soft-core magazines sanitize images to make them suitable to fairly large audiences, by offering substitutes for "the real thing." Arabella Melville's essay, "The Dirty Doctor: A (Brief) Career in Porno," outlines this dynamic. Melville, a Ph.D., became first a photographer's model, then publisher of *Libertine* magazine, a serious English periodical that combined political comment, outrageous opinion, and explicit illustrations. Brought to trial for obscenity in 1977, she was acquitted by a British jury. Melville's essay is included here because she makes the interesting point that soft-core magazine editors and publishers not only have learned to operate within a repressive government system but have also come to support that system because it favors them economically. The hard-core and fetish magazines, then, have served as traditional channels of marginalized discourse, a function that is gradually being taken over by esoteric sites on the Web today. Sex Web sites, in fact, are displacing the magazines, most of which have ended up in secondhand stores, grab-bag specialty packages sold by mail, or landfill. If no scholar ever chronicles the explicit photo sex magazine genres of the last four decades, then they will retain their mystery and their authenticity as low porn.

In 1969, the first time anyone tried to characterize the medium with any thoroughness, the *Report* of the President's Commission on Obscenity and Pornography said that the revenues of combined annual numbers of all hard-core magazines did not equal the sales of one month's issue of *Reader's Digest* (Part Three, Section B). In the early 1980s, each issue of John Milton's *$ex $ense* ranked the photo-magazine best-sellers for a two-month period. The December–January 1982 issue listed *Super Head* (oral), *Slut Orgy* (heterosexual couplings), *Cum Drippers* (semen leaking out of mouths and vaginas), *Best of Cum* (oral sex), *Ero* (a bizarre European import, featuring kinky acts), *Hard TV* (transvestites and transsexuals in intercourse with gay or straight partners), *Pleasure Production* (Vanessa del Rio, Sue Nero, Lisa Deleeuw, and Tawny Pearl in stills from their movies), *Erotic World of Seka* (mostly stills from the star's movies), *Pleasure* (another import, featuring garden-variety sex along with fellatio, cunnilingus, and anal intercourse), and *Sulka and Her Friends* (the reigning postop transsexual of the time, in intercourse with various genders), in that order, at prices ranging from $7.50 to $12.50. *Screw* magazine still regularly reports on hard-core magazines, usually to note a new series or a particularly bizarre periodical. Despite a market rapidly collapsing because of competition from the Internet, some are still available by mail, while many can be found in the larger adult bookstores, and the massive list of magazines in the attorney general's report can help the interested find them (see Chapter 4, **Bibliographies and**

Reference Tools). That list in itself is a significant cultural document, since it attests to low pornography's power to resist categorization and classification (it is just a list of almost 3,000 titles.) In its way, the sexual chaos the magazines represent is both astonishing and wonderful.

ROMANCE, CONFESSION, AND WOMEN'S MAGAZINES

Romance fiction is a staple of women's magazines. Like soft-core men's magazines, these include—in addition to articles of general interest on many subjects—essays and photos dealing with the battle of the sexes, fashion, sexual advice, romance, medical problems, pop psychology, and other matters less obviously erotic. Perhaps because it has itself so often been the target of feminist derision, *Playboy* over the years has bashed periodicals for females. Typical is "A Man's Guide to Women's Magazines," an amusing review of *Cosmopolitan, Vogue, Glamour, Elle, Woman's Day*, and *Ms*, which feature departments similar to *Playboy*'s own. More pointed is William Iverson's "The Pious Pornographers Revisited," a two-part update of Iverson's book-length *The Pious Pornographers*, an investigation of often explicitly detailed coverage of sexual matters to be found in *Redbook, Ladies' Home Journal*, and *Cosmopolitan*. Worth noting is Jennifer Scanlon's *Inarticulate Longings: The Ladies' Home Journal, Gender, and the Promises of Consumer Culture*. While much of the appeal of the early *Ladies' Home Journal* was simply consumerism, says Scanlon, the magazine also spoke to women's need for sensuality. Janice Winship's *Inside Women's Magazines* is a broader survey with some American examples amid the British journals she studies. Like Winship, Eva Illouz says in "Reason within Passion: Love in Women's Magazines" that romance fiction in magazines such as *Cosmopolitan* and *Woman* hold utilitarian and therapeutic value for their readers, who know very well the differences between fantasy and reality—an observation that can be extended to audiences for all types of pornography. Katharine McMahon's "The *Cosmopolitan* Ideology and the Management of Desire" analyzes a dozen years' worth of articles in *Cosmopolitan*, often linked with *Playboy* as a female "candy-sex" magazine, to demonstrate that the journal is one medium by which sex and gender are socially constructed in America. According to Angela McRobbie, however, magazines such as *Elle, Marie Clare, 19*, and *More!* also exhibit a growing sexual frankness; McRobbie's "*More!*: New Sexualities in Girls' and Women's Magazines" discusses what she calls the "ironic spaces" that such periodicals occupy in the political economy.

The sexuality inherent in these formats was covered some years ago in "The Social Role of the Confession Magazine," by George Gerbner, and "Content Analysis of the World of Confession Magazines," by Wilbur Schramm. In the late 1960s David Sonenschein and his colleagues surveyed the form in "A Study of Mass Media Erotica: The 'Romance' or 'Confession' Magazine" for the *Technical Report of the Commission on Obscenity and Pornography*; they decided that if the intent was salacious, the content was pretty innocuous. Sonenschein analyzed tropes in "Love and Sex in the Romance Magazines" (which says that marriage, family, and religion eventually domesticate love and sex in the typical story); in "Process in the Production of Popular Culture: The Romance Magazine" (which interviews editors of some of the forty-three magazines surveyed for the commission); and (with Mark Ross) in "Sex Information in the 'Romance' and 'Confession' Magazines" (which finds that most stories contain little sex information). Though similarly dated, the funniest analysis is Amy Gross' "Woman as Sex Object: 'I'm Fragile, I'm Female, I Confess': Life as It's Lived (More or Less) in the Confession Magazines." Gross identifies the dominant stereotype as a lower-class uneducated housewife burdened with children and domestic chores; either she or her auto-mechanic husband has an affair, repents, and together "they find God." Since then, increased explicitness has compelled scholars to look more closely. Carole Spitzach's "The Confession Mirror: Plastic Images for Surgery" concludes that confession magazines are purveyors of wish fulfillment, as does Jerry Stahl's "Adventures in the Sin Trade," on newsstand fixtures such as *Modern Love Confessions*, *Intimate Story*, and *Uncensored Confessions*.

FANZINES

Fascinating pornographic fiction has evolved from science fiction fanzines, called variously "slash/zines," or "K/S (Kirk/Spock)," a sort of American variation on the Russian samizdat. Here authors deliberately subvert the artifacts of popular culture by resexualizing them. The subversiveness of such enterprises should lay to rest myths of passive audiences rooted in front of a screen that simply programs Americans. Fanzines can be traced back to the 1930s in the United States but flourished in the 1970s. Frederick Wertham, who attacked comic books in the 1950s, was mesmerized by fanzines, whose amateurishness struck him as an index of authenticity on the part of publishers and contributors. His *The World of Fanzines* (1973), the first study of the genre, is a good historical starting point. Fantasy fiction written today by mostly female fans on typed or cheaply printed sheets stapled together circulates by hand or mail. Not all fanzines are pornographic, of course, but of those that are, the ones based on *Star Trek*, now numbering in the *thousands*, have received the most critical attention. Camille Bacon-Smith's article, "Spock among the Women," is a brief introduction to the more than 30,000 pieces of art, fiction, poetry, songs, criticism, and commentary authored by some 10,000 fans, most of them women. As Bacon-Smith points out, the phenomenon illustrates a need for communication of desire and a hunger for narrative stretched within flexible, but familiar, popular forms that are fundamental to pornographic expression. Bacon-Smith's *Enterprising Women: Television Fandom and the Creation of Popular Myth* notes that "the fan women's erotic engagement with visual media . . . seems to be less dependent on the graphic detailing of genitalia than on the presence of an object of sexual focus in the frame" (195), a response quite different from the male gaze. Bacon-Smith's reflections on eroticism are mandatory for those seeking to understand new genres.

Like Bacon-Smith's texts, Judith Spector's "Science Fiction and the Sex War: A Womb of One's Own" speculates on the reasons that most fan writing thus far has centered on science fiction, whose form and content in the past have marginalized women. Both suggest that the popular media narratives leave gaps that can be claimed by women and eroticized by feminine sensibilities, often in extended, branching stories ideally suited to zines. Typical are *Star Trek* story-trees, to which episodes can be added as writer after writer joins the collective endeavor. Stories in *Trek*-zines may portray Spock in homosexual intercourse with Captain Kirk, for example, or invent other gender- and species-bending encounters between crew members and aliens. A somewhat circumspect, but highly informative, overview is Henry Jenkins' *"Star Trek* Rerun, Reread, Re-written: Fan Writing as Textual Poaching," a reflection on authorship and copyright occasioned by litigation by Lucasfilm that drove some zines deeper underground. Jenkins expanded his observations into *Textual Poaching: Television Fans and Participatory Culture*, which examines a wider field of television characters and images transformed into erotic fantasies. "Romantic Myth, Transcendence, and *Star Trek* Zines," by Patricia F. Lamb and Diana Veith, studies fanzines as a new subgenre of romance. The science-fiction writer Joanna Russ' "Pornography by Women for Women, with Love" also deals with the sexualization and regendering of Kirk, Spock, and other characters. In this regard, Karin Blair's "Sex and *Star Trek*," while not about zines, does consider the eroticism implicit in the television series and thus helps explain the sexual experimentation that zines enshrine.

Katharine Gates treats slash/zines as a fetish in *Deviant Desires: Incredibly Strange Sex*, a text that also covers sploshing, crushing, ponygirling, body inflating, balloon-popping, and a host of other strange sexual obsessions, along with "niche-kink internet communities." The swelling volume of slash/zines, especially as they have mutated and spread on the Internet, has attracted popular journalism. Reporters seem more stunned by the perversity of slash/zines subverting mainstream icons—sacred prime-time television programs—than by the gender of their authors. One prominent article to marvel at slash/zines, or "fanfic," as some adherents now call the genre, is Austin Bunn's "The X-rated Files." Additional information and sources can be found on the webpage "Fanfic."

Some of the essays in Donald Palumbo's *Erotic Universe: Sexuality and Fantastic Literature* cover science-fiction zines, but the most erudite discussion of feminist slash/zines is Constance Penley's "Feminism, Psychoanalysis, and the Study of Popular Culture," which looks at many examples of fan-generated erotic encounters and ranges beyond the *Trek*-inspired fantasies to others based on prime-time programs or films. Casey Finch uses illustrations from *Heavy Metal* and other popular science-fiction magazines as soft-core kitsch derivations of painterly traditions in "Two of a Kind."

In decades past, fan magazines mixed celebrity worship with advice on intimate problems, a combination treated in Gaylyn Studlar's "The Perils of Pleasure: Fan Magazine Discourse as Women's Commodified Culture in the 1920s" and Jane Gaines' "War, Women, and Lipstick: Fan Magazines in the Forties." Some contributors to Martin Levin's *Hollywood and the Great Fan Magazines* note that the erotic appeal derived from pinup photos and the occasionally risqué stories of celebrity love-lives. Contemporary gender-bending variants include gay fanzines, the subject of two essays by Matias Viegener: "Gay Fanzines: 'There's Trouble in That Body' " and "Kinky Escapes, Bedroom Techniques, Unbridled Passion and Secret Sex Codes" and still another by Mark Fenster: "Queer Punk Fanzines: Identity, Community, and the Articulation of Homosexuality." The titles signpost approaches.

OTHER ZINES

Zine increasingly refers to small, specialized, modestly financed, more or less periodic publication. Zine writers and audiences communicate electronically through *Datazine*, an electronic bulletin board updated bimonthly. Zines are forums for controversy, and publishers often argue with other zines. *The Taste of Latex* regularly reviews other zines; issue 1:4 (1990/1991) covers *Diseased Pariah News* (HIV updates), *Libido* (upscale arty), *Mentertainment* (go-go dancers), *On Our Rag* (lesbian menstruation), and *Scream Box* (lesbian kinkiness), some of which may already be defunct. The best reviews are provided by *Factsheet Five*, published from 1982 to 1991 by Mike Gunderloy and since 1992 by Seth Friedman, which deals with a large range of zines, some of them pornographic. *Factsheet Five* can be accessed electronically, and subscribers can participate in discussion on the WELL teleconferencing system. V. Vale has edited a first volume of *Zines*, with more volumes to follow; included are zines of various kinds, including the sexually explicit, with comment on the phenomenon of demotic publication. The Zine Exchange Network will swap zines. James Romenesko surveys some of the more outrageous, from *ROC* (Rock Out Censorship) to *Slut Mag* in "The Zine Explosion." Romenesko himself edits a zine called *Obscure Publications* (Milwaukee) to chronicle the rise and decline of specific zines. Jeremy Mindich's "Soap Box Samurai" also provides an excellent overview of the economics (most zines lose money) of zines, the psychology of their publishers (alienated or enraged people determined to explore truly "alternative" lifestyles and communications), the loose connections between them (like the San Francisco Zine Publishers Collective), and outlets for distribution (e.g., Tower Records stores in major cities, Amok Bookstore in Los Angeles, See Hear in New York, Quimby's in Chicago). Johnny Marr tells Mindich that Gunderloy's editing of *Factsheet Five* was like "walking into a firing squad in the round" (99), so intense is the passion behind views of sex and reality.

Erotic zines as a category differ from run-of-the-mill pornographic photo magazines in the quality of their self-reflection; zines typically include stories of erotic experimentation, comment, and analysis. One notable example, *Erotic Fiction Quarterly: A Journal of Erotic and Other Sexual Fiction*, edited by Richard Hiller, had only one issue. Better-established erotic zines include *Yellow Silk: Journal of the Erotic Arts*, whose sensibility is so ethereal that it is difficult to gauge its eroticism for humans; *Libido: The Journal of Sex and Sensibility*, whose pages are fairly tame; *Frighten the Horses: A Journal of the Sexual Revolution*, which assaults frontiers more vigorously; *Poppin' Zits!*, whose collages defy description; *P.O.N.Y. X-Press*, which focuses on the sex workers of New York; *Whorezine*, which also covers sex trades; *Taste of Latex*, which espouses pansexuality; *EIDOS*, whose range is catholic and raunchy; and *PURE*, which specializes in photography and fiction by and for women. Most of these can be characterized as defenses of radical sexual theory, with essays and commentary from social and political fringes.

GAY AND LESBIAN PAPERS, PERIODICALS, AND ZINES

Gays and lesbians have struggled to make their voices heard in the din of American culture because journalism has so often distorted reportage on their orientation and concerns. As Frank Pearce points out in "How to Be Immoral and Ill, Pathetic and Dangerous, All at the Same Time: Mass Media and Homosexuality," even sympathetic representations of homosexuality in news media have been contradictory and deformed. Edward Alwood makes similar points in *Straight News: Gays, Lesbians, and the News Media* but is much more thorough, with numerous citations to mainstream media. Michelle A. Wolf and Alfred P. Kielwasser have gathered essays on gay audiences in *Gay People, Sex and the Media*. In the early part of the century publishing magazines devoted to homosexuality was dangerous. Lillian Faderman discusses lesbian magazines such as *The Ladder* (1956–1972) at length in her *Odd Girls and Twilight Lovers: A History of Lesbian Life in Twentieth-Century America* and *Surpassing the Love of Men: Romantic Friendship and Love between Women from the Renaissance to the Present*. Faderman observes that such magazines emphasized socially sanctioned romantic friendships rather than physical contact and that periodicals helped establish a sense of community among lesbians. *Lesbian Lives: Biographies of Women from "The Ladder,"* edited by Barbara Grier and Coletta Reid, supports Faderman's arguments by presenting often poignant accounts of the isolation felt by lesbians seeking comradeship and common interests.

The most thorough history of gay and lesbian journalism is Roger Streitmatter's *Unspeakable: The Rise of the Gay and Lesbian Press in America*, premised on a cultural dynamic that views information as arising to build community and combat prejudice. In a similar vein, Jim Kepner has gathered unusual articles for *Rough News—Daring Views: 1950s Pioneer Gay Press Journalism*, an important period in America for the formation of a gay community, especially since discrimination against gays went hand in hand with repression of their views and representations. Ed Jackson and Stan Persky have edited material from one of the best-known gay periodicals in *Flaunting It: A Decade of Gay Journalism from the Body Politic*. Winston Leyland has done the same for another leading magazine in *Gay Roots: Twenty Years of Gay Sunshine*, an anthology of fiction, essays, humor, cartoons, and so on from the original issues (1970–1982) published by Gay Sunshine Press. In some ways, this collection and its companion volume, *Gay Roots: An Anthology of Gay History, Sex, Politics, and Culture, Volume 2*, provide deeper insight into gay sexuality than academic histories and commentaries devoted to the subject. Among writers represented are Tennessee Williams, Allen Ginsberg, and John Rechy, but even more interesting are articles such as one on a possible gay connection between George Washington and the Marquis de Lafayette, one on gay life in Harlem in the 1920s, and one on homosexuality among Native Americans. Emmanuel Cooper's *The Sexual Perspective: Homosexuality and Art in the Last 100 Years in the West* surveys gay and lesbian magazines such as *The Advocate* and *Heresies* and discusses writers and artists appearing in their pages. Cooper is particularly informative on George Quaintance and Tom of Finland, both of whom drew the cover art for early homosexual magazines.

Comprehensive in its look at the "muscle" genre is F. Valentine Hooven's *Beefcake: The Muscle Magazines of America, 1950–1970*, which also explores the contributions of Quaintance, Tom of Finland, and Bruce of Los Angeles in a discussion of major publishers such as AMG Studios. Probably the most historically important "beefcake" magazine was *Physique Pictorial*, though its chief rivals had titles like *Grecian Guild Pictorial* and *Vim: America's Best Built Physiques*, all of which flourished in the 1950s until superseded by the more explicit *Male Man* in the 1960s. Timothy Lewis' *Physique: A Pictorial History of the Athletic Model Guild* reproduces photos and covers from *Physique Pictorial*, published by AMG from 1951 on. Taschen has reprinted every issue as *The Complete Reprint of Physique Pictorial, 1951–1990*. Vince Aletti's "Boys on Film" profiles Robert Mizer, founder of the Athletic Model Guild and producer of more than 1 million gay nude photos during a career that began in the 1940s. Mizer's chief rivals, notes Aletti, were Bruce Bellas of Bruce of Los Angeles, Constantine of Spartan, and Don Whitman of the Western Photography Guild. Aletti has also written "Physique Pictorial: The Rise, Fall, and Revival of Lon of New York," a neglected physique photographer and publisher now coming into his own. (See also **Gender Disputations: The Male Nude, the Male Pinup, and the Lesbian Photograph** in Chapter 12.)

A. Block samples publications in "Scanning the 'Zine Scene: Rumblings from the New Gay Underground," and *Holy Titclamps* keeps track of "queer-zines." More raucous are *Slippery When Wet*, "the Little Sex Zine That Does," which specializes in "queer" fiction and comment; *On Our Backs*, founded by Debi Sundahl and Susie Bright, subtitled "Entertainment for the Adventurous Lesbian"; *Bad Attitude*, another lesbian journal heavy on smut; *Girljock*, which deals explicitly with the "athletic lesbian"; and *Yoni: Lesbian Erotica*, which features photography, poems, fiction, and commentary. *Out/Look: The National Lesbian and Gay Quarterly* and *OutWeek: The Lesbian and Gay News Magazine* strive for a national audience. (For additional information on gay and lesbian magazines, see **Magazines, Newspapers, and Comics** in Chapter 4, especially Clardy, Copley, Dynes, Garber, Gunderloy and Janice, Humphreys, Husni, Kadrey, Kehoe, Owens, Parker, Potter, Richards, Rutledge, *Queer Zine Explosion*, Saunders, Searing, Vida, Weinberg and Bell; see also Chapter 7, **Major Research Collections**, McEnroe.)

EROTICISM IN ADVERTISING

Although virtually all texts on advertising mention eroticism, most offer shopworn illustrations and trite observations. Jackson Lears deals intelligently with advertising's intrusions into personal realms in *Fables of Abundance: A Cultural History of Advertising in America*, especially in the chapter called "The Merger of Intimacy and Publicity" (137–161), which covers the selling of intimate items from corsets to patent medicines. Lois Banner's *American Beauty* and Martha Banta's *Imaging American Women: Idea and Ideals in Cultural History* are also excellent sources on advertising that exploited women as images and consumers. (See also **Concepts of Beauty** and subsequent sections in Chapter 9.) *Channels of Desire: Mass Images and the Shaping of American Consciousness*, by Stuart Ewen and Elizabeth Ewen, deals, in part, with attempts to lace television advertising with sexual appeal. Torben Vestergaard's *Language of Advertising* discusses predatory aspects of sexualized advertising.

Erving Goffman's wide-ranging study of gender display, *Gender Advertisements*, contains many insights: "Children and women are pictured on floors and beds more than are men" (41). Goffman makes much of the ritualization of gender by American advertising, a practice that may actually subvert the stereotypes of commerce and convention. Similarly, in "A Capital Idea: Gendering in the Mass Media," Lisa Steele insists that the images of women in pornography are often no worse and sometimes preferable to those in mass media advertising. Steele thinks it wise to remember that "commodity fetishism is a two-way street: humans cannot be made into objects without a concurrent 'humanization' of objects taking place. Is a 'sexy' automobile in a television commercial—or a dancing candy bar, for that matter—any less harmful visually and psychically than a fragmented female form displayed on a newsstand shelf?" (59). The conclusions of Trevor Millum's *Images of Woman: Advertising in Women's Magazines*, that the fantasies promoted by women's magazines simply reinforce the status quo, are based on a survey of English, rather than American, magazines and are somewhat dated now because they refer to stereotypes that have changed somewhat, but those having to do with eroticism would appear to be still valid. Millum notes that hairstylists coif blond and brunet models differently for photo shoots. Jane Root's *Pictures of Women* also explores the affinities between advertising and pornography, especially in terms of the ways in which women are presented. *Killing Us Softly III*, the second update of Jean Kilbourne's documentary on the ways in which advertisers sexualize young girls and trivialize older women, impose standards of beauty on different ages and races, and employ aggressive images against women, is an excellent compilation of ads from print, photographic, and electronic media.

Sexual Representation as Allure

Alice E. Courtney and Thomas W. Whipple discuss the seeming permanence of sex roles and gender assumptions in mass media in *Sex Stereotyping in Advertising*, as do M. A. Massé and K. Rosenblum in "Male and Female Created They Them: The Depiction of Gender in the Advertising of Traditional Women's and Men's Magazines." A well-known study on "Women in Magazine Advertisements" by D. E. Sexton and P. Haberman concluded that roughly one-fourth of all magazine ads make use of pictures of "obviously alluring" women and that the number increased from 1951 to 1971. One famous example by G. H. Smith and R. Engel, "Influence of a Female Model on Perceived Characteristics of an Automobile," presented two ads for an automobile to two different groups. One depicted the car by itself; the second added a scantily dressed woman carrying a clearly phallic spear. The males and females in the group exposed to the second ad responded far more favorably than did the members of the group exposed to the first ad (whether approval might translate into increased sales was not measured). "Reactions to Sexy Ads Vary with Age," a study by G. L. Wise, A. L. King, and J. P. Merinski, points out that young viewers generally approved of sexy ads more than did older Americans.

Other academic studies challenge what has become almost an article of folklore—the belief that American advertisers will always choose sexual images and undertones. Many studies indicate that sex does not sell all that well and that sexual images may deflect the viewer's attention away from the product and reduce later recall. A particularly well constructed survey by B. J. Morrison and R. C. Sherman found that the answer to the question "Who Responds to Sex in Advertising?" is complex, depending on gender and other factors mostly having to do with selective perception. Some subjects responded to the sexual images, and some did not; some responded to particular features, and others did not. "Do Nudes in Ads Enhance Brand Recall?" reports that a study by M. Wayne Alexander found that nudity did not enhance brand or product recall and that strong attitudes toward nudity were only a possible reason. The only reliable conclusion was that married men could remember significantly more brand names than single men.

Edward A. McCabe's "Sex in Advertising," a better than ordinary history, contrasts contemporary practice against Madison Avenue's use of sex in the past; the article is notable for its reproduction of historically important ads from about 1919 to the present. Stuart Elliot asks, "Has Madison Avenue Gone Too Far?" in his article on the increasingly naked and /or erotic ads for Calvin Klein and other manufacturers of clothing and perfume. Reporters adore the topic, always good filler for a slow news day, and any number of weightless articles ask similarly rhetorical questions. Americans are beginning to accept public references to penises and the display of penises in art, television, movies, performance, and, above all, advertising, according to Lena Williams in " "Bodies Go Public: The Nature of Privacy Changes for Men, Too." In "Here's the Beef," Benjamin Svetkey also notes the increased appearance of sexy males, clad and undressed, in Pepsi, National Airlines, and Hyundai ads pitched at women. Aaron Botsky's "An Emblem of Crisis Makes the World See the Body Anew" argues that AIDS has encouraged illustrators to use the body more candidly in advertising, design, and visual expression generally.

In the 1950s, Vance Packard's *The Hidden Persuaders* suggested that advertisers used sexual messages unconsciously to influence consumers. Wilson Bryan Key has since raised that assertion to the status of urban myth. Key's several books, especially *The Clam-Plate Orgy: and Other Subliminals the Media Use to Manipulate Your Behavior*, *Media Sexploitation*, and *Subliminal Seduction: Ad Media's Manipulation of a Not So Innocent America*, are perhaps the most sustained attacks on the alleged pervasiveness of sex in modern advertising. Key thinks that advertisers manipulate the consumer's unconscious. He makes much of "subliminal advertising," a concept developed in the 1950s by Jim Vicary, who claimed that his study proved that advertisers were inserting ads in microsecond bursts between frames in motion pictures; audiences would then race to the lobby to buy popcorn and soda. No researcher has been able to replicate this study, and most social scientists consider arguments for subliminal advertising a species of folklore. Lack of evidence has not deterred Key from claiming that advertisers hide messages advocating sexual promiscuity, satanic worship, homosexuality, and deviant behavior in copy and pictures. Key claims to have found the word "sex" baked into Ritz crackers, spotted orgies in the photos of seafood dishes reproduced on place mats in Howard Johnson restaurants, and uncovered the silhouettes of copulating humans in ads for various liquors. The 1990 trial concerning the alleged hidden lyrics in a Judas Priest music album, which Key claimed urged teenagers to commit suicide, damaged the author's reputation (the jury rejected subliminal messages), but he still has a large following.

More defensible are the insights in Judith Williamson's *Decoding Advertisements: Ideology and Meaning in Advertising*. Among these is a clever variation on Claude Lévi-Strauss' raw and cooked theory: the notion that society transforms images from a "raw" to a "cooked" state and that ads are one of the means by which raw sexuality is converted to acceptable eroticism. Because advertisements make up whole strata of American folklore, the scholar can read many texts on their sexual meanings; the model was set by Guiseppe Lo Duca in *Technique de L'erotisme*, an encyclopedic survey of erotic imagery in advertising and magazines published before 1961. A more recent text is Robert Goldman's *Reading Ads Socially*. Goldman frames his arguments with the usual observations about commodity fetishism (a bad thing, according to academics) but ventures on to fresh looks at desire, gender, and the commodification of feminism as an advertising strategy itself. "Sexual Fetishism: An Experimental Analogue" by S. Rachman, and "Experimentally-induced 'Sexual Fetishism' ": Replication and Development" by Rachman and R. J. Hodgson examine folkloristic assumptions about the alleged power of sexual advertising. The articles review an experiment in which researchers failed to convert viewers of specially designed advertisements into boot fetishists. Effective or not, however, sexiness in ads has increased. Tom Reichert, Jacqueline Lambiase, Susan Morgan, Meta Carstarphen, and Susan Zavoina, in "Cheesecake and Beefcake: No Matter How You Slice It, Sexual Explicitness in Advertising Continues to Increase," reported on a study of issues of *Newsweek*, *Time*, *Cosmopolitan*, *Redbook*, *Esquire*, and *Playboy* in 1983 and 1993. They found that 1983 ads depicting a man and a woman rarely (only one percent) pictured or implied intercourse between the models; in 1993, 17 percent did. In 1983 ads only 28 percent of the female models and 11 percent of the males were dressed "provocatively"; in 1993, the numbers increased 40 percent and 18 percent, respectively.

Celebrity and Fashion Nudity in Ads

As the furor over Madonna's high jinks indicates, the craze for celebrity nudity is intense. (See **Films and Videotapes** in Chapter 4, especially Bernard, Hosoda, and Jones.) Michael Angeli and Stephen Klein devote many pages to the psychological appeal of the nude—and pregnant—Demi Moore on the August 1991 cover of *Vanity Fair* in "The Last Pinup." According to another source, the cover triggered "95 separate video pieces, reaching an estimated audience of 110 million people. There were sixty-four radio programs on thirty-one stations and 1,500 newspaper articles."[2] Kathy Myers' "Fashion 'n' Passion" maintains that pornographic elements animate fashion photography. Woody Hochswender's "Pins & Needles" column for *Harper's Bazaar*, which itself capitalizes on nudity, agrees; Hochswender points out that fashion directors can usually make their choices from nude photos of supermodels. He maintains that full-frontal nude shots in *Eileen Ford Models* (1993), the agency listing from which models are selected for shoots, are as raunchy as pictures in *Penthouse*. Eroticism in advertising also figures in Valerie Steele's "Erotic Allure," a brief, but straightforward, look at the merchandising of clothing.

Scholars should note "Fashion with Passion," which appeared in the April 1991 *Penthouse*: a dozen pages depict ultrarevealing fashions by Thierry Mugler, Gianfranco Ferré, Martine Sitbon, Claude Montana, Yves Saint-Laurent, Enrico Coveri, Katharine Hammett, and Christian Dior. What makes the photoessay unusual is that it is not; though featured in a men's magazine, it is no more salacious than a pictorial in *Vogue* or *Harper's Bazaar* or the video footage on a given episode of *Fashion Television*. Richard Avedon's *Versace: The Naked and the Dressed* reviews twenty years of the late designer's revealing fashions, as modeled by Kate Moss, Claudia Schiffer, Stella Tenant, and others. *Top Model*, a magazine devoted to the careers and personal lives of the reigning runway stars, caters to supermodel worship. Books on male models are also beginning to appear. Typical is *Male Super Models: The Men of Boss Models*, for which George Wayne interviews some of the current mannequins. Michael Gross looks at the underside of an industry in *Model: The Ugly Business of Beautiful Women*. Supermodels such as Crawford, Schiffer, and Campbell frequently pose nude and seminude in a variety of media, evidence that high fashion shades easily into pinup venues. Fans have established dozens of Web site archives of nude photos of supermodels. Marco Glaviano's *Sirens* is typical of endless volumes of high-gloss high-fashion supernudity.

Helmut Newton, the German-born fashion photographer who now works in America, is blunt about what he sees as a necessary connection between fashion and eroticism in Margy Rochlin's interview, "20 Questions: Helmut Newton." Newton's several volumes, *Big Nudes, Sleepless Nights, White Women*, and *World without Men*, feature high-fashion nudes with a sharp erotic edge, images that bridge traditional divisions between fashion magazines and those aimed at entertaining men. "The Obsessive Eye of Bruce Weber," a *Playboy* layout by the creator of Calvin Klein "Obsession" ads, profiles another crossover artist. Weber is better known for his male nudes, but he works prolifically in media aimed at different genders. Rosetta Brookes details the "traps for the gaze" set by images of three famous fashion photographers in "The Double-Page Spread: Helmut Newton, Guy Bourdin and Deborah Turbeville." Teal Triggs finds that nude males posed with clothed women are the "fashion signifiers" in the work of Ritts and Weber in "Framing Masculinity: Herb Ritts, Bruce Weber and the Body Perfect." Separating categories was easier in the past, perhaps, though the celebrated Conde-Nast fashion photographer John Rawlings began to blur distinctions in 1951 with publication of his *100 Studies of the Figure*, a collection of studio nudes of favorite fashion model Evelyn Frey. In the 1970s, the renowned fashion photographer George M. Hester published *The Classic Nude*, his studies of professional and amateur models. Deliberately erotic photographs are now common in the work of most contemporary fashion photographers, an increasing number of whom are women. Perhaps the most skilled is Rebecca Blake; the sensuality of the piquant frames in her *Forbidden Dreams* recalls Newton's work. Blake's work might also be compared to that of fashion photographer Juergen Teller, whose *Juergen Teller*, edited by Cornell Windlin, presents erotic shots of supermodels such as Kate Moss and Kristin McMenamy and celebrities such as Courtney Love and Patti Smith. Worth looking at also is Ellen Von Unwerth's *Wicked*. In Von Unwerth's heated frames, taken backstage as designers readied shows for the runways, fashion models self-consciously, even mockingly, display the nipples and bare curves that they know eyes seek out beneath the expensive clothing they wear.

Advertisements for Sex

During the nineteenth century bordellos published *Blue Books*, or pamphlets advertising the specialties of the prostitutes who worked there. Someone has collected the photographic and graphic contents of these pamphlets under the nom de plume Idem Semper as *The Blue Book*. Al Rose's *Storyville, New Orleans: Being an Authentic, Illustrated Account of the Notorious Red-Light District* reproduces ads and photos circulated by prostitutes at the turn of the century. Early prostitutes borrowed circumspect tropes ("relaxation for the stiffly inclined") for the services they offered from pornographic novels, just as their modern sisters borrow blatant photographic representations (a photo of themselves fellating a penis) from hard-core films; scholars might compare the contours.

Carol Stevens focuses on wall displays in "Gutter Graphics," an analysis of urban advertisements for massage parlors. Ads featuring photographs are common in most industrialized countries, with Japanese booklets of call-girl ads the most visible. There seems to be no American counterpart to Patrick Jewell's *Vice Art: An Anthology of London's Prostitute Cards*, which reproduces dozens of heavy-stock examples from his collection ("Nurse Birchbum is now accepting new patients"). Doubtless the same formulas contribute to posters and handouts promoting telephone sex, explicit massage, male and female escorts, and other sexual services in American urban centers. A glance at any alternative paper will elicit ads for various kinds of outcall and in-house sexual services for all genders.

Among variations are explicit "personal" ads. These appear in back pages of magazines and newspapers, not just the sex tabloids but also news weeklies such as the *Village Voice*. Susan Block's *Advertising for Love: How to Play the Personals* is an amusing account of the art of writing ads for companionship, as are Sherri Foxman's *Classified Love: A Guide to the Personals* and Jay Wiseman's *Personal Adventures: How to Meet People through the Personal Ads*. All of them explain the abbreviations, codes, and protocols, suggest ads that will obtain results, list the best places to advertise, and offer advice on how to respond, setting up a first date, avoiding trouble, and so on, but their real value is the overview of an important form of sexual discourse. An analysis of more than 350 ads in the *Advocate* by Mary Riege Laner and G. W. Levi Kamel indicates that the majority of those running the notices were advertising for "husky" or "masculine" partners; their results were published as "Media Mating I: Newspaper 'Personals' Ads of Homosexual Men." Malcolm E. Lumby, looking at the same journal for his "Men Who Advertise for Sex," discovered that advertisers usually represented themselves as endowed with large penises. Sometimes the personals nestle against ads for massage parlors and escort services, though some mainstream papers decline to accept the latter. Kenneth MacDonald asks whether newspapers like the *New York Times* can legitimately refuse ads for sexual enterprises if such businesses operate legally in "Should Newspapers Be Policing Sex?" Finally, Lonny Shavelson's *Personal Ad Portraits* collects photographs of people who have placed "lonely hearts" or sex ads, some of them weird, and reproduces the texts of their original ads. Laura Kipnis studies the photos in personal ads placed by transvestites to discover that ostensibly heterosexual male transvestites sometimes look for homosexual contacts as well in "She-Male Fantasies and the Aesthetics of Pornography."

NOTES

1. C. J. Scheiner to Joseph W. Slade, 14 October 1992.
2. Marianne Macy, *Working Sex: An Odyssey into Our Cultural Underground* (New York: Carroll and Graf, 1996), p. 91.

REFERENCES

Aletti, Vince. "Boys on Film." *Village Voice*, 11 August 1992, p. 95.
———. "Physique Pictorial: The Rise, Fall, and Revival of Lon of New York." *Village Voice*, 2 March 1999, pp. 55–56.
Alexander, M. Wayne. "Do Nudes in Ads Enhance Brand Recall?" *Journal of Advertising Research*, 18: 1 (February 1978): 47–50.
Allen, Frederick Lewis. *Only Yesterday*. New York: 1931.
Alter, Jonathan. "Substance vs. Sex." *Newsweek*, 3 February 1992, pp. 18–20.
Alternative Press Review. Columbia, MO: 1994–.
Alwood, Edward. *Straight News: Gays, Lesbians, and the News Media*. New York: Columbia University Press, 1996.
Angeli, Michael, and Stephen Klein. "The Last Pinup." *Esquire* (May 1993): 80–89.
Anger, Kenneth. *Hollywood Babylon*. San Francisco: Straight Arrow, 1975; rpt. New York: Dell, 1981.
———. *Hollywood Babylon II*. New York: Plume, 1985.
Armstrong, David. *A Trumpet to Arms: Alternative Media in America*. Los Angeles: J. P. Tarcher, 1981.
Attorney General's Commission on Pornography. *Attorney General's Commission on Pornography: Final Report, July 1986*. 2 vols. Washington, DC: Government Printing Office, 1986.
Avedon, Richard. *Versace: The Naked and the Dressed*. New York: Random House, 1998.
Bacon, James. *Made in Hollywood*. New York: Warner Books, 1977.
Bacon-Smith, Camille. *Enterprising Women: Television Fandom and the Creation of Popular Myth*. Philadelphia: University of Pennsylvania Press, 1992.
———. "Spock among the Women." *New York Times Book Review*, 16 November 1986, pp. 1, 26, 28.
Bad Attitude. P.O. Box 390110, Cambridge, MA 02139.
Banes, Sally, Sheldon Frank, and Tem Horowitz. *Our National Passion: 200 Years of Sex in America*. Chicago: Follett, 1976.
Banner, Lois W. *American Beauty*. Chicago: University of Chicago Press, 1983.

Banta, Martha. *Imaging American Women: Idea and Ideals in Cultural History.* New York: Columbia University Press, 1987.

Benedict, Helen. *Virgin or Vamp: How the Press Covers Sex Crimes.* New York: Oxford, 1992.

Bernstein, I. H., et al. "Effect of Attitudes toward Pornography upon Male Judgements of Female Attractiveness." *Perception and Psychophysics,* 39:4 (April 1986): 287–293.

Bessie, Simon Michael. *Jazz Journalism: The Story of the Tabloid Newspapers.* New York: Dutton, 1938.

Betrock, Alan. *Pin-Up Mania: The Golden Age of Men's Magazines (1950–1967).* Brooklyn, NY: Shake Books, 1996.

———. *Unseen America: The Greatest Cult Exploitation Magazines, 1950–1966;* rev. of *One Hundred Greatest Cult Exploitation Magazines, 1950–1965.* Brooklyn, NY: Shake Books, 1990.

Betrock, Alan, and Hillard Schneider. *The Personality Index to Hollywood Scandal Magazines, 1952–1966.* Brooklyn, NY: Shake Books, 1990.

Bird, S. Elizabeth. *For Enquiring Minds: A Cultural Study of Supermarket Tabloids.* Knoxville: University of Tennessee Press, 1992.

Black, Bob. *Beneath the Underground.* Portland, OR: Feral House, 1994.

Blair, Karin. "Sex and *Star Trek.*" *Science Fiction Studies,* 10 (1983): 292–297.

Blake, Rebecca. *Forbidden Dreams.* New York: Quartet, 1984.

Block, A. "Scanning the 'Zine Scene: Rumblings from the New Gay Underground." *Advocate,* no. 543 (1990): 54–55.

Block, Susan. *Advertising for Love: How to Play the Personals.* New York: Quill, 1984.

Botsky, Aaron. "An Emblem of Crisis Makes the World See the Body Anew." *New York Times,* 30 November 1997, sec. 2, pp. 1, 44.

Boulware, Jack. *Sex American Style: An Illustrated Romp through the Golden Age of Heterosexuality.* Venice, CA: Feral House, 1997.

Brachman, Jacob. "The Underground Press." *Playboy,* 14 (August 1967): 83.

Bradbury, Ray, ed. *The Art of Playboy.* New York: Van der Marck, 1985.

Brady, Frank. *Hefner.* New York: Macmillan, 1974.

Brady, John. "Nude Journalism." *Journal of Popular Culture,* 9:1 (Summer 1975): 153–163.

Brookes, Rosetta. "The Double-Page Spread: Helmut Newton, Guy Bourdin and Deborah Turbeville." *Chic Thrills,* ed. Juliet Ash and Elizabeth Wilson. Berkeley: University of California Press, 1993, pp. 17–24.

Bunn, Austin. "The X-rated Files." *Brill's Content,* 3:4 (May 2000): 96–99.

Burstyn, Varda. "Anatomy of a Moral Panic." *FUSE,* 8 (Summer 1984): 29–38.

Byer, Stephen. *Hefner's Going to Kill Me When He Reads This.* Chicago: Allen-Bennett, 1972.

Caputi, Jane E. *The Age of Sex Crime.* Bowling Green, OH: Bowling Green State University Press, 1987.

———. "The Fetishes of Sex-Crime." *Objects of Special Devotion: Fetishes and Fetishism in Popular Culture.* Bowling Green, OH: Bowling Green State University Press, 1982, pp. 4–20.

Cawthorne, Nigel. *Sex Lives of the U.S. Presidents.* New York: Prion, 1996.

Chapple, Steve, and David Talbot. *Burning Desires: Sex in America, a Report from the Field.* New York: Signet, 1990.

Chepesiuk, Ron. "Paul Krassner, Father of the Underground Press." *Sixties Radicals, Then and Now: Candid Conversations with Those Who Shaped the Era*. Jefferson, NC: MacFarland, 1995, pp. 25–40.

Churcher, Sharon. "She's No Barbara Bush." *Penthouse*, 23:7 (March 1992): 22–23.

Clay, Steven, and Rodney Phillips. *A Secret Location on the Lower East Side: Adventures in Writing 1960–1980*. New York: Granary Books/New York Public Library, 1998.

Cohen, Lester. *The New York Daily Graphic: The World's Zaniest Newspaper*. Philadelphia: Chilton, 1964.

Cohen, Patricia Cline. "Editors and Publishers of the Sporting 'Flash' Press." "The 'Sporting' Press in 1840s New York: Three Interpretations." Conference of the American Studies Association/Canadian Association of American Studies, Montreal, 29 October 1999.

Cohen, Roger. "Ms. Playboy." *New York Times Magazine*, 9 June 1991, pp. 32, 55–57, 84. *The Complete Reprint of Physique Pictorial, 1951–1990*. 3 vols. Berlin: Benedikt Taschen, 1997.

Conlin, Joseph R., ed. *The American Radical Press, 1880–1960*. 2 vols. Westport, CT: Greenwood Press, 1974.

Cooper, Emmanuel. *The Sexual Perspective: Homosexuality and Art in the Last 100 Years in the West*. London: Routledge and Kegan Paul, 1986.

Corkery, P. J. "*Enquirer*: An Eyewitness Account." *Rolling Stone*, 11 June 1981, pp. 19–21, 62.

Courtney, Alice E., and Thomas W. Whipple. *Sex Stereotyping in Advertising*. Lexington, MA: Lexington Books, 1983.

Cropsey, Charles, and Jill Browner. *The Shameless Nude*. Topanga, CA: Elysium Growth, 1963; rev. ed., *The Shameless Nude: A Selection of Articles and Stories from Nude Living* (1991).

Csicsery, George Paul. *The Sex Industry*. New York: NAL, 1973.

Davis, L. J. "Double Trouble." *Penthouse*, 22:12 (August 1991): 30–32, 34, 36, 41, 54.

"Debbie Does Swaggart." *Penthouse*, 19:11 (July 1988): 107–122.

Details. Los Angeles, 1989–.

Dietz, Elliott P., Bruce Harry, and Robert Hazelwood. "Detective Magazines: Pornography for the Sexual Sadist?" *Journal of Forensic Sciences*, 31:1 (January 1986): 197–211.

Dines, Gail. " 'I Buy It for the Articles': *Playboy* Magazine and the Sexualization of Consumerism." *Gender, Race and Class in Media: A Text-Reader*, ed. Gail Dines and Jean M. Humez. Thousand Oaks, CA: Sage, 1995, pp. 254–262.

Ditzion, Sidney. *Marriage, Morals, and Sex in America: A History of Ideas*. New York: Bookman Associates, 1953.

Domanick, Joe. "Maybe There Is a God." *Playboy*, 37:8 (August 1990): 110–111.

Douglas, Jason. *The Age of Perversion: A Close-Up View of Sexuality in Our Permissive Society*. London: Canova Press, 1969.

Drop, Mark. *Dateline Hollywood: Sins and Scandals of Yesterday and Today*. New York: Friedman/Fairfax, 1994.

Duncombe, Stephen. *Notes from Underground: Zines and the Politics of Alternative Culture*. New York: Verso, 1997.

Edgren, Gretchen, ed. *The Playboy Book: Forty Years, the Complete Pictorial History*. Santa Monica, CA: General Publishing Corp., 1994.

Ehrenreich, Barbara. "*Playboy* Joins the Battle of the Sexes." *The Hearts of Men.* New York: Anchor, 1983, pp. 42–51.

EIDOS [Everyone Is Doing Outrageous Sex]. P.O. Box 96, Boston 02137.

Eileen Ford Agency. *Eileen Ford Models.* New York: Eileen Ford, 1992.

Elliott, Stuart. "Has Madison Avenue Gone Too Far?" *New York Times,* national ed., 15 December 1991, sec. 3, pp. 1, 6.

Ellis, Albert. *The Folklore of Sex,* aka *Sex Beliefs and Customs.* New York: Charles Boni, 1951; and *The Folklore of Sex.* New York: Grove Press, 1961.

Ernst, Robert. *Weakness Is a Crime: The Life of Bernarr Macfadden.* Syracuse, NY: Syracuse University Press, 1990.

Erotic Fiction Quarterly: A Journal of Erotic and Other Sexual Fiction. San Francisco, 1985.

Ewen, Stuart, and Elizabeth Ewen. *Channels of Desire: Mass Images and the Shaping of American Consciousness.* New York: McGraw-Hill, 1982.

Exner, Judith Campbell, as told to Ovid Demaris. *My Story.* New York: Grove Press, 1977.

Exotique. New York: Burmel Publications, 1957–1963; 36 issues reprinted as *Exotique: A New Magazine of the Bizarre and Unusual.* 3 vols. Cologne: Benedikt Taschen, 1998.

Factsheet Five. 1982–1991, 6 Arizona Avenue, Rensselaer, NY 12144; 1992–present, Box 170099, San Francisco 94117; e-mail: jerod23@well.sf.ca.us.

Faderman, Lillian. *Odd Girls and Twilight Lovers: A History of Lesbian Life in Twentieth-Century America.* New York: Columbia University Press, 1991.

———. *Surpassing the Love of Men: Romantic Friendship and Love between Women from the Renaissance to the Present.* New York: Morrow, 1981.

"Fanfic." http://www.slate.msn.com/Features/fanfic/fanfic.asp.

"Fashion with Passion." *Penthouse,* 22:8 (April 1991): 38–45.

Fenster, Mark. "Queer Punk Fanzines: Identity, Community, and the Articulation of Homosexuality." *Journal of Communication Inquiry,* 17:1 (1993): 73–94.

Ferreira, James M. "Fetishes and Fetishism in Girlie Magazines." *Objects of Special Devotion: Fetishes and Fetishism in Popular Culture.* Bowling Green, OH: Bowling Green State University Press, 1982, pp. 33–44.

Finch, Casey. "Two of a Kind." *Artforum,* 30 (February 1992): 91–94.

Flowers, Gennifer. *Passion and Betrayal.* Del Mar, CA: Emery Dalton Books, 1995.

Flynt, Larry. *An Unseemly Man: My Life as Pornographer, Pundit and Social Outcast.* New York: Penguin/Dove, 1996.

Forcade, Thomas King, comp. *Underground Press Anthology.* New York: Ace Books, 1972.

Ford, Paul Leicester. *Who Was the Mother of Franklin's Son?* New Rochelle, NY: Walpole Printing Office, 1932.

Forman, Milos, dir. *The People vs. Larry Flynt.* Sony Pictures, 1996.

Foxman, Sherri. *Classified Love: A Guide to the Personals.* New York: McGraw-Hill, 1982.

Frankl, George. *The Failure of the Sexual Revolution.* London: Kahn and Averill, 1974.

Freedman, Estelle B. " 'Uncontrolled Desires': The Response to the Sexual Psychopath." *Passion and Power: Sexuality in History,* ed. Kathy Peiss and Christina Simmons, with Robert A. Padgug. Philadelphia: Temple University Press, 1989, pp. 199–225.

Freeman, Gillian. *The Undergrowth of Literature*. London: Nelson and Sons, 1967; rpt. London: Panther, 1969.

Frighten the Horses: A Journal of the Sexual Revolution. 41 Sutter Street #1108, San Francisco 94104.

Gabler, Neal. *Winchell: Gossip, Power and the Culture of Celebrity*. New York: Knopf, 1994.

Gabor, Mark. *The Illustrated History of Girlie Magazines*. New York: Harmony, 1984.

Gaines, Jane. "War, Women, and Lipstick: Fan Magazines in the Forties." *Heresies*, 5: 2 (issue 18; 1984): 42–47.

Gallagher, Neil. *How to Stop the Porno Plague*. Minneapolis: Bethany Fellowship, 1977.

Gamelin, Douglas H., ed. *The Tijuana Bible Reader*. San Diego: Greenleaf, 1969.

Garment, Suzanne. *Scandal: The Culture of Mistrust in American Politics*. New York: Doubleday/Anchor, 1992.

Gates, Henry Louis, Jr. "American Notes: The Naked Republic." *New Yorker*, 25 August and 1 September 1997, pp. 114–118, 120–123.

Gates, Katharine. *Deviant Desires: Incredibly Strange Sex*. New York: Juno Books, 2000.

Gauvreau, Emile. *Hot News*. New York: Macauley, 1931.

Gerbner, George. "The Social Role of the Confession Magazine." *Social Problems*, 5 (1958): 29–40.

Gertzman, Jay A. *Bookleggers and Smuthounds: The Trade in Erotica. 1920–1940*. Philadelphia: University of Pennsylvania Press, 1999.

Gilfoyle, Timothy J. *City of Eros: New York City, Prostitution, and the Commercialization of Sex, 1790–1920*. New York: Norton, 1992.

———. "Politics and 'Sporting Men': The Birth of Pornography in the U.S." "The 'Sporting' Press in 1840s New York: Three Interpretations." Conference of the American Studies Association/Canadian Association of American Studies, Montreal, 29 October 1999.

Ginzburg, Ralph. "Eros on Trial." *Fact*, 2:3 (May–June 1965).

———. "Playboy Interview: Ralph Ginzburg." *Playboy*, 13:7 (July 1966): 47–48, 50, 52–54, 120, 122, 124.

———, ed. *Avant-Garde*. New York, 1968–1971.

———. *Eros*. New York, 1962–1963.

Girljock. Rox-a-Tronic, 2060 Third Street, Berkeley, CA 94710.

Glaviano, Marco. *Sirens*. New York: Warner Books/Callaway, 1997.

Glessing, Robert J. *The Underground Press in America*. Bloomington: Indiana University Press, 1970.

Goffman, Erving. *Gender Advertisements*. New York: Harper, 1979.

Goldberg, Joe. *The Big Bunny*. New York: Ballantine, 1967.

Goldman, Robert. *Reading Ads Socially*. New York: Routledge, 1992.

Goldstein, Al. "Playboy Interview: Al Goldstein." *Playboy*, 21:10 (October 1974): 63–64, 68, 70, 72, 74, 76, 212–216, 218.

Goldstein, Al, and Jim Buckley, eds. *The Screw Reader*. New York: Lyle Stuart, 1971.

Goodstone, Tony. *The Pulps: Fifty Years of American Popular Culture*. New York: Chelsea House, 1970.

Gordon, George N. *Erotic Communications: Studies in Sex, Sin and Censorship*. New York: Hastings House, 1980.

Goulart, Ron. *Cheap Thrills: An Informal History of the Pulp Magazines*. New York: Arlington House, 1972.

Govoni, Steve. "Now It Can Be Told." *American Film*, 15 (February 1990): 28–33, 43.

Grier, Barbara, and Coletta Reid, eds. *Lesbian Lives: Biographies of Women from "The Ladder."* Oakland, CA: Diana Press, 1976.

Grimes, William. "Lurid! Licentious! Collectible! The Flip Side of the 1940's and 50's." *New York Times*, 25 July 1994, p. B3.

Gross, Amy. "Woman as Sex Object: 'I'm Fragile, I'm Female, I Confess': Life as It's Lived (More or Less) in the Confession Magazines." *Mademoiselle*, 75:3 (July 1972): 128–129, 133–134.

Gross, Michael. *Model: The Ugly Business of Beautiful Women.* New York: Warner, 1995.

Guccione, Bob. "Pornography and the First Amendment." Audiocassette no. 03772. New York: Encyclopedia Americana/CBS News Audio Resource Library, 1977.

Hall, Dennis R. "A Note on the Erotic Imagination: *Hustler* as a Secondary Carrier of Working-Class Consciousness." *Journal of Popular Culture*, 15:4 (1982): 150–156.

Handelman, David. "All the Nudes Fit to Print." *Details* (February 1997): 114, 116.

Hardy, Simon. *"The Reader, the Author, His Discursive Woman and Her Lover: A Cyclical Study of the Social Effects Constituted by 'Top-Shelf' Magazines."* Ph.D. dissertation, University of Essex (U.K.), 1995; rpt. *The Reader, The Author, His Woman and Her Lover.* London: Cassell, 1998.

Harris, Sarah. *The Puritan Jungle: America's Sexual Underground.* New York: Putnam, 1969.

Hastings, Deborah. "The Unhappy Hustler." *Charlotte (North Carolina) News and Observer*, 17 August 1995, p. 3E.

Hebditch, David, and Nick Anning. *Porn Gold: Inside the Pornography Business.* Boston: Faber, 1988.

Hefner, Hugh M. "On Playboys and Bunnies." *Up against the Wall, Mother,* ed. Elsie Adams and Mary Louise Briscoe. Beverly Hills, CA: Glencoe Press, 1971, pp. 38–39.

Heidenry, John. *What Wild Ecstasy: The Rise and Fall of the Sexual Revolution.* New York: Simon and Schuster, 1997.

Hellmann, Harald. *The Best of American Girlie Magazines.* Cologne: Benedikt Taschen, 1997.

Hershey, Harold B. *Pulpwood Editor.* New York: Frederick A. Stokes, 1977.

Hester, George M. *The Classic Nude.* Garden City, NY: Amphoto, 1973.

Hoberman, J. "Working-Class Heroes." *Village Voice*, 31 December 1996, p. 59.

Hochswender, Woody. "Pins & Needles." *Harper's Bazaar*, September 1992, p. 411.

Hoddeson, Bob. *The Porn People: A First-Person Documentary Report.* Watertown, MA: American Publishing Co., 1974.

Holland, Patricia, Jo Spence, and Simon Watney, eds. *Photography/Politics: Two.* London: Comedia/Methuen, 1987.

Holy Titclamps. P.O. Box 591257, San Francisco 94159–1275.

Hooven, F. Valentine. *Beefcake: The Muscle Magazines of America, 1950–1970.* Berlin: Benedikt Taschen Verlag, 1995.

Horowitz, Helen Lefkowitz. "Understanding 'Obscenity' in the 1840s." "The 'Sporting' Press in 1840s New York: Three Interpretations." Conference of the American Studies Association/Canadian Association of American Studies, Montreal, 29 October 1999.

Howard, Mel, and Thomas King Forcade, comps. *Underground Reader*. New York: Plume, 1972.

Hugh Hefner: Once upon a Time. Los Angeles: An IRS Release of a Lynch/Frost Production, directed by Robert Heath, 1992.

Hunt, William R. *Body Love: The Amazing Career of Bernarr Macfadden*. Bowling Green, OH: Bowling Green State University Popular Press, 1989.

Ide, Arthur Frederick. *Evangelical Terrorism: Censorship, Falwell, Robertson, and the Seamy Side of Christian Fundamentalism*. Irving, TX: Scholars Books, 1986.

Illouz, Eva. "Reason within Passion: Love in Women's Magazines." *Critical Studies in Mass Communication*, 8:3 (September 1991): 231–248.

Iverson, William. *The Pious Pornographers*. New York: William Morrow, 1963.

———. "The Pious Pornographers Revisited." *Playboy*, 11:9 (September 1964): 92–94, 96, 190–199; 11:10 (October 1964): 110–112, 161–165.

Jackson, Ed, and Stan Persky, eds. *Flaunting It: A Decade of Gay Journalism from the Body Politic*. Vancouver: New Star Books, 1982.

Jenkins, Henry. "*Star Trek* Rerun, Reread, Rewritten: Fan Writing as Textual Poaching." *Critical Studies in Mass Communication*, 5:2 (1988): 85–107.

———. *Textual Poaching: Television Fans and Participatory Culture*. New York: Routledge, 1992.

Jewell, Patrick. *Vice Art: An Anthology of London's Prostitute Cards*. London: Turnaround Distributors, 1994.

Jordan, Pat. "The Creep, the Cop, His Wife, and Her Lovers." *Playboy*, 39:3 (March 1992): 66–70, 80, 162–165.

———. "Hello. This Is Alan Smith of the *National Enquirer . . .*" *New York Times Magazine*, 25 June 1995, pp. 42–46.

———. "The Trash Collector." *Details*, December 1995, pp. 148–153, 199–200.

Kaite, Berkeley. "The Pornographic Body Double: Transgression Is the Law." *Body Invaders: Panic Sex in America*, ed by Arthur Kroker and Marilouise Kroker. Montreal: New World Perspectives, 1987, pp. 150–168.

Kaplan, Michael. "Editing by Desire." *Folio: The Magazine for Magazine Management*, 25:16 (1 November 1996): 50–53.

Kelly, Valerie. *How to Write Erotica for Fun and Profit*. New York: Harmony Books, 1986.

Kelm, Rebecca Sturm. "The Lack of Access to Back Issues of the Weekly Tabloids: Does It Matter?" *Journal of Popular Culture*, 23 (Spring 1990): 45–50.

Kennedy, Philippa. "A Marriage Made in Sleaze." *Bangkok Post*, 1 November 1994, p. 37.

Kepner, Jim. *Rough News—Daring Views: 1950s Pioneer Gay Press Journalism*. Binghamton, NY: Haworth Press, 1997.

Key, Wilson Bryan. *The Clam-Plate Orgy: and Other Subliminals the Media Use to Manipulate Your Behavior*. Englewood Cliffs, NJ: Prentice-Hall, 1980.

———. *Media Sexploitation*. New York: NAL, 1977.

———. *Subliminal Seduction: Ad Media's Manipulation of a Not So Innocent America*. New York: NAL, 1974.

Kilbourne, Jean, director. *Killing Us Softly III*. Northampton, MA: Media Education Foundation, 1999.

Kipnis, Laura. *Bound and Gagged: Pornography and the Politics of Fantasy in America*. New York: Grove Press, 1996.

———. "It's a Wonderful Life." *Village Voice*, 31 December 1996, pp. 37–39.

———. "(Male) Desire and (Female) Disgust: Reading *Hustler*." *Cultural Studies*, ed. Lawrence Grossberg, Cary Nelson, and Paula A. Treichler. New York: Routledge, 1992, pp. 373–391; rpt. in Kipnis's *Ecstasy Unlimited: On Sex, Capital, Gender, and Aesthetics*. Minneapolis: University of Minnesota Press, 1993, pp. 219–242.

———. "She-Male Fantasies and the Aesthetics of Pornography." *Dirty Looks: Women, Pornography, Power*, ed. Pamela Church Gibson and Roma Gibson. London: British Film Institute, 1993, pp. 124–143.

Kirkendall, Lester A., Gina Allen, Albert Ellis, and Helen Colton. "Sex Magazines and Feminism." *Humanist*, 38 (November–December 1978): 44–51.

Kirkendall, Lester A., and Robert N. Whitehurst, eds. *The New Sexual Revolution*. New York: Donald W. Brown, 1971.

Kittay, Eva Feder. "Pornography and the Erotics of Domination." *Beyond Domination: New Perspectives on Women and Philosophy*, ed. Carol C. Gould. Totowa, NJ: Rowman and Allanheld, 1984, pp. 145–174.

Klein, Jeffrey. "Born Again Porn." *Mother Jones* (February–March 1978): 12–23.

Kohn, George C. *Encyclopedia of American Scandal*. New York: Facts on File, 1991.

Krajicek, David J. *Scooped! Mass Media Miss Real Story on Crime While Chasing Sex, Sleaze, and Celebrities*. New York: Columbia University Press, 1998.

Kramer, Mark. "The Mastur Race." *Gauntlet*, 5 (1993): 136–139.

Krassner, Paul. *Confessions of a Raving, Unconfined Nut: Misadventures in the Counterculture*. New York: Simon and Schuster, 1993.

———. *How a Satirical Editor Became a Yippie Conspirator in Ten Easy Years*. New York: Putnam, [1971].

Lamb, Patricia F., and Diana Veith. "Romantic Myth, Transcendence, and *Star Trek* Zines." *Erotic Universe: Sexuality and Fantastic Literature*, ed. Donald Palumbo. Westport, CT: Greenwood Press, 1986, pp. 235–256.

Laner, Mary Riege, and G. W. Levi Kamel. "Media Mating I: Newspaper 'Personals' Ads of Homosexual Men." *Journal of Homosexuality*, 3 (1977): 141–150.

Lange, Ed, and Stan Sohler, eds. *Nudist Magazines of the 50s and 60s*. 2 vols. Topanga, CA: Elysium Growth, 1992.

Leamer, Laurence. *The Paper Revolutionaries: The Rise of the Underground Press*. New York: Simon and Schuster, 1972.

Lears, Jackson. *Fables of Abundance: A Cultural History of Advertising in America*. New York: Basic Books, 1994.

Lehnert, Eileen, and Mary J. Perpich. "An Attitude Segmentation Study of Supermarket Tabloid Readers." *Journalism Quarterly*, 59 (Spring 1982): 104–111.

Leigh, Michael. *The Velvet Underground*. New York: MacFadden, 1966.

Levin, Martin, ed. *Hollywood and the Great Fan Magazines*. New York: Arbor House, 1970.

Lewis, Timothy. *Physique: A Pictorial History of the Athletic Model Guild*. San Francisco: Gay Sunshine Press, 1983.

Leyland, Winston, ed. *Gay Roots: Twenty Years of Gay Sunshine* and *Gay Roots: An Anthology of Gay History, Sex, Politics, and Culture, Volume 2*. San Francisco: Gay Sunshine Press, 1991, 1993.

Libido: The Journal of Sex and Sensibility. P.O. Box 146721, Chicago 60614.

Lo Duca, Guiseppe. *Technique de L'erotisme*. Paris: Pauvert, 1963.

Lukas, J. Anthony. "The 'Alternative Life-Style' of Playboys and Playmates." *New York Times Magazine*, 11 June 1972, pp. 7, 75.

Lull, James, and Stephen Hinerman, eds. *Media Scandals*. New York: Columbia University Press, 1997.

Lumby, Malcolm E. "Men Who Advertise for Sex." *Journal of Homosexuality*, 4 (1978): 63–68.

Lynd, Robert S., and Helen M. Lynd. *Middletown: A Study in Contemporary American Culture*. New York: Harcourt, Brace, 1929.

MacDonald, Kenneth. "Should Newspapers Be Policing Sex?" *Columbia Journalism Review*, 17:1 (May–June 1978): 15–16.

MacDougall, Curtis D. *News Pictures Fit to Print . . . Or Are They?* Stillwater, OK: Journalistic Services, 1971.

MacKinnon, Catharine A. "More than Simply a Magazine: *Playboy*'s Money." *Feminism Unmodified: Discourses on Life and Law*. Cambridge: Harvard University Press, 1987, pp. 134–145.

Malamuth, N. M., and R. D. McIlwraith. "Fantasies and Exposure to Sexually Explicit Magazines." *Communication Research*, 15:6 (December 1988): 753–771.

Malamuth, N. M., and Barry Spinner. "A Longitudinal Content Analysis of Sexual Violence in Best-Selling Erotica Magazines." *Journal of Sex Research*, 16 (1980): 226–237.

"A Man's Guide to Women's Magazines." *Playboy*, 35:8 (August 1988): 104–109.

Margolis, H. E., and Paul Rubenstein. *The Groupsex Tapes*. New York: McKay, 1971.

Martignette, C. G., and L. K. Meisel. *The Best of American Girlie Magazines*. Cologne: Benedikt Taschen, 1998.

Martin, Douglas. "Family Man. No Mansion. This Guy Really Runs Playboy?" *New York Times*, 22 November 1992, p. F10.

Massé, M. A., and K. Rosenblum. "Male and Female Created They Them: The Depiction of Gender in the Advertising of Traditional Women's and Men's Magazines." *Women's Studies International Forum*, 11 (1988): 127–144.

McCabe, Edward A. "Sex in Advertising." *Playboy*, 39:8 (August 1992): 76–83.

McDonough, Kevin. *A Tabloid History of the World*. New York: Hyperion, 1998.

McMahon, Katharine. "The *Cosmopolitan* Ideology and the Management of Desire." *Journal of Sex Research*, 27 (1990): 381–396.

McRobbie, Angela. "*More!*: New Sexualities in Girls' and Women's Magazines." *Cultural Studies and Communications*, ed. James Curran, David Morley, and Valerie Walkerdine. New York: Arnold/St. Martin's, 1996, pp. 172–194.

Melville, Arabella. "The Dirty Doctor: A (Brief) Career in Porno." *Tales from the Clit: A Female Experience of Pornography*, ed. Cherie Matrix. San Francisco: AK Press, 1996, pp. 1–11.

Merrill, Hugh. *ESKY: The Early Years at Esquire*. New Brunswick, NJ: Rutgers University Press, 1995.

Michelson, Peter. *The Aesthetics of Pornography*. New York: Herder and Herder, 1971.

———. "The Pleasures of Commodity, or How to Make the World Safe for Pornography." *Mass Media and Mass Man*, ed. Alan Casty. 2d ed. New York: Holt, Rinehart, and Winston, 1973, pp. 122–131.

Miller, Russell. *Bunny: The Real Story of "Playboy."* New York: NAL-Dutton, 1986.

The Millionaire Pornographers: Adam Special Report 12. Los Angeles: Knight Publishing, February 1977.

Millum, Trevor. *Images of Woman: Advertising in Women's Magazines*. Totowa, NJ: Rowman and Littlefield, 1975.

Milton, John. *$ex $ense*. New York: Milky Way Productions, 1974–1982.

Mindich, Jeremy. "Soap Box Samurai." *Details*, 12:3 (August 1993): 97–101.

Morgan, Robin. "Goodbye to All That." *The American Sisterhood*, ed. Wendy Martin. New York: Harper and Row, 1972.

Morrison, B. J., and R. C. Sherman. "Who Responds to Sex in Advertising?" *Journal of Advertising Research*, 12:2 (1972): 15–19.

Mott, Frank Luther. *A History of American Magazines*. 5 vols. Cambridge: Harvard University Press, 1930–1968.

Mullins, Greg. "Nudes, Prudes, and Pigmies: The Desirability of Disavowal in *Physical Culture*." *Discourse*, 15:1 (Fall 1992): 27–48.

Musto, Michael. "Where the Queers Are." *Village Voice*, 22 July 1991, p. 29.

Myers, Kathy. "Fashion 'n' Passion." *Screen*, 223:3/4 (September/October 1982): 89–97.

New England Watch and Ward Society. *Annual Reports*. Boston: New England Watch and Ward Society, 1905–1939.

Newton, Helmut. *Big Nudes*. New York: Xavier Moreau, 1982.

———. *Sleepless Nights*. New York: Xavier Moreau, 1978.

———. *White Women*. New York: Stonehill, 1976.

———. *World without Men*. New York: Xavier Moreau, 1984.

New York Society for the Suppression of Vice. *Annual Reports*. New York: New York Society for the Suppression of Vice, 1874–1940.

Nixon, Sean. *Hard Looks: Masculinities, Spectatorship, and Contemporary Consumption*. New York: St. Martin's, 1996.

Nobile, Philip. "Inside *Screw*," the New Eroticism: Theories, Vogues, Canons*, ed. Philip Nobile. New York: Random House, 1970, pp. 161–164.

On Our Blacks: Entertainment for the Adventurous Lesbian. 526 Castro Street, San Francisco 94114.

Otto, H. A. "Sex and Violence on the American Newsstand." *Journalism Quarterly*, 40 (1963): 19–26.

Out/Look: The National Lesbian and Gay Quarterly. New York, 1988–.

Out/Week: The Lesbian and Gay News Magazine. New York, 1989–.

Owens, Tuppy. *Politico Frou-Frou: Pornographic Art as Political Protest*. New York: Cassell, 1996.

Packard, Vance. *The Hidden Persuaders*. New York: McKay, 1957.

Palumbo, Donald, ed. *Erotic Universe: Sexuality and Fantastic Literature*. Westport, CT: Greenwood, 1986.

Parfrey, Adam, ed. *Apocalypse Culture*. Portland, OR: Feral House, 1987.

Pearce, Frank. "How to Be Immoral and Ill, Pathetic and Dangerous, All at the Same Time: Mass Media and Homosexuality." *The Manufacture of News*, ed. Stanley Cohen and Jack Young. London: Constable, 1973, pp. 284–301.

Peck, Abe. *Uncovering the Sixties: The Life and Times of the Underground Press*. New York: Pantheon, 1985.

Penley, Constance. "Feminism, Psychoanalysis, and the Study of Popular Culture." *Cultural Studies*, ed. Lawrence Grossberg, Cary Nelson, and Paula A. Treichler. New York: Routledge, 1992, pp. 479–500.

Peterson, Theodore. *Magazines in the Twentieth Century*. Urbana: University of Illinois Press, 1964.

Plummer, Ken. *Telling Sexual Stories*. New York: Routledge, 1995.

P.O.N.Y. X-Press. 25 West 45th Street, New York City 10036.

Poppin' Zits! 1800 Market Street, San Francisco 94102–6227.

President's Commission on Obscenity and Pornography. *Report of the Commission on Obscenity and Pornography*. Washington, D.C.: Government Printing Office, 1970; see also *The Illustrated Presidential Report of the Commission on Obscenity and Pornography*. San Diego: Greenleaf Classics, 1970; see also *The Report of the Commission on Obscenity and Pornography*. New York: Bantam, 1970.

————. *Technical Report of the Commission on Obscenity and Pornography*. 9 vols. Washington, DC: Government Printing Office, 1971–1972.

PURE. 9171 Wilshire Blvd, Beverly Hills, CA 90210.

Rachman, S. "Sexual Fetishism: An Experimental Analogue." *Psychological Record*, 16: 3 (1966): 293–296.

Rachman, S., and R. J. Hodgson. "Experimentally-Induced 'Sexual Fetishism': Replication and Development." *Psychological Record*, 18:1 (1998): 25–27.

Rawlings, John. *100 Studies of the Figure*. New York: Crowell, 1951.

Reeves, Richard. *What the People Know: Freedom and the Press*. Cambridge:Harvard University Press, 1998.

Reichert, Tom, Jacqueline Lambiase, Susan Morgan, Meta Carstarphen, and Susan Zavoina, reporting in "Cheesecake and Beefcake: No Matter How You Slice It, Sexual Explicitness in Advertising Continues to Increase." *Journalism and Mass Communication Quarterly*, 76:1 (Spring 1999): 7–20.

Reisman, Judith A. *"Soft Porn" Plays Hardball: Its Tragic Effects on Women, Children and the Family*. Lafayette, LA: Huntington House, 1991.

Ressner, J. "Enquiring Minds: A Walk on the Sleazy Side with the New Breed of Tabloid Reporters." *Rolling Stone*, 30 June 1988, pp. 53–56, 64.

Rips, Geoffrey. *The Campaign Against the Underground Press*, ed. Anne Janowitz and Nancy J. Peters. San Francisco: City Lights, 1981.

Robins, Natalie. *Alien Ink: The FBI's War on Freedom of Expression*. New York: Morrow, 1992.

Rochlin, Margy. "20 Questions: Helmut Newton." *Playboy*, 39:12 (December 1992): 117, 223–224.

Romenesko, James. "The Zine Explosion." *American Journalism Review*, 15:3 (April 1993): 39–43.

Root, Jane. *Pictures of Women*. Boston: Pandora Press, 1984.

Rose, Al. *Storyville, New Orleans: Being an Authentic, Illustrated Account of the Notorious Red-Light District*. University Station: University of Alabama Press, 1974.

Ross, Shelley. *Fall from Grace: Sex, Scandal and Corruption in American Politics, 1702–1987*. New York: Ballantine, 1988.

Rossi, Lee D. "The Whore vs. the Girl-Next-Door: Stereotypes of Women in *Playboy, Penthouse*, and *Oui*." *Journal of Popular Culture*, 9 (Summer 1975): 90–94.

Roth, Samuel, ed. *American Aphrodite*. New York: Samuel Roth, 1951–1955.

————. *Beau: The Man's Magazine*. New York: Two Worlds Publishing Company, 1924.

————. *Good Times: A Review of the World of Pleasure*. New York: Picadilly Books, 1954–1956.

————. *Two Worlds Monthly: Devoted to the Increase of the Gaiety of Nations*. New York: Two Worlds Publishing Company, 1926–1927.

Rudnitsky, Howard. "How Gene Pope Made Millions in the Newspaper Business." *Forbes*, 16 October 1978, pp. 77–78.

Rugoff, Milton. *Prudery and Passion: Sexuality in Victorian America*. New York: Putnam, 1971.

Russ, Joanna. "Pornography by Women for Women, with Love." *Magic Mommas: Trembling Sisters, Puritans and Perverts: Feminist Essays*. Trumansburg, NY: Crossing Press, 1985, 79–99.

Sachs, Walker. "Sex Magazines: No Business like Show Business." *Business and Society Review*, Winter 1976–1977, pp. 21–25.

Scanlon, Jennifer. *Inarticulate Longings: The Ladies' Home Journal, Gender, and the Promises of Consumer Culture*. New York: Routledge, 1995.

Schramm, Wilbur. "Content Analysis of the World of Confession Magazines." *Popular Conceptions of Mental Health*, ed. J. Nunnall. New York: Holt, Rinehart, and Winston, 1961, pp. 297–307.

Schroeder, F. E. H. "*National Enquirer* Is National Fetish! The Untold Story!" *Objects of Special Devotion: Fetishes and Fetishism in Popular Culture*, ed. Ray B. Browne. Bowling Green, OH: Bowling Green State University Popular Press, 1982, pp. 168–181.

Schroeder, Theodore A., comp. *Free Press Anthology*. New York: Free Speech League and Truth Seeker Publishing, 1909.

Schwarz, Henry, and Anne Balsamo. "Under the Sign of *Semiotext(e)*: The Story according to Sylvere Lotringer and Chris Kraus." *Critique*, 37:3 (Spring 1996): 205–227.

Scott, Gini Graham. *Dominant Women, Submissive Men: An Exploration in Erotic Dominance and Submission*. New York: Praeger, 1983; aka *Erotic Power: An Exploration of Dominance and Submission*. Secaucus, NJ: Citadel Press, 1983.

Scott, Janny. "For the Media, an Unsavory Story Tests Ideals and Stretches Limits." *New York Times*, 1 February 1998, pp. A1, 17.

Scott, Joseph E., and Stephen J. Cuvelier. "Sexual Violence in *Playboy* Magazine: A Longitudinal Content Analysis." *Journal of Sex Research*, 23 (November 1987): 534–539.

Screw. New York, 1969–.

Sears, Hal D. *The Sex Radicals: Free Love in Victorian America*. Lawrence: Regents Press of Kansas, 1977.

See, Carolyn. "Nude Times: 1." *New Times*, 2:4 (22 February 1974): 28–32, 35.

Seligson, Marcia. "Nude Times: 2." *New Times*, 2:4 (22 February 1974): 36–41.

Semiotext(e). New York: Columbia University, 1977–1985; Brooklyn, NY: Autonomedia, 1986–.

Semper, Idem. *The Blue Book*. New Orleans: Privately printed, 1936; see also *The Blue Book: Guide to Pleasures for Visitors to the Gay City*. N.p.: n.p., [1965?]; rpt. of 1890s edition.

Sennott, Charles M. *Broken Covenant*. New York: Simon and Schuster, 1992.

Sensoria from Censorium. 2 vols. Toronto, Ontario: Mangajin Books, 1991, 1993.

Server, Lee. *Danger Is My Business: An Illustrated History of the Fabulous Pulp Magazines. 1896–1953*. San Francisco: Chronicle, 1993.

Sexton, D. E., and P. Haberman. "Women in Magazine Advertisements." *Journal of Advertising Research*, 14:4 (1974): 41–46.

Shavelson, Lonny. *Personal Ad Portraits.* Berkeley, CA: De Novo Press, 1983.

Shepard, Charles E. *Forgiven: The Rise and Fall of Jim Bakker and the PTL Ministry.* New York: Atlantic Monthly, 1991.

Signorile, Michelangelo. "Gossip Watch." *Outweek: New York's Lesbian and Gay News Magazine,* no. 34 (18 February 1990): 47, 49.

Slippery When Wet, aka *Logomotive.* P.O. Box 3101, Berkeley, CA 94703.

Smith, Gene, and Jayne Barry Smith, eds. *The Police Gazette.* New York: Simon and Schuster, 1972.

Smith, G. H., and R. Engel. "Influence of a Female Model on Perceived Characteristics of an Automobile." *Proceedings of the 76th Annual Convention of the American Psychological Association,* 3 (1968): 681–682.

Smolla, Rodney A. *Jerry Falwell v. Larry Flynt: The First Amendment on Trial.* Champaign: University of Illinois Press, 1990.

Sonenschein, David. "Love and Sex in the Romance Magazines." *Journal of Popular Culture,* 4 (Fall 1970): 398–409.

———. "Process in the Production of Popular Culture: The Romance Magazine." *Journal of Popular Culture,* 6 (Fall 1972): 399–406.

Sonenschein, David, and Mark J. M. Ross. "Sex Information in the 'Romance' and 'Confession' Magazines." *Medical Aspects of Human Sexuality,* 5 (1971): 136–159.

Sonenschein, David, et al. "A Study of Mass Media Erotica: The 'Romance' or 'Confession' Magazine." *Technical Report of the Commission on Obscenity and Pornography.* 9 Vols. Washington, DC: Government Printing Office, 1971–1972, IX, 99–164.

Soothill, Keith, and Sylvia Walby. *Sex Crime in the News.* New York: Routledge, Chapman, and Hall, 1991.

Spector, Judith. "Science Fiction and the Sex War: A Womb of One's Own." *Gender Studies: New Directions in Feminist Criticism.* Bowling Green, OH: Bowling Green State University Press, 1986, pp. 161–183.

Spence, Gerry. *Trial by Fire: The True Story of a Woman's Ordeal at the Hands of the Law.* New York: William Morrow, 1986.

Spitzach, Carole. "The Confession Mirror: Plastic Images for Surgery." *The Hysterical Male,* ed. Arthur Kroker and Marilouise Kroker. New York: New World Perspectives, 1991, pp. 56–68.

Stahl, Jerry. "Adventures in the Sin Trade." *Village Voice,* 1 September 1975, p. 102.

Stauffer, John, and Richard Frost. "Male and Female Interest in Sexually-Oriented Magazines." *Journal of Communication,* 26:1 (Winter 1976): 25–30.

Steele, Lisa. "A Capital Idea: Gendering in the Mass Media." *Women against Censorship,* ed. Varda Burstyn. Vancouver: Douglas and McIntyre, 1985, pp. 58–78.

Steele, Valerie. "Erotic Allure." *The Idealizing Vision: The Art of Fashion Photography,* ed. Andrew Wilkes. New York: Aperture, 1991, Introduction.

Stein, Joel. "Larry Flynt, the Sequel." *Time,* 20 April 1998, p. 64.

Steinem, Gloria. "I Was a Playboy Bunny." *Outrageous Acts and Everyday Rebellions.* New York: Holt, Rinehart, and Winston, 1983, pp. 29–69.

Stephens, Mitchel. *A History of News.* London: Penguin, 1989.

Stevens, Carol. "Gutter Graphics," *Print,* 30:1 (January–February 1976): 72–73.

Stewart, Philip G. *"The New-Genre Nude: A New Fine Art Motif Derived from Nudist Magazine Photography."* Ph.D. dissertation, Ohio State University, 1986.

Stoehr, Taylor. *Free Love in America: A Documentary History*. New York: AMS Press, 1979.

Streitmatter, Roger. *Unspeakable: The Rise of the Gay and Lesbian Press in America*. Boston: Faber and Faber, 1995.

Studlar, Gaylyn. "The Perils of Pleasure: Fan Magazine Discourse as Women's Commodified Culture in the 1920s." *Wide Angle*, 13:1 (January 1991): 6–33.

Summers, Anthony. *Official and Confidential: The Secret Life of J. Edgar Hoover*. New York: Putnam, 1993.

Svetkey, Benjamin. "Here's the Beef." *Entertainment Weekly*, 214 (18 March 1994): 26, 28.

Swartz, Louis H. "Erotic Witness: The Rise and Flourishing of Genitally Explicit and Sex Act Explicit Heterosexually Oriented Photographic Magazines in the U.S., 1965–1985." *Porn 101: Eroticism, Pornography, and the First Amendment*, ed. James Elias, Veronica Diehl Elias, Vern L. Bullough, Gwen Brewer, Jeffrey J. Douglas, and Will Jarvis. Amherst, NY: Prometheus Books, 1999, pp. 414–426.

The Taste of Latex. P.O. Box 460122, San Francisco 94146.

Tavris, Carol. "Beware the Incest-Survivor Machine." *New York Times Book Review*, 3 January 1993, pp. 1, 23.

Tebbel, John. *The Media in America*. New York: New American Library, 1974.

Teller, Juergen. *Juergen Teller*, ed. Cornell Windlin. Berlin: Benedikt Taschen Verlag, 1996.

Thomas, Joe A. "(Over) Theorizing Dirty Magazines." *Journal of Sex Research*, 33:4 (1996): 333–335.

Thomas, Sari. "Gender and Social-Class Coding in Popular Photographic Erotica." *Communication Quarterly*, 34:2 (Spring 1986): 103–114.

Top Model. Paris/New York: Top Model, 1994–.

Triggs, Teal. "Framing Masculinity: Herb Ritts, Bruce Weber and the Body Perfect." *Chic Thrills*, ed. Juliet Ash and Elizabeth Wilson. Berkeley: University of California Press, 1993, pp. 25–29.

Tucher, Andie. *Froth and Scum: Truth, Beauty, Goodness, and the Ax-Murder in America's First Mass Medium*. Chapel Hill: University of North Carolina Press, 1994.

Underground Newspaper Microfilm Collection. 147 reels. Wooster, OH: Bell and Howell and the Underground Press Syndicate, 1965–1973.

Vale, V., ed. *Zines*. Vol. I. San Francisco: Re/Search, 1996.

Van Every, Edward. *Sins of America as Exposed by the Police Gazette*. New York: Stokes, 1931.

Vestergaard, Torben. *Language of Advertising*. London: Blackwell, 1985.

Viegener, Matias. "Gay Fanzines: 'There's Trouble in That Body.' " *Afterimage*, 18:5 (January 1991): 12–14.

———. "Kinky Escapes, Bedroom Techniques, Unbridled Passion and Secret Sex Codes." *Camp Grounds*, ed. David Bergman. Amherst: University of Massachusetts Press, 1993, pp. 25–36.

von Unwerth, Ellen. *Wicked*. New York: Le Neues, 1998.

Wachsberger, Ken. *Voices from the Underground: Insider Histories of the Vietnam Era Underground Press, Vol. I*. Tempe, AZ: MICA Press, 1993.

Wagner, Peter. "Pornography in the Courtroom: Trial Reports about Cases of Sexual Crimes and Delinquencies as a Genre of Eighteenth Century Erotica." *Sexuality in Eighteenth-Century Britain*, ed. Paul-Gabriel Bouce. Manchester: Manchester University Press, 1982, pp. 120–140.

———. "The Veil of Medicine and Morality: Some Pornographic Aspects of the *Onania*." *British Journal for Eighteenth-Century Studies*, 6 (1983): 179–184.

Wakefield, Dan. "An Unhurried View of Ralph Ginzburg." *Playboy*, 12:10 (October 1965): 95–96, 172–177.

Wallace, Irving, et al. *The Intimate Sex Lives of Famous People*. New York: Dell, 1982.

Ward, Robert. "Grossing Out with Publishing's Hottest Hustler." *New Times*, 9 January 1976, pp. 11–13.

Wayne, George. *Male Super Models: The Men of Boss Models*. New York: Distributed Art Publishers, 1996.

Weber, Bruce. "The Obsessive Eye of Bruce Weber." *Playboy*, 39:3 (March 1992): 72–79, 146.

Weinberg, Thomas, and G. W. Levi Kamel, eds. *S & M: Studies in Sadomasochism*. Buffalo, NY: Prometheus Books, 1983.

Wertham, Frederick. *The World of Fanzines: A Special Form of Communication*. Carbondale: Southern Illinois University Press, 1973.

Wexler, Neil. "The Master of Leg Art." *Gallery*, 22:9 (September 1994): 36.

Weyr, Thomas. *Reaching for Paradise: The Playboy Vision of America*. New York: Times Books, 1978.

Whiteside, Thomas. "An Unhurried View of Ralph Ginzburg." *Audience*, 1:4 (July–August 1971): 86–99.

Whorezine. 2300 Market Street, Suite 19, San Francisco 94114.

Williams, Lena. "Bodies Go Public: The Nature of Privacy Changes for Men, Too." *New York Times*, national ed., 31 October 1990, pp. B1, 8.

Williamson, Judith. *Decoding Advertisements: Ideology and Meaning in Advertising*. London: Marion Boyars, 1987.

Willie, John [Coutts, J. A. S.]. *Bizarre: The Complete Reprint of John Willie's Bizarre. vols. 1–13*, ed. Eric Kroll. Berlin: Benedikt Taschen Verlag, 1995.

Wilson, Earl. *Show Business Laid Bare*. New York: New American Library, 1974.

———. *The Show Business Nobody Knows*. New York: Cowles, 1971.

Winick, Charles. "A Content Analysis of Sexually Explicit Magazines Sold in an Adult Bookstore." *Journal of Sex Research*, 21:2 (1985): 206–210.

Winkler, Karen. " 'Seductions of Biography': Scholars Delve into New Questions about Race, Class, and Sexuality." *Chronicle of Higher Education*, 27 October 1993, pp. A6–A7, A14.

Winship, Janice. *Inside Women's Magazines*. London: Pandora, 1987.

Wise, G. L., A. L. King, and J. P. Merenski. "Reactions to Sexy Ads Vary with Age." *Journal of Advertising Research*, 14:4 (1974): 11–16.

Wiseman, Jay. *Personal Adventures: How to Meet People through the Personal Ads*. San Francisco: Gentle Persuasion, 1989.

Wolf, Michelle A., and Alfred P. Kielwasser, eds. *Gay People, Sex and the Media*. Binghamton, NY: Haworth Press, 1991.

Wright, Lawrence. "Remembering Satan: Parts 1 and 2." *The New Yorker*, 17 May 1993, pp. 60–66, 68–74, 76–81; 24 May 1993, pp. 54–66, 68–76.

Yellow Silk: Journal of the Erotic Arts. P.O. Box 6374, Albany, CA 94706, 1981–.

Yoni: Lesbian Erotica. P.O. Box 19316, Oakland, CA 94619.

Young, Perry D. *God's Bullies: Power Politics and Religious Tyranny*. New York: Holt, Rinehart, and Winston, 1982.

Zine Exchange Network. P.O. Box 7052, Austin, TX 78713.

Zuckerman, Marvin. "Physiological Measures of Sexual Arousal in the Human." *Psychological Bulletin*, 75 (1971): 297–310.

18

Comics

BACKGROUND: DRAWINGS, CARICATURES, AND COMICS

For background, the scholar should consult general histories. Of several historical surveys, M. Thomas Inge's *Comics as Culture* is an excellent, wide-ranging study, with occasional mention of cartoonists working in erotic/pornographic genres; it contains an annotated bibliography and an especially useful guide to American library collections of comics. Another good survey is Les Daniels' *Comix: A History of Comic Books in America*, although it concludes with the advent of underground comics in the 1960s. William M. Marston's "Why 100,000,000 Americans Read Comics" places cartooning in a specifically American context and is worth a look because of its analysis of classes of readers and the loyalty they bring to the genre. *Comic Book Confidential*, a video chronology of American comic books, includes footage on censorship in the 1950s as well as on underground comix of recent decades, with interviews and narrative by R. Crumb and other artists. Martin Barker's *Comics: Ideology, Power and the Critics* offers an interesting perspective because it compares comic book controversies in the United States with those in Great Britain.

The classic text on sexually explicit pre-twentieth-century examples, Eduard Fuchs' *Das Erotische Element in der Karikatur* (part of his larger history of erotic art), covers mostly European drawings and caricatures of the late nineteenth century, as opposed to the cartoons that became popular later. Some early French examples can be found in John Grand-Carteret's *Die Erotik in der französischen Karikatur*, although, like Fuchs' work, it is more generally concerned with erotic drawings of all sorts. Turn-of-the-century American pornographic cartoons were sporadically produced, though in enough volume to attract the attention of bluenoses. The *Annual Reports* of the New York Society for the

Suppression of Vice from 1874 to about 1915 mention seizures of pornographic drawings and cartoons, though usually not by traceable names or titles. A better indicator of early output is *Die Frühzeit der Erotischen Comics, 1900–1935*, the catalog published by the D. M. Klinger auction house in Nuremberg, Germany; a solid historical essay precedes a list of 878 almost exclusively American pornographic comics from the first decades of this century, though most are clustered in the 1920s and 1930s. In *Sex in the Comics*, Maurice Horn deals with sexual themes and images in comic strips and books from many countries but gives precedence to American forms; neither as scholarly nor as organized as one might wish, it is an essential text. The most authoritative study of American experiments is Mark James Estren's *A History of Underground Comics*, which covers cartoons from Tijuana bibles to *Zap* and *Big Ass*. While it is only slightly updated in its second edition and often neglects to contextualize and date artists and their works, Estren's history is indispensable; an appendix provides a checklist of underground titles compiled by Clay Geerdes. Roger Sabin's *Adult Comics: An Introduction* is a fine history of adult comics from the late nineteenth century on, with discussion of aesthetics, sexual themes, gender roles, and cultural elements in many countries; part II deals with American comics. Robert C. Harvey devotes considerable space to explicit comics in *The Art of the Comic Book: An Aesthetic History*, an equally interesting theoretical work, with insightful observations on the relationship of panels to pacing and other technical matters; Harvey is especially astute on R. Crumb.

The best—if too brief—sociological examination of the genre is "Pornographic Comics: A Content Analysis," in which C. Eddie Palmer isolates cultural differences in comics of different countries, particularly in areas of ethical values and gender concerns. Palmer asserts that while porn comics deal with deviant sex, the effect is to underline "normative" sexual behavior by using reference points that are adult, monogamous, and heterosexual. The essay identifies taxonomical, linguistic, and methodological problems in studying porno comics and sets an agenda for future research. Palmer's "Filthy Funnies, Blue Comics, and Raunchy Records: Dirty Jokes and Obscene Language as Public Entertainment" veers away from comics into wider areas of folklore and music.

William McLean studies erotic comic books as a form of graffiti, or the discourse of urban rebellion, in *Contribution a l'etude de l'iconographie populaire de l'erotisme*. Jacques Sadoul's *L'Enfers des Bulles* compares treatment of erotic themes and degrees of explicitness in French and American comics and is especially good on their cross-pollination in the 1930s and 1940s. Because it appeared a decade later, M. Bourgeois' book on erotic illustration, *Erotisme et pornographie dans la bande dessine*, offers better coverage of American (Crumb and Forest) and French (Crepax) underground cartoonists and greater bibliographic accuracy; the volume has a handy name index. Gillian Freeman's *The Undergrowth of Literature*, a freewheeling survey of periodical subgenres, devotes several pages to sex in comic books, especially those emphasizing fetishes. Porn comics, along with other erotic forms, have contributed to a heightened consciousness of sexuality that, in turn, has redefined the artistic sensibilities of the twentieth century, or so says Peter Gorsen in *Sexualästhetik: Grenzformen der Sinnlichkeit im 20. Jahrhundert*. Gorsen cites Richard Lindner as an artist profoundly influenced by erotic cartoons, as does Joan C. Siegfried, in "The Spirit of the Comics," who traces their influences on pop art of various types. *Comics Journal* (formerly *The Nostalgia Journal* and *New Nostalgia Journal*), edited by Gary Groth, is a source of uneven essays of history and criticism, often enlivened by a penchant for controversy.

TIJUANA BIBLES

In *Love and Death*, Gershon Legman says that the eight-page Tijuana bibles are "America's only original contribution to the development of the comics" (46). The great majority satirize popular icons. These include public celebrities—"Doug Fairybanks" and "Mae Breast" are examples—but also parodies of Moon Mullins, Dagwood Bumstead, Dick Tracy, and Little Orphan Annie. Numerous reprints of American comic-strip Tijuana bibles, most of them published in the 1960s and 1970s and now out of print, are occasionally available in adult book stores. The best have historical introductions or running comment. Easily the most elegantly framed volume is *Tijuana Bibles: Art and Wit in America's Forbidden Funnies, 1930s–1950s*, edited by Bob Adelman, with a whimsical Introduction by the cartoonist Art Spiegelman, an essay on styles of "bibles" by the artist Richard Merkin, and two essays (and a bibliography) on the language of "eight-pagers" by Madeline Kripke. The four volumes of Donald H. Gilmore's *Sex in Comics: A History of the Eight Pagers* are also mandatory for the scholar, despite their having been issued by a publisher better known for slipshod prurience. Gilmore concentrates on the era of the depression, when this most demotic of forms was affordable even in rural areas. According to Gilmore, almost 700 different eight-pagers were produced in the United States during the classic period beginning with the 1920s; the title list in the Klinger catalog suggests that the number was actually higher. Gilmore's text deals with roughly 500 printed between 1930 and 1965.

Also valuable is Otis Raymond's *Sex Comic Classics*, a two-volume history of the Tijuana bible, notable for its character index and bibliography. In his Introduction, Raymond says that dirty comics originated in California. By contrast, Maurice Horn in *Sex in the Comics* argues less persuasively that the eight-pagers owe their beginnings to semipolitical Cuban examples; then, transformed by American cultural imperatives, they began to parody mainstream cartoon characters. Horn is more accurate when he notes that by 1950 "the eight-pagers had become tired and repetitive, every character and every situation had been milked to the fullest, and there were few sexual variations left to explore. The booklets finally petered out in the fifties (when cheap and heavily censored versions were advertised for sale through the mails, in contrast to the real items, which were generally sold under the counter). When the more permissive era of the sixties opened up new fields for the graphic depiction of sex, they simply became objects of curiosity and even nostalgia" (85). Raymond points out that sadomasochism is not common in Tijuana bibles, which almost always depict garden-variety sex, albeit with humorous or ironic twists. R. G. Holt's Introductions to two compilations, *Little "Dirty" Comics* and *More Little "Dirty" Comics* (the first volume is usually listed under Holt's name, while the second gives Terence Atkinson as editor), are solid pieces of work, the first on the 1920s and 1930s, the second on the 1930s and 1940s.

Anthologies of less merit include *Famous Collection of 8 Page Sex Cartoons*, edited by Cecil Barkley, whose sketchy commentary introduces "Tillie the Toiler" and other classics; *Carnal Comics*, edited by Dwain Bryan, whose brief text is overwhelmed by illustrations of eight-pagers of the 1930s and 1940s; *Dirty Little Sex Cartoons*, edited by Jay Gilbey, whose commentary on the compilation of panels from the 1930s and 1940s is modest; *Classic Comics of Yesterday and Today*, compiled by the pseudonymous Cliff Hardman, whose Introduction contains nothing new; *Famous Sex Comics*, edited by John J. Reynolds, whose text is inadequate to a good selection; and *A Treasury of Dirty Little Comics: "The Kind Men Like*," edited by Michael Jennings, whose remarks are conventional. Harder to find are the two volumes of *The Tijuana Bible Revival*, edited by "Robert Murky," whose fake name is matched by fanciful publishers and places; according to C. J. Scheiner, both volumes were printed in New York by a collector clearly not a scholar, but the illustrations are well reproduced. *A Naughty Treasury of Classic Fairy Tales*, a collection of pornographic retellings of fairy tales (Goldilocks, the Three Bears, etc.), includes cartoon illustrations from various periods, none attributed. C. J. Scheiner's annual *Erotica-Curiosa-Sexology Catalogs* and his *Compendium* offer original Tijuana bibles and reprints of classic porn cartoons. Page 31 of the *Compendium*, for example, lists *There's Always Room for a Man*, by "Rhangild (Susan Aguerra?)." According to Scheiner, it is the only Tijuana bible drawn by a woman. The depiction of blacks in Tijuana bibles is the subject of Phyllis R. Klotman's "Racial Stereotypes in Hard-Core Pornography." Klotman discusses blacks as sexual outsiders in American culture, represented as comic, but also sinister, stereotypes capable of provoking sexual anxiety among whites. Volume III of *Technical Reports of the Commission on Obscenity and Pornography* contains a brief and conventional history of pornographic comics during the 1920s and 1930s, with some material on postwar varieties.

MAINSTREAM AND MARGINAL COMICS OF MIDCENTURY

As early as the 1940s, Gershon Legman pointed out that violence had become a staple of mainstream comic books, in part as a substitute for the forbidden depiction of sexuality. A revision of Legman's "The Psychopathology of the Comics" became the "Not for Children" chapter of his classic *Love and Death: A Study in Censorship*. Legman also speaks of the sadism and violence directed against women in popular romances and high literature by writers like Hemingway, themes elaborated in Legman's *The Horn Book*. Legman's argument was taken up, in somewhat less persuasive form, by Frederick Wertham, whose *Seduction of the Innocent* found insidious messages in every comic strip panel, some ferreted out by the author's homophobia (see his discussion of *Batman* comics). Wertham professed to be unconcerned about pornographic comic books for adults, a point generally lost in the rising public furor. Wertham charged that in addition to contributing to illiteracy, comic books conditioned children by distorting reality, encouraging cruelty and criminality, promoting sexual fantasies and deceit; he believed they generally undermined morality and stimulated delinquency. As Shearon Lowery and Melvin L. DeFleur point out in "Seduction of the Innocent: The Great Comic Book Scare," one of the best commentaries on the Wertham thesis, Wertham's anecdotal conclusions were unsupported by evidence or research. The astute Robert Warshow in "Paul, the Horror Comics, and Dr. Wertham" said that the psychiatrist was allowing personal bias to intrude; Warshow's is still the best essay on the Wertham controversy. Wertham set off alarm bells, and obliging journalists of every description took up his themes. N. Muhlen's "Comic Books and Other Horrors: Prep School for Totalitarian Society?" is representative in its sensationalism. Wertham embroidered some of his ideas in *A Sign for Cain: An Exploration of Human Violence*, a rather conventional speculation on the origins of aggression that failed to capture the same public attention.

The debate over comic books coincided with congressional investigations of juvenile delinquency in both houses of Congress, each of which launched investigations that quickly embraced erotic materials (see **Hearings, Panels, Commissions, and Other Forums for Dramatizing Sexual Expression** in Chapter 5). Three-D Zone (Ray Zone) has published *Forbidden 3-D*, a 3-D comic book complete with glasses, on this most paranoid of periods in comic history; its pages cover comic critics Sterling North and Frederick Wertham, the various hearings, and the establishment of the Comics Code Authority with much more panache than scholars are wont to supply. Leslie Fiedler took up the battle on behalf of comic books in "The Middle against Both Ends," still a highly relevant and readable essay in which the critic says that comic book characters reify archetypal patterns and "folk-impulses." From abroad, Geoffrey Wagner joined the fray with *Parade of Pleasure: A Study of Popular Iconography in the U.S.A.*, which is less notable for its criticism of comic books than its attack on popular culture in the United States as a form of control engineered by the upper classes. Amy Kiste Nyberg's extremely useful *Seal of Approval: The History of the Comics Code* recounts much of the controversy, centers disputes in historical context, and outlines the provisions and policies of the code itself. The ferment of opinion also inspired a fine, but forgotten, text, *But That's Unprintable! About the Taboos in Magazine and Newspaper Comic Cartoons*, by David Breger, who discusses prohibited political, social, religious, and sexual themes.

Investigators for the Kefauver committee eventually got around to the fetish cartoons and drawings sold by specialty shops like that of Irving Klaw, who actually commissioned many of them by artists like Ruiz, Stanton, and John Willie; the last was the most talented of all those working in these genres. Willie, the nom de plume of J. A. S. Coutts, an Australian who emigrated to the United States, himself published the magazine *Bizarre* for a time in Montreal. Willie excelled at bondage scenarios, but he could draw panels highlighting leather, exotic lingerie, high heels, and other fetishes. Klaw's encounter with Kefauver is the subject of Chapter 10 of *The Betty Pages Annual*; Chapter 7 reproduces some of the strips drawn by Stanton and others using Page as a model. Bélier Press has published the five-volume *Bizarre Classix*, a collection of drawings and photos on various fetishes, mostly S/M, bondage, and flagellation compiled by J. B. Rund, who drew on originals such as those advertised in Klaw's *Cartoon and Model Parade* catalog. The twenty-four-volume *Bizarre Comix*, also compiled by Rund, reproduces fetish comics from the 1950s and 1960s by Stanton, Mario, Ruiz, Eneg, "Jim," and others. These were serial comics commissioned and published originally by Klaw, the self-styled " 'Pin-Up King' for Artists, Photography Students and Collectors," as he advertised himself.

Bélier Press' edition of Willie's *The Adventures of Sweet Gwendolyn* is now a classic, and it, together with other materials from the Bélier archives, are the basis for a seven-cassette video series of the same title. Willie's two-volume *The Art of John Willie: Sophisticated Bondage 1946–1961*, edited by Stefano Piselli and Riccardo Morrocchi, is dotted with his photographs and drawings. (See **Fetish Photographs** in Chapter 12, Willie.) Eric Stanton's work from the 1950s and 1960s has been collected, with discussion of his technique and cultural context, in the two-volume *The Best of Stanton. The Art of Eric Stanton: For the Man Who Knows His Place* includes an interview with the artist, comment on his work, and many of his illustrations of busty women dominating hapless males. Reprints of classic Stanton fetish serials, *Sweeter Gwen* and *Sweeter Gwen and the Return of Sweeter Gwendoline* (reminiscent of Willie's originals) and *The Dominant Wives and Other Stories*, are also available; the latter is introduced by Rund's bibliographic essay. Stanton is still drawing and sells directly through C. J. Scheiner, the book dealer, who will provide a catalog. The sadomasochistic cartoons of Bob Bishop are collected in the three-volume *Bishop*. Some Americans still remember Bill Ward's cartoons of bazooka-breasted women from garage walls in the 1940s, 1950s, and 1960s. A collection of Ward's drawings have been published as *Ward's Wow*; a section of the volume features similar drawings by Jack Cole, one of Ward's contemporaries. During the late 1970s, Ward drew hundreds of erotic panels for a series of fetishistic narratives written by Joe Doakes and Bart Keister; they illustrate sadomasochism, flagellation, female domination, and bizarre acts of all sorts.

Risqué cartoons were staples of men's magazines at least from the time of the *Police Gazette*, according to Edward Van Every's *Sins of America as Exposed by the Police Gazette*, a classic study of the off-color genre. In *Portrait of an Era as Drawn by C. D. Gibson: A Biography*, Fairfax D. Downey investigates the iconographic "Gibson Girl," the pinup and cartoon character drawn by C. D. Gibson. The influence of the Gibson Girl receives extended treatment in Martha Banta's brilliant *Imaging American Women: Idea and Ideals in Cultural History*. George Petty's art deco–style cartoons have been collected in *A Portfolio from Esquire*. While perhaps more properly considered pinup artists, Petty and Alberto Vargas, another highly stylized illustrator, occasionally ventured cartoon turns. Astrid Rossana-Conte's *Vargas: The Creator of the Pin-Up Girl, 20s–50s* covers some of the latter's. Sexy cartoons sometimes appeared in venues perceived as staid, as "From the Archives: Sex to Sexty," a *New Yorker* piece by Hendrik Hertzberg, makes clear; this charming essay on the "sugar daddy" cartoons by Peter Arno, Richard Taylor, Whitney Darrow, and other cartoonists for the magazine recalls their now politically incorrect attitude toward gender relations.

Ward, Petty, Vargas and many others are represented in the catholic *Playboy Cartoon Album*, a sampling from the magazine's first decade. Drawings and a brief history of a now-famous character in *Playboy's Little Annie Fanny*, by Harvey Kurtzman and Will Elder, fill two volumes. Like other departments in the magazine, *Playboy* cartoons have come under fire over the years. Chapter 9 of Judith Reisman's *"Soft Porn" Plays Hardball: Its Tragic Effects on Women, Children and the Family* attacks cartoons in *Playboy* and other men's magazines as pernicious to family values. A former songwriter for the television show *Captain Kangaroo*, Reisman (aka Judith Bat-Ada) received a $750,000 grant from the Justice Department to survey the pornographic images in *Playboy* and other magazines. As Robert Scheer has noted in "Ed Meese's Dirty Pictures," Reisman counted *each panel* in the *Little Annie Fanny* cartoon strip in *Playboy* as statistical evidence of the magazine's promotion of child porn. Among unhumorous looks at male-magazine cartoons are two complementary analyses. In their often-cited "A Longitudinal Content Analysis of Sexual Violence in Best-Selling Erotica Magazines," Neil Malamuth and Barry Spinner survey photos and cartoons in *Playboy and Penthouse* from 1973 to 1977 to find that while the photographs reflected a modest increase in violent elements (setting, costume, interactions between figures), the cartoons did not. In another study, "Sexual Violence in *Playboy* Magazine: A Longitudinal Content Analysis," Joseph E. Scott and Stephen J. Cuvelier cover all of *Playboy*'s issues from the very first; unlike Malamuth and Spinner, they find very little violence as element or theme in pictorials or cartoons and think that violence has decreased even further since 1978.

The cocreator of *Little Annie Fanny*, Harvey Kurtzman, is a transitional figure, on one hand, a stalwart of *Mad* magazine and, on the other, a dabbler in the erotic, and important as well for his encouragement of artists more outrageous than himself. Kurtzman's autobiography, *My Life as a Cartoonist*, written with Howard Zimmerman, offers an insider's view of his colleagues, his own aspirations, and the ferment that created the new underground genres of the 1960s. A colleague at *Mad* was Wally Wood, whose rebellious energies overflowed into porn parodies of other cartoon strips, most notably, the gloriously excessive drawing called "Disneyland" that Paul Krassner accepted for *The Realist*; here all the major Disney characters copulate, while Dumbo the flying elephant relieves himself in the sky. The pages of Wood's *Gang Bang*! and *Gang Bang! 2* are replete with episodes of "Prince Violate," "Perry and the Privates," "Flasher Gordon," and "So White and the Six Dorks." For Wood's obituary in *Comics Journal*, "Newswatch: Wally Wood Dead at 54," Dwight R. Decker and Gary Groth review his career. A lengthier memoir is Bhob Stewart's "Memories of Wally Wood: There Are Good Guys and Bad Guys," which graphs the pornographic obsessions that increased toward the end of Wood's life. The second issue of *The Betty Pages: The Magazine Dedicated to Tease* covers Wood's "good girl art," and issues 2 through 5 of *Torchy* highlight Wood's "Blonde Bombshell."

UNDERGROUND COMIX

Largely because of their political associations, underground comics have attracted more comment than other forms. Bob Abel's "Comix of the Underground" was one of the first articles on the then-new phenomenon of explicit, socially conscious comics; its value is its fresh perspective and its interviews with pioneers. Similarly useful is David Zack's "Smut for Love, Art, Society," an essay devoted to S. Clay Wilson, with reflections on the history of eight-pagers as compared to the newer styles of *Zap*, *Snatch*, and *Jiz*. Other early looks are the Mad Peck's "The Legendary Comix Ripoff Ruse," on specifically pornographic elements, Mike Barrier's "Notes on the Underground," on comix subcultures, Arthur Berger's "Eroticomics or 'What Are You Doing with That Submachine Gun, Barbarella?,' " on the fusion of erotic and violent elements in some of the slicker magazines, and especially Jacob Brackman's authoritative "The International Comix Conspiracy," on Gilbert Shelton, Harvey Kurtzman, Robert Crumb, Dave Sheridan, "Spain" Rodriquez, S. Clay Wilson, Rick Griffin, and Victor Moscoso. The speed with which these artists garnered audiences is detailed by Paul Buhle in "The New Comics and American Culture," an important essay on the historical, social, and political aspects of underground comics as they impacted on mainstream institutions. Authoritative information is available from two serials, Gary Groth's *Comics Journal* and *David Anthony Kraft's Comics Interview*; the latter zine is devoted to interviews with cartoonists and publishers, while the former has thrived on controversy.

The most important underground cartoonist is Robert Crumb. Many critics credit Crumb with inventing the modern form with the publication of *Zap #1* (1967). *Robert Crumb*, Marjorie Alessandrini's biography (in French), though published in 1974, is the best introduction to Crumb's work and significance, still superior to the more recent *The Life and Times of R. Crumb: Commentary from Contemporaries*, edited by Monte Beauchamp, who gathers evaluations from various artists and critics. Harvey Pekar's "Rapping about Cartoonists,

Particularly Robert Crumb," similarly dated, is a personal evaluation of Crumb's work, with specific attention to *Zap*, the magazine most closely identified with the cartoonist, and a brief and incomplete bibliography of Crumb's publications. (Joseph Witek's *Comic Books as History: The Narrative Art of Jack Jackson, Art Spiegelman, and Harvey Pekar* contains a chapter called "The Underground Roots of Fact-Based Comics" [48–57] on the Comics Code adopted in the 1950s and revised in the 1970s. Otherwise, though he is not concerned with the cartoonist's eroticism per se, Witek is very good on Pekar himself.)

Crumb's own conversation with Bill Griffith in "As the Artist Sees It: Interviews with Comic Artists" offers reflections on his role and insights on the work of his contemporaries. Crumb is, of course, well represented in the various anthologies of underground strips, but those devoted exclusively to him are most useful, particularly Crumb's *Robert Crumb's Carload o' Comics: An Anthology of Choice Strips and Stories—1969 to 1976*, which usually include comment on his artistry and cultural significance. Upset at the results of Ralph Bakshi's shooting of *Fritz the Cat* (1971), Crumb had his name removed from the film's credits; he also dropped the hip feline from his roster of characters. In recent years, Crumb has enjoyed distinguished gallery shows, but the ultimate accolade appears to be his cover for the 21 February 1994 anniversary issue of *The New Yorker*, in which one of Crumb's "scuzzy" characters, studying an ad for a sex shop, replaces Eustace Tilley, the magazine's famous icon. The circumstances behind this editorial decision are the subject of Robert D. McFadden's "Eustace Tilley's on Vacation, and My, What a Stand-In." An even more telling indication of Crumb's contemporary status is Steve Ringgenberg's article, "Gary Groth on *The Complete Crumb*: Where's a Good Censor When You Need One?" on the mild reception of the multivolume works of Crumb as issued by Fantagraphics Books: "It must come as something of a surprise (not to say a disappointment) to Groth that his company's publication of underground cartoonist Robert Crumb's complete underground comics *oeuvre* and sketchbooks has met with as little public outrage and as few censorship problems as it has" (163). The cynical will doubtless agree that putting Crumb's work in museums and turning the artist himself into a cultural icon are society's ultimate revenge on pornographers, a process apparent in *The R. Crumb Coffee Table Art Book: Crumb's Whole Career, from Shack to Chateau*, edited by Peter Poplaski. The volume remakes Crumb as an artist rather than a lowbrow drawer of comics; a selective sampling of his work downplays nasty, raucous adolescence in favor of better-drawn panels with less vitality.

Volumes I through X of *The Complete Crumb* cover the artist's years from early jottings in the 1950s through the shambling figures of Crumb's trademark urban landscapes in the mid-1970s; projected volumes will doubtless record Crumb's rise to comix elder statesman. Crumb himself recently moved to France, a decision that occasioned Terry Zwigoff's feature-length documentary, *Crumb*. Zwigoff follows Crumb and his wife in their preparations but also focuses on the dysfunctional family that produced the weird genius by filming

Crumb with his mother, brothers, children, and associates. In the film, art critic Robert Hughes calls Crumb the Breughel of the latter twentieth century and reminds detractors that offensive art like Crumb's "is not put there for a nice, normative effect." Herself an artist, Crumb's wife, Aline, says that her husband's drawings "depict the id in its pure form." Trina Robbins, Spain Rodriquez, Bill Griffith, Deidre English, and Dian Hanson also comment on camera. Typical of the publicity that greeted release of the film is Owen Gleiberman's "It's Mr. Unnatural." Gleiberman praises Crumb's courage in rendering "a world of lust and anxiety and funk and rage and banality and joy and craziness. A world that's perfectly god-damn delightful" (42). (For works by and about Crumb, see also **Magazines, Newspapers, and Comics** in Chapter 4.)

Much of the critical comment on underground comics, where not superficial, is often desultory, redundant, repetitive, or lame. That is perhaps as it should be, since the form speaks for itself; one of the most demotic of all pornographic types, it seems to shrug off heavy-handed critical approaches. Anyone wishing to study "dirty" comics should begin with the works themselves, and collections sometimes help. S. Clay Wilson contributed many offensive cartoons to *Screw* magazine; these have been collected as *Spots*. Two rich anthologies, *The Apex Treasury of Underground Comics*, edited by Don Donahue and Susan Goodrick, and *The Best of Bijou Funnies*, edited by Jay Lynch, have been reissued in a single volume. Both contain generous reproductions, biographies, and interviews with those represented. *The Best of Drawn and Quarterly* collects artists such as Matt, Doucet, and Dougan from the first ten issues of the press. *Comix Compendium* collects panels by Doucet, Fleener, Diana, Matt, and dozens of others. *The Best of the Rip Off Press*, in two volumes, reprints classics from one of the leading underground publishers. Diana Schutz's "Rip Off Press: The Publishing Company That's a Little Like the Weather [: An Interview with Gilbert Shelton, Fred Todd, and Don Baumgart]" explores a perennial topic among artists, the need for a publisher willing to print questionable material. *The Young Lust Reader*, edited by Bill Griffith and Jay Kinney, gathers some of the more outrageous satirical strips drawn for that magazine. Last Gasp has recently collected perhaps the most popular (and most sexist) installments of Spain Rodriquez's saga, the story of a horny superspy, as *She Comics: An Anthology of Big Bitch*.

Histories and anthologies of the underground press of the 1960s usually put comix in a political perspective. Worth consulting in this regard are *Underground Press Anthology*, compiled by Thomas King Forcade, and *Underground Reader*, compiled by Mel Howard and Forcade; both include underground artists among voices of rebellion. A review in *ArtPress* says that the Parisian show of the work of "Ed Roth, Stanley Mouse, Robert Williams: Galerie Julie Rico 10 décembre 1993–27 février 1994" "demonstrates how sixties underground culture which flourishes in an anti-establishment context becomes mainstream in an art gallery." The observation, of course, can be applied to many genres of pornography.

ALTERNATIVE ADULT COMICS AND GENDER-BENDERS

Some underground comics adopted political positions, while most dealt in satire. With other axes to grind, the newer alternative strains do not always aim clearly at arousal either and often subordinate sex itself to postmodern themes, gender issues, and the stresses of contemporary experience. According to Maurice Horn's *Sex in the Comics*, the first widely circulated gay underground comic book was *Gay Heart Throbs*, which struggled through a few issues in the mid-1970s. Howard Cruse started *Gay Comix* in 1980, and it has been home to many talented artists, including Roberta Gregory, editor of the first lesbian underground serial, *Dynamite Damsels*, and Mary Wings, editor of *Dyke Shorts*. Winston Leyland has edited *Meatmen: An Anthology of Gay Male Comics* and *More Meatmen: An Anthology of Gay Comics*, whose pages include artists ranging from Tom of Finland to American cartoonists. The Tom of Finland Foundation holds the copyright on his works and can provide information on the artist and on the massive sailors, cowboys, and soldiers who insouciantly bugger each other in his voluptuous panels. *Women in the Comics*, by Maurice Horn, treats the roles and images of women in mainstream, underground, and pornographic comics, as does "Bandes dessinees: la revanche de la femme," by Claude Moliterni and G. Amadiu, though the latter gives more attention to European examples. Historians are gradually beginning to discover that women cartoonists have long been interested in sex, according to Alice Sheppard in "There Were Ladies Present: American Women Cartoonists and Comic Artists in the Early Twentieth Century." A more comprehensive history of American women cartoonists from the turn of the century to the present is *Women and the Comics* by Trina Robbins and Catherine Yronwode, who note that women cartoonists tend to use story lines of emotion and psychology rather than action and technology. Robbins has also edited an excellent anthology called *A Century of Women Cartoonists*.

Mary McKenny lists underground comics without the overt sexism of, say, Crumb, that should appeal to women in "Mind Candy for the Ms's." *The Girl Wants To: Women's Representations of Sex and the Body*, edited by Lynn Crosbie, anthologizes thirty-nine contemporary writers and cartoonists. Several female cartoonists have developed serious followings. Researchers may wish to look at *Tits and Clits: Women's Humor Series*, comic volumes featuring the work of women cartoonists like Trina Robbins, Mary Fleener, and Dori Seda. Panels from the pens of recent underground artists such as Julie Doucet and Phoebe Gloeckner fill the pages of Diane Noomin's *Twisted Sisters: A Collection of Bad Girl Art*, a well-edited anthology. Noomin and Aline Kominsky (Robert Crumb's wife) began drawing *Twisted Sisters*, an underground zine, in 1976. Noomin has also pulled together stories by Carol Lay, Debbie Drechsler, Krystine Kryttre, Carol Tyler, Fiona Smith, Dame Darcy, Penny Moran Van Horn, Caryn Leschen, M. K. Brown, Aline Kominsky Crumb, Carel Moiseiwitsch, Mary Fleener, Leslie Sternbergh, Noomin, Carol Swain, and the incomparable Phoebe Gloeckner in *Twisted Sisters: Volume II: Drawing the Line*. In "Comic Strip-Tease: A Revealing Look at Women Cartoon Artists," Jaye Berman Montresor notes that women artists draw from their own experience, that for them cartooning is an autobiographical art form full of female anxieties about menstruation, intercourse, pregnancy, and elimination but, above all, about appearance, expressed in obsessions about diet and beauty. Montresor is also working on a book, *Women Cartoonists: Self-Portraits in a Comics Mirror*.

In "A Look at Love Comics," a soft-core genre, Fran Taylor deplores comics aimed at teenaged girls because of the stereotypes of both male and female characters. Bruce Bailey's "An Inquiry into Love Comic Books: The Token Evolution of a Popular Genre" agrees that the stereotypes are pretty traditional: "because they cater to such intense and culturally well-established daydreams, these comics need not adjust appreciably to relatively subtle shifts in social attitudes" (245), though he notes they have undergone some changes. The basic formula is driven by "the heroine's single-minded scheming on the way to true love, the ultimate expression of which is marriage and absorption by a strong, work-oriented male ego" (245). *Real Love: The Best of the Simon and Kirby Romance Comics, 1940s–1950s*, a collection of examples of the genre by Joe Simon and Jack Kirby, displays tropes and plotlines.

Though she defies categorization as an erotic artist, Lynda Barry is much interested in matters sexual. A profile by Margot Mifflin, "A Not So Perfect Life: The Anxious Humor of Lynda Barry," deals with the sources of her humor. Barry's *Naked Ladies, Naked Ladies Coloring Book* provides some sense of her perspective. A more startling coloring book is Tee Corinne's *Cunt Coloring Book*, a collection of drawings of vaginas designed to be crayoned; the anticipated audience is female; the purpose didactic. Retitled *Labiaflowers* in 1981, it did not sell nearly as well. Patricia Waters' *The Sensuous Coloring Book* also aimed at gently educating women. P. Fleisher's "Conversations with Badanna Zack: A Female View of Sexuality" interviews another cartoonist who has pushed against limits. Roz Warren has compiled work by Shary Flenniken, Roberta Gregory, Nina Paley, Ellen Forney, and others who poke fun at heterosexuality, homosexuality, bisexuality and less conventional variations; the volume is titled *What Is This Thing Called Sex? Cartoons by Women*. Warren has also arranged about forty panels and strips by artists poking fun at penises for her *Weenie-Toons: Women Cartoonists Mock Cocks*.

Alison Bechdel's *Dykes to Watch Out For* and *More Dykes to Watch Out For* are among the best of lesbian cartoons, and her titles are alluded to in Dominique Dibbell's "Dykes and Fags to Look Out For," a review of *The Cartoon Show*, an exhibit of cartoons by forty gays and lesbians at the Lesbian and Gay Community Center, New York City, in May 1990. That show featured erotic comic strips along with others less sexual. Paula Routly critiques Bechdel's work in "A Cartoonist to Watch Out For": "How do Bechdel's characters manage to bash the patriarchy over lentil loaf and raspberry tea without alienating guys . . . ? The same way their maker illustrates female foreplay and post-coital bliss: with equal parts respect and humor" (18). Less respectful are the comix of Diane DiMassa, whose panels attacking mainstream society have been collected as *Hothead Paisan: Homicidal Lesbian Terrorist*. Also notable for their ability to attract loyal readers are gay cartoonist Rupert Kinnard (*B. B. and the Diva*) and lesbian cartoonist Kris Kovick (*What I Love about Lesbian Politics Is Arguing with the People I Agree With*). A funny and comprehensive collection of gay cartoons taken from the pages of the magazine *Christopher Street* has been given the title *Relax! This Book Is Only a Phase You're Going Through* by its editors, Charles Ortleb and Richard Fiala.

Comic strip forms lend themselves to innovations that resist labels. Tomi Ungerer's *Fornicon*, drawings of fantastic pleasure devices, was extremely popular in the 1960s and 1970s. E. Widaen's *What Pornography Does to Women and to Men* is a sort of underground comic, elegantly bound, whose explicit and witty panels studiously avoid answering the question posed in the title. Less sophisticated is Errol Selkirk's *Sex for Beginners*, a cartoon volume that includes reflections on pornography. In *Strip AIDS, USA*, edited by Trina Robbins and others, more than 100 cartoonists offer panels, some explicit, on sex and HIV. Douglas Crimp's "How to Have Promiscuity in an Epidemic" discusses the ways in which explicit ads, pictures, and cartoons can educate gays to the necessity of safe sex. Since so much of their stock-in-trade is parody, comic artists occasionally run into legal difficulties. In "The Chilling Effect of Corporate Extortion on the Arts," Ed Cafasso reports on efforts by Disney and other companies to stifle parodies (some pornographic) of their cartoon characters. Not surprisingly, Disney artists have been known to do a little moonlighting themselves. Shamus Culhane recalls Disney animators who relax in bouts of drawing pornographic frames in his memoir *Talking Animals and Other People*. Michael Fleming's "Freeze Frames: Who Undressed Jessica Rabbit?" reports on the discovery that unknown pranksters surreptitiously redrew a few frames to expose Jessica Rabbit's nipples and vagina for the laser-disc version of the animated movie; Disney executives were embarrassed by the ensuing scandal.

That underground comics have not lost their vitality is evident from the critical attention that greets their occasional surfacing into mainstream culture. The October 1992 issue of *Art? Alternatives* is devoted to artists such as R. Crumb, Ed Hardy, Tod Waters, and Judith Schaechter. Richard Gehr's "Caught Looking: Sex Comics Come Again" cover *Anton's Collected Drek*, which features strips like Anton Drek's *Wendy Whitebread: Undercover Slut*; Mike McCarthy's *Bang Gang*; Gilbert Hernandez's sci-fi parody *Birdland*; Brian S. Eros' *Box*; Dennis P. Eichhorn's *Real Smut*, which also includes the work of artists like Pat Moriarty, Renee French, Holly Tuttle, Joe Zabel, and Gary Dumm; Bob Fingerman's *Skinheads in Love*; M. Scott Campbell's *Spank*; Craig Maynard's *Up from Bondage*; Larry Welz's famous parody of the *Playboy* bunny-type, *Cherry*; Reed Waller and Kate Worley's *Omaha the Cat Dancer*; and some reprints of Tijuana bibles. The best of these continue to twit authority. Worth a look is "Omaha the Cat Dancer: Tip of the Iceberg," in which Worley and Waller take on the Supreme Court's decision to "outlaw nipples" in the *Barnes* case. *Erotic Art of Reed Waller* contains a sprightly commentary by Dave Schreiner.

An even better indicator of the power of comics to arouse controversy is the 1994 Diana case. Michael Diana has been prosecuted and convicted for drawing the explicit zine *Boiled Angel*, whose comics, say Florida authorities, are obscene (his conviction has been upheld). Sources for information are Chuck Shepherd's "The Playboy Forum: Loony Toons" and Peter Kuper's "It's Obscene!" The latter is a cartoon page depicting the artist's arrest and trial. Jay Allen Sanford decries hostile reactions to comic book artists who take on unpopular or explicit themes in "Don't Be Scared, It's Just a Comic Book." Like other writers and artists, says Sanford, those who produce comics deal with social, cultural, and political issues, and like those others they are protected by the First Amendment, despite the recent rise of censors.

Regarding an entirely unrelated case, *Rate It X*, a videotape documentary by Lucy Winer and Paula Koenigsberg, contains an interview with Dwaine Tinsley, creator of "Chester the Molester" cartoons for *Hustler*, who was convicted in 1989 for sexual abuse of his daughter (see *Washington Times*, 22 May 1989). "Hot Comics," by Barry Janoff, briefly notes new titles like *The Bill Clinton Story*, *The Gennifer Flowers Story*, and another on Amy Fisher and Joey Buttafuoco (First Amendment Publishing), a grouping that attests to quick satirical response to scandal by contemporary cartoonists. Mark Kernes' article on the Glamourcons (Glamour Conventions), "Adult Industry Ogles T & A at Glamourcon II," explores the lively trade in adult comix. These are attended by dealers, collectors, and cartoonists such as Larry Welz (*Cherry*) but also by porn movie stars who have followed Annie Sprinkle's lead in launching comic books drawn around herself as a fetish character (Rip Off Press). Sarah Jane Hamilton (aka Victoria Secret), a specialist in female ejaculation, anal intercourse, and bondage and discipline, is the latest to have a comic book series of her own (*Golden Apple Comics* from Renegade Press). *Penthouse Comix*, an offshoot of *Penthouse*, first appeared in April 1994; it is a bimonthly devoted to erotic strips. Fetish fare in the tradition of John Willie is reappearing; typical is *Miranda the Tease*, drawn by Miss Mercy Van Vlack, who specializes in the erotic appeal of feet. Ironically, postmodern comix, as the emerging genre is sometimes called, can be as violent as the mainstream comics of the 1950s. Even the most cursory glance at contemporary comics will reveal cultural currents of great complexity. Finally, Andrea Juno has gathered conversations with leading underground figures for *Dangerous Drawings: Interviews with Comix & Graphic Artists*.

REFERENCES

Abel, Bob. "Comix of the Underground." *Cavalier*, 19:5 (April 1969): 34–36, 38–40, 52–54.

Adelman, Bob, ed. *Tijuana Bibles: Art and Wit in America's Forbidden Funnies, 1930s–1950s*. New York: Simon and Schuster, 1997.

Alessandrini, Marjorie. *Robert Crumb*. Paris: Albin Michel, 1974.

Art? Alternatives, 1:2 (October 1992).

Atkinson, Terence, ed. *More Little "Dirty" Comics*. San Diego: Socio Library, 1971.

Bailey, Bruce. "An Inquiry into Love Comic Books: The Token Evolution of a Popular Genre." *Journal of Popular Culture*, 10 (Summer 1976): 245–248.

Banta, Martha. *Imaging American Women: Idea and Ideals in Cultural History*. New York: Columbia University Press, 1987.

Barker, Martin. *Comics: Ideology, Power and the Critics*. New York: St. Martin's, 1989.

Barkley, Cecil, ed. *Famous Collection of 8 Page Sex Cartoons*. N.p.: Cameo, 1975.

Barrier, Mike. "Notes on the Underground." *Funnyworld*, 1 (Summer 1970): 5–9.

Barry, Lynda. *Naked Ladies, Naked Ladies Coloring Book*. Seattle: Real Comet Press, 1984.

Beauchamp, Monte, ed. *The Life and Times of R. Crumb: Commentary from Contemporaries*. New York: St. Martin's/Griffin, 1998.

Bechdel, Alison. *Dykes to Watch Out For* and *More Dykes to Watch Out For*. Ithaca, NY: Firebrand, 1989, 1990.

Berger, Arthur. "Eroticomics or 'What Are You Doing with That Submachine Gun, Barbarella?'" *Social Policy*, 1:3 (September/October 1970): 42–44.

The Best of Drawn and Quarterly. Montreal: Drawn and Quarterly, 1993.

The Best of the Rip Off Press. 2 vols. San Francisco: Rip Off Press, 1973, 1974.

The Betty Pages: The Magazine Dedicated to Tease. New York: Pure Imagination/Black Cat, 1988–.

Betty Pages Annual. New York: Black Cat Books, 1991.

Bishop, Bob. *Bishop*. 3 vols. Los Angeles: House of Milan, n.d.

Bizarre Classix. 5 vols. New York: Bélier Press, 1977–1982.

Bizarre Comix. 24 vols. New York: Bélier Press, 1975–1987.

Bourgeois, M. *Erotisme et pornographie dans la bande desinee*. Grenoble, France: Glenat, 1978.

Brackman, Jacob. "The International Comix Conspiracy." *Playboy*, 17:12 (December 1970): 195–199, 328–332, 334.

Breger, David. *But That's Unprintable! About the Taboos in Magazine and Newspaper Comic Cartoons*. New York: Bantam, 1955.

Bryan, Dwain. *Carnal Comics*. N.p.: N.p., n.d.

Buhle, Paul. "The New Comics and American Culture." *Tri-Quarterly*, 23/24 (Winter–Spring 1972): 367–402, 408–411.

Cafasso, Ed. "The Chilling Effect of Corporate Extortion on the Arts." *Gauntlet*, 1:5 (1993): 146–162.

Comic Book Confidential. Los Angeles: Pacific Arts, 1993.

Comix Compendium. Toronto: Mangajin, 1992.

Corinne, Tee. *Cunt Coloring Book*. San Francisco: Last Gasp, 1975; rpt. *Labiaflowers*, 1981.

Crimp, Douglas. "How to Have Promiscuity in an Epidemic." *October*, 43 (Winter 1987): 237–271.

Crosbie, Lynn, ed. *The Girl Wants To: Women's Representations of Sex and the Body*. Toronto: Coach House, 1993.

Crumb, Robert. *The Complete Crumb*. 10 vols. Seattle: Fantagraphics, 1986–1994.

————. *Fritz the Cat.* Directed by Ralph Bakshi. Produced by Steve Krantz. Los Angeles: Jerry Gross/Cinemation Industries, 1971.

————. *The R. Crumb Coffee Table Art Book: Crumb's Whole Career, from Shack to Chateau*, ed. Peter Poplaski. Boston: Little, Brown, 1997.

————. *Robert Crumb's Carload o' Comics: An Anthology of Choice Strips and Stories—1969 to 1976.* New York: Bélier Press, 1976.

Crumb, Robert, and Bill Griffith. "As the Artist Sees It: Interviews with Comic Artists." *Popular Culture in America*, ed. Paul Buhle. Minneapolis: University of Minnesota Press, 1987, pp. 132–135.

Culhane, Shamus. *Talking Animals and Other People.* New York: St. Martin's, 1986.

Daniels, Les. *Comix: A History of Comic Books in America.* New York: Outerbridge and Dienstfrey, 1971.

Decker, Dwight R., and Gary Groth. "Newswatch: Wally Wood Dead at 54." *Comics Journal*, 69 (December 1981): 8–10.

Dibbell, Dominique. "Dykes and Fags to Look Out For." *Outweek*, 23 May 1990, pp. 67, 73.

DiMassa, Diane. *Hothead Paisan: Homicidal Lesbian Terrorist.* Pittsburgh: Cleis Press, 1993.

Donahue, Don, and Susan Goodrick, eds. *The Apex Treasury of Underground Comics* (1974); bound with *The Best of Bijou Funnies*, ed. Jay Lynch (1975). New York: Quick Fox, 1981.

Downey, Fairfax D. *Portrait of an Era as Drawn by C. D. Gibson: A Biography.* New York: Scribner's, 1936.

"Ed Roth, Stanley Mouse, Robert Williams: Galerie Julie Rico 10 décembre 1993–27 février 1994." *ArtPress*, 192 (June 1994): ii.

Estren, Mark James. *A History of Underground Comics.* San Francisco: Straight Arrow Books, 1974; 3d ed. Berkeley, CA: Ronin, 1993.

Fiedler, Leslie. "The Middle against Both Ends." *Literary Censorship: Principles, Cases, Problems*, ed. Kinsley Widmer and Eleanor Widmer. San Francisco: Wadsworth, 1961, pp. 84–91.

Fleisher, P. "Conversations with Badanna Zack: A Female View of Sexuality." *Art Magazine*, 7:24 (December 1975): 24–25.

Fleming, Michael. "Freeze Frames: Who Undressed Jessica Rabbit?" *Variety*, 14–20 March 1994, p. 2.

Forbidden 3-D. Los Angeles: Three-D Zone, 1993.

Forcade, Thomas King, comp. *Underground Press Anthology.* New York: Ace Books, 1972.

Freeman, Gillian. *The Undergrowth of Literature.* London: Thomas Nelson and Sons, 1967.

Fuchs, Eduard. *Das Erotische Element in der Karikatur.* Munich: Albert Langen, 1904; rpt. and enlarged *Geschichte der Erotischen Kunst, Erw. und Neubearb. des Werkes, das Erotische Element in der Karikatur, mit Einschluss der Ernsten Kunst.* Munich: Albert Langen, [1912]; enlarged *Geschichte der Erotischen Kunst.* 3 vols. Munich: Albert Langen, 1912–26.

Gehr, Richard. "Caught Looking: Sex Comics Come Again." *Village Voice*, December 1992 Voice Literary Supplement, 8 December 1992, pp. 28–29.

Gilbey, Jay. *Dirty Little Sex Cartoons.* Los Angeles: Argyle, 1972.

Gilmore, Donald H. *Sex in Comics: A History of the Eight Pagers*. 4 vols. San Diego: Greenleaf Classics, 1971.

Gleiberman, Owen. "It's Mr. Unnatural." *Entertainment Weekly*, 272 (28 April 1995): 38–39, 42.

Gorsen, Peter. *Sexualästhetik: Grenzformen der Sinnlichkeit im 20. Jahrhundert*. Hamburg: Rowohlt, 1987.

Grand-Carteret, John. *Die Erotik in der französischen Karikatur*. Vienna: C. W. Stern, 1909.

Griffith, Bill, and Jay Kinney, ed. *The Young Lust Reader*. Berkeley, CA: And/Or Press, 1974.

Groth, Gary, ed. *Comics Journal* (formerly *The Nostalgia Journal* and *New Nostalgia Journal*). Seattle: Fantagraphics, 1977–.

Hardman, Cliff, ed. *Classic Comics of Yesterday and Today*. N.p.: N.p., n.d.

Harvey, Robert C. *The Art of the Comic Book: An Aesthetic History*. Jackson: University Press of Mississippi, 1996.

Hertzberg, Hendrik. "From the Archives: Sex to Sexty." *New Yorker*, 7, 14 December 1998, 144–149.

Holt, R. G., ed. *Little "Dirty" Comics*. San Diego: Socio Library, 1971.

Horn, Maurice. *Sex in the Comics*. New York: Chelsea House, 1985.

———. *Women in the Comics*. New York: Chelsea House, 1981.

Howard, Mel, and Thomas King Forcade, comps. *Underground Reader*. New York: Plume Books, 1972.

Inge, M. Thomas. *Comics as Culture*. Jackson: University Press of Mississippi, 1990.

Janoff, Barry. "Hot Comics." *Gallery*, 22:8 (August 1994): 92–94.

Jennings, Michael. *A Treasury of Dirty Little Comics: "The Kind Men Like."* New York: Valiant Books, 1972.

Juno, Andrea, ed. *Dangerous Drawings: Interviews with Comix & Graphic Artists*. New York: Juno Books, 1997.

Kernes, Mark. "Adult Industry Ogles T & A at Glamourcon II." *Adult Video News*, 9:6 (May 1994): 16.

Kinnard, Rupert. *B. B. and the Diva*. Boston: Alyson Press, 1992.

Klinger, D. M. *Die Frühzeit der Erotischen Comics, 1900–1935*. Auction catalog no. 8. Nuremberg, Germany: D. M. Klinger, 1985.

Klotman, Phyllis R. "Racial Stereotypes in Hard-Core Pornography." *Journal of Popular Culture*, 5:1 (Summer 1971): 221–235.

Kovick, Kris. *What I Love about Lesbian Politics Is Arguing with the People I Agree With*. Boston: Alyson Press, 1995.

Kraft, David Anthony. *David Anthony Kraft's Comics Interview*. New York: Fictioneer Books, 1983–.

Kuper, Peter. "It's Obscene!" *Village Voice*, 24 May 1994, 37.

Kurtzman, Harvey, with Howard Zimmerman. *My Life as a Cartoonist*. New York: Minstrel Books, 1988.

Kurtzman, Harvey, and Will Elder. *Playboy's Little Annie Fanny*. 2 vols. Chicago: Playboy Press, 1966, 1972.

Legman, Gershon. *The Horn Book: Studies in Erotic Folklore and Bibliography*. New Hyde Park, NY: University Books, 1964.

———. *Love and Death: A Study in Censorship*. New York: Breaking Point, 1949.

———. "The Psychopathology of the Comics." *Neurotica*, 1:3 (Autumn 1948): 3–30.

Leyland, Winston, ed. *Meatmen: An Anthology of Gay Male Comics*. San Francisco: G. S. Press, 1986.

———. *More Meatmen: An Anthology of Gay Comics*. San Francisco: G. S. Press, [1987?].

Lowery, Shearon, and Melvin L. DeFleur. "Seduction of the Innocent: The Great Comic Book Scare." *Milestones in Mass Communication Research: Media Effects*. New York: Longman, 1983, pp. 233–266.

The Mad Peck. "The Legendary Comix Ripoff Ruse." *Creem*, 18 (October 1970): 22–25.

Malamuth, Neil, and Barry Spinner. "A Longitudinal Content Analysis of Sexual Violence in Best-Selling Erotica Magazines." *Journal of Sex Research*, 16 (1980): 226–237.

Marston, William Moulton. "Why 100,000,000 Americans Read Comics." *American Scholar* (September 1943): 35–44.

McFadden, Robert D. "Eustace Tilley's on Vacation, and My, What a Stand-In." *New York Times*, 15 February 1994, p. B3.

McKenny, Mary. "Mind Candy for the Ms's." *Booklegger*, 1 (September–October 1974): 16–19; rpt. *New Women's Survival Sourcebook*, ed. Susan Rennie and Kirsten Grimstad. New York: Knopf, 1975, pp. 134–137.

McLean, William. *Contribution a l'etude de l'iconographie populaire de l'erotisme*. Paris: Maisonneuve et Larose, 1970.

Mifflin, Margot. "A Not So Perfect Life: The Anxious Humor of Lynda Barry." *Elle*, 7: 8 (April 1992): 122, 130.

Moliterni, Claude, and G. Amadiu. "Bandes dessinees: la revanche de la femme." *Opus International*, 13/14 (November 1969):58–65.

Montresor, Jaye Berman. "Comic Strip-Tease: A Revealing Look at Women Cartoon Artists." *Look Who's Laughing: Women and Gender*, ed. Gail Finney. Langhorne, PA: Gordon and Breach, 1994.

Muhlen, N. "Comic Books and Other Horrors: Prep School for Totalitarian Society?" *Commentary*, 68:1 (January 1949): 80–87.

Murky, Robert. *The Tijuana Bible Revival*. 2 vols. Vol. I: Blue Balls, PA: Penetrating, 1977; Vol. II: Hooker, CA: Paramounds, 1977.

A Naughty Treasury of Classic Fairy Tales. N.p.: N.p., n.d.

New York Society for the Suppression of Vice. *Annual Reports*. New York: New York Society for the Suppression of Vice, 1874–1940.

Noomin, Diane, ed. *Twisted Sisters: A Collection of Bad Girl Art*. New York: Penguin, 1991.

———. *Twisted Sisters: Volume II: Drawing the Line*. Northampton, MA: Kitchen Sink, 1995.

Nyberg, Amy Kiste. *Seal of Approval: The History of the Comics Code*. Jackson: University of Mississippi Press, 1998.

Ortleb, Charles, and Richard Fiala, eds. *Relax! This Book Is Only a Phase You're Going Through*. New York: St. Martin's, 1978.

Palmer, C. Eddie. "Filthy Funnies, Blue Comics, and Raunchy Records: Dirty Jokes and Obscene Language as Public Entertainment." *Sexual Deviancy in Social Context*, ed. Clifton D. Bryant. New York: New Viewpoints, 1977, pp. 82–101.

———. "Pornographic Comics: A Content Analysis." *Journal of Sex Research*, 15:4 (November 1979): 285–298.

Pekar, Harvey. "Rapping about Cartoonists, Particularly Robert Crumb." *Journal of Popular Culture*, 3 (1970): 677–688.

Petty, George. *A Portfolio from Esquire*. Chicago: Esquire, 1937.

Playboy Cartoon Album. New York: Crown Publishers, 1959.

Raymond, Otis. *Sex Comic Classics*. 2 vols. New York: Comic Classics, 1972.

Reisman, Judith A. *"Soft Porn" Plays Hardball: Its Tragic Effects on Women, Children and the Family*. Lafayette, LA: Huntington House, 1991.

Reynolds, John J. *Famous Sex Comics*. San Diego: Socio Library, 1975.

Ringgenberg, Steve. "Gary Groth on *The Complete Crumb*: Where's a Good Censor When You Need One?" *Gauntlet*, 1:5 (1993): 163–166.

Robbins, Trina, ed. *A Century of Women Cartoonists*. Princeton, WI: Kitchen Sink Press, 1992.

Robbins, Trina, and Catherine Yronwode. *Women and the Comics*. Forestville, CA: Eclipse Press, 1990.

Robbins, Trina, et al. *Strip AIDS, USA*. San Juan, CA: Shanti Project, 1988.

Rodriquez, Spain. *She Comics: An Anthology of Big Bitch*. San Francisco: Last Gasp, 1994.

Rossana-Conte, Astrid. *Vargas: The Creator of the Pin-Up Girl, 20s–50s*. Berlin: Benedikt Taschen, 1990.

Routly, Paula. "A Cartoonist to Watch Out For." *Oberlin Alumni Magazine*, 90:1 (Winter/Spring 1994): 16–18.

Sabin, Roger. *Adult Comics: An Introduction*. New York: Routledge, 1993.

Sadoul, Jacques. *L'Enfers des Bulles*. Paris: Pauvert, 1968.

Sanford, Jay Allen. "Don't Be Scared, It's Just a Comic Book." *Gauntlet*, 14 (1997): 95–100.

Scheer, Robert. "Ed Meese's Dirty Pictures." *Thinking Tuna Fish, Talking Death: Essays on the Pornography of Power*. New York: Hill and Wang, 1988, pp. 63–85.

Scheiner, C. J. *Compendium: Being a List of All the Books (Erotica, Curiosa, & Sexology) Listed in Our Catalogs 1:6 (1978–1988)*. Brooklyn, NY: C. J. Scheiner, 1989.

———. *Erotica-Curiosa-Sexology Catalog* of C. J. Scheiner Books, 275 Linden Blvd. Brooklyn, NY: C. J. Scheiner, 1977–present.

Schutz, Diana. "Rip Off Press: The Publishing Company That's a Little like the Weather [: An Interview with Gilbert Shelton, Fred Todd, and Don Baumgart]." *Comics Journal*, 92 (August 1984):69–83.

Scott, Joseph E., and Stephen J. Cuvelier. "Sexual Violence in *Playboy* Magazine: A Longitudinal Content Analysis." *Journal of Sex Research*, 23 (November 1987): 534–539.

Selkirk, Errol. *Sex for Beginners*. New York: Writers and Researchers, 1987.

Shepherd, Chuck. "The Playboy Forum: Loony Toons." *Playboy*, 41:8 (August 1994): 41–43.

Sheppard, Alice. "There Were Ladies Present: American Women Cartoonists and Comic Artists in the Early Twentieth Century." *Journal of American Culture*, 7 (Fall 1984): 34–48.

Siegfried, Joan C. "The Spirit of the Comics." *Art and Artists*, 4:9 (December 1969): 18–21.

Simon, Joe, and Jack Kirby. *Real Love: The Best of the Simon and Kirby Romance Comics, 1940s–1950s*, ed. Richard Howell. Forestville, CA: Eclipse, 198?.

Stanton, Eric. *The Art of Eric Stanton: For the Man Who Knows His Place*, ed. Eric Kroll. Berlin: Benedikt Taschen, 1997.

———. *The Best of Stanton.* 2 vols. Paris: Collection Vertiges Graphiques, 1979.

———. *The Dominant Wives and Other Stories.* Cologne: Benedikt Taschen, 1999.

———. *Sweeter Gwen.* Delaware: Unique Publications, 1975; *Sweeter Gwen and the Return of Sweeter Gwendoline.* New York: Bélier Press, 1976.

Stewart, Bhob. "Memories of Wally Wood: There Are Good Guys and Bad Guys." *Comics Journal*, 70 (January 1982): 50–67.

Taylor, Fran. "A Look at Love Comics." *Second Wave: A Magazine of the New Feminism*, 2:1 (1972): 16–19.

Technical Reports of the Commission on Obscenity and Pornography. 9 vols. Washington, DC: Government Printing Office, 1971–1972.

Tits and Clits: Women's Humor Series. Laguna Beach, CA: Nanny Goat, 1975–present.

Tom of Finland. Tom of Finland Foundation, 1421 Laveta Terrace, Los Angeles 90026.

Torchy. New York: Pure Imagination/Black Cat, 1988–.

Ungerer, Tomi. *Fornicon.* New York: Grove Press, 1969.

Van Every, Edward. *Sins of America as Exposed by the Police Gazette.* New York: Stokes, 1931.

Van Vlack, Miss Mercy. *Miranda the Tease.* Maugansville, MD: Forbidden Fruit (Box 699, zip 21767), 1993–.

Wagner, Geoffrey. *Parade of Pleasure: A Study of Popular Iconography in the U.S.A.* London: Verschoyle, 1954.

Waller, Reed. *Erotic Art of Reed Waller*, ed. Dave Schreiner. Princeton, WI: Kitchen Sink, 1990.

Ward, Bill, illus. *Bertha*, written by Joe Doakes and Bart Keister. Paris: Collection Vertiges Graphiques, 1978; others in the series, all by Ward and the same writers for the same publisher, are *Le Secret de Belinda*, 1980; *Ludovic Exile*, 1979; *Pascaline*, 1978; and *Rose Mary Chevrotine*, 1978.

Ward, Bill, and Jack Cole. *Ward's Wow.* New York: Allied American Artists, 1990.

Warren, Roz, ed. *Weenie-Toons: Women Cartoonists Mock Cocks.* Bala Cynwyd, PA: Laugh Lines Press, 1992.

———. *What Is This Thing Called Sex? Cartoons by Women.* Freedom, CA: Crossing Press, 1994.

Warshow, Robert. "Paul, the Horror Comics, and Dr. Wertham." *The Immediate Experience: Movies, Comics, Theatre and Other Aspects of Modern Culture.* Garden City, NY: Doubleday, 1962, pp. 44–62.

Waters, Patricia. *The Sensuous Coloring Book.* Burlingame, CA: Down There Press, 1980.

Wertham, Fredrick. *Seduction of the Innocent.* New York: Rinehart, 1954; rpt. Port Washington, NY: Kennikat Press, 1972.

———. *A Sign for Cain: An Exploration of Human Violence.* New York: Macmillan, 1966.

Widaen, E. *What Pornography Does to Women and to Men.* [Staten Island, NY]: E. Widaen, 1982.

Willie, John [J. A. S. Coutts]. *The Adventures of Sweet Gwendolyn.* New York: Bélier Press, 1974. Now (1993) available in seven video cassettes from Alain Siritzky, ASP 29, rue de Marignan, Paris 75008.

————. *The Art of John Willie: Sophisticated Bondage 1946–1961*, ed. Stefano Piselli and Riccardo Morrocchi. 2 vols. Milan: Glittering Images, 1990.

Wilson, S. Clay. *Spots*. San Francisco: Last Gasp, 1985.

Winer, Lucy, and Paula Koenigsberg. *Rate It X*. New York: International Video, 1985.

Witek, Joseph. *Comic Books as History: The Narrative Art of Jack Jackson, Art Spiegelman, and Harvey Pekar*. Jackson: University of Mississippi Press, 1989.

Wood, Wallace. *Gang Bang*! and *Gang Bang! 2* N.p.: Nuance, 1980.

Worley, Kate and Reed Waller. "Omaha the Cat Dancer: Tip of the Iceberg." *Gauntlet*, 1:5 (1993): 72–77.

Zack, David. "Smut for Love, Art, Society." *Art and Artists*, 4:9 (December 1969): 12–17.

Zwigoff, Terry, dir. *Crumb*. Los Angeles: Columbia Tristar Pictures, 1994.

19

Research on Pornography in the Medical and Social Sciences

THE "INVENTION" OF SEXOLOGY

It would not be accurate to say that sexologists invented either sexuality or pornography, but they have certainly shaped conceptions of both. "Sex Research and Social Change," by John Gagnon, attributes the origins of sexology (the science of sexuality) to Havelock Ellis and Sigmund Freud. Others date the inception later. In "Sexology Struggling to Establish Itself amid Wide Hostility," Edwin Haeberle tells Philip M. Boffey that sexology actually began in Germany after the turn of the century and flourished until it was suppressed by the Nazis. Now, says Haeberle, an early theorist in the field and one of several thousand researchers to attend the 6th World Congress of Sexology held in Washington in 1993, "the field is in total confusion. It's like the state criminology was in 80 years ago, when it was just getting started. But I would still call sexology a science, an interdisciplinary effort where the natural sciences and the humanities have to work together" (C1). Haeberle has selected and annotated excerpts from the work of sexologists like Iwan Bloch, Albert Moll, Magnus Hirschfeld, and Max Marcuse for *The Birth of Sexology: A Brief History in Documents.* Gert Heckma's "A History of Sexology" is an excellent, succinct chronicle of those and other pioneers. Most luminaries in other countries are beyond our scope here, but volume III (*Sexualwissenschaft*) of the *Bilderlexicon der Erotik* introduces figures of international significance, and Charlotte Woolf's *Magnus Hirschfeld: A Portrait of a Pioneer in Sexology,* though necessarily focused on Germany, traces lines of influence radiating from Berlin to America.

More comprehensive is the coverage of trends, issues, breakthroughs, and controversies in Vern L. Bullough's *Science in the Bedroom: A History of Sex Research.* On a different note, the scientist Paul R. Abramson asks whether rigor

can be introduced to a field grown sloppy because of the crowding of disciplinary agendas in "Sexual Science: Emerging Discipline or Oxymoron?" Since
evolution may suggest progress rather than mere change, *development* may be
a more neutral term to describe the establishment of the discipline. Of the several
histories of sexual science, the most comprehensive is Lawrence Birken's *Consuming Desire: Sexual Science and the Emergence of a Culture of Abundance,
1871–1914*, whose dateline begins three decades before Haeberle's. Birken details the economic, psychological, and biological factors that accelerated the
study of sex in the latter half of the nineteenth century. Birken's thesis is that
a new emphasis on pleasure and consumption triggered the growth of sexual
science. One of the purposes of sexology is to counter the folklore that is the
stock-in-trade of genres of pornography and antipornography. At the same time,
like other bodies of knowledge, sexology articulates social, political, and economic forces impinging upon researchers.

Edward M. Brecher's *The Sex Researchers* covers the personalities and careers of key scholars in America, beginning with Havelock Ellis and running
through Masters and Johnson, with overdue attention to the contributions of
women researchers. Personal accounts of their experience in the field of sexology by Clive Davis, Albert Ellis, Robert Francoeur, Paul Gebhard, Naomi Mc-
Cormick, John Prendergast, and Ira Reiss fill the pages of *How I Got into Sex*,
edited by Bonnie Bullough and Vern Bullough and others. *The Modernization
of Sex: Havelock Ellis, Alfred Kinsey, William Masters, and Virginia Johnson*,
by Paul Robinson, concentrates on the work of those named in the title and uses
them as illustrations of the agendas that researchers borrow from the culture at
large. Robinson's *The Sex Radicals* deals with personalities such as Wilhelm
Reich, Geza Roheim, and Herbert Marcuse as they defined phases of cultural
awareness. The essays in *Sex and Scientific Inquiry*, edited by Sandra Harding
and Jean F. O'Barr, question sexology's claim to objectivity and advance various
theories of social construction to explain gendered bias. The always refreshing
John Money offers his own take on recent debates in *Venuses, Penises: Sexology, Sexosophy, and Exigency Theory*.

One consequence of the Kinsey reports was that scientist and institute passed
into folklore, the one as crusader against ignorance, the second as archive of
sexual knowledge. Stanley Elkin's "Alfred Kinsey: The Patron Saint of Sex,"
originally printed in *Esquire* in the 1950s, was an admiring portrait that gave
the man credit for expanding the sexual boundaries of discourse and widening
the experiences of Americans. *Dr. Kinsey and the Institute for Sex Research*,
by Wardell Pomeroy, one of Kinsey's associates, recounts the institute's struggle
to become a privileged archive and details the battles the staff had to fight with
U.S. Customs, which seized erotica sent from abroad, before authorities accepted
the idea of a repository that would be closed to all but scholars. Once clothed
in legitimacy, the institute began to receive for study materials confiscated by
police departments around the country. Ernest Havemann described the politically astute policies that added to the holdings of what by the 1960s had become

the nation's premiere sex research facility in "The Sex Institute." Cornelia Christenson's *Kinsey: A Biography* is dated but still serviceable, especially on the institute's early years. Probably the most trenchant and certainly the most important revisionist study of Kinsey is James H. Jones' *Alfred C. Kinsey: A Public/Private Life*, which attributes the man's sometimes "anguished" methods to his conflicted homosexuality and voyeurism. Jones covers Kinsey's "management" of the publicity surrounding the institute, his orchestration of the publication of the two famous reports, his personal sexual behavior, his idiosyncratic habits, and his practice of personally filming scenes of intercourse, including some involving his own staff.

Paul Gebhard, a close associate, succeeded Kinsey as director. When June Reinisch became director, the name changed to the Kinsey Institute of Sex, Gender, and Reproduction, and the institute reached out to a society more respectful of its expertise. Philip Nobile reports on Reinisch's tenure as director and the discomfort that new agendas caused the staff in "Intrigue at the Kinsey Institute." Reinisch herself wrote *The Kinsey Institute New Report on Sex*, partly as a way of establishing her own leadership and distinguishing it from Kinsey's. (The current head is John Bancroft.)

Conservatives remain convinced that by introducing sexual discourse into the mainstream, Kinsey opened the floodgates of immorality. Chief among exponents of this belief is Judith A. Reisman. In 1990 Reisman and Edward W. Eichel published *Kinsey, Sex and Fraud: An Indoctrination of a People: an Investigation into the Human Sexuality Research of Alfred C. Kinsey et al*, which charged, among other things, that Kinsey "cooked" the statistics on homosexuality in the United States, that he molested young boys, and that his political agenda was to promote bisexuality. Reisman continued her attack in *"Soft Porn" Plays Hardball: Its Tragic Effects on Women, Children and the Family* (1991), in which she linked Kinsey to *Playboy* publisher Hugh Hefner, a man she compares, in turn, to Adolf Hitler; Kinsey and Hefner are proponents, she says, of a secular humanism that undermines family values and saps the spiritual well-being of the nation. A former songwriter for the television show *Captain Kangaroo*, Reisman received a large grant from the Justice Department to survey images of children in *Playboy*, *Penthouse*, and *Hustler*. Philip Nobile's "Was Kinsey a Fake and a Pervert?" says that the Reisman and Eichel book is one phase of a right-wing effort to create a myth of sexual conspiracy. Nobile claims that Reisman's survey of cartoons in the magazines cost $734,000, more than the entire budget for the Meese Commission, and that the Justice Department, embarrassed by the bizarre methodology, shelved the report in 1986. Nobile also notes that Al Regnery, head of the Juvenile Justice and Delinquency prevention program in the Justice Department, gave Reisman the grant; Regnery had to resign from the Meese Commission because the *New York Post* discovered that he "kept porno magazines around the house" (39). Whatever the merits of these charges and countercharges, the exchange is fascinating as an example of folklore in the making. Cultural imperatives make celebrities out of sex researchers, censors, and their opponents, presumably for the same reason that *Playboy* appends brief biographies to its photos of Playmates; the additional information gives substance to otherwise invisible personalities.

The dynamic continues. William H. Masters and Virginia E. Johnson are celebrated for three texts, *Human Sexual Inadequacy*, *Human Sexual Response*, and *The Pleasure Bond*. Like the Kinsey reports, these works were popularized, and their findings, sometimes oversimplified and misinterpreted, become part of the nation's folklore. One of the best popularizations, Nat Lehrman's *Masters and Johnson Explained*, splices an intelligent reading of their work to a fascinating interview with Masters and Johnson themselves. Two other readable glosses on the first work by Masters and Johnson are *Understanding Human Sexual Inadequacy*, by Rollin C. Belliveau, and *An Analysis of Human Sexual Inadequacy*, a collection of essays edited by Edward M. Brecher and Ruth Brecher. Both works stress the historical importance of the pioneering study and translate its tables and charts into popularized narrative. *The New Sex Therapy*, by Helen Singer Kaplan, is perhaps the most informative of many books based on the Masters and Johnson studies.

Jeffrey Weeks remains skeptical about the nature of sexology, seeing in its pronouncements the residue of social and political prejudices. Weeks says in *Sexuality and Its Discontents: Meanings, Myth and Modern Sexualities* that he would settle for a clear-cut statement of sexuality as socially constructed. Sexology mirrors fashion, and that, says Joanna Russ in "Pornography and the Sexuality Debates: Examining the History," has a lot to do with continuing debate. Russ observes that the split between pro- and antisex feminists continues a schism begun around the turn of the century, when male sexologists like Ernest van der Velde and Havelock Ellis tried to liberalize and reform sex as a consequence of the feminist movements of that earlier time. Janice Irvine brings a somewhat different perspective to this point by structuring her history of the discipline, *Disorders of Desire: Sex and Gender in Modern American Sexology*, around the politics of research, its gender biases, and its achievements and shortcomings. Hers may be the most trenchant gender reading of a field whose outlines are continually remapped by cultural critics on one side and scientists on the other.

Historians are just beginning to sift through the mistaken gender assumptions that colored scientific research in the past. Scholars should regard *Science and Homosexualities*, edited by Vernon Rosario, as required reading. Although all of the essays in that volume are first-rate, Margaret Gibson's "Clitoral Corruption: Body Metaphors and American Doctors' Constructions of Female Homosexuality, 1870–1900," is an example of what a gifted historian can do with sources. Almost as good is Gibson's "The Masculine Degenerate: American Doctors' Portrayal of the Lesbian Intellect," which reviews the contributions of phrenology, craniology, endocrinology, urology, and psychology to construction of a bizarre lesbian identity. Two other sources, selected from a huge corpus of new investigations, are Jennifer Terry's "Lesbians Under the Medical Gaze:

Scientists Search for Remarkable Differences," which discusses the significance of early studies and documents, and Londa L. Schiebinger's *The Mind Has No Sex? Women in the Origins of Modern Science*, which reveals brain and anatomy research on genders. One could, of course, find similar, though even larger, bodies of scientific literature on gays and other sexual minorities, each now largely obsolete, if not downright dangerous, as Bullough's *Science in the Bedroom* makes clear. The point is not to sneer at these often-earnest investigations of "difference," "degeneracy," and "deviance" in the past: it is to be cautious about research in present and future.

Other excellent texts, from a field currently exploding with publications, include *Researching Sexual Behavior: Methodological Issues*, edited by John Bancroft, one of the Kinsey Institute series on tools for studying gender, sexual networks and interactions, and cross-cultural issues, and *Thinking Critically about Research on Sex and Gender*, by Paula J. Caplan and Jeremy B. Caplan, a text designed for students interested in the wide range of theories. Finally, it is useful to compare Edward Sagarin's "Sex Research and Sociology: Retrospective and Prospective," published in 1971, and Richard G. Parker and John H. Gagnon's *Conceiving Sexuality: Approaches to Sex Research in a Postmodern World*, published in 1995, in terms of what specialists thought were the most pressing research agendas then and now. (See also **The "Invention" of Sexuality** in Chapter 5.)

ETHNOGRAPHIC RESEARCH

Ethnographers study sexual behavior and communication directly, as it takes place, in different contexts and subcultures. One of the standard texts is *Human Sexual Behavior: Variations in the Ethnographic Spectrum*, edited by Donald S. Marshall and Robert C. Suggs. Its essays are chiefly concerned with remote cultures rather than American communities, but the reader will learn a good deal about the principles and methodology of this type of research; the bibliography of related texts is excellent. Another good introduction to ethnographic fieldwork, despite its having little to do with the United States, is Gilbert Herdt and Robert J. Stoller's *Intimate Communications: Erotics and the Study of Culture*, a text devoted to comparative ethnographic examinations of sexuality in various cultures. The essays in *Taboo: Sex, Identity and Erotic Subjectivity in Anthropological Fieldwork*, edited by Don Kulick and Margaret Willson, deal with the difficulties of evaluating the erotic imagination in anthropological studies, though the sexuality thus exposed can generate folklores that complement our own. Increasingly, ethnographers study the group dynamics and the folklore of sexual situations and events, some involving pornography but all involving specific tropes of behavior.

Notable in this regard is the work of Erving Goffman, whose *Behavior in Public Places* has become a bible for ethnographers. Goffman, the father of situationism, reflects on what happens to site-specific behavior, such as intimate physical contact normally associated with bedrooms, as it moves to other venues. His influence is obvious in articles such as "Behavior in Private Places: Sustaining Definitions of Realities in Gynecological Examinations," by Joan P. Emerson, and "Dramaturgical Desexualization: The Sociology of the Vaginal Examination," by James M. Henslin and Mae A. Briggs, both of which use Goffmanesque approaches to trace the dramatic phases of examinations and analyze the roles of doctors, patients, and nurses in what is really a form of representational theater. Terri Kapsalis goes further, looking at gynecology as medicine, history, ethnography, performance, and art in *Public Privates: Performing Gynecology from Both Ends of the Speculum*. Similar concerns structure "Cruising the Truckers: Sexual Encounters in a Highway Rest Area" by Jay Corzine and Richard Kirby, and it is worth noting that such investigation can shift the study of pornography away from sterile concepts of textuality toward the more fruitful concepts of performance and agency.

Ethnographic and anthropological methods enliven Jack Weatherford's *Porn Row*, probably the most authoritative field study of adult bookstores and arcades (see **Fetishes** in chapter 9). The "sexual dilemma" of American culture piqued Weatherford's attention and stimulated his research: "On the one hand, it is a society whose people have fewer sexual opportunities than almost any other people in the world. On the other hand, it constantly bombards its members with messages promoting sex as the way to happiness, ego fulfillment, balanced character, fun, love, liberation and everything else good" (208). Americans typically react to this dilemma, he says, by denouncing sexual mythologies, embracing hedonism, or withdrawing into chastity, alcohol, or drugs. Weatherford is more interested, of course, in those who pursue their obsessions in pornography. Michael Stein's *The Ethnography of an Adult Bookstore* is a Goffman-like study of the private and public spaces of a combined adult bookstore and theater in a midsized midwestern city, the result of the author's having clerked in the business for some months so that he could observe the clientele and their habits. In addition to his insights on gay and straight behavior in such settings, Stein demonstrates that pornography has become a significant component of popular culture.

David A. Karp found peculiar dynamics at work in the furtive environment described in "Hiding in Pornographic Bookstores: A Reconsideration of the Nature of Urban Anonymity." Patrons respect each other's privacy, avoid contact, verbal or physical, and closely adhere to the social protocols of the stores. Harold Nawy's survey of patrons of adult stores, "In the Pursuit of Happiness? Consumers of Erotica in San Francisco," revealed that habitual consumers of porn are no more deviant than the general population. They are college-educated, white, white-collar, middle-class, married, and middle-aged. John Lindquist and Howard L. Cane agree; their "Myths and Realities of Dirty Book Buyers" confirms that "ordinary" people purchase such materials. So does "The Pulp Voyeur: A Peek at Pornography in Public Places," for which William McKinstry observed the strategies adopted by browsers and customers to minimize embarrassment and conform to prevailing spatial segregation and traffic patterns within the stores. To conduct the research for his *Thy Brother's Wife*, Gay Talese worked as a clerk in a bookstore and as the manager of a massage parlor, from both of which vantage points he could observe the interaction of patrons in these settings. In one of the few such accounts by a woman, Sallie Tisdale speaks of her visits to adult bookstores, first in company with other women, then, as she grew more comfortable, by herself, in *Talk Dirty to Me: An Intimate Philosophy of Sex*. She found clerks determined to be helpful and did not find male patrons threatening or threatened.

According to Kyle Knowles and Houshang Poorkaj in "Attitudes and Behavior on Viewing Sexual Activities in Public Places," the majority of audience members at explicit sexual performance adopt demeanors and postures that provide protective coloration at the same time that their anonymity facilitates voyeurism. Pat Califia's *Public Sex: The Culture of Radical Sex* theorizes about sex in "contested areas," especially gay and lesbian gathering places, but also trendy clubs and other venues. Graphic, if authoritative is Laud Humphreys' *Tearoom Trade: Impersonal Sex in Public Places*, an ethnographic study of voyeurism and exhibitionism behind the public sex in gay toilets and gathering places, based on the researcher's direct observation of glory holes and blow jobs. (For studies of audiences in striptease theaters, public sex scenes, and other venues, see **Sexuality in Public: Exhibitionism** in Chapter 10.)

Two studies conducted by Charles Winick for the President's Commission are models of research. These are "Some Observations on Characteristics of Patrons of Adult Theaters and Bookstores," for which Winick observed styles of dress, behavior, age, and ethnicity in patrons, and "A Study of Consumers of Explicitly Sexual Materials: Some Functions Served by Adult Movies," for which Winick conducted more than 100 interviews to discover why men went to theaters (older patrons sought out fantasies, while younger ones found them partly educational). Winick's follow-up studies, conducted for City University of New York's West 42nd Street Study Team, have been published in *Sex Industries in New York City* and in another City University project, *West 42nd Street Study: The Bright Light Zone*, edited by William Kornblum. These are massive data-gathering expeditions to massage parlors, strip, peep, and sex shows, bookstores, prostitutes, swing clubs, gay baths, street cluster patterns, and so on. Winick's "Licit Sex Industries and Services" contains very precise information on thirteen gay baths, sixteen massage parlors, and seven spas in New York City.

Cultural and/or ethnographic studies of hard-core porn theaters and their audiences during the 1970s include Joseph Slade's "Pornographic Theatres off Times Square," Peter Donnelly's "Running the Gauntlet: The Moral Order of Pornographic Movie Theaters," and Roger B. Rollin's "Triple-X: Erotic Movies and Their Audiences." All three discuss the classes of customers, their expectations, their preferences, and their behavior in theaters. Reporter John Corry brings journalistic hauteur to descriptions of rituals of alienation in movie houses and adult bookstores in Times Square in "The Selling of Sex: A Look through a Solemn Sodom." By contrast, Charles A. Sundholm disdains to patronize viewers in "loop-film" booths in arcades in "The Pornographic Arcade: Ethnographic Notes on Moral Men in Immoral Places." Sundholm catalogs activities that begin with entering the arcade, searching for change for machines, using the viewers, and exiting. Goffman's theories structure Robert P. McNamara's "Dramaturgy and the Social Organization of Peep Shows," which provides "thick" descriptions of the cues, signs, and signals of customers and hustlers in and out of booths.

Though hampered by postmodern jargon, Christian Hansen, Catherine Needham, and Bill Nichols offer an interesting comparison of ethnography and pornography as scales of authenticity in "Skin Flicks: Pornography, Ethnography, and the Discourses of Power." James Ridgeway and Sylvia Plachy enter the subculture of fetishes in *Red Light*, which interviews in startling detail mistresses and their slaves, sex performers, strippers, hustlers, pornographers, and many others. Marianne Macy avoids the grittiness but still gets close to denizens of similar scenes in *Working Sex: An Odyssey into Our Cultural Underworld*; she talks with pornographers, performers, prostitutes. Steven Chapple and David Talbot visit orgies and other sex scenes but mostly interview fairly well known figures in the sex industry (and in the antiporn industry) in *Burning Desires: Sex in America—A Report from the Field*. "Eurydice" visits lesbian, straight, and gay subcultures in *Satyricon USA: A Journey across the New Sexual Frontier*, a highly readable, intimate, and astute tour of "scenes" enlivened by the author's reflections on sexuality and gender.

PORNOGRAPHY AS GENERATOR OF FANTASIES

We know so little about the role of fantasy in human sexuality that much of what passes for research on that aspect of pornography is mere speculation. We do not know how arousal works, let alone what triggers it, nor do we understand the mechanisms by which desire is sustained. Like more socially acceptable forms of discourse (the average prime-time television program, for instance), pornography both reproduces and (presumably) generates fantasies. Despite the ubiquity of fantasy in human sexuality, its functions have scarcely been mapped, though it may well be that pornography is simply one of the names we give to this clearly essential component of sexual experience.

One function may be ontological. In their authoritative essay "Fantasy and the Origins of Sexuality," Jean Laplanche and J. B. Pontalis explore fantasy's crucial role in the shaping of sexuality by providing "settings for desire." Fantasy, say the authors, *enables* sexuality: it "is not the object of desire, but its setting." Beverley Brown concentrates on the properties of pornography in her "A Feminist Interest in Pornography—Some Modest Proposals":

Insofar as fantasy does not work without material, there must be *some* object, arbitrary but not random. If that object is already connected with the sexual, so much the better. Pornography essentially provides a stock of visual repertoires constructed out of elements of the everyday, using objects, including elements of the feminine, already placed within definite cultural practices. In re-placing these objects, in making them available or special, as objects around which sexual fantasy can operate without too much wit or effort, pornography simultaneously opens up the possibility of a reversal, of seeing objects return to their cultural niches with a certain afterglow. (11)

While a great deal of research assumes that humans are passive recipients of sexual stimuli, quasi automatons whose glands moisten at the sight of movie stars, say, logic suggests—and the history of communication research confirms—that individuals themselves invest texts, images, and events with erotic meaning and that they reeroticize them at will. Audiences, in short, are *not* passive, and actively seek pleasure. We all have stored memories that can trigger erotic reveries; we need not call them fetishes. They may be memorable acts of intercourse, recalled to spur better performance with the partner of a moment, a fleeting glimpse of a face or body recalled to similar effect, or a microsecond suddenly flooded with sensory overload; any or all of these may be subject to volition. As the physician John Money says again and again, especially in "Pornography in the Home: A Topic in Medical Education": "Pornography does not automatically have the power to incite behavior. It does not have the power to turn people into sexual maniacs who rush out in the street in order to copulate with the first living thing they see, whether on two legs or four. In fact, it doesn't have the power even to turn you into a 'picture freak' " (419). Valerie Steele endorses such common sense in *Fetish*: "Human sexuality involves more than an instinctual response to a programmed stimulus; we do not go into 'heat' and mate like animals. Human sexuality is constructed. But contrary to what many feminists believe, it is not learned in the sense of acquiring new roles. Boys do not look at *Playboy* and learn to like big breasts and view sex objects any more than girls look at *Vogue* and learn to become anorexic and passive" (167).

Second, pornographic fantasy augments and enlivens sexual experience, a position advanced by Eberhard Kronhausen and Phyllis Kronhausen in *Erotic Fantasies: A Study of the Sexual Imagination* and "The Psychology of Pornography." At the other extreme are neo-Puritans who believe that intercourse should be free of the baggage of erotic reverie, that the act should be mediated only by the physical attraction between the two people who remain for the time at least fixated on each other; otherwise, such critics think, the sex lacks authenticity. Those who disingenuously profess astonishment that anyone could possibly enjoy a "representation" of the sexual act are willfully oblivious to the habits of the millions who enjoy representations of "real life" on television or in books—at the same time that they also enjoy normal pursuits. The Kronhausens believe that fantasy enhances any sexual act, that one might, in fact, make love to a concatenation of images or scripts that *include* those specifically focused on the partner. In this interpretation, pornography advances sexual pleasure and meaning by furnishing or burnishing fantasies. Of course, pornography can stimulate solitary masturbation as well as mutual desire. Here, as with every other aspect of sex and pornography, politics reigns. Many conservatives and fundamentalists believe that masturbation is misguided, wasteful, or immoral, although some might make exceptions for men or women who have no mates and no hope of one. By contrast, millions of Americans routinely practice masturbation for relief or for recreation.

Third, pornography helps us to articulate fantasies that have been shrouded in mystery or guilt. That viewpoint has been succinctly expressed as a sorites by Christopher Lehmann-Haupt in his review of Maurice Girodias' *The Frog Prince*: "After all, without sexual constraint, there would be no frustration. Without frustration, there would be no fantasy. Without fantasy, there would be no pornography."[1] Therapists report that more and more "normal" people experience fantasies once regarded as perverse or even violent. Most interesting is the evidence that women experience similar fantasies and compulsions, albeit in subtle forms. The danger is that they can substitute for life by becoming necessary to sexual arousal, says Daniel Goleman in "New View of Fantasy: Much Is Found Perverse," an article on the functions of fantasy. Goleman quotes therapist Louise Kaplan as saying that "the erotic pleasure in a perverse act is secondary to the emotional reassurance it offers" (B7). A study by David Sue indicates that sexual fantasies during intercourse enhance arousal. Sue's "Erotic Fantasies of College Students during Coitus" says that males report more incidences of fantasy lovers; women report more fantasies of being forced into sexual relationships. William E. Masters and Virginia H. Johnson compare fantasies among different genders as part of their *Homosexuality in Perspective*. Their survey indicates that among homosexuals the fantasy of being forced to engage in sex is more common than forcing someone else to have sex.

Popular treatises on sexual fantasy far outnumber academic publications. Some of these are feel-good texts, such as *Dr. Ruth's Guide to Good Sex*, in which Ruth Westheimer advises using pornography in order to enrich fantasy life, and *Joys of Fantasy: The Book for Loving Couples*, an illustrated volume of fantasies by Siv Cedering Fox, a prizewinning poet. Daniel Goleman and Sherida Bush offer a broad look at various special interest groups clustered around standard and marginal fantasies and fetishes in "The Liberation of Sexual Fantasy." Avodah K. Offit's *Night Thoughts: Reflections of a Sex Therapist* is a balanced consideration of pornography and various forms of behavior, without theoretical fanfare, elitist assumptions, or laments about sexual anxieties. Her bottom line is that sexual fantasies are essential to health, useful in sexual performance, and gloriously human. Fantasies are similar to play, claims Eric Berne in *Games People Play: The Psychology of Human Relationships*, which analyzes games, pastimes, and roles, many of them self-consciously erotic. Even more specific are the role-playing activities advanced by Rolf Milonas in *Fantasex: A Book of Erotic Games for the Adult Couple*.

One of the first Americans to promote fantasy for women was "J. Aphrodite," the penname of Carol Livingston, whose *To Turn You On: 39 Sex Fantasies for Women* became quite popular. Interviewed by *Hustler*, Livingston described her goal as educational; too many women do not realize that they share fantasies. Lonnie Barbach tells women that the key to sexual liberation is the freedom to choose one's fantasies and behavior in *For Yourself: The Fulfillment of Female Sexuality*, a guide to writing one's own sexual scripts. Karen Shanor also maintains that fantasy is important to a rich erotic life in *The Fantasy Files: A Study of the Sexual Fantasies of Contemporary Women*. One of the more prolific interpreters of women's fantasies is Nancy Friday. The success of her collection, *My Secret Garden: Women's Sexual Fantasies*, led to *Forbidden Flowers: More Women's Sexual Fantasies*, and *Women on Top: How Real Life Has Changed Women's Sexual Fantasies*. Complementing these volumes is Friday's *Men in Love: Men's Sexual Fantasies: The Triumph of Love over Rage*, in which the most prevalent male sexual fantasies turn out not to be violent, as so many Americans so often think, but fairly conventional scenarios of exotic sex mixed with affection. William J. Slattery discovers similar patterns in *The Erotic Imagination: Sexual Fantasies of the Adult Male*, a serious analysis of archetypal sexual scripts. Psychologist Peter Dally discusses the fantasies he had encountered over years of practice in *The Fantasy Factor: How Male and Female Sexual Fantasies Affect Our Lives*.

Academics are powerfully attracted to the cheap-labor studies that elicit fantasies from samples of volunteers and college students. These range from the old "Effects of Erotic Films on Sexual Behavior of Married Couples" study conducted by Jay Mann, Jack Sidman, and Sheldon Starr for the President's Commission to "College Men and Women Respond to X-Rated Videos Intended for Male or Female Audiences: Gender and Sexual Scripts" by Donald Mosher and P. Maclan and "Gender Differences in Sexual Fantasy and Behavior in a College Population: A Ten-Year Replication" by B. Hsu, A. Kling, C. Kessler, K. Knape, P. Diefenbach, and J. Elias. All of these, and more studies like them, found that males exhibit and prefer fantasies of numerous young and beautiful women eager to engage in sex with little commitment, while women exhibit and prefer fantasies involving a powerful male of high status and income who may display aggression toward others and couple frequently but settle down to monogamy with, and kindness toward, his chosen mate. B. Ellis and D. Symons conclude in "Sex Differences in Sexual Fantasy" that women are drawn toward softer, more romantic tropes, while males are aroused by graphic sex that is uncontextualized by emotional involvement but that these categories are not impermeable and are affected by external factors such as economics and class. (See also **Film Content: Violence and Sex** in Chapter 13.) The idea that women are indifferent to images or repelled by graphic discourse, textual or otherwise, is reiterated in Robert May's *Sex and Fantasy: Patterns of Male and Female Development*. Though May makes little reference to pornographic representations, his somewhat romantic discussion of gender differences in eroticism turns on what has by now become a cliché: that males are subject to "undifferentiated lust," while females respond to "emotional investment in another person." These stereotypes, says May, are culturally constructed from social expectations. His point is echoed by Rosalind Coward, whose *Female Desires: How They Are Sought, Bought, and Packaged* is a study of what corporations *suppose* that women will enjoy. In *The Secrets of Sexual Fantasy* and *The Great Sex Divide: A Study of Male—Female Differences*, psychologist Glenn Wilson reports that men are more susceptible to visual stimuli, more prone to voyeurism and fetishism, and more likely to fantasize about sexual images and themes than women. Graham Masterton's *1001 Erotic Dreams Interpreted* is a more literary, than psychological, analysis, but it is also more interesting, reputable, and fun than the title would indicate. Edward Thorne identifies standard scenarios that recur in the similarly popular *Your Erotic Fantasies: In 25 Real-Life Interviews, the Hidden Sexual Yearnings That All of Us Have.*

Feminists sometimes contend that pornography masks a fear of women. The best-known exponent of this view is Susan Griffin, whose *Pornography and Silence: Culture's Revenge against Nature* suggests that male hatred of women is cosmic. According to Griffin, the fantasies that animate pornography are akin to the male's technological rape of a nature that he sees as feminine. The Freudian thesis of Susan Lurie's "Pornography and the Dread of Women: The Dilemma of Male Sexuality" also holds that fear of women drives male eroticism; dread begins with a boy's separation from his mother, a trauma compensated for only by the possession of a weaponlike penis that is given free rein to terrorize women in pornography. Scott G. McNall argues in "Pornography: The Structure of Domination and the Mode of Reproduction" that Western cultures use pornography as a means to "mystify" macho behavior; pornography is thus one of many discourses that persuade humans to accept male dominance. Stephen G. Smith considers Susan Griffin's argument that masculinity takes its revenge on motherhood—a theme she sees expressed in porn—as itself a source of misunderstanding. From a Kantian ethical perspective, Smith says in "Pornography and Other Pathologies of Gender Valuation," it is impossible to tell whether pornography denigrates or exalts the feminine side of the psyche. In "Pornography and the Mechanisms of Defense," a famous essay that is mandatory reading for scholars, Norman Holland discusses the ways in which fantasies in pornography impact on the reader's own fantasies; such fantasies, he argues, result in adaptation but no permanent alteration in the recipient.

Some scholars try to extrapolate the psychological significance of fantasies from their content. In a version of catharsis theory, C. Crepault suggests in "Sexual Fantasies and Visualization of 'Pornographic Scenes' " that pornography helps society in that it encourages the aggressive to masturbate instead of acting out urges with innocent victims, on the premise that masturbation provides relief when intercourse is not an option. According to many psychologists, humans seek in pornography fantasies that match "sexual scripts" they carry inside their heads. Getting a fix on such scripts is difficult, however, because it is impossible to know whether the fantasies in a particular pornographic example are aligned with fantasies that the reader/viewer has already made iconographic, or whether the pornographic source reveals it for the first time. On one hand, a male who enjoys seeing red-haired women performing oral sex may be disappointed if the red-haired actress in a porn film engages instead in something else; on the other, the scene he does see may help him to expand his erotic horizons.

In *Observing the Erotic Imagination*, the late Robert J. Stoller noted in pornography created by individuals "a script, the principal purpose of which is to undo childhood traumas, conflicts, and frustrations by converting those earlier painful experiences to present (fantasized) triumphs" (vii). The scripts, according to Stoller, are always precise, so that fueling sexual excitement are "meanings, scripts, interpretations, tales, myths, memories, beliefs, melodramas, and built like a playwright's plot, with exquisite care, no matter how casual and spontaneous the product appears" (49). In *Sexual Excitement: The Dynamics of Erotic Life* and *Perversion: The Erotic Form of Hatred*, perhaps his most controversial books, Stoller argued that anger, cruelty, humiliation, and desire for revenge may be components of a hostility that he thinks is integral to sexual excitement and that the sadism that results is not limited to one gender. Some brutality is always a component in fantasies leading to potency, Stoller thinks, even when those fantasies are loving. He argued that hostility is inherent in pornography and that the more perverse the pornographic vision, the more hostile it is. Stoller's "Pornography and Perversion" observes that pornography for women tends to be successful (i.e., arousing) if it has a story line that reaches narrative closure—as opposed to more open-ended plots preferred by males. *True Confessions* and *True Love* are never explicit about sexual acts or nudity, but they are romantic, sentimental, satisfying, and complete. Pornographic depictions of activities like sadism satisfy people whose psychological dynamics were shaped in childhood and help (primarily) males resolve conflicts. What is porn to one person may not be to another, and hostility can be disguised in the message.

Other theorists think the dynamic both more complex and more benign. William Simon advances the idea that the cultural context of sexual scripts, that is, codes that determine meaning, can be altered in healthy directions in "The Social, the Erotic, and the Sensual: The Complexities of Sexual Scripts." Simon and John H. Gagnon develop this concept further in "Sexual Scripts: Permanence and Change." Carol G. Wells' *Right Brain Sex: Using Creative Visualization to Enhance Sexual Pleasure* is a sort of manual on creating and controlling erotic mental scripts. Elizabeth Cowie draws on Freud and Pat Califia to discuss the multiple meanings and complexities of fantasy in "Pornography and Fantasy: Psychoanalytic Perspectives." Seymour Fisher observes in *Sexual Images of the Self: The Psychology of Erotic Sensations and Illusions* that sexuality is "framed by illusion"; examples are the belief that "masturbation produces weakness" or "men are weakened by ejaculation" or "women are uninterested in and incapable of being sexually aroused" (270–271). Implicit is the notion that there is no "normal" sex, because we are early implanted with "sexual fictions." Paula Webster, one of the best and most honest writers about pornography, explores fantasies nonjudgmentally in "The Forbidden: Eroticism and Taboo," an essay that asserts the value of what Webster calls an "erotic heritage."

Some psychologists worry about fantasies becoming too prominent. In *Lacan, Discourse, and Social Change: A Psychoanalytic Cultural Criticism*, Mark Bracher says that porn presents "a multifaceted array of desire in which the desire of the other (in various forms) is central, and in which both men and women figure as subjects and objects" (85) and that "pornography works to suppress love in general, including the only kind of love that, according to Lacan, can coexist with desire: a love that exists beyond the law, a love of difference and otherness, which psychoanalytic treatment makes possible" (100). Therapist Terry A. Kupers suggests in "Pornography and Intimacy" that excessive reliance on pornographic images may work against an ideal relationship between husband and wife. On the positive side, pornography can, on occasion, help heal damaged male psyches. Another therapist, Joseph Glenmuller, writes of a case in which a man's "addiction" to pornography interfered with his relationship with his companion and led to enormous guilt in the title narrative of *The Pornographer's Grief, and Other Tales of Human Sexuality*. The subject's fondness for explicit magazines, however, also helped him "recover" a bond with his father, who also enjoyed pornography. Subjects shown common, nonviolent pornography for a study called "Pornography's Impact on Sexual Satisfaction," conducted by Dolf Zillmann and Jennings Bryant, reported increased dissatisfaction with their partners in terms of the latter's appearance, performance, affection, and curiosity. The viewers apparently found that the fantasy performers were more exciting than their own partners, but the researchers did not investigate mainstream movies to see if the viewers would feel similar dissatisfaction with their partners after seeing, say, Cindy Crawford or Richard Gere; in any case they stop short of blaming porn for the dissatisfaction. In *Media, Children, and the Family: Social Scientific, Psychodynamic, and Clinical Perspectives*, however, Zillmann, Bryant, and Aletha C. Huston suggest that porn may have deleterious effects on children and that it may be destructive of family relationships.

RESEARCH ON AUDIENCES: GENDERED RESPONSES

Research on *actual*—rather than experimental or theorized—audiences for pornography is just beginning, pioneered by Larry Gross in "Marginal Texts, Marginal Audiences." Gross points out that "the public" condemns pornography and believes that the government should regulate it at the same time that millions of Americans consume it. He examines the messages of a porn film as they mutate—the conceived text, the production text, the produced text, the transmitted text, the received text, the perceived text, the social/public text—on their way to an audience that Gross believes is average and normal. No text remains stable as it moves through communication channels. At each point of interchange, as it crosses cultural synapses, the text will be perceived and interpreted differently. A pornographic text may thus be arousing at one juncture but not at another. Despite this mutability, the great power of pornography nevertheless derives from a shared secret: almost no one will admit to finding it arousing. Clearly, humans lie about pornography as often as they lie about sex itself.

Probably the most intriguing statistics are those indicating that women rent large numbers of explicit films and thus form a sizable percentage of porn audiences. Of a host of sources, two, one dated, one recent, will serve to indicate a continuous trend: Karen Haehne's "Confessions of a Feminist Porn Programmer" puts the women's share of the audience at 60 percent; Linda Williams' *Hard Core: Power, Pleasure, and the Frenzy of the Visible* says that 50 percent of American women watch porn and that they as a group watch 40 percent of all such videos. (See **Films and Videotapes** in Chapter 21.) Such authorities point out the obvious: women consume pornography for the same reason men do—pleasure—and they may lie about their pleasure just as often as male counterparts.

Women as well as men subscribe to pornographic stereotypes, says Mariana Valverde in "Pornography: Not for Women Only," and women must be free to advance their own ideas of sexuality as a way of empowering themselves; society cannot deal with pornography by isolating or banning it, because eroticization is part of culture. Bernice Faust's *Women, Sex and Pornography: A Controversial Study* maintains that women are less stimulated by explicit pornography because they are more responsive to tactile, than visual, stimulation; that it is shallow to assume that all porn is an expression of male power; and that both sexes should work toward achieving erotic expression that is real communication. In this regard, Faust explicitly opposes the feminist, antiporn position, in part because she thinks that such groups do not really look at pornography, let alone try to understand sexuality. Faust advances well beyond Lois Gould's pioneering "Pornography for Women," an early (1975), but still important, consideration of the different reactions of men and women to erotica. Gould thinks that women and men are attracted to pornography of different kinds, partly because men think of sex as recreational, while women see it as relational behavior. Men prefer images, have less need for social context, are not bothered by a lack of characterization, and do not object to raw and graphic language. By contrast, says Gould, women are not so visual, rely more on their imaginations, are drawn to more romantic plots, and need to identify with the people in scenarios and fantasies. Taking note of magazines like *Playgirl* purportedly aimed at women, Gould says that most women seem uninterested and concludes that the fantasies in such genres are insufficiently romantic. An even earlier (1970) article by the indefatigable Joyce Brothers, "What Women Think of Pornography," pertinent as a relic of a more liberal period, observes that women have become more aggressively interested in sexuality and in male sexual attributes, though they still prefer contexts of romance. Christine Pickard says in "A Perspective on Female Response to Sexual Material" that women are indifferent to porn because they are socially compelled to be.

Celia Barbour's "Looking at Pictures" insists that women are as influenced as men by every other kind of image and should be just as responsive to sexual ones. She thinks women should demand pornography that caters to varieties of female taste: "Adolescent girls need sexy magazines that are passed along by their sisters and given as gift subscriptions by maiden aunts, with nudges and winks all around. Magazines that encourage them to look without shame at dirty pictures." Gertrud Koch believes that with time and exposure to explicit material women will be able to appreciate (and even to change) pornography. As Koch puts it in "The Body's Shadow Realm," "The fact that women react ambivalently to pornographic films, torn between fascination and disappointment, may not always be because of a prudish upbringing, which forbids an open view and leads to repulsion and a defensive attitude toward sexuality. It may still be possible for women, in spite of their criticism, to take a utopian view of Pornotopia" (43).

To the question "What Turns Women On?" Germaine Greer responds that women don't need to see men sporting enormous erections or clutching their crotches, though some focus on buttocks or musculature would be nice; she thinks that women do respond to visual cues but that artists should strive for sexual appeal that does not rely exclusively on genitals or gender. A confident Susie Bright believes that women can construct a powerful pornography of their own. In her charming Introduction to *Herotica: A Collection of Women's Erotic Fiction*, Bright observes:

There's still a lot of confusion about what the label "women's erotica" means. At its worst, it's a commercial term for vapid femininity, a Harlequin romance with a G-string. The very word "erotic" implies superior value, fine art, an aesthetic which elevates the mind and incidentally stimulates the body. "Women's pornography," on the other hand, is a contradiction in terms for many people, so convinced are they that pornography represents the darker, gutter side of lust. We are enmeshed in a semantic struggle for which words will describe our sexual creativity. What turns women on? And why have we been silent on the subject for so long? As we begin to reveal, in detail, the complexity and scope of our sexual desires, the appropriate language will evolve. (3)

Women have only to seize the opportunity, Bright says:

At least we can get one thing straight before we wander down the path of feminine hedonism: some women want the stars, some the sleaze. Some desire the nostalgia of the ordinary, some the punch of the kinky. And some want all of it. Our sexual minds travel everywhere, and embrace every emotion. Our sexual fiction is not so different from men's in terms of physical content. Its uniqueness lies in the detail of our physical description, our vulnerability and the often confessional quality of our speech in this new territory. Above all, because we have had so little of women's sexual fiction, there is absolutely no formula to follow. (3)

That generational difference is telling. In the 1970s, Margaret Mead worried that women would never find an erotic voice. In "Women and the 'New' Pornography," Mead generally approved of discourse aimed at recognizing women as sexual creatures who can make their own decisions but thought that vulgarity blunted the genuine messages that women could contribute.

Although Bright often plays the cultural role of "bad girl" (the title of one of her books is *Susie Bright's Sexwise: America's Favorite X-Rated Intellectual Does Dan Quayle, Catharine MacKinnon, Stephen King, Camille Paglia, Nicholson Baker, Madonna, the Black Panthers, and the GOP*), she has been joined by feminists who know that sexual representation, sexual expression, and sexual stimulation are complex and essential assets of the women's movement, too necessary for realizing identity, and too valuable to be dismissed in ideological diatribes. Anthropologist Carole S. Vance intelligently foregrounds what she calls "Vance's One-Third Rule: show any personally favored erotic image to a group of women, and one-third will find it disgusting, one-third will find it ridiculous, and one-third will find it hot." The remarks are part of the epilogue (433) of *Pleasure and Danger: Exploring Female Sexuality*, a collection of essays edited by Vance. In the "Current Controversies" section (417–418) of *Powers of Desire: The Politics of Sexuality*, edited by Ann Snitow, Christine Stansell, and Sharon Thompson, the editors ask whether men's and women's sexual natures are quintessentially different. In "The New Feminism of Yin and Yang," one of the essays in that volume, Alice Echols says those feminists generally associated with the antipornography campaign

answer in the affirmative, positing maleness and femaleness as essential psychic qualities based in biology. Conversely, critics of the anti-pornography movement are characterized not only by their sexual libertarianism but by a skeptical attitude to the question of sexual identity, arguing that differences between the sexes are not dichotomous and constant but arbitrary, relative, and subject to change. Is it only men who prefer and perpetuate pornography, who enjoy its imagery of subordination, domination, extreme sexual excitement, and promiscuity, or who are interested in sexual expression that includes aggression and penetration? Are such pleasures inherently violent and misogynist? (418)

Feminists may very well have displaced fears of rape onto erotic images, but the anxieties are real, and males who associate sex with romantic ideals of freedom, rebellion, and individuality are not always sensitive to the dangers that unrestricted sex holds for women. Judith Levine makes these points well in "Perils of Desire," a review of *Pleasure and Danger*. Levine agrees with the pro-sex contributors to that volume that the rhetoric of the antiporn radicals is often misinformed and that it discriminates against sexual minorities but is "distressed" that liberals do not always acknowledge the dangers of sexuality for women. "Vague and downright wrong as antiporn theory may be," she says, it does try to make connections "among porn, misogynist porn, and misogyny in general, between consensual pain and assault, and (the most extreme conflation) between consensual heterosexual intercourse and rape" and notes that the theory "rings true to a lot of women" (13).

It might be useful, nonetheless, to imagine a politically perfect pornography. First, it would not be antisocial, raucous, or nasty; the representations would be warm, sweet, and nurturing, totally without aggression, and completely safe, perhaps accompanied by a nonsectarian prayer; its expression would violate no taboos and would offend no one. Second, it would not be masculine. It might not even involve sex as we know it: no nudity by which women could be objectified, no penetration, perhaps no exchange of fluids, probably no friction, but tons of respect. It would be, in short, the product of corporate America, the public fantasy of a committee. Mark Bracher, for instance, calls for a sort of Republican/feminist cultural and symbolic "reconstruction" of "the desiring masculine body" to promote the unity of love and sex in "Writing and Imaging the Body in Pornography: The Desire of the Other and Its Implications for Feminism." In their efforts to end the dispute over nature and nurture, some gender theorists view pornography as the site where gender is constructed. From their behaviorist perspective, a perfect pornography would subvert hegemonic order by depicting humans in intercourse with males *and* females (and perhaps other species) on a nondiscriminatory basis and would thus encourage all of us to experiment with a pansexuality free from biological imperatives that we erroneously believe drive us. Mariana Valverde lampoons these ideas as academic folklore in "Lesbiantics: The True Joy of Sex": "Some people think that eroticism in a feminist utopia would be androgynous, non-violent, soft and fuzzy, and perfectly symmetrical, with both partners doing exactly the same thing for the same amount of time at precisely the same time. You know the myth: two happy significant others of no particular gender meet, like each other, talk, quietly kiss, and disappear between the sheets as the light fades. No lust; no sweat; no power struggle."

Many studies have noted that the age of subjects is a significant factor in response to pornography. C. Gary Merritt, Joel E. Gerstl, and Leonard A. LoSciuto, for instance, discovered in a survey of more than 2,000 people reported in "Age and Perceived Effects of Erotica-Pornography: A National Sample Study" that attitudes shift toward conservatism as sexual urges diminish. Gender responses are more difficult to assess. Mary Burt's invaluable summation, "Use of Pornography by Women: A Critical Review of the Literature," concludes that research from 1965 to 1972 indicates that women seem less interested in pornography than men because of the roles assigned them by culture, not because of physiology or psychology. The need, she says, is for more research into the emotional and physiological responses by men *and* women. "Male–Female Differences in Sexual Arousal and Behavior during and after Exposure to Sexually Explicit Stimuli," by Gunter Schmidt, and "Sex Differences in Response to Psychosexual Stimulation by Films and Slides," by Schmidt and Volkman Sigusch, found that differences in response to explicit films and slides from groups of men and women were not so great as expected; women reported being aroused to masturbation also, but more women than men found some examples repellent. Since their subjects were German, however, the authors allow that American subjects might respond differently. Their point is that women can be aroused by visual erotica. In another study by Schmidt, Sigusch, and S. Schaefer, "Responses to Reading Erotic Stories: Male–Female Differences," women as well as men acknowledged genital responses to explicit stories. J. H. Geer and M. S. McGlone report in "Sex Differences in Memory for Erotica" that women tend to recall the romantic elements of erotic stories, where males tend to recall more graphic detail.

William Masters and Virginia Johnson insist in "The Sexual Response, Cycle I" and "The Sexual Response, Cycle II" that instrumentation must be supplemented by direct observation where women are concerned. Masters and Johnson also note that a good deal of patience is required: "Providing [female] subjects with pornographic material to read while the vagina is under direct observation [with instruments] soon produces a most successful vaginal lubrication reaction [the so-called sweating phenomenon of vaginal walls]" (I, 72), though clitoral reaction takes longer; "A minimum of one half-hour of exposure to pornographic literature was necessary to produce an observable tumescent reaction of the clitoral glans" (II, 102). Julia R. Heiman points out in "Women's Sexual Arousal: The Physiology of Erotica" that using the photoplethysmograph (which is inserted into the vagina of subjects) permits researchers to measure arousal even when the women subjects do not admit to being stimulated. The technology indicates that women are aroused (albeit more slowly than men) by explicit porn, whether with romantic context or not, particularly if the focus was on women who initiated the intercourse; the results appear to undermine the theory that women are drawn only to soft, romantic subjects.

N. McConaghy's "Penile Volume Changes to Moving Pictures of Male and Female Nudes in Heterosexual and Homosexual Males" found that images of nude males aroused homosexuals but that the same images caused detumescence among heterosexual males, a finding usually cited in support of heterosexual fear of homosexuality. A follow-up study by McConaghy, "Penile Volume Responses to Moving and Still Pictures of Male and Female Nudes," concluded that heterosexual males responded sexually to pictures of females but not of males and that responses to specific pictures were idiosyncratic. William A. Fisher and Donn Byrne report in "Sex Differences in Response to Erotica: Love versus Lust" that images and themes of casual sex arouse men and women to about the same degree. Donald L. Mosher and Paul R. Abramson find in "Subjective Sexual Arousal to Films of Masturbation" that males prefer films of females masturbating, but females respond to films of masturbation by either sex. Mosher's "Sex Differences, Sex Experience, Sex Guilt and Explicitly Sexual Films" finds that women experience more negative responses than men and thinks that masculine guilt enhances the appeal of such films to men. Donn Byrne, Fran Cherry, John Lamerth, and Herman E. Mitchell discovered in "Husband–Wife Similarity in Response to Erotic Stimuli" that spouses tend to respond to the same kinds of material and to share attitudes toward pornography and legal issues concerning it.

Zillmann and Bryant found in "Shifting Preferences in Pornography Consumption" that experimental subjects who had been exposed to large quantities of garden-variety pornography exhibited a preference for more exotic types (sadomasochism, bestiality, bondage), though the researchers could not determine whether the preference stemmed from genuine desire or boredom consequent on repetition. For her study, "*The Relationship between Pornography Use by Male Spouses and Women's Experiences of Marital Interaction and Satisfaction*," Shirley Rae Fuller found no significant differences among couples in which the male partners enjoyed pornography and those in which the male partners used none. Correlated on scales indicating dominance, independence, connection, and other factors as indices of marital satisfaction, those who viewed lots of porn seemed no better as lovers than those who viewed none, or vice versa. There was no indication of negative effects on the males fond of erotica. Zillmann and Bryant's "Effects of Prolonged Consumption of Pornography on Family Values" concluded that extensive exposure to sexually explicit materials encouraged greater acceptance of premarital and extramarital sex; such exposure also increased the likelihood that subjects would believe that both sexes are promiscuous and that repression of sexual desires may be harmful. These ideas, the authors concede, seem to undermine traditional regard for marriage. In "Repeated Exposure to Pornography and Arousal Levels of Subjects Varying in Guilt," Thomas Schill, Mark Van Tuinen, and Don Doty attempted to determine whether guilt reduced sexual arousal, as some researchers have suggested, and conclude that it might not, since other kinds of inhibitions may be at work. The authors note that subjects may just be reporting what they think researchers want to hear.

James Weaver's "Responding to Erotica: Perceptional Processes and Dispositional Implications," an excellent, objective survey of research, outlines the difficulty of isolating and distinguishing messages in erotica and speculates on how audiences extract them from the welter of messages that media carry. The inconsistencies and contradictions of content are thus certain to generate controversies, some of which Weaver sketches. Since real-life relationships, pedestrian or otherwise, require a great deal of emotional and intellectual investment, the "irresponsible" fantasies of pornography would seem to offer relief by serving as safety valves. The question then becomes, Do those fantasies merely vent the pressures of everyday routine, do they function as primers of superficiality, or do they reinforce stereotypes that are dangerous? Critics divide along lines drawn by their own moral assumptions and by their assessment of audiences. Some critiques implicitly postulate audiences who are passive and unaware, while others envision them as intelligent and active interpreters; neither group is likely to convince the other. Ellen Willis' well-known essay, "Feminism, Moralism, and Pornography," points out, "The erotica-versus-porn approach evades the (embarrassing?) question of how porn is *used*. It endorses the portrayal of sex as we might like it to be and condemns the portrayal of sex as it too often is, whether in action or only in fantasy. But if pornography is to arouse, it must appeal to the feelings we have, not those that by some utopian standard we ought to have. Sex in this culture has been so deeply politicized that it is impossible to make clear-cut distinctions between 'authentic' sexual impulses and those conditioned by patriarchy. Between, say, *Ulysses* at one end and *Snuff* at the other, erotica/pornography conveys all sorts of mixed messages that elicit complicated and private responses." (463). (See also **Sex and Pornography Surveys** in Chapter 5.)

PORNOGRAPHY AS THERAPY

Common sense suggests that exposure to sexual materials can lead to masturbation and thus lessen the tendency of individuals predisposed to aggression to act upon their desires. Unfortunately, few studies examine the "catharsis" effect, as such channeling toward release is sometimes called. Several factors explain why this theory is ignored. First, conventional wisdom holds that pornography is by definition antisocial. Second, discussion of masturbation is still virtually taboo in our culture, despite ample evidence that its practice, assisted by pornography or not, is widespread among Americans of all classes, ethnicities, and genders. Third, short of an arrest for a sexual crime, by which time any test would be invalid, it is difficult to identify individuals predisposed toward sexual aggression. Fourth and most important, it is virtually impossible to design a study that would test the premise. Since researchers have yet to design a credible experiment demonstrating that exposure to properly and carefully defined sexual expression leads to visible, recordable, or measurable aggressive effects, it seems unlikely that anyone can construct a test for registering what would be—in effect—*no effect*. Despite the low repute in which it is thus held by social scientists under heavy pressure to experiment, then, catharsis theory remains a strong, but untestable, concept. Changing fashions in research will inevitably bring it to the fore in the future.

In the meantime, some researchers find modest variations on the theory persuasive. Sexual materials, correctly presented, can help reduce anxieties and guilt, according to Dorothy M. Dallas' "The Use of Visual Materials in Sex Education." Those conclusions are echoed by Patricia Gilland's "Therapeutic Use of Obscenity" and by Maurice Yaffé's "Therapeutic Uses of Sexually Explicit Material." Both Gilland and Yaffé point out that pornography works with some patients, not with others, but that it definitely has a place in the doctor's tool kit. Wendy Melillo reviews the practice of treating disorders with the "new genre of adult film" used by therapists in "Visualizing Erotica." These include "The Better Sex Video Series" produced by Learning Corporation of Pompano

Beach, Florida, and the equally explicit videos of Candida Royalle, a well-known woman director of erotica. Melillo quotes Dr. Susan Cole of the University of Michigan Medical Center as saying: "These films are not made for prurient exploitation but for sexual satisfaction." Pornography can often provide valuable models of experience, says Dr. Marty Klein, a California sex therapist also interviewed by Melillo: "One hallmark of healthy adult sexuality is the ability to choose to lose yourself in a sexual situation under the appropriate circumstances, and it is that experience that most of pornography depicts." Most of the therapists told Melillo that erotica can counter sexual boredom. "In Defense of Sexy Videos," a similar article by Michael Baroni, points to benefits for males: some pornography helps men control sexual urges, helps single males to experience sex without a partner, and helps men in general to become better lovers.

Probably the chief exponent of the therapeutic value of pornography is the psychiatrist John Money, who observes in "The Positive and Constructive Approach to Pornography: In General Sex Education, in the Home, and in Sexological Counseling" that erotica properly handled can serve beneficially to educate children and adults. In "Pornography in the Home: A Topic in Medical Education," Money elaborates: "Let's not forget that it is indeed part of Nature's major and grand design to use perceptual imagery in order to procreate the race" (420). The sight of arousing images—real, dreamed, or reproduced—is important to males at puberty: "When the young male is confronted with these images, since he has no power or voluntary choice of them, especially those that appear in his dreams, he learns something about his own capacity for sexual arousal. This indeed can be, for many males who have a problem with regard to psychosexual arousal, the first time that the problem is actually presented to them very vividly." In contrast to young males, "the female at puberty does not have erotic dreams, wet dreams, in the way the boy does" (420–421). If ideal images are not available, says Money, then males can spin fantasies out of Sears Roebuck catalogs or anything else at hand (412). Other therapists agree. Because pornography helps stimulate healthy fantasies, says Helen Singer Kaplan in *The New Sex Therapy: Active Treatment of Sexual Dysfunctions*, it can be prescribed by professionals treating dysfunctions. Some critics demur at going so far. In "On Obscenity and Pornography," a nostalgic, even wistful essay, Edward Sagarin concludes that the traditional benefits of pornography, such as its ability to counter sexual ignorance and dispel erotic anxieties, are offset by its unseemliness and its association with criminals and slums.

Any number of critics, however, believe that however unpleasant some erotic materials can be, recourse to them as inspiration to masturbation is preferable to promiscuity in an age of AIDS. Pornography-induced pleasure is a form of "safe sex" for consumers. Properly produced, pornography can be safe for performers as well.

EFFECTS RESEARCH

Social scientists—a large group that can include psychologists, sociologists, anthropologists, communication specialists, and even medical doctors and pathologists—carry out research on pornography. Social scientists emulate scientists in other disciplines by attempting to design experiments that can be verified by statistical data. Working on erotic expression in these disciplines is problematic because of the enormous number of variables, many of them entirely subjective, governing human sexual behavior; controlling for all but one variable and properly interpreting the data raise difficulties that beggar imagination. For example, Vera Dunwoody and Kathy Pezdek discovered in "Factors Affecting the Sexual Arousal Value of Pictures" that "micro-variables that change from picture to picture"—factors such as the position, view, clothing, or nudity of a model—work against examinations of "global aspects of erotic stimuli" (276). Quantification can scarcely recognize, let alone register, nuances in erotic representation, arguably its most important single aspect.

Many other problems arise, not the least of which is inconclusive result. Both the profession and the public tend to ignore studies that find nothing measurable, as in the little-known report by James L. Howard, Myron B. Liptzin, and Clifford B. Reifler entitled "Is Pornography a Problem?" Their answer, after subjecting twenty-three subjects to massive exposure for two weeks, is a straightforward *no*. Exposure actually reduces the ability of later encounters to arouse, they found, and they could discover no deleterious results. It fact, for every study purporting to discover causal connections between exposure to pornography and antisocial behavior, there is another denying such connections. Sometimes the proportions of the research already carried out can color new experiments: social scientists must exercise caution that the data used to form a hypothesis are not then used to test the hypothesis.

Such contradictions are inherent in any discipline. Differing conclusions do not necessarily cancel each other out, though they suggest that both erotic materials *and* the research on them give off diametrically opposed messages simultaneously and that researchers (and recipients) may be unaware of many of them. Agendas and assumptions conflict, and at some point they shade into folklore. Bogus studies are rare, but when released, they can leave a lasting impression that deepens myth. In "Not So Naughty," for example, Gary Chapman takes Philip Elmer-Dewitt to task for publishing a seriously flawed article in *Time* based on the strange Martin Rimm study of pornography on the Internet (see **The Internet** in Chapter 14) and thus perpetuating fabricated estimates of vast traffic in pornographic images. Similarly, in "How *Time* Fed the Internet Porn Panic," *Harpers* magazine editorialized on the perniciousness of spreading disinformation, much of which will never be corrected in the public mind. Researchers themselves are sometimes to blame for public misconceptions. In promoting their research at UCLA in "Sex and Aggression: Proving the Link," written for a popular magazine, Seymour Feshbach and Neil Malamuth intemperately asserted that sexually explicit materials can cause aggression and thus helped to create a myth that has been widely accepted. Generally speaking, the more adamant the assertion of connections between a globally defined pornography and social violence, the more suspect are the data.

At the very least, the scholar seeking to extrapolate from the research literature must be cautious. Most conclusions are highly qualified, and taking statements out of context, let alone translating them across disciplinary boundaries, can be especially misleading. About all that social science can say at this point is a variation on a famous dictum: some pornography under some circumstances may affect some people in some ways some of the time. No one can predict the type of material, the circumstances, the individuals, or the effects. Gut feeling may hold that some pornography could be one trigger for people already predisposed to violence, in the same way that some religious messages can be said to switch on violence in similarly disposed individuals, but we can rarely prove the connection and cannot extend the effect beyond those specific individuals and messages.

OVERVIEWS AND SUMMARIES

The number of social science studies on pornography is now so large that only broad patterns seem worth discussing. The bottom line is clear enough: *no reputable researcher holds that generic pornography has a clear causal effect on antisocial behavior.* In its spring 1998 (38:2) issue, the prestigious *Journal of Communication* ran conflicting reports under the heading "Uneasy Bedfellows: Social Science and Pornography," an admission that social scientists may have ventured into waters too murky for conclusions to be visible. While some studies indicate that sexual images that also exhibit violence or aggression may contribute to heightened levels of aggressiveness in certain subjects, there is virtually no evidence supporting a causal link between the much larger number of plain-vanilla sexual images (soft- or hard-core). Marcia Pally's "Standard Deviation: Research Literature on Sexually Explicit Material and Social Harms," a review of major studies of many areas of erotica research, is one of the most straightforward. Pally enlivens her account by quoting the often hostile remarks by researchers on the credentials and integrity of their colleagues. F. M. Christensen's *Pornography: The Other Side* demystifies sociological and psychological research to an even greater degree; it is an excellent guide to the vicissitudes of investigating what is, after all, a vast, complex phenomenon. Christensen deals at length with various studies and finds them riddled with improper assumptions, improperly used materials, slipshod definitions, naive methodologies, and conflated conclusions. No serious scholar of the subject can fail to take Christensen's arguments into account.

Probably the best short survey is Alison King's "Mystery and Imagination: The Case of Pornography Effects Studies." Misunderstanding of research, says

King, results when laypeople, especially antiporn zealots, misinterpret the lab studies. One of the most common errors is to equate the terms "arousal," which can be measured, though imperfectly, and "aggression," for which there is no intelligible scale. King is especially mistrustful of studies in which the experimenter annoys or angers subjects and then shows them pornographic materials; the assumption, she points out, is that "an external arousing stimulus can increase a subject's aggression. This obviously means that *any* arousing stimulus [not just pornography] will have a similar effect" (59). Moreover, she points out (as do Pally and Christensen), researchers often ignore a "parallel phenomenon in aggression research called pro-social effects." King notes that a female researcher, Kathryn Kelley (one of the most careful and reliable investigators), has demonstrated that males exposed to pornography are often more quick to help a female subject perceived as suffering than those not exposed to such materials. According to King, "experiments which demonstrate that pornography leads to violence do so because they are constructed in such a way that there can be no other outcome; if we change the options in the experiment we find that pornography can and does produce pro-social effects" (59).

In 1983 the Toronto Task Force on Violence against Women commissioned "Making Sense of Research on Pornography" but quickly rejected it because it did not bear out the group's faith that sexual materials cause violence. Said author Thelma McCormack: "To summarize, the recent studies of pornography and aggression have shed little light on the effects of pornography, but have sensitized us to the deeper problems men have about aggression. They alter our perception of the type of person who would commit rape, from a male whose sexual development has been disturbed leading to a strong sense of self-hatred and sex-guilt, to a male who lacks the inhibitions that might deter him" (195). In McCormack's reading of the literature, most males are turned off by violent pornography, and she characterizes research by Donnerstein, Malamuth, and others hoping to discover connections between viewing horror movies and aggression as "mindless." Another agency, the Canadian Select Committee of Inquiry into Pornography and Prostitution, rejected *The Impact of Pornography: An Analysis of Research and Summary of Findings*, by H. B. McKay and D. J. Dolff, who reached conclusions similar to those of McCormack.

Avedon Carol in *Nudes, Prudes and Attitudes: Pornography and Censorship* maintains that evidence is insufficient to establish harm or justify repressive legislation; Robert Athanasiou concludes in "Pornography: A Review of Research" that data do not support the assumption that pornography represents a danger to society, certainly not in the ways that alcohol or tobacco does; and Edward C. Nelson concludes in "Pornography and Sexual Aggression" that effects of exposure to explicit sexual materials "are extremely variable and belief in absolutes in this as in most other fields is clearly untenable" (237). Similarly, Lynne Segal's "Introduction" to *Sex Exposed: Sexuality and the Pornography Debate*, a concise and masterly summary of research, asserts that "empirical research on soft-core pornography has almost without exception failed to reveal *changes* of any significance in the behaviour of its consumers, whether affecting sexual practices, attitudes about, or behaviour towards, women. Indeed, its most characteristic effect, were we to feel confident generalizing from laboratory research on aggression to behaviour generally, has been to *lower* aggression levels" (6). In support, she cites research by Robert Baron, Edward Donnerstein, Kathryn Kelley, Thompson and Annetts, and Howitt and Cumberbatch. Chapter 4 of *Pornography in a Free Society*, by Gordon Hawkins and Franklin E. Zimring, is also essentially an overview of research; at best, say the authors, research into effects is inconclusive. *Media, Children, and the Family: Social Scientific, Psychodynamic, and Clinical Perspectives*, by Dolf Zillmann, James Bryant, and Aletha C. Huston, contains a chapter on "Effects of Erotica and Pornography," which reluctantly says the same thing. Attorney Alan M. Dershowitz flatly dismisses studies purporting to establish links between pornography and violence as "junk science" in "Justice: Connecting Pornography with Violence Is Junk Science, Which Doesn't Belong in Courts."

RESEARCH AS A SOCIALLY CONSTRUCTED ENDEAVOR

Doing pornography research is itself a socially constructed activity. Michael Altimore points out in "The Social Construction of a Scientific Myth: Pornography and Violence" that there is little science in the studies purporting to establish links. In fact, says Altimore, the very assertion of links between the pornographic and the aggressive is itself a socially constructed ploy that "obscures the most accurate representation of violence in the United States, which involves social class and race" (118). As demonstrated by the relatively short period of time required to persuade the public that pornography causes violent behavior, the concept of pornography seems eminently mutable, the pawn of groups with the strongest voices and the most alliances. Ian Jarvie makes similar points in "The Sociology of the Pornography Debate," which examines major texts and assumptions by the participants to conclude that the antiporn posture is constructed from zeal and misinformation, not from curiosity and understanding.

In a volume with considerable relevance to social science's investigations of pornography, Willard Rowland Jr. has noticed in *The Politics of TV Violence: Policy Uses of Communication Research* that money gravitates toward research into violence on television, an issue that flares every few years and that often leads to federal commissions, because the public's need for drama meshes with scientists' need for self-promotion. If it could be "proved" that violence on television did not cause antisocial behavior, says Rowland, then funds for research would dry up. In fact, any definitive conclusion would have the same effect, so researchers carefully avoid them in the interest of keeping open sources of money. Given the First Amendment, which forbids government censorship, it seems obvious that the research on televised violence and the commissions politicians establish are not intended to reach closure or come up with answers, merely to dramatize those concerns symbolically, as a way of asserting that Americans "care." Believing that violence on television causes antisocial behavior and expressing that concern in national forums, says Rowland, are socially constructed strategies crucial to a culture that has neither the will nor the means actually to deal with matters of race, poverty, and class.

Research into pornography ages rapidly, a factor that underscores the social construction of the discipline. The dozens of studies in the *Technical Reports* of the President's Commission on Pornography and Obscenity, probably the most systematic research endeavor ever undertaken on the subject, are dated, and those in the more recent Attorney General's *Report*, though much less authoritative, are on their way to becoming so. One reason is that as technologies of communication supersede each other, as different groups make particular issues trendy, or as moral panics sweep the media, then researchers must construct new agendas and methodologies to stay in fashion.

RESEARCHER AND VOLUNTEER BIAS

Some social scientists acknowledge that the artifice of a laboratory cannot be equated with the environment outside and acknowledge also that they observe experiments through the lenses of their own personalities and assumptions. Textbooks warn of a long-recognized phenomenon: that subjects of surveys and experiments often try to tell researchers what the subjects think they want to hear. Leading questions, statistically inappropriate samples, the presence of uncontrolled variables, and a great many other factors can contribute to flawed conclusions. The "Rosenthal effect," as the syndrome is sometimes called, is the social science equivalent of the Heisenberg principle: that the observer, to some extent, determines the outcome of the experiment. Two collections of essays edited by Robert Rosenthal and Ralph L. Rosnow, *Artifact in Behavioral Research*, and *The Volunteer Subject*, sketch the challenges to objectivity. Contributors to those volumes note that too many experiments employ students as easily assembled experimental populations that may not represent cross-sections of Americans at large. A classic social learning study suggests that merely conducting a study may skew the results. Jay Mann, Jack Sidman, and Sheldon Starr surveyed eighty-three couples viewing erotic films for "Evaluating Social Consequences of Erotic Films: An Experimental Approach." Subjects reported significantly more sexual activity on film-viewing nights and exhibited a growing tolerance of the legal exhibition of such films. Closer examination, however, revealed that filling out the survey questionnaires actually led to more sexual activity than the films themselves.

Moreover, subjects may *volunteer* for experiments from motives of their own. The ways in which volunteer self-selectivity and bias corrupt experiments involving erotic materials are so numerous as to have established a subcategory of research literature. In 1985, for example, D. W. Saunders et al. attempted to design filters for the most pronounced biases in "A Method for Empirically

Assessing Volunteer Selection Effects: Recruitment Procedures and Responses to Erotica." Numerous researchers have grappled with the problems raised by volunteers since. G. M. Farkas, L. F. Sine, and I. M. Evans studied male subjects who volunteer for exposure-to-erotica experiments in "Personality, Sexuality, and Demographic Differences between Volunteers and Nonvolunteers for a Laboratory Study of Male Sexual Behavior." They found that volunteers, who must undress to be fitted with a strain-gauge device to measure erections, are less fearful and less guilty about sex, more experienced, and generally older than nonvolunteers. Volunteers tend to be white or racially mixed (but not Oriental) and reported higher incidences of erection difficulties. Nevertheless, say the researchers, subjects are not markedly different from nonvolunteers. Sharlene A. Wolchik, S. Lee Spencer, and Iris S. Lise conducted a similar survey of female volunteers who volunteer to have their levels of arousal measured by vaginal photoplethysmographs—which register vagina opacity and liquidity—to find that the subjects have usually experienced more exposure to erotic materials, generally find them less objectionable than do other women, masturbate more often, and suffer from less sexual fear. In "Volunteer Bias in Erotica Research Employing Vaginal Measures of Sexual Arousal," Wolchik, Spencer, and Lise say that researchers should be cautious in accepting volunteer responses as typical. Vaginal photoplethysmographs are sensitive enough to register the differences between exposure to erotic romances and erotic films, but they must be inserted, and the physical contact may skew responses. Put bluntly, the issue is whether one can trust data elicited from males with constriction bands around their penises or from females with tamponlike active devices in their vaginas. (See also **Sexual Aids, Toys, Contrivances, and Implements** in Chapter 9.)

RESEARCH DEFINITIONS OF PORNOGRAPHY

Research definitions of pornography remain problematic. Even Diana E. H. Russell, who thinks that pornography is socially dangerous, acknowledges confusion in *Sexual Exploitation: Rape, Child Sexual Abuse, and Workplace Harassment*: "First, distinctions are rarely made between 'explicit, sexual materials,' 'erotica,' and 'pornography.' Second, precise descriptions of the films, pictures, or stories used in experiments are usually lacking, making it impossible to know whether the findings are relevant to the effects of pornography or not. Third, although many researchers have focused on the effects of 'erotica' on sexual behavior, a distinction is rarely made between degrading images of sex and respectful, tender images." Making that last distinction meaningful to any audience is probably impossible, since almost any act will be viewed differently by any two people. To some people, the depiction of oral sex will always be degrading, however it is staged, while to others it will seem distasteful only when force is involved, and to still others questionable merely because one partner is depicted kneeling before the other, and to yet others beautiful, loving, and uplifting under most circumstances. Perhaps the least detectable bias is that of the researcher who subtly "criminalizes" the pleasure of others.

Donald M. Amoroso and Marvin Brown write in "Problems in Studying the Effects of Erotic Material" that errors in effects research are likely because investigators do not subscribe to uniform definitions of the erotic or the pornographic; because they have no standardized systems of measurement of arousal; because they cannot psychologically screen the control and test groups of subjects; and because they carry out experiments in the nonrealistic, artificial surroundings of the laboratory. Susan H. Gray also observes in "Exposure to Pornography and Aggression toward Women" that experiments designed to elicit evidence of causal relationships of necessity are limited to artificial constructs and can measure only short-term effects. Gray does summarize studies in which hard-core pornography appears to enhance aggression in already-angered (deliberately provoked) males. Her article is a good guide to research conducted between 1970 and 1980.

Another source of confusion stems from the definitions that researchers bring to their studies: thinking of certain sexual practices as "deviant" will color their findings, whereas people who think of, say, anal intercourse as an occasional, but entirely "normal," practice will view the matter from a diametrically opposed perspective. A study of homosexual themes in a pornographic genre conducted before 1973, when the American Psychiatric Association declared homosexuality no longer a category of the aberrant, will reach substantially different results and be informed by substantially different semantics than one conducted after that date. Few studies attempt to grapple with what definitions *subjects* bring to experimental research. One that does, albeit in limited fashion, is "The Semantic Meaning of Pornographic Stimuli," conducted by Edward E. Ware et al. The researchers found that subjects exposed to explicit slides were more apt to characterize them as "bad, unpleasant, dirty and harmful" than less explicit versions.

"Photograph Characteristics Influencing the Judgement of Obscenity," a study conducted by M. Katzman, indicated that while features like degrees of explicitness, "deviant" behavior, depiction of organs of excretion, violence, posture, and so on might be expected to affect judgment, pictures across a large scale usually elicit no consensus even among groups chosen for similar education, class, and background. Another problem has to do with the approach to the artifact itself. A sample of fewer than 100 hard-core films or magazines is hopelessly small if one is trying to draw conclusions about something so complex and many-genred as pornography, but surveys based on minuscule samples (when the annual American output of hard-core videos exceeds 10,000 videotapes) are the norm. Merely counting acts of intercourse in a hard-core porn film tells us little about pornography or sexuality; saying that oral sex occurs in 90 percent of such films is like saying that 90 percent of automobiles have radios. Moreover, to assume that an oral act like fellatio is automatically a sign of male dominance—all too common—may ignore the visual imperatives of a scenario. In short, studies of pornography usually reveal at least as much about the researchers as about the material studied.

RESEARCH ASSUMPTIONS AND METHODOLOGIES

Researchers are supposed to park their biases and assumptions at the door of the laboratory, but some do not. Among the strange assumptions masked in some kinds of research are the conviction (1) that the average person may not be able to distinguish between representation and reality; (2) that most males harbor a secret desire to rape; (3) that only people with damaged psyches could possibly enjoy pornography; (4) that people who masturbate after being stimulated by pornography are sick; (5) that depictions of sex are uniformly nasty; (6) that depictions carried by older media, such as print, are less dangerous than visual and electronic ones (7) that seeing a representation of a "deviant" act will transform the viewer into a deviant; (8) that all pornography is violent; (9) that pornography is monolithic, its examples without genre differences; (10) that the content of pornography is incoherent, that is, that any example is merely a train of separate, unlinked, blindly arousing images; (11) that all pornography is anti-female; (12) that it appeals only to people of lower classes; (13) that it is an upper-class phenomenon; (14) that it is a means of holding down the masses; (15) that it has no history; (16) that any kind of pornography causes harm; (17) that all pornography is inhuman or dehumanizing; (18) that pornography has nothing to do with love; (19) that pornography is immoral because people make money from it; (20) that the traffic in pornography dwarfs that in other kinds of information. To this score the alert reader can doubtless add many more. It would be pointless to try to match all these biases with studies here, especially since critics are beginning to do so (a case in point is Larry Gross' "Marginal Texts, Marginal Audiences," which suggests that Neil Malamuth's pornography research has been affected by childhood neuroses), but we can indicate some. We need only observe that much research into pornography's alleged nature and effects can best be characterized as "folklore in, folklore out." Keeping cultural dynamics in mind helps to explain why the debate over pornography rarely progresses beyond the level of the bumper sticker.

Methodologies differ widely, despite their having been refined repeatedly over decades. In 1929 the Payne Fund sponsored the first major studies of media. One, by Herbert George Blumer, became notorious as a methodological disaster because of its grounding in what we now call the simple "stimulus-response" or "magic bullet" theory of media effects: that media have a direct message-response effect on audiences. Arthur R. Jarvis' "The Payne Fund Reports: A Discussion of Their Content, Public Reaction, and Effect on the Motion Picture Industry, 1930–1940" reviews these early efforts to study the behavioral effects of the cinema and their role in prompting the movie industry to censor itself. Blumer himself reported in his two books, *Movies and Conduct* and *Movies, Delinquency, and Crime* that movies powerfully influenced teenagers, because when he asked teenagers, they *said* that the movies powerfully influenced them. This simple-minded approach still tempts researchers. More recent studies, for example, have asked men if they would rape if they knew they would not be caught or punished. Not surprisingly, a fair number of subjects so questioned have said that they would. The results, says Michael Altimore in "The Social Construction of a Scientific Myth: Pornography and Violence," can have little validity because they do not establish an actual probability of men raping women (123).

In *Sex, Violence, and the Media*, a 1978 evaluation of research in several related fields, H. J. Eysenck and D. K. B. Nias discuss pornography—defined largely as sexual material with very low levels of violence—as an adjunct to mainstream conflations of sex and violence (standard network programming, say) not normally called pornographic. Research in any of these areas, say the authors, rarely arrives at any coherent or comprehensible conclusions, in part because so many studies are carried out by sociologists on subject matter that is psychological. The two psychologists argue that hormones are important, neglected factors in behavior and that sociologists (and many psychologists) are unaware of the complexity of effects studies. Eysenck and Nias do believe that evidence suggests that visual representations of sexual violence affect viewers, though individual differences, hormonal and otherwise, mean that establishing direct causal links is unlikely. Americans commonly assume that advertising causes behavioral change, say Eysenck and Nias, and pornography may well do the same: "Pornography, although probably less serious in its effects [than mainstream media], cannot escape blame entirely" (274).

Barbara J. Wilson, Daniel Linz, and Barbara Randall examine the assumptions behind the Motion Picture Association of America's (MPAA's) ratings for commercial films in "Applying Social Science Research to Film Ratings: A Shift from Offensiveness to Harmful Effects." The assumptions include convictions (1) that age is a guide to sensibilities, (2) that younger children are more profoundly affected by depictions of violence and sex, (3) that films should be rated on the basis of the quantity or explicitness of sex or violence, and, most important, (4) that excessive and/or explicit sex is more troubling than excessive violence, all assumptions challenged by social scientists. The authors suggest that a more realistic rating scheme would focus on violence rather than sex and on exploitative sex rather than on sex or nudity rendered humanistically. Such assumptions often have to be teased out of the methodologies, but the point is that, more often than not, researchers are talking about different things—not just to laypeople but also to their colleagues. What is erotic or pornographic to one person is simply not to another, and social scientists demonstrate every day the immutability of that confusion. Worse, such assumptions introduce uncontrollable variables.

In "Does Pornography Cause Violence? The Search for Evidence," Lynne Segal believes that confusion may arise when researchers such as Edward Donnerstein say one thing in scholarly papers and another thing in their remarks to the popular press. While researchers find that *some* men can be aroused by depictions of rape, especially if the depiction is of the woman's enjoying it, other studies indicate that men as a group "list violence as the least titillating aspect of pornography, react to it with distress rather than pleasure, and have become less, rather than more, tolerant towards violent pornography" (12). Segal notes that Daniel Linz and Edward Donnerstein, in separate studies, found that narrative context counts: when male audiences see a *complete* film, rather than excerpts, they are no more tolerant of violence than any other group.

OTHER MODELS

Pornography research typically falls into two categories, says Thelma McCormack in "The Censorship of Pornography: Catharsis or Learning?": a behaviorist approach that collects statistics for a theoretical model that interests the researcher or a Freudian approach that assumes that pornography furnishes some sort of release or allays some sort of anxiety. Pauline Bart and Margaret Jozsa reject catharsis and imitation models in "Dirty Books, Dirty Films, and Dirty Data," an essay that promotes instead a conflict model in which pornography is studied as an arena in which males and females have different interests. Daniel Linz and Neil Malamuth identify other models in *Pornography*, a broad survey of sociological research, conclusions, and limitations. They categorize research using three perspectives: authoritarian/conservative-moralistic, libertarian/liberal, and social responsibility/feminist models. Using passages from *Story of O*, Neil Malamuth and V. Billings apply different models of pornography's functions. Their "Why Pornography?" categorizes the therapeutic/educational model, which suggests that pornography's effects are beneficial and didactic; the psychoanalytic model, which suggests that pornography encapsulates fantasies representing childhood conflicts; the Marxist model, which suggests that pornography serves as a tool of the ruling class for subordinating the workers; the feminist model, which suggests that pornography represents and causes male oppression of women; and the sociological model, which suggests that pornography operates as an agent of social change. Researchers may employ other models less clearly articulated.

W. Cody Wilson and Herbert I. Abelson indicate in "Experience with and Attitudes toward Explicit Sexual Materials" that a large majority of adults report being exposed at some time to explicit materials, but reactions appear to be determined as much by personality factors as by degrees of explicitness. They note that their data do not support a "contemporary community standard" for judging such materials. W. Wilson and V. Liedtke's "Movie-Inspired Sexual Practices" examined the effects of the mainstream films *10, Endless Love, The Blue Lagoon*, and *Saturday Night Fever* (rather than porn films) to find that increased frequency of masturbation, intercourse, and oral-genital contact apparently results among women viewers as well as among men, though menstruation cycles are also a factor. A study of 200 San Francisco prostitutes published by M. H. Silbert and A. M. Pines as "Pornography and Sexual Abuse of Women" elicited the belief (on the part of the prostitutes) that customers had been influenced by pornography to ask for certain acts. The authors say that while their data are probably not reliable, they seem to support the "imitation theory" of pornography and possible effects.

Dolf Zillmann's "Effects of Prolonged Consumption of Pornography" summarized research to find that sexual stimulation and pleasure decrease with prolonged consumption, as does any initial repulsion by the materials; only less common acts seem to rekindle interest; prolonged consumption appears to alter perceptions of sexuality itself and may encourage acceptance of premarital or extramarital sex; prolonged exposure to either violent or nonviolent pornography increases desensitization to victims of sexual violence (this point is disputed by others); males who habitually are exposed—in large amounts—to pornography are at greater risk of becoming desensitized to victims and to becoming sexual aggressors themselves than the occasional male consumer (this point also disputed). When Dolf Zillmann and Jennings Bryant studied long-term (defined as more than one hour) exposure to nonviolent pornography for "Effects of Massive Exposure to Pornography," they found that subjects exhibited sexually callous attitudes and decreased support for the "women's liberation movement."

Perhaps reacting against criticism of most quantitative research on erotica (especially that on alleged violent effects—see later) as simplistic and flawed, Neil Malamuth has moved toward an "evolutionary paradigm" to explain gender differences in reactions to sexual materials. His "Sexually Explicit Media, Gender Differences, and Evolutionary Theory" makes a case for the effects of biology on the ways that humans become aroused and how they respond to the fantasies embodied in sexual representation. Malamuth tries to see beyond popular versions of social Darwinism and gender stereotypes, though the issue is clearly one of daunting complexity, by drawing on research on gendered fantasies reinforced by pornography. Although fantasy categories are not airtight, they indicate that heterosexual males dream of unfettered sex with as many fertile (shapely, well-endowed) women as possible, a presumed genetic imperative to spread semen widely and impregnate as many females as possible. Pornography for males gratifies such biological programming. By contrast, women dream of a powerful (wealthy, dominant) male who can aggress and couple at will (a sign of valuable sperm) but who eventually professes love and affection for one mate, after which, also presumably, he guards and protects the family that results. Pornography for women gratifies this type of biological programming. (See **Pornography as Generator of Fantasies**, in this chapter). Viewed dispassionately from a sociobiological perspective, although few researchers make this argument, pornography might well reinforce monogamy and family values by siphoning off through masturbation the sexual energies of males who would otherwise attempt to impregnate as many women as they could. Representing erotic images thus might contribute to social stability by reducing sexual chaos. This version of catharsis theory aside, other researchers have also tried to build sociobiological models. "Sex without Emotional Involvement: An Evolutionary Interpretation of Sex Differences" by J. M. Townsend reviews sociobiological arguments (evolutionary strategies) for gendered interpretations of the meaning of different kinds of sex, such as those depicted in porn. Scholars interested in further exploring intersections between cultural and scientific models should look at Kathryn Kelley's *Females, Males, and Sexuality: Theories and Research*, which is slightly dated, and David M. Buss and Neil M. Malamuth's *Sex, Power and Conflict: Evolutionary and Feminist Perspectives*. (For other sources on nature-nurture polarities, see **The Social Construction of Sexuality and Gender** in Chapter 5.)

PORNOGRAPHY AND VIOLENCE

Americans and Canadians accept a connection between sexual expression and violence more readily than do people of other nations, in part, one suspects, because they have so long used violent metaphors to represent sex. In *Love and Death*, an investigation of the relationship between pornography and mainstream culture, Gershon Legman points out that when depictions of sexuality are suppressed, they reappear as depictions of violence, at least in American culture: "there is *no* mundane substitute for sex except sadism" (9). In other words, according to Legman, violence as a melodramatic element is the socially acceptable surrogate of sex in fiction, movies, television, and so on. Michael Leach appears to agree in his exploration of the ambiguities of pornography for *I Know It When I See It: Pornography, Violence, and Public Sensitivity* when he remarks that the sexual couplings of hard-core movies can seem morally superior to the maimings, dismemberments, and murders of mainstream films. Leach is also excellent on his discussion of the ways in which different pornographic genres shade into one another; he refers to pornography as an ever-shifting "frontier."

In this regard, a text not about pornography but useful for its discussion of the inextricable connections between sex and violence is Rene Girard's *Violence and the Sacred*. Girard's thesis is that violence lies at the heart of spirituality:

Sexuality is one of those primary forces whose sovereignty over man is assured by man's firm belief in his sovereignty over it. The most extreme forms of violence can never be directly sexual because they are collective in nature. The group is quite capable of perpetrating a single, coherent act of violence, whose force is increased with the addition of each individual quotient of violence; but sexuality is never truly collective. That fact alone explains why sexual interpretations of the sacred invariably ignore or play down the role of violence, whereas an interpretation based on violence readily grants sexuality the prominent role it plays in all primitive religions. We are tempted to conclude that violence is impure because of its relation to sexuality. Yet only the reverse proposition can withstand close scrutiny. Sexuality is impure because it has to do with violence. (34).

Somewhat further afield but still pertinent to pornographic genres is Richard Slotkin's *Regeneration through Violence*, a study of the mythos of American violence as cleansing force, a theme Slotkin detects in the literature and culture of the United States. Probably the most trenchant explanation of violence in performance or in other media can be found in *Violence in the Arts*, where John Fraser observes that "in a culture as starved of physicality as ours, the enduring appeal of a good many violent works is not just that they are violent but that they re-immerse us vicariously in physical action" (63). Fraser discusses mimetic, cathartic, and dramatic uses of violence. What is surprising, perhaps, is that there is not more violence in sexual expression as a whole, says Joseph Slade in "Violence in the Hard-Core Pornographic Film: A Historical Survey," which notes that hard-core film and videotapes have generally avoided violent content in favor of graphic sex. It would appear that pornography may *sometimes* represent sex violently but just as often eschew aggression. Sadomasochism, bondage, and discipline are violent by definition, even if the aggression is static, theatrical, and statistically more likely to be directed toward men than women. Richard B. Miller's "Violent Pornography: Mimetic Nihilism and the Eclipse of Difference" attempts to link violent porn with contemporary nihilism and aggression against women but notes some of the many contradictions that occur in genres such as sadomasochism, in which women commit violence against males.

The premise of works such as "Sexual Excitement" and *Perversion: The Erotic Form of Hatred* by Robert J. Stoller is that sexual excitement is often associated with hostility, a linkage pronounced where fetishistic "scripts" drive "deviants," though hostility may inform even "normal" sexual relationships, that is, those that depend to some degree on fetishizing the object of desire through fantasy. Stoller has often been attacked, and he moderated his views toward the end of his life, but his premise aligns nicely with poststructuralist assertions that we know reality and each other only though language and image, which is decidedly a fetishistic association. Men and women are alike in this regard, differing only in degrees of hostility, says Stoller. Jessica Benjamin suggests in "The Bonds of Love: Rational Violence and Erotic Domination" that denial of needs in infancy leads to linkages between violence and eroticism; Benjamin expands similar reflections in *Like Subjects, Love Objects*, a lengthier exploration of relationships among gender and sexuality, love and aggression.

At one extreme are radical feminists who equate sex and violence. From that perspective, any representation of sex, no matter how innocuous, is by definition violent. Extreme antiporn feminists believe that virtually every media representation of women promotes violence toward women and excoriate images in mainstream advertising, movies, television, and so on. Those are the views of the contributors to *Making Violence Sexy: Feminist Views on Pornography*, edited by Diana E. H. Russell, and there are many such texts. One curious text often cited is *Pornography and Sexual Violence: Evidence of the Links*, a transcript of the Minneapolis Hearings on 12 and 13 December 1983; it shrilly misappropriates inconclusive and often badly designed research. Several unremarkable essays have been gathered as "Sexuality, Violence and Pornography." Gary E. McCuen's *Pornography and Sexual Violence* assumes linkages as well. The more aggressively the critic insists on the linkage between sex and violence, the less concerned he or she seems to be with proof. *Power Surge: Sex, Violence and Pornography*, by Susan G. Cole, for example, sees sinister implications in Madonna, surrogate mothers, feminine hygiene, and pornography, the latter of which she associates with violence. Micheline Carrier's *La Danse Macabre: Violence et Pornographie*, another collection of Canadian journalistic pieces, does not offer much evidence. Because many of the essays in *Pornography: Women, Violence and Civil Liberties*, edited by Catherine Itzin, are concerned with antiporn feminist attacks on other feminists, they are more entertaining than illuminating.

Extremists oppose extremists: Camille Paglia chides the antiporn crusaders in "The Return of Carry Nation": "MacKinnon and Dworkin are victim-mongers, ambulance chasers, addicts. MacKinnon begins every argument from big, flawed premises such as 'male supremacy' or 'misogyny,' while Dworkin spouts glib Auschwitz metaphors at the drop of a bra. Here's one of their typical maxims: 'The pornographers rank with Nazis and Klansmen in promoting hatred and violence.' Anyone who could write such a sentence knows nothing about pornography *or* Nazism" (38). As such criticisms indicate, extremism disturbs many women, who worry that antiporn feminists reduce all women to the status of victimized children who must become wards of the state. Though women inevitably will sympathize with strategies to counter very real sexual oppression, says Ellen Willis in "Feminism, Moralism, and Pornography," the antiporn movement falsely identifies violence with sex: "Since porn is by definition overtly sexual, while most of it is not overtly violent, this equation requires some fancy explaining . . . [which] doesn't hold up" (463).

Varda Burstyn, filing a dissent against antiporn feminists entitled "Who the Hell Is We?," points out that censorship always operates against the powerless and ends by attacking the arts. She observes that when Edward Donnerstein and other social scientists show violent pornography (a very specific genre) to young males, the subjects do experience attitudinal changes and misunderstandings about female consent, *but* when the same subjects discuss what they have seen, especially the myth that women "really want to be raped," these same men actually experience a better understanding of issues of consent and dignity than groups that have not undergone the same educational process. The obvious conclusion, she says, is education—using those kinds of pornography, not trying to suppress them. Similarly, Ian Vine's *Liberty, Morality and Sexual Censorship: The Politics of Pornography* says that education is sufficient to counter any deleterious messages. Vine says that in an information age we cannot afford to tolerate censorship of sexual materials but that we can teach people, especially the young, to understand that pornography is not "a script for courtship," a source of happiness, or a blueprint for sexual morality.

In "Sexual Violence and Sexuality," Rosalind Coward says that it is possible to code many kinds of representations, even those of naked female bodies, as porn or nonporn and that we need to know far more about both sex and violence before we endorse simplistic equations: "Unless we refine our ways of talking about sexist codes in general, how they operate and produce their meanings, and why they are offensive, we run the risk of constantly being misunderstood" (309). Jacqueline N. Zita's "Pornography and the Male Imaginary" outlines some of the codes with which male-oriented pornography constructs images of women. Zita thinks that certain features define eroticism for heterosexual males: sex divorced from reproduction, women presented as insatiable and masculinized, and—less often—sexuality packaged as violation. Moreover, even where pornography *is* "about" violence in the antiporn, feminist sense, it can also be "about" a great many other things: curiosity, pleasure, lawlessness, dissent, rebellion, spirituality, and the quotidian nature of the body. Dany Lacombe, writing in *Ideology and Public Policy: The Case against Pornography*, says that, in any case, it is clear that sex seems to be distancing itself from violence in most porn genres. Penetration of a female body and postures which accommodate penetration are not in and of themselves expressions of power and even still less of aggression; though it is clear, says Lacombe, that many antiporn feminists "read" such images in that way. That assumption, that penetration itself is demeaning, is too often unspoken in critiques of pornography and sexuality. To receive a penis is not necessarily to be inferior or subordinate, especially since many genres of porn seem bent on teaching women how to extract pleasure from different positions. Ironically, if so many mainstream representations do reduce the freedom of women, the irony is that what most people call pornography—the explicit novel or videotape, for example—may be one of the few venues in which sexual freedom for women can be imagined.

As usual, definitions are at issue. What some antiporn feminists call violence in pornography, say some critics, is simply masculine dominance or hegemony, the legacy of traditional gender differentiation and historical inequity, that is reflected in representations of any aspect of culture. To call pornography inherently violent on those grounds, say the critics, is like calling a corporation violent merely because it symbolically and literally arranges people in hierarchies of power. In *The Jaguar and the Anteater: Pornography Degree Zero*, Bernard Arcand locates the source of confusion in an inability to distinguish between sexism and aggression, a point echoed by increasing numbers of pro-sex feminists. Marcia Pally's "X-Rated Feminism: Ban Sexism, Not Pornography" says flatly that while some pornography is sexist, not all erotic expression is. Material that gratifies fantasies is one thing; behaving like a sexist is another, and conflating the two moves the state into the arena of thought-control. The most succinct outline of the syndrome can be found in Michael Altimore's "The Social Construction of a Scientific Myth: Pornography and Violence," a careful, well-documented, and well-reasoned exploration of the reasons why believing in a causal connection between pornography and violence is so comforting, despite ample evidence that the real factors behind sexual violence are race, class, and crime.

Thelma McCormack's "Machismo in Media Research: A Critical Review of Research on Violence and Pornography" notes that in the 1960s, sex seemed progressive and violence regressive, so the liberal assumptions privileged sex, a bias that might have affected findings from that period. Now, in an era in which feminists wish to redefine sex as violence, says McCormack, masculine anxieties, assumptions, and tools still shape the research, and it is still not possible to equate sex and violence. McCormack has in mind studies such as "Evaluating Social Consequences of Erotic Films: An Experimental Approach," by Jay Mann, Jack Sidman, and Sheldon Starr, who admitted the difficulty of making judgments but could find few deleterious effects of pornography. McCormack thinks that the major national studies between 1969 and 1972 were biased and believes that reference-group theory would be more useful.

PORNOGRAPHY AND ACCEPTANCE OF RAPE MYTHS

In the early 1980s, when researchers thought that they could make certain statements about the effects on male subjects of exposure to what they called aggressive pornography, laypeople frequently cited their studies in calls for censorship of sexual materials. Such studies indicated that males exposed to pornography exhibited callousness about rape, sometimes expressed as denigration of rape victims. Among the researchers to pursue these directions were Edward Donnerstein, Daniel Linz, Dolf Zillmann, and Jennings Bryant. Donnerstein's "Aggressive Erotica and Violence against Women" and Donnerstein and L. Berkowitz's "Victim Reactions in Aggressive Erotic Films as a Factor in Violence against Women" concluded that males so exposed were more likely to act aggressively. The method was to show subjects films, and artificially anger them, then try to assess the impact of the films on any subsequent aggression. The inference was that aggression against females is caused by the higher aggression directed against women in films. The Donnerstein and Berkowitz report refined matters by pointing out that films appear to have negative effects *only* when sexual content is combined with violence, although media reports tended to omit those qualifications. A. Brannigan and S. Goldenberg in "The Study of Aggressive Pornography: The Vicissitudes of Relevance" assert that most behavior research in this area is deficient because there is confusion between the effects of the stimuli and the anger induced in the subjects; nearly all conclusions are ambiguous and open to conflicting interpretation; statistical norms and scales are flawed; and the studies themselves are rarely applicable to reality. Society can base its censorship on morality or ideology, say Brannigan and Goldenberg, but laboratory studies cannot justify it.

The Donnerstein (and similar) studies have been widely criticized. F. M. Christensen's "Effects of Pornography: The Debate Continues: A Critique" and "Sexual Callousness Revisited: A Critique," for example, take issue with the methodology and the artificiality of the laboratory settings, as do Larry Gross' "Pornography and Social Science Research: Serious Questions: A Critique" and A. Brannigan's "Pornography and Behavior: Alternative Explanations: A Critique." Of these, Gross raises the most trenchant ethical issue: if Donnerstein and his colleagues believe that pornography does cause people to become sexual monsters, then how can they justify exposing experimental subjects to such materials? It is a double-bind, since so exposing subjects suggests either hypocrisy or lack of conviction on the part of the researchers.

The theory that some behavior is learned from others, articulated by Albert Bandura in *Social Learning Theory*, is often appropriated to model effects research today. The most controversial studies of pornography and aggression, for example, rest on a version of social learning advanced by Bandura, Underwood, and Fromson in "Disinhibition of Aggression through Diffusion of Responsibility and Dehumanization of Victims." The theory holds that dehumanizing some people—as in media portrayals—will "disinhibit" others from viewing aggression toward the victims as cruel. In such studies, the assumption is that pornography routinely dehumanizes women. That assumption, say many critics, is misleading in view of the depiction of males as more dehumanized than their female counterparts in the typical hard-core pornographic scenario. In "Pornography and Sexual Aggression: A Social Learning Theory Analysis," J. V. P. Check and Neil Malamuth apply a "social learning" model by assuming that pornography symbolically codes a message that aggression is acceptable. According to this argument, exposure to a pornographic scenario first raises expectations that rape is something to be enjoyed, then depicts the rape as indeed pleasurable, reinforces the message by depicting the victim as involuntarily enjoying the aggression, and finally rewards the behavior by not punishing the transgressor. That is a beguiling argument, though it would apply only to erotic materials that employ aggressive formulas.

Some critics think it more likely that culture at large desensitizes Americans to acts of violence. Others point out that when researchers actually identify the "pornography" they show to their subjects, the "aggressive-erotic" films usually turn out to be "slasher" films, not a category that most Americans would recognize as either erotic or pornographic and about which perceptions are wildly misleading (see **Film Content: Violence and Sex** in Chapter 13). Deciding what actually turns the viewers on is problematic: since American audiences understand that violence is the most acceptable way of presenting nudity, it is difficult to know whether subjects are responding to the aggression or merely to the nudity. Other variables are equally tricky. For example, Allan Fenigstein and Ronald G. Heyduk tried first to induce aggressive fantasies in subjects as a way of testing whether such subjects would then choose videotaped scenes of aggression for a study called "Sexual-Aggressive Fantasies and Attraction to Pornography." When nothing happened, the authors concluded that perhaps they had not induced fantasies specific enough. In "The Effects of Alcohol and Anger on Interest in Violence, Erotica, and Deviance," W. H. George and G. A. Marlatt found that the expectation of alcohol, even more than anger (provoked by researchers), seemed to increase interest in violent-erotic slides.

Studies have proliferated, nevertheless, as in "Physiological Desensitization and Judgments about Female Victims of Violence," by Daniel G. Linz, Edward Donnerstein, and S. M. Adams; "The Effects of Multiple Exposures to Filmed Violence against Women," by Daniel G. Linz, Edward Donnerstein, and S. Penrod; "The Effects of Long-Term Exposure to Violent and Sexually Degrading Depictions of Women," also by Linz, Donnerstein, and Penrod; *The Question of Pornography: Research Findings and Policy Implications*, again by Donnerstein, Linz, and Penrod; and *Pornography and Sexual Aggression*, edited by Neil Malamuth and Edward Donnerstein. Dolf Zillmann and Jennings Bryant's "Pornography, Sexual Callousness, and the Trivialization of Rape" made the strongest statements and is perhaps the most controversial such experiment. Zillmann and Bryant said that massive exposure to pornography appears to foster a callousness toward women, especially noticeable in attitudes toward rape, which comes to seem a "trivial" matter to those so exposed. The "pornography" used in their study, however, appears to be mainstream films (as opposed to hard-core or even soft-core genres).

Other researchers could not duplicate these results. When Vernon R. Padgett Jr., Jo Ann Brislin-Slütz, and James A. Neal tried to replicate the study by Zillmann and Bryant in "Pornography, Erotica, and Attitudes Toward Women: The Effects of Repeated Exposure," they found that exposure to nonviolent porn has no significant effect on attitudes toward women or toward women's organizations. In fact, the researchers say, exposure to pornography may increase positive attitudes toward women and may be otherwise socially beneficial because pornography can assist masturbation. They cite the common observation that Japan has a small incidence of rape despite pervasive, extremely violent pornography. Kathryn Kelley and her associates observe in "Three Faces of Sexual Explicitness; The Good, the Bad, and the Useful" that while there do seem to be some antisocial effects of pornography, there are also pro-social and educational effects: men exposed to pornographic materials are more quick to come to the aid of women perceived as victims than those unexposed.

Neil M. Malamuth and J. V. P. Check showed mainstream (not pornographic by most definitions) films to subjects for "The Effects of Mass Media Exposure on Acceptance of Violence against Women: A Field Experiment." Reactions indicated that exposure made violence directed against women more acceptable to normal males, increased their acceptance of rape myths, and reinforced violent attitudes toward women. Malamuth and Check's "Sexual Arousal to Rape and Consenting Depictions: The Importance of the Woman's Arousal" reported that men who view aggressive behavior toward women in mainstream films in which such activities as rape take place are more likely to accept the myth that women enjoy rape when the female film characters appear to become involuntarily aroused. "Rape Fantasies as a Function of Exposure to Violent Sexual Stimuli," by Neil M. Malamuth, and "Sexual Responsiveness of College Students to Rape

Depictions: Inhibitory and Disinhibitory Effects," by Malamuth, M. Heim, and S. Feschbach, found that male and female subjects tend to become aroused after watching "pornographic" (i.e., R-rated) films in which aggression toward women takes place—but *not* if the woman in the scenario is depicted as actually hurt or abused. In "Reported Proclivity for Coercive Sex following Repeated Exposure to Sexually Violent Pornography, Nonviolent Dehumanizing Pornography, and Erotica," J. V. P. Check and T. H. Guloien conclude that exposure to nonviolent erotica seems to have few antisocial effects and that subjects with preexisting psychoses are more likely to be affected by exposure to any kind of pornography. Other personality traits also seem important in subjects who do appear affected.

In a study called "Repeated Exposure to Sexually Explicit Stimuli: Novelty, Sex, and Sexual Attitudes," Kathryn Kelley and D. Musialowski discovered that exposure to erotica every day for four days led not to increased negative attitudes toward women but to a decrease in sexual arousal and boredom with the films. Many additional studies have reported no increase for males in negative attitudes toward women and no increased acceptance of rape myths after prolonged exposure to feature-length, nonviolent, plain-vanilla pornographic videotapes, even if these contained "degrading" portrayals of women. These include C. L. Krafka's "Sexually Explicit, Sexually Violent, and Violent Media: Effects of Multiple Naturalistic Exposures and Debriefing on Female Viewers" and other studies cited in Donnerstein, Linz, and Penrod's *The Question of Pornography: Research Findings and Policy Implications* and in Vernon R. Padgett, Jo Ann Brislin-Slütz, and James A. Neal's "Pornography, Erotica, and Attitudes toward Women: The Effects of Repeated Exposure."

When one treats erotica as a carrier of messages, say Daniel Linz and Edward Donnerstein in "The Effects of Counter-Information on the Acceptance of Rape Myths," then it becomes apparent that exploding the myth that women actually enjoy being ravished depends directly on better education. The researchers believe that young people can be taught about the dangers of accepting myths about rape (such as "they really want it") in a variety of ways. Margaret Jean Intons-Peterson, Margaret Jean, and Beverly Roskos-Ewoldsen observe in "Mitigating the Effects of Violent Pornography" that "debriefing" viewers after or briefing them before showing them violent sexual materials counteracts some of the effects of exposure. The key distinction is violence, not sexuality. In "The Effects of Long-Term Exposure to Violent and Sexually Degrading Depictions of Women," Daniel Linz, Edward Donnerstein, and Stephen Penrod did not find a correlation or a significant relationship between exposure to nonviolent pornography and the tendency to view women as sex objects or even the tendency to believe in traditional sex roles. Subjects with prolonged exposure to R-rated violent films exhibited some desensitization toward rape and the objectification of women.

After reviewing the literature in the field, Daniel Linz says in "Exposure to Sexually Explicit Materials and Attitudes toward Rape: A Comparison of Study

Results" that the experimental results are so mixed as to cancel each other out and that it is clear only that individuals exposed to "violent (slasher) films" can be said consistently to exhibit reduced sensitivity toward rape victims immediately after exposure. In other words, the effects are short-term. Vernon R. Padgett Jr., Jo Ann Brislin-Slütz, and James A. Neal used 184 psychology students and twenty patrons at an adult theater as subjects for "Pornography, Erotica, and Attitudes toward Women: The Effects of Repeated Exposure." Multiple linear regressions suggest that number of hours of viewing provides no indicator of attitudes toward women in either group. In general, however, the patrons of the movie theater seemed to manifest more favorable attitudes toward women than did the college students. Padgett, Brislin-Slütz, and Neal discovered no correlation between exposure to nonviolent pornography and hostile or negative attitudes toward women or women's issues.

Understandably frustrated at the confusion, Mike Allen, Tara Emmers, Lisa Gebhardt, and Mary A. Giery adopted a "meta-analysis" of more than 1,000 experimental and nonexperimental studies in "Exposure to Pornography and Acceptance of Rape Myths." They concluded that such an evaluation gave a slight edge to studies that indicated a relationship between exposure and the acceptance of rape myths. Since the studies they tabulated included many of questionable validity, ludicrous design, bizarre definitions, and runaway variables, however, the result is reminiscent of stories in which instructors weigh term papers in order to give an "A" to the heaviest. In any case, the ambiguity of so many studies has led psychologists Daniel Linz and Edward Donnerstein, whose research is most often advanced as demonstrating a connection between pornography and violence, explicitly to reject the inferences that many critics draw from the vast number of studies. Writing in "Research Can Help Us Explain Violence and Pornography," they insist on three points: (1) "Little proof exists that sexual aggression, as measured in the laboratory, is representative of aggression in actual sexual assaults"; (2) "Antisocial attitudes and callousness toward women are more likely to occur following exposure to *violent* materials, *regardless* of whether they are also obscene"; and (3) "No scientifically reputable data exist that indicate a pornography-violence connection in serial murders" (B3). Daniel Goleman's "Researchers Dispute Pornography Report on Its Use of Data" includes complaints by Donnerstein and others that their findings have been distorted to support the attorney general's report attributing a causality to pornography that is not borne out by their studies or, for that matter, by any clear evidence. Indeed, in his testimony before the Meese Commission, Donnerstein said flatly that no reputable researchers had linked ordinary hard-core films, that is, those primarily concerned with depicting sexual intercourse, with violent behavioral effects. According to Robert Scheer's report on the commission's deliberations, "Ed Meese's Dirty Pictures," the statement caused visible consternation among commissioners hoping for evidence that evil could be traced to representations of sex alone (73).

Reputable researchers insist on the Linz–Donnerstein distinction. Although most believe that sexual images alone cannot be linked to antisocial behavior, since there is almost no evidence of causation, they suspect that when sex and violence are *combined* as images in film, the consequences may be increased desensitization to reports of rape—though none would construe desensitization as an increased likelihood *to* rape. In "Mass Media Sexual Violence and Male Viewers," Donnerstein and Linz ask: "Does pornography influence behaviors and attitudes toward women?" Their conclusion: "The answer is difficult and centers on the definition of pornography. There is no evidence for any 'harm'-related effects from sexually explicit materials. But research may support potential harm effects from aggressive materials. *Aggressive* images are the issue, not sexual images. The message about violence and the sexualized nature of violence is crucial. Although these messages may be part of some forms of pornography, they are also pervasive media messages in general, from prime-time TV to popular films" (615–616). *Pornography and Sexual Aggression*, edited by Neil H. Malamuth and Edward Donnerstein, collects studies whose import is that negative effects occur only when sex is combined with violence. The researchers believe that depictions of violence can desensitize men to violence against women but stop well short of asserting causal links between representations of violence, however sexualized, and actual behavior. Similarly, *The Question of Pornography: Research Findings and Policy Implications*, edited by Donnerstein, Daniel Linz, and Stephen Penrod, broadly reviews the formulation of questions regarding the possible social effects of pornography. The research suggests that there is no link between sexually explicit material and sexual crimes *unless* the material includes images of violence; the latter type may contribute to aberrant behavior. Moreover, if violent content might increase aggression, exposure to porn without violent content might actually diminish it. Linkages between sex and violence occur far more frequently in mainstream representations than in materials obviously aimed at sexual arousal.

According to recent studies, in the absence of very specific factors, most males do not respond erotically to depictions of sex involving violence done to women. As Daniel Goleman reports in "New Studies Map the Mind of the Rapist," men who are already disturbed or men made momentarily angry at women by researchers—according to one experiment—can find violent depictions arousing. The artificial circumstances of many studies, in which the researchers *create* the precise conditions they want, may thus skew the results. With that possibility in mind, M. D. Smith and C. Hand mounted a longitudinal self-report (outside the laboratory) study of 230 college women for "The Pornography/Aggression Linkage: Results from a Field Study." These subjects reported no significant increase in aggression from a group of males who were shown a pornographic movie.

In the 1970s, Robert A. Baron and Paul A. Bell found in "Sexual Arousal and Aggression by Males: Effects of Type of Erotic Stimuli and Prior Provocation" that exposure to erotica actually inhibited males from behaving aggressively. Baron ran a similar study five years later on women. His "Heightened

Sexual Arousal and Physical Aggression: An Extension to Females" first made the female subjects angry, then showed them erotic material, then encouraged them to aggress against other females. Mild erotica appeared to inhibit aggression, whereas more explicit material (that the females deemed disgusting or repellent—though not necessarily the type of interest to males) increased aggression. In "Men's Interactions with Women after Viewing Sexually Explicit Films: Does Degradation Make a Difference?" L. L. Jansma, D. G. Linz, A. Mulac, and D. J. Imrich find that sexually explicit films that might be said to degrade women have no effect on the behavior of male subjects toward women.

Antiporn feminists dispute this view, of course. Radical feminists believe that sex is inherently violent and that sex is the origin of all injustice toward women. For them, any representation of sex will therefore be violent by definition. Diana E. H. Russell advances what she calls "Pornography and Rape: A Causal Model." In building this model, she theorizes that pornography may predispose some males to rape, may act as well on those already predisposed, may reduce the inhibitions of those not normally predisposed, or may undercut the social inhibitions against rape of still others. Russell points out that some sexual criminals report that they were motivated by pornography, that some college students say they would rape after seeing violent pornography, and that still other groups admit imitating scenes from X-rated movies. She also cites the usual Milgram-type studies in which subjects are persuaded to "shock" others, a phenomenon often used in support of assertions that exposure to violent materials heightens levels of aggression against females. The real problem, as Russell sees it, is that *all* men are predisposed to rape, by definition. (See **Feminist Positions on Pornography** in Chapter 6, especially Russell.)

As many scholars have pointed out, Milgram studies are suspect. In "Erotica and Aggression: The Influence of Sexual Arousal, Positive Affect, and Negative Affect on Aggressive Behavior," Leonard A. White presents the results of an experiment in which subjects were encouraged to express anger toward a volunteer and to apply electrical shocks to the volunteer (as in usual Milgram studies, the subjects do not know, of course, that no real shock is administered). If the subject is first shown pornographic pictures, then he may or may not shock the volunteer as hard. White's conclusion is that whether erotica has anything to do with aggression depends on the individual. If the subject attributes positive value to the material, pornography may actually lessen aggression, but pornography with high aggressive content *may* correlate with increased acting-out of hostility. Neil M. Malamuth's "Sexually Violent Media, Thought Patterns, and Antisocial Behavior" finesses such issues by suggesting that pornography has indirect effects: cumulations of sexually violent images might influence thought patterns normally shaped by community, family, and other pressures and lead to consequences like date and stranger rape.

STATISTICAL CORRELATIONS BETWEEN NUMBER OF REPORTED CRIMES AND AVAILABILITY OF PORNOGRAPHIC MATERIALS

Researchers for the 1970 President's Commission were influenced by the Danish experiment in legalizing pornography. Berl Kutchinsky's *Studies in Pornography and Sex Crimes in Denmark. A Report to the U.S. Presidential Commission on Obscenity and Pornography* asserted that Danish legalization led to a drop in sex crimes, especially the molestation of children, and doubtless affected the commission's recommendation that pornography be legalized for adults in America. Some parts of the study have since been questioned, but its conclusions may yet be valid. For example, Victor Bachy's "Danish 'Permissiveness' Revisited" claimed that statistics do not indicate that sexual crime rates in Denmark were affected one way or the other. Kutchinsky's "Pornography and Its Effects in Denmark and the United States: A Rejoinder and Beyond" points out that legalization led to a surge in production of explicit materials that began just as rapidly to fall off and that sex crimes in that country seemed to drop as well, depending on how one defined such crimes. The scholar may wish to look at Kutchinsky's most recent statement in "Legalized Pornography in Denmark." Here Kutchinsky maintains that pornography remains a "trifling issue": "In Denmark, most people dislike pornography and therefore stay away from it. In the United States, many of those who dislike pornography want *others* to stay away from it. That is a blemish on one of the freest nations in the world" (245).

Perhaps aware that their livelihood is threatened by such ideas, researchers sometimes attempt to correlate crime rates in specific states with the sales or circulation figures of materials that some people think of as pornographic. The hypothesis here is that while it may be impossible to establish a causal connection between sexual materials and sex crimes committed by individuals, a comparison of gross statistics may indicate some sort of relationship between the volume of such materials in circulation and particular kinds of crime. The most extreme advocate of this position is the Australian John H. Court, who claims in "Pornography and Sex Crimes: A Reevaluation in Light of Recent Trends around the World" that the increased availability of porn is responsible for the rise of rapes around the planet. Most statisticians reject Court's thesis, which has occasionally been adopted by law enforcement agencies in this country, but not by the FBI (see Marcia Pally's "Standard Deviation: Research Literature on Sexually Explicit Material and Social Harms"). A. Brannigan and A. Kapardis maintain in "The Controversy over Pornography and Sex Crimes: The Criminological Evidence and Beyond" that the distribution of pornographic materials appears unrelated to the frequency of sexual offenses like rape in recent periods when pornography appeared to spread more widely (and child molestation may actually decline during such periods). Legal systems, community pressures, and the characteristics of offender and victim seem to be more plausible factors than the possible effects of pornography alleged by antiporn feminists and funda-mentalists. (None of the studies deal with male rapes in American prisons, whose horrendous numbers rival the figures for rape of women annually in this country. That phenomenon awaits social construction as a topic of interest, presumably when pornography loses its glamour as a potential cause of evil.)

In "Rape and Pornography," George C. Thomas correlates the availability of pornography with the Justice Department's crime statistics, the National Crime Survey (NCS), to conclude that the FBI's Uniform Crime Reports (UCR) con-cerning rape (the figures that pornography opponents use to make causal con-nections between sexual expression and rape) are probably inaccurate. According to Thomas' study, which covered the years 1973 to 1992, the inci-dence of rape actually *drops* as pornography begins to become more available in 1981. Georgette Bennett's "Purveying Prurience" reached similar conclusions several years earlier than Thomas' study. The Audit Bureau of Circulation's figures for 1973 and 1983 for men's magazines, for instance, when correlated with the number of rapes (reported and unreported) given by the National Crime Survey for those years, provide ratios that reveal nothing; on the other hand, if the ratios do mean anything, says Bennett, then the incidence of rape has de-clined ever since 1973, when men's magazines first became widely available (194–195).

In *Sexual Science and the Law*, Richard Green notes that in the years from 1970 until 1978, a period during which pornographic films spread around the United States, the reported incidence of rape swelled from 20 incidents per 100,000 population to 30 per 100,000 but that the incidence of aggravated as-sault rose from 150 incidents per 100,000 to 230 per 100,000. The rise in rape may therefore have been "a nonspecific correlate" of the rise in assaults, and, if one factors in the heightened awareness of the importance of reporting rape promoted by the feminist movement, the rate of rape might possibly have fallen. Moreover, says Green, "regional analyses of the relation between the availability of sexual materials and sex-crime rates do not support a positive relationship between the two" (123–124). Other variables, says Green, can be more inti-mately connected: "These include alcohol consumption, the percentage of poor in a region, and the circulation of another type of magazine, 'outdoor' publications such as *Field and Stream* and *Guns and Ammo*. Although a prelim-inary study found that states with a higher circulation of sex magazines also had higher rape rates, three other variables were found to correlate more closely with rape: the number of divorced men, the degree of economic inequality, and urbanization" (124).

Larry Baron and Murray A. Straus, writing in *Four Theories of Rape in American Society: A State-Level Analysis*, review four theories as explanations of high rates of rape—gender inequity, pornography, social disorganization, and legitimate violence—but find that the presence of so many variables raises the likelihood of spurious relationships, not the least of which stems from trying to correlate such gross statistics. On that gross level, Baron and Straus do find a high correlation between the circulation of eight sex magazines (all soft-core, ranging from *Playboy* to *Gallery*) and the rape rate in various states. (They draw on annual *Sourcebook of Criminal Justice Statistics* published by the Justice Department and National Crime Surveys with Audit Bureau of Circulation figures for magazines.) Alaskans buy four times as many copies of *Playboy* than West Virginians and eight times as many of *Hustler* as residents of Utah (119), and Alaska has ranked high in rapes per 100,000 population: First in 1960 (before most of the magazines were published), fifth in 1970, and second in 1980 (42).

In "Pornography and Gender Equality: An Empirical Analysis," however, Baron finds that such quantitative methodologies indicate—contrary to initial supposition—that pornography and gender equality both flourish in politically tolerant societies. Baron observes that antiporn sentiment seems to flourish most readily in those states where religious intolerance and obvious gender inequity are stongest. In other words, pornography probably does not substantially contribute to sexual discrimination, nor does it seem to contribute to rape or violent behavior. This seems to be the case globally: in general, pornography is far more prevalent in countries in which women have attained higher measures of equality. Gender equality is higher in social contexts where magazines such as *Playboy* circulate freely. J. Bryant and D. Brown, in "Uses of Pornography," point out that Americans are loath to speak openly about their exposure to pornography or to participate in surveys, but of those who do, few report involuntary exposure. Among other factors, peer pressure is important, with most respondents reporting exposure by high school years. Bryant and Brown note that social influences and the male-oriented nature of the distribution system usually combine to deny females the same access to, or enjoyment of, pornography.

STUDIES OF SEX CRIMINALS

Several researchers have investigated possible connections between pornography and convicted sex criminals. The question is, Are males more likely to commit sexual crimes or simply motivated to engage in deviant behavior after being exposed to sexual materials? In "Personality Characteristics of Sex Offenders," S. Levin and L. Stava conclude that pornography acts as a stimulus to a very small group of sexual offenders. Royer F. Cook, Robert H. Fosen, and H. Asher Pacht compared the prior exposure to pornography of a group of convicted sex offenders and a control group of other criminals for "Pornography and the Sex Offender: Patterns of Previous Exposure and Arousal Effects of Pornographic Stimuli." The investigators found that sex offenders were less likely to have been exposed to erotic materials as children and that there appeared to be no correlation between exposure and sex crimes (perhaps even the reverse, e.g., that those so exposed were less likely to commit violent sex crimes). They believe that it is not really possible to talk about effects without very specific examples of crimes and very specific, highly individualized responses to very specific stimuli. Robert G. Meyer's "Pornography and the Sexual Deviations" makes similar points.

A classic study by Keith E. Davis and G. Nicholas Braucht, "Exposure to Pornography, Character and Deviance: A Retrospective Survey," found a positive link between sexual deviance and exposure to pornography at all age-of-exposure levels. Davis and Braucht thought that attraction to pornography might even be a predictor, since early (before age ten) exposure can be correlated with higher rates of deviance or offense. But they suggest that a more refined assessment might show that it is not the mere presentation of naked bodies or intercourse that has any detrimental effect; rather, it is the person's attitude toward the body and toward sex that is critical. In other words, sexually deviant attitudes probably precede interest in pornography. Davis and Braucht found little evidence that, over the long run, pornography contributes to pathology in its consumers. Another study of the same period by Michael J. Goldstein, Harold S. Kant, and John J. Hartman established no clear patterns. Their *Pornography and Sexual Deviance: A Report of the Legal and Behavioral Institute* compares consumers of porn, convicted sexual offenders, and homosexuals and transsexuals with control groups. They noted that while some sexual criminals have been exposed to pornography, they generally came to it later in life than non-sexual-offenders and were more likely to have been punished for looking at it as teenagers. Changes in the definitions of deviance, mutations in media technology, and the dated surveys that Goldstein and Kant cite make their volume less useful now, especially since they rejected definitive conclusions.

W. L. Marshall's study, "The Use of Sexually Explicit Stimuli by Rapists, Child Molesters, and Non-Offender Males" generally confirms those by Goldstein, Kant, and others. Marshall's follow-up, "Pornography and Sex Offenders," allows that pornography *might* have some relationship to offenders who sexually attack women or children despite data that thus far show only vague correlations. Most studies aimed at establishing linkages between sexual materials and sexual offenders, Marshall says, are methodologically naive or invalid. A study by Glen A. Kercher and C. Eugene Walker, "Reactions of Convicted Rapists to Sexually Explicit Stimuli," found that physical responses of offenders, as measured by penile volume, did not differ from those of a control group and that the rapists found the erotic material unpleasant or threatening. There is some evidence that men who have been repressed sexually or denied sexual socialization are more likely to have their behavior altered by exposure to sexual materials than are males who have experienced a more "normal" childhood and adolescence, or so say W. A. Fisher and D. Byrne in "Individual Differences in Affective and Behavioral Responses to an Erotic Film." E. K. Sommers and J. V. P. Check find in "An Empirical Investigation of the Role of Pornography in the Verbal and Physical Abuse of Women" that sexually aggressive partners of battered women were more likely to be consumers of pornography than a control group of males. Scholars may wish to consult "The Influence of Pornography on Sex Crimes," by Mary R. Murrin and D. R. Laws, for other information.

In what is easily the most thorough investigation of serial killers, *The Serial Killer: A Study in the Psychology of Violence*, C. Wilson and D. Seaman quote FBI spokesmen as observing that pornography does not come first; rather, the violent nature of such criminals makes them seek out pornography. They are not first exposed to pornography, which then incites murderous behavior. No legitimate researcher takes seriously the sly remarks of serial killer Ted Bundy to a fundamentalist minister that pornography led him to kill women, despite the prominence of the anecdote in our sexual folklore. Wilson and Seaman insist that Ted Bundy began to blame pornography only when his death sentence was confirmed: "Bundy may have blamed pornography for his obsessions but that is typical of a serial killer. He always blamed someone else or something else for what he has done; he is not to blame, it is never his fault" (201). Police found magazines about cheerleaders when they arrested him; no one found pornography in his possession. Wilson and Seaman also observe that many of the alleged studies "proving" a link between pornography and sex crimes are simply a species of urban myth. As Linz and Donnerstein insist in "Research Can Help Us Explain Violence and Pornography," there is simply no credible evidence that pornography is causally connected to serial murder.

NOTES

1. Christopher Lehmann-Haupt, "Books of the Times," *New York Times*, 11 December 1980, p. C25.

REFERENCES

Abramson, Paul R. "Sexual Science: Emerging Discipline or Oxymoron?" *Journal of Sex Research*, 27 (1990): 147–165.

Allen, Mike, Tara Emmers, Lisa Gebhardt, and Mary A. Giery. "Exposure to Pornography and Acceptance of Rape Myths." *Journal of Communication*, 45:1 (Winter 1995): 5–26.

Altimore, Michael. "The Social Construction of a Scientific Myth: Pornography and Violence." *Journal of Communication Inquiry*, 15: 1 (Winter 1991): 117–133.

Amoroso, Donald M., and Marvin Brown. "Problems in Studying the Effects of Erotic Material." *Journal of Sex Research*, 9 (August 1973): 187–195.

Aphrodite, J. [Carol Livingston]. *To Turn You On: 39 Sex Fantasies for Women*. Secaucus, NJ: Lyle Stuart, 1975.

Arcand, Bernard. *The Jaguar and the Anteater: Pornography Degree Zero*, trans. Wayne Grady. New York: Verso, 1993.

Athanasiou, Robert. "Pornography: A Review of Research." *Handbook of Human Sexuality*, ed. Benjamin B. Wolman and John Money. Northvale, NJ: Aronson, 1993, pp. 251–268.

Attorney General's Commission on Pornography. *Final Report*. 2 vols. Washington, DC: Government Printing Office, 1986.

Bachy, Victor. "Danish 'Permissiveness' Revisited." *Journal of Communication*, 26 (Winter 1976): 40–43.

Bancroft, John, ed. *Researching Sexual Behavior: Methodological Issues*. Bloomington: Indiana University Press, 1997.

Bandura, Albert. *Social Learning Theory*. Englewood Cliffs, NJ: Prentice-Hall, 1977.

Bandura, Albert, B. Underwood, and M. E. Fromson. "Disinhibition of Aggression through Diffusion of Responsibility and Dehumanization of Victims." *Journal of Research in Personality*, 9 (1975): 253–269.

Barbach, Lonnie. *For Yourself: The Fulfillment of Female Sexuality*. New York: Doubleday, 1975.

Barbour, Celia. "Looking at Pictures." *New York Times*, 23 April 1994, p. 15.

Baron, Larry. "Pornography and Gender Equality: An Empirical Analysis." *Journal of Sex Research*, 27:3 (August 1990): 363–380.

Baron, Larry, and Murray A. Straus. *Four Theories of Rape in American Society: A State-Level Analysis*. New Haven, CT: Yale University Press, 1989.

Baron, Robert A. "Heightened Sexual Arousal and Physical Aggression: An Extension to Females." *Journal of Research in Personality*, 13 (March 1979): 91–102.

Baron, Robert A., and Paul A. Bell. "Sexual Arousal and Aggression by Males: Effects of Type of Erotic Stimuli and Prior Provocation." *Journal of Personality and Social Psychology*, 29 (1974): 111–116.

Baroni, Michael. "In Defense of Sexy Videos." *Cosmopolitan*, 220:5 (May 1996): 140.

Bart, Pauline, and Margaret Jozsa. "Dirty Books, Dirty Films, and Dirty Data." *Take Back the Night: Women on Pornography*, ed. Laura Lederer. New York: William Morrow, 1980, pp. 204–217.

Belliveau, Rollin C. *Understanding Human Sexual Inadequacy*. Boston: Little, Brown, 1970.

Benjamin, Jessica. "The Bonds of Love: Rational Violence and Erotic Domination." *Feminist Studies*, 6 (1980): 144–174.

―――. *Like Subjects, Love Objects*. New Haven, CT: Yale University Press, 1995.

Bennett, Georgette. "Purveying Prurience." *Crime Warps: The Future of Crime in America*. Garden City, NY: Anchor Press/Doubleday, 1987, pp. 188–200.

Berne, Eric. *Games People Play: The Psychology of Human Relationships*. New York: Grove Press, 1966.

Bilderlexicon der Erotik. 6 vols. Vienna and Hamburg: Verlag für Kulturforschung, 1928–1931, 1963. Edited by Leo Schidrowitz: I: *Kulturgeschichte*; II: *Literatur und Kunst*; III: *Sexualwissenschaft*; IV: *Ergänzungsband*. Edited by Armand Mergen: V and VI: *Sexualforschung: Stichwort und Bild*.

Birken, Lawrence. *Consuming Desire: Sexual Science and the Emergence of a Culture of Abundance, 1871–1914*. Ithaca, NY: Cornell University Press, 1988.

Blumer, Herbert George. *Movies and Conduct*. New York: Macmillan, 1933.

―――. *Movies, Delinquency, and Crime*. New York: Macmillan, 1933.

Boffey, Philip M. "Sexology Struggling to Establish Itself amid Wide Hostility." *New York Times*, 31 May 1993, pp. C1, 3.

Bracher, Mark. *Lacan, Discourse, and Social Change: A Psychoanalytic Cultural Criticism*. Ithaca, NY: Cornell University Press, 1993, pp. 83–102.

―――. "Writing and Imaging the Body in Pornography: The Desire of the Other and

Its Implications for Feminism." *American Journal of Semiotics*, 8:4 (1991): 105–130.

Brannigan, Augustine. "Pornography and Behavior: Alternative Explanations: A Critique." *Journal of Communication*, 37:3 (Summer 1987): 185–189.

Brannigan, Augustine, and Sheldon Goldenberg. "The Study of Aggressive Pornography: The Vicissitudes of Relevance." *Critical Studies in Mass Communications*, 4:3 (1987): 262–283.

Brannigan, Augustine, and A. Kapardis. "The Controversy over Pornography and Sex Crimes: The Criminological Evidence and Beyond." *Australian and New Zealand Journal of Criminology*, 19:4 (December 1986): 259–284.

Brecher, Edward M. *The Sex Researchers*. London: Andre Deutsch, 1970.

Brecher, Edward M., and Ruth Brecher, eds. *An Analysis of Human Sexual Inadequacy*. New York: Bantam, 1970.

Bright, Susie. *Herotica: A Collection of Women's Erotic Fiction*, ed. Susie Bright. Burlingame, CA: Down There Press, 1988.

———. *Susie Bright's Sexwise: America's Favorite X-Rated Intellectual Does Dan Quayle, Catharine MacKinnon, Stephen King, Camille Paglia, Nicholson Baker, Madonna, the Black Panthers, and the GOP*. Pittsburgh: Cleis Press, 1995.

Brothers, Joyce. "What Women Think of Pornography." *Good Housekeeping*, May 1970, pp. 54–55.

Brown, Beverley. "A Feminist Interest in Pornography—Some Modest Proposals." *m/f*, no. 5–6 (1981): 5–12.

Bryant, J., and D. Brown. "Uses of Pornography." *Pornography: Research Advances and Policy Considerations*, ed. Dolf Zillmann and Jennings Bryant. Hillsdale, NJ: Lawrence Erlbaum Associates, 1989, pp. 25–55.

Bullough, Bonnie, Vern L. Bullough, Marilyn A. Fithian, William E. Hartman, and Randy Sue Klein, eds. *How I Got into Sex*. Amherst, NY: Prometheus Books, 1997.

Bullough, Vern L. *Science in the Bedroom: A History of Sex Research*. New York: Basic Books, 1994.

Burstyn, Varda. "Who the Hell Is 'We'?" *Good Girls/Bad Girls: Feminists and Sex Trade Workers Face to Face*, ed. Laurie Bell. Seattle: Seal Press, 1987, pp. 163–172.

Burt, Mary. "Use of Pornography by Women: A Critical Review of the Literature." *Case Western Reserve Journal of Sociology*, 8 (September 1976): 1–16.

Buss, David M., and Neil M. Malamuth, eds. *Sex, Power and Conflict: Evolutionary and Feminist Perspectives*. New York: Oxford University Press, 1996.

Byrne, Donn, Fran Cherry, John Lamerth, and Herman E. Mitchell. "Husband–Wife Similarity in Response to Erotic Stimuli." *Journal of Personality*, 41 (September 1973): 385–394.

Califia, Pat. *Public Sex: The Culture of Radical Sex*. Pittsburgh: Cleis Press, 1994.

Caplan, Paula J., and Jeremy B. Caplan. *Thinking Critically about Research on Sex and Gender*. New York: HarperCollins, 1994.

Carol, Avedon. *Nudes, Prudes and Attitudes: Pornography and Censorship*, with cartoons by Lee Kennedy. Cheltenham: New Clarion Press, 1994.

Carrier, Micheline. *La Danse Macabre: Violence et Pornographie*. Quebec: Apostrophe, 1984.

Chapman, Gary. "Not So Naughty." *New Republic*, 31 July 1995, p. 11.

Chapple, Steven, and David Talbot. *Burning Desires: Sex in America—A Report from the Field.* New York: Signet, 1990.

Check, J. V. P., and T. H. Guloien. "Reported Proclivity for Coercive Sex following Repeated Exposure to Sexually Violent Pornography, Nonviolent Dehumanizing Pornography, and Erotica." *Pornography: Research Advances and Policy Considerations*, ed. Dolf Zillmann and Jennings Bryant. Hillsdale, NJ: Lawrence Erlbaum Associates, 1989, pp. 159–184.

Check, J. V. P., and N. M. Malamuth. "Pornography and Sexual Aggression: A Social Learning Theory Analysis." *Communication Yearbook 9*, ed. M. L. McLaughlin. Beverly Hills, CA: Sage, 1986, pp. 181–213.

Christensen, F. M. "Effects of Pornography: The Debate Continues: A Critique." *Journal of Communication*, 37:1 (Winter 1987): 186–187.

———. *Pornography: The Other Side.* New York: Praeger, 1990.

———. "Sexual Callousness Revisited: A Critique." *Journal of Communication*, 36:1 (Winter 1986): 174–184.

Christenson, Cornelia. *Kinsey: A Biography.* Bloomington: Indiana University Press, 1971.

Cole, Susan G. *Power Surge: Sex, Violence and Pornography.* Toronto: Second Story Press, 1995.

Cook, Royer F., Robert H. Fosen, and Asher Pacht. "Pornography and the Sex Offender: Patterns of Previous Exposure and Arousal Effects of Pornographic Stimuli." *Journal of Applied Psychology*, 55 (December 1971): 503–511.

Corry, John. "The Selling of Sex: A Look through a Solemn Sodom." *New York Times*, 10 October 1972, p. 47.

Corzine, Jay, and Richard Kirby. "Cruising the Truckers: Sexual Encounters in a Highway Rest Area." *Urban Life*, 6 (July 1977): 171–192.

Court, John H. "Pornography and Sex Crimes: A Reevaluation in Light of Recent Trends around the World." *International Journal of Criminology and Penology*, 5 (May 1977): 129–157.

Coward, Rosalind. *Female Desires: How They Are Sought, Bought, and Packaged.* New York: Grove Press, 1985.

———. "Sexual Violence and Sexuality." *Sexuality: A Reader*, ed. editors of *Feminist Review*. London: Virago Press, 1987, pp. 307–325.

Cowie, Elizabeth. "Pornography and Fantasy: Psychoanalytic Perspectives." *Sex Exposed: Sexuality and the Pornography Debate*, ed. Lynne Segal and Mary McIntosh. New Brunswick, NJ: Rutgers University Press, 1993, pp. 132–152.

Crepault, Claude. "Sexual Fantasies and Visualization of 'Pornographic Scenes." *Journal of Sex Research*, 8 (1972): 154–155.

Dallas, Dorothy M. "The Use of Visual Materials in Sex Education." *The Influence of Pornography on Behavior*, ed. Maurice Yaffé and Edward C. Nelson. London: Academic Press, 1982, pp. 65–79.

Dally, Peter. *The Fantasy Factor: How Male and Female Sexual Fantasies Affect Our Lives.* London: Weidenfeld and Nicolson, 1975.

Davis, Keith E., and G. Nicholas Braucht. "Exposure to Pornography, Character and Deviance: A Retrospective Survey." *Journal of Social Issues* 29:3 (1973): 183–196.

Dershowitz, Alan M. "Justice: Connecting Pornography with Violence Is Junk Science, Which Doesn't Belong in Courts." *Penthouse*, 29: 6 (February 1998): 128.

Donnelly, Peter. "Running the Gauntlet: The Moral Order of Pornographic Movie Theaters." *Urban Life*, 10:3 (October 1981): 239–264.

Donnerstein, Edward. "Aggressive Erotica and Violence against Women." *Journal of Personality and Social Psychology*, 39:2 (August 1980): 269–277.

Donnerstein, Edward, and L. Berkowitz. "Victim Reactions in Aggressive Erotic Films as a Factor in Violence against Women." *Journal of Personality and Social Psychology*, 41:4 (1981): 710–724.

Donnerstein, Edward, and Daniel Linz. "Mass Media Sexual Violence and Male Viewers." *American Behavioral Scientist*, 29: 5 (May/June 1986): 601–618.

Donnerstein, Edward, Daniel Linz, and Stephen Penrod. *The Question of Pornography: Research Findings and Policy Implications*. New York: Free Press, 1987.

Dunwoody, Vera, and Kathy Pezdek. "Factors Affecting the Sexual Arousal Value of Pictures."*Journal of Sex Research*, 15:4 (November 1979): 276–284.

Echols, Alice. "The New Feminism of Yin and Yang." *Powers of Desire: The Politics of Sexuality*, ed. Ann Snitow, Christine Stansell, and Sharon Thompson. New York: Monthly Review Press, 1983, pp. 439–459.

Elkin, Stanley. "Alfred Kinsey: The Patron Saint of Sex." *Esquire: 1933–1983* (December 1983): 48–59.

Ellis, B., and D. Symons. "Sex Differences in Sexual Fantasy." *Journal of Sex Research*, 27 (1989): 527–555.

Ellis, Havelock. *Studies in the Psychology of Sex*. 7 vols. Philadelphia: F. A. Davis, 1925–1930; rpt. 7 vols. in 2. New York: Random House, 1942.

Emerson, Joan P. "Behavior in Private Places: Sustaining Definitions of Realities in Gynecological Examinations." *Recent Sociology: Patterns of Communicative Behavior*, ed. Hans Peter Dreitzel. New York: Macmillan, 1970, pp. 74–97.

Eurydice. *Satyricon USA: A Journey across the New Sexual Frontier*. New York: Scribner's, 1999.

Eysenek, Hans J., and D. K. B. Nias. *Sex, Violence, and the Media*. New York: St. Martin's, 1978.

Farkas, G. M., L. F. Sine, and I. M. Evans. "Personality, Sexuality, and Demographic Differences between Volunteers and Nonvolunteers for a Laboratory Study of Male Sexual Behavior." *Archives of Sexual Behavior*, 7 (November 1978): 513–520.

Faust, Bernice. *Women, Sex and Pornography: A Controversial Study*. New York: Macmillan, 1980.

Fenigstein, Allan, and Ronald G. Heyduk. "Sexual-Aggressive Fantasies and Attraction to Pornography." *Selective Exposure to Communication*, ed. Dolf Zillmann and Jennings Bryant. Hillsdale, NJ: Lawrence Erlbaum Associates, 1985, pp. 123–126.

Feshbach, Seymour, and Neil Malamuth. "Sex and Aggression: Proving the Link."*Psychology Today* (November 1978): 111–122.

Fisher, Seymour. *Sexual Images of the Self: The Psychology of Erotic Sensations and Illusions*. Hillsdale, NJ: Lawrence Erlbaum Associates, 1989.

Fisher, William A., and Donn Byrne. "Individual Differences in Affective and Behavioral Responses to an Erotic Film." *Journal of Applied Social Psychology*, 8 (1978): 355–365.

———. "Sex Differences in Response to Erotica: Love versus Lust." *Journal of Personality and Social Psychology*, 36 (February 1987): 117–125.

Fox, Siv Cedering. *Joys of Fantasy: The Book for Loving Couples*. Chelsea, MI: Scarborough House, 1978.

Fraser, John. *Violence in the Arts*. New York: Cambridge University Press, 1974.

Friday, Nancy. *Forbidden Flowers: More Women's Sexual Fantasies*. New York: Pocket Books, 1975.

———. *Men in Love: Men's Sexual Fantasies: The Triumph of Love over Rage*. New York: Delacorte, 1980.

———. *My Secret Garden: Women's Sexual Fantasies*. New York: Pocket Books, 1974.

———. *Women on Top: How Real Life Has Changed Women's Sexual Fantasies*. New York: Simon and Schuster, 1991.

Fuller, Shirley Rae. "The Relationship between Pornography Use by Male Spouses and Women's Experiences of Marital Interaction and Satisfaction." Ph.D. dissertation, Pacific Graduate School of Psychology, 1995.

Gagnon, John. "Sex Research and Social Change." *Archives of Sexual Behavior*, 4 (1975): 111–141.

Geer, J. H., and M. S. McGlone. "Sex Differences in Memory for Erotica." *Cognition and Emotion*, 4 (1990): 71–78.

George, W. H., and G. A. Marlatt. "The Effects of Alcohol and Anger on Interest in Violence, Erotica, and Deviance." *Journal of Abnormal Psychology*, 95:2 (May 1986): 150–158.

Gibson, Margaret. "Clitoral Corruption: Body Metaphors and American Doctors' Constructions of Female Homosexuality, 1870–1900." *Science and Homosexualities*, ed. Vernon Rosario II. New York: Routledge, 1996, pp. 177–196.

———. "The Masculine Degenerate: American Doctors' Portrayal of the Lesbian Intellect." *Journal of Women's History*, 9:4 (Winter 1998): 78–103.

Gilland, Patricia. "Therapeutic Use of Obscenity."*Censorship and Obscenity*, ed. Rajeev Dhavan and Christie Davies. London: Martin Robertson, 1978, pp. 127–147.

Girard, Rene. *Violence and the Sacred*, trans. Patrick Gregory. Baltimore: Johns Hopkins University Press, 1977.

Glenmuller, Joseph. *The Pornographer's Grief, and Other Tales of Human Sexuality*. New York: HarperCollins, 1993.

Goffman, Erving. *Behavior in Public Places*. Glencoe, IL: Free Press, 1963.

Goldstein, Michael J., Harold S. Kant, and John J. Hartman. *Pornography and Sexual Deviance: A Report of the Legal and Behavioral Institute*. Berkeley: University of California Press, 1973.

Goleman, Daniel. "New Studies Map the Mind of the Rapist." *New York Times*, national ed., 10 December 1991, pp. B5, 8.

———. "New View of Fantasy: Much Is Found Perverse." *New York Times*, 7 May 1991, pp. B5, B7.

———. "Researchers Dispute Pornography Report on Its Use of Data." *New York Times*, 17 May 1986, pp. A1, A35.

Goleman, Daniel, and Sherida Bush. "The Liberation of Sexual Fantasy." *Psychology Today* 11:5 (1977): 48–53, 104–107.

Gould, Lois. "Pornography for Women." *New York Times Magazine* (2 March 1975), 10–11, 50–51, 54, 57, 60, 62.

Gray, Susan H. "Exposure to Pornography and Aggression toward Women: The Case of the Angry Male." *Social Problems*, 29 (April 1982): 387–398.

Green, Richard. *Sexual Science and the Law*. Cambridge: Harvard University Press, 1992.

Greer, Germaine. "What Turns Women On?" *Esquire*, 80:1 (July 1973): 88–91, 150, 152.

Griffin, Susan. *Pornography and Silence: Culture's Revenge against Nature*. New York: Harper and Row, 1981.

Gross, Larry. "Marginal Texts, Marginal Audiences." *The Audience and Its Landscape*, ed. James Hay, Lawrence Grossberg, and Ellen Wartella. Boulder, CO: Westview, 1996, pp. 161–176.

———. "Pornography and Social Science Research: Serious Questions: A Critique." *Journal of Communication*, 33:4 (Autumn 1983): 107–111.

Haeberle, Erwin J., ed. *The Birth of Sexology: A Brief History in Documents*. Bloomington IN: Kinsey Institute for Sex, Gender, and Reproduction/World Association for Sexology, 1983.

Haehne, Karen. "Confessions of a Feminist Porn Programmer." *Film Quarterly*, 37:1 (Autumn 1983): 9–16.

Hansen, Christian, Catherine Needham, and Bill Nichols. "Skin Flicks: Pornography, Ethnography, and the Discourses of Power." *Discourse: Journal for Theoretical Studies in Media and Culture*, 11:2 (Spring–Summer 1989): 65–79; rpt. *Representing Reality: Issues and Concepts in Documentary*, by Bill Nichols. Bloomington: Indiana University Press, 1991, pp. 201–228.

Harding, Sandra, and Jean F. O'Barr, eds. *Sex and Scientific Inquiry*. Chicago: University of Chicago Press, 1987.

Havemann, Ernest. "The Sex Institute." *Playboy*, 12:9 (September 1965): 139, 152, 164, 194, 196, 198, 200, 207.

Hawkins, Gordon, and Franklin E. Zimring. *Pornography in a Free Society*. New York: Cambridge University Press, 1989.

Heckma, Gert. "A History of Sexology." *From Sappho to de Sade: Moments in the History of Sexuality*, ed. Jan Bremmer. New York: Routledge, 1991, pp. 176–186.

Heiman, Julia R. "Women's Sexual Arousal: The Physiology of Erotica." *Psychology Today*, 8: 11 (April 1975): 90–94.

Henslin, James M., and Mae A. Briggs. "Dramaturgical Desexualization: The Sociology of the Vaginal Examination." *Studies in the Sociology of Sex*, ed. James M. Henslin. New York: Appleton-Century-Crofts, 1971, pp. 243–272.

Herdt, Gilbert, and Robert J. Stoller. *Intimate Communications: Erotics and the Study of Culture*. New York: Columbia University Press, 1990.

Holland, Norman. "Pornography and the Mechanisms of Defense." *Technical Reports of the Commission on Obscenity and Pornography*. 9 vols. Washington, DC: Government Printing Office, 1971–1972, I: 115–129.

"How *Time* Fed the Internet Porn Panic." *Harpers*, 291 (September 1995): 11–15.

Howard, James L., Myron B. Liptzin, and Clifford B. Reifler. "Is Pornography a Problem?" *Journal of Social Issues*, 29 (1973): 133–145.

Hsu, B., A. Kling, C. Kessler, K. Knape, P. Diefenbach, and J. Elias. "Gender Differences in Sexual Fantasy and Behavior in A College Population: A Ten-Year Replication." *Journal of Sex and Marital Therapy*, 20 (1994): 103–118.

Humphreys, Laud. *Tearoom Trade: Impersonal Sex in Public Places*. Chicago: Aldine, 1970.

Intons-Peterson, Margaret Jean, and Beverly Roskos-Ewoldsen. "Mitigating the Effects of Violent Pornography." *For Adult Users Only: The Dilemma of Violent Por-*

nography, ed. Susan Gubar and Joan Hoff. Bloomington: Indiana University Press, 1989, pp. 218–239.

Irvine, Janice. *Disorders of Desire: Sex and Gender in Modern American Sexology.* Philadelphia: Temple University Press, 1990.

Itzin, Catherine, ed. *Pornography: Women, Violence and Civil Liberties.* New York: Oxford, 1992.

Jansma, L. L., D. G. Linz, A. Mulac, and D. J. Imrich. "Men's Interactions with Women after Viewing Sexually Explicit Films: Does Degradation Make a Difference?" *Communication Monographs*, 64 (1997).

Jarvie, Ian. "The Sociology of the Pornography Debate." *Philosophy of the Social Sciences*, 17 (1987): 257–275.

Jarvis, Arthur R. "The Payne Fund Reports: A Discussion of Their Content, Public Reaction, and Effect on the Motion Picture Industry, 1930–1940." *Journal of Popular Culture*, 25:2 (Fall 1991): 127–140.

Jones, James H. *Alfred C. Kinsey: A Public/Private Life.* New York: Norton, 1997.

Kaplan, Helen Singer. *The New Sex Therapy: Active Treatment of Sexual Dysfunctions.* New York: Times Books, 1974.

Kapsalis, Terri. *Public Privates: Performing Gynecology from Both Ends of the Speculum.* Durham, NC: Duke University Press, 1997.

Karp, David A. "Hiding in Pornographic Bookstores: A Reconsideration of the Nature of Urban Anonymity." *Urban Life and Culture*, 1 (January 1973): 427–451.

Katzman, M. "Photograph Characteristics Influencing the Judgement of Obscenity." *Technical Reports of the Commission on Obscenity and Pornography.* 9 vols. Washington, DC: Government Printing Office, 1970.

Kelley, Kathryn, ed. *Females, Males, and Sexuality: Theories and Research.* Albany: State University Press of New York, 1987.

Kelley, Kathryn, and D. Musialowski. "Repeated Exposure to Sexually Explicit Stimuli: Novelty, Sex, and Sexual Attitudes." *Archives of Sexual Behavior*, 15 (1986): 487–498.

Kelley, Kathryn, et al. "Three Faces of Sexual Explicitness: The Good, the Bad, and the Useful." *Pornography: Research Advances and Policy Considerations*, ed. Dolf Zillmann and Jennings Bryant. Hillsdale, NJ: Lawrence Erlbaum Associates, 1989, pp. 57–91.

Kercher, Glen A., and C. Eugene Walker. "Reactions of Convicted Rapists to Sexually Explicit Stimuli." *Journal of Abnormal Psychology*, 81 (February 1973): 46–50.

King, Alison. "Mystery and Imagination: The Case of Pornography Effects Studies." *Bad Girls and Dirty Pictures: The Challenge to Reclaim Feminism*, ed. Alison Assiter and Avedon Carol. Boulder, CO: Pluto Press, 1993, pp. 57–87.

Knowles, Kyle, and Houshang Poorkaj. "Attitudes and Behavior on Viewing Sexual Activities in Public Places." *Sociology and Social Research*, 58:2 (January 1974): 130–135.

Koch, Gertrud. "The Body's Shadow Realm," trans. Jan-Christopher Horak. *Jump Cut*, 35 (April 1990): 17–29; rpt. *Dirty Looks: Women, Pornography, Power*, ed. Pamela Church Gibson and Roma Gibson. London: British Film Institute, 1993, pp. 22–45.

Kornblum, William, ed. *West 42nd Street Study: The Bright Light Zone.* New York: Graduate School and University Center of the City University of New York, 1978.

Krafka, C. L. "Sexually Explicit, Sexually Violent, and Violent Media: Effects of Multiple Naturalistic Exposures and Debriefing on Female Viewers." Ph.D. dissertation, University of Wisconsin, 1985.

Kronhausen, Eberhard, and Phyllis Kronhausen. *Erotic Fantasies: A Study of the Sexual Imagination.* New York: Grove Press, 1969.

———. "The Psychology of Pornography." *The Encyclopedia of Sexual Behavior,* ed. Albert Ellis and A. Abarbanel. New York: Hawthorne Books, 1961.

Kulick, Don, and Margaret Willson, eds. *Taboo: Sex, Identity and Erotic Subjectivity in Anthropological Fieldwork.* New York: Routledge, 1995.

Kupers, Terry A. "Pornography and Intimacy." *Revisioning Men's Lives: Gender, Intimacy, and Power.* New York: Guilford Press, 1993, pp. 76–91.

Kutchinsky, Berl. "Legalized Pornography in Denmark." *Men Confront Pornography,* ed. Michael S. Kimmel. New York: Crown, 1990, pp. 233–245.

———. "Pornography and Its Effects in Denmark and the United States: A Rejoinder and Beyond." *Comparative Social Research, an Annual (Vol. 8).* Greenwich, CT: JAI Press, 1985.

———. *Studies in Pornography and Sex Crimes in Denmark. A Report to the U.S. Presidential Commission on Obscenity and Pornography.* Copenhagen: Nyt fra Samfundsvidenshaberne, eksp: DBK, 1970.

Lacombe, Dany. *Ideology and Public Policy: The Case against Pornography.* Toronto: Garamond Press, 1988.

Laplanche, Jean, and J. B. Pontalis. "Fantasy and the Origins of Sexuality." *International Journal of Psycho-Analysis,* 49:1 (1968): 1–18; rpt. in *The Language of Psychoanalysis,* trans. Donald Nicholson-Smith. New York: Norton, 1973; rpt. in *Formations of Fantasy,* ed. Victor Burgin, James Donald, and Cora Kaplan. New York: Methuen, 1986.

Leach, Michael. *I Know It When I See It: Pornography, Violence, and Public Sensitivity.* Philadelphia: Westminster Press, 1975.

Legman, Gershon. *Love and Death: A Study in Censorship.* New York: Breaking Point, 1949; New York: Hacker Art Books, 1963.

Lehrman, Nat. *Masters and Johnson Explained.* Chicago: Playboy Press, 1970.

Levin, S., and L. Stava. "Personality Characteristics of Sex Offenders." *Archives of Sexual Behavior,* 16 (1987): 57–79.

Levine, Judith. "Perils of Desire." *Village Voice Literary Supplement,* March 1985, pp. 1, 12–15.

Lindquist, John, and Howard L. Cane. "Myths and Realities of Dirty Book Buyers." *Free Inquiry in Creative Sociology,* 7:1 (May 1979): 51.

Linz, Daniel. "Exposure to Sexually Explicit Materials and Attitudes toward Rape: A Comparison of Study Results." *Journal of Sex Research,* 26 (February 1989): 50–84.

Linz, Daniel, and Edward Donnerstein. "The Effects of Counter-Information on the Acceptance of Rape Myths." *Pornography: Research Advances and Policy Considerations,* ed. Dolf Zillmann and Jennings Bryant. Hillsdale, NJ: Lawrence Erlbaum Associates, 1989, pp. 259–288.

———. "Research Can Help Us Explain Violence and Pornography." *The Chronicle of Higher Education,* 30 September 1992, pp. B3–B4.

Linz, Daniel, Edward Donnerstein, and S. M. Adams. "Physiological Desensitization and Judgments about Female Victims of Violence." *Human Communication Research,* 15 (1989): 509–522.

Linz, Daniel, and Neil Malamuth. *Pornography*. Newbury, Park, CA: Sage, 1993.

Linz, Daniel, Edward Donnerstein, and Stephen Penrod. "The Effects of Long-Term Exposure to Violent and Sexually Degrading Depictions of Women." *Journal of Personality and Social Psychology*, 55 (1988): 758–768.

———. "The Effects of Multiple Exposures to Filmed Violence against Women." *Journal of Communication*, 34:3 (1984): 130–147.

Livingston, Carol. Interview. *Hustler*, 2:11 (May 1976): 44–46, 49–50.

Lurie, Susan. "Pornography and the Dread of Women: The Dilemma of Male Sexuality." *Take Back the Night: Women on Pornography*, ed. Laura Lederer. New York: Morrow, 1980, I, 159–173.

Macy, Marianne. *Working Sex: An Odyssey into Our Cultural Underworld*. New York: Carroll and Graf, 1996.

Malamuth, Neil M. "Rape Fantasies as a Function of Exposure to Violent Sexual Stimuli." *Archives of Sexual Behavior*, 10 (1981): 33–47.

———. "Sexually Explicit Media, Gender Differences, and Evolutionary Theory." *Journal of Communication*, 46:3 (Summer 1996): 8–31.

———. "Sexually Violent Media, Thought Patterns, and Antisocial Behavior." *Public Communication and Behavior*, ed. G. Comstock. 2 vols. San Diego: Academic Press, 1989, I, 159–204.

Malamuth, Neil M., and V. Billings. "Why Pornography? Models of Functions and Effects." *Journal of Communication*, 34:3 (Summer 1984): 117–129.

Malamuth, Neil M., and J. V. P. Check. "The Effects of Mass Media Exposure on Acceptance of Violence against Women: A Field Experiment." *Journal of Research in Personality*, 15 (1981): 436–446.

———. "Sexual Arousal to Rape and Consenting Depictions: The Importance of the Woman's Arousal." *Journal of Abnormal Psychology*, 89 (1980): 763–766.

Malamuth, Neil M., and Edward Donnerstein, eds. *Pornography and Sexual Aggression*. Orlando, FL: Academic Press, 1984.

Malamuth, Neil M., M. Heim, and S. Feschbach. "Sexual Responsiveness of College Students to Rape Depictions: Inhibitory and Disinhibitory Effects." *Journal of Personality and Social Psychology*, 38 (1980): 399–408.

Mann, Jay, Jack Sidman, and Sheldon Starr. "Effects of Erotic Films on Sexual Behavior of Married Couples." *Technical Reports of the Commission on Obscenity and Pornography*. 9 vols. Washington, DC: Government Printing Office, 1971–1972, VIII: pp. 170–254.

———. "Evaluating Social Consequences of Erotic Films: An Experimental Approach." *Journal of Social Issues*, 29:3 (1973): 113–131.

Marshall, Donald S., and Robert C. Suggs, eds. *Human Sexual Behavior: Variations in the Ethnographic Spectrum*. New York: Basic Books, 1971.

Marshall, W. L. "Pornography and Sex Offenders." *Pornography: Research Advances and Policy Considerations*, ed. Dolf Zillmann and Jennings Bryant. Hillsdale, NJ: Lawrence Erlbaum Associates, 1989, pp. 185–214.

———. "The Use of Sexually Explicit Stimuli by Rapists, Child Molesters, and Non-Offender Males." *Journal of Sex Research*, 25:2 (1988): 267–288.

Masters, William H., and Virginia E. Johnson. *Homosexuality in Perspective*. Boston: Little, Brown, 1979, pp. 188–189.

———. *Human Sexual Inadequacy*. Boston: Little, Brown, 1970.

———. *Human Sexual Response*. Boston: Little, Brown, 1966.

————. *The Pleasure Bond*. Boston: Little, Brown, 1975.

————. "The Sexual Response, Cycle I" and "The Sexual Response, Cycle II." *Sex Research: New Developments*, ed. John Money. New York: Holt, Rinehart, and Winston, 1965, pp. 53–112.

Masterton, Graham. *1001 Erotic Dreams Interpreted*. Chicago: H. Regnery, 1976.

May, Robert. *Sex and Fantasy: Patterns of Male and Female Development*. New York: Norton, 1980.

McConaghy, N. "Penile Volume Changes to Moving Pictures of Male and Female Nudes in Heterosexual and Homosexual Males." *Behaviour Research and Therapy*, 5 (1967): 43–48.

————. "Penile Volume Responses to Moving and Still Pictures of Male and Female Nudes." *Archives of Sexual Behavior*, 3 (November 1974): 565–570.

McCormack, Thelma. "The Censorship of Pornography: Catharsis or Learning?" *American Journal of Orthopsychology*, 5: 8 (October 1988): 492–504.

————. "Machismo in Media Research: A Critical Review of Research on Violence and Pornography." *Social Problems*, 25: 5 (1977–1978): 544–555.

————. "Making Sense of Research on Pornography." Appendix I of *Women against Censorship*, ed. Varda Burstyn. Vancouver: Douglas and McIntyre, 1985, pp. 181–205.

McCuen, Gary E. *Pornography and Sexual Violence*. Hudson, WI: Gary E. McCuen Publisher, 1985.

McKay, H. B., and D. J. Dolff. *The Impact of Pornography: An Analysis of Research and Summary of Findings*. Working Papers on Pornography and Prostitution: Report 13. Ottawa: Federal Department of Justice, 1985.

McKinstry, William. "The Pulp Voyeur: A Peek at Pornography in Public Places." *Deviance: Field Studies and Self Disclosures*, ed. Jerry Jacobs. Palo Alto, CA: National Press Books, 1974, pp. 30–40.

McNall, Scott G. "Pornography: The Structure of Domination and the Mode of Reproduction." *Current Perspectives in Social Theory*, 4 (1983): 181–203.

McNamara, Robert P. "Dramaturgy and the Social Organization of Peep Shows." *Sex, Scams, and Street Life: The Sociology of New York City's Times Square*. Westport, CT: Praeger, 1995, pp. 57–66.

Mead, Margaret. "Women and the 'New' Pornography." *Redbook*, February 1976, pp. 29–32.

Melillo, Wendy. "Visualizing Erotica." *Washington Post*, 21 July 1992, "Health" section, p. 13.

Merritt, C. Gary, Joel E. Gerstl, and Leonard A. LoSciuto. "Age and Perceived Effects of Erotica-Pornography: A National Sample Study." *Archives of Sexual Behavior*, 4 (November 1975): 605–621.

Meyer, Robert G. "Pornography and the Sexual Deviations." *Abnormal Behavior and the Criminal Justice System*. New York: Lexington Books, 1992, pp. 99–101.

Miller, Richard B. "Violent Pornography: Mimetic Nihilism and the Eclipse of Difference." *For Adult Users Only: The Dilemma of Violent Pornography*, ed. Susan Gubar and Joan Hoff. Bloomington: Indiana University Press, 1989, pp. 147–162.

Milonas, Rolf. *Fantasex: A Book of Erotic Games for the Adult Couple*. Rev. ed. New York: Putnam/Perigee, 1983.

Money, John. "Pornography in the Home: A Topic in Medical Education." *Contemporary*

Sexual Behavior: Critical Issues in the 1970s, ed. Joseph Zubin and John Money. Baltimore: Johns Hopkins University Press, 1973, pp. 409–440.

———. "The Positive and Constructive Approach to Pornography: In General Sex Education, in the Home, and in Sexological Counseling." *Technical Report of the Commission on Obscenity and Pornography*. 9 vols. Washington, DC: Government Printing Office, 1970–1971. V: *Societal Control Mechanisms*, pp. 339–353.

———. *Venuses, Penises: Sexology, Sexosophy, and Exigency Theory*. Amherst, NY: Prometheus Books, 1995.

Mosher, Donald L. "Sex Differences, Sex Experience, Sex Guilt and Explicitly Sexual Films." *Journal of Social Issues*, 29 (1973): 95–112.

Mosher, Donald L., and Paul R. Abramson. "Subjective Sexual Arousal to Films of Masturbation." *Journal of Consulting and Clinical Psychology*, 45: 5 (October 1977): 796–807.

Mosher, Donald L., and P. Maclan. "College Men and Women Respond to X-Rated Videos Intended for Male or Female Audiences: Gender and Sexual Scripts." *Journal of Sex Research*, 31 (1994): 99–113.

Murrin, Mary R., and D. R. Laws. "The Influence of Pornography on Sex Crimes." *Handbook of Sexual Assault: Issues, Theories, and Treatment of the Offender*, ed. W. L. Marshall, D. R. Laws, and H. E. Barbaree. New York: Plenum Press, 1990, pp. 73–91.

Nawy, Harold. "In the Pursuit of Happiness? Consumers of Erotica in San Francisco." *Journal of Social Issues*, 29 (1973): 147–161.

Nelson, Edward C. "Pornography and Sexual Aggression." *The Influence of Pornography on Behaviour*, ed. Maurice Yaffé and Edward C. Nelson. New York: Academic Press, 1982, pp. 171–248.

Nobile, Philip. "Intrigue at the Kinsey Institute." *Village Voice*, 19 January 1993, p. 29.

———. "Was Kinsey a Fake and a Pervert?" *Village Voice*, 11 December 1990, pp. 39–41.

Offit, Avodah K. *Night Thoughts: Reflections of a Sex Therapist*. New York: Congdon and Lattes, 1981.

Padgett, Vernon R., Jr., Jo Ann Brislin-Slütz, and James A. Neal. "Pornography, Erotica, and Attitudes toward Women: The Effects of Repeated Exposure." *Journal of Sex Research*, 26: 4 (November 1989): 479–491.

Paglia, Camille. "The Return of Carry Nation." *Playboy*, 39: 10 (October 1992): 36–38.

Pally, Marcia. "Standard Deviation: Research Literature on Sexually Explicit Material and Social Harms." *Sex and Sensibility: Reflections on Forbidden Mirrors and the Will to Censor*. Hopewell, NJ: Ecco Press, 1994, pp. 25–61.

———. "X-Rated Feminism: Ban Sexism, Not Pornography." *The Nation*, 29 June 1985, pp. 794–796.

Parker, Richard G., and John H. Gagnon, eds. *Conceiving Sexuality: Approaches to Sex Research in a Postmodern World*. New York: Routledge, 1995.

Pickard, Christine. "A Perspective on Female Response to Sexual Material." *The Influence of Pornography on Behaviour*, ed. Maurice Yaffé and Edward C. Nelson. New York: Academic Press, 1982, pp. 91–118.

Pomeroy, Wardell. *Dr. Kinsey and the Institute for Sex Research*. New York: Harper and Row, 1972.

Pornography and Sexual Violence: Evidence of the Links. London: Everywoman, 1988.

President's Commission on Obscenity and Pornography. *Technical Report*. 9 vols. Washington, DC: Government Printing Office, 1971–1972.

Reinisch, June. *The Kinsey Institute New Report on Sex*. New York: St. Martin's, 1990.

Reisman, Judith A. *"Soft Porn" Plays Hardball: Its Tragic Effects on Women, Children and the Family*. Lafayette, LA: Huntington House, 1991.

Reisman, Judith, and Edward W. Eichel. *Kinsey, Sex and Fraud: An Indoctrination of a People: An Investigation into the Human Sexuality Research of Alfred C. Kinsey et al*. Lafayette, LA: Lochinvar-Huntington House, 1990.

Ridgeway, James, and Sylvia Plachy. *Red Light*. New York: powerHouse, 1996.

Robinson, Paul A. *The Modernization of Sex: Havelock Ellis, Alfred Kinsey, William Masters, and Virginia Johnson*. New York: Harper and Row, 1976.

———. *The Sex Radicals*. London: Palladin, 1970.

Rollin, R. B. "Triple-X: Erotic Movies and Their Audiences." *Journal of Popular Film and Television*, 10: 1 (Spring 1982): 2–21.

Rosario, Vernon, II, ed. *Science and Homosexualities*. New York: Routledge, 1996.

Rosenthal, Robert, and Ralph L. Rosnow, eds. *Artifact in Behavioral Research*. New York: Academic, 1969.

———. *The Volunteer Subject*. New York: Wiley-Interscience, 1975.

Rowland, Willard D., Jr. *The Politics of TV Violence: Policy Uses of Communication Research*. Beverly Hills, CA: Sage, 1983.

Russ, Joanna. "Pornography and the Sexuality Debates: Examining the History." *Gay Community News*, 7 September 1986, p. 5.

Russell, Diana E. H. "Pornography and Rape: A Causal Model." *Political Psychology*, 9 (1988): 41–73; rpt. *Pornography: Women, Violence and Civil Liberties*, ed. Catherine Itzin. New York: Oxford University Press, 1992, pp. 310–349.

———. *Sexual Exploitation: Rape, Child Sexual Abuse, and Workplace Harassment*. Beverly Hills, CA: Sage, 1984.

———, ed. *Making Violence Sexy: Feminist Views on Pornography*. New York: Teachers College Press, 1993.

Sagarin, Edward. "On Obscenity and Pornography." *The New Sexual Revolution*, ed. Lester A. Kirkendall and Robert N. Whitehurst. New York: Donald W. Brown, 1971, pp. 105–113.

———. "Sex Research and Sociology: Retrospective and Prospective." *Studies in the Sociology of Sex*, ed. James M. Henslin. New York: Appleton-Century-Crofts, 1971, pp. 377–408.

Saunders, D. M., W. A. Fisher, E. C. Hewitt, and J. P. Clayton. "A Method for Empirically Assessing Volunteer Selection Effects: Recruitment Procedures and Responses to Erotica." *Journal of Personality and Social Psychology*, 49 (1985): 1703–1712.

Schiebinger, Londa L. *The Mind Has No Sex? Women in the Origins of Modern Science*. Cambridge: Harvard University Press, 1989.

Schill, Thomas, Mark Van Tuinen, and Don Doty. "Repeated Exposure to Pornography and Arousal Levels of Subjects Varying in Guilt." *Psychological Reports*, 46:2 (1980): 467–471.

Schmidt, Gunter. "Male–Female Differences in Sexual Arousal and Behavior during and after Exposure to Sexually Explicit Stimuli." *Archives of Sexual Behavior*, 4 (1975): 353–365.

Schmidt, Gunter, and Volkman Sigusch. "Sex Differences in Response to Psychosexual Stimulation by Films and Slides." *Journal of Sex Research*, 6 (November 1970): 268–283.

Schmidt, Gunter, Volkman Sigusch, and S. Schaefer. "Responses to Reading Erotic Stories: Male–Female Differences." *Archives of Sexual Behavior*, 2 (1973): 181–199.

Segal, Lynne. "Does Pornography Cause Violence?: The Search for Evidence." *Dirty Looks: Women, Pornography, Power*, ed. Pamela Church Gibson and Roma Gibson. London: British Film Institute, 1993, pp. 5–21.

———. "Introduction." *Sex Exposed: Sexuality and the Pornography Debate*. New Brunswick, NJ: Rutgers University Press, 1993, pp. 1–11.

"Sexuality, Violence and Pornography." Special issue. *Humanities in Society*, 7:1/2 (Winter–Spring 1984).

Shanor, Karen. *The Fantasy Files: A Study of the Sexual Fantasies of Contemporary Women*. New York: Dial Press, 1977.

Silbert, M. H., and A. M. Pines. "Pornography and Sexual Abuse of Women." *Sex Roles*, 10: 11/12 (June 1984): 857–868.

Simon, William. "The Social, the Erotic, and the Sensual: The Complexities of Sexual Scripts." *Nebraska Symposium on Motivation*, 21 (1973): 61–82.

Simon, William, and John H. Gagnon. "Sexual Scripts: Permanence and Change." *Archives of Sexual Behavior*, 15 (1986): 97–120.

Slade, Joseph W. "Pornographic Theatres off Times Square." *Transaction*, 9 (November/December 1971): 35–43, 79.

———. "Violence in the Hard-Core Pornographic Film: A Historical Survey." *Journal of Communication*, 34: 3 (Summer 1984): 148–163.

Slattery, William J. *The Erotic Imagination: Sexual Fantasies of the Adult Male*. Chicago: Henry Regnery, 1975.

Slotkin, Richard. *Regeneration through Violence*. Middletown, CT: Wesleyan University Press, 1973.

Smith, M. D., and C. Hand. "The Pornography/Aggression Linkage: Results from a Field Study." *Deviant Behavior*, 8: 4 (1987): 389–400.

Smith, Stephen G. "Pornography and Other Pathologies of Gender Valuation." *Gender Thinking*. Philadelphia: Temple University Press, 1992, pp. 175–182.

Snitow, Ann, Christine Stansell, and Sharon Thompson. "Current Controversies." *Powers of Desire: The Politics of Sexuality*, ed. Ann Snitow, Christine Stansell, and Sharon Thompson. New York: Monthly Review Press, 1983, pp. 417–418.

Sommers, E. K., and J. V. P. Check. "An Empirical Investigation of the Role of Pornography in the Verbal and Physical Abuse of Women." *Violence and Victims*, 2 (1987): 189–209.

Steele, Valerie. *Fetish: Fashion, Sex and Power*. New York: Oxford University Press, 1995.

Stein, Michael. *The Ethnography of an Adult Bookstore: Private Scenes, Public Places*. Lewiston, NY: Edwin Mellen Press, 1990.

Stoller, Robert J. *Observing the Erotic Imagination*. New Haven, CT: Yale University Press, 1985.

———. *Perversion: The Erotic Form of Hatred*. New York: Pantheon, 1975.

———. "Pornography and Perversion." *Archives of General Psychiatry*, 22 (1970): 490–499.

———. "Sexual Excitement." *Archives of General Psychiatry*, 33 (1976): 899–909.

―――. *Sexual Excitement: The Dynamics of Erotic Life*. New York: Pantheon, 1970.

Sue, David. "Erotic Fantasies of College Students during Coitus." *Journal of Sex Research*, 15:4 (November 1979): 299–305.

Sundholm, Charles A. "The Pornographic Arcade: Ethnographic Notes on Moral Men in Immoral Places." *Urban Life and Culture*, 2 (1973): 85–104; rpt. *Sexual Deviancy in Social Context*, ed. C. D. Bryant. New York: New Viewpoints, 1977, pp. 45–61.

Talese, Gay. *Thy Brother's Wife*. New York: Dell, 1981.

Terry, Jennifer. "Lesbians under the Medical Gaze: Scientists Search for Remarkable Differences." *Journal of Sex Research*, 27 (1990): 317–339.

Thomas, George C., III. "Rape and Pornography." *Maryland Law Review*, 52 (1993): 119–161.

Thorne, Edward. *Your Erotic Fantasies: In 25 Real-Life Interviews, the Hidden Sexual Yearnings That All of Us Have*. London: Spearman, 1971.

Tisdale, Sallie. *Talk Dirty to Me: An Intimate Philosophy of Sex*. New York: Doubleday, 1994.

Townsend, J. M. "Sex without Emotional Involvement: An Evolutionary Interpretation of Sex Differences." *Archives of Sexual Behavior*, 24 (1995): 173–206.

"Uneasy Bedfellows: Social Science and Pornography." A suite of articles: "British, Canadian, and U.S. Commissions," by Edna F. Einsiedel; "Pornography, Politics, and the Press: The U.S. Attorney General's Commission on Pornography," by David L. Paletz; and "Methods and Merits of Research," by Daniel Linz, Edward Donnerstein, Dolf Zillmann, and Jennings Bryant. *Journal of Communication*, 38: 2 (Spring 1998): 107–136.

Valverde, Mariana. "Lesbiantics: The True Joy of Sex." *Rites for Lesbian and Gay Liberation*, 1 (June 1984): 17.

―――. "Pornography: Not for Women Only." *Sex, Power and Pleasure*. Philadelphia: New Society, 1987; rpt. Toronto: Women's Press, 1985, pp. 121–146.

Vance, Carole S. "Epilogue." *Pleasure and Danger: Exploring Female Sexuality*, ed. Carole S. Vance. Boston: Routledge and Kegan Paul, 1984, pp. 431–439.

Vine, Ian. *Liberty, Morality and Sexual Censorship: The Politics of Pornography*. New York: Cassell, 1997.

Ware, Edward E., Marvin Brown, Donald M. Amoroso, Dennis W. Pilkey, and Manfred Pruesse. "The Semantic Meaning of Pornographic Stimuli." *Canadian Journal of Behavioural Science*, 4 (July 1972): 204–209.

Weatherford, Jack. *Porn Row*. New York: Arbor House, 1986.

Weaver, James. "Responding to Erotica: Perceptional Processes and Dispositional Implications." *Responding to the Screen: Reception and Reaction Processes*, ed. Jennings Bryant and Dolf Zillmann. Hillsdale, NJ: Lawrence Erlbaum Associates, 1991, pp. 329–354.

Webster, Paula. "The Forbidden: Eroticism and Taboo." *Pleasure and Danger: Exploring Female Sexuality*, ed. Carole S. Vance. Boston: Routledge and Kegan Paul, 1984, pp. 385–398.

Weeks, Jeffrey. *Sexuality and Its Discontents: Meanings, Myth and Modern Sexualities*. London: Routledge, 1985.

Wells, Carol G. *Right Brain Sex: Using Creative Visualization to Enhance Sexual Pleasure*. New York: Prentice-Hall, 1989.

West 42nd Street Study Team. *Sex Industries in New York City*. New York: City University of New York, 1980.

Westheimer, Ruth. *Dr. Ruth's Guide to Good Sex*. New York: Grammercy Publishing, 1987.

White, Leonard A. "Erotica and Aggression: The Influence of Sexual Arousal, Positive Affect, and Negative Affect on Aggressive Behavior." *Journal of Personality and Social Psychology*, 37 (April 1979): 591–601.

Williams, Linda. *Hard Core: Power, Pleasure, and the Frenzy of the Visible*. Berkeley: University of California Press, 1989.

Willis, Ellen. "Feminism, Moralism, and Pornography." *Powers of Desire: The Politics of Sexuality*, ed. Ann Snitow, Christine Stansell, and Sharon Thompson. New York: Monthly Review Press, 1983, pp. 460–467.

Wilson, Barbara J., Daniel Linz, and Barbara Randall. "Applying Social Science Research to Film Ratings: A Shift from Offensiveness to Harmful Effects." *Journal of Broadcasting and Electronic Media*, 34:4 (Fall 1990): 443–468.

Wilson, C., and D. Seaman. *The Serial Killer: A Study in the Psychology of Violence*. London: W. H. Allen, 1990.

Wilson, Glenn. *The Great Sex Divide: A Study of Male–Female Differences*. London: Peter Owen, 1989.

———. *The Secrets of Sexual Fantasy*. London: Dent, 1978.

Wilson, W. Cody, and Herbert I. Abelson. "Experience with and Attitudes toward Explicit Sexual Materials." *Journal of Social Issues*, 29:3 (1973): 19–39.

Wilson, W., and V. Liedtke. "Movie-Inspired Sexual Practices." *Psychological Reports*, 54:1 (February 1984): 328.

Winick, Charles. "Licit Sex Industries and Services." *The Apple Sliced: Sociological Studies of New York City*, ed. Vernon Boggs, Gerald Handel, and Sylvia F. Fava. New York: Praeger, 1984, pp. 151–162.

———. "Some Observations on Characteristics of Patrons of Adult Theaters and Bookstores." *Technical Report of the Commission on Obscenity and Pornography*. 9 vols. Washington, DC: Government Printing Office, 1971–1972, IV:225–244.

———. "A Study of Consumers of Explicitly Sexual Materials: Some Functions Served by Adult Movies." *Technical Report of the Commission on Obscenity and Pornography*. 9 vols. Washington, DC: Government Printing Office, 1971–1972, IV: 245–262.

Wolchik, Sharlene A., S. Lee Spencer, and Iris S. Lise. "Volunteer Bias in Erotica Research Employing Vaginal Measures of Sexual Arousal." *Archives of Sexual Behavior*, 12 (October 1983): 399–408.

Woolf, Charlotte. *Magnus Hirschfeld: A Portrait of a Pioneer in Sexology*. London: Quartet, 1986.

Yaffé, Maurice. "Therapeutic Uses of Sexually Explicit Material." *The Influence of Pornography on Behavior*, ed. Maurice Yaffé and Edward C. Nelson. London: Academic Press, 1982, pp. 119–150.

Zillmann, Dolf. "Effects of Prolonged Consumption of Pornography." *Pornography: Research Advances and Policy Considerations*, ed. Dolf Zillmann and Jennings Bryant. Hillsdale, NJ: Lawrence Erlbaum Associates, 1989, pp. 127–157.

Zillmann, Dolf, and Jennings Bryant. "Effects of Massive Exposure to Pornography." *Pornography and Sexual Aggression*, ed. N. Malamuth and E. Donnerstein. Orlando, FL: Academic Press, 1984, pp. 115–138.

———. "Effects of Prolonged Consumption of Pornography on Family Values." *Journal of Family Issues*, 9:4 (December 1988): 518–544.

———. "Pornography, Sexual Callousness, and the Trivialization of Rape." *Journal of Communication*, 32:4 (Fall 1982): 10–21.

———. "Pornography's Impact on Sexual Satisfaction." *Journal of Applied Social Psychology*, 18:5 (April 1988): 438–453.

———. "Shifting Preferences in Pornography Consumption." *Communication Research*, 13:4 (October 1986): 560–578.

Zillmann, Dolf, Jennings Bryant, and Aletha C. Huston. *Media, Children, and the Family: Social Scientific, Psychodynamic, and Clinical Perspectives.* Hillsdale, NJ: Lawrence Erlbaum Associates, 1994.

Zita, Jacqueline N. "Pornography and the Male Imaginary." *Enclitic*, 9 (1987): 28–44.

20

Pornography and Law

HISTORY AND THEORY OF CENSORSHIP

Histories of censorship exhibit formulas and tropes. Chroniclers of suppression have dealt overwhelmingly with "high pornography" such as books, rather than "low" varieties such as comic strips and photos: modern readers can thus shake their heads at the intolerance that once savaged now-respectable works. Histories of censorship differ less in terms of the outrages they list than in the care with which they contextualize the legal climate, parse the finer points of law, and delineate the personalities involved. The best treat the law as a continuum that mutates with advancing knowledge and new technologies and, above all, with shifting moralities and changing tastes.

But there is another history, mostly anonymous, almost invisible, whose vestiges are the courthouse records of the trial of the Boston street-lamp lighter sentenced to the stocks for selling bawdy chapbooks on the side, of peddlers arrested for selling copies of *Confessions of a Washington Belle* from a pushcart, of waiters fined for selling Tijuana bibles from the kitchen of a greasy spoon, of "foreigners" sent to the workhouse for selling two obscene photographs during the depression, of a stag filmmaker caught with six reels at a truck stop, of the heroin-addicted woman imprisoned for fellating her boyfriend in one of the films, while her partner got off with a reprimand. A rural arrest would make the front page of a local paper, but big-city reporters gave headlines only to the occasional large busts orchestrated by Comstock or a district attorney trying to become mayor, not the arrests of small-time colporteurs and distributors. These usually plea-bargained for short time or were sentenced by a magistrate without benefit of a jury's decision on the First Amendment status of their contraband.

Newspaper indexes rarely mention these spots on the police blotter, and the researcher can find them, if at all, only by cranking through reels of microfilm.

It is well to remember, of course, that one of pornography's most significant functions is to serve as an outlet for antisocial impulses. Pornographic genres not only violate sexual and cultural taboos but continually redefine and defile them. Reasonable Americans can take offense at depictions of sexuality that strike them as demeaning, degrading to women or children, socially hostile, spiritually bankrupt, or otherwise insulting to individual, group, or community— at least at a certain time in a certain place. Trying to call such depictions *obscene*, rather than pornographic, usually muddles, rather than clarifies, such distinctions. Better legal histories acknowledge the pornographer's need to speak the unspeakable; the best make clear that the unspeakable, once spoken, can reshape the law.

Even so, historians rarely seem to know that the best source of stag films or spicy photos was the local sheriff who could not bring himself to burn those he had seized and who saw no harm in sharing them at the Elks Lodge. Alfred Kinsey did know. At his request, several police departments around the country began sending seized materials to what became the Kinsey Institute, a practice that continued into the 1960s. The film cannisters and photographs still bear docket numbers, dates, and, less frequently, names, but the historic record is otherwise mute on these hidden, lower-class, criminal enterprises. Historians often ignore the ubiquity of a sexual raucousness that levels and democratizes, cannot register the longing embedded in artifacts, cannot comprehend the blessings of pornography-inspired masturbation that enables a housewife to get through a day. Histories of censorship are not about the ultrahuman need to shock, to subvert, to seem inhuman. They trace the development of law, its majesty, its rationale, its philosophy—as manifest in cases involving sexual expression whose prosecution seems, in retrospect, to have been mistaken. Such histories implicitly acknowledge the power of the "real thing," that is, low, vulgar, anonymous pornography, by keeping it at a distance. Distance is essential to "real" pornography's power. Once it leaves margins for the center of a society, authentic pornography becomes sanitized into something else, call it "high" pornography or erotica or popular culture. If this "other" low history is ever to be recovered, it will be found in America's folklore. It will not be found in recollections of dealers in buckram-bound volumes of high-class erotica, in decisions of the Supreme Court, or in trendy theories advanced by academics. Low pornography affronts. The affront may reveal unpleasant truths about ourselves, or it may simply be gratuitous and nasty.

In short, histories of censorship serve a different purpose: they are cultural documents, forms of discourse that dramatize and interpret the collision of groups and individuals. Pornography, Walter Kendrick notes, is not so much a thing as an *argument*.[1] It is one of the permanent contentions by which a society determines normative standards of conduct, permissible levels of eroticism, the roles of class, ethnicity, and gender, the contours of sexuality—and only secondarily the limits of expression. In America, moreover, prosecution of sexual expression has often functioned as a safety valve for a society in which otherwise free speech can lead to tension. Clearly political speech might be protected, but in a kind of inversion of catharsis theory, those frustrated by freedoms granted to others have always been permitted to attack the sexuality of people they feared and mistrusted. In their turn, restrictive statutes can lead to contempt for the law among groups and individuals who know from their own experience that most sexual representation is harmless and know that officials often prosecute the discourse of others for personal political gain. Although many histories emphasize these dynamics by way of explaining how laws evolve, few have improved upon Justice Potter Stewart's observation that censorship is the mark of a society that has lost confidence in itself.

The best broad introduction is *Censorship: 500 Years of Conflict*, a collection of essays edited by William Zeisel. As one might expect from a book that grew out of censorship exhibits at the New York Public Library, the essays occasionally branch into the difficulties encountered by archivists but otherwise make clear that the suppression of speech—political, religious, and sexual—has been common to virtually all cultures for the last half millennium. David Tribe reinforces that theme in his survey of suppression of political and sexual speech in various nations from the USSR to the United States in *Questions of Censorship*, though the volume is dated by the international upheavals of the last decade. The ironic title of *There's No Such Thing as Free Speech, and It's a Good Thing, Too* is not entirely borne out by Stanley Fish's review of attacks on all forms of speech, including pornography. While Fish maintains that Americans have always tried to censor each other, and while they continue to do so with great ingenuity, he points out that abridgments of speech cannot *logically* be justified on grounds of hate, dissent, or postulated harm. Censors and censored argue at cross-purposes: Fish observes that First Amendment absolutists assume that protection is content-neutral, while in practice courts have always tended to judge expression on the content itself.

As Martha Alshuler demonstrates in "Origins of the Law of Obscenity," censorship in earlier periods almost always aimed at preserving the status of political and religious institutions, a point echoed in Karin Dovring's "Troubles with Mass Communication and Semantic Differentials in 1744 and Today." The Hicklin principle, the chief obscenity argument used in the United States until the twentieth century, implicitly and explicitly characterized obscenity as a trespass against religion. The confusion still clouds debate. As Jeffrey Weeks points out in *Against Nature: Essays on History, Sexuality and Identity*, all religions regulate the degree of pleasure they permit their adherents, a principle that carries over into the legislation of sexuality and obscenity; the question is to what extent states should do the same for their citizens. In "Obscenity—Forget It," Charles Rembar, who long specialized in obscenity cases, favors abandoning obscenity as a legal concept as hopelessly vague. He proposes instead that courts concentrate on the protection of minors, on shielding citizens from unwelcome exposure to sex materials, and on clearly dangerous sexual behavior. Richard R. Reynolds says in "Our Misplaced Reliance on Early Obscenity Cases" that British obscenity laws of the previous century, especially *Hicklin*, were deigned to suppress political dissent, not sexual expression, and thinks that the precedents we rely on today are faulty. The American reprint of a 1945 British text, G. R. Scott's *"Into Whose Hands": An Examination of Obscene Libel in Its Legal, Sociological, and Literary Aspects* is an excellent dissertation on the persistence of the Hicklin decision.

Students in search of lucidity will prize three authorities. The first is Daniel S. Moretti, whose *Obscenity and Pornography: The Law under the First Amendment* best maps the intersections of law and culture. Moretti cuts through thickets of legal jargon: "It must be remembered that although obscenity is very similar to pornography, in the eyes of the law, these terms are not synonymous. Material which is pornographic is generally protected by the First Amendment. In most instances, only if material is first judged obscene may it be prohibited" (xii). Moretti outlines the major judicial decisions in terms of the justices' intent, critiques the rulings, points out the special features of cases, and emphasizes the role of precedents. For example, according to Moretti, in *United States v. Kennerly* (209 F. 119, [1913]), Judge Learned Hand wrote that the *Hicklin* test was too narrow and restrictive, first, in that it judged literature by the standards of those most vulnerable. The consequence would be that libraries would be reduced to collections of children's books. Second, Hand knew that the *Hicklin* test isolated passages, thus distorting the author's intent and destroying the effect of the whole work. But, says Moretti, Hand felt, nevertheless, that he had to apply the test because of precedent. Moretti also carefully distinguishes among laws applied to different media.

The second authority is Edward de Grazia, whose *Censorship Landmarks* was itself a landmark text, one of the first thorough examinations of important state and federal cases; it is still mandatory. De Grazia writes out of genuine feeling for the law as a humane instrument, fascinated by its evolution. De Grazia's more recent *Girls Lean Back Everywhere: The Law of Obscenity and the Assault on Genius* argues that the danger of censorship is that it stifles the gifted, the novel, and the radical. De Grazia details the strategies of defense attorneys like Morris Ernst, whose savvy had to equal that of Comstock and Sumner in efforts to fix the outcome of cases. Ernst engineered a series of postponements, for example, until he got Judge Woolsey to preside over the *Ulysses* trial. One of the subtexts is that muddles, evasions, self-deceptions, and bad faith are common to both sides in obscenity disputes. *Girls Lean Back* (the title is borrowed from Jane Heap's defense of her publishing parts of *Ulysses* in *The Little Review*) covers censorship of literature and art in cases ranging from Lawrence and Joyce to Karen Finley and 2 Live Crew today.

Almost as important a resource is Arthur S. Leonard's *Sexuality and the Law: An Encyclopedia of Major Legal Cases*, a comprehensive and extremely well written guide. Leonard arranges his comment in categories: reproduction, sexual conduct, family, speech, discrimination, military and national security issues, educational institutions, immigration and naturalization, and estates and trusts. The book's virtue is that it frames issues of speech in terms of sexual behavior stratified by gender, race, class, age, and custom; selected cases illustrate controversies and resolutions. Like Moretti and de Grazia, Leonard avoids legalese in favor of plain speech. The value of *Obscenity: The Complete Oral Arguments before the Supreme Court in the Major Obscenity Cases*, edited by Leon Friedman, is apparent from the title. For laypeople, it is a valuable sourcebook of the most significant cases. Especially relevant are *Roth v. U.S.*; *Alberts v. California*; *Kingsley International Pictures Corporation v. Regents*; *Manual Enterprises v. Day*; *Jacobellis v. Ohio*; *Freedman v. Maryland*; *Ginzburg v. U.S.*; *Mishkin v. New York*; *Memoirs v. Massachusetts*; *Ginsburg v. New York*; and *Stanley v. Georgia*. Friedman's Introduction and commentary are unobtrusive but first-rate. Many books offer excerpts from major legal decisions regarding sexual expression; a typical example is Margaret C. Jasper's *The Law of Obscenity and Pornography*. James Jackson Kilpatrick's *The Smut Peddlers: The Pornography Racket and the Law Dealing with Obscenity Censorship*, a rather philistine account of American traffic in pornography during the late 1950s and mid 1960s, based chiefly on the work of the Kefauver Commission, contains a valuable appendix of court cases.

In *Censorship: The Knot That Binds Power and Knowledge*, Sue Curry Jansen views censorship as both political surveillance and economic force: these are ways of stabilizing nations and ensuring proprietary interests in information and thus acquiring and securing the clout that knowledge brings. While it is possible to construe sexual censorship as one of the costs of democracy, restrictions in an information economy are the costs of doing business. Jansen contrasts commodity censorship with strategies of totalitarian repression, especially as it affects information flow; her book offers a fresh and provocative perspective on the issue. Those themes are taken up by the essayists in Theodore R. Kupferman's *Censorship, Secrecy, Access, and Obscenity*, which construes censorship in terms of restricting access to information that empowers, and, similarly, by some of the essayists in Ithiel de Sola Pool's *On Free Speech in the Electronic Age: Technologies of Freedom*, who view communication technologies themselves as demotic. Behind these arguments is the variously articulated recognition that economic forces shape our concepts of expression. In the process of commodifying expression, an information economy establishes a price structure for every kind of discourse by cheapening some forms and making others more expensive. The discussions of censorship in Jane M. Gaines' *Contested Culture: The Image, the Voice, and the Law* are also illuminating because of her analysis of intellectual property law. Two decades ago, in fact, conservatives tried to deny copyright to pornographic works as a way of driving them out of the market. In "Authority of the Register of Copyrights to Deny Registration of a Claim to Copyright on the Ground of Obscenity," Dan W. Schneder argued that the copyright office should not be vested with that authority, since obscenity is a matter only courts can decide. Steve Redhead offers a fresh look at collisions between law as an instrument of, and frequently a foe of, popular enthusiasms in *Unpopular Cultures: The Birth of Law and Popular Culture*, which covers issues as diverse as copyright law, computer games, pornography, youth culture, mass media, sports, and a host of artistic endeavors such as rap music.

Robert A. Liston discusses censorship as a form of warfare between classes in *The Right to Know: Censorship in America* but structures the conflict in terms of beliefs about what constitutes morally appropriate knowledge, which he construes as stretched between reprehensible obscenity and morally neutral information. One of the effects of imposing censorship is to vest police, Customs inspectors, postal workers, and lower-echelon bureaucrats of lower-class origins and limited education with the power to interdict works of high art and expression, says Gershon Legman in "Sex Censorship in the U.S.A." Legman's tract, full of outrage by the greatest American authority on pornography, details the measures used to suppress expression, especially by the Catholic Church and the Post Office.

Essays by Charles Keating, Judith Crist, Hollis Alpert, Eugene McCarthy, Max Lerner, and others were put together by Harold Hart as *Censorship for and Against*. *Censorship and Obscenity*, edited by Rajeev Dhavan and Christian Davies, is another useful, if conventional, anthology of articles pro and con, including pieces by Hans Eysenck, John Trevelyan, and Berl Kutschinsky. The essays in *Pornography and Censorship*, edited by David Copp and Susan Wendell, are less concerned with legalities than with philosophical and social science considerations. The essays in *Obscenity and Freedom of Expression*, edited by Haig A. Bosmajian, cover a large group of court cases and opinions, with specific reference to landmark decisions regarding various media of expression until 1973; it has an excellent bibliography. The passions evoked by censorship are the subjects of a chapter on pornography in *Taking Sides: Clashing Views on Controversial Issues in Human Life*, by George McKenna and Stanley Feingold. The second edition, edited by Alison Alexander and Janice Hanson, adds a piece by James Dobson, who lists nine ways in which he thinks society is harmed by pornography and calls for massive repression. *Censorship: Opposing Viewpoints* aims its essays at young adults. Edited by Terry O'Neill, the volume covers issues of political bias, religious prejudice, and ideological intolerance as they manifest themselves in cases of libel, textbook censorship, and questions of national security as well as pornography.

A decade of warfare over sexual and political expression, as evident from attacks by both liberals and conservatives, is the subject of Nat Hentoff's *Free Speech for Me but Not for Thee: How the American Left and Right Relentlessly Censor Each Other*, a volume remarkable for its reminders that "liberals" are just as intolerant as their colleagues across the aisle. Among other things, Hentoff rejects the argument that the First Amendment injures women and points out that accepting the claim that free speech violates the civil rights of women would make possible the suppression of many kinds of expression as different groups assert the same kind of damage. He provides recent examples of absurd censorship in the name of liberal and conservative principles and generally demonstrates how easy it is for ideologies to warp common sense.

Jurists have developed any number of absolutist or near-absolutist positions regarding the First Amendment. Typical is M. J. Perry's "Freedom of Expression: An Essay on Theory and Doctrine." Perry says that both the "democratic" conception (political) and the "epistemic" conception (self-realization) of free speech provide the basis for protection of literary, artistic, scientific, and political expression, despite subversive or antisocial aspects, because the public has a "right to know." Excepting "obscenity" from protection is impossible. Walter Gellhorn's *Individual Freedom and Governmental Restraints* is an elegant First Amendment study that holds up well. So does *Free Speech in the United States*, perhaps the best of several books by Zechariah Chaffee to discuss censorship from historical and philosophical perspectives. William W. Van Alstyne's *Interpretations of the First Amendment* is valuable because of its reference to many different media, as is Olga G. Hoyt and Edwin P. Hoyt's *Censorship in America*, which covers cases involving literature, radio, movies, television, and theater up until the 1960s. Ithiel de Sola Pool's *On Free Speech in the Electronic Age: Technologies of Freedom* contains superb essays on official and cultural efforts to control modern channels of communication and the difficulties of doing so as new technologies challenge concepts such as obscenity and First Amendment principles. Rodney A. Smolla's position in *Free Speech in an Open Society* is that freedom of speech, even when it takes the form of pornography and obscenity, defines the human spirit itself, not just the politics of a given state. Legal philosophers and scholars are drawn to reflection on the First Amendment because curtailment of any kind of speech presents one of the most dangerous challenges to the moral and political validity of a democracy.

Commitment to the First Amendment does not require absolutism, of course; most of the older texts listed here discuss possible exceptions, situations in which absolutes may not apply, or other distinctions that make the law an evolutionary process, and they are still to be found in libraries. The conservative Harry M. Clor supported narrowly defined censorship and advanced legal arguments for it in *Obscenity and Public Morality: Censorship in a Liberal Society. Censorship and Freedom of Expression: Essays on Obscenity and the Law*, edited by Clor, presented essays for and against, with Clor and Richard Kuhn arguing for censorship and Charles Rembar, Richard Hettlinger, and Willard Gaylin against. In *The Death of Discourse*, using a juxtaposition of fragments of opinions from various authorities (the graphic design was "produced" by Bruce Mau), Ronald Collins and David M. Skover advance various challenges to the First Amendment. The format and style of the book make it more cute than illuminating, but the authors do point to important considerations: the First Amendment today chiefly serves commercial interests and often monopoly itself, especially in media enterprises; new technologies undermine old principles of law, especially those that, on one hand, guarantee freedom of political expression and, on the other, condemn obscenity; and new political realities collapse distinctions between high forms of discourse (art) and low (pornography) and thereby erase meaningful standards of taste and intelligence. Collins and Skover conclude that the Madisonian principles behind the First Amendment are no longer viable, though their vision of the future seems relentlessly postmodern, that is, fuzzy.

CENSORSHIP OF BOOKS AND MAGAZINES

Most histories of censorship deal with literature. Those included here concentrate primarily on print media in the United States or, where relevant—since early American courts based their decisions on English common-law precedent, specifically the *Hicklin* test—on Great Britain. Thus, while Alec Craig's *Above All Liberties* surveys book censorship in Great Britain, the scholar will find numerous American parallels. Norman St. John-Stevas' *Obscenity and the Law* is helpful for the same reason; it is an excellent source for information on English publishers, some of whom supplied Americans during "the great period for pornography" during the Victorian era. Roger Thompson's *Unfit for Modest Ears* and Donald Thomas' *A Long Time Burning: The History of Literary Censorship in England* are also standard works on English prosecutions. Thomas elaborates the details of court cases; Thompson is particularly good on the origins of English libel law in the seventeenth century. Similarly, Alec Craig's *Suppressed Books: A History of the Conception of Literary Obscenity*, though again concerned with events across the Atlantic, draws careful comparisons with jurisprudence in the United States; the books discussed were available in the United States.

Due for yet another revision is Anne Lyon Haight's justly famous *Banned Books: Informal Notes on Some Books Banned for Various Reasons at Various Times and in Various Places*; the fourth edition was revised and enlarged by Chandler B. Grannis. Its broad, international reach distinguishes between political, religious, and sexual censorship, a necessity since courts did not often separate explicit sexuality from sacrilege; Haight chronicles assaults on libraries as well. *Banned Books*, a four-volume set recently published, goes beyond Haight in addressing the whole of Western culture and uses similar categories. In volume I, *Literature Suppressed on Political Grounds*, Nicholas J. Karolides covers works as diverse as *Das Kapital* and works denying the Holocaust; in volume II, *Literature Repressed on Religious Grounds*, Margaret Bald ranges over Martin Luther, Salman Rushdie, and the New Testament; in volume III, *Literature Suppressed on Social Grounds*, Dawn B. Sova tackles books on race, homosexuality, drugs, abortion, and almost anything else found objectionable by school boards; and in volume IV, *Literature Suppressed on Sexual Grounds*, Sova deals impressively with materials deemed pornographic or obscene. All entries on books contain summaries in addition to chronologies of attacks on them. Banned Books Online is an electronic exhibit/gallery of mostly contemporary books that censors have tried to suppress, regularly updated.

"To Deprave and Corrupt . . ."; Original Studies in the Nature and Definition of "Obscenity," edited by John Chandos, anthologizes essays by Walter Allen, Lord Birkett, Ernest van den Haag, Chandos himself, Maurice Girodias, William B. Lockhart, Robert C. McClure, Clair and William Russell, and Norman St. John Stevas. Still of interest is a book prompted by the Kefauver hearings, *The Impact of Literature: A Psychological Discussion of Some Assumptions in the Censorship Debate* by the research psychologist Marie Jahoda. Jahoda's volume is a reminder of the power Americans once attributed to printed pornography, an assumption now evident in the influence attributed to imagery in more modern media. Jahoda pointed out that no evidence demonstrated causality between obscene literature and antisocial behavior, an observation that she knew was beside the point in a debate where facts are irrelevant.

The classic text on American literature anathematized as pornography is *Pornography and the Law*, by Eberhard Kronhausen and Phyllis Kronhausen. The Kronhausens bring common sense to a study ranging over American editions of *Fanny Hill*, to Edmund Wilson's *Memoirs of Hecate County*; they classify such books as examples of "erotic realism" in order to distinguish them from other proscribed works. Almost as valuable is Felice Flanery Lewis' *Literature, Obscenity, and the Law*, published in the 1970s but helpful because the decade distilled the major arguments over literary erotica. Lewis' comment on major cases of suppression, especially those of works by Lawrence and Miller, reveals scholarship of a subtlety still unsurpassed; she is excellent on legal, aesthetic, and social ramifications and also on the degree to which American consciousness has been shaped by public reaction to bold literary texts. Eleanor Widmer's college casebook, *Freedom and Culture: Literary Censorship in the 70s*, contains three dozen articles on notable American cases, with excerpts ranging back to Plato. Michael Moscato and Leslie Le Blanc have collected essays on perhaps the most important landmark case in *The United States of America v. One Book Entitled Ulysses by James Joyce*. The attorney who won the *Ulysses* decision was Morris Ernst; his *The Best Is Yet* charts the changing cultural climate that permitted publication of questionable books. *Censorship: The Search for the Obscene*, by Ernst and Alan U. Schwartz, isolates issues in the trials of *Ulysses* and *Lady Chatterley's Lover*, as does *The End of Obscenity: The Trials of Lady Chatterley, Tropic of Cancer and Fanny Hill*, by Charles Rembar. Jay Gertzman has mined Ernst's archives for information on the trials of publishers Esar Levine and Ben Rebkuhn in *Bookleggers and Smuthounds: The Trade in Erotica, 1920–1940*. Gertzman's "Erotic Novel, Liberal Lawyer, and 'Censor-Moron': 'Sex for Its Own Sake' and Some Literary Censorship Adjudications of the 1930s" explores the motivations and tactics of attorneys like Ernst in opposing Comstockery in the 1930s; here Gertzman focuses on Esar Levine of Panurge Press.

Gertzman's *A Descriptive Bibliography of Lady Chatterley's Lover: With Essays toward a Publishing History of the Novel* includes important information on the novel's prosecutions in America, on the role of censorship organizations like the National Organization for Decent Literature (NODL), and on the novel's influence on obscenity law. Gertzman's superlative bibliographic essays cover the publication history of various editions, piracies, parodies, and so on, with fine discussion of publishers and prosecutors. Lawrence's responses to suppression of *Lady Chatterley* in both Britain and the United States have been reprinted in various editions, the most useful of which is his *Sex, Literature, and Censorship. The End of Obscenity: The Trials of Lady Chatterley, Tropic of Cancer and Fanny Hill by the Lawyer Who Defended Them* is Charles Rembar's narrative of the judicial process in three celebrated litigations (partial transcripts included). The volume documents what would become apparent: that literature—as distinct from other media—would henceforth rarely be prosecuted as obscene in the United States. Courts would refuse to convict because literary works belonged to the category of "high" pornography, whereas newer technologies appeared to foster "low" forms; the law thus enshrines distinctions predicated on class, education, and alleged intelligence. E. R. Hutchison's *Tropic of Cancer on Trial: A Case History of Censorship* is a useful chronicle of the multiple American prosecutions of Miller's novel, the "most censored book in American history." The indispensable reference guide to major American literary trials, however, is Edward de Grazia's *Girls Lean Back Everywhere: The Law of Obscenity and the Assault on Genius*. The book interviews many of the principals in the cases: defense attorneys, witnesses, judges, and so on; de Grazia begins with the case of Ida Craddock, imprisoned in 1902 for sending a sex guide, *The Wedding Night*, through the mails, moves on through Margaret Anderson's defenses of Joyce's *Ulysses*, and ranges across attacks on authors on up to Anne Rice in the present. A valuable, up-to-date survey of the status of literary obscenity in the United States is the comprehensive *On Pornography: Literature, Sexuality and Obscenity Law* by Ian Hunter, David Saunders, and Dugald Williamson. The March 1996 issue of *Index on Censorship* focuses on publishing censorship of many kinds.

Representing Women: Law, Literature, and Feminism, edited by Susan Sage Heinzelman and Zipporah Batshaw Wiseman, is an offbeat group of essays on the ways in which law and literature have responded to feminism, the changing images of women as legal entities, and related matters. Like their male counterparts, female attorneys adopt diametrically opposed views of erotica. Anne B. Goldstein's "Representing the Lesbian in Literature and Law" maintains that she has found lesbian novels such as *The Well of Loneliness, The Color Purple*, and others regarded as pornographic useful in representing lesbian clients before the law because of the insights into character and choices that fiction offers. Presumably to soothe fears that antiporn feminists would ban expression across a wide spectrum, Carol Sawyer in "Less than Pornography: The Power of Popular Fiction" comments on the ambiguity of representations in Miller's *The*

Good Mother and Turow's *Presumed Innocent*, both best-sellers about trials that chart women's roles as simplistically good and bad before the law. While these two works are disgusting, says the charitable Sawyer, she would not recommend banning them despite the "subliminal sexism" (76) that she thinks pervades them.

There is no comprehensive history of censorship of magazines whose primary content is sexual. Over the years *Playboy* has been the target of zealots and politicians; keyword searches of databases will produce many hits. Gains Hawkins' "Common Sense and Censorship" attacks the hyperbole of Morality in Media in its efforts to force businesses to remove men's magazines. Worth noting is Robert H. Yoakum's "An Obscene, Lewd, Lascivious, Indecent, Filthy, and Vile Tabloid Entitled *Screw*." Yoakum dramatizes the comedy played out in the 1977 obscenity trial of *Screw* magazine in Wichita, Kansas (which ended in a mistrial); the title refers to the indictment. Yoakum subordinates bemused comment on the grandstanding ambitions of prosecutors to discussions of the political functions of porn. Although Yoakum stops short of saying that the tabloid should be cherished, he does insist that *Screw* "spends most of its time giving people the finger" (49), a fact that ensures First Amendment protection precisely because the tabloid is at least as political as it is sexual. Alan Dershowitz's "Screwing Around with the First Amendment" remarks on the sleaziness of the Justice Department's prosecuting and convicting Al Goldstein, publisher of *Screw*, in Wichita, Kansas, a notoriously conservative city, even though the tabloid rarely circulates outside New York City. Yoakum discovers similar patterns in "The Great *Hustler* Debate," a report on the prosecution of that magazine.

Chapter 5 of *Comics: Anatomy of a Mass Medium*, by Reinhold Reitberger and Wolfgang Fuchs, follows the censorship debates over comic books in the 1950s to the evolution of the Comics Code of Ethics to counter governmental intervention. Fearing that passions raised by the Kefauver hearings were out of control, the American Civil Liberties Union enlisted various authorities to urge common sense in its *Censorship of Comic Books: A Statement in Opposition on Civil Liberties Grounds* (1955). *Censorship in the Comics* videotapes comment by Paul Stockton of the Comic Legends Legal Defense Fund, cartoonist John Callahan, film director David Cronenberg, and several editors and writers of comic books and fantasy fiction. A "Short History of Comics Censorship" is available on the Internet. For up-to-date information on the legal problems faced by cartoonists, the Comic Book Legal Defense Fund maintains a Web site. A recent case involves Mike Diana's *Boiled Angel*. At the site one can learn that Mike Diana's publisher, Michael Hunt Publications, plans an anthology of comic artists outraged by Diana's conviction to be entitled *Fuck Florida*. "Comics under Fire," on prosecutions in Oklahoma, Oregon, and California, points out that prosecutors do not have to prove obscenity, merely extend litigation until retailers run out of money.

At present, in theory if not always in fact, pornography—defined as sexual expression—*is* shielded by the First Amendment; obscenity is not. Even so, as Daniel Eisenberg warns in "Toward a Bibliography of Erotic Pulps": "It should be remembered that the disappearance of censorship of erotic fiction in the United States was primarily due to the impossibility of defining what should be prohibited, rather than any finding that pornography is entitled to First Amendment protection" (183). Finally, impressions that the government has relaxed efforts to censor writers and publishers are dispelled by Donna A. Demac, of PEN, the national writers' organization, who says that the government's systematic attempts to restrict expression during the Reagan years in *Liberty Denied: The Current Rise of Censorship in America* resurfaced, albeit in different form, in the 1990s.

CENSORSHIP OF ART

Jane Clapp's unique *Art Censorship* is a chronology of centuries of suppression in Western culture, with entries on hundreds of images that have offended someone. Its more than 600 citations include about 200 American entries, and scholars looking for individual cases before the 1970s will usually find them here. Almost as valuable is Moshe Carmilly-Weinberger's *Fear of Art: Censorship and Freedom of Expression in Art*. In an excellent section on "American Morality" (183–186), Carmilly-Weinberger traces modern censorship to the 1930 tariff act and cites many interdictions, court cases, and individual artists and their works. His analysis of the class and economic assumptions behind attempts to censor is astute. Still valuable are the essays in *Suppressed: Seven Key Essays Publishers Dared Not Print*, by Albert Ellis, who inveighs against censorship of various forms of art.

Occasionally heavy-handed essays in *Culture Wars: Documents from the Recent Controversies in the Arts*, edited by Richard Bolton, raise serious questions about the limits of permissible representations of sexuality in the arts and detail attempts to censor those that encroach upon boundaries. Typical of the dozens of articles generated by the controversies over Mapplethorpe, Serrano, Finley, and others recently pilloried by conservatives is Hilton Kramer's "Is Art above the Laws of Decency?" Kramer's answer is inconclusive. The Brooklyn Museum's *The Brooklyn Museum Collection: The Play of the Unmentionable* is based on a show curated by the conceptual artist Joseph Kosuth in 1990. The museum assembled a vast number of works—paintings, drawings, photographs, sculpture, and artifacts—whose sexual content has offended the prudish or the political; the ensemble was moving, its selections brilliant, and the whole stunning in its magnitude. Roberta Smith praises the sweep and the rationale of the show in " 'Unmentionable Art' through the Ages." While she notes that the demise of more conservative schools of thought has defused many of the works, she is still struck by the power of others to shock and to challenge and by the continuing obsessions of censors; the notes in the show's catalog are extremely helpful. As his title promises, Steven C. Dubin also deals with the controversy engendered by exhibits (e.g., of Mapplethorpe photos) in *Arresting Images: Impolitic Art and Uncivil Actions* but turns primarily on confrontations between conservatives and the avant-garde. Douglas Davis' "Art and Contradiction: Helms, Censorship, and the Serpent" traces Jesse Helms' attacks on art to traditional American mistrust of intellectuals and artists, while Tom Mathews' "Fine Art or Foul?" offers an overview of the furor over the limits of permissible art. Wendy Steiner's impressive *The Scandal of Pleasure*, which argues that pleasure justifies art, finds many recent cases of those who think it does not.

Articles on embattled artists who ran afoul of pressure groups in the 1990s run into the hundreds. Bruce Selcraig's "Reverend Wildmon's War on the Arts" chronicles the efforts of the Tupelo, Mississippi, minister and his action group, the American Family Association, to censor materials ranging from Mapplethorpe photographs to the film *The Last Temptation of Christ* and the television show *Cheers*. "Arts Endowment's Opponents Are Fighting Fire with Fire," Richard Bernstein's report on Donald Wildmon's American Family Association and Louis Sheldon's Coalition for Traditional Values, outlines efforts by these groups to combat pornography, abortion, homosexuality, and blasphemy, elements they believe the National Endowment for the Arts promotes. William H. Honan notes that the letter-writing campaigns of these groups have left supporters of the NEA in disarray in "Arts Endowment Backers Are Split on Strategy." Elizabeth Hess' "Artist Doesn't Turn the Other Cheek: Wojnarowicz to Sue Reverend Wildmon" refers to David Wojnarowicz's suit against Donald Wildmon for removing images from the artists's "Tongues of Flame" exhibition catalog and reprinting them out of context in a newsletter sent to congresspeople. The minister printed the images under the heading "Your Tax Dollars Helped Pay for These 'Works of Art' " and thereby, said the artist, turned his serious artistic presentation into "pornography." In "Judge Halts Publication of Pamphlet," Richard Bernstein reports that courts did grant an injunction against Wildmon's American Family Association on grounds that the group violated Wojnarowicz's copyright. *Damned in the USA*, a documentary by Paul Yule and Jonathan Stack, depicted the rancor of debate; the Reverend Donald Wildmon, one of the subjects, tried with no sense of irony to have it banned in the United States.

When organizers of a feminist conference at the University of Michigan Law School seized an exhibit of videotapes and photos by five artists, including two former prostitutes, Tamar Lewin called it censorship in "Furor on Exhibit at Law School Splits Feminists." Ted C. Fishman's "Dangerous Art" is another account of the show, originally intended to complement a symposium on prostitution at the Michigan conference, as savaged by the antiporn feminists on campus. Carol Jacobsen's "Fighting for Visibility: Notes on the Censorship Battle of 'Porn'im'age'ry: Picturing Prostitutes" covers the same events. The May 1996 issue of *Index on Censorship* deals with American censorship of the arts in the 1990s. See web sites in **Courtrooms and Jurists**, later, for other examples.

CENSORSHIP OF PHOTOGRAPHS

It would be difficult to list all the arrests for obscene photos in the United States over the years. Most were scarcely noticed by the press, though scholars cranking through rolls of newspaper microfilms will find that large hauls of prints sometimes made the back pages in large metropolitan dailies. While there is no systematic catalog of banned photos, the Photo Archive at the Kinsey Institute contains thousands of images seized by local and state police, many with docket numbers stamped on the reverse. Gene Slabaugh tried to correlate some of the photographs with stag films in the institute's film collection in his Card Catalog and Stag Film Analyses and listed arrests and prosecutions. Chapter 10 of Abigail Solomon-Godeau's *Photography at the Dock: Essays on Photographic History, Institutions, and Practices* discusses legal distinctions between obscenity and photographic realism. Several essays in Richard Bolton's *The Contest of Meaning: Critical Histories of Photography* also examine particular cases, as do some in Carol Squires' *The Critical Image: Essays on Contemporary Photography*.

Jane Clapp's *Art Censorship: A Chronology of Proscribed and Prescribed Art* covers photographs less often than paintings but is still helpful. Paul Boyer's *Purity in Print: The Vice-Society Movement and Book Censorship in America* includes digressions on suppressed photographs, as does Robert Haney's *Comstockery in America: Patterns of Censorship and Control*. Jay Gertzman's " 'Esoterica' and 'The Good of the Race': Mail-Order Distribution of Erotica in the 1930s," although more concerned with book publishers, comments on mail-order traffic in photos in the 1930s, also in relation to vice crusaders. The U.S. Postmaster General's *Annual Reports* contain some information on photos destroyed or prosecuted, as does Dorothy Ganfield Fowler's *Unmailable: Congress and the Post Office*, which is based on those records. One chapter of George N. Gordon's *Erotic Communications: Studies in Sex, Sin and Censorship* deals with pornographic pictures as a spur to official censorship. The Feminist Anti-Censorship Task Force (FACT) reproduces many images censored in the United States in *Caught Looking: Feminism, Pornography, and Censorship*, although the book does not contain much comment on legal issues. By contrast, Jane M. Gaines reviews the law as it applies to images in a work focused on disputation, *Contested Culture: The Image, the Voice, and the Law*; its arguments are meticulous and lucid.

Kenneth R. Stevens reviews a famous case in "*United States v. 31 Photographs*: Dr. Alfred Kinsey and Obscenity Law." Stevens points out that the 1957 decision freeing photographs imported by the Kinsey Institute from Customs inspectors who had seized them was based on an interesting concept called "variable obscenity." The concept did not establish precedent, however, because of the subjective nature of the reasoning: that obscenity can be determined by the nature and qualifications of the audience. *Sex and Censorship in the Visual Arts*, by the indefatigable Donald H. Gilmore, an academic who turned out illustrated books over a period of several years, covers comics, painting, sculpture, and photos, the latter Scandinavian and American. Gilmore also published the two-volume *Sex, Censorship, and Pornography*, a lightweight history that depicts the very things that upset the censors, photographs being high on the list. Similar is William E. Sprague's *Sex, Pornography and the Law*. Despite the publisher's designing the text to show off explicit photos and paintings, the two volumes are better written than they first appear. In the same category is Alfred Ellison's *Oral Sex and the Law*, a listing of state laws forbidding oral sex, used as an excuse to print explicit photos of fellatio and cunnilingus.

Peter Carlyle-Gordge's "An Erotic Error That Titillates" is an amusing account of a Joe Borowski photograph, part of an Ottawa exhibit mounted by the Canada Council Art Bank, that was seized by police as obscene. A court dropped the charge because the complaint read "fellatio" rather than "cunnilingus"; the magistrate ruled that if police could not tell the difference, they were hardly capable of distinguishing between art and pornography. Robert Atkins writes of the problems encountered by art journals and museums when nervous printers refuse to print controversial illustrations for their pages or catalogs in "Some Print, Others Won't." Those circumstances inspired *The Body in Question*, a special issue of *Aperture* magazine. Its valuable, illustrated discussion focuses on photographs by Robert Mapplethorpe, Jock Sturges, Sally Mann, Donna Ferato, Lutz Bacher, and Sylvia Plachy, with commentary by Karen Finley, Allen Ginsberg, Carole S. Vance, and others. The anxiety over images, especially those in which children are depicted, says Amy Adler in "Photography on Trial," has reached such a pitch that legitimate photographers such as Sally Mann and Larry Clark are constantly menaced by zealots and politically ambitious prosecutors. Anne Higonnet's "Conclusions Based on Observation," an important essay on the 1995 *Knox* decision, stresses the threat to First Amendment protection of *all* images growing out of the interpretation of child pornography statutes (see also Chapter 8, **Child Pornography**).

CENSORSHIP OF FILM AND VIDEO

Speaking strictly, movie censorship for the first six decades of this century applied to mainstream cinema rather than the clandestine, hard-core stag films, which were forbidden outright and prosecuted under different statutes, a distinction implicit in most histories of film censorship. Moreover, early censors were as affronted by scenes of prizefighting and gambling as they were by nudity or sexual behavior, so the term "indecency" is not always an indicator of sexual content. Richard S. Randall's *Censorship of the Movies: The Social and Political Control of a Mass Medium*, a fine sociological history of constraints on the seventh art, is useful as background. In a separate essay, "Censorship: From 'The Miracle' to 'Deep Throat,' " Randall establishes the significance of his topic: "The narrowing of what is legally proscribable as obscenity [especially as it applies to movies] . . . is one of the true revolutions of our time and is, of course, part of a larger cultural change in sexual attitudes and behavior, which it unquestionably helped to bring about" (439). Randall observes that although they are widely advertised to mass audiences, modern movies (as distinct from television) also serve elites and thus suffer from a "cultural disequilibrium" that subjects them to censorship (456–457).

Neville M. Hunnings' exceptional scholarship is visible in *Film Censors and the Law*, a comparative study of censorship in many countries, including the United States, until the 1960s. Ira H. Carmen's *Movies, Censorship, and the Law*, a compendium of legal action on the federal, state, and local level up through the mid-1960s, has been enriched with interviews with censors, subject indexes, and bibliographies. Volumes concerned with suppression of legitimate films are *Movies in Society: Sex, Crime, and Censorship* by Mark Koenigil, which is pretty dated, though good on historical periods, on misinformed opinions, and on early codes, and *Banned Films: Movies, Censors and the First Amendment*, by Edward de Grazia and Roger K. Newman, which is indispensable for understanding movie censorship in this country. De Grazia's *Censorship Landmarks* treats selected cases in a larger cultural context, arguing that suppression has historically targeted intellectual and aesthetic radicalism. James L. Limbacher lists numerous cases of specific film censorship in his comprehensive *Sexuality in World Cinema*, as does Frank Manchell in *Film Study: An Analytical Bibliography*. The four volumes of *Current Research in Film: Audiences, Economics, and Law*, edited by Bruce A. Austin, present occasional case studies of censorship, mostly of mainstream films.

Cinema, Censorship, and Sexuality 1909–1925, by Annette Kuhn, finds that censorship shaped conceptions of sexuality on- and off-screen in cinema's early decades; Kuhn is one of the great scholars of this period. In "Film Censorship and Progressive Reform: The National Board of Censorship of Motion Pictures," Robert Fisher traces the evolution of the New York Board of Censorship, founded in 1909, later called the National Board of Censorship and then the National Board of Review. A weak precursor of production code offices, the "board" was an industry ploy; financed by the major studios to deflect public outrage, it had no legal authority but was influential nonetheless. That influence was not strong enough for the censors of the New York Society for the Suppression of Vice, who prosecuted every film they could persuade police to seize. Contemporary viewers puzzled by the actions of the New York censorship board will be more confused than ever after consulting *What Shocked the Censors: A Complete Record of Cuts in Motion Picture Films Ordered by the New York State Censors*, a list of excisions compiled by the American Civil Liberties Union in 1933; most of the scenes and references were to fights, juvenile delinquency, and blasphemy.

Outside New York, movie censorship was local and powerful, as Kathleen D. McCarthy points out in "Nickel Vice and Virtue: Movie Censorship in Chicago, 1907–1915." McCarthy studies the establishment of the Chicago movie censorship board (1909), the model for review panels in Pennsylvania (1911),

Ohio (1913), and Kansas (1914). The Chicago board, formed to protect minors from the alleged pernicious effects of cinema, claimed considerable authority. Ford H. MacGregor's "Official Censorship Legislation," a contemporary view of the law during the 1920s, credits the Payne studies on the presumed effects of motion pictures with encouraging censors. Particularly interesting is *The Public and the Motion Picture Industry* (1926), by William M. Seabury, counsel first to the Motion Picture Board of Trade and then to the National Association of the Motion Picture Industry; Seabury analyzes state and federal laws then in force, all of which he thought futile. Gregory D. Black's study of the Legion of Decency in the 1930s, *Hollywood Censored: Morality Codes, Catholics, and the Movies*, is essential to understanding the role of religious pressure groups. "Hollywood, Censorship, and American Culture," a special issue of *American Quarterly*, contains several essays on censorship in the first decades of the movies. Frank Miller includes illustrations in his popular *Censored Hollywood: Sex, Sin and Violence on Screen*, an otherwise unremarkable text.

In *The Movies on Trial*, William Perlman gives a lively account of the public concern with reports of gambling, drugs, rampant sexuality, and high living by movie professionals that forced Hollywood to become circumspect during the 1920s and 1930s. Martin Quigley's *Decency in Motion Pictures*, published at the same time, cites similar rumors in his justification of the need for careful oversight of so powerful a medium; Quigley was one of the two Catholic authors of the Revised Production Code, adopted under pressure by the industry in 1934. The movie industry's self-censorship over the years, from older codes to current rating systems, has generated an irony much apparent in *The Memoirs of Will H. Hays*, a book memorable for the moral obtuseness of America's first full-fledged movie censor. It can be read with Olga J. Martin's guide for professionals during the 1930s, when the industry policed itself most rigorously; her *Hollywood's Movie Commandments: A Handbook for Motion Picture Writers and Reviewers* translated the code into practical dos and don'ts (e.g., couples shown on a bed must keep one foot on the floor). The most hilarious absurdities inflicted on mainstream cinema by its agents of propriety have been collected by Gerald Gardner as *Movie Censorship: Letters from the Hays Office, 1934 to 1968*. Sober by contrast, Raymond Moley's *The Hays Office* is a straightforward account of the industry institution during the 1940s, with a careful explication of the codes and the people who enforced them. The annual volumes of the *International Motion Picture Almanac* have always carried the current "Industry Code of Self Regulation." In *The Dame in the Kimono: Hollywood, Censorship, and the Production Code from the 1920s to the 1960s*, Leonard J. Leff and Jerold L. Simmons laugh at how chief censor Joseph Breen was undone by *The Bicycle Thief* (1948), an Italian film with subtextual references to urination and prostitution. Also exceptional is *The Wages of Sin: Censorship and the Fallen Woman Film, 1928–1942*, in which Lea Jacobs deals with Hollywood's treatment of prostitution. Jacobs points out that the Hays Office and pressure groups like the Catholic Legion of Decency forced filmmakers to visit retribution on women who transgressed sexual mores. Scholars of these periods will find Anthony Slide's detailed *Banned in the U.S.A.: British Films in the United States and Their Censorship, 1933–1966* useful in pinpointing the responses of American Production Code censors to language and images in imported films, especially those involving toilet humor.

The industry's internal censor underwent several name changes: from 1922 to 1945, it was known as the Motion Picture Producers and Distributors of America (MPPDA), but commonly called the Hays Office, after the first enforcer of the Production Code, since 1930; from 1945 to 1990, it was known as the Motion Picture Producers' Association (MPPA); from 1990 to the present, it has been known as the Motion Picture Association of America (MPAA).

The "confessional" format of Jack Vizzard's *See No Evil: Life Inside a Hollywood Censor* recalls footage or language that offended, or was presumed to offend, the public, the Hays Office, and the studio heads. Equally anecdotal is Murray Schumach's *The Face on the Cutting Room Floor: The Story of Movie and Television Censorship*; the volume devotes more space to movies than television. Stephen Farber, who worked for the ratings panel in its early days, admits to disillusionment, concluding in *The Movie Rating Game* that ratings are arbitrary and hypocritical. As a student intern, Farber saw bias and subjectivity at work, especially, he says, in the case of Dr. Aaron Stern, who became chairman in 1971. Jack Valenti wrote *The Voluntary Movie Rating System: How It Began, Its Purpose, the Public Reaction* to explain the MPAA coding system's operations. In "Guidance or Censorship? New Debate on Rating Films," Glenn Collins reflects on the inappropriateness of an "X" rating for serious films and notes that over the years the MPAA adopted a strategy of isolating hard-core pornography. Larry Rohter's "New MPAA Rating" explains the new NC-17 rating as a way of distinguishing meritorious mature films from triple-X fare. The MPAA had not trademarked the "X" rating, which was then appropriated by pornographers to hype their films; by the same token, serious producers and directors shunned the "X" rating.

Morris L. Ernst and Pare Lorentz combine perspectives as attorney and anthropologist to satirize the antics of American censors during the 1920s in *Censored: The Private Life of the Movie*. Garth Jowett's magisterial history of the shaping of cinema content and metaphysics by studios, censors, and cultural forces is appropriately called *Film: The Democratic Art*. The space that Jowett devotes to censorship of the 1920s and 1930s is as generous as George N. Gordon's in *Erotic Communications: Studies in Sex, Sin and Censorship* is slight. In *Sex, Pornography and Justice*, Albert B. Gerber ventures beyond legalese into the realm of censorship folklore and connects efforts to censor movies with forces directed at the culture itself. Numerous cases involving literature, radio, movies, television, and theater pace *Censorship in America*, by Olga Hoyt and Edwin Hoyt. Finally, the essays in *Forbidden Films: The Filmmaker and Human Rights* cover the political, cultural, and sexual censorship faced by filmmakers in various cultures; the collection is a guide to a festival of forbidden films held in Canada in 1984, before that country became so conflicted about sexual representations. Charles Lyons studies opposition by feminists to films such as *Snuff!*, by gays and lesbians to films such as *Basic Instinct*, and by fundamentalists to films such as *The Last Temptation of Christ* in *The New Censors: Movies and the Culture Wars*.

The trials of *Deep Throat* in New York and Tennessee are historically interesting as reactions against "porno-chic," a term coined to describe the phenomenon of middle-class audiences flocking to see it. Richard Smith assesses the cultural impact and its legal consequences in *Getting into Deep Throat*. By contrast, *The Deep Throat Papers*, though it is crammed with legal depositions from the New York State trial that banned it, is a scruffy volume laced with soft-core photos of scenes. Probably the best article, Richard Rhodes' " 'Deep Throat' Goes Down in Memphis," incisively profiled Larry Parrish, the prosecutor, and Harry Reems, the actor/defendant, against a local conservatism that led to a guilty verdict. Memphis' prosecution of Reems is also discussed by Edward de Grazia and Roger K. Newman in *Banned Films: Movies, Censors and the First Amendment* (140–143).

The Child Protection and Obscenity Enforcement Act of 1988, which grew out of the Meese Commission's recommendations that the Justice Department harass and intimidate everyone who produces or distributes sexual materials of any kind, established record-keeping provisions for visual depictions of sexual conduct. These were draconian: everyone who handled such visual depictions had independently to secure and maintain records on every performer, not merely those who seemed young but even those clearly past their fifties. A coalition of organizations including the American Library Association and various artists' groups challenged the requirement in *American Library Association v. Thornburgh*, 713 F. Supp. 469 (1989) on the grounds that such requirements would throttle visual production of any kind. A librarian, for example, would have been required to verify the age of, and keep a birth certificate on file for, every performer in, say, Bertolucci's *Last Tango in Paris* or a skimpily clad model in *Cosmopolitan*, before those items could be checked out by anyone. A Federal District Court judge in Washington enjoined the law in 1989, and Congress in 1990 altered the requirement while the case was on appeal to apply only to those involved in the actual hiring and production supervision of performers and to be applicable only to "lascivious" productions. In 1992 a justice questioned the record-keeping requirement (he said that if the act applied only to the underage—rather than people of all ages—it would be constitutional); see "Judge Overturns Part of Child-Pornography Law." Further challenges are likely, but producers of X-rated films and cable television documentaries, fearing publicity-hungry prosecutors, are nevertheless careful to keep proofs of age under section 2257 (h)(1).

Information on contemporary prosecutions, legal strategies, and points of law are the staple of *Adult Video News*. This is one of the most reliable sources of information on legal issues confronting the industry, whose attorneys monthly review important cases and advise video rental stores. That function was served in the past by the *Bulletin of the Adult Film Association of America*, also a mine of information on censorship attempts, some of which never reached the courts, and *TAB (The Adult Business) Report*, whose pages recorded attacks on adult businesses in all the states during the 1970s. These sources also list episodes of official harassment, local prosecutions, and plea bargains.

CENSORSHIP OF ELECTRONIC MEDIA

Broadcasting

Broadcast regulation covering explicit expression has evolved slowly, attended by conflicting interpretations. The 1934 Communications Act made a distinction between *common carriers* such as telephone and telegraph systems and non-common carriers such as radio and television. Common carriers must transmit any message so long as the sender has the money to pay for it. That being the case, the government can regulate messages on a common carrier only to the extent that the content is actually obscene. Determining what is obscene is as difficult there as elsewhere, of course.

The regulation of broadcasting is predicated on the scarcity of a natural resource, the electromagnetic spectrum, that must be shared by everyone, though the opening of more frequencies over the years has made the argument less compelling. Because the spectrum is "owned" by the public, and broadcast frequencies are merely franchised, the Federal Communications Commission licenses broadcasters to operate "in the public interest, convenience and necessity," and that injunction, while never precisely defined, gives the FCC greater power to control speech; broadcasters do not enjoy all of the First Amendment protections accorded print media. The problem, however, is this: Section 1464 of the U.S. Criminal Code provides sanctions against profane, indecent, or obscene language over a broadcast medium. At the same time, Section 326 of the 1934 Communications Act, written to comply with the First Amendment, forbids the FCC from censoring program content; the contradiction is evident.

Perhaps the most famous case in radio broadcasting is *FCC v. Pacifica* (1978), sometimes called the "George Carlin Case," the "Seven Dirty Words Case," or just "Pacifica," after the 1973 broadcast of a comic routine (a funny disquisition on what makes words taboo) over New York's WBAI-FM (Pacifica Broadcasting). A father filed a complaint because his son was listening, and the FCC imposed sanctions on the station. In its review, the Supreme Court reversed a lower-court decision in favor of Pacifica. The justices ruled that the FCC did have the authority to impose sanctions against material that was indecent on several grounds: (1) that the FCC had not edited the broadcast in advance, which would have constituted prior restraint, (2) that broadcasting confronts the individual in the home (or car) and that prior warnings about content cannot protect a station-hopping listener, and (3) that broadcasting is "uniquely accessible to children." Jeff Demas' "Seven Dirty Words: Did They Help Define Indecency?" concludes that the stipulations of the WBAI decision were too narrow to provide much guidance. The best source on the case and its aftermath, however, is Matthew L. Spitzer's *Seven Dirty Words and Six Other Stories: Controlling the Content of Print and Broadcast.*

Both the FCC and the courts have shied away from characterizing specific broadcasts as *obscene*—rather than indecent—because of the greater difficulty of defining the former. Nonetheless, the definition of obscenity that currently applies is *Miller v. California* (1973), the so-called community standards test. This is a three-pronged test. To be obscene, a program, taken as a whole, (1) has to include material that depicts or details in an obviously offensive way acts that a state legislature has defined as objectionable; (2) has to appeal to the prurient interest of an average citizen, applying contemporary community standards; and (3) has to lack serious artistic, literary, political, or scientific merit. The closest the FCC has come to defining indecency is to say that while it may not be material that is obscene or pornographic, it does depict "sexual or excretory activities or organs" in terms that "are patently offensive as measured by contemporary community standards for the broadcast medium."[2] Except for the seven dirty words (shit, piss, cunt, fuck, cocksucker, motherfucker, and tits), profanity as such, the other form of expression forbidden by Section 1464, is generally ignored by the FCC because it raises religious questions the government would rather avoid.

Among standard texts on legislation governing radio and television broadcasting, the most journalistic is Don Pember's *Mass Media Law*, now in its fifth edition. Others include *The First Amendment and the Fourth Estate: Regulation of Electronic Mass Media*, edited by T. Barton Carter, M. A. Franklin, and J. B. Wright; and *Major Principles of Media Law*, by Wayne Overbeck with Rick D. Pullen. Both *Mass Communication Law: Cases and Comment*, by Donald Gilmor and Jerome Barron, and *Broadcast Regulation: Selected Cases and Decisions*, by Marvin Bensman, look at specific cases, though both could use updates. The most current sources available are *Media Law Reporter* (quarterly) and *Congressional Quarterly*, loose-leaf newsletter formats carrying news and citations to media materials (e.g., see the 30 June 1995 issue of *CQ* on computers, sex, privacy, and related matters). Jeremy H. Lipschultz has written a short history on the difficulties of defining indecency in "Conceptual Problems of Broadcast Indecency Policy and Application"; those interested in broadcast law might look at it before other items. Still more helpful is Lipschultz's *Broadcast Indecency: F.C.C. Regulation and the First Amendment*, which is perhaps the most up-to-date volume on the subject now; it reprints nonpublic FCC documents on indecency that Lipschultz obtained under the Freedom of Information law.

The evolution of early radio regulation, most of it is concerned with issues (e.g., military) other than indecency, can be traced in the papers gathered by Harrison B. Summers in *Radio Censorship*. Louise M. Benjamin's "Defining the Public Interest and Protecting the Public Welfare in the 1920s: Parallels between Radio and Movie Regulation" contrasts indecency regulations as applied to radio and similar strictures applied to motion pictures. D. L. Brenner interprets the recurrent ramifications of a famous case in "Censoring the Airwaves: The Supreme Court's *Pacifica* Decision." In 1987 Irvin Molotsky's "F.C.C. Rules on Indecent Programming" reported that the agency would permit radio broadcasters to air adult material during a "safe harbor" period late at night, as did a *Time* article, "Midnight Blue: An FCC Time Limit for Raunch."

Reports were premature. Using three cases (a Howard Stern show, a college station's airing of bawdy songs, and a play about gay phone sex), L. A. Powe Jr. argues in "Consistency over Time: The FCC's Indecency Rerun" that the FCC has revived repressiveness and that the cases embody three consistencies: (1) the decisions are political, most recently as a sop to Republicans; (2) they affirm the Pacifica ruling as justified by the need to protect minors and the naive; and (3) they restrict program diversity by privileging the bland and the conventional. The importance of precedent figures in most discussions of censorship. In "A Solution to Indecency on the Airwaves," H. T. Schrier observes that if there is to be continued or even augmented regulation, then the FCC must precisely define what constitutes indecency, since its vague public descriptions actually contravene the Supreme Court's decision upholding the original *Pacifica* decision. Howard Fields points out that legislation governing common carrier media does not necessarily govern broadcast media in "Dial-a-Porn Decision Poses Contradictions for Indecent Broadcasts."

The Federal Communications Commission in 1975 issued *Report on the Broadcast of Violent, Indecent and Obscene Material*. It claimed that because television was "a guest in the American home," the broadcaster had a "responsibility to provide some measure of support to concerned parents" (423). The issue, of course, is the degree of support. The stance of the FCC on candor depends almost entirely on the political orientation of the individual commissioners. In 1984 the editors of the trade journal *Broadcasting* observed in "Mark Fowler's Great Experiment: Setting His People Free" that the chair of the FCC seemed determined to force broadcasters to toe a moral line. Chairman Fowler was reimposing what is usually called "the newsprint model" on electronic media, which meant reducing expressions of candor to blandness.

Edmund L. Andrews reports in "Government Seeks to Extend Ban on Broadcast of Offensive Shows" (1990) that the FCC was seeking to extend the ban of indecency on radio and television broadcast (cable television exempted) for twenty-four hours a day on the grounds that at least some children are listening or watching at all hours. The FCC refused to comment on assertions that the rule could result in fines for television shows like *L.A. Law* and *Thirty Something*, both of which frequently discussed sexual matters, despite their airing after 10 P.M. A year later, in "Indecency Ban Nixed," the trade journal

Electronic Media breathed relief that the Federal Appeals Court in Washington ruled the FCC's position unconstitutional. The article points out that indecency refers in this context to material that parents might find inappropriate to children; it is not to be equated with obscenity in either a legal or a social sense. Prodded by a conservative Congress, the FCC kept trying, but two years later, as Neil Lewis writes in "U.S. Restrictions on Adult-TV Fare Are Struck Down," the same Federal Court of Appeals in the District of Columbia struck down as unconstitutional another FCC regulation prohibiting indecent television programs broadcast between midnight and 6 A.M. The latest ruling asserted that the FCC had not adequately considered the rights of adults—as opposed to children—to view such programs. The legal maneuvering provoked scholarly debate. In "An Alternative Justification for Regulating Broadcast Indecency," Sharon Docter argues that the government's position is not that indecent broadcasting in any way harms children, which cannot be proved or even supported, but that parents have a right to raise children as they see fit; that means that the FCC can regulate the *hours* at which indecent material can be broadcast.

Though dated now, Charles Winick's *Taste and the Censor in Television* defines the issues as those of propriety rather than law. In *See No Evil: The Backstage Battle over Sex and Violence in Television*, Geoffrey Cowan, legal counsel to Norman Lear and the Writers Guild of America in their struggle against the networks' "Family Viewing Policy" of 1975, writes about efforts by broadcasters to ward off federal interference by policing entertainment shown during prime time. Cowan recalls negotiations between producer and network censors concerning Lear's *All in the Family*, which offended many viewers. A more recent and more comprehensive historical survey of shifts in network policy is John T. Weispfenning's "Changing Standards: Self-Regulation and the Evolution of the Roles of the Network Television Censors." Weispfenning outlines the rationale behind broadcasting self-censorship and the role of economics and social pressures in gradually liberalizing those standards over the years.

Sexual imagery sometimes characterized as pornographic in advertising itself is the subject of occasional debate. Some jurists believe that "commercial speech" is substantially different from individual speech and therefore cannot be accorded the same First Amendment safeguards. Extremes can test the limits, says Marc S. Charisse in "Brothels in the Marketplace of Ideas: Defining Commercial Speech." His article deals with the question of how far "commercial speech" should be protected in a discussion of court cases involving Nevada brothels that advertise. The issue has implications for television ads for dial-a-porn services.

The Communications Decency Act of 1996 mandated that V-chips capable of being programmed to block objectionable content for children be installed in all American television sets manufactured after 1997 and that broadcast and cable networks agree on codes to be electronically attached to the header of every program. The civil liberties issues have not been resolved, and the alleged effectiveness of the system is still hotly disputed, as is obvious in the Showtime video documentary *Ratings, Morals, and Sex on TV*, featuring interviews with a variety of television producers, critics, fundamentalists, and other interested parties. Lawrie Mifflin's "F.C.C. Approves Ratings System for TV; Sets with Blockers Will Be on Market within a Year" reports that as of March 1998 only NBC and the Black Entertainment Network have declined to add the content codes V(violence), S(sexual content), L(foul language), and D(sexually sugges-tive dialogue) to the six age-group designations ranging from Y(suitable for all children) to TV-MA (unsuitable for those under 17) ratings that will be keyed to V-chip technology in sets. As the designations indicate, issues of violence often cloud issues of sexual expression. For a broad overview of thinking on filtering technologies, scholars should consult Monroe Price's *The V-Chip De-bate: Content Filtering from Television to the Internet*. Though more careful than most such arguments, Kevin W. Saunders' *Violence as Obscenity: Limiting the Media's First Amendment Protection* questions assumptions that the Con-stitution shields violence and suggests prosecuting it under the obscenity excep-tion to the First Amendment. The problem, already manifest in endless litigation, is that many Americans equate sex and violence and improperly treat both as obscenity.

Cable and Satellite Transmission

Ronald Garay's *Cable Television: A Reference Guide to Information* is an excellent sourcebook on all things having to do with cable. *Cable Television Law*, by C. D. Ferris, F. W. Lloyd, and T. J. Casey, takes a broad view of various aspects of cable legislation, including issues of sexuality and indecency. Patrick R. Parsons' *Cable Television and the First Amendment* is the standard textbook on the evolution of regulation of speech on cable media.

In the mid-1970s, very explicit programs transmitted on cable public-access in Manhattan led to calls for censorship by legislators (though rarely by citizens). In 1975 Cliff Jahr reported on the collision between rigid FCC positions and local tolerance in "Porn on Cable TV: Is There Excess?" Jahr observed, "The only form of cable censorship that is fair to all is the one now operating in Toledo, Ohio, where parents can turn off cable reception with a 'censor plug' in the back of the set" (13). The next year, as noted by Carol F. Brown in "Cable TV Censorship: Black Out 'Midnight Blue,' " the FCC pushed Manhat-tan Cable hard, leading the system operator to remove "Midnight Blue" from the public-access channel, despite New York state laws forbidding censorship of public-access program content. In fact, "Midnight Blue" simply moved to a leased-access channel.

Almost a decade later, FCC enthusiasm for cable censorship crested again. In "Obscenity, Cable Television, and the First Amendment: Will FCC Regulation Impair the Marketplace of Ideas?" G. P. Faines gauged increasing pressure to suppress sexual expression on cable as a threat to diversified speech. In his analysis of the rights of cablecasters to offer material that might be offensive in

" 'Cableporn' and the First Amendment: Perspectives on Content Regulation of Cable Television," D. L. Hofbauer pointed out that the real issues are the legal definition of cable television, which is neither a common carrier nor a franchise of a limited resource, like the broadcasting spectrum, and whether or not it can be said to intrude into private areas regardless of the consumer's right to control its entry. In this regard, T. G. Krattenmeker and M. L. Esterow in "Censoring Indecent Cable Programs: The New Morality Meets the New Media" assert "It is inconceivable that [cable] could be viewed as an unwelcome intruder without similarly classifying home-delivered newspapers or subscription services for books and records" (631).

Similarly, V. H. Robbins' "Indecency on Cable Television: A Barren Battleground for Regulation of Programming Content" argues that the *Pacifica* decision limiting indecency in broadcasting cannot be applied to cable, which is fundamentally different from over-the-air sources. J. E. Wallace frames the issues in terms of freedom of speech versus the privacy of others and argues that it should be possible to avoid unconstitutional regulations and still protect those not wishing to view indecent materials through technology (codes and filters) in "Contextual Regulation of Indecency: A Happy Medium for Cable Television." L. D. Wardle sorts through cases in "Cable Comes of Age: A Constitutional Analysis of the Regulation of 'Indecent' Cable Television Programming." J. Sporn's "Content Regulation of Cable Television: 'Indecency' Statutes and the First Amendment" discusses two cases holding unconstitutional regulations designed to restrict indecency on cable and concludes that encouraging diversity on cable overrides concerns about sexual materials appearing on the medium.

In an authoritative monograph, *Cable Television and the First Amendment: The Post-Preferred Cases*, Patrick Parsons says that when the Supreme Court decided to wait for more facts in *Los Angeles v. Preferred Communications* (1986), the justices left the cable industry without constitutional guidelines in dealing with First Amendment issues, especially indecency. Richard D. Heffner, the former head of the film industry's rating system, feared that this limbo would bring fresh calls for censorship by extremists. His "Here Come the Video Censors" says that ratings similar to film categories are inadequate for the pornography looming on electronic media like cable and computer networks. Howard M. Kleiman's "Indecent Programming on Cable Television: Legal and Social Dimensions" described the legal climate of 1986 as oppressive, primarily because of the Meese Commission. Kleiman recommended that the cable industry should consider voluntary restraints on hours and on the manner in which it distributes sex-oriented programming. The 1986 Meese Commission urged states and federal prosecutors to curtail sexual expression by fair means or foul. In 1990 the trade journal *Television Broadcast* noted the success of this "lowest common denominator" censorship when a conservative local community (Montgomery County, Alabama) imposed its standards on a national distributor in "Alabama Indictments Force Satellite Porn Programmer Out of Business." Further information on the distributor of American Exxstacy, Home Dish Satellite

Corporation, can be found in Mark Schone's article "Satellite of Lust: Feds Dog TV Pornographers," which reported on the demise of the satellite-carried, hard-core porn channel because of attacks by the state of Alabama and federal obscenity units created in the wake of the Meese Commission.

The 1984 Cable Communications Policy Act guaranteed cable operators immunity from prosecution for obscene materials appearing on public-access channels and leased-access channels because it prohibited operators from exercising any editorial control over content. (The act did hold franchise authorities vaguely accountable, but court decisions chipped away at local authority and liability.) To counter that approach, Senator Jesse Helms added an amendment to the 1992 Cable Television Consumer Protection and Competition Act that gave operators the right to ban indecent programming and held them accountable if they did not. Two cable operators, joined by numerous other groups, filed a challenge. Drawing on a series of court decisions holding that parents have a responsibility to police their children's viewing, the operators argue that the act unconstitutionally restricts free speech in order to accomplish a goal that could be met by using lock-out boxes that cable companies provide on request. The Supreme Court accepted the case, as Linda Greenhouse reports in "Justices to Rule on Whether Cable TV's Sexually Explicit Programs Can Be Restricted." The issue may be moot.

Censorship of Dial-a-Porn

Section 223 of the Communications Act specifies that it is illegal to use the telephone to make comments or statements that are "obscene, lewd, lascivious, filthy, or indecent." The framers of that section never anticipated the 900-number porn services advertised everywhere today, so in 1983 Congress added section 223 (b) to restrict telephone transmission of obscene or indecent messages to minors. In 1988 it amended that section to prohibit such messages entirely. That year, as Stuart Taylor reported in "Ban on Dial-a-Porn Is Allowed to Stand," the Supreme Court upheld a lower court's ruling in favor of the Mountain States Telephone and Telegraph Company's refusal to carry services offering pornographic phone messages. At the same time, the Court struck down a law that prohibited "indecent" messages—which are protected—along with "obscene" ones. Congress then passed a new law, sponsored by Senator Jesse Helms, requiring that telephone companies block access to adult message services unless the subscriber requested it in writing; required credit card authorization, access codes, or scrambling to further limit the service to subscribers; and required that message companies inform telephone companies that they are providing an adults-only service. Neil A. Lewis' article, "F.C.C. Adopts Dial-a-Porn Rules," says that the intent of the law was to prevent minors from listening to sexually explicit telephone recordings but also pointed out that telecommunications experts do not know how many minors actually use such services.

Carlos Briceno noted that the regulation that companies require subscribers to identify themselves in writing led dial-a-porn entrepreneurs to file numerous lawsuits on the grounds that the requirement violated the First Amendment in " 'Dial-a-Porn' Industry Battles U.S. Restrictions." According to Briceno, gay and lesbian groups claimed that the law restricted the flow of information to the gay and lesbian community, especially in a time when fear of AIDS leads people to seek nonphysical forms of sexuality. Despite such protests, Andrew Pollack reported in "Court Allows Limited Access to 'Dial-a-Porn' Phone Lines" that a Federal Appeals Court in San Francisco in 1991 upheld federal regulations denying minors access to porn services by requiring phone companies to block access at the request of parents.

Leaving aside the eroticism itself, dial-a-porn presents interesting challenges to a culture being transformed by ubiquitous and instantaneous communication. Judicial restraint has guided even what most people have thought of as a conservative Supreme Court, or so say John L. Huffman and Denise M. Trauth in "Obscenity, Indecency, and the Rehnquist Court," which reviews *Sable Communications v. FCC* (1989), a decision that permitted dial-a-porn under certain conditions. Another interesting issue is addressed by Juliet L. Dee's "From 'Pure Speech' to Dial-a-Porn: Negligence, First Amendment Law and the Hierarchy of Protected Speech," on the question of possible liability arising from suits attributing causality in aberrant sexual behavior cases to erotic magazines and records and other media such as telephones.

Two useful historical surveys of dial-a-porn legislation are "First Amendment Constraints on the Regulation of Telephone Pornography," by E. L. Nagel, who thinks that existing laws are quite sufficient to protect minors and that rights to speech and privacy should govern where adults are concerned; and "Telephones, Sex, and the First Amendment," by E. J. Mann, who believes that blocking mechanisms can protect minors; in any case, he argues, efforts to control obscenity should be the least restrictive possible to safeguard First Amendment rights. In "Aural Sex: Has Congress Gone Too Far by Going All the Way with Dial-a-Porn?" H. S. Maretz says that the 1988 amendment is unconstitutional and that the rights and interests of porn providers, telephone companies, consumers, and states must be balanced. The right of the state to act in the absence of state legislation leads M. W. Tovey in "Dial-a-Porn and the First Amendment: The State Action Loophole" to challenge the Ninth Circuit Court decision permitting a telephone company to deny access to dial-a-porn services on the grounds that blocking technology and number prefixes safeguard minors and are preferable means of regulation. By contrast, H. C. Jassem suggests in "Scrambling the Telephone: The FCC's Dial-a-Porn Regulations" that the principles aimed at protecting children enunciated in the *Ginzburg* and *Pacifica* decisions will probably be successful in restricting sexual material because telephones are addressable and pervasive.

Censorship of Computers and the Internet

In the mid-1980s, after Congress began investigations of alleged pornographic uses of various electronic technologies, the Justice Department began subjecting obscenity and indecency on computer networks to scrutiny and asking for litigation, usually in the name of protecting children. The journal *New Media* put out a special issue in April 1993 called "Digital Sex: Technology, Law and Censorship," tracing the evolution of digitalized sexual material and reflecting on issues of broadband censorship. When the courts maintained that year that the FCC cannot take away the First Amendment rights of adults in order to shield children from violent or sexual television programming, William Safire wrote in "The Porn Is Green" that the same ruling should apply to computer networks. Where content is concerned, Safire argues, pornographic elements must be separated from violent elements; the latter are troublesome. Nudity should not be an issue at all. "Plain private porn is no big deal. It's a fact of life that has this constructive aspect: Porno films launched the videotape revolution, and while we computer illiterates sleep, multimedia porn—interactive yet—is giving the new world of PC-ROM its initial commercial impetus. (They aren't buying those triple-speed players for the encyclopedias.)" Safire says that if parents don't want their children to watch certain material, they can lock it out on their receivers and code their sets to punch the stuff up later for adult viewing.

Casey B. Mulligan suggests that legislation is misguided because the unregulated Internet—still relatively uncommercialized—is itself "a powerful antipornography tool." Mulligan's "Pornography, Profits and the Internet" observes (rather naively) that the electronically sophisticated can obtain sexual material at little cost because the system encourages piracy and that market forces will dry up porn because there will be little profit in producing it—as opposed to posting existing images. That argument may be valid only until marketing becomes more sophisticated. Suzanne Stefanac's "Playboy Opens WWW Emporium" notes that Playboy Enterprises will market only tangible goods (such as T-shirts) until it can figure out how to protect its images from duplication. The issue of *Georgetown Law Review* (83 [June 1995]) that carried the bogus study of pornography on the Internet by Martin Rimm also carried an excellent article on the futility of censoring the Net even as it reviewed various options for attempting to restrict electronic pornography. This is Carlin Meyer's "Reclaiming Sex from the Pornographers: Cybersexual Possibilities," which argues that the benefits of enhanced access, even to minors, far outweigh the dangers. In "A Crusader against Cyberporn Who Was Once Involved in a Sex Scandal," Edmund L. Andrews notes that Enough Is Enough (www.enough.org), a censorship group, is run by Donna Rice Hughes, the paramour whose discovery scuttled the 1988 presidential run of Senator Gary Hart. Hughes has traded her tabloid cover-girl image for that of crusader against obscenity on the Internet and promotes her proposed constraints as a buffer against those who would destroy the Internet altogether. (See chapter 8, **Child Pornography**, Hughes.)

Burt Rapp's *Sex Crimes Investigation: A Practical Manual*, a Big Brother guide to snooping on pornographers, offers advice on conducting mail entrapment schemes, investigating and enticing homosexuals, and infiltrating computer sex networks. The story of attempts by the Secret Service to track illegal activities of hackers is told by Bruce Sterling in *The Hacker Crackdown*. Sterling outlines the role of the Electronic Frontier Foundation (established by Mitch Kapor, the inventor of Lotus, and John Perry Barlow, a songwriter for the Grateful Dead) in countering the excesses of government officials. Wendy Cole's "The Marquis de Cyberspace" profiles Robert Thomas and Carleen Thomas, operators of Amateur Action, an on-line service offering 25,000 images to subscribers. The Thomases were convicted of obscenity when they sent images from their California business to a government agent in Memphis, Tennessee; the Justice Department used its frequent venue-shopping ploy of seeking local convictions of entrepreneurs whose activities would be acceptable in their own communities.

The novelist Erica Jong worries about such censors and state control of individuals in the electronic world of the future in "The Electronic Anti-Sex League Wants Your Number." Given the number of potential Big Brothers, which include corporations as well as government agencies, all of whom hope to employ electronic surveillance to track Americans, Jong's fears are realistic. Newer communication technologies pose a threat to established institutions, which at first seek to preserve their authority by enforcing older regulations, says Stephen Labaton in "Old Laws Have a Way of Learning New Tricks": "This year, the Justice Department said it plans to crack down on pornography in computer programs. Even though no Federal laws have been written with precisely that problem in mind, prosecutors say they intend to apply existing provisions in the criminal code as stringently as they can. Just as the courts have developed detailed procedures for the legal use of telephone wiretaps, prosecutors are looking at ways these rules can be applied to surreptitiously monitor personal computers and fax machines" (E14).

"Cyberspace under Lock and Key," by John Markoff, reports on proposals to put a "clipper chip" inside computers and ancillary equipment. The chip, which would embody a data scrambling standard, would enable law enforcement agencies with warrants to decode consumer computer codes. Manufacturers and hackers are resisting. " 'They're asking us to ship millions of computers abroad with a chip stamped J. Edgar Hoover inside,' " says a spokesman for Sun Microsystems; " 'We refuse to do it.' " Lawrie Mifflin, in "Spurned by Industry, V-Chip Retains Some Mighty Friends," recounts the Senate's successful effort to require television sets to come equipped with a V-chip that can do for broadcast signals what cable devices can already do: block programming some Americans might find offensive. That led to filters such as SurfWatch that block potentially objectionable Web sites. The problem, as "See No Evil?" points out, is that filtering Web sites on the Internet blocks perfectly innocent information as well. In striking down the Communications Decency Act in 1997, however, the Supreme Court listed filtering software and Web site ratings as possible alternatives to the destructive provisions envisioned by Congress in passing the act.

As Amy Harmon points out in "The Self-Appointed Cops of the Information Age," however, the danger is that private filtering devices will become public filters and thus destroy the most participatory medium ever invented. No filters or blockers currently available can distinguish innocuous information from obscene material; the result is to reduce what is available behind such filters to bland uselessness. The ACLU and other civil libertarian agencies worry that lack of concern for the First Amendment among electronic code-writers will Disney-fy the Net. Monroe Price has edited essays from different points of view into *The V-Chip Debate: Content Filtering from Television to the Internet*, which broadens the debate to include discussion of the dangers of commercialization as entrepreneurs ride roughshod over consumers. "Freedom of Cyberspeech," by Stephen Rohde, covers the Supreme Court's affirmation of a lower-court ruling that sections of the Communications Decency Act (CDA) violated the First Amendment. The District Court pointed out that there is no way to verify the age of a user without violating an individual's right to privacy, that the precedents cited by the framers of the CDA did not apply, that the standards of the CDA were so vague that birth control information or discussions of homosexuality would have been prohibited, that sexual expression that is indecent but not obscene is protected (despite congressional attempts to outlaw the former), that under the act's provisions a parent could be jailed for asking her child to do research on sophisticated topics, and that the act would inhibit the growth of the Internet. In "Netspeech 97: Free Speech Issues and Incidents on the Internet in 1997," Russ Kick reminds readers that Congress is gearing up for another assault on unfettered speech. He reviews computer V-chips, encryption, rating and filtering devices, domain names, and selected Web sites.

Censorship of Audio Recordings

In 1986, frightened by congressional hearings, the Recording Industry Association of America (RIAA) (comprising companies responsible for 95 percent of U.S. record sales) asked its members either to adopt warning labels or to print lyrics that might be construed as offensive on the album jacket. Louis P. Sheinfeld's "Ratings: The Big Chill" canvassed responses from the industry. By 1990 the RIAA had approved a voluntary black-and-white label with the legend "PARENTAL ADVISORY EXPLICIT LYRICS." That was not enough for conservative legislators in fourteen states, who wanted huge, mandatory labels printed in fluorescent yellow announcing that the lyrics *might* contain references to "suicide, incest, sadomasochism, sexual activity in a violent context, murder and bestiality." As a college journalist reports in "Down Boy! Censorship Bites Back," all fourteen states rejected it, though Louisiana required the governor's veto to do so. Jon Pareles still found plenty to laugh at in "Legislating the Imagination" on record labeling practices in states like Pennsylvania, Florida, and Missouri; Pareles thought each label was, in effect, a blatant endorsement of politicians who liked to promote themselves as antismut. In "After Lyrics,

What?" Tom Wicker attacked the Pennsylvania "parental warning" labels on certain records as censorship, though the legislators maintain that it is just information for consumers. Wicker claimed that the labels "chill" expression by persuading record stores (especially chains, often the only stores in a region) not to stock the records. Jeffrey Ressner's "To Sticker or Not to Sticker" notes that the choice is difficult: some companies use a uniform label, while others are distressed by it.

Steve Jones' "Ban(ned) in the U.S.A.: Popular Music and Censorship," on recent efforts to censor rap music, touches on precedents such as campaigns aimed at jazz and early rock; Jones notes that warning labels may actually enhance a recording's appeal. Dave Marsh's *You've Got a Right to Rock*, however, is a better history of attacks on rock and roll. S. Wishnia's article, "Rockin' with the First Amendment," documents widespread attempts to censor rock music. Because so many battles are local, the best sources are publications by organizations formed to fight censors. Dave Marsh's *Rock and Roll Confidential*, a monthly devoted to the industry, recently changed its name to *Rock & Rap Confidential*; it reports on legal proceedings in all the states. Mary Morello's newsletter, *Parents for Rock and Rap*, also combats censorship by reporting on cases around the country. Marsh's *50 Ways to Fight Censorship; and Important Facts to Know about the Censors* identifies pressure groups that attempt to suppress any kind of speech, with special sections on music censors. Marsh provides names and addresses of the principal groups, discusses their philosophies and political agendas, and suggests tactics for resistance. A zine called *The ROC: Voice of Rock Out Censorship* lists what it considers the most dangerous censorship groups and their counterparts on the side of free expression as well as other zines such as *U.S. Rocker*. Two other information sources are *GRIP* (Group for Rap Industry Protection), a newsletter, and *The Source*, a monthly magazine, both concerned with rap genres. The late Frank Zappa used to provide a "Z-Pac" containing information on music censorship; copies can still be useful.

In "A Rap Group's Lyrics Venture Close to the Edge of Obscenity," Jon Pareles discusses the ruling by a Federal District Court judge that 2 Live Crew's "As Nasty as They Wanna Be" is obscene, the first such recording ever to be declared obscene from the federal bench. Pareles points out that popular music has always had a hard time defending itself in the United States; that there are elements of racism involved, since similar material has made the white performer Andrew Dice Clay into a celebrity; and that the street language of the lyrics has deep roots in the ethnic community. Doug Simmons' "Gangsta Was the Case" reports on the Senate hearings that accused rap of obscene and misogynistic content. Marcia Pally says that those worried about the alleged effects of rock and rap should instead examine documented cases of religious-inspired sexual perversion and child abuse in "Minors and Media Minotaurs: Sexual Material, Rock, and Rap." The number of cases almost overwhelms Pally's effort to detail them.

CENSORSHIP OF PERFORMANCE

As in the case of photographs and magazines, the history of American censorship of performance has yet to be written. One reason is legal semantics, since performances have been prosecuted as instances of "obscenity," "gross indecency," "public indecency," "exhibitionism," "lewdness," "prostitution," "soliciting," actions that might "corrupt minors," or even violations of liquor or building codes—depending on which statutes applied—rather than dramatic license onstage. Newspaper accounts are fugitive, awaiting historians in archives and newspaper morgues. T. Allston Brown's three-volume *A History of the New York Stage from 1732 to 1901*, a sober and unentertaining chronicle, pauses only briefly over episodes scandalous enough to involve the law but can be a useful starting point. Alarmed by fairly constant official harassment of drama during the 1920s and 1930s, the National Committee against Censorship of the Theatre Arts, comprising actors, directors, producers, and attorneys, published essays under the auspices of the ACLU in 1935; the volume was simply called *Censorship*. Albert B. Gerber devotes a great deal of space to the busts that greeted Lenny Bruce's performances in *Sex, Pornography and Justice* (which covers other media also), as does Edward de Grazia in *Girls Lean Back Everywhere* (444–479).

Lennox Raphael, the playwright of *Che!* (1969), recounts the story of the arrest of himself, the performers, and the theater managers for obscenity when the principal actress grasped the penises of two performers in "Notes from the Underground: Censorship." A documentary film by Eberhard Kronhausen and Phyllis Kronhausen, *Freedom to Love* (1970) includes excerpts from McClure's *The Beard* and Bowen's *Word Play* and interviews Kenneth Tynan, Hugh Hefner, and John Trevelyan, Britain's film censor at the time. J. Nathan details official reaction to McClure's *The Beard* in "Notes from the Underground: San Francisco Censorship," an article representative of the many to appear in newspapers and magazines across the country as various theatrical companies encountered problems with candor. Since 1969, *High Performance* (now defunct), the journal of performance art, routinely carried notices of busts by zealots in various venues. De Grazia also reviews the legal difficulties encountered by performance artists such as Holly Hughes and Karen Finley in *Girls Lean Back Everywhere* (622–688).

Arthur S. Leonard's *Sexuality and the Law: An Encyclopedia of Major Legal Cases* covers a few significant performance trials. The chapter "Doing 'It' on Stage: Theatrical Oral Sex" (103–105) discusses *Commonwealth v. Bonadio*, 415 A.2nd 47 (PA 1980), a ruling by the Pennsylvania Supreme Court upholding a lower court's dismissal of a case against two dancers who performed oral sex on members of the audience in an adult theater. Leonard also addresses *Barnes v. Glen Theatre*, 111 S. Ct. 2456 (1991), the most celebrated restriction on performance in recent years. In that Indiana case, Justice Rehnquist and his conservative majority upheld the right of states that choose to require pasties and G-strings on performers. In "Ode on a G-String," William Safire quotes Justice Souter, one of several justices to write an opinion in the case: "Pasties and a G-string moderate the expression to some degree, to be sure, but . . . the limitation is minor when measured against the dancer's remaining capacity and opportunity to express the erotic message," and concludes that such hair-splitting over so insignificant a matter wastes the republic's time. Unfortunately, no legal opinion explains just why the sight of the female breast should be so taboo, though sooner or later an academic will doubtless employ nipple theory to illuminate late twentieth-century jurisprudence.

Jay Gertzman's comment on *Barnes* is worth noting. In "Postal Service Guardians of Public Morals and Erotica Mail Order Dealers of the Thirties: A Study in Administrative Authority in the United States," Gertzman observes that arguments founded on "public order" are currently powerful: "Judge Scalia wrote that the state may prohibit 'expressive conduct,' at least a version of it which is not essential to expressing an idea, if it has a 'rational basis' [i.e., 'public order'] for so doing. (It is easier to prove such essential significance in the case of historical or political expression than in fiction, poetry or artwork. Thus flag-burning merits First Amendment protection; nude dancing does not)" (106, n. 41). Similarly, in "First Amendment Protection for Gays," C. Edwin Baker points out inconsistencies between the "topless dancing" decision in *Barnes* that nude dancing is entitled to some First Amendment protection as communication and the Court's rejection of a constitutional challenge brought five years previously against a Georgia ban on homosexual sodomy between two consenting adults.

CENSORSHIP OF THE MAILS

Two major histories of the agency that censored expression for longer than any other provide essential background. The first is *Federal Censorship: Obscenity in the Mail*, by James C. N. Paul and Murray L. Schwartz, who chronicle the postal service's interdictions of sexually explicit and obscene materials; it is a fine source of information on postal inspectors, entrapment, mail blocks, charges of fraud as a tool to suppress porn, and so on. More up-to-date but less focused on obscenity and pornography is *Unmailable: Congress and the Post Office*, by Dorothy Ganfield Fowler, another comprehensive review of attempts by the Post Office to censor objectionable and politically suspect material. The Post Office often ignored court decisions, says Edward de Grazia, whose article "Obscenity, Censorship and the Mails I" asserts that authorities paid no attention to *Walker v. Popenoe* (1945), a ruling that even suspect mail must be permitted to circulate until a determination as to its obscenity is made.

Jane M. Friedman studies the agency's use of mail covers—blanket "watches" on an individual's mail—and the illegal opening of sealed, first-class mail as weapons against distributors in "Erotica, Censorship, and the United States Post Office Department." Chapters 5 and 6 of Jay A. Gertzman's *Bookleggers and*

Smuthounds cover cases of postal censorship of marginal publishers such as Falstaff Press and Panurge Press before World War II. Gertzman points out that postal inspectors often shut down publishers using regulations governing fraud, arguing that they did not deliver the salacious material that they advertised. According to Gertzman, harassment and intimidation of distributors or booksellers on a special list proved more effective than mail covers. Gertzman finds constitutionality lacking in the actions of the Post Office in "Postal Service Guardians of Public Morals and Erotica Mail Order Dealers of the Thirties: A Study in Administrative Authority in the United States." The article also documents Catholic influence on postal policy and, always the case with Gertzman's scholarship, sets these actions in a carefully researched social context. Jon Bekken expands on these tactics in " 'These Great and Dangerous Powers': Postal Censorship of the Press," an article devoted chiefly to the Post Office's fixation on alleged subversion but germane to its targeting of sexual materials also. With William Seagle, Morris Ernst published *To the Pure . . . : A Study of Obscenity and the Censor*, which is as notable for its delineation of the Post Office's abuse of power in the absence of federal obscenity legislation as for its condemnation of notable censors.

Jay Gertzman's " 'Esoterica' and 'The Good of the Race': Mail-Order Distribution of Erotica in the 1930s" is the best single source of information on the distribution of pornography through the mail in the 1930s; he draws extensively on postal records. Patricia E. Robertus' dissertation, "Postal Control of Obscene Literature, 1942–1957," focuses on the most intense period of censorship by the Post Office, when it used a variety of techniques, including mail blocks and entrapment, to prevent consumers from purchasing birth control information and other interdicted materials by mail. Desperate postal censors redoubled their zeal in a fruitless effort to stop Congress from shifting the power to censor away from the Post Office. The agency's power to censor continued to erode, despite the case of Ralph Ginzburg, whose conviction for using the mails to distribute *Eros* magazine was upheld by the Supreme Court (1966) on grounds that while the magazine itself was not obscene, Ginzburg had used the mails to pander through advertisements. The legalities seemed irregular: the material itself was not obscene, and the Post Office seemed both a bully and a panderer itself. In any case, the Ginzburg case left a bad taste in the national consciousness. That may have been the motivation for publication of "Mailing Lists and Pornography," by J. Edward Day, the postmaster general. Although Day endorsed the Ginzburg decision, he admitted that his predecessor as postmaster general (under whose authority *Eros* had been seized) seemed obsessed by pornography. John N. Makris offers a different view in *The Silent Investigators: The Great Untold Story of the United States Postal Inspection Service*. Makris presents postal inspectors as a misunderstood, yet tireless, corps intent on stemming a flood tide of filth.

In *Crime Warps: The Future of Crime in America*, Georgette Bennett says that the Post Office fielded over 284,000 complaints about obscenity in 1970 as opposed to approximately 5,000 in 1984. The falloff led postal authorities to instruct inspectors to pursue only major cases and organized crime links. The investigations resulted in few convictions. "By 1982," Bennett points out, "the number of dealers convicted was only 5. But even prior to the policy change, when small-timers were included, convicted dealers never totalled more than 36" (190). One postal law still in force is the Pandering Advertisement Act of 1968, which grew out of the Ginzburg decision. The act allows the individual receiving mailed advertisements or material to determine what is obscene or pornographic. Under the terms of the act, if the addressee affirms that he or she has been offended or aroused by a circular promoting sexuality *or* religion, animal rights, antismoking, feminism, or the Republican Party—in short, anything at all—the Post Office must inform the mailer, and the mailer must cease sending it and any similar materials to the complainant or face proceedings and penalties. Comparatively few Americans exercise this option, but it does give individuals the power to keep potentially offensive expression out of their mailbox, and it leaves the right to determine what is offensive entirely up to the person.

FEMINIST CHALLENGES TO FIRST AMENDMENT AND PRIVACY INTERPRETATIONS

In the 1980s, the antiporn (sometimes called the "antisex") wing of the feminist movement opened discussion of individual freedoms versus group or class rights, a polarity as old as politics. The effort led to a new round of theories seeking to find exceptions to the First Amendment in an effort to regulate speech that a particular group sees as either inimical to women or a barrier to their achieving full rights of citizenship. One argument is that women *believe* that pornography causes them harm and thus ought to be humored whether it does or not; others say that porn *does* cause harm, though they point to research that is, at best, highly ambiguous; still others assert that groups traditionally discriminated against should claim rights that outweigh individual freedoms.

As always, issues devolve upon definitions. Women against Pornography (WAP), an activist organization, has published *Where We Stand on the First Amendment: Women against Pornography Position Paper*, which says that WAP wants to "change the definition of obscenity so that it focuses on violence, not on sex." Most American producers of porn would instantly subscribe to that revised definition, of course, but in practice the task is much more complicated, since WAP usually defines as "violent" any depiction of women as sexual beings. The chief legal theorist of the antiporn feminists is Catharine MacKinnon. The most useful among her many explanations of her position are three texts. "Not a Moral Issue" argues that pornography is not a moral issue but a political one. The First Amendment, she says, has never been absolute and is in any case only an abstraction. "Pornography, Civil Rights, and Speech" claims that pornography is "central in creating and maintaining the civil inequality of the sexes" and therefore violates the civil rights of women. *Feminism Unmodified: Discourses on Life and Law* consolidates and extends these arguments. (See **Feminist Positions on Pornography** in Chapter 6 and **Language, Genders, and Subcultures** in Chapter 15.) MacKinnon's arguments have spawned elaborations by others on a patriarchal system whose only significant reason for being, they say, is the domination of women through the instrument of pornography. Typical in this category is Robin West's "Pornography as a Legal Text: Comments from a Legal Perspective," which holds that unlike "liberal legal texts" that "convey their promises directly to the subordinate class," "pornography controls behavior by defining a conception of women *for men*. . . . What men think *of* women becomes what women think of women; in a system of total dominance, what men think of women becomes what women are" (118).

In 1984 MacKinnon and Andrea Dworkin wrote an antipornography ordinance passed by the city council of Minneapolis. Dworkin and MacKinnon collaborated on *Pornography and Civil Rights; A New Day for Women's Equality*, a pamphlet recounting the strategy behind their legal position. When the courts declared a similar Indianapolis ordinance unconstitutional, says Penelope Seator's "Judicial Indifference to Pornography's Harm: *American Booksellers v. Hudnut* (Women's Law Forum)," the decision was political in that the courts refused to recognize that pornography discriminates against women; the decision merely upheld "male hegemony." In "Anti-Pornography Legislation as Viewpoint-Discrimination," Geoffrey R. Stone rejects arguments (like Seator's) on the grounds that antipornography legislation based on the concept of discrimination against women depends on a particular viewpoint and that male viewpoints are not necessarily privileged in First Amendment rights. Robert G. Meyer's "Sex, Sin, and Women's Liberation: Against Porn-Suppression" observes that while women's groups insist that they are not censors, they do collude at suppression. E. A. Carr's "Feminism, Pornography, and the First Amendment: An Obscenity-Based Analysis of Proposed Antipornography Laws" reviews the Minneapolis and Indianapolis ordinances urged by antiporn feminist groups. Carr sides with such groups because he believes advocates of free speech ignore the harm that pornography causes women. Carr thinks that the ordinances in their present form may violate First Amendment principles but could probably be modified along the Supreme Court's obscenity guidelines so as to succeed.

Advocates of free speech must recognize the contention of feminists that pornography causes physical harm and must redefine the obscenity issue to take harm into account, without restricting free speech, says W. K. Layman in "Violent Pornography and the Obscenity Doctrine: The Road Not Taken." Rosemarie Tong analyzes the Indianapolis ordinance in "Women, Pornography, and the Law," some of which appears in her *Women, Sex and the Law*, a broader consideration of feminist legislative initiatives. Tong maintains that women's sexuality puts them at risk before the law, which has traditionally treated females as subordinate and inferior. The book is valuable because it categorizes feminist legal positions. The problem, as many scholars have been quick to notice, is that only a fraction of what *some* people consider pornography is violent and that the evidence that even that fraction causes antisocial behavior is equivocal. They caution against legislating on the basis of what is essentially folklore. The distinguished jurist Fred B. Berger, for example, reiterates that data do not support the thesis that typical pornography degrades or defames women. He allows that violent sexual material may *sometimes* lead to antisocial behavior but that even if such an effect were more common, it would not justify suppression. In *Freedom, Rights, and Pornography: A Collection of Papers*, Berger opposes censorship on the grounds that paternalism is paternalism whether exercised by allegedly hegemonic males or a feminist-inspired state and that it always restricts access to ideas.

Robert G. Meyer speaks for many jurists in "Pornography and the Sexual Deviations" when he says that given the widespread market for pornography, "it is clear that pornography does not stimulate criminal or grossly deviant behavior in the great majority of users" (100) but notes that some studies indicate that certain kinds of pornography may stimulate certain kinds of deviant behavior in certain kinds of people. Pornography can incorporate and speak to paraphilias, that is, sexual disorders, among them transvestism, fetishism, zoophilia, pedophilia, incest, exhibitionism, voyeurism, sadomasochism, and arousal by odors. That being the case, the issues raised by abuse of the First Amendment should remain uppermost, argues Meyer, since otherwise censorship penalizes the "normal" individual. Put another way: every year a few children watch *Superman* on television, don a pillowcase for a cape, and jump out a window. Would society be justified in banning the fantasy from television altogether? (See **Pornography and Violence** in Chapter 19.)

Priscilla Alexander challenges Andrea Dworkin's contempt for the First Amendment as having been written by white males to protect only white males. In "Speaking Out: A Response to Andrea Dworkin," Alexander asserts that democratic law evolves toward greater justice for all groups, slow and uneven though the process might be. The theories of MacKinnon and Dworkin require continuous revision of the ways in which law and behavior interact, and that contributes to a permanent instability, says Frances Ferguson in "Pornography: The Theory." Lisa Duggan, Nan Hunter, and Carole S. Vance examine the Minneapolis and Indianapolis ordinances in "False Promises: Feminist Anti-Pornography Legislation." They point out that women are already protected against harassment by means of pornography under Title VII of the 1964 Civil Rights Act and that new laws proposed by radical feminists make no distinction between actual sexual assault and the display of sexually explicit images that may merely be offensive to some women. Moreover, proponents of restrictions mistakenly assume that pornography is wholly devoid of ideas and cannot qualify as a species of speech. Even worse, antiporn advocates treat women only as victims rather than as agents of sexuality.

Helen E. Longino's "Pornography, Oppression and Freedom: A Closer Look" calls for a return to the original rationale for obscenity law, which was that obscenity either blasphemes or libels. Longino claims, "Pornography is the vehicle for the dissemination of a deep and vicious lie about women. It is defamatory and libelous" (48). This is a variation on what critics sometimes call the "Ayatollah offense," named after the Ayatollah Khomeini. Khomeini condemned the writer Salman Rushdie to death for having blasphemed against the Koran (as interpreted, of course, by Khomeini) on the grounds that Rushdie defamed the faith of Muslims and thus injured the entire group. What makes the argument especially questionable is the lack of evidence that anybody is, in fact, injured, let alone a whole class—or whether such an offense should matter in the first place. It might be possible to prove that individuals are injured, say opponents, but not a whole class.

As most histories of censorship point out, the concept of obscenity was closely identified with blasphemy in both English common law and in early America. The American legal system, by and large, rejected blasphemy as an element of obscenity (though it still resonates in FCC broadcast indecency regulations). The separation of church and state had much to do with that rejection; more important still was that the recognition that insisting that so large a group could be defamed unnecessarily curtailed free speech. Unlike Great Britain, which not only refused to ban Rushdie's book but also officially protected his person against assassination attempts, Canada declined to ensure circulation of *The Satanic Verses*, let alone protection for the author. Not surprisingly, then, the Canadian government accepted the idea that group rights might outweigh individual rights and passed a porn law that embodied the contention that pornography harms women. Tamar Lewin's "Canada Court Says Pornography Harms Women and Can Be Banned" (1992) reports that the Supreme Court of Canada redefined pornography as discourse that discriminates against women and opened the way for seizures and prosecutions, "ruling that though the antipornography law infringes on the freedom of expression, it is legitimate to suppress materials that harm women" (A1). The redefinition of pornography adopted in Canada, says Lewin, is similar to the Indianapolis ordinance struck down by the Federal Court of Appeals in Chicago and affirmed by the Supreme Court as an unwarranted restriction of freedom of expression.

In *Against Nature: Essays on History, Sexuality and Identity*, Jeffrey Weeks confronts the Rushdie issue, pointing out that groups may certainly advocate constraints, though the need for them changes over time, but that individual rights must be respected also; the only answer is continuous debate in the political arena, not legislation directed *at* one group in the name of another ("The Value of Difference," 184–196). Wendy Steiner's *The Scandal of Pleasure* also notes that free expression can collide with Islamic fundamentalists who take as an article of faith the limitations of representation and compares this principle with the current feminist antiporn position. Mariana Valverde and Linda Weir predict that antiporn legislation will hinder the construction of a sexually pluralistic society because such laws will be used against lesbians, as has happened in Canada, in "Thrills, Chills and the 'Lesbian Threat.' " Similarly, Varda Burstyn in "Women, Sex and the State" outlined the dangers to women of state control of expression. Her predictions came to pass when Canadian Customs, acting under the feminist-designed pornography law adopted by Canada, seized Andrea Dworkin's own explicit books.

Leanne Katz's "Censors' Helpers" followed up on the Canadian seizures of lesbian literature and the two Andrea Dworkin works (the latter were released after fanfare and as a special exception to a fellow censor). Katz quotes Thelma McCormack, a sociologist: "The Supreme Court of Canada doesn't give a damn about gender equality. It is concerned about control, and was pleased to have a feminist gloss put on it"; and Lenore Tiefer, a psychologist: "The Canadian situation has made it unambiguous that the sex wars have entered a new phase. There's nothing like a little taste of state repression to put one back in touch with reality" (15). (*Playboy* noted with some glee the seizure of Dworkin's *Pornography: Men Possessing Women* and *Women Hating* as obscene by Canadian customs.[3]) One of the best perspectives on Canadian experimentation with repression is Dany Lacombe's *Blue Politics: Pornography in the Age of Feminism*, which suggests that the politicization of sexuality has damaged discourse and civility. Lacombe's critique: "[The feminist and conservative] attempt to go beyond liberal individualism to questions of justice, equality, and the community is certainly a necessary step in the development of a radical plural diversity," but the attempt is flawed because "both the feminist and the conservative common good is conceived of existing prior to, and independent of, individual freedoms, desires, and interests. Consequently, neither common good allows for diversity" (153).

Jack Glascock examines the Canadian case in "*Regina v. Butler*: The Harms Approach and Freedom of Expression" by sifting through the scientific literature on the alleged violent effects of pornography and finds that the evidence is not compelling. The analysis of the *Butler* decision by Brenda Cossman, Shannon Bell, Lise Gotell, and Becki L. Ross is trenchant; they point out in *Bad Attitude/s on Trial: Pornography, Feminism, and the Butler Decision* that the decision (1992) legitimated censorship of many kinds of sexual expression and unleashed continuing witch-hunts against feminists by antipornography zealots in Canada. As if to confirm such fears, Stephen Rohde's "We Have Seen a Land of Censorship, and It Is Canada" discusses defensive measures by writers, publishers, and booksellers against Canadian government censors who have seized works by Hubert Selby, John Steinbeck, Oscar Wilde, John Irving, bell hooks, Ambrose Bierce, and many others. The chapter on "Obscenity" in Kent Greenawalt's *Fighting Words: Individuals, Communities, and Liberties of Speech* is a careful and concise examination of the feminist, conservative, and Canadian antiporn arguments and the most persuasive in its conclusion that all, on balance, are mistaken. Greenawalt's logic is incisive when he points out that because advocates of censorship make no distinction between sexual and violent materials, using obscenity as a test would suppress materials that socially benefit citizens and leave the violent materials untouched.

Elizabeth Wolgast offers a version of the argument that groups possess inherent rights in "Pornography and the Tyranny of the Majority." Wolgast denigrates the "atomism" of individual freedom in favor of the ethics of the group as a basis for legislation. She argues for "a carefully plotted middle way between broad and oppressive controls and reckless liberty" (444). Like some conservative theorists, she thinks that newer communication technologies are more dangerous than older ones; she accepts the legitimacy of the word but not the picture. Wolgast believes that language differs from representation; she tries to distinguish between pornographic literature as acceptable "expression" of opinion and images that are devoid of ideas worthy of protection. Twiss Butler's "Abortion and Pornography: The Sexual Liberals' 'Gotcha' against Women's Equality" argues that when liberals conflate the right to abortion and the right to enjoy sexual representations, they overlook one salient consideration, that pregnancy is the ultimate form of pornography in our society, since women do not truly have the right to escape it; pregnancy is a form of subordination, just as pornography is. The Constitution is simply an "exclusive men's club" (117); the right to privacy when used as a defense merely shields the oppression of women, makes it possible for males to impregnate women and to degrade them through sexual expression, and should be abandoned in favor of the Equal Rights Amendment.

Richard Delgado and Jean Stefancic are in favor of suppressing speech thought by some groups to be offensive and include pornography in this category in "Overcoming Legal Barriers to Regulating Hate Speech on Campuses." In "Pornography and Harm to Women: 'No Empirical Evidence'?" Delgado and Stefancic launch an ad hominem attack on the motives of researchers who point out the lack of evidence for causal relationships between depictions of sexuality and harm to women. Delgado and Stefancic patronize those who resist a feminist ideology they think will surely triumph and characterize advocates of free speech as reactionaries soon to be condemned to the ash-heap of history. The feminist, antiporn argument, say the two, is rooted "in postmodernism and the social construction of reality" and therefore should not be subject to empirical standards of proof (88). Delgado and Stefancic chide extreme antiporn feminists who "do in fact preach against the evils of patriarchy, do speak unkindly of some men's sexual intentions" (89), apparently to make their case more palatable.

Similarly, the essays in *The Price We Pay: The Case against Racist Speech, Hate Propaganda, and Pornography*, edited by Laura Lederer and Richard Delgado, maintain that the harm caused by pornography is self-evident and that people whose speech hurts other people should not be protected by concepts of free expression. Going even further, Robin Yeamans asserts in "A Political-Legal Analysis of Pornography" that courts did not require proof that segregation was unjust and upheld laws forbidding it. So, too, no one should require proof that pornography harms women, and courts should uphold laws censoring it. Lederer's *Speech, Equality, and Harm: New Legal Paradigms* gathers essays (by MacKinnon, Catherine Itzin, Elisabeth de Feis, Frederick Schauer, and others) urging that concern for equality must take precedence over principles of free speech, especially when the loudest advocates of free speech are those who disagree with the authors. Owen Fiss' *The Irony of Free Speech* also attacks "civil libertarian rhetoric" on the First Amendment. Still other approaches, from the politically correct to more thoughtful analyses, are gathered by Karen Maschke in *Pornography, Sex Work, and Hate Speech.*

Ruth Colker focuses on what she thinks is the false legal shield of privacy often used as a defense of the individual's freedom to read or view pornography. "Pornography and Privacy: Towards the Development of a Group-Based Theory for Sex-Based Intrusions of Privacy" asserts that an oppressive act toward any woman (which is how some feminists define pornography) is an attack on all women, because it encourages all males to behave that way, and that the law equates abuse of women with normal sexual practice. David R. Carlin Jr. posits the outcome of such an approach in "Hegel and Pornography: The Limits of Personal Taste," a succinct statement of the issue of sexual expression as one of taste. If privacy is a right, then no one can restrict pornography for another, no matter how disgusting or demeaning it might be to women or anybody else; if there is no such right, then society can police the taste of males or anyone else. Patricia Hughes says in "Pornography: Alternatives to Censorship" that pornography, defined as sex linked to violence or humiliation, *is* a political, rather than a moral, issue. Since direct censorship of expression is offensive to many people, antiporn crusaders should carefully endorse municipal regulations on sexual expression, urge consecutive penalties for offenses, work for revisions of the criminal code along feminist lines, and engage in activism generally.

One antiporn, feminist position recycles an argument long espoused by religious opponents of erotica: that sexual expression cannot contain ideas. In *Free Speech: A Philosophical Enquiry*, Frederick F. Schauer points out that using the absolutism of free speech as a defense against pornography is something of an anomaly because we routinely accept restrictions on expression such as advertising, commercial endeavors, and perjury. Schauer also suggests that some hardcore pornography exists only for the sake of masturbation and therefore cannot be said to be a form of communication or speech (178–188). Haig A. Bosmajian argues in "Obscenity, Sexism, and Freedom of Speech" that censorship, allegedly motivated by an effort to reduce the sexual crimes of males, actually discriminates against women by denying them sexual materials. Kenneth L. Karst takes up that notion in "Pornography and Law as Images of Power." Law, says Karst, is "an image of order and power." "For both the moralists and the antipornography feminists, the enactment of new legislation appears to have a value of its own as a cultural totem" (50); such a symbolic victory, however, would be Pyrrhic. Karst asserts convincingly that pornography does encapsulate thought and that many women look for ideas there.

Anthony Grey's "Pornography and Free Speech" warns that censorship is at least as harmful as the availability and possible effects of porn, while W. A. Linsley's "The Case against Censorship of Pornography" says that censorship poses one immutable danger: enforced conformity. Daniel Linz, Stephen Penrod, and Edward Donnerstein, researchers whose studies are often cited as evidence of harm to women, insist that their findings have been distorted, and they worry that their research may be improperly co-opted by those who would stifle speech and thought. In "Issues Bearing on the Legal Regulation of Violent and Sexually Violent Media," Linz, Penrod, and Donnerstein hope courts do not try to counter *alleged* harm to women—especially that based on imperfect research—with *genuine* harm to free speech. Wendy Kaminer's "Pornography and the First Amendment: Prior Restraint and Private Action" warns feminists that the First Amendment is a shield against governmental abuse, *not* a protection for pornographers, and that to redefine issues of speech would be to lose many other rights: "Legislative or judicial control is simply not possible without breaking down the legal principles and procedures that are essential to our own right to speak and, ultimately, our freedom to control our own lives" (247). Besides, Kaminer continues, characterizing pornography as "a clear and present danger" to a specific group (such as women) would make it political in fact, not just in theory, and therefore ensure its protection as political speech.

Others agree. The dangers to the First Amendment posed by the arguments of a group of antiporn and antihate speech legal scholars meeting at the University of Chicago Law School in March 1993 prompted Nadine Strossen's "Legal Scholars Who Would Limit Free Speech," in which Strossen marvels at the willingness of feminist legal scholars to abandon constitutional protections in the belief that doing so will advance the status of women. In her book, *Defending Pornography: Free Speech, Sex and the Fight for Women's Rights*, Strossen deals authoritatively with issues of consent versus coercion regarding people who pose for pictures or movies, rejects as myth the radical, feminist position that pornographers invariably force women to appear in visual porn, and says that Constitution and common sense deny that the Fourteenth Amendment can take precedence over the First. Using exhaustive references, she also points out that if pornography must be considered a form of political oppression, as radical feminists assert, then the Constitution would absolutely protect it precisely because political expression is guaranteed. Dorothy Atcheson interviews Strossen in "Defending Pornography: Face-to-Face with the President of the ACLU." Here Strossen asks, that "if freedom of expression doesn't include the right to talk about sex, to look at pornography, to pose for it, to perform in it, to defend it, how do I have free speech?" (108).

E. Hoffman maintains in "Feminism, Pornography and Law" that current law governing pornography already embodies a compromise between liberal and conservative positions. Hoffman says that while feminist assertions that pornography shapes social values may have merit and that while continued efforts to enact antiporn laws may help educate, feminists should avoid promoting state regulation of pornography since to do so is dangerous for political reasons. Another trenchant feminist critique is that of Drucilla Cornell, who argues in *The Imaginary Domain: Abortion, Pornography and Sexual Harassment* that feminists should concentrate on political, rather than legal, action to counter production of pornography. Instead of treating sex workers as victims, feminists should help them organize for economic self-protection in an industry that— like other industries—tends to exploit its labor force. Cornell's concern is the exploitation that occurs when less celebrated sex workers (nonstars, say) are paid off the books and subjected to poor working conditions. Sexual representation otherwise should be safeguarded, and in the same spirit newer forms of expression (for gender and ethnic minorities, say) should be fostered. The object should not be to constrain men but to encourage women's sexuality. Legal restrictions tend to reinforce retrograde stereotypes of women and halt experimentation on the part of women, though Cornell does endorse zoning as a legitimate function of law.

That the arguments cross and recross familiar ground attests to the importance of the issue. A Gresham's law-justification of censorship articulated by Frank Michelman in "Conceptions of Democracy in American Constitutional Argument: The Case of Pornography Legislation" is that some forms of speech, such as pornography, actually make it impossible for other voices to be heard. In response, Ronald Dworkin answers the question "Do We Have a Right to Pornography?" in the affirmative: access to pornography must be guaranteed, he says, on the grounds that restrictions, however formulated, will still forestall exposure to all possible ideas. Feminists cannot justify censorship of pornography on the grounds that it "silences" women; to do so merely means suppressing some ideas to make way for others, and the Constitution forbids that. In "Women and Pornography," Dworkin says that if one really believes that pornography oppresses women and denies them a voice, then one must speak out in order to restore balance and combat bias, something women are, in fact, doing. Because he is one of the world's leading constitutional authorities, Dworkin's position incensed radical feminists. Ronald Dworkin and Catharine MacKinnon went head-to-head in "Pornography: An Exchange," which has the virtue of conciseness, though disciples of one or the other will probably not have their minds changed. (Dworkin has also edited *Morality, Harm, and the Law*, whose topics include sexual behavior, nude dancing, flag burning, and other pertinent legal issues.) Susan W. Easton, drawing on mostly British examples in *The Problem of Pornography: Regulation and the Right to Free Speech*, tries to counter Dworkin's endorsement of the right to pornography with discussion of the alleged harm pornography causes. As Easton sees it, pornography is "a testing ground for the use of law as a feminist strategy" (175). She thinks that restrictions on sexual speech are justifiable on the same grounds as regulations applied to national security, official secrets, and racial intolerance.

Noting such disputes in "The Apologetics of Suppression: The Regulation of Pornography as Act and Idea," S. G. Gey observes that current efforts to ban pornography stem from a "tolerance" model of expression that relies on moral certainty; permitted speech must serve a useful purpose, as determined by politicians or judges. A better basis for First Amendment protection of expression, he says, would be a scientific model that emphasizes skepticism as an ongoing process. Cass R. Sunstein proposes making distinctions among kinds of speech in "Pornography and the First Amendment." Since pornography is a substantial social problem (even if there is only a very modest correlation between expression and aggression against women), and pornographic expression is "low-value" speech and thus not entitled to the same degree of First Amendment protection, the law should not be neutral. The problem is defining pornography narrowly enough so that it can be regulated, but the certainty that some "viewpoints" would thereby be eliminated should not prevent legal action. Actually, says the author in a bold Orwellian argument, antipornography laws would enhance free speech, since they would ensure more room for the kinds of speech he prefers. Other useful essays by feminists for and against interdiction of sexual materials can be found in *Feminism and Censorship: The Current Debate*, edited by Gail Chester and Julienne Dickey, and in *Applications of Feminist Legal Theory to Women's Lives*, edited by D. Kelly Weisberg.

Leaving aside the dangers of defining pornography as exclusively male expression and leaving aside as well the dangers of curtailing the rights of males to protect females who may or may not be harmed by such expression, antisex feminists have called for the suppression of free speech at a period in which affirmative action and similar legislative initiatives are in retreat, if not disarray. The trend has not halted the flood of books and articles arguing for censorship on these grounds, however, and scholars will surely locate other texts.

COMMUNITY STANDARDS

In *Roth v. United States*, 354 U.S. 476 (1957), the Warren Court established the "redeeming social value" test. A work could be proscribed if "to the average person, applying contemporary community standards, the dominant theme of the material taken as a whole appeals to the prurient interests" and had no redeeming value. Community standards thus occupied the President's Commission on Obscenity and Pornography; several studies in volume IX of the *Technical Report*, entitled *The Consumer and the Community*, deal with different cities, but the overall assumption was that the standards were national, rather than local. In *Miller v. California*, 413 U.S. 15 (1973), the Burger Court redefined the test as "whether the work depicts or describes, in a patently offensive way, sexual conduct specifically defined by state law," which invited states to prohibit certain conduct, and "whether the work, taken as a whole, lacks serious literary, artistic, political or scientific value," a much weaker statement of the standard of *any* redeeming value set by *Roth*. The Burger opinion did make clear, however, that the majority had in mind *local* standards.

Sociologists immediately tried to discover whether the concept was feasible.

Tabulating responses by Detroit adults to explicit pictures, D. H. Wallace asserts in "A Survey on Obscenity and Contemporary Community Standards" that it is difficult to assess community response because there is no single standard by which people evaluate the material. Similarly, W. C. Wilson and H. I. Abelson said that while a large majority of adults reported being exposed at some time to explicit materials, reactions appeared to be determined as much by personality factors as by degrees of explicitness. Accordingly, data collected for their study, as reported in "Experience with and Attitudes toward Explicit Sexual Materials," did not support a "contemporary community standard" for judging such materials. Disturbed by such ambiguity, lawyers urged social scientists to use ever more precise public opinion polls to establish prevailing community standards regarding sex and its representation, as did Roderick A. Bell in "Determining Community Standards."

In "Community Standards, Conservatism, and Judgements of Pornography," Coke Brown, Joan Anderson, Linda Burggraf, and Neal Thompson concluded from their experiment that community standards can be established only in a very small community and that conservatism is the most reliable predictor of attitudes. Marc B. Glassman's "Community Standards of Patent Offensiveness: Public Opinion Data and Obscenity Law" analyzes opinion polls to find that none were reliable even in establishing that metropolitan areas are more liberal than smaller communities. D. Pritchard, J. P. Dilts, and D. Berkowitz sent questionnaires to local prosecutors in Indiana for their study "Prosecutors' Use of External Agendas in Prosecuting Pornography Cases." The results suggest that prosecutors are more likely to initiate cases if they perceive pornography to be high on citizen agendas or if the local press has an interest in running stories—not whether it is the right thing to do.

In *Ain't Nobody's Business If You Do: The Absurdity of Consensual Crimes in a Free Society*, Peter McWilliams underlines the waste, the futility, and, above all, the expense of attempting to punish and/or incarcerate those charged with acts to which the various parties have agreed. McWilliams includes a section entitled "Pornography, Obscenity, Etc." (585–596) as a particularly relevant illustration. A case in point is the subject of Leslie Maitland's article, "Bestiality Found of Little Appeal, Jury Acquits Movie Wholesaler." In the 1977 case in which a film distributor was charged with obscenity, the Manhattan jury viewed two films, *Man's Best Friend* and *Every Dog Has His Day*, in which men had sexual contact with German shepherds. The members of the jury applied the standard test, whether the material in question would "appeal to the prurient interest of average people," and found that bestiality did not. As Maitland reported, the judge, in acquitting the distributor, said to the jury, "if you're not aroused, it's not obscene." Given the community standards in Manhattan, there has not been an obscenity prosecution there since 1983, when yet another jury found that magazines and videos seized by police were not legally obscene, a fact noted by Steven Lee Meyers in "Obscenity Laws Exist, but What Breaks Them?" John Stossel's *Sex, Drugs, and Consenting Adults*, originally run on

ABC, decries the hypocrisy of laws and prosecutions of those society will not tolerate.

Richard L. Abel's *Speaking Respect, Respecting Speech* suggests that Americans argue continuously about the limits of speech because issues of identity overshadow many others. Abel explores gender, racial, and religious divisions and tries to steer a course between civil libertarians and "regulatory enthusiasts" by proposing a climate of discourse that amplifies silenced voices and soothes the injuries caused by extreme speech (such as pornography) through ceremonies of apology constructed by various communities. In "Is It Time to Overturn the Miller Standard?" Lloyd K. Stires insists that issues of obscene speech should be subject to considerations of whether it does harm, rather than whether it is popular or not, as the Miller standard holds.

Edward J. Shaughnessy and Diana Trebbi statistically computed community standards in *A Standard for Miller: A Community Response to Pornography* (1980), a report on averages in the community of Clinton (Manhattan), adjacent to Times Square, an area replete with adult bookstores, massage parlors, topless and bottomless bars, and so on. Asked for their opinions, people generally expressed more opposition to topless dancing and massage parlors than to adult bookstores. They mixed a general tolerance for adult expression with a desire to reduce the aggressive display of sexually explicit materials, to lessen harassment of passersby, to counter a perceived offensiveness to minors, and to combat the deterioration of the neighborhood. The study is interesting because of the variety of responses; some were absolutely opposed to explicit materials, but most supported the First Amendment rights of porn producers and distributors provided that they did not push the materials on others. "Regulating Pornography: A Public Dilemma," a survey conducted in 1990 by Margaret E. Thompson, Steven H. Chafee, and Hayg H. Oshagan, found that respondents of modestly sized communities in the West who feel most strongly that pornography has negative effects, particularly those involving male–female relationships, are also those most opposed to the regulation of pornography. Most respondents worried about the effects on other people, not themselves, but most felt that additional regulations were not the answer. The study is difficult to evaluate, however, because television shows like *Dynasty* and *Hill Street Blues*, not the sort of entertainment many Americans would call pornographic, were some of the examples used. A more persuasive study of the often-noted "other fellow" syndrome is Albert C. Gunther's "Overrating the X-Rating: The Third-Person Perception and Support for Censorship of Pornography." Using a large survey population, Gunther established that many Americans worried not about their own exposure to triple-X materials but about neighbors (real or imagined) who were perceived as mentally weak or morally deficient; suppressing such materials might prevent their fellow citizens from behaving badly.

Despite the Supreme Court's emphasis on local community standards, says P. J. Stevens in "Community Standards and Federal Obscenity Prosecutions," federal prosecutions against those accused of sending obscene materials through the mails create a *federal* standard of intolerance that the author believes chills free speech. Stevens reviews legal arguments regarding community standards to conclude that the only legitimate purpose of a national standard should be to permit states to enforce their own obscenity laws. But the smaller the community and the smaller the number of materials involved, the more problematic is the case based on community standards. In "A Bookstore Perishes: How an Obscenity Law Victimized a Respectable Business Woman," Beverly Jacobson tells the story of Carole Grant, owner of the only bookstore in Orem, Utah, who was forced out of business for selling books adjudged obscene (a very small fraction of her stock) by local standards. While the charges were later dropped, the expense killed the store, and the actual damage to the community's intellectual life was incalculable.

More disturbing is a prosecutorial tactic given legitimacy when the Court refused to review *Novick, Haim and Unique Specialities, Inc. v. U.S. District Court*, 423 U.S. 911 (1975). In that case, Louisiana applied its conservative local standards to seize materials passing through the state in transit from California to New York. The conviction opened the door for prosecutors to "shop for forums" in conservative communities where they could obtain convictions. One of the most celebrated recent cases involved the Thomases, operators of a California adult business, when they sent images that would be legal in California via the Internet to Memphis, Tennessee, where a jury decided that the images were illegal. Used to harass and persecute, forum shopping makes a joke out of the community standards test and raises ethical questions that the Justice Department declines to confront. (See also **Sex and Pornography Surveys** and **Hearings, Panels, Commissions, and Other Forums for Dramatizing Sexual Expression** in Chapter 5.)

NUISANCE LAWS

In 1977 Doug Rendleman's "Civilizing Pornography: The Case for an Exclusive Obscenity Nuisance Statute" identified one advantage of nuisance laws used against sexually oriented establishments: they provide civil sanctions rather than the severe criminal penalties that result from other types of obscenity prosecutions. Rendleman proposes a nuisance law he thinks will pass constitutional muster. "The New Weapons Being Used in Waging War against Pornography," a 1978 article by Harold P. Fahringer and Paul J. Cambria, discussed zoning regulations, building code violations, police harassment campaigns, and nuisance laws as low-profile, low-visibility, practical methods designed to avoid formal constitutional challenges. Fahringer and Cambria pointed out that all were open to abuse, especially by police using nuisance laws. T. L. Davis' "Defects in Indiana's Pornographic Nuisance Act" (1974) pointed out that nuisance laws do not provide adequate First Amendment safeguards, do not go to jury trials, and are a form of prior restraint that can inhibit expression; they are generally more vague than the standards established in *Miller v. California*. Even so, nuisance laws enjoyed a vogue in the early 1980s as a backstairs means of closing adult businesses. Denise M. Trauth and John L. Huffman's "Public Nuisance Laws: A New Mechanism for Film Censorship" focuses on North Carolina's attempt to use nuisance laws to restrict sexually explicit movies in 1982. R. L. Hughes worried that overzealous authorities would sweep away clearly protected material along with obscenity. In "Abating Obscenity as a Nuisance: An Easy Procedural Road for Prior Restraints," Hughes argued that enforcing civil nuisance laws to regulate obscenity is an exception to the rule that government must demonstrate the unprotected nature of any form of speech in that it proceeds from a relaxed burden of proof. In *Arcara v. Cloud Books, Inc.*, 478 U.S. 697 (1986), the Supreme Court upheld the use of nuisance-abatement ordinances to shutter adult emporiums in which sexual contact took place, but only after less drastic measures had been advanced. (Even so, says Arthur Leonard in *Sexuality and the Law*, the higher court's upholding of the *Arcara* decision on grounds of improper "safety and sanitation" led the New York State Supreme Court to reconsider the case; the lower court held that the First Amendment was in jeopardy.) The Supreme Court was more prone, however, to greenlight the use of zoning regulations to control adult businesses; two decisions, *Young v. American Mini Theaters*, 327 U.S. 50 (1976), and *City of Renton v. Playtime Theatres, Inc.*, 475 U.S. 41 (1986), were crucial.

ANTIDISPLAY ORDINANCES AND ZONING LEGISLATION

"What Is a Civil Libertarian to Do When Pornography Becomes So Bold?" asked Paul Goodman of archliberal Gay Talese and archconservative Ernest van den Haag in 1976. Van den Haag admitted that he supported government intervention in private matters—very much against his conservative principles—on the grounds that family structure has deteriorated to the point that parents cannot supervise their children. For his part, Talese—opposed to intervention in private life—admitted that pornography can assault the senses indiscriminately and that governments might have a case for regulating the *public* display of sexual materials, where children might be exposed, so long as there was no intent to prevent private access to such materials by adults. Courts in recent years have tended to uphold laws designed to shield unwilling or unwitting citizens rather than prohibit expression; such statutes, say their advocates, do the least harm to the First Amendment and to the free circulation of ideas. In some cases, the issues usually come down to what constitutes a *public* venue. As William E. Brigman points out in "Pornography or Group Libel: The Indianapolis Sex Discrimination Ordinance," the forcing of pornography on unwilling audiences in the workplace might constitute sexual harassment and a violation of civil rights, and generally courts have moved in that direction. Large-scale regulation usually takes the form of zoning ordinances, which can be concerned with quality-of-life matters but must not be attacks on expression—a point that inspires contention. W. M. Sunkel, reviewing the Rehnquist majority opinion and the

Brennan dissent in *"City of Renton v. Playtime Theatres, Inc*: Court-Approved Censorship through Zoning," concluded that the Renton ordinance should have been struck down because it is not a content-neutral regulation.

One of the first comprehensive texts on zoning and licensing sex-related enterprises was William Toner's *Regulating Sex Businesses*. Case studies included Norwalk, California; New Orleans; Boston; Fairfax County, Virginia; and Santa Maria, California. Toner pointed out that most zoning experiments stem from Detroit's original "anti-skid-row" ordinances adopted in 1962. The Supreme Court upheld these ordinances in 1976 (*Young v. American Mini Theaters*), ruling that neither the due process clause nor the equal protection clause of the Fourteenth Amendment was violated. The First Amendment was not at issue because the city made no moral judgment on the sex business and did not attempt to prosecute on grounds of expression; it simply listed the kinds of activities that were to be kept distant from other businesses, residential neighborhoods, and institutions such as schools and churches. Nonetheless, Toner observed, cities must be careful to adapt Court decisions to conditions applicable in their communities, to separate intent to censor from zoning, to pass no judgment on the content of expression, and—most important—actually to provide accessible zones where such businesses may operate. Zoning may take two forms: concentration of sex businesses into one area or dispersal to outlying regions. Although a more constitutionally ambiguous strategy, licensing of businesses may regulate operating hours, safety, cleanliness, and so on, but, again, may not pass judgment on content.

The same year Toner published his book, Jane M. Friedman pointed out in "Zoning 'Adult' Movies: The Potential Impact of *Young v. American Mini Theaters*," that zoning concerning adult theaters turns on the difficulty of defining an adult theater, so that in theory any theater that showed films aimed at mature audiences could be zoned away. Her article is interesting because it illustrates how technology can render a question largely moot, since video recorders have pretty much killed off theaters specializing in pornographic films. The spread of sexual expression on the Internet will doubtless also take some of the sting out of zoning regulations. Still, zoning laws can obviously be abused by zealots or unscrupulous prosecutors seeking to remove bookstores vulnerable because they sell a few books the censors do not like; if the history of sexual expression teaches anything, it is that there is no form so innocent that it will not invoke the ire of a censor. In 1981 the Supreme Court placed limits on zoning of sex-related businesses in *Schad v. Mt. Ephraim*, 452 U.S. 61, by forbidding a municipality to eliminate such businesses entirely.

In 1986, when the Supreme Court killed the antiporn, feminist-inspired Indianapolis ordinance, it upheld local laws zoning sex enterprises. Stuart Taylor reports on the latter decision in "High Court Backs Use of Zoning to Regulate Showing of Sex Films": the Court reaffirmed the right of municipalities to zone adult theaters showing sexual films. Arthur S. Leonard points out in *Sexuality and the Law: An Encyclopedia of Major Legal Cases* that the assumptions behind the decision in that case (*City of Renton v. Playtime Theatres, Inc.*) have withstood scrutiny. In "Putting Porno in Its Place," *The Wall Street Journal* predicted that the First Amendment will continue to shield expression but that local communities, especially small or rural ones, will increasingly resort to zoning to restrict the distribution of explicit material. In "The Legal Case for Restricting Pornography," A. E. Sears also estimates that the most successful attempts to regulate sexual materials will involve measures like zoning and antidisplay ordinances; Sears thinks that myriad regulations already in force can satisfy the public's concern. Curtis J. Sitomer provides an overview of censorship campaigns in cities such as Indianapolis and Minneapolis but also in Los Angeles and New York, with particular reference to the 1986 law in New York prohibiting the open display of sex-oriented materials in "Sifting Out Pornography from Free Speech." Legal justifications for suppressing speech are shaped by the political environment, says H. L. Schachter in "The Pornography Debate in the United States: Politics, Law and Justification." He reviews antiporn, feminist (civil rights) rationales and zoning (land-use) ordinances and finds that while both are expedients adopted by their advocates to sway officials, the latter are more pragmatic. Charles Millard proposes that New York City also pass a zoning law restricting sex-related businesses like adult bookstores and topless bars in residential areas in "Stop the Porn Explosion." Millard does not oppose pornography but sees the spread of such enterprises as a "quality-of-life" issue. In fact, New York has applied zoning regulations in its effort to "clean up" Times Square and has exempted very few sex-oriented businesses; court challenges involving the degree of access—whether citizens who wish to visit adult bookstores, for example, will have to travel too far—slowed, but did not stop, this form of regulation.

COURTROOMS AND JURISTS

Many biographies of eminent justices include comment on famous obscenity rulings. Gerald Gunther writes about perhaps the most pivotal justice in the evolution of American law on sexual materials in *Learned Hand: The Man and the Judge*, an admiring look at the intellectual power the jurist could marshal. Moretti, de Grazia, and Leonard (see earlier) present finely wrought portraits of jurists such as Augustus and Learned Hand, John M. Woolsey, Earl Warren, and William Douglas. Warren himself reviews the evolution of obscenity law toward a realistic appraisal of the prominent place of sexual expression in American culture in "Obscenity Laws: A Shift to Reality." Walter Berns launches a very literate attack on "libertarian" jurists in *Freedom, Virtue and the First Amendment*; Berns' favorite target is Supreme Court Justice William Douglas. The late Justice Douglas was (with Hugo Black) a First Amendment absolutist on the Court; he argued that the statement "Congress shall make no law abridging freedom of speech . . ." allowed for no exceptions for sexual expression. Douglas' *The Douglas Opinions* includes excerpts from the justice's many dissents from the majority in cases of censorship. In "Justice Brennan's Struggle with Obscenity Law: The Evolution of Supreme Court Doctrine, 1957–1973," W. McKeen traces the mutations in Brennan's early position, which was that obscenity was not protected by the First Amendment. Trying to impose logic, Brennan adopted the doctrine of "redeeming social importance," which mitigated obscenity, developed most of the language used in the Court's decisions, and eventually, despairing of ever sufficiently defining what obscenity was, joined those who took an absolutist position: that the First Amendment *did* protect *all* expression. Bruce Murphy recaps how the perceived liberal position of Abe Fortas on sexual materials contributed to his failure to win confirmation as chief justice in *Fortas: The Rise and Ruin of a Supreme Court Justice.* Richard F. Hixson patiently breaks out opinions and delineates personalities in *Pornography and the Justices: The Supreme Court and the Intractable Obscenity Problem.*

Lawyers such as Morris Ernst have extracted drama from courtroom performances. With his partner Alexander Lindey, Ernst wrote *Hold Your Tongue: Adventures in Libel and Slander,* a discussion of libel law in Britain and the United States, with some reference to obscenity, with which libel had traditionally been conflated. Ernst and Alan U. Schwartz wrote *Censorship: The Search for the Obscene* to document the expansion of protections afforded by the First Amendment through key court decisions. Two of Ernst's colleagues, Arthur Garfield Hayes and Paul Blanchard, also published defenses of the First Amendment, though Hayes' *Let Freedom Ring* and Blanchard's *The Right to Read* lack the verve of Ernst's volumes. (See also **Period Commentaries** in Chapter 16, Rembar.) More recently, Martin Garbus with Stanley Cohen has published his memoir, *Tough Talk: How I Fought for Writers, Comics, Bigots, and the American Way,* to recount his defenses of Lenny Bruce, Samuel Beckett, and other victims of censorship. Even when they win, prosecutors of First Amendment cases, perhaps conscious that history will not deal kindly with them, rarely write about successful suppressions. An exception is *Foolish Figleaves? Pornography in—and Out of—Court,* written by Richard Kuh, a New York district attorney who recommends measures against the public display of sexually explicit materials and for shielding minors from alleged effects. The book is curious in its ambivalence and is essential for understanding the degree to which political ambition and motivation have traditionally framed the issue of censorship.

Historically pertinent are Theodore Schroeder's *Freedom of the Press and "Obscene" Literature* and *"Obscene" Literature and Constitutional Law.* The first, published in 1906, argues that obscenity exists in the eye of the beholder and that it should not be recognized in law as having any objective status. The second, published in 1911, is a primer for defense lawyers of the period; the citations indicate just how long prosecution had been going on and how necessary were effective countermeasures for those accused. That Schroeder published the books privately is a reminder that defending marginal literature was a touchy subject in the first decade of the century. The strategies Schroeder recommended—employing expert witnesses, arguing that single passages did not taint a whole work, and standing firm on the First Amendment—were novel for the time but set patterns for future courtroom practice. By 1926 defense attorneys were beginning to prevail. *Criminal Obscenity: A Plea for Its Suppression*, by John Ford, is a New York State judge's tract against "hedonistic" texts that lobbies for "clean books" and swift prosecution of those that are not; it is notable because it calls for forbidding "expert witnesses" to testify in behalf of evil literature and for revising statutes to permit condemning a book on the basis of a single passage. Ford was responding to *Halsey v. New York Society for the Suppression of Vice* (180 N.Y.S. 836), a ruling that a book should be evaluated as a whole, not just in terms of isolated passages, and that qualified critics rather than smut-hunters should be asked for their opinions.

Three texts from the 1970s contain information of use to lawyers. William E. Ringel's *Obscenity Law Today* was a handbook for lawyers defending cases in various media. Frederick F. Schauer's *The Law of Obscenity* covered every kind of legislation from mail regulations to a host of other statutes. It listed all the acts that individual states considered obscene and was useful, since the depiction of an act that Oregon considered obscene might not distress the citizens of California. Donald B. Sharp's collection, *Commentaries on Obscenity*, was also aimed at lawyers. Nathaniel Sheppard's 1977 article "Bar Group Debates Pornography and Effects That It Has on Society" reported on a group of attorneys arguing various aspects of pornography and alleged effects outside of court; it is a good barometer of legal opinion during that period.

Laws governing sexual behavior always shimmer in the background of obscenity cases; because they prescribe levels of "normality," their influence is muted but significant. Scholars may thus wish to consult works such as Walter Barnett's *Sexual Freedom and the Constitution* and Samuel D. Kling's *Sexual Behavior and the Law*. Both are now dated dissertations on the scope and constitutionality of state and federal laws governing sexual behavior and, more tangentially, sexual representation and expression; both break down notable cases. Justice Richard A. Posner calls for greater rationality in the legal arena in his examination of the sometimes-illogical laws governing both sexual behavior and sexual expression in *Sexual Reason*. For example, in responding to antiporn, feminist claims that pornography is the ideological expression of patriarchy and misogyny, Posner observes that such messages would then be *doubly* protected as both sexual and political discourse (381–382). G. Sidney Buchanan asks whether government can regulate sexual behavior, homosexuality in particular, in *Morality, Sex, and the Constitution: A Christian Perspective on the Power of Government to Regulate Private Sexual Conduct between Consenting Adults*. Buchanan notes that decriminalization of many forms of behavior is an established fact but argues that moral suasion is still useful.

The relevance of expert witnesses continues to arise, as indicated by William E. Brigman's "The Controversial Role of the Expert in Obscenity Legislation." Despite problems, says Brigman, experts should be allowed to testify in obscenity trials in order to help jurors interpret often vague guidelines. The opinions of the expert witness, a staple in courtrooms since the turn of the century, are usually ignored, says Ruth McGaffey in "A Realistic Look at Expert Witnesses in Obscenity Cases." *Sexual Science and the Law*, by Richard Green, is a fascinating study of how the findings of sex researchers, including those who investigate pornography, can inform debate on all aspects of sexuality and the law, from abortion prostitution, homosexuality, and transsexualism, to pornography and related issues. Green also delivered a paper called "The Expert Witness" to the World Conference on Pornography in 1998. His paper, and two others, Marilyn A. Fithian's "Importance of Knowledge as an Expert Witness," and William Simon's "The Social Scientist as Expert Witness," all of which recount the experience of serving as witnesses, are included in *Porn 101: Eroticism, Pornography, and the First Amendment*, edited by James Elias, Veronica Diehl Elias, Vern L. Bullough, Gwen Brewer, Jeffrey J. Douglas, and Will Jarvis. Fithian's essay contains a splendid bibliography on the subject, but many other essays in the volume, especially those on issues of law, are short on substance.

Chapters in Dave Marsh's *Fifty Ways to Fight Censorship; and Important Facts to Know about the Censors* list addresses and phone numbers of organizations committed to constitutional protection of expression, sources of information on censorship groups, and strategies for combating them, from joining local libraries to checking on the tax-exempt status of extremist groups. Pages 26–29 of *The Meese Commission Exposed*, edited by Arlene Carmen et al., list ways for concerned citizens to combat censorship in their communities. The National Coalition against Censorship publishes *Censorship News*, a newsletter on recent attempts by various groups to suppress expression in schools, libraries, or other venues. Several organizations maintain Web sites in favor of free expression and offer information about specific cases of suppression or harassment. Among those dedicated to combating censorship are Feminists for Free Expression; the American Civil Liberties Union; Free Expression Clearinghouse (which speaks for some thirty groups); Institute for First Amendment Studies; People for the American Way; and Playboy Forum.

Experience in successful prosecutions by opponents of pornography is encapsulated in two reference tools published by the National Obscenity Law Center, a division of Morality in Media, Inc. The first is the *Obscenity Law Reporter*, whose two volumes summarize successful prosecutions in the United States, and George Weaver's *Handbook on the Prosecution of Obscenity Cases*, a guide for would-be censors. "The Porn Fighters" (1974) announced the establishment of the National Legal Data Center, which serves local prosecutors who wish to censor. The National Family Legal Foundation offers municipalities help in developing "stringent and constitutionally-sound ordinances to control adult businesses." Robert D. Reed and Danek S. Kaus have written *Pornography: How and Where to Find Facts and Get Help*. Among Web sites devoted to opposing pornography are American Family Association; the Andrea Dworkin Web Site;

Christian Coalition; Eagle Forum (Phyllis Schlafly); Traditional Values Coalition; Struggling with Pornography; and the Institute for Media Education (Judith Reisman).

Beyond the Pornography Commission: The Federal Response, by the U.S. Justice Department, contains proposals for implementing the ninety-two recommendations for combating pornography made by the Meese Commission. These recommendations included formation of citizens' pressure groups, the use of RICO legislation, creation of a National Obscenity Enforcement Unit, the filing of multiple, simultaneous prosecutions in different states so that at least one will stick, and so on. Philip Shenon's article, "Justice Department Plans Anti-Racketeering Drive against Pornographers," covered Attorney General Meese's plans to use the Racketeer Influenced and Corrupt Organizations statute, or RICO, against "major distributors" of pornography. The statute permits authorities to seize all of the assets of individuals or businesses, even if only a small number of materials are found to be obscene. Civil libertarians oppose the move, says Shenon, but the Reverend Donald Wildmon of the American Family Association praises it. In "X-Rated Raids," Stephen Rae describes such operations, noting that from 1987 to 1990, obscenity prosecutions jumped 400 percent. In 1991 officials arrested James Wasson, a director of gay films, Paul Thomas (real name Phil Toubus), a director of straight films, and Steven Hirsch and David James, owners of Vivid Films, charging them with conspiracy to distribute obscene films. Rae suggests that the real conspirators are the members of National Obscenity Enforcement Unit, orchestrators of the busts, who carefully set up video shops in conservative local areas, ordered hard-core films from distributors like Vivid, and then charged them with violating the standards of the small communities. Rae points out that the FBI itself is concerned about the zealousness of these self-appointed prosecutors, especially their contempt for civil rights and individual liberties. The American Civil Liberties Union calls the National Obscenity Enforcement Unit antiporn crusade "a constitutionally renegade operation" in *Above the Law: The Justice Department's War against the First Amendment*. The courts themselves worry about authorities' overstepping the law, reports Stephen Labaton in "Justices Restrict Ability to Seize Suspects' Goods." Ruling in *Alexander v. United States*, the Supreme Court in 1993 undercut RICO tactics by restricting the ability of prosecutors to seize property in obscenity cases on Eighth Amendment, but not First Amendment, grounds.

CURRENT STATE OF THE LAW

Two excellent and succinct reviews of the current state of pornography legislation are Lauren Robel's "Pornography and Existing Law: What the Law Can Do," written from a feminist perspective, and William Brigman's "Politics and the Pornography Wars," written from a civil libertarian perspective. Both cite numerous court cases that will be unfamiliar to many Americans, the first to indicate the steps that antiporn feminists have taken to revise concepts of free speech, the second to document the abuses of government in suppressing expression. Current decisions of U.S. Courts of Appeals for all districts can be found in the *Federal Reporter*. Decisions by the Supreme Court are reprinted in *United States Reports*. Some information on prosecutions of pornography can be found in *Crime in the United States*, the Uniform Crime Reports published annually by the FBI. More recently, *Gauntlet: Exploring the Limits of Free Expression* has come to serve as a popular clearinghouse of information on notable cases.

NOTES

1. *The Secret Museum: Pornography in Modern Culture* (New York: Viking, 1987).
2. Neil A. Lewis, "U.S. Restrictions on Adult-TV Fare Are Struck Down," *New York Times*, 24 November 1993, p. A1.
3. "Forum," *Playboy*, 40:9 (September 1993): 54–55.

REFERENCES

Abel, Richard L. *Speaking Respect, Respecting Speech*. Chicago: University of Chicago Press, 1998.

Adler, Amy. "Photography on Trial." *Index on Censorship*, 25: 3 (May 1996): 141–146.

Adult Video News. Upper Darby, PA, 1983–1996; Van Nuys, CA, 1996–.

"Alabama Indictments Force Satellite Porn Programmer Out of Business." *Television Broadcast*, 13 June 1990, p. 13.

Alexander, Alison, and Janice Hanson, eds. *Taking Sides: Clashing Views on Controversial Issues in Mass Media and Society*. 2d ed. Guilford, CT: Dushkin, 1993.

Alexander, Priscilla. "Speaking Out: A Response to Andrea Dworkin." *Gay Community News*, 8 February 1986, p. 5.

Alshuler, Martha. "Origins of the Law of Obscenity." *Technical Report of the Commission on Obscenity and Pornography*. 9 Vols. Washington: Government Printing Office, 1971–1972, II, 65–71.

American Civil Liberties Union. *Above the Law: The Justice Department's War against the First Amendment*. New York: ACLU, 1991.

———. *Censorship of Comic Books: A Statement in Opposition on Civil Liberties Grounds*. New York: ACLU, 1955.

———. *What Shocked the Censors: A Complete Record of Cuts in Motion Picture Films Ordered by the New York State Censors*. New York: National Council on Freedom Forum/ACLU, 1933.

American Civil Liberties Union. http://www.aclu.org.

American Family Association. http://www.afa.net.

Andrea Dworkin Web Site. http://www.igc.apc.org/womensnet/dworkin.

Andrews, Edmund L. "A Crusader against Cyberporn Who Was Once Involved in a Sex Scandal." *New York Times*, 27 November 1995, p. A8.

———. "Government Seeks to Extend Ban on Broadcast of Offensive Shows." *New York Times*, 13 July 1990, pp. A1, B6.

Aperture. The Body in Question, issue no. 121 (1990).

Atcheson, Dorothy. "Defending Pornography: Face-to-Face with the President of the ACLU." *Playboy*, 42:2 (February 1995): 37–39, 108.

Atkins, Robert. "Some Print, Others Won't." *Village Voice*, 19 February 1991, p. 105.

Attorney General's Commission. *Attorney General's Commission on Pornography: Final Report*. 2 vols. Washington, DC: Government Printing Office, 1986.

Austin, Bruce A., ed. *Current Research in Film: Audiences, Economics, and Law*. 4 vols. Norwood, NJ: Ablex, 1985.

Baker, C. Edwin. "First Amendment Protection for Gays." *New York Times*, 27 July 1991, p. 15.

Banned Books. 4 vols. New York: Facts on File, 1998. Vol. I: Nicholas J. Karolides. *Literature Suppressed on Political Grounds*; vol. II: Margaret Bald. *Literature Repressed on Religious Grounds*; vol. III: Dawn B. Sova. *Literature Suppressed on Social Grounds*; vol. IV: Dawn B. Sova. *Literature Suppressed on Sexual Grounds*.

Banned Books Online. www.cs.cmu.edu/Web/People/spok/

Barnett, Walter. *Sexual Freedom and the Constitution*. Albuquerque: University of New Mexico Press, 1973.

Bekken, Jon. " 'These Great and Dangerous Powers': Postal Censorship of the Press." *Journal of Communication Inquiry*, 15:1 (Winter 1991): 55–71.

Bell, Roderick A. "Determining Community Standards." *ABA Journal*, 63 (September 1977): 1202–1207.

Benjamin, Louise M. "Defining the Public Interest and Protecting the Public Welfare in the 1920s: Parallels between Radio and Movie Regulation." *Historical Journal of Film, Radio and Television*, 12:1 (1992): 87–101.

Bennett, Georgette. "Purveying Prurience." *Crime Warps: The Future of Crime in America*. Garden City, NY: Anchor Press/Doubleday, 1987, pp. 188–200.

Bensman, Marvin R. *Broadcast Regulation: Selected Cases and Decisions*. 3d ed. Lanham, MD: University Press of America, 1990.

Berger, Fred R. *Freedom, Rights, and Pornography: A Collection of Papers*, ed. Bruce Russell. Dordrecht, Netherlands: Kluwer Academic Publishers, 1991.

Berns, Walter. *Freedom, Virtue and the First Amendment*. Chicago: Henry Regnery, 1965.

Bernstein, Richard. "Arts Endowment's Opponents Are Fighting Fire with Fire." *New York Times*, 30 May 1990, pp. C13, 15.

———. "Judge Halts Publication of Pamphlet." *New York Times*, 26 June 1990, p. C20.

Black, Gregory D. *Hollywood Censored: Morality Codes, Catholics, and the Movies*. Cambridge, England: Cambridge University Press, 1994.

Blanchard, Paul. *The Right to Read*. Boston: Beacon Press, 1956.

Bolton, Richard, ed. *The Contest of Meaning: Critical Histories of Photography*. Cambridge: MIT Press, 1989.

———. *Culture Wars: Documents from the Recent Controversies in the Arts*. New York: New Press, 1992.

Bosmajian, Haig A. "Obscenity, Sexism, and Freedom of Speech." *College English*, 39 (March 1978): 812–819.

———, ed. *Obscenity and Freedom of Expression*. New York: Burt Franklin, 1976.

Boyer, Paul S. *Purity in Print: The Vice-Society Movement and Book Censorship in America*. New York: Scribner's, 1968.

Brenner, D. L. "Censoring the Airwaves: The Supreme Court's *Pacifica* Decision." *Free but Regulated,* ed. D. L. Brenner and W. L. Rivers. Ames: Iowa State University Press, 1982, pp. 175–181.

Briceno, Carlos. " 'Dial-a-Porn' Industry Battles U.S. Restrictions." *New York Times,* 13 April 1990, p. B5.

Brigman, William E. "The Controversial Role of the Expert in Obscenity Legislation." *Capital University Law Review,* 7 (1978): 519–551.

———. "Politics and the Pornography Wars." *Wide Angle,* 19:3 (1997): 149–170.

———. "Pornography or Group Libel: The Indianapolis Sex Discrimination Ordinance." *Indiana Law Review,* 18:2 (1985): 479–505.

The Brooklyn Museum. *The Brooklyn Museum Collection: The Play of the Unmentionable,* curated by Joseph Kosuth. Brooklyn, NY: Brooklyn Museum, 1990.

Brown, Carol F. "Cable TV Censorship: Black Out 'Midnight Blue.' " *Village Voice,* 4 May 1976, p. 126.

Brown, Coke, Joan Anderson, Linda Burggraf, and Neal Thompson. "Community Standards, Conservatism, and Judgments of Pornography." *Journal of Sex Research,* 14 (May 1978): 81–95.

Brown, T. Allston. *A History of the New York Stage from 1732 to 1901.* 3 vols. New York: Dodd, Mead, 1903.

Buchanan, G. Sidney. *Morality, Sex, and the Constitution: A Christian Perspective on the Power of Government to Regulate Private Sexual Conduct between Consenting Adults.* Lanham, MD: University Press of America, 1985.

Bulletin of the Adult Film Association of America. Los Angeles, 1979–1982.

Burstyn, Varda. "Women, Sex and the State." *Women against Censorship,* ed. Varda Burstyn. Vancouver: Douglas and McIntyre, 1985, pp. 4–31.

Butler, Twiss. "Abortion and Pornography: The Sexual Liberals' 'Gotcha' against Women's Equality." *The Sexual Liberals and the Attack on Feminism,* ed. Dorchen Leidholdt and Janice G. Raymond. New York: Pergamon Press, 1990, pp. 114–122.

Carlin, David R., Jr. "Hegel and Pornography: The Limits of Personal Taste." *Commonweal,* 1 November 1985, pp. 599–600.

Carlyle-Gordge, Peter. "An Erotic Error That Titillates." *Macleans,* 93:6 (30 June 1980): 19–20.

Carmen, Arlene, et al. *The Meese Commission Exposed: Proceedings of a National Coalition against Censorship Public Information Briefing on the Attorney General's Commission on Pornography, January 16, 1986.* New York: National Coalition against Censorship [1322 West 43d Street, New York City 10036], 1987.

Carmen, Ira H. *Movies, Censorship, and the Law.* Ann Arbor: University of Michigan Press, 1966.

Carmilly-Weinberger, Moshe. *Fear of Art: Censorship and Freedom of Expression in Art.* New York: Bowker, 1986.

Carr, E. A. "Feminism, Pornography, and the First Amendment: An Obscenity-Based Analysis of Proposed Antipornography Laws." *UCLA Law Review,* 34:4 (April 1987): 1265–1304.

Carter, T. Barton, M. A. Franklin, and J. B. Wright. *The First Amendment and the Fourth Estate: Regulation of Electronic Mass Media.* 2d ed. Westbury, NY: Foundation Press, 1989.

Censorship in the Comics. Princeton, NJ: Films for the Humanities and Sciences, 1994.

Chaffee, Zechariah. *Free Speech in the United States*. Cambridge: Harvard University Press, 1941.

Chandos, John, ed. *"To Deprave and Corrupt . . .": Original Studies in the Nature and Definition of "Obscenity."* London: Souvenir Press, 1962.

Charisse, Marc S. "Brothels in the Marketplace of Ideas: Defining Commercial Speech." *Communications and the Law*, 12:3 (September 1990): 3–19.

Chester, Gail, and Julienne Dickey, eds. *Feminism and Censorship: The Current Debate*. Bridgeport, CT: Prism Press, 1988.

Christian Coalition. http://cc.org.

Clapp, Jane. *Art Censorship: A Chronology of Proscribed and Prescribed Art*. Metuchen, NJ: Scarecrow Press, 1972.

Clor, Harry M. *Obscenity and Public Morality: Censorship in a Liberal Society*. Chicago: University of Chicago Press, 1969.

———, ed. *Censorship and Freedom of Expression: Essays on Obscenity and the Law*. Chicago: Rand-McNally, 1971.

Cole, Wendy. "The Marquis de Cyberspace." *Time*, 3 July 1995, p. 43.

Colker, Ruth. "Pornography and Privacy: Towards the Development of a Group-Based Theory for Sex-Based Intrusions of Privacy." *Law and Inequality: A Journal of Theory and Practice*, 1 (1983): 191, 201–205.

Collins, Glenn. "Guidance or Censorship? New Debate on Rating Films." *New York Times*, 9 April 1990, pp. C11, C17.

Collins, Ronald K. L., and David M. Skover, produced by Bruce Mau. *The Death of Discourse*. Boulder, CO: Westview Press, 1996.

Comic Book Legal Defense Fund. http://www.edgeglobal.com/cbldf.

"Comics under Fire." *Playboy*, 43:9 (September 1996): 45.

Congressional Quarterly. Washington, DC, 1972–.

Copp, David, and Susan Wendell, eds. *Pornography and Censorship*. Buffalo, NY: Prometheus Books, 1983.

Cornell, Drucilla. *The Imaginary Domain: Abortion, Pornography and Sexual Harassment*. New York: Routledge, 1995.

Cossman, Brenda, Shannon Bell, Lise Gotell, and Becki L. Ross. *Bad Attitude/s on Trial: Pornography, Feminism, and the Butler Decision*. Toronto: University of Toronto Press, 1997.

"Court Rejects U.S. Appeal on Obscenity Ban." *New York Times*, national ed. 30 August 1991, p. A18.

Cowan, Geoffrey. *See No Evil: The Backstage Battle over Sex and Violence in Television*. New York: Simon and Schuster, 1979.

Craig, Alec. *Above All Liberties*. London: Allen and Unwin, 1942.

———. *Suppressed Books: A History of the Conception of Literary Obscenity*. Cleveland: World Publishing, 1963.

Davis, Douglas. "Art and Contradiction: Helms, Censorship, and the Serpent." *Art in America*, 78:5 (May 1990): 55–61.

Davis, T. L. "Defects in Indiana's Pornographic Nuisance Act." *Indiana Law Journal*, 49 (1974): 320–333.

Day, J. Edward. "Mailing Lists and Pornography." *American Bar Association Journal*, 52:12 (December 1966): 1103–1109.

de Grazia, Edward. *Censorship Landmarks*. New York: Bowker, 1969.

————. *Girls Lean Back Everywhere: The Law of Obscenity and the Assault on Genius*. New York: Random House, 1992.

————. "Obscenity, Censorship and the Mails I." *The New Republic*, 23 January 1956, p. 16.

de Grazia, Edward, and Roger K. Newman. *Banned Films: Movies, Censors and the First Amendment*. New York: Bowker, 1982.

Dee, Juliet L. "From 'Pure Speech' to Dial-a-Porn: Negligence, First Amendment Law and the Hierarchy of Protected Speech." *Communication and the Law*, 13:4 (December 1991): 27–73.

The Deep Throat Papers. New York: Manor Books, 1973.

Delgado, Richard, and Jean Stefancic. "Overcoming Legal Barriers to Regulating Hate Speech on Campuses." *Chronicle of Higher Education*, 11 August 1993, pp. B1–B3.

————. "Pornography and Harm to Women: 'No Empirical Evidence'?" *Failed Revolutions: Social Reform and the Limits of Legal Imagination*. Boulder, CO: Westview Press, 1994, pp. 81–92.

Demac, Donna A. *Liberty Denied: The Current Rise of Censorship in America*. New York: PEN, 1989.

Demas, Jeff. "Seven Dirty Words: Did They Help Define Indecency?" *Communication and the Law*, 20:3 (September 1998): 39–52.

Dershowitz, Alan. "Screwing Around with the First Amendment." *Penthouse*, 8: 5 (January 1977): 106–107, 142–143.

Dhavan, Rajeev, and Christian Davies, eds. *Censorship and Obscenity*. Totowa, NJ: Rowman and Littlefield, 1978.

"Digital Sex: Technology, Law and Censorship." Special issue of *New Media*, 3:4 (April 1993).

Docter, Sharon. "An Alternative Justification for Regulating Broadcast Indecency." *Journal of Broadcasting and Electronic Media*, 36: 2 (Spring 1992): 245–247.

Douglas, William. *The Douglas Opinions*, ed. Vern Countryman. New York: Random House, 1977.

Dovring, Karin. "Troubles with Mass Communication and Semantic Differentials in 1744 and Today." *American Behavioral Scientist*, 8:1 (1965): 9–14.

"Down Boy! Censorship Bites Back." *Inside Out: Ohio's College Magazine* (Summer 1992): 12.

Dubin, Steven C. *Arresting Images: Impolitic Art and Uncivil Actions*. New York: Routledge, 1992.

Duggan, Lisa, Nan D. Hunter, and Carole S. Vance. "False Promises: Feminist Antipornography Legislation." *Women against Censorship*, ed. Varda Burstyn. Vancouver: Douglas and McIntyre, 1985, pp. 130–151; rpt. *Caught Looking: Feminism, Pornography, and Censorship*, by the Feminist Anti-Censorship Task Force. New York: Caught Looking, 1986, pp. 72–84.

Dworkin, Andrea. *Pornography: Men Possessing Women*. New York: Putnam's, 1980.

————. *Woman Hating*. New York: Dutton, 1974.

Dworkin, Andrea, and Catharine A. MacKinnon. *Pornography and Civil Rights: A New Day for Women's Equality*. Minneapolis: Organizing against Pornography, 1988.

Dworkin, Ronald. "Do We Have a Right to Pornography?" *A Matter of Principle*. New York: Oxford University Press, 1986, pp. 335–372; rpt. *The Problem of Pornography*, ed. Susan Dwyer. Belmont, CA: Wadsworth, 1995, pp. 77–90.

————. *Morality, Harm, and the Law*. Boulder, CO: Westview, 1994.

————. "Women and Pornography." *The New York Review of Books*, 21 October 1993, pp. 15–21.

Dworkin, Ronald, and Catharine MacKinnon. "Pornography: An Exchange." *The New York Review of Books*, 3 March 1994, pp. 47–49.

Eagle Forum. http://www.basenet.net/~eagle.

Easton, Susan W. *The Problem of Pornography: Regulation and the Right to Free Speech*. New York: Routledge, 1994.

Eisenberg, Daniel. "Toward a Bibliography of Erotic Pulps." *Journal of Popular Culture*, 15:4 (Spring 1982): 175–184.

Elias, James, Veronica Diehl Elias, Vern L. Bullough, Gwen Brewer, Jeffrey J. Douglas, and Will Jarvis, eds. *Porn 101: Eroticism, Pornography, and the First Amendment*. Amherst, NY: Prometheus Books, 1999.

Ellis, Albert. *Suppressed: Seven Key Essays Publishers Dared Not Print*. New York: New Classics House, 1965.

Ellison, Alfred. *Oral Sex and the Law*. San Diego: Academy Press, 1970.

Ernst, Morris L. *The Best Is Yet*. New York: Harper and Brothers, 1945.

Ernst, Morris L., and Alexander Lindey. *Hold Your Tongue: Adventures in Libel and Slander*. London: Methuen, 1936.

Ernst, Morris L., and Pare Lorentz. *Censored: The Private Life of the Movie*. New York: Jonathan Cape, 1930.

Ernst, Morris L., and Alan U. Schwartz. *Censorship: The Search for the Obscene*. New York: Macmillan, 1965.

Ernst, Morris L., and William Seagle. *To the Pure . . . : A Study of Obscenity and the Censor*. New York: Viking, 1928.

Fahringer, Harold P., and Paul J. Cambria. "The New Weapons Being Used in Waging War against Pornography." *Capital University Law Review*, 7 (1978): 553–578.

Faines, G. P. "Obscenity, Cable Television, and the First Amendment: Will FCC Regulation Impair the Marketplace of Ideas?" *Duquesne Law Review*, 21 (1983): 965–993.

Farber, Stephen. *The Movie Rating Game*. Washington, DC: Public Affairs Press, 1972.

Federal Bureau of Investigation. Uniform Crime Reports. *Crime in the United States*. Washington, DC: Government Printing Office, annual.

Federal Communications Commission. *Report on the Broadcast of Violent, Indecent and Obscene Material*. Washington, DC: FCC 2d 418, 1975.

Federal Reporter. Washington, DC: Government Printing Office, current.

Feminist Anti-Censorship Task Force (FACT). *Caught Looking: Feminism, Pornography, and Censorship*. New York: Caught Looking, 1986.

Feminists for Free Expression. 2525 Times Square Station, New York 10108. http://www.well.com/user/freedom.

Ferguson, Frances. "Pornography: The Theory." *Critical Inquiry*, 21:3 (Spring 1995): 670–695.

Ferris, C. D., F. W. Lloyd, and T. J. Casey. *Cable Television Law*. New York: Bender, 1987.

Fields, Howard. "Dial-a-Porn Decision Poses Contradictions for Indecent Broadcasts." *Television/Radio Age*, 10 July 1989, p. 86.

Fish, Stanley. *There's No Such Thing as Free Speech, and It's a Good Thing, Too*. New York: Oxford University Press, 1993.

Fisher, Robert. "Film Censorship and Progressive Reform: The National Board of Censorship of Motion Pictures." *Journal of Popular Film*, 4 (1975): 143–156.

Fishman, Ted C. "Dangerous Art." *Playboy*, 41:3 (March 1994): 42–43.

Fiss, Owen M. *The Irony of Free Speech*. Cambridge: Harvard University Press, 1996.

Fithian, Marilyn A. "Importance of Knowledge as an Expert Witness." *Porn 101: Eroticism, Pornography, and the First Amendment*, ed. James Elias, Veronica Diehl Elias, Vern L. Bullough, Gwen Brewer, Jeffrey J. Douglas, and Will Jarvis. Amherst, NY: Prometheus Books, 1999, pp. 117–136.

Forbidden Films: The Filmmaker and Human Rights. Toronto: Toronto Arts Group for Human Rights, 1984.

Ford, John. *Criminal Obscenity: A Plea for Its Suppression*. New York: Revell, 1926.

Fowler, Dorothy Ganfield. *Unmailable: Congress and the Post Office*. Athens: University of Georgia Press, 1977.

Free Expression Clearinghouse. http://www.freeexpression.org.

Friedman, Jane M. "Erotica, Censorship, and the United States Post Office Department." *The Michigan Academician*, 4:1 (Summer 1971): 8–10.

———. "Zoning 'Adult' Movies: The Potential Impact of *Young v. American Mini Theaters*." *Hastings Law Journal*, 28 (July 1977): 1293–1304.

Friedman, Leon, ed. *Obscenity: The Complete Oral Arguments before the Supreme Court in the Major Obscenity Cases*. New York: Chelsea House, 1970.

Gaines, Jane M. *Contested Culture: The Image, the Voice, and the Law*. Chapel Hill: University of North Carolina Press, 1995.

Garay, Ronald. *Cable Television: A Reference Guide to Information*. Westport, CT: Greenwood, 1988.

Garbus, Martin, with Stanley Cohen. *Tough Talk: How I Fought for Writers, Comics, Bigots, and the American Way*. New York: Times Books/Random House, 1998.

Gardner, Gerald. *Movie Censorship: Letters from the Hays Office, 1934 to 1968*. New York: Dodd, Mead, 1987.

Gauntlet: Exploring the Limits of Free Expression. Springfield, PA: 1992–.

Gellhorn, Walter. *Individual Freedom and Governmental Restraints*. Baton Rouge: Louisiana State University Press, 1956.

Gerber, Albert B. *Sex, Pornography and Justice*. New York: Lyle Stuart, 1965.

Gertzman, Jay A. *Bookleggers and Smuthounds: The Trade in Erotica, 1920–1940*. Philadelphia: University of Pennsylvania Press, 1999.

———. *A Descriptive Bibliography of Lady Chatterley's Lover: With Essays toward a Publishing History of the Novel*. Westport, CT: Greenwood Press, 1989.

———. "Erotic Novel, Liberal Lawyer, and 'Censor-Moron': 'Sex for Its Own Sake' and Some Literary Censorship Adjudications of the 1930s." *D. H. Lawrence Review*, 24:3 (Fall 1992): 217–227.

———. " 'Esoterica' and 'The Good of the Race': Mail-Order Distribution of Erotica in the 1930s." *The Papers of the Bibliographical Society of America*, 86:3 (September 1992): 295–340.

———. "Postal Service Guardians of Public Morals and Erotica Mail Order Dealers of the Thirties: A Study in Administrative Authority in the United States." *Publishing History*, 37 (1995): 83–110.

Gey, S. G. "The Apologetics of Suppression: The Regulation of Pornography as Act and Idea." *Michigan Law Review*, 86:7 (June 1988): 1564–1634.

Gilmor, Donald M., and Jerome A. Barron. *Mass Communication Law: Cases and Comment*. 4th ed. St. Paul, MN: West, 1984.

Gilmore, Donald H. *Sex, Censorship, and Pornography*. 2 vols. San Diego: Greenleaf Classics, 1969.

———. *Sex and Censorship in the Visual Arts*. San Diego: Greenleaf Classics, 1970.

Glascock, Jack. "*Regina v. Butler*: The Harms Approach and Freedom of Expression." *Communication Law and Policy*, 1:1 (Winter 1996): 117–138.

Glassman, Marc B. "Community Standards of Patent Offensiveness: Public Opinion Data and Obscenity Law." *Public Opinion Quarterly*, 42 (Summer 1978): 161–170.

Goldstein, Anne B. "Representing the Lesbian in Literature and Law." *Representing Women: Law, Literature, and Feminism*, ed. Susan Sage Heinzelman and Zipporah Batshaw Wiseman. Durham, NC: Duke University Press, 1994, pp. 356–385.

Goodman, Paul. "What Is a Civil Libertarian to Do When Pornography Becomes So Bold?"*New York Times*, 21 November 1976, Sec. 2, pp. 1, 26.

Gordon, George N. *Erotic Communications: Studies in Sex, Sin and Censorship*. New York: Hastings House, 1980.

Green, Richard. "The Expert Witness." *Porn 101: Eroticism, Pornography, and the First Amendment*, ed. James Elias, Veronica Diehl Elias, Vern L. Bullough, Gwen Brewer, Jeffrey J. Douglas, and Will Jarvis. Amherst, NY: Prometheus Books, 1999, pp. 105–116.

———. *Sexual Science and the Law*. Cambridge: Harvard University Press, 1992.

Greenawalt, Kent. *Fighting Words: Individuals, Communities, and Liberties of Speech*. Princeton, NJ: Princeton University Press, 1995.

Greenhouse, Linda. "Justices to Rule on Whether Cable TV's Sexually Explicit Programs Can Be Restricted." *New York Times*, 14 November 1995, p. C17.

Grey, Anthony. "Pornography and Free Speech." *The Influence of Pornography on Behaviour*, ed. Maurice Yaffé and Edward C. Nelson. New York: Academic Press, 1982, pp. 47–64.

GRIP (Group for Rap Industry Protection). P.O. Box 4856, Berkeley, CA 94704.

Gunther, Albert C. "Overrating the X-Rating: The Third-Person Perception and Support for Censorship of Pornography." *Journal of Communication*, 45:1 (Winter 1995): 27–38.

Gunther, Gerald. *Learned Hand: The Man and the Judge*. Cambridge: Harvard University Press, 1995.

Haight, Anne Lyon. *Banned Books: Informal Notes on Some Books Banned for Various Reasons at Various Times and in Various Places*. 4th ed., rev. and enl. by Chandler B. Grannis. New York: R. R. Bowker, 1978.

Haney, Robert W. *Comstockery in America: Patterns of Censorship and Control*. Boston: Beacon Press, 1960.

Harmon, Amy. "The Self-Appointed Cops of the Information Age." *New York Times*, 7 December 1997 sec. 4, pp. 1, 6.

Hart, Harold H., ed. *Censorship for and Against*. New York: Hart, 1971.

Hawkins, Gains. "Common Sense and Censorship." *Publishers Weekly*, 5 July 1985, pp. 33–34.

Hayes, Arthur Garfield. *Let Freedom Ring*. New York: Liveright, 1937.

Hays, W. H. *The Memoirs of Will H. Hays*. New York: Doubleday, 1955.

Heffner, Richard D. "Here Come the Video Censors." *New York Times*, 1 May 1994, p. 17.

Heins, Marjorie. *Above the Law: The Justice Department's War against the First Amendment.* New York: ACLU, 1991.

Heinzelman, Susan Sage, and Zipporah Batshaw Wiseman, eds. *Representing Women: Law, Literature, and Feminism.* Durham, NC: Duke University Press, 1994.

Hentoff, Nat. *Free Speech for Me But Not for Thee: How the American Left and Right Relentlessly Censor Each Other.* New York: HarperCollins, 1993.

Hess, Elizabeth. "Artist Doesn't Turn the Other Cheek: Wojnarowicz to Sue Reverend Wildmon." *Village Voice,* 22 May 1990, pp. 98–99.

High Performance: A Quarterly Magazine for the New Arts Audience. Los Angeles, 1969–1997.

Higonnet, Anne. "Conclusions Based on Observation." *Yale Journal of Criticism,* 9:1 (1996): 1–18.

Hixson, Richard F. *Pornography and the Justices: The Supreme Court and the Intractable Obscenity Problem.* Carbondale: Southern Illinois University Press, 1996.

Hofbauer, D. L. " 'Cableporn' and the First Amendment: Perspectives on Content Regulation of Cable Television." *Federal Communications Law Journal,* 35 (1983): 139–208.

Hoffman, E. "Feminism, Pornography and Law." *University of Pennsylvania Law Review,* 133:2 (January 1985): 497–534.

"Hollywood, Censorship, and American Culture." Special issue of *American Quarterly,* 44:4 (1992).

Honan, William H. "Arts Endowment Backers Are Split on Strategy." *New York Times,* 17 May 1990, p. C20.

Hoyt, Olga G., and Edwin P. Hoyt. *Censorship in America.* New York: Seabury, 1970.

Huffman, John L., and Denise M. Trauth. "Obscenity, Indecency, and the Rehnquist Court." *Communications and the Law,* 13:1 (March 1991): 3–23.

Hughes, Patricia. "Pornography: Alternatives to Censorship." *Canadian Journal of Political and Social Theory,* 9 (Winter–Spring 1985): 96–126.

Hughes, R. L. "Abating Obscenity as a Nuisance: An Easy Procedural Road for Prior Restraints." *Communications and the Law,* 5:4 (Fall 1983): 39–50.

Hunnings, Neville M. *Film Censors and the Law.* London: Allen and Unwin, 1967.

Hunter, Ian, David Saunders, and Dugald Williamson. *On Pornography: Literature, Sexuality and Obscenity Law.* New York: St. Martin's, 1993.

Hutchison, E. R. *Tropic of Cancer on Trial: A Case History of Censorship.* New York: Grove Press, 1968.

"Indecency Ban Nixed." *Electronic Media,* 10:21 (20 May 1991): 1.

Index on Censorship. New York: Cassell, 1972–.

Institute for First Amendment Studies. http://www.berkshire.net/~ifas/fw.

Institute for Media Education. http://www.iglou.com/first~principles.

Jacobs, Lea. *The Wages of Sin: Censorship and the Fallen Woman Film, 1928–1942.* Madison: University of Wisconsin Press, 1991.

Jacobsen, Carol. "Fighting for Visibility: Notes on the Censorship Battle of 'Porn'im'age'ry: Picturing Prostitutes." *Social Text,* 37 (Winter 1993): 135–141.

Jacobson, Beverly. "A Bookstore Perishes: How an Obscenity Law Victimized a Respectable Business Woman." *Christian Century,* 91 (23 October 1974): 990–992.

Jahoda, Marie. *The Impact of Literature: A Psychological Discussion of Some Assumptions in the Censorship Debate.* New York: Research Center for Human Relations, New York University, 1954.

Jahr, Cliff. "Porn on Cable TV: Is There Excess?" *Village Voice*, 20 October 1975, pp. 12–13.

Jansen, Sue Curry. *Censorship: The Knot That Binds Power and Knowledge*. New York: Oxford University Press, 1988.

Jasper, Margaret C. *The Law of Obscenity and Pornography*. Dobbs Ferry, NY: Oceana Publications, 1996.

Jassem, H. C. "Scrambling the Telephone: The FCC's Dial-a-Porn Regulations." *Communications and the Law*, 10:6 (December 1988): 3–14.

Jones, Steve. "Ban(ned) in the U.S.A.: Popular Music and Censorship," *Journal of Communication Inquiry*, 15:1 (Winter 1991): 73–87.

Jong, Erica. "The Electronic Anti-Sex League Wants Your Number." *Penthouse*, 25:2 (October 1993): 88–89, 128.

Jowett, Garth. *Film: The Democratic Art*. Boston: Little, Brown, 1976.

"Judge Overturns Part of Child-Pornography Law." *New York Times*, 28 May 1992, p. A7.

Kaminer, Wendy. "Pornography and the First Amendment: Prior Restraint and Private Action." *Take Back the Night: Women on Pornography*, ed. Laura Lederer. New York: William Morrow, 1980, pp. 241–247.

Karst, Kenneth L. "Pornography and Law as Images of Power." *Law's Promise, Law's Expression: Visions of Power in the Politics of Race, Gender, and Religion*. New Haven, CT: Yale University Press, 1993, pp. 43–49.

Katz, Leanne. "Censors' Helpers." *New York Times*, 4 December 1993, p. 15.

Kick, Russ. "Netspeech 97: Free Speech Issues and Incidents on the Internet in 1997." *Gauntlet*, 15 (1998): 108–116.

Kilpatrick, James J. *The Smut Peddlers: The Pornography Racket and the Law Dealing with Obscenity Censorship*. Garden City, NY: Doubleday, 1960.

Kleiman, Howard M. "Indecent Programming on Cable Television: Legal and Social Dimensions." *Journal of Broadcasting and Electronic Media*, 30:3 (Summer 1986): 275–294.

Kling, Samuel D. *Sexual Behavior and the Law*. New York: Bernard Geis, 1965.

Koenigil, Mark. *Movies in Society: Sex, Crime, and Censorship*. New York: Robert Spekker and Sons, 1962.

Kramer, Hilton. "Is Art above the Laws of Decency?" *New York Times*, 22 July 1989, II, pp. 1, 7.

Krattenmeker, T. G., and M. L. Esterow. "Censoring Indecent Cable Programs: The New Morality Meets the New Media." *Fordham Law Review*, 51 (1983); 606–636.

Kronhausen, Eberhard, and Phyllis Kronhausen. *Freedom to Love: A Film by Drs. Phyllis and Eberhard Kronhausen*. New York: Grove Press, 1970.

———. *Pornography and the Law*. New York: Ballantine Books, 1959; rev. ed. New York: Bell Publishers, [1975].

Kuh, Richard. *Foolish Figleaves? Pornography in—and Out of—Court*. New York: Macmillan, 1967.

Kuhn, Annette. *Cinema, Censorship, and Sexuality 1909–1925*. London: Routledge, 1988.

Kupferman, Theodore R., ed. *Censorship, Secrecy, Access, and Obscenity*. Vol. III of *Readings from Communications and the Law*. Westport, CT: Meckler, 1990.

Labaton, Stephen. "Justices Restrict Ability to Seize Suspects' Goods." *New York Times*, 29 June 1993, pp. Al, A8.

————. "Old Laws Have a Way of Learning New Tricks." *New York Times*, 19 December 1993, p. E14.

Lacombe, Dany. *Blue Politics: Pornography in the Age of Feminism.* Toronto: University of Toronto Press, 1994.

Lawrence, D. H. *Sex, Literature, and Censorship*, ed. Harry T. Moore. New York: Irvington, 1953.

Layman, W. K. "Violent Pornography and the Obscenity Doctrine: The Road Not Taken." *Georgetown Law Journal*, 75:4 (April 1987): 1475–1508.

Lederer, Laura, ed. *Speech, Equality, and Harm: New Legal Paradigms.* Boulder, CO: Westview, 1997.

Lederer, Laura, and Richard Delgado, eds. *The Price We Pay: The Case against Racist Speech, Hate Propaganda, and Pornography.* New York: Hill and Wang, 1995.

Leff, Leonard J., and Jerold L. Simmons. *The Dame in the Kimono: Hollywood, Censorship, and the Production Code from the 1920s to the 1960s.* New York: Grove Weidenfeld, 1990.

Legman, Gershon. *Love and Death: A Study in Censorship.* New York: Breaking Point, 1949.

————. "Sex Censorship in the U.S.A." *PLAN: Organization of the British Progressive League* (London), 2:1 (January 1945): 2–9.

Leonard, Arthur S. *Sexuality and the Law: An Encyclopedia of Major Legal Cases.* New York: Garland, 1993.

Lewin, Tamar. "Canada Court Says Pornography Harms Women and Can Be Banned." *New York Times*, 28 February 1992, pp. A1, B9.

————. "Furor on Exhibit at Law School Splits Feminists." *New York Times*, 13 November 1992, p. B9.

Lewis, Felice Flanery. *Literature, Obscenity, and the Law.* Carbondale: Southern Illinois University Press, 1976.

Lewis, Neil A. "F.C.C. Adopts Dial-a-Porn Rules." *New York Times*, 15 June 1990, p. A17.

————. "U.S. Restrictions on Adult-TV Fare Are Struck Down." *New York Times*, 24 November 1993, pp. A1, A12.

Limbacher, James L. *Sexuality in World Cinema.* 2 vols. Metuchen, NJ: Scarecrow Press, 1983.

Linsley, W. A. "The Case against Censorship of Pornography." *Pornography: Research Advances and Policy Considerations*, ed. Dolf Zillmann and Jennings Bryant. Hillsdale, NJ: Lawrence Erlbaum Associates, 1989, pp. 343–359.

Linz, Daniel, Stephen Penrod, and Edward Donnerstein. "Issues Bearing on the Legal Regulation of Violent and Sexually Violent Media." *Journal of Social Issues*, 42:3 (1986): 171–194.

Lipschultz, Jeremy H. *Broadcast Indecency: F.C.C. Regulation and the First Amendment.* Woburn, MA: Focal Press, 1996.

————. "Conceptual Problems of Broadcast Indecency Policy and Application." *Communications and the Law*, 14:2 (June 1992): 3–29.

Liston, Robert A. *The Right to Know: Censorship in America.* New York: Franklin Watts, 1973.

Longino, Helen E. "Pornography, Oppression and Freedom: A Closer Look." *Take Back the Night: Women on Pornography*, ed. Laura Lederer. New York: William Morrow, 1980, pp. 40–54.

Lyons, Charles. *The New Censors: Movies and the Culture Wars*. Philadelphia: Temple University Press, 1997.

MacGregor, Ford H. "Official Censorship Legislation." *Annals of the American Academy of Political and Social Science*, 128 (November 1926): 163–174.

MacKinnon, Catharine A. *Feminism Unmodified: Discourses on Life and Law*. Cambridge: Harvard University Press, 1987.

———. "Not a Moral Issue." *Yale Law and Policy Review*, 2 (Spring 1984): 321–345.

———. "Pornography, Civil Rights, and Speech." *Harvard Civil Rights—Civil Liberties Law Review*, 20 (Winter 1985): 1–70.

Maitland, Leslie. "Bestiality Found of Little Appeal, Jury Acquits Movie Wholesaler." *New York Times*, 18 December 1977, p. 72.

Makris, John N. *The Silent Investigators: The Great Untold Story of the United States Postal Inspection Service*. New York: Dutton, 1959.

Manchell, Frank. *Film Study: An Analytical Bibliography*. 4 vols. Rutherford, NJ: Fairleigh Dickinson Press, 1970.

Mann, E. J. "Telephones, Sex, and the First Amendment." *UCLA Law Review*, 33:4 (April 1986): 1221–1236.

Maretz, H. S. "Aural Sex: Has Congress Gone Too Far by Going All the Way with Dial-a-Porn?" *Communication/Entertainment*, 11:3 (Spring 1989): 493–526.

"Mark Fowler's Great Experiment: Setting His People Free." *Broadcasting*, 30 April 1984, pp. 116–128.

Markoff, John. "Cyberspace under Lock and Key." *New York Times*, 13 February 1994, p. E3.

Marsh, Dave. *Fifty Ways to Fight Censorship; and Important Facts to Know about the Censors*. New York: Thunder's Mouth Press, 1991.

———. *You've Got a Right to Rock*. Los Angeles: Rock and Roll Confidential, 1990.

———, ed. *Rock and Roll Confidential*, aka *Rock & Rap Confidential*. P.O. Box 341305. Los Angeles 90034.

Martin, Olga Johanna. *Hollywood's Movie Commandments: A Handbook for Motion Picture Writers and Reviewers*. New York: H. W. Wilson, 1937.

Maschke, Karen, ed. *Pornography, Sex Work, and Hate Speech: Part I*. New York: Garland, 1997.

Mathews, Tom. "Fine Art or Foul?" *Newsweek*, 2 July 1990, pp. 46–52.

McCarthy, Kathleen D. "Nickel Vice and Virtue: Movie Censorship in Chicago, 1907–1915." *Journal of Popular Film*, 5 (1976): 37–55.

McGaffey, Ruth. "A Realistic Look at Expert Witnesses in Obscenity Cases." *Northwestern University Law Review*, 69:2 (May/June 1974): 218–232.

McKeen, W. "Justice Brennan's Struggle with Obscenity Law: The Evolution of Supreme Court Doctrine, 1957–1973." *Southwestern Mass Communication Journal*, 1:1 (June 1985): 1–16.

McKenna, George, and Stanley Feingold, eds. *Taking Sides: Clashing Views on Controversial Issues in Human Life*. Guilford, CT: Dushkin Press, 1987.

McWilliams, Peter. *Ain't Nobody's Business If You Do: The Absurdity of Consensual Crimes in a Free Society*. Los Angeles: Prelude Press, 1993.

Media Law Reporter. Washington, DC, 1967–.

Meyer, Carlin. "Reclaiming Sex from the Pornographers: Cybersexual Possibilities." *Georgetown Law Review*, 83 (June 1995): 1969–2009.

Meyer, Robert G. "Pornography and the Sexual Deviations." *Abnormal Behavior and the Criminal Justice System.* New York: Lexington Books, 1992, pp. 99–101.

———. "Sex, Sin, and Women's Liberation: Against Porn-Suppression." *Texas Law Review,* 72 (1994): 1112–1115.

Meyers, Steven Lee. "Obscenity Laws Exist, but What Breaks Them?" *New York Times,* 19 January 1992, p. E4.

Michelman, Frank. "Conceptions of Democracy in American Constitutional Argument: The Case of Pornography Legislation." *Tennessee Law Review,* 56:291 (1989): 303–304.

"Midnight Blue: An FCC Time Limit for Raunch." *Time,* 7 December 1987, p. 61.

Mifflin, Lawrie. "F.C.C. Approves Ratings System for TV; Sets with Blockers Will Be on Market within a Year." *New York Times,* 13 March 1998, p. A14.

———. "Spurned by Industry, V-Chip Retains Some Mighty Friends." *New York Times,* 17 July 1995, p. C7.

Millard, Charles. "Stop the Porn Explosion." *New York Times,* 29 January 1993, p. A13.

Miller, Frank. *Censored Hollywood: Sex, Sin and Violence on Screen.* Atlanta: Turner Publishing, 1994.

Moley, Raymond. *The Hays Office.* Indianapolis: Bobbs-Merrill, 1945.

Molotsky, Irvin. "F.C.C. Rules on Indecent Programming." *New York Times,* 25 November 1987, p. C25.

Morello, Mary, ed. *Parents for Rock and Rap.* P.O. Box 53, Libertyville, IL 60048.

Moretti, Daniel S. *Obscenity and Pornography: The Law under the First Amendment.* New York: Ocean, 1984.

Moscato, Michael, and Leslie Le Blanc, eds. *The United States of America v. One Book Entitled Ulysses by James Joyce.* Frederick, MD: University Publications, 1984.

Motion Picture Association of America. "Industry Code of Self Regulation." *International Motion Picture Almanac.* Los Angeles: Quigley Publications, annual.

Mulligan, Casey B. "Pornography, Profits and the Internet." *Chicago Tribune,* 28 June 1995, sec. 1, p. 19.

Murphy, Bruce. *Fortas: The Rise and Ruin of a Supreme Court Justice.* New York: Morrow, 1988.

Nagel, E. L. "First Amendment Constraints on the Regulation of Telephone Pornography." *University of Cincinnati Law Review,* 55:1 (1986): 237–255.

Nathan, J. "Notes from the Underground: San Francisco Censorship." *Evergreen Review,* 45 (February 1967): 16–20.

National Coalition against Censorship. *Censorship News.* 275 Seventh Avenue, New York City 10001.

National Committee against Censorship of the Theatre Arts. *Censorship.* New York: American Civil Liberties Union, 1935.

National Family Legal Foundation. 11000 North Scottsdale Road, Scottsdale, AZ 85254.

Obscenity Law Reporter. 2 vols. New York: National Obscenity Law Center, 1986.

O'Neill, Terry, ed. *Censorship: Opposing Viewpoints.* St. Paul, MN: Greenhaven Press, 1985.

Overbeck, Wayne, with Rick D. Pullen. *Major Principles of Media Law.* New York: Harcourt, Brace, 1994.

Pally, Marcia. "Minors and Media Minotaurs: Sexual Material, Rock, and Rap." *Sex and Sensibility: Reflections on Forbidden Mirrors and the Will to Censor.* Hopewell, NJ: Ecco Press, 1994, pp. 81–115.

Pareles, Jon. "Legislating the Imagination." *New York Times*, 11 February 1990, p. H30.
———. "A Rap Group's Lyrics Venture Close to the Edge of Obscenity." *New York Times*, 14 June 1990, pp. C15, 19.
Parsons, Patrick R. *Cable Television and the First Amendment*. Lexington, MA: Lexington Books, 1987.
———. *Cable Television and the First Amendment: The Post-Preferred Cases*. University Park, PA: National Cable Television Center and Museum, 1989.
Paul, James C. N., and Murray L. Schwartz. *Federal Censorship: Obscenity in the Mail*. New York: Free Press, 1961.
Pember, Don R. *Mass Media Law*. 5th ed. Dubuque, IA: Brown, 1990.
People for the American Way. http://www.pfaw.org.
Perlman, William. *The Movies on Trial*. New York: Macmillan, 1936.
Perry, M. J. "Freedom of Expression: An Essay on Theory and Doctrine." *Northwestern University Law Review*, 78:5 (December 1983): 1137–1211.
Playboy Forum. http://www.playboy.com/forum.
Pollack, Andrew. "Court Allows Limited Access to 'Dial-a-Porn' Phone Lines." *New York Times*, 22 March 1991, p. A11.
Pool, Ithiel de Sola, ed. *On Free Speech in the Electronic Age: Technologies of Freedom*. Cambridge: Harvard University Press, 1983.
"The Porn Fighters." *Newsweek*, 9 December 1974, pp. 74–79.
Posner, Richard A. *Sexual Reason*. Cambridge: Harvard University Press, 1992.
Powe, L. A., Jr. "Consistency over Time: The FCC's Indecency Rerun." *Communication/ Entertainment*, 10:2 (Winter 1988): 571–578.
President's Commission on Obscenity and Pornography. *Report of the Commission on Obscenity and Pornography*. Washington, DC: Government Printing Office, 1970.
———. *Technical Report of the Commission on Obscenity and Pornography*. 9 vols. Washington, DC: Government Printing Office, 1971–1972. Vol. I: *Preliminary Studies*; vol. II: *Legal Analysis*; vol. III: *The Marketplace: The Industry*; vol. IV: *The Marketplace: Empirical Studies*; vol. V: *Societal Control Mechanisms*; vol. VI: *National Survey*; vol. VII: *Erotica and Antisocial Behavior*; vol. VIII: *Erotica and Social Behavior*; vol. IX: *The Consumer and the Community* (and index of authors).
Price, Monroe E., ed. *The V-Chip Debate: Content Filtering from Television to the Internet*. Mahwah, NJ: Lawrence Erlbaum Associates, 1998.
Pritchard, D., J. P. Dilts, and D. Berkowitz. "Prosecutors' Use of External Agendas in Prosecuting Pornography Cases." *Journalism Quarterly*, 64: 2/3 (Summer/Autumn 1987): 392–398.
"Putting Porno in its Place." *Wall Street Journal*, eastern ed., 28 February 1986, p. 24.
Quigley, Martin. *Decency in Motion Pictures*. New York: Macmillan, 1937.
Rae, Stephen. "X-Rated Raids." *Playboy*, 39:6 (June 1992): 44–45.
Randall, Richard S. "Censorship: From 'The Miracle' to 'Deep Throat.' " *The American Film Industry*, ed. Tino Balio. Madison: University of Wisconsin Press, 1976, pp. 432–457.
———. *Censorship of the Movies: The Social and Political Control of a Mass Medium*. Madison: University of Wisconsin Press, 1968.
Raphael, Lennox. "Notes from the Underground: Censorship." *Evergreen Review*, 67 (June 1969): 20–21, 92.

Rapp, Burt. *Sex Crimes Investigation: A Practical Manual.* Port Townsend, WA: Loompanics, 1988.

Ratings, Morals, and Sex on TV. New York: New York Times/Showtime, 1998.

Redhead, Steve. *Unpopular Cultures: The Birth of Law and Popular Culture.* New York: Manchester University Press/St. Martin's, 1995.

Reed, Robert D., and Danek S. Kaus. *Pornography: How and Where to Find Facts and Get Help.* Saratoga, CA: R & E Publishers, 1993.

Reitberger, Reinhold, and Wolfgang Fuchs. *Comics: Anatomy of a Mass Medium.* Boston: Little, Brown, 1972.

Rembar, Charles. *The End of Obscenity: The Trials of Lady Chatterley, Tropic of Cancer and Fanny Hill by the Lawyer Who Defended Them.* New York: Random House, 1968.

———. "Obscenity—Forget It." *Atlantic Monthly*, May 1977, pp. 37–41.

Rendleman, Doug. "Civilizing Pornography: The Case for an Exclusive Obscenity Nuisance Statute." *University of Chicago Law Review*, 44 (Spring 1977): 509–560.

Ressner, Jeffrey. "To Sticker or Not to Sticker." *Rolling Stone*, 7 February 1991, pp. 14–15.

Reynolds, Richard R. "Our Misplaced Reliance on Early Obscenity Cases." *ABA Journal*, 61 (February 1975): 220–222.

Rhodes, Richard. " 'Deep Throat' Goes Down in Memphis." *Playboy*, 23: 10 (October 1976): 106–108, 181–192.

Ringel, William E. *Obscenity Law Today.* Jamaica, NY: Gould Publications, 1970.

Robel, Lauren. "Pornography and Existing Law: What the Law Can Do." *For Adult Users Only: The Dilemma of Violent Pornography*, ed. Susan Gubar and Joan Hoff. Bloomington: Indiana University Press, 1989, pp. 178–197.

Robbins, V. H. "Indecency on Cable Television: A Barren Battleground for Regulation of Programming Content." *St. Mary's Law Journal*, 15:2 (1984): 417–441.

Robertus, Patricia E. "Postal Control of Obscene Literature, 1942–1957." Ph.D. dissertation, University of Washington, 1974.

The ROC: Voice of Rock Out Censorship. Jewett, OH, 1991–.

Rohde, Stephen. "Freedom of Cyberspeech." *Gauntlet*, 14 (1997): 75–80.

———. "We Have Seen a Land of Censorship, and It Is Canada." *Gauntlet*, 14 (1997): 81–84.

Rohter, Larry. "New MPAA Rating." *New York Times*, 27 September 1990, pp. 1, B2.

Safire, William. "Ode on a G-String." *New York Times Magazine*, 4 August 1991, p. 12.

———. "The Porn Is Green." *New York Times*, 5 November 1993, p. A21.

Saunders, Kevin W. *Violence as Obscenity: Limiting the Media's First Amendment Protection.* Durham, NC: Duke University Press, 1996.

Sawyer, Carol. "Less than Pornography: The Power of Popular Fiction." *Representing Women: Law, Literature, and Feminism*, ed. Susan Sage Heinzelman and Zipporah Batshaw Wiseman. Durham, NC: Duke University Press, 1994, pp. 75–100.

Schachter, H. L. "The Pornography Debate in the United States: Politics, Law and Justification." *Gazette*, 42:2 (1988/1989): 93–104.

Schauer, Frederick F. *Free Speech: A Philosophical Enquiry.* Cambridge: Cambridge University Press, 1982.

———. *The Law of Obscenity.* Washington, DC: Bureau of National Affairs, 1976.

Schneder, Dan W. "Authority of the Register of Copyrights to Deny Registration of a Claim to Copyright on the Ground of Obscenity." *Chicago-Kent Law Review*, 51 (1975): 691–724.

Schone, Mark. "Satellite of Lust: Feds Dog TV Pornographers." *Village Voice*, 9 April 1991, p. 47.

Schrier, H. T. "A Solution to Indecency on the Airwaves." *Federal Communications Law Journal*, 41:1 (November 1988): 69–107.

Schroeder, Theodore. *Freedom of the Press and "Obscene" Literature*. Cos Cob, CT: Printed by author, 1906.

———. *"Obscene" Literature and Constitutional Law*. New York: Privately printed for Forensic Uses, 1911.

Schumach, Murray. *The Face on the Cutting Room Floor: The Story of Movie and Television Censorship*. New York: Morrow, 1964.

Scott, G. R. *"Into Whose Hands": An Examination of Obscene Libel in Its Legal, Sociological, and Literary Aspects*. Brooklyn, NY: Warron, 1961.

Seabury, William M. *The Public and the Motion Picture Industry*. New York: Macmillan, 1926; rpt. New York: Jerome Ozer, 1971.

Sears, A. E. "The Legal Case for Restricting Pornography." *Pornography: Research Advances and Policy Considerations*, ed. Dolf Zillmann and Jennings Bryant. Hillsdale, NJ: Lawrence Erlbaum Associates, 1989, pp. 323–342.

Seator, Penelope. "Judicial Indifference to Pornography's Harm: *American Booksellers v. Hudnut* (Women's Law Forum)." *Golden Gate University Law Review*, 17 (1987): 297–358.

"See No Evil?" *Time*, 12 May 1997, p. 21.

Selcraig, Bruce. "Reverend Wildmon's War on the Arts." *New York Times Magazine*, 2 September 1990, pp. 22–25, 43, 52–53.

Sharp, Donald B., ed. *Commentaries on Obscenity*. Metuchen, NJ: Scarecrow Press, 1970.

Shaughnessy, Edward J., and Diana Trebbi. *A Standard for Miller: A Community Response to Pornography*. Washington, DC: University Press of America, 1980.

Sheinfeld, Louis P. "Ratings: The Big Chill." *Film Comment*, 22:3 (May–June 1986): 10.

Shenon, Philip. "Justice Department Plans Anti-Racketeering Drive against Pornographers." *New York Times*, 12 January 1988, p. 2.

Sheppard, Nathaniel. "Bar Group Debates Pornography and Effects That It Has on Society." *New York Times*, 30 October 1977, p. 26.

"Short History of Comics Censorship." http://www.insv.com/cblds/history.html.

Simmons, Doug. "Gangsta Was the Case." *Village Voice*, 8 March 1994, pp. 63, 66.

Simon, William. "The Social Scientist as Expert Witness." *Porn 101: Eroticism, Pornography, and the First Amendment*, ed. James Elias, Veronica Diehl Elias, Vern L. Bullough, Gwen Brewer, Jeffrey J. Douglas, and Will Jarvis. Amherst, NY: Prometheus Books, 1999, pp. 137–142.

Sitomer, Curtis J. "Sifting Out Pornography from Free Speech." *Christian Science Monitor*, national ed., 14 May 1986, p. 21.

Slabaugh, Eugene. Card Catalog, Erotic Film Archives. Kinsey Institute for Sex, Gender, and Reproduction, Indiana University, Bloomington.

———. Stag Film Analyses. 3 Notebooks. 1960–1967. Erotic Film Archives. Kinsey Institute for Sex, Gender, and Reproduction, Indiana University, Bloomington.

Slide, Anthony. *Banned in the U.S.A.: British Films in the United States and Their Censorship, 1933–1966.* New York: I. B. Tauris/St. Martin's 1998.

Smith, Richard. *Getting into Deep Throat.* Chicago: Playboy Press, 1973.

Smith, Roberta. " 'Unmentionable Art' through the Ages." *New York Times,* 11 November 1990, pp. H39, H43.

Smolla, Rodney A. *Free Speech in an Open Society.* New York: Knopf, 1992.

Solomon-Godeau, Abigail. *Photography at the Dock: Essays on Photographic History, Institutions, and Practices.* Minneapolis: University of Minnesota Press, 1991.

The Source. 594 Broadway, New York 10012.

Spitzer, Matthew L. *Seven Dirty Words and Six Other Stories: Controlling the Content of Print and Broadcast.* New Haven, CT: Yale University Press, 1986.

Sporn, J. "Content Regulation of Cable Television: 'Indecency' Statutes and the First Amendment." *Rutgers Computer and Technology Law Journal,* 11:1 (1985): 141–170.

Sprague, William E. *Sex, Pornography and the Law.* 2 vols. San Diego: Academy Press, 1970.

Squires, Carol, ed. *The Critical Image: Essays on Contemporary Photography.* Seattle: Bay Press, 1990.

Stefanac, Suzanne. "Playboy Opens WWW Emporium." *New Media,* 4:11 (November 1994): 58.

Steiner, Wendy. *The Scandal of Pleasure.* Chicago: University of Chicago Press, 1995.

Sterling, Bruce. *The Hacker Crackdown.* New York: Bantam, 1992.

Stevens, Kenneth R. "*United States v. 31 Photographs*: Dr. Alfred Kinsey and Obscenity Law." *Indiana Magazine of History,* 71 (December 1975): 299–318.

Stevens, P. J. "Community Standards and Federal Obscenity Prosecutions." *Southern California Law Review,* 55:3 (March 1982): 693–726.

Stires, Lloyd K. "Is It Time to Overturn the Miller Standard?" *Gauntlet,* 14 (1997): 85–89.

St. John-Stevas, Norman. *Obscenity and the Law.* London: Secker and Warburg, 1956.

Stone, Goeffrey R. "Anti-Pornography Legislation as Viewpoint-Discrimination." *Harvard Journal of Law and Public Policy,* 9:2 (1986): 461–480.

Stossel, John. *Sex, Drugs, and Consenting Adults.* San Francisco: Laissez Faire, 1998.

Strossen, Nadine. *Defending Pornography: Free Speech, Sex and the Fight for Women's Rights.* New York: Scribner's, 1995.

———. "Legal Scholars Who Would Limit Free Speech." *Chronicle of Higher Education,* 7 July 1993, pp. B1–B2.

Struggling with Pornography. http://www.rsts.net/topics/porn.html.

Summers, Harrison B., ed. *Radio Censorship.* New York: H. H. Wilson, 1939; rpt. New York: Arno Press, 1971.

Sunkel, W. M. "*City of Renton v. Playtime Theatres, Inc*: Court-Approved Censorship through Zoning." *Pace Law Review,* 7:1 (Fall 1986): 251–290.

Sunstein, Cass R. "Pornography and the First Amendment." *Duke Law Journal,* 4 (1986): 589–627.

TAB (The Adult Business) Report, Washington, DC, 1978–1985.

Taylor, Stuart. "Ban on Dial-a-Porn Is Allowed to Stand." *New York Times,* 26 April 1988, p. A23.

———. "High Court Backs Use of Zoning to Regulate Showing of Sex Films." *New York Times,* 26 February 1986, pp. A1, A20.

Thomas, Donald. *A Long Time Burning: The History of Literary Censorship in England*. London: Routledge and Kegan Paul, 1969; New York: Praeger, 1969.

Thompson, Margaret E., Steven H. Chafee, and Hayg H. Oshagan. "Regulating Pornography: A Public Dilemma." *Journal of Communication*, 40 (Summer 1990): 73–83.

Thompson, Roger. *Unfit for Modest Ears: A Study of Pornographic, Obscene, and Bawdy Works*. Totowa, NJ: Rowman and Littlefield, 1979.

Toner, William. *Regulating Sex Businesses*. Chicago: American Society of Planning Officials, 1977.

Tong, Rosemarie. "Women, Pornography, and the Law." *Academe* (September-October 1987): 14–22.

———. *Women, Sex and the Law*. Totowa, NJ: Rowman and Allenheld, 1984.

Tovey, M. W. "Dial-a-Porn and the First Amendment: The State Action Loophole." *Federal Communications Law Journal*, 40:2 (April 1988): 267–294.

Traditional Values Coalition. http://www.traditionalvalues.org.

Trauth, Denise M., and John L. Huffman. "Public Nuisance Laws: A New Mechanism for Film Censorship." *Current Research in Film: Audiences, Economics, and Law*, ed. Bruce A. Austin. 4 vols. Norwood, NJ: Ablex, 1985, I: 197–207.

Tribe, David. *Questions of Censorship*. New York: St. Martin's, 1973.

United States Reports. Washington, DC: Government Printing Office, current.

U.S. Department of Justice. *Beyond the Pornography Commission: The Federal Response*. Washington, DC: National Obscenity Enforcement Unit, 1987.

U.S. Postal Service. *Annual Report of the Postmaster General*. Washington, DC: Government Printing Office, 1898–present.

U.S. Rocker. Cleveland, OH, 1989.

Valenti, Jack. *The Voluntary Movie Rating System: How It Began, Its Purpose, the Public Reaction*. Los Angeles: Motion Picture Association of America, 1987.

Valverde, Mariana, and Linda Weir. "Thrills, Chills and the 'Lesbian Threat.' " *Women against Censorship*, ed. Varda Burstyn. Vancouver: Douglas and McIntyre, 1985, pp. 99–106.

Van Alstyne, William W. *Interpretations of the First Amendment*. Durham, NC: Duke University Press, 1990.

Vizzard, Jack. *See No Evil: Life Inside a Hollywood Censor*. New York: Simon and Schuster, 1970.

Wallace, D. H. "A Survey on Obscenity and Contemporary Community Standards." *Journal of Social Issues*, 29:3 (1973): 53–67.

Wallace, J. E. "Contextual Regulation of Indecency: A Happy Medium for Cable Television." *Valparaiso University Law Review*, 21:4 (Fall 1986): 193–220.

Wardle, L. D. "Cable Comes of Age: A Constitutional Analysis of the Regulation of 'Indecent' Cable Television Programming." *Denver University Law Review*, 63: 4 (1986): 621–696.

Warren, Earl, Jr. "Obscenity Laws: A Shift to Reality." *The Pornography Controversy: Changing Moral Standards in American Life*, ed. Ray C. Rist. New Brunswick, NJ: Transaction Books, 1975, pp. 96–116.

Weaver, George M. *Handbook on the Prosecution of Obscenity Cases*. New York: National Obscenity Law Center, 1985.

Weeks, Jeffrey. *Against Nature: Essays on History, Sexuality and Identity*. London: Rivers Oram Press, 1991.

Weisberg, D. Kelly, ed. *Applications of Feminist Legal Theory to Women's Lives*. Philadelphia: Temple University Press, 1996.

Weispfenning, John T. "Changing Standards: Self-Regulation and the Evolution of the Roles of the Network Television Censors." Ph.D. dissertation, Purdue University, 1992.

West, Robin. "Pornography as a Legal Text: Comments from a Legal Perspective." *For Adult Users Only: The Dilemma of Violent Pornography*, ed. Susan Gubar and Joan Hoff. Bloomington: Indiana University Press, 1989, pp. 108–130.

Wicker, Tom. "After Lyrics, What?" *New York Times*, 5 February 1990, p. A19.

Widmer, Eleanor, ed. *Freedom and Culture: Literary Censorship in the 70s*. Belmont, CA: Wadsworth, 1970; revision of *Literary Censorship: Principles, Cases, Problems*, ed. Kingsley Widmer and Eleanor Widmer. Belmont, CA: Wadsworth, 1961.

Wilson, W. C., and H. I. Abelson, "Experience with and Attitudes toward Explicit Sexual Materials." *Journal of Social Issues*, 29:3 (1973): 19–39.

Winick, Charles. *Taste and the Censor in Television*. New York: Fund for the Republic, 1959.

Wishnia, S. "Rockin' with the First Amendment." *Nation*, 24 October 1987, pp. 444–446.

Wolgast, Elizabeth. "Pornography and the Tyranny of the Majority." *Feminist Jurisprudence*, ed. Patricia Smith. New York: Oxford University Press, 1993, pp. 431–448.

Women against Pornography. *Where We Stand on the First Amendment: Women against Pornography Position Paper*. New York 10036: WAP, 579 Ninth Avenue, 1982.

Yeamans, Robin. "A Political-Legal Analysis of Pornography." *Take Back the Night: Women on Pornography*, ed. Laura Lederer. New York: William Morrow, 1980, pp. 248–251.

Yoakum, Robert H. "The Great *Hustler* Debate." *Columbia Journalism Review*, 16:1 (May/June 1977): 53–58.

———. "An Obscene, Lewd, Lascivious, Indecent, Filthy, and Vile Tabloid Entitled *Screw*." *Columbia Journalism Review*, 15:6 (March/April 1977): 38–49.

Yule, Paul, and Jonathan Stack. *Damned in the USA*. New York: DIUSA Releasing, 1991.

Zappa, Frank. *Z-Pac*. P.O. Box 5265, North Hollywood, CA 91616.

Zeisel, William, ed. *Censorship: 500 Years of Conflict*. New York: New York Public Library, 1984.

21

The Economics of Pornography

As if to demonstrate the cultural importance of pornography, journalists usually stress that sexual expression is a multibillion-dollar industry. Newspapers and magazines frequently run exposés of pornographic entrepreneurs; few are trustworthy, especially when they venture into economics, a subject that seems to afflict journalists with either reticence or hyperbole. Most economists dismiss Andrea Dworkin's claim in *Pornography: Men Possessing Women* that "in the United States, the pornography industry is larger than the record and film industries combined" (201) as incredible on its face, but *all* estimates of the traffic in pornography should be read with caution, if not downright skepticism.

Just how large the "industry" is remains a matter of constant dispute, for the simple reason that few statisticians agree on what products are to be included. High estimates of revenues often lump conventional magazines (such as *Vogue* and *Harper's Bazaar*), mainstream films (*Halloween* and *Friday the 13th*), best-selling novels (*Vox*), network television programs (*Married with Children*), and items like condoms with hard-core videotapes, authentic fetish magazines, sleazy paperbacks, and sex toys. Additional complications stem from the difficulty of tracing fly-by-night operations of companies that go in and out of business, of mail-order enterprises, and of Mafia money-laundering schemes and other high cash-flow business scams, and from traditional exaggeration on the part of law enforcement officials. Another source of confusion is a failure to recognize that the market for all media changes from year to year as a consequence of evolving technology and mutating tastes. That is the reason that even careful essays like those collected by Robert M. Baird and Stuart E. Rosenbaum for *Pornography: Private Right or Public Menace?* reproduce old statistics; the claim that Americans purchase 2 million tickets to X-rated movie theaters every week (62, 70) ignores the fact that the videotape industry has so steadily diminished the number of X-rated movie houses that the figure could not possibly have been valid when the book was published (1991).

Market analysis suggests that the high volume of sexual materials fills a need for expression in the United States in much the same way that the much larger annual volume of religious materials satisfies a need for spiritual discourse. In other words, the pornographic industry—whatever its dimensions—cannot be characterized as aberrant capitalism or as a force-feeding of the public; the demand—however one wishes to describe it—is clear. A fascinating attempt to understand erotica in terms of standard capitalist theory is Linda W. Dutcher's "Scarcity and Erotica: An Examination of Commodity Theory Dynamics." If erotica is simply a commodity, says Dutcher, then its scarcity should increase demand for the product. But supply is apparently affected by many other variables, including the gender, sexual preference, and background of the consumer, not to mention technology. In "A Commodity Theory Analysis of the Effects of Age Restrictions upon Pornographic Materials," David A. Zellinger, Howard L. Fromkin, Donald E. Speller, and Carol A. Kohn apply economic theory to find that restricting pornographic materials to adults makes them more attractive (or valuable) to minors but that the same thing seems to be true of other materials restricted to older people, like cigarettes; otherwise, labeling materials pornographic did not seem to enhance their desirability. Using similar methodology, R. N. Jones and V. C. Joe found little evidence for the hypothesis that limiting materials to adults enhanced their appeal to minors in "Pornographic Materials and Commodity Theory."

Jay Gertzman believes that print erotica and photographs proliferated during the depression because these materials provided cheap entertainment for Americans who could not afford anything else. His *Bookleggers and Smuthounds: The Trade in Erotica, 1920–1940* details the finances of publishers in the late 1920s and early 1930s, the revenues of drugstore lending libraries of smutty novels, and other aspects of the economics of sex materials. Many commentators have noticed that women in particular turn to sex industries when ordinary opportunities pay too little. Susan Faludi notes in her "The Money Shot" that women (not the male performers) make most of the money in porn films today, that the stars often appear in hard-core as a way of building audiences for their primary occupation of stripping in lounges across America. To a certain degree, of course, sex industries persist whatever the health of the larger economy, but it probably does vary according to available capital and, in particular, according to the financial well-being of the middle and lower classes. By most estimates, the real income of the middle class has declined steadily for more than two decades, and that trend has almost certainly made pornography attractive to many workers at the lower end of economic scales. However exploited sex workers may be, sex industries by most reckonings pay better than fast-food franchises and in some cases offer better working conditions. But not always, says George Gurtner in "Noonie Smith: Shrines to Two Different Worlds," the story of a seventy-three-year-old woman who owns both a chapel and a porn shop on the Louisiana Highway 1 and who is just scraping along.

HISTORICAL ESTIMATES

The real problem is accurate statistics, as indicated by the history of attempts to quantify investments and profits. Now very much out-of-date, James J. Kilpatrick's *The Smut Peddlers: The Pornography Racket and the Law Dealing with Obscenity Censorship* raised no real alarms when it was published in 1960 because few Americans could see much evidence of the tidal wave of smut Kirlpatrick saw looming. Much of his material was taken from Post Office and state legislature reports and borrowed its edge from the usual alleged menace to the young. The message of Richard Kyle-Keith's *The High Price of Pornography*, published the following year, was similar. Kyle-Keith estimated the economic and (mostly) social cost (he believed that porn increased deviancy and sex crimes) of traffic in pornography in millions of dollars; he did not break out his figures, but did identify some of the corporate players he thought responsible. The title essay of E. J. Mishan's *Making the World Safe for Pornography and Other Intellectual Fashions* (107–150), a rational, but disapproving, critique, focused on the need for controlling porn through legislation in Britain that he thought could be extended to America as well; Mishan's chapter on "The Economics of Sex Pollution" (151–160) suggested segregating porn and sex industries in isolated areas for purposes of taxation, a strategy adopted soon after by cities such as Boston and New York. Like Kilpatrick and Kyle-Keith, however, Mishan concentrated on nebulous social costs rather than hard figures.

John Austin surveyed sexual advertisements, bookstores, massage parlors, and so on at the onset of the sexual revolution of the 1960s for his 1967 *Sex Is Big Business*; it was weak on statistics and was, in any case, more interested in prostitution than in pornography. Considerably more authoritative was the 1970 *Report* of the Presidential Commission on Obscenity and Pornography. The commission's studies, though dated now, were the most extensive ever undertaken; no government agency since has attempted, let alone achieved, its degree of accuracy. Volumes III and IX of the *Technical Reports* broke out figures for the various sectors of the adult industries at the time. John J. Sampson's "Commercial Traffic in Sexually Oriented Materials in the United States (1969–1970)," included in volume III, and Morris Massey's "A Marketing Analysis of Sex-Oriented Materials: A Pilot Study in Denver, August 1969," in volume IV, studied market trends and sales. Sampson pointed out that the traffic was enormous, though categorized by degrees of explicit representation; Massey noted, however, that individual retail outlets were small and that most were supplied by only a few distributors. Researchers for the commission noted that tracking the economics of the many different pornographic genres and their respective markets was extremely difficult and that virtually all previous estimates, especially those that spoke of the "pornography industry" as if it were monolithic, were unreliable, even "meaningless" (*Technical Reports* [3:4]). The researchers dismissed journalistic accounts pegging the traffic of the "industry" at between $500 million and $2.5 billion as inadequately supported (4). Part I of the general *Report* was devoted to commerce, mostly in books, photographs, motion pictures, and magazines. Volumes III, IV, and IX provided supporting detail on producers, distributors, jobbers, retailers, and consumers.

More concerned with cultural aspects of erotica was George Csicsery's *The Sex Industry*, published in 1973. Csicsery gives a few statistics, such as those for massage parlors in large cities like New York and Los Angeles, but contented himself with observing that a lot of money was being made from once-illegal activities. That year *Newsweek*'s "Sexploitation: Sin's Wages" reported that large pornographic enterprises were pulling in a lot of money. The title of Carolyn See's *Blue Money: Pornography and the Pornographers, an Intimate Look at the Two-Billion Dollar Fantasy Industry*, one of the very best journalistic treatments of pornography, foregrounds the figure she thought was accurate. Her estimates are derived, in part, from interviews with insiders such as publisher Marvin Miller, producer Matt Cimber, actress Linda Lovelace, historian Jim Holliday, and attorney Burton Marks. *The Millionaire Pornographers: Adam Special Report 12* contained information on the holdings of Hugh Hefner, Bob Guccione, Larry Flynt, Ralph Ginzberg, Douglas Lambert, Al Goldstein, Marvin Miller, Lyle Stuart, Gerard Damiano, and Bill Osco but is not very detailed.

James Cook's "The X-Rated Economy," though also dated (1978), remains one of the best explorations of the economics of porn because its author, a skilled financial reporter, actually examined markets, technology, and connections with organized crime. Cook quoted the California Department of Justice's estimate that pornography was a $4 billion a year business in the United States, noting that despite the absence of supporting evidence, the figure was never challenged. Cook himself computed that the ten leading sexually oriented magazines—*Playboy, Penthouse, Hustler, Oui, Playgirl, Club, Gallery, Chic, Genesis*, and *High Society*—grossed $475 million a year; estimated that the nation's 708 adult theaters sold 2 million tickets a week for an annual gross of $365 million (these are the figures quoted by the essayists in Baird and Rosenbaum, cited earlier); and guessed that marital aids and sex toys accounted for another $100 million a year. Cook cited the Los Angeles Police Department as saying that porn enterprises in that city grossed $125 million annually. Cook himself calculated that an adult shop with film loops in New York City could take in as much as $10,000 a day in 1978.

Using Cook's figures as the starting point for two 1981 articles, "Sex Is a Growing Multibillion Dollar Business" and "Opponents of Flourishing Sex Industry Hindered by Its Open Public Acceptance," William Serrin probed further. Serrin interviewed people like Father Bruce Ritter of Covenant House (before he resigned because of charges of child molestation); Al Goldstein, publisher of *Screw*; Ted Williams, developer of the enormously successful Prelude 3 vibrator;

David Friedman, chair of the Adult Film Association (Los Angeles); Duane Colglazier, head of *Pleasure Chest* (purveyors of erotic accoutrements); Dennis Sobin, publisher of *Adult Business Report* (Washington, DC); Manhattan district attorney Robert Morgenthau, and assorted law enforcement officials. While Serrin did not doubt that the demand for sex and ancillary products at the onset of the 1980s was huge, he observed that industry spokespeople tended to overestimate the size of the market to make the business seem more respectable, just as opponents tended to inflate the profits to make adult enterprises seem more sinister. When Sobin said that Americans spent $5 billion annually on sex, Serrin was skeptical, pointing out that the figure would represent twice what Americans spent on breakfast cereal, 20 percent of what they spent on fresh fruit and vegetables, or 25 percent of what they gave to churches per year ("Sex Is a Growing," B6). "Pornography: Obscene Profits at the Expense of Women," whose 1978 context was that pornography was antifemale, boosted estimates even higher. Paul Siebenand's analysis of the gay porn industry, completed in 1980 as *The Beginnings of Gay Cinema in Los Angeles: The Industry and the Audience*, noticed that the once-underground gay market was attracting revenues in the millions. A study published in 1980 by the West 42d Street Study Team as *Sex Industries in New York City* is perhaps the most reliable survey of the period; figures are modest—and credible—by comparison with journalistic accounts, but they are localized.

In 1984 Abt Associates, Inc., an agency commissioned by the government, published *Unreported Taxable Income from Selected Illegal Activities*; some of the estimates were used in the *Final Report* of the Attorney General's Commission. Volume II of *Final Report* provided an extensive overview of production, distribution, and sales of pornographic and sexually oriented materials. The estimate here was that the American pornography industry *netted* around $7 billion a year, though it is not clear even that all members of the commission agreed with that figure, which is clearly inflated. Gordon Hawkins and Franklin E. Zimring compare the Johnson and the Meese Commission reports on the economics of porn in "The Nature and Distribution of Pornography in the United States." Real economists do not often look at porn, but when they do, their attention can illuminate. In 1983 Stephen A. Kurkjian and his colleagues noticed that some porn theater owners were forming chains to cut costs and increase profits, while publishers and adult businesses were doing market studies of their clientele, and other companies were jockeying for cable and satellite channels, as detailed in "Pornography Industry Finds Big Profits in New Markets."

In 1986 Helen Reynolds attempted to deal with pornography as an adjunct to prostitution in Nevada, Texas, California, and Massachusetts but gives few statistics in her *The Economics of Prostitution*. John Leo's "Romantic Porn in the Boudoir" counted the rentals of more than 100 million porn videotapes and other materials to estimate gross sales of the entire American porn industry at $8 billion, another high wild guess. More realistic figures were provided a year later by David Hebditch and Nick Anning in their volume *Porn Gold: Inside the Pornography Business*, easily the best popular investigation of the industry. In 1988 Hebditch and Anning pegged the annual *worldwide* sales revenues of sexually explicit materials at somewhere in excess of $5 billion, of which the lion's share came from consumer demand for videotapes. Hebditch and Anning pointed out that sex industries typically flourish when real income sinks; video- tapes become a cheap form of entertainment for the masses. The financial sta- tistics provided by Roger Faligot and Rémi Kauffer for their *Porno Business* are similar to those of Hebditch and Anning, though the former are more inter- ested in the Continental and Japanese markets; less sexually paranoid Europeans generally define pornography more narrowly than Americans, of course, and simply do not include some materials—fashion magazines or prime-time tele- vision shows, for example—that Americans consider overly sexualized.

In late 1989, "Prosecute Porn? It's on the Decline," an article in the *Wall Street Journal*, noted that the number of porn theaters in the United States had dropped below 250, that the income of the erotic video industry had fallen from $430 million in 1986 to $380 million in 1989, that sales of *Playboy*, *Gallery*, and *High Society* were in a tailspin, and that dial-a-porn calls had fallen off by 40 percent. "The stricken market for sexual materials cannot justify the bal- looning costs of prosecuting pornographers" (1), said the newspaper. Since that year, revenues have fluctuated: the video industry is doing well, but magazines are not, and dial-a-porn revenues, after initial surges, by most estimates are now flat.

Another reason that the economics are so complicated is evident in "The Porn Broker," for which William Bastone investigates the finances of William Bas- ciano, a real estate mogul and porn king who stands to make money by selling Times Square properties as New York tries to redevelop that area. As Bastone's analysis indicates, researchers have a tendency to conflate income from pornog- raphy and that from other enterprises when the same people are involved. Jour- nalists and government prosecutors do not make distinctions, and the Justice Department routinely employs RICO provisions to seize any assets that a por- nographer might have, even though those assets may have been derived legiti- mately. Joe Pichirallo chronicles the beginnings of that ploy in "FBI Targets Owners, Profits of Sex Businesses in D.C. Area," an article on FBI attempts to prosecute owners of sex industry businesses under RICO legislation. According to some critics, the government simply wants to share in profits it considers insufficiently taxed. To Candida Royalle, speaking to Don Vaughn for "An Interview with Candida Royalle," federal prosecutors are self-serving, hypocrit- ical, and self-perpetuating: "they are targeting the very big companies, and they are usually walking away with $500,000 to $2 million in damages. That's what they'll sue the company for. With VCA, for example, the owner had to go to prison for a year and pay $2 million. But VCA is still in business. So in a way this is just extortion, and it's a way for the government to fund its continued attacks on the industry" (103). It is hard to resist the conclusion that federal obscenity units are themselves extremely profitable businesses, since successfully prosecuting $100 worth of sexual material can enable an agency to seize millions of dollars of assets under RICO statutes.

THE CURRENT BOTTOM LINE

Eric Schlosser's "The Business of Pornography" for *U.S. News and World Report* asserts that Americans in 1996 spent $8 billion "on hard-core videos, peep shows, live sex acts, adult cable programming, sexual devices, computer porn, and sex magazines" (44). Schlosser says that the $8 billion is "an amount much larger than Hollywood's domestic box office receipts and larger than all the revenues generated by rock and country music recordings" (44). These are figures selected for color rather than illumination. According to the Veronis, Suhler and Associates *Communications Industry Forecast*, published annually in July, the total revenues of U.S. media industries break out as follows for 1997, the most recent year for which "hard" figures are available: book publishing $28 billion, newspapers $55 billion, television $49 billion, magazines $26 billion, radio $13 billion, movies $35 billion (includes world sales), and recordings $14 billion. Better indicators can be found in media trade journals and in *U.S. Industrial Outlook*, published annually by the Department of Commerce to project annual income of industries, including media businesses. Those inclined toward hyperbolic estimates should also consult the latest *Statistical Abstract of the United States*, which does not report sales figures for pornographic industries but does provide them for other businesses. In 1991, for example, liquor stores in the United States took in $21.4 billion, a total that does not include sales of liquor in restaurants or bars. Such numbers are sobering because even the wildest estimates of the revenues of the pornographic industries pale beside them.

Homelier comparisons are even more appropriate. As Sally Johnson has pointed out in "Reaping What the Boomers Sow: Getting Down and Dirty in the Garden Is Big Business," Americans spent $22.2 billion in 1995 just on home gardening supplies. Still another figure is illuminating: "Industry statistics have it that Americans spent $2.5 billion shoving quarters in pinball machines, half what they spent going to the movies," says Douglas Martin in the 1990 article "Barroom Wizard Sure Plays Up a Pinball Mien." "Just the Facts," on the American Meat Institute's Web site, indicates that Americans spent about $4 billion on hot dogs in 1996. Schlosser's figures omit print porn such as women's romances (about $1 billion a year—see later), but if we accept his $8 billion as authoritative, then Americans spend on pornography about twice what they spend on frankfurters, three times what they spend on pinball games, and about a third of what they spend on their gardens.

In "The Sex Industry" (1998), *The Economist* conservatively estimates the worldwide sex industry, which includes far more enterprises than pornography, at $20 billion a year (21). The article points out that the "bottom of the [pornography] market is hopelessly oversupplied" with cheap products (22), which has led producers to go upscale or to find niche markets for fetishes. It also discusses the falling demand for sex magazines, the threat to established businesses by Internet sites offering images for free, the going rates for performers, and the pressures of global competition. The magazine predicts that governments will increase penalties for child porn as a way of legitimating sexual materials for adults. Growing tolerance and liberal legislation will put most sectors of the sex business "where it ultimately belongs—as just another branch of the global entertainment industry." It should be noted, however, than neither the *U.S. News and World Report* nor *The Economist* articles take sufficient account of Internet sex services, which are rising too fast to chart (see later).

PRINT

Bernard Arcand points out in *The Jaguar and the Anteater: Pornography Degree Zero* that *Playboy* and *Penthouse* each lost more than a million readers in the years between 1979 and 1984 (39), that their seemingly large circulation figures are roughly the same as those for *Good Housekeeping, Redbook*, and *Mademoiselle* and far below those for *Ladies Home Journal, Better Homes and Gardens*, and *Reader's Digest* (43), and that the stock of Playboy Enterprises fell from 30 to 7 (it has bounced back to 20 [1999]). In 1991 Roger Cohen's "Ms. Playboy" examined the efforts of Christie Hefner, daughter of Hugh, to improve the fortunes of Playboy Enterprises. As head of the company, she must deal with a track record of declining revenues. Magazines such as *Penthouse* and *Hustler* are privately owned, but *Playboy* is publicly held. According to its *Annual Report*, Playboy Enterprises in 1995 netted $629,000, a figure that reflects an upswing in the company's fortunes. The magazine itself accounted for only part of its revenues. Analyzing the magazine's revenues in 1996, Noreen O'Leary's "The Old Bunny Trick" points out that while domestic sales have slumped, *Playboy* abroad occupies a cultural status similar to Disney's and appeals to Europeans as an icon of American lifestyles, a circumstance that bodes well for *Playboy*'s aggressive marketing of international editions and cable television fare. Michael Kaplan's dispassionate look at the finances of Larry Flynt's $100 million a year (1993) empire furnishes information on the thirty magazines (e.g., *Maternity Fashion* as well as *Hustler*) Flynt publishes plus the eighty he distributes in "The Resurrection of Larry Flynt." In 1993, according to Philippa Kennedy in "A Marriage Made in Sleaze," General Media International, the privately held parent company of *Penthouse*, grossed $200 million. As for other soft-core, hard-core, and fetish magazines, the *Final Report* of the Attorney General's Commission lists more than 2,500 published in the United States and roughly estimates their revenues in the tens of millions. In "Looking for the Holy Grail: Publishing and Advertising Strategies and Contemporary Men's Magazines," S. Nixon discusses the process by which editors and owners identify markets, shape them, and achieve success.

Sylvia Plachy and James Ridgeway unearth statistics in *Red Light: Inside the*

Sex Industry, which covers the revenues of media such as Masquerade Books, a porn house, *Screw* magazine, and cybersex providers. Any number of sources have graphed the sales of romance novels over the last fifteen years. In 1980, S. Grover alerted readers of the *Wall Street Journal* to the rising revenues of "The Bodice Busters." "Romance Publishing and the Production of Culture," by John Markert, considers the phenomenal growth of romances in the 1980s in terms of six factors: law, technology, industry structure, organizational structure, occupational careers, and market, all of which, to one degree or another, explain the increase in sexual explicitness. In 1990 "A Man's Guide to Heaving-Bosom Women's Fiction," an amusing review of "bodice-ripping" fiction by Judith Krantz, Jackie Collins, Kathleen E. Woodiwiss, Johanna Lindsey, and others, reproduced statistics from *Publishers Weekly*, which indicated that 40 percent of all mass-market paperbacks printed in America were romance novels, and from *Romantic Times* magazine, which said that 100–200 romance novels were published every month in the United States. By 1993 David L. Langford's Associated Press story, "Romance Novels Are Hot!," increased those figures. According to Langford, romances accounted for 46 percent of the American paperback market, a $750 million a year business. Consumers could choose from 120 new novels each month, of which heavy consumers may read twenty to forty. Langford observes that explicit bedroom scenes became a staple in the historical romance with Kathleen Woodiwiss' *The Flame and the Flower* (Avon, 1972). Avon advanced $100,000 for three novels to be written by Fabio, who is ordinarily a popular male model for book covers. Like stars of pornographic movies, Fabio was branching out into posters, calendars, and 900 telephone numbers for women who need to see more of him or to seek his advice. By 1994, said Edith Updike's "Publishers of Romance Novels Add Color to Their Lines," "Romance novels account for nearly 50 percent of mass market paperback sales. In 1992, readers spent $885 million on 177 million romance books. Harlequin alone puts out 62 new titles each month, almost 750 a year. Romance readers are insatiable. Many spend more than $1,000 a year, purchasing as many as 30 paperbacks a month" (23). The industry chugs on: U.S. revenues in 1999 exceed $1 billion annually, says E. Graham in "Romances, Long Denied Reviews, Get Some Respect," a figure confirmed by the reporter in "Words of Love."

Jay A. Gertzman examines the costs and revenues of publishers ranging from Ben Rebkuhn in the 1930s to Samuel Roth in the 1950s in *Bookleggers and Smuthounds: The Trade in Erotica, 1920–1940*. The mania for collecting sleaze from the past, such as pulp paperbacks, scandal magazines, pinups, and any kind of cheesecake, is the subject of William Grimes' "Lurid! Licentious! Collectible! The Flip Side of the 1940's and 50's." Consumer guides to sex materials are rare and unreliable. *Screw* magazine built its reputation, in large part, on its attempt to judge the merits of pornographic genres and report on the prices of adult bookstores, massage parlors, movie theaters, magazines, sex novels, and mail-order dealers. For some years one of *Screw*'s columnists, John Milton, edited $ex $ense, one of the tabloid's secondary publications. Billed as "a consumer's guide to mail-order sex products," this newsletter included information on books, magazines, and films and listed "safe sellers" as well as "dirty dealers," that is, merchants who did not deliver what customers ordered. It is useful today because it indicates going prices during the late 1970s. Richard Ellis discusses the publishing strategies of Grove Press, the upscale publisher of erotica in the 1960s and 1970s, in "Disseminating Desire: Grove Press and 'The End[s] of Obscenity,' " and Robert S. Boynton does the same for Routledge in "The Routledge Revolution: Has Academic Publishing Gone Too Far?" William E. Geist reports on the lively market for sexual advice in "Merchandising Dr. Ruth." "The Selling of Sex," by John Leland et al., a *Newsweek* review, argues that the expanding sales of sexual materials, as typified by Madonna's *Sex*, indicates that such photographs encourage voyeurism as a form of "safe sex" in an age of AIDS but also generate big bucks. The merchandising is increasingly respectable. Bloomingdale's now sells Tom of Finland fashions, says Lynn Yaeger in "Commercial Art." Porn star Jenteal models sunglasses and clothing, and other actresses make personal appearances at chain stores selling a variety of products.

FILMS AND VIDEOTAPES

The interviews with pornographic film producers conducted by Eugene Slabaugh and George Hutchinson indicate that stag films shot before the 1960s did not make much money, in large part because (1) they were difficult to copy, (2) few people had projectors until the advent of the 8mm format, (3) there were no distribution systems of any size, (4) the market itself was limited to specialty entertainment requested by male groups such as American Legion Posts and local Elks Clubs, and (5) police, postal inspectors, and other agents regularly interdicted or seized reels. The Presidential Commission's 1970 *Report* said that the 8mm-format stag film was a small industry revolving around localized production; only a few individuals made more than $10,000 per year in making them (18).

There are few figures for the market in exploitation films over the years, primarily because of the many genres—some of them nonsexual—involved. Feature-length porn films appeared first in the late 1960s and took off with the advent of *Deep Throat* and *Behind the Green Door* (both 1972). By the mid-1970s, the weekly trade journal *Variety* regularly reported the revenues of porn features. In the 3 February 1977 issue, for instance, the "50 Top-Grossing Films" of the week listed *Through the Looking Glass* in sixteenth place, *Chatterbox*, a French import, in twentieth, *Autobiography of a Flea* in twenty-seventh, *Lollipop Girls in Hard Candy* in twenty-eighth, and *Kinky Ladies of Bourbon Street* in fortieth. *Lollipop Girls* had been on the chart for eighteen weeks, grossing $1,096,050, as compared to the legitimate film *The Last Tycoon*, in fourteenth place, which had been on the chart for fourteen weeks with a total gross of

$1,058,510 (9). At the same time, such figures can be misleading. *Deep Throat*, surely the most famous porn feature of all time, has grossed in theater runs and video rentals many millions of dollars. The exact figure is unknown but would surely pale beside the grosses of, say, *Terminator II* especially if inflation were factored in.

Once they became quasi-legitimate, American pornographic films were marketed worldwide. "L'Erotisme en Question," a special issue of *Cinema D'Aujourd'Hui* published in the mid-1970s, includes a report on the debate in the French National Assembly over the influx of American porn. The discussion led to the French government's imposing duties on American imports in order to foster the domestic French porn industry. Sophie Bordes and Daniel Serceau's "L'irrésistible marginalisation du cinéma pornographique" analyzes the taxation strategy. Karen Thorsen noted in "The State of French Porn: Up 'n Coming" that American porn films continued to attract large audiences in France despite the high tariff, though protectionism could be credited with stimulating French products such as Davy's *Exhibition*, which was shown in New York at the Lincoln Center Film Festival in 1975.

By the mid-1970s, at the peak of production, prior to the boom in videocassette recorder/players, the demand for hard-core *features* began to fall. In 1976 Addison Verrill reported that "Parisi Sees Porn Market Off, Now Averages $150,000–$300,000," an article that provides some information about the Mob's financing of *Deep Throat* but that is really about declining demand. Using the director Jonas Middleton as his focus, Joseph W. Slade took a close look at the returns a pornographer could expect in "The Pornographic Film Market and Pornographic Formulas" (1976). Here Slade dealt with foreign distribution of American movies as well, drawing on articles like "U.S. Porn Producer Goes O'Seas for Fresh Faces, More Natural Attitudes." By 1978 Dave Goldberg of the Associated Press said in "No Longer a Novelty, Porno Movies Put Their Makers on Economic Skids" that porn theaters were closing down and that producers, facing diminished profits, were shooting hardcore, cable, and R-versions in order to reach the widest possible venues. In retrospect, the decline appears to have been a readjustment occasioned by the inroads of videocassettes. To some at the time the industry still seemed pretty healthy. Jill Stewart wrote in "The Bottom Line in Blue Movies" that in 1977 the porn film industry "brought in $3.5 million in weekly box-office gross nationwide, nearly one-tenth the total film industry gross per week" (16). San Francisco officials had stopped prosecuting pornography, she said, because juries would not convict: "They just don't think it's obscene" (18). The city's police insisted that while Los Angeles' porn industry was connected with the Mafia, San Francisco's was not. By 1981, said David Chute in "Tumescent Market for One-Armed Video-philes," profits of the average porn feature released in the saturated market worked out to $40,000–$60,000, figures not even close to the much higher receipts for comparable legitimate films. For a quick, but accurate, look at the economics of the porn videocassette in 1984, the introductory chapters of Robert

H. Rimmer's first *The X-Rated Video Guide* (1984) is excellent. He provides information on capitalization and grosses.

The *Attorney General's Commission on Pornography: Final Report* of 1986 said that between twelve and twenty-four production companies made about 100 feature-length (16mm and 35mm) hard-core films in 1985; these were distributed to a national total of about 700 adult movie theaters, which sold about 2 million tickets per week for gross receipts of about $500 million for the year. In thus reproducing Cook's 1978 figures, the commission implied that theatrical exhibition—already in a nosedive—was still generating substantial revenues. On the other hand, the commission admitted that the number of 8mm films had dropped to an insignificant fraction of the market (1384–1385). As agents of the Attorney General's Commission began themselves to harass adult businesses, many entrepreneurs ran for cover. Attacks by fundamentalists allied with antiporn feminists caused some video stores to stop renting explicit tapes, said Nicholas D. Kristof in "X-Rated Industry in a Slump." Kristof noticed that women seemed entrenched as renters, perhaps accounting for 32 percent (as opposed to the 37 percent rented by males) of all porn tape rentals (the balance were rented by heterosexual couples together). Jami Bernard also began his "The Way of All Flesh" with the suggestion that conservative, religious, and law enforcement pressure might be killing off the porn tape industry. When Bernard interviewed John Weston, legal counsel for the Adult Video Association, however, he learned that Americans were expected to rent 200 million erotic tapes in 1988, as opposed to only 54 million in 1984. Bernard did note that some rental stores were stocking more "classy" porn as a way of defusing complaints from opponents.

Reporting has in the past been sketchy. Prior to 1983, researchers usually had to depend on *Variety*, which noted gross box office receipts. *TAB (The Adult Business) Report*, published from 1978 to 1985, carried material on many aspects of the adult business, from novelties and sex aids to films and videotapes. The *Bulletin of the Adult Film Association of America*, published from 1979 until 1982, as the title suggests, was devoted to visual media. In "Rape and Pornography," George C. Thomas notes a jump in porn revenues from 1982 to 1983 of $38 million to $340 million but thinks that the rise in part probably has to do with better reporting of sales figures. Reliable canvassing began with the advent of the current bible of the industry, *Adult Video News*, which began publication in 1983. "Charting the Adult Video Market," a 1989 *AVN* report for video rental stores, said that wholesale sales were close to $400 million in the United States and that some 1,250 tapes had been released that year, 500 of them new. Every issue of *AVN* deals with sales, but occasional supplements, such as *Special Supplement Summer 1994: Marketing Gay Video*, list trends, popular performers, and "must-stock" tape recommendations.

From the mid-1970s to the mid-1980s, the Adult Film Association held annual awards, which are still sponsored by the trade journal *Adult Video News*, which also sells videocassettes of each year's event. "Porn to Win" is Michele Capozzi's account of her visit to the 1990 X-Rated Critics Awards ceremony in Santa Monica, California, with directors, stars, and fans in attendance. Although *Adult Video News* runs more comprehensive accounts of awards ceremonies, similar articles appear from time to time in various magazines and are revealing because they indicate the rituals of a subculture. The adult film industry mimics (often raucously) Hollywood's handing out Oscars by bestowing prizes to Best Actor, Best Actress, Best Picture, best oral sex scene, and so on before audiences composed of agents, distributors, performers, directors, producers, publicists, and assorted professionals. As is the case in the legitimate business, the awards figure in advertising and do boost sales and rentals. The *Tenth Anniversary Supplement* to *Adult Video News* (1993) contains very good historical essays and prognostications for the future of the adult film industry. *Adult Video News* reported that the number of rentals of hard-core videotapes had risen 1.2 billion over three years to 2.1 billion in 1993, beggaring the predictions of John Weston cited by Bernard earlier. Beginning in May 1993, each issue of *Adult Video News* has reported in depth on adult business retailing in major cities: Los Angeles (May 1993), New York (June 1993), Boston (November 1993), Tampa Bay (May 1994), and so on. "Porno Goes Mainstream," Eric Hollreiser's 1995 article on adult video emporiums in various cities, charts a growth industry with useful figures. "The Sex Industry," by the authoritative *The Economist*, puts the American adult video industry's revenues for 1997 at $2.5 billion. (But note Joel Stein's estimate later.)

Some confusion has arisen over the years as a consequence of mutations in the marketplace due to changes in format and as a result of fluctuations in exports. Few hard-core pornographic films are shot for theatrical release today, and only a few cassettes are mastered on film stock because of the high cost. Productions are commonly videotaped in three versions: hard-core (graphic intercourse) for X-rated sale or rent; hard-R (simulated sex) for cable television; and soft-R (implied sex) for hotels. According to Nick Ravo's "A Fact of Life: Sex-Video Rentals," pornographic videotapes in 1990 accounted for 20 percent of video rentals nationwide; of that percentage, 40 percent are rented by men alone, 29 percent by men and women together, 15 percent by individual women, 13 percent by two men together, and 3 percent by two women together. Ravo suggests that the steady rental rates reflect the fear of AIDS, since those who might otherwise engage in sex can find masturbatory pleasure, singly or with partners, in voyeurism. Ravo notes as well the increased popularity of amateur productions and finishes off the article by quoting directors Henri Pachard (real name Ron Sullivan) and Candida Royalle and several video store owners on increased efforts by local censors to suppress tapes. Molly Colin furnishes a list of the porn films women rent most often in "Women Tuning into Porn." More recent rental figures from *Adult Video News*, as Patti Britton notes in "Women Who Make Porn: The Influence of Gender on the Content and Approach of Porn Videos," indicate that 71 percent of renters in 1998 were men alone; women alone and couples together are still renting, but their percentages have fallen.

According to a *Time* article of late 1998, Joel Stein's "Porn Goes Mainstream," video sales and rentals now stand at 4.2 billion (a number that seems inflated to account for any kind of sex in any kind of movie) and account for 14 percent of all rentals and almost 50 percent of the rental industry (54). The "Big Four" video companies (Metro, Vivid, VCA, Wicked) dominate distribution. Of these, Vivid is the largest, with sales estimated at between $25 million annually (according to Stein's "Porn Goes Mainstream") and $50 million (according to Jeffrey Gettleman's "L.A. Economy's Dirty Secret: Porn Is Thriving"). (These figures, when properly extrapolated for other companies, make *The Economist*'s estimates, given earlier, seem more credible. One cannot help thinking that producers and opponents all have a vested interest in boosting statistics.) Vivid markets its products through increasingly upscale outlets and mail-order, co-owns with *Playboy* the AdulTVision cable channel, and is working on virtual reality and interactive systems. Metro Video already trades on Wall Street on the NASDAQ exchange.

Even experts have disagreed as to the number of porn videos produced annually. Al Goldstein's "Making Your Own Erotic Video" puts the total number of porn films at 5,000 for 1993, but that figure would have to include R-rated and European adult fare, because *AVN*, a much more authoritative source, pegs it at 2,200 in 1992, for aggregate revenues of $1.6 billion for all rental-sales outlets except all-adult shops (see *AVN*'s *Adult Entertainment Guide 1993*). Eric Schlosser in "The Business of Pornography" accepts AVN's estimate of 8,000 for 1996, but this may be slightly misleading given the many older films then being transferred onto videotape in an effort to avoid the records-keeping requirement of section 2257 of the U.S. Code. The industry is nonetheless robust. The *Adult Video News* website reports that aggregate sales and rentals for 1998 were $4.1 billion (down slightly from $4.2 billion in 1997), of which approximately one-third came from foreign business. American studios turned out 10,000 new titles in 1999. The percentage of offshore revenues is also telling. America leads the world in production. According to John Nadler's " 'X' Marks the Spot," European producers turn out only 100 hard-core videos per month. Joseph W. Slade discusses global markets, worldwide video and cable demand, and competition from European producers in "Pornography in the Late Nineties." Laurence O'Toole sketches the history and revenues of American production houses such as Vivid in *Pornocopia: Porn, Sex, Technology and Desire*.

CABLE AND SATELLITE TELEVISION AND TELEPHONE SEX

By the early 1980s, according to Howard Polskin's "Love and Money," softcore sexual programming had become entrenched on American cable television systems. Polskin quoted David Friedman, then chair of the Adult Film Association of America, to the effect that in 1982 producers of X-rated films on average earned $350,000 in theaters, $35,000 on videocassette, and $35,000 on cable

(32). X-rated films and videotapes are shot in various hard- and soft-core versions for the different markets, notes Tony Schwartz in "The TV Pornography Boom," a historically important article that covers VCR tapes and soft-core programming on cable and satellite here and abroad. The Playboy Channel began as a cable service in the early 1980s as a subsidiary of the corporation that markets the magazine. *TV Guide* critic David Handler asked, "Now the Playmates Move—But Will America Pay to Watch?" in an article on the inauguration of the channel, distributed by satellite and carried by various cable systems. Early statistics, said Handler, indicated that 40 percent of the audience were couples, while another 20 percent were women watching alone. Three years later, Mark Frankel noted that the soft-core fare had thus far proved unprofitable in "Can Playboy Save Its Skin?" Since then, under Hefner's daughter Christine, the finances have improved, thanks, in part, to aggressive marketing overseas. Competition for shares of developing European broadcasting markets has led many Western European stations to show erotic fare. Michael Williams points out in "Latenight Libido Rules Euro TV" that cable companies have virtually exhausted the world's stock of soft-core films, which means that European broadcasters are turning increasingly to hard-core films, more often than not American, that American cable operators cannot carry. French subscribers to satellite services prefer American hard-core to the domestic variety, according to Williams, because French performers aren't "pretty enough" (52).

Subscribers to premium American cable services such as the Playboy Channel, American Exxxtasy, and Tuxxedo Channel (the latter two now defunct) in 1989 numbered about half a million, according to "Cable Stats," published by a trade journal. Subscription fees for those services are difficult to compute, in part because they are usually add-ons to tiered cable services. If one makes the unlikely assumption that subscribers subscribe to a multitier service *only* in order to receive sexually explicit programming, as does James Weaver in "Responding to Erotica: Perceptional Processes and Dispositional Implications," then the figure is high; Weaver puts it at more than $75 million (331). In 1994, according to *Cable Television Developments*, the only sexually explicit pay channels were Adam and Eve Channel (begun 1994, number of subscribers unavailable), Playboy (1982, PPV 1989, 500,000 subscribers), Spice and Spice 2 (1994, 7.3 million subscribers); all carried soft-core fare. Kim Mitchell and Eric Glick of *Cable World* estimate that 1996 cable erotica revenue was $95 million. The advent of hard-core has raised the ante. Playboy bought the Spice Channel in 1998, and its soft erotica is now lagging well behind harder material offered by New Frontier Media, which owns two cable channels (Erotic Network and Pleasure) and three Direct Broadcast Satellite channels (Exctasy, TrueBlue, and Gonzo X). According to "Playboy Weathers 505 Storm," New Frontier markets its erotica to some 165,000 customers at subscription rates between $6 and $14.95 per month for annual revenues exceeding $80 million.

Religious, inspirational, family-value, and parenting channels far outnumber the adult channels. Those persuaded that cable television is rife with sexuality will point to the R-rated movies carried by HBO and Showtime, of course, but assigning an economic value to those would be impossible, since these movies are (1) not necessarily regarded as adult in nature by subscribers, (2) mixed in with innocuous fare, and (3) are often R-rated because of violence, not sex. Class distinctions also cloud financial estimates, since less affluent Americans, unable to pay the monthly subscription fees, may instead rent the occasional adult film to play on a VCR, whose initial cost can be amortized over several years. To put matters in perspective, it is useful to remember that the broadcast *rights* (not the network revenues) to National Football League (NFL) football in 1990 went for *$3.6 billion* ("Year in Review: Sports").

C. Richard King's "The Siren Scream of Telesex: Speech, Seduction and Stimulation," a Baudrillardian speculation on the hyperreality of dial-a-porn messages, contains up-to-date figures on the dial-a-porn industry. More dated are the statistics collected by the House Committee on Energy and Commerce for *Telephone Decency Act of 1987: Hearing on H.R. 1786 before the Subcommittee on Telecommunications and Finance of the House Committee on Energy and Commerce* and by the House Subcommittee on Criminal Law for *Cable Porn and Dial-a-Porn Control Act: Hearing before the Subcommittee on Criminal Law of the Committee on the Judiciary* (1986). Among other government documents, the *Attorney General's Commission on Pornography: Final Report* contains estimates of the revenues of telephone sex (vol. II). Schlosser's "The Business of Pornography" estimates that dial-a-porn services brought in between $750 million and $1 billion in 1996 (49).

INCOME OF SEX WORKERS

Even more elusive are figures on the income of sex workers themselves. *Playboy* pays its Playmates upward of $50,000, with additional income likely from personal appearances; the Playmate of the Year receives many times that. *Penthouse* follows a similar practice, but the women and men models in run-of-the-mill, soft-core and hard-core, or gay porn magazines are paid nowhere near such sums. As in most endeavors, disparities between the average performers and the headliners seem to be large; stars, in short, get paid far more. Because they are so often targeted by the IRS, porn stars rarely allude to salaries even in their autobiographies (see **Female Performers** and **Male Performers** in Chapter 13). In 1985 David T. Friendly visited the set of *A Coming of Angels—The Sequel*, starring Annette Haven and Jaime Gillis, for his *Newsweek* article, "This Isn't Shakespeare." Gillis, reported Friendly, got $750 a day; Haven $1,500. The budget for the film was $120,000. Gillis has been working in films since 1972, but has never earned as much as $50,000 a year. (Friendly pointed out that annual box-office receipts for hard-core features in 1985 were $500 million before video sales and rentals.) By contrast, the Attorney General's *Final Report* claimed that in 1986 Annette Haven (and Seka, a star of comparable stature) made $17,000 a day (870). Most people in the industry found the figures provided by Friendly much more credible. Sylvia Plachy and James Ridgeway's *Red Light: Inside the Sex Industry* pegs the numbers much lower. Susan Faludi's "The Money Shot" reports on inequities in the salaries of women and men performers in video, with those for the former far outpacing those for the latter.

Two excellent 1993 articles review working conditions, safety standards (e.g., a lamentable lack of concern for condoms), salaries, profits, performer motivations, and industry practices in the production of hard-core videos. These are Gary Indiana's "A Day in the Life of Hollywood's Sex Factory" and Lisa Katzman's "The Women of Porn: They're Not in It for the Moneyshot." Katzman notes that Candida Royalle shot *Revelations* for $115,000. In an amusing 1994 piece occasioned by the John Wayne Bobbitt case, Bruce Handy tried to calculate the value of a penis in "What's It Worth to You?" Handy asked agent Jim South and actor William Margold about the earnings of male porn stars. Although South claimed that the most successful can earn $100,000 a year, Margold said that $50,000 to $75,000 is a more realistic figure. Moreover, Margold predicated his reply on the performer's being able to complete two sex scenes per day for three to five days a week—" 'truly a gift,' Margold added, 'that very few men will attain.' " Celebrated actresses can gross considerably more. According to Robert Rimmer, Traci Lords made $150,000 annually before her exposure as a minor forced her to leave the business some years ago.[1] Some performers, such as Ron Jeremy, make money from endorsing products like cigars and beer and dildos, says Joel Stein in "Porn Goes Mainstream." On the other hand, many actresses are regularly ripped off when their images are used without recompense in ads for telephone sex or other products.

Roger Trilling interviews Madison, a porn star anxious that Americans know that the porn industry is "respectable" as a form of safe sex in "Madison: Ex-High School Cheerleader: Hapless Romantic. Porn Star." Trilling's question: " 'What kind of money do you make?' 'It depends on who you are and what you're doing. About seven hundred to a thousand dollars a day. Boy/girl is more money than a lesbian scene, and doing two men is more than one. I just finished shooting a twenty-five-girl orgy—my goodness!—and they paid me a lot. But then, there was a lot to be done" (126). Jeffrey Gettleman's 1999 article "L.A. Economy's Dirty Secret: Porn Is Thriving" says that male performers average $500 per sex scene, while women receive three to ten times that much, although stars such as Jenna Jameson, Anna Malle, Jenteal, and Lexus can command $5,000. The stars earn far more than that stripping in clubs across the country.

At the other end of the scale, "Mondo Washington," by James Ridgeway, puts the income of a Florida telephone sex operator at $400 a week.

PERFORMANCE

Serious performance art, explicit or not, is a marginal enterprise and thus impervious to economic analysis. Given zoning legislation and the threat of AIDS, commercial, live-sex shows have virtually disappeared from America's urban areas. "It's Hard to Stay Hot," a 1976 article on Rod Swenson, a low-rent impresario of Times Square sex by Howard Smith and Brian Van Der Horst, observed that Swenson's "Sex Fantasy Theatre" shows grossed $20,000 a week. Swenson did not say how much he paid his performers. (Swenson moved out of porn to manage the career of one of his performers, Wendy O. Williams, the lead singer for the Plasmatics.) Four years later, examining the Show World theater complex (42d Street at Eighth Avenue) where Swenson mounted his shows, Henry Schipper found that most people who worked there made very little. Schipper's "Filthy Lucre" put the salary of a woman who performed sex in front of audiences at $130 a week. The supply of willing performers, says Schipper, outstripped the demand, and exploitation was the result.

By contrast, strip shows in other venues have become steadily more profitable for operators and dancers, though with marked disparities that are typical of the sex industries. In 1967 Libby Jones estimated the number of stripteasers in the United States at 7,000 for her study of the profession, *Striptease*. In 1991, according to D. Keith Mano, 62,000 women were currently dancing topless in the United States, and some 750,000 had been dancers at one time or another. Mano's "Playboy after Hours" piece estimated that topless and nude dancing generated revenues in excess of $2 billion annually. According to Eric Schlosser's "The Business of Pornography," the number of strip clubs has doubled since 1987, and their patrons now spend more on them annually than Americans spend on the theater, opera, ballet, and classical and jazz concerts combined—that in spite of a reclassification of strippers as employees instead of independent contractors—by the Labor Department and the IRS—so that the agencies could hold clubs liable for back Social Security payments, a move that forced many clubs into bankruptcy. *Strippers: The Naked Stages*, an HBO documentary, follows novice dancers and discusses working conditions, longevity of performers, and the marketplace. By 1998, the producers claim, more than 2,500 men's clubs employed more than 250,000 women. They also point out that "good" strippers, that is, those skilled at eye contact and lap dancing, can make thousands of dollars a night. Like athletes, dancers have short careers, but they can be lucrative. That was the reason that the IRS, smelling revenue, began to tax dancers' tips and wages. The IRS has also gone after many porn movie performers on similar grounds, a story that indicates the degree to which sex industries have been co-opted by some government agencies. "Strip Clubs under Fire: Erotic Dance Clubs down for the Count?" contains a suite of articles on issues of management and unionization, although the dancers who have written them do not report income.

A contemporary article on the increasing numbers of male and female students who work their way through college as strippers and the growing respectability of such pursuits is Nancy Donisi's "Dancers Make Big Bucks in the Buff." More recently, *Sales and Marketing Management* devoted several articles to what its editors call a growth industry. Bob Zeigler estimates in "Dancers: They're Not Here to Fall in Love" that the annual income of these "independent contractors" is $70,000, mostly in cash, mostly from table or lap dancing. In another article in the issue, "Topless Bars Dress Up Their Act," Andy Cohen noted that topless bars in major convention cities have gone upscale to attract large business groups. In "Risky Business," David Dorsey found that in 1991–1992 company policy dictated that members of the Xerox sales force take clients to topless bars. In still another article, "How Topless Bars Shut Me Out," Mary MacKinnon protested the discrimination this practice causes. A former sales-women, MacKinnon found herself excluded from these events because of the hostile attitude to women created by holding business meetings in topless bars. Marianne Macy visits strip bars in *Working Sex: An Odyssey into Our Cultural Underworld* and notes that the income of dancers ranges widely depending on the neighborhood. Sylvia Plachy and James Ridgeway note in *Red Light: Inside the Sex Industry* that New Jersey has more than 200 strip clubs, more than any other state, and that strippers prefer working there because they can make more money; Plachy and Ridgeway provide lots of figures. Social and personal costs aside, women dancing in urban entertainment centers, especially Las Vegas, can make huge amounts. A chapter on strip clubs in Texas in Eurydice's *Satyricon USA: A Journey Across the New Sexual Frontier* contains reliable figures on income for owners and performers.

THE INTERNET

"How Pivotal Is Porn in Developing the Market for CD-ROM?" asks Martin Tucker, and he concludes that erotic movies and images are crucial to growth in that sector of the computer industry. Internet entrepreneurs must take erotic applications into account. At the very least, says Kayte Van Scoy in "Sex Sells, So Learn a Thing or Two from It," Internet professionals should remember the cautionary tale of the VCR. JVC readily licensed its format to makers of por-nographic videos in the 1970s; when Sony refused to do so, it doomed the Beta home VCR. In "Sex Sells—Young Ambitious Seth Warshavsky Is the Bob Guccione of the 1990s," Frank Rose points out that pornographers have invented many Internet technologies and innovations. For example, Internet Entertain-ment Group, the porn company, pioneered the "transaction technologies" now widely copied by legitimate businesses to secure credit card purchases, and also the technologies similarly used by websites to "stream" audio and video signals.

The real money, however, will probably come from merchandising, although some states will doubtless attempt to legislate against sexual representation. Al-abama, for example, has prohibited the sale or distribution of sexual devices, apparently in the hope that legislators can keep southern women pure by pre-venting them from using vibrators. But Internet sales of vibrators have boosted the revenues of San Francisco's Good Vibrations store, a cooperative enterprise run by women, to $5 million a year, says David Kushner in "Joystick Nation." Given the soaring number of Web sites, any figures on pornographic represen-tations on the Internet are premature. Small entrepreneurs can quickly become large if they appeal. For an example, Gerard Van Der Leun interviews David Messner, his wife, Cherie, and her sister Jill for "Take My Wife, Please—Over and Over!" The three post pictures of themselves in intercourse on an interactive commercial site that receives more than 300 hits a day.

Rachel Shteir's "Behind the Screen: Online Stripping Takes Off" explores the explosive growth of downloadable "live" (interactive) striptease performances by men and women via the Internet; these, says Shteir, produce very lucrative incomes. David Kushner reports in "Debbie Does HTML" on porn stars such as Asia Carrera, Jenteal, Mimi Miyagi, and Vanessa Del Rio, who have moved from video to the Internet, where their Web sites can make them up to $0.5 million a year, five times what video work brought in. Although some complain about debugging programs and carpal tunnel syndrome, the performers enjoy the greater sense of control, the safe sex, and the opportunity to present themselves to fans as "real" women.

In "The Body Electric," Julian Dibbell says that "adult websites are a nearly $1 billion-a-year business. That's almost a tenth of the entire sex industry. At their current rate of growth, they will soon claim the lion's share" (27). The figures for Web sites are impressive, though, as is always the case where sexual representation is concerned, they are a guess. Dibbell does interview executives David James and Steven Hirsch of Vivid Video for the article. Both are convinced that electronics are transforming the porn business and that huge opportunities await the entrepreneur. Ernest Moore's "Adult Content Grabs Lion's Share of Revenue" goes further; Moore says that sexual representation accounts for 69 percent (or roughly one billion dollars worth) of total Internet content sales. Karl Greenfeld's "Taking Stock in Smut" reports on Seth Warshavsky, CEO of Internet Entertainment Group (ieg), and other entrepreneurs as they prepare to take their sex on-line companies public. The process involves a dance of brokers, underwriters, and consumers in a minuet that should be extremely profitable for investors. From the standpoint of researchers, the public offerings solicitations aimed at investors will provide accountant-verified data and bottom lines for such companies.

ORGANIZED CRIME LINKS

Despite the fact that explicit sexual expression has been illegal in the United States for most of the nation's history, it has attracted the interest of organized crime only relatively recently, when profits began to rise with quasi legitimacy. So long as pornographic pictures or Tijuana bibles were traded at truck stops, and blue movies were exhibited by the same people who made them, the Mafia was not much interested: the scale was not large enough. James Kilpatrick's *The Smut Peddlers* attempted to identify and trace mob connections in the 1950s but could not find much evidence. Similarly, in "The San Francisco Erotic Marketplace" study for the *Technical Report* of the President's Commission, Harold Nawy could find little trace of organized crime in the porn industry in the 1960s.

From that point on, however, the mob learned to pirate films from masters but, as a rule, did not front the money for production. In fact, porn "loops," the little 8mm films that sprocketed through the coin-operated projectors, were made in the late 1960s mostly by small Los Angeles entrepreneurs who recruited performers from the ranks of hippies. The entrepreneurs sold the masters to distributors, and that is where the Mafia found the pressure point: not in production but in distribution. There was one major exception: just as the 1970s opened, Gerard Damiano, a former hairdresser from Queens, borrowed $25,000 from Louis Peraino, called "Butchie" by the Colombo family, to shoot a feature-length film starring an unknown actress named Linda Lovelace in Florida. The Colombo crime family blundered into big-time commercial pornography by accident. The family moved into peep-show arcades in Times Square in the 1970s for the same reason that it had established beachheads in the dry cleaners and pizza parlors in New York: mobsters were attracted to ownership of peep arcades because the huge numbers of quarters that customers dropped in the slots make it easy to launder money and evade taxes.

William Knoedelseder sums up the episode succinctly in *Stiffed: A True Story of MCA, the Music Business, and the Mafia*:

In the 1970s, members of New York's Colombo crime family ran untold millions in cash profits from the porno movie *Deep Throat* through a legitimate Hollywood movie company they set up called Bryanston Pictures, which released the modern horror classic *Texas Chainsaw Massacre* as well as *Devil's Rain*, the debut film of John Travolta, and *Echoes of a Summer*, which starred a precocious pre-teen named Jodie Foster. Bryanston president Louis ("Butchie") Peraino, a graduate of the Times Square peep-show school of moviemaking, became a well-known Hollywood figure for a time, employing scores of legitimate film executives, writers, and producers. He gave speeches to gatherings of movie theater owners and distributors and was quoted constantly in the trade papers announcing his plans to make "family-oriented movies," including one about the Pope. Instead, Bryanston went out of business owing millions in 1976, and, three years later, Peraino went to prison on pornography charges. (76–77)

The charges were racketeering and obscenity.

Carolyn See noted some obvious mob connections in *Blue Money: Pornography and the Pornographers, an Intimate look at the Two-Billion Dollar Fantasy Industry*, published in 1974. In 1975 Nicholas Gage reported on the infiltration of pornography distribution by the mob in "Organized Crime Reaps Huge Profits from Dealing in Pornographic Films." Gage names principal figures and the crime families they are tied to; he also interviews producers of films who have made deals with the Mafia. Gage is a particularly good source on Louis Peraino and the backing of *Deep Throat*. Wendell Rawls describes a sweep of mobsters in "55 Indicted by U.S. as Pornographers and in Film Piracy." *Children in Chains*, by Clifford L. Linedecker, covers some mob connections certified by the Justice Department. The degree of organized crime's involvement in pornography—as opposed to prostitution, for example—remains somewhat speculative, as is evident in a text such as *Goombata: The Improbable Rise and Fall of John Gotti and His Gang*, by John Cummings and Ernest Volkman, who devote only a couple of pages to imprecise information. The *Final Report* of the Attorney General's Commission on Pornography provides data about mob infiltration of the industry in the 1980s taken directly from Justice Department files; the information is doubtless accurate.

John H. Davis identifies the Gambino family as another Mafia group involved in pornography in *Mafia Dynasty: The Rise and Fall of the Gambino Crime Family*. According to Davis, the family controls Star Distributors, the nation's largest distributor of explicit materials, through Robert "Di B" DiBernardo. DiBernardo's offices were for years located in a building in lower Manhattan owned by John Zaccaro, husband of Geraldine Ferraro, the former Democratic candidate for vice president, who received, according to Davis, about $350,000 in campaign funds funneled through DiBernardo (257). *New York News* reporter Milton Moskowitz's "Porno and the $4 Billion Bad Business" challenges Cook's report for *Forbes* by pointing out that the figures are speculative. Moskowitz does say that *Dollars and Sense*, a journal published by economists, agrees with Forbes that the three biggest dealers of pornography are Parliament News of Los Angeles, founded by Milton Luros, Peachtree Enterprises of Atlanta, founded by Michael Thevis, and Sovereign News of Cleveland, founded by Reuben Sturman; all have mob connections. Sturman, generally acknowledged to be in first place, owns Automatic Vending, a company that manufactures peep machines; Western Amusements, a chain of peep arcades; *Eros*, a magazine (not to be confused with Ralph Ginzburg's journal); and a chain of 800 adult bookstore outlets.

Many journalistic articles on these entrepreneurs have appeared; the attributions of profits vary greatly. Typical is George Denison's "Sultan of Smut," a somewhat sensational *Reader's Digest* article on Michael Thevis, who built a porn empire with connections to both legitimate businesses and organized crime. Jim Michaels' "Mike Thevis: Smut Sultan, behind Closed Doors" also profiled Thevis and his associates. Similarly, David May and Mark Hosenball sketch a profile of Reuben Sturman, sometimes called "the King of Porn," and his business activities in "Worldwide Tentacles of Mr. Porn." The article describes how operations in different cities branch out from Sturman's base in Cleveland, Ohio, where his Sovereign News Company is parent to companies like Bon-Jay Sales of Baltimore. The tropes here are familiar; porn distributors almost always have "tentacles." Eric Schlosser's "The Bill Gates of Porn: How Reuben Sturman Shaped the Sex Industry" credits Sturman with inventing the peep-show arcade in 1974, notes that he has used some twenty aliases in owning the retail stores that made him wealthy, and reports on the tax evasion trials that finally imprisoned the entrepreneur.

"An Investigation of Racketeer Infiltration into the Sex-Oriented Materials Industry in New York City," conducted by the New York State Commission of Investigation, had already identified these men and other mob-connected figures in its study of the penetration of the industry by gangsters; the report looked at the economics of films, photos, and adult bookstores in an effort to discover profit margins. Gary W. Potter concentrates on connections between organized crime and pornography and lists major distributors of some forms of pornography over a ten-year period ending in 1985 in *The Porn Merchants*, a text assembled by the author chiefly from newspaper stories and Justice Department sources. The prosecutions of Michelson, Sturman, and others during the 1970s are covered by Ted Morgan in "United States versus the Princes of Porn." In "Peep Porn $$ Titillate Mob," Dick Brass lists still other underworld figures involved in the Mafia's control of peep shows, which show loops of 8mm film: Edward Mishkin, owner of Wholesale Book Corporation of Manhattan, reputedly a front for the Gambino crime family; Theodore Snyder of Queens, allegedly connected with the Joseph Colombo family; Martin Hodas, credited with bringing the peep show to New York, but who lost his protection when Joe Colombo was murdered and was himself convicted of income tax evasion; Sid Levine, a porn movie producer; and Anthony Peraino, suspected of pirating porn films for distribution. The "Mob Controls Distribution of Porno Press," says Nicholas Gage, because respectable distributors will not handle magazines like *Screw*, and the publishers are forced to deal with criminal enterprises.

The profits of video rental stores proved irresistible to organized crime, though it is unclear which was first more attractive, the laundering of cash that such enterprises made possible by renting vast numbers of family and specialty tapes or the profits to be made from pirating X-rated fare. Paul Meskil's "How the Mob Controls Video Piracy and Pornography" identifies major figures in crime families with connections to video porn, though Meskil points out that many filmmakers and distributors have no ties with organized crime. Lester A. Sobel offers a quasi-economic analysis of the role of organized crime in the distribution of pornography in *Pornography, Obscenity and the Law*, and William A. Stanmeyer discusses the hidden costs attributable to criminal involvement in *The Seduction of Society: Pornography and Its Impact on American Life*. Finally, in their *Porn Gold*, David Hebditch and Nick Anning say flatly that there is no Mafia involvement in European porn and—given the size of the market—less organized crime involvement in porn industries in the United States than might be expected. The FBI agrees. In one of its reports to the Meese Commission, the FBI noted that the connections are tangential, mostly "agreements" that allow adult businesses to operate in certain areas.

The influence and power of organized crime in pornography in the United States have been much reduced by (1) vigorous prosecutions that have left the mobs weakened, by (2) competition that has cheapened most types of erotic materials, by (3) distribution of such materials through the Internet, and by (4) growing demand that has legitimated most forms of sexual expression. Luke Ford constantly updates information on the role of organized crime in pornography at his Web site. Ford is especially helpful on the 1970s and 1980s and has reviewed the histories of Thevis, Sturman, Harry Virgil Mohney, Star Distributors of New York City (owned by the Calvancante family), and many other players; he usually provides sources. Ford's investigations have convinced him that organized crime still exerts powerful influence on the pornographic industries; he documents some criminal roles in *The Story of X: 100 Years of Sex in Film.*

NOTE

1. Robert H. Rimmer, "A Connoisseur's Selection of X-Rated Videotapes for the Library," *Libraries, Erotica, Pornography*, ed. Martha Cornog (Phoenix, AZ: Oryx Press, 1991), p. 242.

REFERENCES

Abt Associates. *Unreported Taxable Income from Selected Illegal Activities.* Washington, DC: Government Printing Office, 1984.

Adult Video News. Upper Darby, PA, 1983–1996; Van Nuys, CA, 1996–.

———. *Special Supplement Summer 1994: Marketing Gay Video.* Upper Darby, PA, 1994.

Adult Video News Online. http://www.avn.com.

American Meat Institute. "Just the Facts." *AMI OnLine* (www.meatami.org), August 1997.

Arcand, Bernard. *The Jaguar and the Anteater: Pornography Degree Zero.* New York: Verso, 1993.

Attorney General's Commission. *Attorney General's Commission on Pornography: Final Report.* 2 vols. Washington, DC: Government Printing Office, 1986.

Austin, Bruce A., ed. *Current Research in Film: Audiences, Economics, and Law.* 4 vols. Norwood, NJ: Ablex, 1985.

Austin, John. *Sex Is Big Business.* New York: Tower Books, 1967.

Baird, Robert M., and Stuart E. Rosenbaum, eds. *Pornography: Private Right or Public Menace?* Buffalo, NY: Prometheus Books, 1991.

Bastone, William. "The Porn Broker." *Village Voice*, 18 July 1997, p. 13.

Bernard, Jami. "The Way of All Flesh." *New York Post*, 9 May 1988, p. 21.

Bordes, Sophie, and Daniel Serceau. "L'irrésistible marginalisation du cinéma pornographique." *Érotisme et cinéma: Themes et variations*, ed. Daniel Serceau. Paris: Atlas L'Herminier, 1986, pp. 155–172.

Boynton, Robert S. "The Routledge Revolution: Has Academic Publishing Gone Too Far?" *Lingua Franca*, 5:3 (March/April 1995): 24–32.

Brass, Dick. "Peep Porn $$ Titillate Mob." *New York Post*, 15 October 1975, pp. 4, 15.

Britton, Patti. "Women Who Make Porn: The Influence of Gender on the Content and Approach of Porn Videos." *Porn 101: Eroticism, Pornography, and the First Amendment*, ed. James Elias, Veronica Diehl Elias, Vern L. Bullough, Gwen Brewer, Jeffrey J. Douglas, and Will Jarvis. Amherst, NY: Prometheus Books, 1999, pp. 211–216.

Bulletin of the Adult Film Association of America. Los Angeles, 1979–1982.

"Cable Stats." *CableVision*, 8 May 1989, pp. 71–73.

Cable Television Developments. Washington, DC: National Cable Television Association, 1994.

Capozzi, Michele. "Porn to Win." *Details*, 8:10 (May 1990): 90–91.

"Charting the Adult Video Market." *Adult Video News: 1989 Buyer's Guide*, pp. 6–7.

Chute, David. "Tumescent Market for One-Armed Videophiles." *Film Comment*, 17:5 (September–October 1981): 66, 68.

Cohen, Andy. "Topless Bars Dress Up Their Act." *Sales and Marketing Management*, 147:7 (July 1995): 54.

Cohen, Roger. "Ms. Playboy." *New York Times Magazine*, 9 June 1991, pp. 32, 55–57, 84.

Colin, Molly. "Women Tuning into Porn." *Mother Jones*, January 1985, p. 13.

Cook, James. "The X-Rated Economy." *Forbes*, 18 September 1978, pp. 81–92.

Csicsery, George Paul. *The Sex Industry*. New York: New American Library, 1973.

Cummings, John, and Ernest Volkman. *Goombata: The Improbable Rise and Fall of John Gotti and His Gang*. Boston: Little, Brown, 1990.

Davis, John H. *Mafia Dynasty: The Rise and Fall of the Gambino Crime Family*. New York: HarperCollins, 1993.

Denison, George. "Sultan of Smut." *Reader's Digest*, November 1975, pp. 105–109.

Department of Commerce. *U.S. Industrial Outlook*. Washington, DC: Government Printing Office, annual.

Dibbell, Julian. "The Body Electric." *Time Digital*, 12 April 1999, pp. 24–27.

Donisi, Nancy. "Dancers Make Big Bucks in the Buff." *U: The National College Newspaper*, February 1992, p. 9.

Dorsey, David. "Risky Business." *Sales and Marketing Management*, 147:7 (July 1995): 128.

Dutcher, Linda W. "Scarcity and Erotica: An Examination of Commodity Theory Dynamics." Ph.D. dissertation, Southern Illinois University, 1975.

Dworkin, Andrea. *Pornography: Men Possessing Women*. New York: Putnam's, 1980.

Ellis, Richard. "Disseminating Desire: Grove Press and 'The End[s] of Obscenity.' " *Perspectives on Pornography: Sexuality in Film and Literature*, ed. Gary Day and Clive Bloom. New York: St. Martin's, 1988, 26–43.

Eurydice. *Satyricon USA: A Journey across the New Sexual Frontier*. New York: Scribner's, 1999.

Faligot, Roger, and Rémi Kauffer. *Porno Business*. Paris: Fayard, 1987.

Faludi, Susan. "The Money Shot." *The New Yorker*, 30 October 1995, pp. 64–70, 72–76, 78–82, 84–87.

Ford, Luke. http://www.lukeford.com/a80.html.

———. *The Story of X: 100 Years of Sex in Film*. Amherst, NY: Prometheus Books, 1999.

Frankel, Mark. "Can Playboy Save Its Skin?" *Channels* 6:7 (November 1986): 37–40.

Friendly, David T. "This Isn't Shakespeare." *Newsweek*, 18 March 1985, p. 62.

Gage, Nicholas. "Mob Controls Distribution of Porno Press." *Toronto Globe and Mail*, 13, 14 October 1975, pp. 12, 16.

———. "Organized Crime Reaps Huge Profits from Dealing in Pornographic Films." *New York Times*, 12 October 1975, pp. 1, 68.

Geist, William E. "Merchandising Dr. Ruth." *New York Times Magazine*, 1 December 1985, pp. 17–20.

Gertzman, Jay A. *Bookleggers and Smuthounds: The Trade in Erotica, 1920–1940*. Philadelphia: University of Pennsylvania Press, 1999.

Gettleman, Jeffrey. "L.A. Economy's Dirty Secret: Porn Is Thriving," *Los Angeles Times*, 1 September 1999, pp. A1, A20.

Goldberg, Dave. "No Longer a Novelty, Porno Movies Put Their Makers on Economic Skids." *(Louisville) Courier-Journal*, 30 July 1978, p. H2.

Goldstein, Al. "Making Your Own Erotic Video." *Penthouse*, 24:7 (March 1993): 91, 110, 124, 126.

Graham, E. "Romances, Long Denied Reviews, Get Some Respect." *Wall Street Journal*, 28 June 1995, pp. B1–B2.

Greenfeld, Karl Taro. "Taking Stock in Smut." *Time*, 19 April 1999, p. 43.

Grimes, William. "Lurid! Licentious! Collectible! The Flip Side of the 1940's and 50's." *New York Times*, 25 July 1994, p. B3.

Grover, S. "The Bodice Busters." *Wall Street Journal*, 5 November 1980, pp. 1, 14.

Gurtner, George. "Noonie Smith: Shrines to Two Different Worlds." *New Orleans*, 30: 6 (March 1996): 90–91.

Handler, David. "Now the Playmates Move—But Will America Pay to Watch?" *TV Guide*, 25 June 1983, pp. 45–48.

Handy, Bruce. "What's It Worth to You?" *New York Times Magazine*, 13 February 1994, p. 82.

Hawkins, Gordon, and Franklin E. Zimring. "The Nature and Distribution of Pornography in the United States." *Pornography in a Free Society*. New York: Cambridge University Press, 1988, pp. 30–73.

Hebditch, David, and Nick Anning. *Porn Gold: Inside the Pornography Business*. London: Faber and Faber, 1988.

Hollreiser, Eric. "Porno Goes Mainstream." *Brandweek*, 36:14 (3 April 1995): 38–39.

Indiana, Gary. "A Day in the Life of Hollywood's Sex Factory." *Village Voice*, 24 August 1993, pp. 27–37.

Johnson, Sally. "Reaping What the Boomers Sow: Getting Down and Dirty in the Garden Is Big Business." *New York Times*, 28 September 1996, pp. 21, 23.

Jones, Libby. *Striptease*. New York: Simon and Schuster, 1967.

Jones, R. N., and V. C. Joe. "Pornographic Materials and Commodity Theory." *Journal of Applied Social Psychology*, 10:4 (July/August 1980): 311–322.

Kaplan, Michael. "The Resurrection of Larry Flynt, Owner of Larry Flynt Publications, Inc." *Folio: The Magazine for Magazine Management* (15 June 1993): 36–38, 89–90.

Katzman, Lisa. "The Women of Porn: They're Not in It for the Moneyshot." *Village Voice*, 24 August 1993, pp. 17, 31.

Kennedy, Philippa. "A Marriage Made in Sleaze," *Bangkok Post*, 1 November 1994, p. 37; reprinted from the *London Express*.

Kilpatrick, James J. *The Smut Peddlers: The Pornography Racket and the Law Dealing with Obscenity Censorship*. Garden City, NY: Doubleday, 1960.

King, C. Richard. "The Siren Scream of Telesex: Speech, Seduction and Stimulation." *Journal of Popular Culture*, 30:3 (Winter 1996): 91–101.

Knoedelseder, William. *Stiffed: A True Story of MCA, the Music Business, and the Mafia*. New York: HarperCollins, 1993.

Kristof, Nicholas D. "X-Rated Industry in a Slump." *New York Times*, 5 October 1986, sec. 3, pp. 1, 6.

Kurkjian, Stephen A., et al. "Pornography Industry Finds Big Profits in New Markets." *Boston Globe*, 13–18 February 1983, pp. 1, 6.

Kushner, David. "Debbie Does HTML." *Village Voice*, 6 October 1998, p. 47.

———. "Joystick Nation." *Village Voice*, 30 March 1999, p. 34.

Kyle-Keith, Richard. *The High Price of Pornography*. Washington, DC: Public Affairs Press, 1961.

Langford, David L. "Romance Novels Are Hot!" *Columbus Dispatch*, 16 December 1993, p. 8G.

Leland, John, et al. "The Selling of Sex." *Newsweek*, 2 November 1992, pp. 94–96, 101–103.

Leo, John. "Romantic Porn in the Boudoir." *Time*, 30 March 1987, p. 63.

"L'Erotisme en Question." Special issue of *Cinema D'Aujourd'Hui*, 4 (Winter 1975–1976).

Linedecker, Clifford L. *Children in Chains*. New York: Everest House, 1981.

MacKinnon, Mary. "How Topless Bars Shut Me Out." *Sales and Marketing Management*, 147:7 (July 1995): 52–53.

Macy, Marianne. *Working Sex: An Odyssey into Our Cultural Underworld*. New York: Carroll and Graf, 1996.

"A Man's Guide to Heaving-Bosom Women's Fiction." *Playboy*, 37:5 (May 1990): 72–75.

Mano, D. Keith. "Playboy after Hours." *Playboy*, 38:12 (December 1991):27.

Markert, John. "Romance Publishing and the Production of Culture." *Poetics*, 14:1/2 (April 1985): 69–93.

Martin, Douglas. "Barroom Wizard Sure Plays Up a Pinball Mien." *New York Times*, 13 January 1990, p. 29.

Massey, Morris. "A Marketing Analysis of Sex-Oriented Materials: A Pilot Study in Denver, August 1969." *Technical Reports of the Commission on Obscenity and Pornography*. 9 vols. Washington, DC: Government Printing Office, 1971–1972, IV:3–96.

May, David, and Mark Hosenball. "Worldwide Tentacles of Mr. Porn." *(London) Sunday Times*, 16 July 1981, p. 16.

Meskil, Paul. "How the Mob Controls Video Piracy and Pornography." *Home Video*, 2:1 (January 1981): 28–33.

Michaels, Jim. "Mike Thevis: Smut Sultan, behind Closed Doors." *Hustler*, 2:11 (May 1976): 83–84, 86, 90–92.

The Millionaire Pornographers: Adam Special Report 12. Los Angeles: Knight Publishing, February 1977.

Milton, John. *$ex $ense*. New York: Milky Way Productions, 1974–1982.

Mishan, E. J. *Making the World Safe for Pornography and Other Intellectual Fashions*. Lasalle, IL: Library Press International, 1973.

Mitchell, Kim, and Eric Glick. "MSOs Scrambling after Court Ruling." *Cable World*, 9: 13 (31 March 1997): 1, 98.

Moore, Ernest. "Adult Content Grabs Lion's Share of Revenue." *Adult Video News Online* (May 1999): http://www.avn.com.

Morgan, Ted. "United States versus the Princes of Porn." *New York Times Magazine* (16 March 1977): 16–17, 26, 28, 30, 33–34, 36, 38.

Moskowitz, Milton. "Porno and the $4 Billion Bad Business." *New York News*, 15 October 1978, p. B9.

Nadler, John. " 'X' Marks the Spot." *Variety*, 9–15 October 1995, pp. 40–41.

Nawy, Harold. "The San Francisco Erotic Marketplace." *Technical Report of the Commission on Obscenity and Pornography*. 9 vols. Washington, DC: Government Printing Office, 1971–1972, IV:155–224.

New York State Commission of Investigation. "An Investigation of Racketeer Infiltration into the Sex-Oriented Materials Industry in New York City." Albany: New York State Printing Office, 1970.

Nixon, S. "Looking for the Holy Grail: Publishing and Advertising Strategies and Contemporary Men's Magazines." *Cultural Studies*, 7:3 (1993): 466–493.

O'Leary, Noreen. "The Old Bunny Trick." *Brandweek*, 37:12 (18 March 1996): 26–30.

O'Toole, Laurence. *Pornocopia: Porn, Sex, Technology and Desire*. London: Serpent's Tail, 1998.

Pichirallo, Joe. "FBI Targets Owners, Profits of Sex Businesses in D.C. Area." *Washington Post*, 14 February 1981, p. 3.

Plachy, Sylvia, and James Ridgeway. *Red Light: Inside the Sex Industry*. New York: Powerhouse Books, 1996.

Playboy Enterprises. *Annual Report*. Chicago: Playboy Enterprises, 1995.

"Playboy Weathers 505 Storm." *Cable World* (Pay Per View Special Report), 6 December 1999, pp. 38A–39A.

Polskin, Howard. "Love and Money." *Home Video*, 3:1 (January 1982): 30–33.

"Pornography: Obscene Profits at the Expense of Women." *Dollars & Sense*, 39 (September 1978): 12–14.

Potter, Gary W. *The Porn Merchants*. Dubuque, IA: Kendall/Hunt, 1986.

President's Commission on Obscenity and Pornography. *Report of the Commission on Obscenity and Pornography*. Washington, DC: Government Printing Office, 1970.

———. *Technical Report*. 9 vols. Washington, DC: Government Printing Office, 1971–1972.

"Prosecute Porn? It's on the Decline." *Wall Street Journal*, 28 December 1989, pp. 1, 16.

Ravo, Nick. "A Fact of Life: Sex-Video Rentals." *New York Times*, 16 May 1990, pp. C1, 8.

Rawls, Wendell. "55 Indicted by U.S. as Pornographers and in Film Piracy." *New York Times*, 15 February 1980, pp. 1, 15.

Reynolds, Helen. *The Economics of Prostitution*. Springfield, IL: Charles C. Thomas, 1986.

Ridgeway, James. "Mondo Washington," *Village Voice*, 30 November 1999, p. 42.

Rimmer, Robert M. *The X-Rated Video Guide*. New York: Arlington House, 1984.

Rose, Frank. "Sex Sells—Young Ambitious Seth Warshavsky Is the Bob Guccione of the 1990s." *Wired* (12 December 1997): 5.

Sampson, John J. "Commercial Traffic in Sexually Oriented Materials in the United States (1969–1970)." *Technical Report of the Commission on Obscenity and Pornography*. 9 vols. Washington, DC: Government Printing Office, 1971, III: 1–208.

Schipper, Henry. "Filthy Lucre." *Mother Jones*, 5 (April 1980), pp. 30–33, 60–62.

Schlosser, Eric. "The Bill Gates of Porn: How Reuben Sturman Shaped the Sex Industry." *U.S. News and World Report*, 10 February 1997, pp. 51–52.

———. "The Business of Pornography." *U.S. News and World Report*, 10 February 1997, pp. 42–50.

Schwartz, Tony. "The TV Pornography Boom." *New York Times Magazine*, 13 September 1981, pp. 44, 120–122, 127, 129, 131–132, 136.

See, Carolyn. *Blue Money: Pornography and the Pornographers, an Intimate Look at the Two-Billion Dollar Fantasy Industry*. New York: David McKay, 1974.

Serceau, Daniel, ed. *Érotisme et cinéma: Themes et variations*. Paris: Atlas L'Herminier, 1986.

Serrin, William. "Opponents of Flourishing Sex Industry Hindered by Its Open Public Acceptance." *New York Times*, 10 February 1981, p. B6.

———. "Sex Is a Growing Multibillion Dollar Business." *New York Times*, 9 February 1981, pp. B1, B6.

"The Sex Industry." *The Economist*, 346 (14–20 February 1998): 21–23.

"Sexploitation: Sin's Wages." *Newsweek*, 12 February 1973, pp. 78–80.

Shteir, Rachel. "Behind the Screen: Online Stripping Takes Off." *Village Voice*, 2 December 1997, p. 29.

Siebenand, Paul Alcuin. *The Beginnings of Gay Cinema in Los Angeles: The Industry and the Audience*. Ann Arbor, MI: UMI Press, 1980.

Slabaugh, Eugene, and George Huntington. "Producers of and Nature of Stag Films." Audiorecording, 1966, in the Erotic Film Archives, Kinsey Institute for Sex, Gender, and Reproduction, Indiana University, Bloomington.

Slade, Joseph W. "The Pornographic Film Market and Pornographic Formulas." *Journal of Popular Film*, 6 (1978): 168–186.

———. "Pornography in the Late Nineties." *Wide Angle*, 19:3 (1997): 1–12.

Smith, Howard, and Brian Van Der Horst. "It's Hard to Stay Hot." *Village Voice*, 25 October 1976, p. 26.

Sobel, Lester A. *Pornography, Obscenity and the Law*. New York: Facts on File, 1979.

Stanmeyer, William A. *The Seduction of Society: Pornography and Its Impact on American Life*. Ann Arbor, MI: Serant Books, 1984.

Stein, Joel. "Porn Goes Mainstream." *Time*, 7 September 1998, pp. 54–55.

Stewart, Jill. "The Bottom Line in Blue Movies." *San Francisco Examiner and Chronicle Sunday Magazine*, 20 August 1978, pp. 16–18.

"Strip Clubs under Fire: Erotic Dance Clubs down for the Count?" Special issue of *Gauntlet*, I: 17 (1999).

Strippers: The Naked Stages. HBO America Undercover Series. Produced by Anthony Radziwill. New York: HBO, 1998.

TAB (The Adult Business) Report. Washington, DC, 1978–1985.

Thomas, George C., III. "Rape and Pornography." *Maryland Law Review*, 52 (1993): 119–161.

Thorsen, Karen. "The State of French Porn: Up 'n' Coming." *Village Voice*, 1 September 1975, p. 23.

Trilling, Roger. "Madison: Ex–High School Cheerleader. Hapless Romantic. Porn Star." *Details*, 12: 1 (June 1993): 126.

Tucker, Martin Jay. "How Pivotal Is Porn in Developing the Market for CD-ROM?" *CD-ROM Professional*, 8:11 (November 1995): 64–72.

Updike, Edith. "Publishers of Romance Novels Add Color to Their Lines." *New York Newsday*, 25 July 1994, pp. 23–24.

U.S. Congress. House Committee on Energy and Commerce. *Telephone Decency Act of 1987: Hearing on H. R. 1786 before the Subcommittee on Telecommunications and Finance of the House Committee on Energy and Commerce.* 100th Congress, 1st session. Washington, DC: Government Printing Office, 1987.

———. House Subcommittee on Criminal Law. *Cable Porn and Dial-a-Porn Control Act: Hearing before the Subcommittee on Criminal Law of the Committee on the Judiciary.* 99th Congress, 2d session. Washington, DC: Government Printing Office, 1986.

"U.S. Porn Producer Goes O'Seas for Fresh Faces, More Natural Attitudes." *Variety,* 4 November 1976, p. 23.

Van Der Leun, Gerard. "Take My Wife, Please—Over and Over!" *Penthouse,* 30:5 (January 1999): 171–173.

Van Scoy, Kayte. "Sex Sells, So Learn a Thing or Two from It." *PC Computing,* 13:1 (January 2000): 64.

Variety. Los Angeles, 1922–.

Vaughn, Don. "An Interview with Candida Royalle." *Gauntlet: Exploring the Limits of Free Expression,* 5 (1993): 99–107.

Veronis, Suhler, and Associates. *Communications Industry Forecast.* New York, 1989–; also http://www.usacomm.com.

Verrill, Addison. "Parisi Sees Porn Market Off, Now Averages $150,000–$300,000." *Variety,* 9 June 1976, p. 4.

Weaver, James. "Responding to Erotica: Perceptional Processes and Dispositional Implications." *Responding to the Screen: Reception and Reaction Processes,* ed. Jennings Bryant and Dolf Zillmann. Hillsdale, NJ: Lawrence Erlbaum Associates, 1991, pp. 329–354.

West 42d Street Study Team. *Sex Industries in New York City.* New York: City University of New York, 1980.

Williams, Michael. "Latenight Libido Rules Euro TV." *Variety,* 18 November 1991, pp. 1, 52.

"Words of Love." *New York Times Magazine,* 7 February 1999, p. 21.

Yaeger, Lynn. "Commercial Art." *Village Voice,* 30 March 1999, p. 14.

"Year in Review: Sports." *Electronic Media,* 10:2 (7 January 1991): 54.

Zeigler, Bob. "Dancers: They're Not Here to Fall in Love." *Sales and Marketing Management,* 147:7 (July 1995): 56.

Zellinger, David A., Howard L. Fromkin, Donald E. Speller, and Carol A. Kohn. "A Commodity Theory Analysis of the Effects of Age Restrictions upon Pornographic Materials." *Journal of Applied Psychology,* 60 (February 1975): 94–99.

Index